Trade Unions in Ireland 1894-1960

by the same author

The Distasteful Challenge

The Decade of Upheaval: Irish Trade Unions in the Nineteen Sixties

Trade Unions in Ireland 1894-1960

CHARLES McCARTHY

INSTITUTE OF PUBLIC ADMINISTRATION
DUBLIN

© Charles McCarthy 1977

Published by

Institute of Public Administration
59 Lansdowne Road
Dublin 4, Ireland

ISBN 0 902173 79 0

Direct Reproduction Series 1

Printed and bound in the Republic of Ireland by
A. Folens & Company Ltd., Tallaght, County Dublin.

CONTENTS

PART ONE

From the Foundation of Congress
to its Division in 1945

Chapter One	The Early Years	1
Chapter Two	Endeavour	29
Chapter Three	Stress	92
Chapter Four	The Trade Union Commission	142
Chapter Five	The Act of 1941	178
Chapter Six	Schism	229

PART TWO

From the End of the War to 1960 and the
Unification of the Trade Union Movement

Chapter Seven	Post-War Ireland	292
Chapter Eight	The North	313
Chapter Nine	Division	358
Chapter Ten	Reconciliation	426
Chapter Eleven	The New Congress	453
Chapter Twelve	The Courts	482
Chapter Thirteen	Parliament and Government	524
Chapter Fourteen	Linking Ahead	556
APPENDICES		588
CLASSIFIED LIST OF SOURCES		640
INDEX		648

APPENDICES

Appendix One	The 1919 reorganisation proposals	588
Appendix Two	The Mortished classification 1926	590
Appendix Three	Sam Kyle's summary of trade union organisation 1939	594
Appendix Four	The proposals of the 1939 Commission of Inquiry	595
Appendix Five	Trade union membership in Ireland 1970	597
Appendix Six	Extract from *Trade Union Information* March 1953 on number and membership of trade unions in Ireland and names of trade unions in Ireland	598
Appendix Seven	Extract from *Trade Union Information* April 1953 on trade unions in Ireland north and south	609
Appendix Eight	Joint memorandum on trade union unity 1954: extract showing list of unions affiliated to the CIU and the ITUC	615
Appendix Nine	The Judge classification of trade unions 1951	618
Appendix Ten	Figures of affiliations to Congress 1922-1951	621A
Appendix Eleven	Trade union membership 1945 to 1970: the Hillery and Kelly classification	622
Appendix Twelve	Membership of British-based unions in the Republic 1945 to 1970, as prepared by Hillery and Kelly	623
Appendix Thirteen	Trade union membership in Northern Ireland 1953 (from D.W. Bleakley)	624
Appendix Fourteen	Letter from the Minister for Industry and Commerce proposing new legislation on trade unions, April 1947	629
Appendix Fifteen	Owens Hynes's proposals 1947	631
Appendix Sixteen	The national wage rounds 1946-1975	633
Appendix Seventeen	Affiliated membership ITUC 1922 to 1945, and CIU to 1958 (from R. Roberts)	635
Appendix Eighteen	ILO conventions 87 and 98	636

ACKNOWLEDGEMENTS

I acknowledge with gratitude the facilities provided me by the library of Trinity College, and by the National Library of Ireland. I am greatly in the debt of Mr Ruaidhri Roberts of the Irish Congress of Trade Unions for making material available to me, Mr Donal Nevin, also of Congress, and Mr. N.C. McGrath of the Irish Graphical Society. Mr William Blease of the Northern Ireland Committee of the Irish Congress of Trade Unions provided me with invaluable help, and I am also much indebted to Mr Harold Binks of the Clerical and Administrative Workers' Union.

Mr. Paul Alexander of the Irish Shoe and Leather Workers Union and Mr.W.T. Chapman of the National Association of Transport Employees were kind enough to provide me with personal material and reminiscences which could not be obtained from any other source.

I am most grateful to Dr Frank Drechsler of the Department of Business Studies of Trinity College for his encouragement. And to Mrs Siobhan Allison I pay tribute for the skill and cheerfulness with which she typed an intractable manuscript. My thanks go as well to Mr Thomas Dunne of the Copying Services, Trinity College for his many kindnesses.

This study was greatly aided by funds provided initially through the Player-Wills research fellowship and later through the Irish Management Institute, and the Trinity College Dublin Trust. I also sincerely thank the President, General Secretary and the Executive Council of the Teachers Union of Ireland for all the facilities they offered me, and also the Irish Productivity Centre.

Finally, and most importantly, I wish to thank most sincerely, for his unfailing support, advice and encouragement, Professor W.J.L. Ryan of Trinity College Dublin. Nor can I thank sufficiently my friends in the Institute of Public Administration, Mr Colm O Nuallain, Mr T.J. Barrington, Mr.James O'Donnell and, in particular, Mr Jonathan Williams.

Charles McCarthy

Preface

This is an attempt to plot the shape of the trade union
movement in Ireland. It is a study of form and development,
the purpose of which is to present a reasonable picture of
the trade unions as they had evolved in 1960, at the point
when Irish society began to be confronted with the great social
and economic problems of our time. 1960 was very much a
watershed year, and in the south we would soon plunge
into the years of turbulent economic development, and in
the north we would see the early promise of O'Neill's
premiership give way by the end of the decade to the shocking
and squalid violence that we now experience.

In 1960 the Irish Congress of Trade Unions, as we know it now,
had just been created, resolving the obsessive problem of
division that had lasted from the war's end. We can see
its form clearly, before it entered into the difficult decade
that followed. But we shall find it to be a congress which
had been very much shaped by the past, complex in structure,
heavy with tradition, reflecting a trade union movement which
had certain strengths but also great weaknesses which the
problems of the ensuing years would exacerbate.

These structural weaknesses were obvious to all, and as the
trade unions became more and more significant in national
terms, there was much pressure for reform. The trade unions
themselves had been attempting reform of their structures
from a very early date; and the achievement of unity in
1959 gave some trade union leaders high hopes of their being
able to achieve a more logical and more efficient system of
organisation. All has so far ended in failure. This study
may help to explain why. We shall see, in the course of the
study, proposals for reform that were ingenious and elegant,
and yet came to nothing. Indeed it is clear that before any
such proposal becomes operational, it must, in a real way,

be seen as legitimate by those whom it is deemed to affect.
Such legitimacy does not depend on logic necessarily, nor
on advisability, although such things are highly important.
It seems to depend on a widespread feeling of appropriateness,
which has its roots in traditional thinking as much as anything else. It is not of course unchanging; it can be
both developed and lost, and organisations once unchallenged
in their influence can be left high and dry by a changing
view of their legitimacy. This is why the study has a
certain historical form, although it is an account as much of
ideas as of events, attempting to explore in this manner how
current trade union thinking is organised.

It follows of course that although trade unions can be
examined as distinct subjects, they are best understood for
our purposes as an aspect of the society in which they exist.
Walter Kendall puts the point well: 'The worker's view
of himself and his patterns of socio-political and
organisational behaviour cannot be arbitrarily separated from
the history of the society or state, and of the classes, of
which, independently of his will, he is an integral part.'[*]
Therefore, as we consider the development of the trade union
movement itself, we must continuously keep in focus the
social, political and economic development in the country
both north and south. In the early chapters, because of the
political cast of the trade union movement and because of
its rudimentary structure, this wider focus is quite strongly
present; but as the trade union structure divided from the
political wing of the movement in 1930 and began to develop
as a clearly separate institution, we shall find the
specific problems of trade union organisation and trade union
objectives becoming much more dominant. Nevertheless, in
large measure, they will continue to derive their significance
from the movements and prejudices within Irish society as
a whole.

---

[*] Walter Kendall: The Labour Movement in Europe p.9

This approach is a necessary one in the circumstances; but
it also provides us with an opportunity of seeing Irish
society north and south in an alternative way, through the
eyes as it were of working-class leaders struggling with
the great problems of nationalism and religion, and
attempting to shape their organisations in a manner which
sometimes fostered such movements and sometimes bitterly
resisted them.

Finally a word on the sources of the study. Because the
period from 1930 onwards was a quarrelsome and unhappy time,
it has received little attention. Those who dominated
the period, men such as William O'Brien of the Irish
Transport, look in their memoirs to earlier days, to the
days of high nationalist fervour, seeing in the later
years a period that was humdrum and dark with disputes.
For example, although O'Brien's reminiscences were
published in Dublin in 1969 (as told to Edward MacLysaght
under the title Forth the Banners Go) the account ends in
1922; and MacLysaght himself comments: 'William O'Brien
was disinclined to discuss at length the events and problems
which belong to the years after 1922.'[*] John Swift in
History of the Dublin Bakers and Others published by the
Irish Bakers, Confectionery and Allied Workers Union in 1948
devotes only a few pages in the final chapter to recent trade
union affairs, although in fairness he might have strayed
beyond his brief had he done more. Emmet Larkin in his
authoritative biography James Larkin: Irish Labour Leader:
1876-1947 (Routledge and Kegan Paul), London 1965, gives
little attention to the period from 1928 onwards. 'To
chronicle nearly twenty years of decline is depressing.'
No doubt this was so, but in the organisational affairs of
the trade union movement, the enmity between Larkin and O'Brien
was of the first importance. R.M. Fox in his biography

---

[*] William O'Brien: Edward MacLysaght: Forth the Banners
Go: The Three Candles. Dublin 1969 pp. 228-229.

Louie Bennett: Her Life and Times (Talbot Press Dublin 1958)
does treat of the thirties and forties, but not in any
depth. Academic studies have not moved beyond the end of
the twenties, with the exception of Jerome J. Judge. An
unpublished thesis for the Degree of Master of Economic
Science in University College Dublin in 1951 deals with
trade union organisation in the Republic of Ireland; his
Ph.D. thesis, 1955, The Labour Movement in the Republic of
Ireland, while helpful, is largely concerned with an
evaluation and criticism of Labour and Nationalism in Ireland
by J.D. Clarkson, Columbia University, 1925. Neither the
work of Arthur H. Mitchell nor that of J.W. Boyle, both
scholars in the field, has been taken beyond the division of
the labour movement in 1930, and David Bleakley's 1955 thesis
(for the Queen's University, Belfast) on the Belfast and
District United Trades Council does not go beyond 1900. The
other Northern Ireland scholar Gordon McMullan, in a 1972
Ph.D. thesis submitted to the Queen's University Belfast,
does indeed bring his study quite up to date, but it is in
the very specialised field of clerical trade unionism in
the north. There are also a number of articles, some rather
specialised, which we shall encounter from time to time,
but the only one of general significance is that by Donal
Nevin, in Ireland in the War Years and After 1939 - 1951
edited by Nowlan and Williams and published in 1969 by
Gill and Macmillan.

For the period from 1930 onwards, therefore, we must rely
on trade union and Labour Party reports, some contemporary
newspaper accounts, such private papers as have been
deposited in the National Library, court judgements,
parliamentary debates and occasional articles in contemporary
journals. We are particularly fortunate in that the reports
of all the trade union congresses contain not only the annual
reports of the executives, but a very full reporting of the
proceedings of each of the conferences. They are not entirely
reliable since, in the nature of things, some editing
has occurred in the accounts of the proceedings, and some

selection in the reports of the various executive councils.
However, two independent congresses existed from 1945
to 1959 and one account can be used to validate the other.
But even for the earlier years, their reliability is quite
high, and I have made considerable use of them for that
reason.

Finally, a number of those who were prominent in this
period, and particularly in the years since the war, are
of course still active, or perhaps only recently retired,
and their assistance has been considerable. As for myself,
I was a delegate at one time or another to each of the
congresses, the old Irish Trade Union Congress, the
Congress of Irish Unions, and the present organisation,
the Irish Congress of Trade Unions.

Part One

*From the Foundation of
Congress to its Division
in 1945*

Chapter One

The Early Years

-i-

An understanding of the Irish trade union movement is an
understanding of two cities, Dublin and Belfast. This is
not the whole story, but it is an essential part of it, and
inevitably, therefore, experiments in trade union unity were
dominated by the way these two cities from time to time
regarded one another, politically and socially. There is
a great gulf in understanding between the two cities, a
radical difference in the way society is understood, and
even a certain perversity of mind regarding one another
made more difficult for a current age by the deliberate
foreignness which was cultivated north and south from the
early thirties until very recent times. And yet they are
bound together, perhaps because of the common lot of an
island people, perhaps for deeper reasons. It is true
that during the thirties and forties the Free State tried to
excise the north under the guise of expelling British-based
unions, and so achieve a Dublin-based unity which derived
its impetus from nationalist sentiment. But as chauvinism
died away, the old polarity reasserted itself, requiring
that the solution be found in its terms.

Trade unions, being essentially of the working class, could
be expected to reflect traditional views on politics and
on social and religious groupings; and the stresses within
the trade union movement do in fact reflect these views.
But what is surprising is the toughness of the bonds which
held the unions together, deriving perhaps from a shared
class feeling (something which is now on the wane), from
the frequent fact of common membership of the large
amalgamated or English-based unions, but deriving as well

from the unifying force of socialism, with its uncompromising international ethic, which seemed to be so strong
an influence on many of the trade union leaders down through
the years, despite the fact that very many of the rank and
file members were not only indifferent to such ideas but
were often hostile to them.

But while such men might hold the trade union movement
together in times of stress, some far more general impetus
was necessary before progress towards a closer-knit structure
could be made. From time to time we shall see such an
impetus arising, making the time fruitful. Without such
an impetus the most attractive of schemes for restructuring
run into the sand. Furthermore the impetus, when it does
arise, seems to spring as much from self-interest as anything
else. The noble socialism of some trade union leaders
must coincide with motives much more self-centred and
immediate among the generality of trade union members.

-ii-

A handful of years before the turn of the century, in 1894,
the Irish Trades Union Congress was founded. It was a most
significant step, radical and successful, and although
the new congress received the blessing of the British
Trades Union Congress, many of the great amalgamated unions
viewed it with some reserve, and for years made no contribution to its funds. Let us examine how this came about.

The eighteen eighties had been a difficult time. Emigration
soared, agriculture and industry were in distress, and
perhaps apart from the Belfast area, population stagnated
or fell; and there was the great economic war conducted
by Michael Davitt and the Land League, attended by bitterness and evictions. But from 1890 onwards things began to
improve. The Congested Districts Board was established,

farm prices recovered and the Wyndham Act greatly increased the facilities for tenant purchase. In industry
this was a period of great reorganisation, the growth of
large firms which were export orientated even in areas where
markets were declining, and the proportion of industrial
output exported was remarkably high, the principal exports
being linen, shipbuilding, distilling and brewing. The
craft trades had suffered from cheap goods from England,
and the early efforts to promote Irish industry, which
received a powerful impetus from Arthur Griffith and Sinn
Fein, gradually developed a protectionist aspect. But as
L.M. Cullen points out, Ireland was in many respects a
highly developed country by the end of the century. 'About
a half of its output - industrial and agricultural - was
exported. Its major industries had an international renown,
Belfast liners and linen, Irish whiskey and Dublin beer
and biscuits having an unrivalled name. The country had an
extensive banking and transport system. The paradox to
contemporaries was that, despite these circumstances,
Ireland was not as prosperous as they would like to see it,
and incomes compared with England and Scotland were
relatively low.'[1] But if urban living conditions had
improved somewhat they were still appallingly bad. In
Dublin for example, the more well-to-do had abandoned the
centre of the city to the impoverished tenement dwellers,
the birth rate was high, disease was endemic and the improvement in public hygiene in Britain generally was not
reflected here. The labourer's wage was such that thousands
were virtually condemned to this way of living.

And what of our two cities, Dublin and Belfast? In the
past sixty years, Belfast had leaped up in importance, its
population increasing from 75,000 in 1841 to 350,000 in
1901, which Dublin matched only if one included the suburbs
of Pembroke, Rathmines and Rathgar. Some of the Belfast
population increase arose because of the centralisation of
the linen industry which by the end of the century was in
decline, but in fact its most spectacular development it

owed to shipbuilding during the last decade of the nineteenth century and the first decade of the twentieth when
its population increased by half. As a result many Scots
and English skilled workers came to and went from Belfast,
fostering in the city a strong socialist tradition. But
Belfast was very active commercially as well, possessing
from the eighteen fifties the largest port in Ireland.
Belfast people like to think that they possess a special
entrepreneurial spirit which is absent from the rest of
Ireland; this was probably not so if one is to judge by
the diversity of economic activity elsewhere, particularly
in Dublin, but whether it was or not, the fact remained that
Belfast, sharing as it did in the great industrial expansion
of the 19th century had become by 1900 the commercial and
industrial centre of the country. Dublin had also grown
over the years but more slowly; nevertheless in the last
half of the 19th century its population had increased by
100,000. We find there the large food, drink and tobacco
industries, now amalgamating and restructuring, a widespread distributive trade and a multiplicity of small-scale
manufacturers, vulnerable to cheap goods from England and
anxious for protection. It is not surprising then that the
characteristic of Belfast trade unionism should be protection
in industrial disputes, while in Dublin it should rather
be the campaigning against the purchase of foreign manufactures.[2]

The trade union movement of the time was dominated by the
great British unions, or amalgamated unions as they were
called, to which, in the second half of the 19th
century the small local Irish unions affiliated, in such
goodly numbers that at the close of the century the great
majority of Irish trade unionists were members of the
amalgamated unions. The 1943 Commission on Vocational
Organisation[3] speaks of the invasion of the country by the
large English unions, but it is most unlikely that the people
of the time saw it in that way. Irish immigrant workers in
Britain had taken a very prominent part in trade union affairs,
and in the eighteen eighties in particular many Irish names
were prominent in the lists of delegates to the British

trade union congresses. Furthermore, workers returning
from England popularised the amalgamated unions here, as
did also the visiting craftsmen to the Belfast shipyards.
But while this was so, a key point to our understanding of
the trade union movement of the time was the importance
of the trades councils, the Belfast council dating from
1881, the Dublin council from 1886 (although it was heir
to an earlier body) and councils being important as well
in Cork, Newry and Drogheda; and indeed it was lack of
representation of these bodies on the British congress
that really confirmed in existence the rather shaky and
uncertain Irish congress in its early years.

But the trade union movement had an uncompromising hard-
hatted respectability, consisting in particular of
associations of tradesmen, carpenters and joiners, bakers
and printers, painters and tailors; the impoverished
labourers, usually organised on a purely local basis, had
little influence, and the 1864 Dublin Exhibition found the
Dublin group proposing some general federation largely for
the purpose of promoting trade.[4] Nor did the establishing
of the British Trades Union Congress in Manchester in 1868
contribute much immediately to the Irish movement. Irish
participation was always small, and resolutions on Irish
matters were usually found clinging precariously to the
end of the agenda. Indeed when the British congress met
in Dublin in 1880, while there was a good attendance from
the city itself, there was none from Belfast.[5] However,
it is significant that the Belfast United Trades Council
was formed in the following year, and in 1893 they were
themselves hosts to the British congress.

The instinct for a wider united movement was much influenced, particularly in the south, by the political
climate of the times, by the Parnellites and the Land
League, by Plunkett's gospel of cooperation and by the
protectionism of Sinn Fein, and also by the new unionism
with its growing concern for the oppressed and the impoverished. The success of the Irish National League,

the rank and file organisation of Parnell's parliamentary
party, inspired T.J. O'Reilly, a printer, to attempt some
Irish organisation, and the Irish Federated Trade and Labour
Union held its first conference in the Angel Hotel Dublin
in May 1889; it was supported by both Irish and amalgamated unions, the British congress sent its blessing,
and, most important of all, it was supported, although
after cautious consideration, by the Belfast council.
But within a few months all was in disarray, when the
Belfast council reacted bitterly to a request from the Dublin
council concerning contributions to a Sunday sports meeting.
This question of Sunday observance captures the unique
character of the Belfast situation, and it was to become a
major issue once again in 1893 when the British congress
came to Belfast and when it was suggested that May day
celebrations should take place on Sunday; it was a
position almost always underestimated in the south, and
often totally misunderstood by the English labour leaders
who tended to dismiss it as bigotry or hypocrisy, as indeed
they did at the 1893 congress. Quite apart from the row
over Sunday observance, other events, not least the controversy over Parnell's leadership of the Irish party,
were too much for the fragile Irish Federated Trade and
Labour Union.

But now there was a great sense of movement in the air.
Michael Canty, the Irish organiser of Will Thorne's Gas
Workers, no doubt under the influence of the new unionism,
called a conference of general labourers in the Ancient
Concert Rooms in Dublin in 1891, at which Parnell was
enthusiastically received, and arising from it formed the
Irish Labour League. The skilled trades held aloof because
of their reluctance to become involved politically (a
very typical posture of the Dublin council of the time);
nonetheless they joined with the labourers in a great May
day parade to the Phoenix park, where 10,000 attended with
banners and bands. There was however a strong Parnellite
tone to some of the speeches. Michael Davitt was also
anxious to improve politically the influence of labour,

and had presided at the formation in Cork in January 1890
of the Irish Democratic Trade and Labour Federation with
the object of organising agricultural labourers and workers
in country towns. In these circumstances John Martin of
the Dublin trades council called a general conference in
the fine new premises in Capel Street, which was attended
both by tradesmen and labourers. While Belfast was
reluctant, it might well have played its part, but Martin
died in August and the organisation with him.

Belfast in the meantime was concerned with more explicitly
trade union matters, and this always seemed to be the unifying agency. It was so within the city itself in 1892 when
the Belfast council held a labour demonstration in support
of striking linenlappers and a monster procession included
thirty or more protestant and catholic bands; 'orange and
green rosettes decked the breast of the District Master
of the Orange Lodge in common with that of the vice-
president of the Irish National Federation.'[6] In contrast
a similar demonstration which was attempted the following
year at the time of the meeting of the British congress
ended in rioting and disorder; the second home rule bill
(which of course Burns and Hardie had voted for) had been
defeated by the Lords the day before. But Belfast and
Dublin had built up valuable cooperation in trade union
matters, as for example when they blacked a Belfast newspaper whose print was set in Dublin. Furthermore, Belfast
workers must have found the British labour movement very
disturbing politically,[7] not only because of their support
for home rule and their impatience with the constitutional
privileges which were the bulwark of protestant Belfast,
but because of the insensitivity as well of rugged socialists
when faced with a clamouring anxiety about religious practice.

It is not surprising then that the initiative of the Dublin
council in the following year, 1894, met with success. It was
appropriate to the time; there were no good reasons against
it, and many for it; in no sense was the movement seen as
a rival to the British congress; and the Dublin council,
heavily influenced by the trades, could be relied on to
keep politics out of the way. Indeed a reference to the

deceased Parnell at the official lunch of the first conference was heckled as being political and contentious.

Thus in the trades hall in Capel Street, Dublin, in 1894
was launched the Irish Trades Union Congress. Twenty-one
thousand workers were directly represented and 39,000
indirectly through the trades councils of Belfast, Dublin,
Cork, Limerick and Drogheda. The Irish branches of the
amalgamated unions gave their full support, and the constitution was modelled on that of the British congress.

But the tone of the conference was very respectable and
responsible and was to remain so for many years: 'an Irish
version', as Boyle remarks, 'of lib-lab reformism'. The
parliamentary committee of eight members and a secretary
(which, following the British practice, was the elected
representative body) were not only all from trades councils
but were also all from the skilled trades. The unskilled
workers gained a seat in 1895 and again in 1896 but on the
whole they were badly represented. Indeed so close was the
idea of federation to industrial promotion that in-
dustrialists and business people contributed substantially
to the expenses of the first conference, and so prominent
among them were the breweries and the vintners that the
Glasgow trade unionists spoke caustically of an unholy
alliance with the publicans of Dublin.

The British Trades Union Congress of 1894 also mended its
hand a little with regard to Ireland and made special
provision for Irish representation, but the following year,
1895, in an effort to bar socialist influence, the British
congress excluded trades councils from future meetings,
and it also rescinded their decision concerning Irish
representation. This confirmed the need for an Irish trade
union centre, a centre which nonetheless continued to
emphasise that its existence constituted in no way any dis-
loyalty to the British congress.

Now that a united trade union centre had been created in Ireland, the tensions within the trade union movement began to develop in two ways. The first concerned the political posture of the trade unions: whether they should be nationalist or socialist, or perhaps - in the socialist context - whether they should be nationalist as well. The second, which was related to the first, concerned the tensions between the amalgamated unions and the Irish unions, that is to say, in our modern phrase, between the British-based and the Irish-based unions. These tensions found expression in particular in the relations between Belfast and Dublin.

The fact of the matter was that the members of the trade union movement had consciously to look two ways, the first being local, political and often sectarian, and the other being nation-wide, indeed kingdom-wide, non-sectarian and non-political in the context of the Irish parties, concentrating instead on explicitly trade union matters. The trades councils tended to fulfil the first role; the Trades Union Congress the second. In Dublin the tension was less evident than in Belfast. Officially the council had to **eschew party politics** if it were to remain on good relations with Belfast, and it was extremely careful on that account; but in fact it supported the nationalist position and 'took a part in the temperance and Gaelic language movements in addition to sending representatives to ceremonies commemorating the patriot dead.'[8] Indeed national sentiment appeared to wash back and forward - from the eighteen thirties when the Dublin trade unions turned out with banners and bands to support Repeal, to the particularism and individualism of the trades at the close of the century when they gathered their skirts in from the labouring and unskilled groups and looked to their own advancement. Now, however, the explicit nationalism of Sinn Fein, and its angry impatience with all things British, was beginning to influence strongly the Dublin council, leading to the sharp de**bate** on the amalgamated unions

at the congress of 1905. Belfast had a much more difficult
task. There was the crisis of the mid eighteen eighties
when Alexander Bowman of the Belfast trades council, who
had been the first Labour candidate elected in Belfast,
supported Gladstone's home rule bill. In 1886 when the
bill was defeated in its second reading in the Commons,
there were bitter riots and some loss of life. A number
of unions disaffiliated from the council, and Bowman had to
resign as its secretary. Whatever about local elections,
there was not another parliamentary candidate for twenty
years when the handsome young Willie Walker threw his hat
in the ring. He was president of the Trades Congress
in 1904 in Kilkenny but the following year his assurances,
for political purposes, to the Belfast Protestant Association
caused great bitterness in catholic and nationalist circles.
By 1905 things were beginning to break up, those complacent
and respectable days where even in the heat of discussion
the delegates were careful to address one another politely
and in a parliamentary manner, where they laughed to scorn
the Wexford burghers for fearing trade unionism, where they
listened with enthusiasm to the masterful addresses in Newry
of **Keir Hardie** and Ramsay MacDonald and proudly recognised
the response of Redmond and the Irish party to their
representations on the great issue of the Taff Vale case and
the other trade union judgements. The peace within the
trade union movement was a peace which derived something
from the exclusion of the major problems of the time, the
growth of Sinn Fein in the south with its vituperative anti-
British sentiment, and the appalling poverty of the unskilled workers and the tenement dwellers. In a few years
all this was to change dramatically.

Before going on to deal with these changes, however, with
the growing nationalism and the thunderous impact of Larkinism,
it is necessary to look briefly at that small voice of
radical dissent, which although it was hardly heard at the
time, greatly influenced the men who were later to give
the cast to the trade union movement. 'Radical views', says
Clarkson,[9] 'were confined to a small assorted group of
socialists, atheists, anarchists, and stray Fenians whose

claim to notice consists in the single fact that among
their number was the author of the "Red Flag".'   Thus it
was throughout the latter part of the nineteenth century;
and in 1896, when Connolly came to Dublin at the age of
twenty-six, he had only a handful of supporters in the
launching of the Irish Socialist Republican Party. His
great strength lay in his continuous writings, and the
Worker's Republic appeared with reasonable regularity until
1903, when he left for the United States. But although the
party very nearly died, there were some remnants that
William O'Brien could pull together in 1908, and this new
body, the Socialist Party of Ireland, was the one that invited Connolly to return from the United States in 1910,
launching him on a course which placed him in the centre
of the passionate events that were to follow. And in Belfast
too William Walker edited for some months the socialist
Labour Chronicle before the Belfast Socialist Party went
over to the Independent Labour Party; but if in the south
Connolly's socialism was nationalist, Walker's was explicitly
unionist.

However, radicalism of that kind was a minor matter. The
great driving force was Sinn Fein, dominating, with its
sharp and uncompromising separatism, two of the debates at
the Athlone Congress of 1906, breaking to the surface really
for the first time just when the trade union movement appeared
to have reached the peak of its achievement. The general
election of January 1906 had brought a change of ministry,
an 'awakening of the British democracy' and - in practical
trade union terms - the introduction of the trade disputes
bill of 1906. It was the crowning of the policies of the
trade unions, who had determined on a policy not of strikes,
nor of expensive law-suits, but of parliamentary representation in order to overcome by legislation the prejudice of
judge and employer. It stimulated support both in Belfast
and Dublin for the Labour Representation Committee, now the
Labour Party, something which in the past had caused Redmond
much concern. Congress had given its support for the idea both
in 1904 and 1905; yet when it came before the 1906 Congress,
it was defeated, some as usual claiming that the Irish

party was in fact a Labour party, but Sinn Fein now
calling a plague on both houses, and clearly favouring
an entirely Irish party. Sinn Fein sentiment came in
particular from the Limerick delegates, who spoke in terms
that were to be soon only too familiar, of a sacred
allegiance to the land of their birth, and of a country
fighting for its independence from an alien government.
'He could quite agree', said one Limerick delegate, 'with
the mover of the resolution if he confined his scheme to
the North of Ireland, whose representatives had in all
cases voted against the interests of labour', and a
colleague of his declared that there was a greater cause to
be achieved in this country than the cause of Labour. It is
difficult to judge the impact of such speeches. There were
more balanced and more urbane contributions made, but such
views had not been expressed in these terms before. Of
course the debate was not helped by Walker's election
assurances to the Belfast protestants; he was not there to
explain his position himself - although there were others
who tried to put what he had done in a reasonable perspective.
But it was in the earlier debate at the same Congress, the
debate on the question of an Irish federation, that we see
the clear impact of Sinn Fein on trade union structures.
The Dublin council had discussed the question of joining
the General Federation of Trade Unions, a body that had
been established some years before in Britain when the
Amalgamated Engineers' strike collapsed, its object being
to build up and control a fund for strike purposes; in the
event it never lived up to expectations. A committee of
the Dublin council favoured joining, but P.T. Daly, the
chairman of the council on a casting vote, had the proposal
referred back in order that the idea of forming an Irish
federation could be considered. At the 1906 Congress the
following June, the Limerick delegates, supported by
P.T. Daly and others from Dublin (who had by no means the
unanimous support of their own delegates) proposed that
Congress should promote 'some scheme of federation among
them',[10] and although the object was declared to be to
prevent non-trade unionists from benefiting from trade union
activity and although the amalgamated societies were invited

to help, it was clearly seen to be a nationalist and
separatist ploy. It was not a well-worked-out scheme and
it was understood by everybody there to be in effect an
attack on the idea of amalgamated unions, which were
defended by many delegates who were in politics supporters
of the Irish party. Belfast in any event wished to
strengthen, not weaken, its relations with the British unions.
The proposal was defeated comfortably, only the Sinn Fein
delegates supporting it, but from the debate the Sinn Fein
position became clear enough: their impatience with the
British-based unions, and their determination to form some
Irish counterparts, that is to say full amalgamations or
federations for particular trades, within the overall context of a Congress which had more deliberative functions.
It would seem as well that they tended to exclude Belfast
from such a development, although the logic of such a
position would be partition, which the Congress would condemn;
and in this they touched on the very heart of the Irish
dilemma. But it is doubtful if they were thinking primarily
of the trade union structure at all. The Sinn Fein
delegates reflected very much the ideas of Arthur Griffith,
that there could be no improvement socially or economically
until British domination was ended in all spheres of Irish
life; and in taking this view they rendered **irrelevant the
trade union movement as it was then organised, firstly**
because being British influenced, it was inherently inadequate, and secondly even if it were reformed, it would
be ineffective in any real sense in the absence of a
political solution. The call for an Irish federation of
trades therefore must be seen more as a political declaration
than a practical programme for restructuring, although
its impact on trade union thinking would continue to grow
until the crisis years of the forties.

-iv-

But the following year there was Larkin and Belfast, there
was the new unionism arriving in Ireland a generation late,

and there was what amounted to a civil revolt rather than
a trade union strike, a sudden upsurge of feeling in response
to the 'strike organiser'. And all at once, a new dimension
was given to trade union affairs. From this grew the
Irish Transport and General Workers Union, dominating the
trade union movement with its vigour and its numbers.
Despite Arthur Griffith's dislike of the new unionism, and
his suspicious hostility to the English organiser (as he
called Larkin) the Transport Union, as it grew, fostered
Sinn Fein sentiment both in politics and in trade union
organisation; through Connolly it fostered syndicalism
and gave a further impetus to the idea of the organisation
of trade unions on industrial lines, and because it began
itself by splintering from an amalgamated union, it introduced a restless, volatile principle into the stable conservative association of trades. While Belfast opinion was
alarmed at any weakening of the amalgamated unions, there
was nevertheless in all this something difficult to deny:
the socialism of the new endeavour, its proletarian character,
and the sheer demagogic commitment of Larkin to the improvement of the lot of the unskilled and the deprived.

Larkin was a delegate from Belfast at the 1907 Congress in
Dublin, and in a typical manner he 'respectfully recommended'
the case of the locked-out Belfast dockers to the trades
unions of Ireland while at the same time condemning the
'tyrannical action' and 'despicable conduct' of the tobacco
king Mr T. Gallagher; this rougher acerbic note was not
unwelcome to delegates in these changing times, although
they still had refreshments on the Hill of Howth, and
travelled free with the compliments of the Dublin United
Tramways Company.[11] But events, under Larkin's leadership,
swiftly ran to crisis in Belfast. On June 26 the dockers'
strike began, the carters struck in sympathy, on July 10
there were reports of rioting; and the coal men were locked
out by their employers over the weekend of July 12. The
result was that on the great Orange day, 'irrespective of
creed or party the workers paraded through the streets of
Belfast and listened to an address by Jim Larkin at the
Custom House.'[12] As the crisis mounted, labour representatives

came in large numbers to Belfast; the police fell into
dispute because of the dismissal of a colleague; an army
expeditionary force was called in; there were riots in the
Falls, and cavalry and bayonet charges. James Sexton, who was
General Secretary of the National Union of Dock Labourers
and Larkin's superior, managed to conclude through the
General Federation of Trade Unions what he described as an
honourable settlement, but which in fact was a capitulation;
and refused to pay any further strike pay. Sexton's background was similar to Larkin's; he was Liverpool Irish and
had himself worked in the docks, but the relations between
the two men had always been strained. The mood now was that
Larkin and the Irish workers had been let down by the English
executives. Larkinism, as it came to be called, began to
sweep the country, and the following June, Larkin, as a
representative of the Dockers Union, but now from Dublin,
was elected to the parliamentary committee of the Irish
Trades Union Congress, which that year met in the city where
these extraordinary events had taken place. In December
1908 the Dublin carters asked Larkin to lead their strike.
His union would have none of it, and eventually refused
to accept further responsibility, suspending Larkin from
office. Early in January of the following year, 1909,
Larkin founded the Irish Transport Workers' Union.[13]

In June of the same year 140 quay labourers in Cork
struck because of the employment of three labourers who
were members of a body called the Workers Union (it was also
known apparently as Stevedore O'Rourke's scab union). The
principle of tainted goods, that is to say of the sympathetic
strike (the significance of which we shall discuss in a
moment), extended the dispute to the railways, and the
Cork Employers' Association, determined not to tolerate
this development, set out to crush the strike. The Cork
trades council gave the strikers its support, and so also did
the councils in Dublin and Belfast; but the employers held
firm, refusing point blank to accept mediation of any
kind, and locking out the workers who supported the new
union. Eventually the men began to drift back to work, but

the significance of the Transport Union was recognised; and
when Larkin later was prosecuted and imprisoned for
collecting contributions which it was claimed should have
gone to the Dockers Union, his reputation was further enhanced.

But now Larkin was in trouble with Congress, although he
was a member of its parliamentary committee. The new Irish
Transport Workers Union, which had sprung up in Belfast
Dublin and Cork, initiated an inter-union dispute when they
asked the Congress to investigate a charge that members of
the National Union of Dock Labourers in Belfast were black-
legging on the union. The parliamentary committee of
Congress decided to refer the matter to the Belfast Trades
Council and in the meantime to send no invitation to attend
the forthcoming Congress to the Irish Transport Workers'
Union. Larkin was effectively expelled from the Congress.
At the annual conference in Limerick in the early summer,
the parliamentary committee was supported but by no great
majority. Larkin was recognised to be a tempestuous
character; some claimed that he had fallen into the hands
of socialists and Sinn Feiners; and there was great anxiety
about the fractionalising of the trade union movement, and
the usurpation of executive authority. But on the other
hand there was the overwhelming fact of Larkin's influence
among the workers. His exclusion seemed to be an excessive
step in all the circumstances, and when D.R. Campbell of
the Belfast council proposed that a committee be set up to
go into the whole affair it was readily agreed. The
following year the committee of investigation reported to
the annual meeting in Dundalk that there was no justification
for the secession of members from the National Union of Dock
Labourers but at the same time 'as it is accepted on all
sides that there is no objection to the formation and
existence of Irish union, we are of opinion that the Irish
Transport Workers Union is a <u>bona fide</u> labour union, and
entitled to recognition in the Trade Union Movement.'[14]
But there were many who felt that the committee had gone
beyond its brief in recommending that the new union be recognised,

including the chairman of Congress, James M'Carron, an
impressive Redmondite, who had little patience with Larkin,
socialism or Sinn Fein. Running through the debate there
was some anxiety as well about the creation of breakaway
Irish bodies from the amalgamated unions; but even when
the drift of the opinion was clearly in favour of readmitting
Larkin and seating the Irish Transport, the chairman fought
it personally all the way, so much so that Willie Walker
protested that he was making a martyr of Larkin who should
now be admitted. The chairman wished to postpone the matter
further until the parliamentary committee met over lunch,
and this brought Larkin, who had been sitting fuming in
the gallery, plunging on to the floor of Congress demanding
to know why he should be now debarred when there were
sitting in Congress notorious blacklegs and enemies of
trade unionism. Walker insisted that the wishes of the
delegates be implemented immediately and this was done,
Larkin and the Irish Transport being admitted. In view of
all that had been said about him in the debate, Larkin,
while apologising for his hastiness, was anxious to make
his political position clear: 'He did not belong to any
party - Sinn Fein, Unionist or United Irish League. In no
country could a person point a finger of scorn at Jim
Larkin (applause).'[15]

It was a difficult congress for the old guard of the trade
union movement. E.L. Richardson, who had been secretary
of the Congress since 1901, resigned in March to accept a
government post; although a young man,[16] he had summarised
in his approach and in his person the old unionism and had
earned the contempt of Arthur Griffith who accused him of
going off to important functions 'with his London tall silk
hat' while the poor of Dublin festered. The delegates
elected P.T. Daly to this key office, a known Sinn Feiner,
and a vigorous supporter of Larkin, whose influence on the
committee of investigation had no doubt greatly helped the
Larkin cause. He was later to join the Irish Transport
Workers Union as an official. All this however, was too
much for the chairman M'Carron who in despair said he was
severing his connection with the Trades Congress.

It was to such an Ireland that Connolly returned in 1910 as organiser for the Socialist Party of Ireland, soon becoming secretary and Ulster organiser for Larkin's union. Connolly's syndicalism, which at this point was a tiny minority view, had later a substantial influence. It was part of a larger international movement of the time, owing more however to the US and the Industrial Workers of the World, with their ideas of centralised structures, than it did to the more anarchic European model. Where orthodox marxism looked to a revolutionary proletariat, syndicalism saw the trade unions as the instrument of revolution, striking by their economic power at the industrial roots of society. The trade union would initially provide the worker with his education and ideology, and would later become the means by which, through a mounting series of strikes, domination would be secured by la grève générale. Syndicalism therefore had two objects: a militant working class, and industrial trade unionism. There was an important distinction however between the French and the US models, the first being local in character, and the second being explicitly centralist in aim; and this latter was the system preferred by the British syndicalists. In Britain itself however, the movement had no impact, being powerfully resisted by the British labour movement. But it formed the basis of Connolly's thinking. However he was careful to point out that 'socialism properly implies above all things the cooperative control by the workers of the machinery of production; without this cooperative control the public ownership by the State is not Socialism - it is only State capitalism.'[17] Connolly saw the administration of society placed in the hands of the representatives of the various industries of the nation; 'that the workers in the shops and factories would organise themselves into unions, each union comprising all the workers at a given industry.'[18] Therefore 'the enrollment of the workers in unions patterned closely after the structure of modern industries, and following the organic lines of industrial development is par excellence the swiftest, safest and most peaceful form of constructive work the Socialist can engage in.'[19] When the day would come when Labour would finally

break with capitalism 'the shops and factories so manned
by Industrial Unionists will be taken charge of by the
workers there employed.'[20] But in this he had no time
for the 'old, narrow, sectional'[21] craft unionism, nor
huge powerful amalgamations if they lost the fraternal
spirit. He preached militancy and the effectiveness of
sporadic strikes. Here then was the origin of the One Big
Union, the OBU which is still the legend on the badges of
the Irish Transport and General Workers Union; here too
was the early pressure for the reform of the trade union
movement on industrial lines.

One can readily see as well the impact of Larkinism, the key
to which was the sympathetic strike, the making of common
cause right throughout the chains of industry and leading
logically to the possibility both of industry wide strikes
and of general strikes. Larkin's campaign for the wretched
and the impoverished had no doctrinaire roots, but it
fitted well into this syndicalist development. In its own
right Larkinism was seen as dangerously revolutionary;
it had created turmoil in Belfast; the Cork employers had
resisted it with immense determination; and this year, 1911,
following the Cork example, a Dublin Employers' Federation
was founded with the object of combating its development.

The syndicalist idea too was not unattractive to certain Sinn
Fein opinion. In 1909 P.T. Daly had moved for a declaration
'that the industrial independence of the workers in this
country should be insisted upon, and as a means to that end
all trades unions should be worked upon a national basis
and federated with the workers of other countries'. While
he did not object to membership in an amalgamated society
he saw no reason why the workers of Ireland should not be
members of Irish trade union organisations. Despite this
obscure point, many of the delegates, including M'Carron
of Derry deplored the move as introducing racial and party
divisions into trade unions, and it was roundly defeated.

Larkin's creation of an Irish union, therefore, and Connolly's
syndicalism with its emphasis on trade union reorganisation

on industrial lines were both forces which weakened the
British connection, and were no doubt seen by Sinn Fein
as such.

In 1911 Congress met in Galway in early June. While
politically things were peaceful enough since it now
appeared certain that, with the curbing of the House of
Lords, home rule would come soon, in industrial matters on the
other hand both Britain and Ireland became deeply troubled
by labour unrest. It spread from Britain into the port of
Dublin, and in the autumn it spread to the railways. Troops
were brought in, there were extensive lockouts, and eventually
the men capitulated. In June therefore, there was some
anxiety about the growing crisis of unrest and also about
the effect of the judgement in the Osborne case, which
concerned the use of trade union funds for political purposes.
It was against this background then that a proposal by
John Good of Cork, seconded by William O'Brien of Dublin
was unanimously adopted. It declared 'that this Congress
is of the opinion that the present system of sectional
Trades Unionism is unable to successfully combat the en-
croachments of modern capitalism, and realises that much
greater achievements are possible and the redemption of the
working class would be hastened if all existing unions
were amalgamated by industries, with one central executive
elected by the combined unions, with power to act unitedly
whenever there is a strike or lock-out in any industry,
thus making the grievance of one the concern of all. This
Congress therefore instructs the Parliamentary Committee to
use its influence and co-operate with the English and Scottish
Trade Union Congresses in any effort that may be made to bring
this about.'[22]. While this had a ring of OBU about it, and
was also a first step towards syndicalism, it was probably
the reference to the Scottish and British Congresses that
made it acceptable. Certainly when Larkin the following
year in Clonmel proposed that an Irish Federation of Trades
should be established, he was defeated, although by a small
majority. Congress on the whole took the view that federations
in the past had never worked, and that in any event the trade
union movement should be international. There was no great

debate on the question;   it was probably ill-judged, and
an attempt by William O'Brien to modify it by way of
amendment was refused by the chairman.

But it was the desire to take political, not industrial,
action which changed radically the structure of the Irish
trade union movement, a change as significant as the creation
in the first instance of the Irish Congress.   The trade union
movement had tried to keep clear of party politics but in
these hectic days, the individual members of Congress and
of the trade unions had often deep political commitments.
In the early years of the century there was a sense in
which Congress could be above party politics;   now it was
somehow below them - below them in that for quite a number,
their political posture was the important consideration,
and their avoidance of party politics at Congress had a
certain artificiality.   In 1909 E.W. Stewart, a well-
known Sinn Feiner,was reported as saying to Redmond when on
a trade union deputation, that he was speaking on behalf
of Sinn Feiners;   and when he was challenged at annual
conference on this, he made a reply, quite satisfactory to
his querist, which gives the quality of Congress at the time;
he said 'that in speaking on behalf of the Trades Union
Congress he said to Mr Redmond and his colleagues that they
represented a very composite body of men, that they
represented men who were trade unionists in the ordinary sense
of the word, men who were Socialists, Sinn Feiners, United
Irish Leaguers, Tories and Orangemen, and in appealing to
them to take action in Parliament, to secure the passage of
measures that this Congress demanded, they were representing
the views of all these bodies - the views of all sections
of labour in Ireland.'[23]   But there could be little vigour
or drive on great issues of state with such a diversity
of strongly held opinion.   Larkin's achievement - and it
was certainly Larkin's much more than Connolly's, despite
latter-day opinion - was to raise the whole of industrial
trade union activity to a high level of significance, to
involve not merely the professional trade unionists but the
great mass of the people, with the result that the trade union
organisation, the Congress, could declare itself to be as

well the independent Labour Party of Ireland, as long as
it held firmly to the principle that all its representatives
must be trade union members and authorised to act by the
trade unions. Larkin had instinctively found the answer;
if one could not come to terms with the diverse party
political tensions, then one set out to dominate them.
In later years, in the foreword to the reports of the Irish
Congress of the thirties, Connolly is given credit for
proposing in Clonmel in 1912 the independent representation
of labour upon all public boards, and thereby with launching
the Irish Trades Union Congress and Labour Party. From this
the present Labour Party traces its origin. This indeed is
so, but it was not as unique a proposal as it might appear.
In 1911, the year prior to that, Thomas Murphy of Dublin had
proposed a properly federated and controlled Labour Party in
Ireland, which was seconded by William O'Brien and vigorously
supported by Larkin. William Walker proposed an amendment
which urged affiliation with the British Labour Party in
order to promote independent labour representation in Ireland,
and while this was carried, the majority was a slender one,
32 votes to 29.[24] On the one hand, a separate Labour
party might be seen by the British party as a hostile act;
but on the other hand, the British Labour Party took its
advice on all Irish matters from the Irish party; and this
was annoying to all sides. Home rule now appeared to be only
a matter of time; and there was therefore a question of
labour representation not only at the Imperial parliament
but at the home parliament as well. The fact remained that
neither the Irish party nor the British Labour Party had
initiated any legislation in Ireland's cause. There was a
very pointed example of all this in the exclusion of Ireland
from the medical benefits under the recent national health
insurance act. There was a great deal of force therefore
in Connolly's question in 1912: 'When the representatives
of Ireland came to meet in the old historic building in
Dublin, which they had heard so much about, were the workers
to be the only class that was not to be represented.'[25]
Those who opposed the motion spoke of its disturbing effect, and
that it was premature - weak enough in all conscience as a
counter to the working-class sense of mission which Larkin

offered. The resolution was made more explicit in 1913 in
Cork, making the point additionally that **conference should
support** the United Trades Congress on all matters affecting the
United Kingdom; and when it was included as a principle
of action by Larkin in his extraordinary address to the
1914 annual congress it was all affirmed overwhelmingly
by acclamation.

The idea of an explicit trade union party, entirely Irish-
based, held together, therefore, despite the growing revolt
in the north against the idea of home rule; and despite
the fact too that by early 1914 an Ulster unionist labour
association had been founded 'to combat disloyal thoughts
among the workers.'[26] Once again it was Larkin's demagogic
appeal as a great labour leader during the bitter and
extended strike in Dublin in 1913, and his vituperative
condemnation of British labour leaders for their lack of
aid during the strike, that maintained the idea of separate
Irish trade union political representation. In any event
there was no intention of breaking with the British party;
the Irish Congress had a long consultation with them in
July of 1913 on the question of political representation;
but they had no intention of being subservient to them in
matters affecting Ireland. The activities of Larkin seemed
to give a validity to the idea that working-class opinion
and interest was a separate and distinct force in Ireland,
an idea that found expression in the support for P.T. Daly
who was imprisoned during the industrial dispute in Wexford
in 1911, when as Larkin more than once remarked, Carson
had remained untouched for uttering much more seditious matter.
This became not a matter of Sinn Feiner and unionist, but
rather of working class and capitalist, a case of discrimination
exercised by the class that held power in society.

The six months lock-out in Dublin in 1913 and early 1914
is one of those large events from which much tradition,
much shared trade union solidarity springs. Larkin was
chairman of Congress at the time, over thirty unions were
involved, and it was a source of considerable international
interest. A special conference of the British congress was

called to consider Larkin's urging that there should be
a sympathetic strike in appropriate British industries.
Indeed he had toured Britain, demanding this over the
heads of the British officials, about whom he had been
frequently abusive. When he rose to address the special
congress in London in December 1913 he did not help matters
by beginning: 'Mr Chairman and human beings..'[27] and in fact
was almost howled off the platform. Early in 1914 the
British labour movement ceased to help financially and the
strike collapsed in bitter exhaustion.

Larkin's address to the 1914 Irish Congress in early June
was quite unparalleled, entirely extempore, full of power
and in the reading, after all these years, full of consistent
and exciting purpose, quite in contrast with his chairmanship
during the Congress when he tried to fight delegates into
the ground despite their best efforts to respect the chair.
His address was full of hope and of inspiration that, with
the Labour Party, they were on the threshold of a newer
movement 'a new party - a labour party - an industrial
army; a political party whose politics would be the
assurance of bread and butter for all.'[28] The question of
home rule had been settled by the Government of Ireland Bill;
religion was a personal matter. 'Intolerance had been the
curse of our country. It is for us to preach the gospel
of toleration and comradeship for all women and men. The
day has come for us of the Irish working class to reconsider
our position. Whatever other classes in Ireland might do,
we must march forward to the complete conquest of Ireland,
not as representing sections, sects or parties, but as
representatives of the organised working class as a whole.'[29]
There was neither unionist nor nationalist among the
working class and but two camps, employers and workers.
'We found no Redmonites, Carsonites or O'Brienites then.
The enemy were all employers ..'. 'One union,' he said,
'one union is the only way out - one union for all industry.
One might say when they hear this suggestion that it is the
term of a madman - that it is Larkin again. It is however
the only sound, logical method and the only way that makes
for success. One union is the way out ... those who would

not assist in this one-union movement were on the side of
the capitalist ... Let us be comrades in the true sense of
the word and join with our brothers the world over to advance
the cause of the class to which we belong.'[30]

While Larkin was thus evolving a quality of working class
unity which he tried to give to the trade union movement,
he believed that home rule was now resolved; and this was the
key both to the idea of an Irish labour party and to the new
working class solidarity. Unlike Connolly who had become
anxious about the course of events, the capitulation of
Asquith to northern opinion, and Redmond's agreement to partition
for a period of six years, came as a great shock to him. Then
a month later in August 1914, the great war commenced, and
Redmond in declaring vigorously for Britain appeared to be
expressing the overwhelming view of the Irish people. Larkin
inveighed against the war; Liberty Hall carried a banner
declaring that they served neither King nor Kaiser; but
Larkin's own behaviour, always random and difficult, became
markedly worse, and before the year was out he set off to the
United States for a brief trip to raise funds. The union had
been badly shaken by the dispute in 1913 and he himself was
very much on edge. He was not to return for many years. He
left in charge James Connolly, who in the logic of his thinking,
moved gradually towards the revolution of 1916 and his common
lot with Irish national sentiment. There was no Congress in
1915, because, it is reported, people were preoccupied with
the war, and when the Congress met again in Sligo in August
1916 the rising had taken place and Connolly was dead. Now
however the body that met was the Irish Trades Union Congress
and Labour Party, developing a dominant political posture, made
all the more explicit when its name was further changed in
1918 to the Irish Labour Party and Trade Union Congress.

-v-

In this first twenty years of the life of the Irish Congress
the changes that we have noted were not merely episodes
in trade unionism on the one hand and in Irish nationalism
on the other; they were in fact part of a breaking-up of
the old ways, the cracking of the cake of custom, and

surging upwards was not only the energy but the violence
of our time, our experience in this island being part of
a wider European experience, and mirroring it, just as
Larkinism in Ireland mirrored the widespread industrial
unrest in Britain twenty years earlier. Protest is one thing,
violence quite another, and there are some who see in the
feminist movement of those years the beginning of something
qualitatively different, depending as it did on minor violence
and hooliganism characteristic of a society which was
abandoning reliance on equitable discussion and consensus
to resolve social problems; and if in Ireland much the
same denial of normal procedures and the greater reliance
on violent confrontation characterised the contribution
of a number of great women nationalists, it accorded well
with a growing sense of impatience and a hunger for catharsis.
It was a time when the very foundations of the British
constitution were under challenge even from members of
the British establishment, when the House of Lords was defending
itself against the rising power of the Commons in a rather
vehement and hysterical manner, when Bonar Law could, on the
part of Ulster, counsel armed revolt in Dublin to the army in
the Curragh and where indeed the whole of society seemed
about to break up in civil unrest. Thus, the great war
came at a time when this social restlessness was building up
to a dangerous level, and in a sense may have been a consequence
of it; in any event it provided a vast and terrible conflict
into which the minor conflicts were subsumed.

But among all the various conflicting interests, among all
the separatist social movements of the time, there was one
in Ireland, the Sinn Fein movement, which survived the
sweep of Armageddon, which rose to unify the greater part
of Ireland against Britain, and which emerged eventually
as the particularly Irish polarity. The Irish Transport
union was to be the vehicle for this feeling as well, combining therefore urban revolt against privilege and high
national sentiment with its own special syndicalist ideas;
and since the Irish Transport in turn dominated the old-
fashioned trade union respectabilities of the past, it
imported its views into the whole trade union movement, giving
it its special structure and its special character.

Notes on Chapter **One**

Abbreviations are used as follows. ITUC followed for example by 1906 refers to the annual report and annual conference proceedings of the Irish Trades Union Congress for that year; ITUC & LP refers in a similar manner to the Irish Trade Union Congress and Labour Party; ILP and TUC to the Irish Labour Party and Trade Union Congress; CIU to the Congress of Irish Unions established in 1945 and ICTU to the Irish Congress of Trade Unions which became the sole organisation in 1959.

1.   L.M. Cullen: An Economic History of Ireland since 1660: London 1972, p.167.

2.   cf. J.W. Boyle: The Rise of the Irish Labour Movement 1887-1907: Dublin 1961.

3.   Report: Commission on Vocational Organisation: Dublin 1943, p.182.

4.   These were not dissimilar to those that made up the influential Junta in England, as described by the Webbs, unions which the Chartists dismissed as 'the pompous trades and proud mechanics.' (See Edmund Frow and Michael Katanka: 1868 Year of the Unions: London 1968, p.11).

5.   Some important Dublin trades were also not represented, possibly because of the militant reputation of the British trade union movement, which its president attempted to play down. (see J. Dunsmore Clarkson: Labour and Nationalism in Ireland: New York 1925, p.177).

6.   Belfast trades council minutes Sept.26, 1891: quoted by Boyle op.cit., p.140, to whom I am indebted for much of the material in this section.

7.   Even as early as 1883 they tended to look to the Parnellites in Westminster for advice on Irish matters. cf. Clarkson op.cit. p.185.

8.   Boyle op.cit. p.302.

9.   J. Dunsmore Clarkson: Labour and Nationalism in Ireland, New York 1925, p.176.

10. ITUC 1906, p.61.

11. ITUC 14th Annual Report, 1907.

12. Clarkson op.cit., p.217.

13. This was the original title, the words 'and General' being added at the suggestion of William O'Brien - with considerable consequences. (See Irish Transport and General Workers' Union: Fifty Years of Liberty Hall: Dublin 1959, p.16).

14. ITUC 1910, p.24

15. ibid. p.30

16. He was still alive at the 50th anniversary of the foundation of the Congress. See ITUC 1944, p.23.

17. James Connolly: The New Evangel: in Erin's Hope The End and the Means, and The New Evangel: 1972 edition p.27.

18. James Connolly: The Axe to the Root: Dublin 1921 p.18.

19. ibid. pp.20-21.

20. ibid. p.20-21.

21. ibid. p.37

22. ITUC 1911, p.45

23. ITUC 1909, p.39

24. ITUC 1911, p.42

25. ITUC 1912, p.13

26. cf. Emile Strauss: Irish Nationalism and British Democracy London 1951.

27. cf. Emmet Larkin: James Larkin Irish labour leader 1876-1947 London 1965.

28. ITUC 1914 p.32

29. idem p.32.

30. idem p.35-36

Chapter Two

Endeavour

-i-

When the Irish Trades Union Congress and Labour Party met
in Sligo in 1916, they did so in the shadow of great events,
in which many of their prominent members had been involved.
Connolly, who was a member of the National Executive at the
time, had been executed; P.T. Daly, secretary of Congress
had been arrested and all records and papers seized; so
also had William O'Brien, then secretary of the Dublin
Trades Council, and Thomas Foran, President of the Irish
Transport and General Workers Union, whose headquarters,
Liberty Hall, had been shelled in a manner which Congress
regarded as wanton and unnecessary. Tom Johnson the President
of Congress and R.D. Campbell, a traditional nationalist,
both from Belfast, appealed for their release through
R.D. Henderson of the British Labour Party; but when the
Congress met in July, P.T. Daly, the secretary, was still in
gaol, and the Congress had to proceed without him.

Tom Johnson began to emerge at this point as the man who
somehow or other made sense of the vast conflicting movements
in the country which were tossing the trade union movement,
as well as many other institutions, into quite new shapes
and postures. Johnson was an Englishman originally, who
had worked for years in Belfast. His attitude to
Republicanism was cautious; he was a little old-fashioned in
his trade unionism, neither marxist nor nationalist, and
shared this attitude with other influential Belfast trade
unionists such as Sam Kyle and David Campbell. He had,
therefore, the capacity to understand both north and south,
both Dublin and Belfast. Larkin, although he had appeared,

for a period, to have bridged the religious divide, in
fact had little appreciation of Belfast, and after 1908 had
probably never visited it again, sending Connolly there
instead. To people like William O'Brien, the north, and
particularly Belfast was a large blank, a vast piece of
philosophical and political discounting. But Johnson was
always sensitive to the complexity of Irish society and
Irish aspirations, and this was very clear from his rather
remarkable speech in Sligo in 1916 as President of Congress
where he honoured James Connolly '... we mourn his death, we
honour his work, we revere his memory',[1] and went on:
'And while laying these wreaths on the graves of our comrades
who gave their lives for what they believed to be the Cause
of Ireland's Freedom - let us also remember those many others
(some of whom had been chosen in years past to attend our
Congresses) who have laid down their lives in another field,
also for what they believed to be the Cause of Liberty and
Democracy, and the Love of their Country.'[2] He skilfully
reminded the delegates of James Connolly's prayer for the
men of the execution party 'who do their duty according to
their lights'and said: 'In that spirit I ask all present,
whatever their views may be in regard to the war or the
rebellion, to rise for a moment in token of respect for all
our comrades who have been brave enough to give their lives
for the cause they believed in.'[3]

At this stage the Congress was not markedly different from
what it had been for many years; true, in 1913 the executive
had been increased from 8 to 12 but a slender majority
still lay with the amalgamated unions, even though the number
of delegates from the north had much diminished. The
sudden leap in numbers in the south was not yet in evidence.
Consequently at the time Johnson pursued a course that was
not only perceptive but courageous. Lloyd George was already
beginning to seek a solution and very soon after the rebellion,
talk of partition was very much in the air. Johnson and the
Congress executive, following their 1914 declaration,deplored
the idea, and from Belfast Johnson wrote to Lloyd George,
to Redmond, to Carson and to others to this effect. More than

that, on July 7   1916 the Congress and the Dublin Council
met Lloyd George[4] to express 'their intense opposition'[5]
to the proposal.   Interestingly, while doing so, the
deputation claimed to represent the organised workers from
the whole of Ireland 'and while not claiming to speak for
the large number of Ulster Trade Unionists who were opposed
to any form of Home Rule, he(Johnson) said that many even
of those were opposed, on trade union grounds, to any
proposal to divide Ireland.'[6]   The Congress in August was
vigorous in its   endorsement of this policy of opposition
to partition.   There were many also who were appreciative
of Johnson's approach.   H.T. Whitley from Belfast, representing
the Typographical Association, in supporting the vote of
thanks, said: 'They were there as trades delegates from
various parts of Ireland, and one of the best features of
Mr. Johnson's address was the manner in which he avoided
wounding the susceptibilities of any of them.'

As we look, at this time, for indications of structural
reform in the trade union movement, we find at this 1916
annual conference of Congress a resolution [7] on 'sectional
unions', a resolution which called for one strong, national
union for each industry.   In substance, it was accepted,
but its suggestion that Congress should in the future refuse
admission to sectional unions had to be withdrawn.   The
matter, in fact, received little discussion and it would
be wrong to place too much emphasis on it.   When a much
more comprehensive debate was undertaken three years later
in 1919, the Irish trade union movement had become quite
a different organisation.   The whole country indeed had been
convulsed in a new beginning.

Towards the end of 1916 and all through 1917[8] both Sinn Fein
and also the militant labour movement leaped upwards in
vigour and in numbers.   It was particularly so in the case
of the Irish Transport.   'At the time of the Rising,' says
Clarkson,[9] 'the Transport Union had ten branches scattered
from Belfast to Killarney, from Sligo to Waterford, and a
membership of 5,000.   By the Autumn of 1917 the number of

branches had increased to thirty-two, with 12,000 members.
A census of the Union taken on June 30 1918 showed a
membership of 43,788. By the end of that year the Union
claimed 67,827 members organised in 210 branches. In the
course of the following year the membership reached 100,000,
exclusive of those casual labourers who were able to pay
dues for only a few months of the year.' The trades councils
in particular sprang into life as centres of local
republican and labour sentiment; and indeed many trade
unions appeared to benefit from this quite dramatic change.
While between 1916 and 1918 the number of unions sending
delegates to annual conferences of Congress did not change
very much (35 in 1916 and 44 in 1918) the number of trades
councils trebled from 5 to 15 and the number of delegates
leaped up from 81 in 1916 (perhaps slightly less than the
usual number) to an unprecedented 240 in 1918. While the
number of delegates from the amalgamated unions had doubled,
the delegates from the Irish based unions had trebled, and
while in 1918 the Irish Transport sent only 37 (they had
sent only 10 in 1916) within three years they sent 102 of
the total delegates of 250.[10]

In the rural areas at the turn of the century labourers
and small farmers had combined in local organisations for
political purposes; they were known as Land and Labour
Associations and had considerable success in rural elections.[11]
Now the agricultural labourers flocked in unprecedented
numbers into the unions, particularly the Irish Transport,
who in all probability built on the associations that were
already there. Clerical workers and women also joined in
substantial numbers.[12] It was a heady time. The Russian
revolution seemed to catch at the very spirit of the labour
movement, not only in its destruction of capitalism and in
its celebration of the proletariat, but also in its emphasis
on self-determination and although Johnson and Campbell
were refused passports to attend the Stockholm conference
in 1917, they received an assurance from Litvinoff of Russia's
full support for the admitting of Ireland as a nation to the
International. The Derry annual conference in August congratulated the Russian people, and Thomas MacPartlin the

President declared that the only bright spot in a period
of awful carnage was the effort that was being made 'by the
organised working class of Russia, which, let us hope, in the
near future will extend to the other belligerents, to bring
about a speedy conclusion to this war.'[13] The Russian
revolution, then, represented the awakening of the working
classes of all lands, casting aside 'the greedy capitalists
of all the belligerent nations' who had caused the war,
offering peace, self-determination in the international
family, and a vigorous anti-militarism to reflect the growing
horror at the destruction of the war.

MacPartlin went on to reject in very comprehensive terms
indeed the idea of partition as a solution to Ireland's
political problems, although looking forward confidently to
self-determination: 'We would prefer to carry on the fight
for another fifty years than consent to any dividing up of
the country (hear, hear). We are told that Ulster wants
partition. We do not believe it (hear, hear)! On the
contrary we are convinced that Ulster does not want it, as
is instanced by the fact that, with the exception of two
delegates, all the workers' representatives from Ulster
voted against partition at our Congress in 1914, although
a number of them were in opposition to Home Rule (hear, hear).'[14]

MacPartlin was from Dublin, and these remarks of his probably
missed the whole point of the partition discussion, since
there was a strong conviction in the north (and likely
enough throughout the country) that Ireland could not survive
economically if they lost Ulster. Those who opposed Home
Rule therefore could reasonably oppose partition as well.
Nevertheless this Congress of 1917, at which MacPartlin spoke,
was held in Derry, and the majority of delegates were from
amalgamated unions, who also held a substantial majority
on the executive council.

It was in these circumstances, with a great nationalist
stirring at the grass roots, and a Congress still cautious
and conservative, that O'Brien tossed in the proposal once
again that an Irish Federation of Labour should be established.

He was not too explicit about its functions but he was
careful to try to come to terms with the amalgamated unions:
'There are two kinds of organisations in Ireland,' he said[15]
'those with headquarters in Ireland and those that were
amalgamated with Unions across the water. Any scheme of
Federation that might be adopted should not divide the two,
but should bind them together. The door should be open to
make it possible for both kinds of Unions to come in.' But
there was great reserve about the whole idea. M'Carron said
quite bluntly that it would mean wiping out the amalgamated
societies in the country,[16] and Tom Johnson capped it by
saying that if it were intended to establish the Federation
for political reasons (and some delegates saw it as having
a parliamentary role) it would wipe out the Irish Trades
Congress and the Irish Labour Party.[17] O'Brien's move had
caused a great deal of concern, much more than was warranted
by his rather ingenuous introduction. Indeed, Whitley
from the Typographical Union spoke of a feeling abroad that
it was the intention later on to have resolutions passed
making it illegal for societies in Ireland to be affiliated
with societies across the channel.[18] In the circumstances
O'Brien accepted that the resolution should be referred to
the executive committee for a report.

In any event he himself had been elected chairman for the
coming year. It is perhaps not too surprising therefore
that quite a remarkable proposal came before the next
annual Congress in 1918 in Waterford, demonstrating among
other things the effect of the extraordinary growth of
membership and the inability of the existing societies to
respond to it, particularly in the rural areas. An
organisation scheme had been launched by the Congress of
1917 but while this was all very well where trade union
organisation already existed, the national executive found
'that in many places in the country calling out for
organisation there was absolutely none, gauged on the
Trades Union basis.'[19] They reported that many towns of
one thousand to ten thousand inhabitants had no trades union
branches whatever. Others had a branch of two or three
societies, perhaps the Typographical, or the Drapers'

Assistants or the NUR. 'The remaining workers are quite
outside, and being so few in each, skilled Trade Unions
consider the expense of organisation is not warranted by
the possible result.'[20] The national executive considered
it its duty to look after the work of organisation in these
places. They had considered introducing 'mixed locals' on
the lines of the American Federation of Labour, but they
believed they needed a mandate from the annual conference.
They proposed that in the small towns where they found local
trades and labour councils 'instead of affiliating branches
of Unions, as is usual in the cities, we join up the
individual workers. These might be grouped in sections
according to the industry followed, say:- Distributive
Trades Section, Building Trades Section, Transport Trades
Section, Agricultural Section. And an executive appointed
from the Sections.'[21] The councils might be regarded as
trades councils for the purpose of affiliating and sending
representatives to Congress. Their duties would be both
industrial and political within their districts. There
should be no question however of their competing with
established societies. 'It should be a condition of
membership', said the national executive, 'that where a
branch of an affiliated society exists or is established,
all members of the council of that particular trade or
calling must forthwith become members of the Union.'[22]
Thus Congress would in fact organise the small towns on
behalf of the unions. To carry out this programme they
anticipated that they would require a permanent organising
secretary. But all this was taking place in a whirl of
great political events, in which both Sinn Fein and also
the labour movement were giving leadership. As we have
seen the labour movement generally had almost doubled its
membership by 1918, and its growing popularity was confirmed
and indeed increased by its dramatic opposition to conscription. The Government in April 1918, despite the
protests of all Irish parties, with the exception of the
Unionists, decided to extend conscription to Ireland.
An 'Extraordinary Labour Conference' was held in Dublin
on April 20, and 1,500 delegates attended from all over

Ireland.[23] Apparently there had never been anything quite
like it in size or enthusiasm. 'Amid scenes of indescribable
enthusiasm',says a later report, 'the Conference declared
the resolute will of the workers to resist a blood levy to
which no popular or representative consent had been asked
or given.'[24] A twenty-four hour general strike was decided
upon and was launched within four days, on April 23. Everything stopped, except in the Unionist districts in Ulster.
Both public services and private industry were affected - even
the government munitions factories. Of course the labour
movement was, in this, merely a part of a national protest
in which the other political leaders were also involved,
Republican, Home Rule and All-for-Ireland as the great
Mansion House conference demonstrated. But they took great
pride in the fact that Ireland had been preserved as the
only unconscripted country in Europe.

When William O'Brien rose on August 6 1918 to address the
Waterford annual conference there were present, as we have
already seen, 240 delegates, more than twice the number
of delegates at any previous conference in the Congress
history. And here we begin to see the celebration of
Connolly as saint and martyr, much in contrast with Johnson's
earlier caution. O'Brien paid tribute to both Connolly and
Larkin and then went on: 'But of James Connolly, one
of whose oldest friends in the Labour movement I can proudly
claim to be, I am bound to say this: his life and his death
were the inspiration to which are due the splendid enthusiasm,
the strong determination, the manly independence, and in
a large measure the wholehearted allegiance of the many
thousands of workers who have joined our ranks within the
past two years. His are the ideals we follow, his the
principles we adopt, his the plans and methods upon which we
organise, his the memory and the inspiration from which we
draw our strength and our place in the forefront of the
fighting army of Labour and in the battle for freedom and
justice in this and all other lands. May the sod rest
lightly upon you, old comrade, murdered at the hands of a
tyranny, and may peace be yours in death ... we who remain
to carry on your battles promise you that we shall not

lower your flag, but through success and reverse shall
travel the road you cut out for us, and battle on until
we have built up in Ireland that Workers' Republic for
which you worked and fought and died.'[25]

There were two things that were very clear from this. In
the first place, there was an instinct for the greatness
of the events, an awareness that all this was being
worked out on a world stage. This was particularly marked
in the relations of Congress with the world socialist movement.
Congress delegates had been refused passports to attend the
International Congress the year before, but they had resumed
international relations with organised labour in other
countries, particularly with the labour and socialist parties
of Russia, France and Great Britain, the last especially,
whose relations with Ireland we shall discuss in a later
paragraph.[26] It was through the British Labour Party that
O'Brien and Johnson met Litvinoff, the Bolshevik pleni-
potentiary, and the 1918 Congress renewed its adherence
to the Russian Peace Formula. All this was much in accord
with the campaign against conscription, which the Irish
labour movement offered as an outstanding contribution in
the cause of peace. Irish self-determination therefore
had a considerable ring of internationalism about it,
and had not as yet become circumscribed with chauvinist
imperatives.

The second and rather overwhelming point is the commitment
to Connolly's teaching regarding a workers' republic, and
the practical steps necessary to bring this about. The
great surge in membership gave point to all this, not
only because of the vast numbers of agricultural workers
who were joining, but also because of the affiliation of
the national teachers, and many clerical workers, giving
the movement a broad national complexion. O'Brien was
swept away with enthusiasm. He urged that the unions
should be organised in departments in accordance with
occupations. He spoke romantically of dreams coming true.
'We have not yet, indeed, the One Big Union, containing
within its shelter the whole working class of Ireland,

but it is fast approaching us, and we have already a great
solidifying of the forces of Labour, and are marching
steadily and swiftly towards unification and the great
bond of brotherhood.'[27]

O'Brien was conscious too of the fact that with the extension of the Franchise Acts, a great number of new
voters, particularly women, would now come on the register,
and in this millenarian mood, a special Congress was
called in November 1918 with the object of adopting a
far more explicit socialist constitution, a constitution
which sought the public ownership of land and industry,
a free and united Ireland, in a word a workers' republic.
This also was the Congress which, startlingly if logically,
decided not to contest the critical post-war election of 1918.

Nineteen-eighteen found Ireland a very changed society indeed.
The last general election had taken place in 1910 and then
the Irish Parliamentary Party was secure in its dominance;
now it was everywhere being displaced by Sinn Fein, with
perhaps the exception of the north. By March 1918 John
Redmond was dead. The Irish convention under Horace Plunkett,
which sat in 1917 and 1918, failed because of Ulster's
determination to remain apart; and Sinn Fein, conscious
of its growing strength, put aside its more general
"Hungarian" policy and explicitly declared itself for an
independent Irish republic, fusing itself thereby with the
mystical bloodletting of 1916; and significantly, Arthur
Griffith yielded the leadership to de Valera, a surviving
commandant of Easter week. Sinn Fein won a number of by-
elections in 1917; and there was a great stir of self-
determination in the air. Indeed it is difficult to distinguish between the labour movement in certain of its
leadership and Sinn Fein during this time. O'Brien spoke
in August of the 'recent proclamation against gatherings
and assemblies, the forcible suppression of meetings,
including our own trade union meetings, sports, concerts
and amusements, the extension of martial law and the
application of the Coercion Acts, the declarations against
political, social and language societies, the trials by

courts-martial and special juries, the division of the
country into ten areas for military purposes, the planting
of a military occupation in almost every square mile of
Irish soil'[28] and while he linked this to the ever-present
danger of conscription it was in fact an expression of
straightforward national concern. There was great unity
of purpose therefore between the leaders of Sinn Fein and
the leaders of the labour movement in the matter of self-
determination. Consequently when the national executive
announced to the special congress in November that they
had decided to recommend the withdrawal from this election
of all labour candidates, the decision was greeted with
applause.[29] They did so in the hope that 'the democratic
demand for self-determination to which the Irish Labour
Party and its candidates give their unqualified adherence,
will thereby obtain the freest chance of expression at the
polls.'[30] Johnson was the one who presented the recommendation to the Congress; he himself had considerable reserve
about Sinn Fein, but it no doubt seemed wiser to him and
to the other traditional trade union representatives to
avoid involvement in that general election, since there
was a serious danger of becoming identified explicitly with
Sinn Fein in view of the mood of the time. By not con-
testing the election, Sinn Fein would have a clear run,
while at the same time, the wider political character of
the Labour Party, its relevance to north as well as south
could be preserved, at least in theory.[31]

It was for these reasons then that Congress at the very
highest peak of its political consciousness decided to
cast its seed aside. But the act intensified its sense of
political mission. Johnson presented their decision as
one of mature political self-sacrifice (as indeed in many
ways it was) sacrificing party in the interests of nation;
but as a result 'their business would be to go ahead with
redoubled energy with the organisation of the Irish Labour
Movement in the political field'[32] particularly in local
elections of all kinds. Congress, in the light of its new

constitution and its new political role, changed its title
from the Irish Trade Union Congress and Labour Party to
the Irish Labour Party and Trade Union Congress. Thus was
the special syndicalist character given to the Irish
labour movement, where Labour politicians tended to be
trade unionists rather than socialists, where status rather
than policy was their major characteristic, and where, to
make matters more complex still, they secured election to
parliament and to other public bodies, neither on the
basis of their trade union activity nor on the basis of
their political philosophy, but because of a largely
personal following in their constituencies.[33] This character
of the Irish labour movement remained after 1930, when the
Labour Party and the trade union congress divided, and
indeed has continued to a substantial extent to the present
time. That it should do so was made easier by the fact that
the other two parties, Fianna Fail and Fine Gael, in the
years between, were distinguished not on philosophical
grounds but rather on the posture taken up during the
rather appalling civil strife in 1922-23. Irish political
parties draw their strength from historical and social
phenomena, making a discussion of left and right a rather
theoretical business at the best of times. It seems extraordinary that it should be so, despite the great fervour of
these times, despite the powerful socialist and syndicalist
convictions of the leaders like O'Brien who were to remain
dominant for a further thirty years, and despite the considerable political leadership which Johnson offered in
parliament in the twenties, when Labour, in the absence of
de Valera's party, were the party of opposition. On the
other hand, the Irish dilemma faded from the world scene
and became a domestic wrangle, ridden with shabby
personality conflicts; economic dreariness blunted the
feeling of high endeavour, and the aftermath of the vast
chiliasm of the time was an empty and purposeless sense
of irritation throughout the whole of society. Perhaps
this was the reason why persons and not policies were to
become the feature of the Irish political scene.

But as yet Ireland was gripped by great events. The
election of December 1918 was the beginning of the great
political cleavage. An overwhelming 73 Sinn Fein candidates
were returned, as against the Unionist 26. The old
parliamentary party returned only **six, four by agreement**
with Sinn Fein. In these circumstances, the Sinn Fein
representatives, commanding the overwhelming majority of
Irish representatives, called a conference in Dublin in
January 1919 inviting the Unionists and Nationalist
members as well, who naturally enough did not attend. This
conference constituted itself the Irish Parliament, the
first Dail, and its first act was to ratify the declaration
of the Republic. It sent a message to the free nations of
the world, seeking independent representation at the Peace
Conference, and it adopted a democratic programme that was
markedly socialist in character, which, some have claimed
subsequently, was not taken very seriously by the majority
of those at the meeting. The Dail established an elementary
form of government, and its overwhelming success in the
local elections of March 1919 confirmed its hegemony in all
areas except the north which remained either Unionist or
Nationalist. They went on to establish law courts, and
even to raise a loan. The Westminster government vacillated
between conciliation and repression, and later in 1919, as
guerilla warfare began to develop, they introduced an armed
auxiliary force, the Black and Tans. In September 1919
Dail Eireann was suppressed.

These were quite extraordinary times. Although Ireland
and Britain were locked in this conflict, never had
Ireland benefited more fruitfully from its trading agreements.
'The first world war', says Cullen,[34] 'and especially the
two years after it, were the most hectic period of
agricultural prosperity in Ireland's history, surpassing
even the best years of the Napoleonic wars.' And

businessmen, whose stocks continuously gained value as prices
leaped up, also profited from the absence of competition
from the British war economy. The boom collapsed in
1920 but there was still a marked tendency towards affluent
living right into the mid-twenties. In the midst of this
rather ostentatious affluence of farmer and businessman,
however, the wage earner, whether urban or rural, did
badly; wages inevitably lagged behind rising prices,
emigration was no longer a ready solution and in the rural
areas in particular unemployment grew. Cullen remarks:
'Underemployed young men who in peacetime might have
emigrated supplied the rural recruits for the Irish
Republican Army in 1918 and later. Social disaffection
was rife among the rural labourers in several parts of
Ireland in the early 1920s.'[35]

There was also industrial unrest throughout the country,
a great deal of it due to the falling value of wages but
taking from time to time a political flavour as in the case
of the strike in local government in Limerick against the
enforcement of military permits. Congress responded by a
special delegate conference on February 8 1919, seeking not
only wage increases and a minimum wage, but, in order to
combat unemployment, a reduction in hours of work as well; and
Tom Cassidy, remarking on this unrest in his presidential
address to the annual conference of Congress in August 1919,
declared that until profiteering in all things was abolished
there could be no industrial peace. Economic inequities
therefore added their own special nastiness to the chiliastic
politics of the time.

When we turn to Belfast we find that the war had brought
sectarian peace. There was a great demand for labour, so
much so that 'no exception was taken to the indiscriminate
employment by shipbuilders and linen merchants of Catholics
and Protestants alike.'[36] Probably for the same reason,
the socialism, indeed the syndicalism, that appeared to fire
many in the south, had little impact in the north, where,
for the moment, politics appeared to be inert and where
instead we see the straightforward industrial action of shipyard workers, who impatiently snapped into a widespread

strike on the question of hours of work in February 1919
just at the time when the Congress was debating the question
in Dublin. At this time there were good working relations
between the protestants and catholics, and although the
majority of the strikers were protestant, the chairman of
the strike committee was a catholic.[37] This was all to
collapse the following year in the sectarian bitterness
and rioting that followed Carson's inflammatory speech
of July 12 1920. It is doubtful if it could have survived
in any event the return from the war of the thousands
who had enlisted.

The Congress regarded their participation at the International Labour and Socialist Conference at Berne in early
1919 as a considerable achievement, where, as the Irish
Labour Party, they were seated as a separate unit. The
British Labour Party had rather sourly come to terms with
these nationalist aspirations the year before when Henderson
wrote to the Irish congress 'and we have also been aware of
your desire to run your own Labour Party independent of
everything British, as was very frankly stated when I
was in conference with your representatives four years ago.'[38]
But the separate representation at Berne was seen as having
far greater significance in view of the Dail's efforts to
gain international recognition. The Congress called a
mass meeting in the Mansion House in Dublin on April 7 1919,
to which the delegates reported. They declared for a League
of Nations which should be a free society of peoples,'not a
League of rulers, governments or cabinets but a Society
fully and directly representative of the Parliaments and
the Sovereign peoples, an association of the working masses
of all nations organised in self-governing republics.'[39]
And they reported as well that 'one definite and valuable
result of these activities is that Ireland as a national
unit and the Irish Labour Movement as distinct and separate
from other national and Labour movements, have been
recognised and accepted by the Labour and Socialist parties
of the whole world.'[40]

One of the recommendations of the Berne International
Congress was that the May day celebrations should be
associated with the demand for a democratic league of
peoples based upon national self-determination; and the
Executive decided to call for a general stoppage of work on
that day, both to demonstrate solidarity and also to reaffirm
the principle of self-determination. They were immensely
pleased with the result. The whole country, with the exception of Belfast, kept holiday, and outside Dublin, where
public meetings and processions had been prohibited, there
were many enthusiastic demonstrations and resolutions adopted
in favour of socialism, self-determination and a league of
free peoples. There were a few cases of 'victimisation' as
a result of the stoppage of work; and the Congress report
on the occasion concluded sadly: 'The spirit of tyranny
is still active in the land, and it is not monopolised by
an alien government.'[41]

The annual Congress in Drogheda in early August 1919 was
very conscious of the greatness of the time, and the greatness
of its own role, in a way which it would not experience
again. The bitterness of the conflict with Britain had
not fully developed, the shattering misery of the civil war
and the sectarian terror in the north were yet to come.
'Labour in Ireland', they reported,[42] 'has helped to give
the finishing blow to the menace of conscription, assisted
in demonstrating to the world the electoral demand of the
majority of the people to choose and form their government
after their own will, taken to itself a new, noble and
closely knit political, industrial and social constitution
designed to be the foundation upon which the organisation
of the working class shall march to its goal, carried the
demands of the people and proletariat of Ireland into the
councils of the International and won for those demands
the fullest and most complete recognition from every
Labour and Socialist movement in Europe, America and the
British Dominion, demonstrated its faith and its purpose as
never before in the great general strike on Labour Day,

held its own and more than its own against militarism
and capitalism at home and proven itself a formidable
force both in national and international affairs in the
political and social fields.' They recognised that these
might appear small beside the great political events of the
time, 'but', they continued proudly, 'to the workers and
people of Ireland they are big in their own way and they
do not prevent a right appreciation of the greater world
events. In those world events, Labour in Ireland has not
been a silent spectator but an active and not ineffective
agent within its own sphere'. There was a sort of breathless
promise about the time, after the devastation of the war
and the misery of the past. W.P. Ryan writing at the time
caught the mood well: 'Indeed the end of the struggle
is mental and spiritual, though it may not seem so yet.
The breaking of the chains, the unloading of the degrading
burdens that we know, will inevitably lead to the
resurrection and the flowering of the workers' deeper
natures, now blunted or buried. Then they may be artists
and creators.'[43] And in the peroration to his book:[44]
'We bring our record to a close at a time when inner and
outer kingdoms and orders of the world, after violent and
tragic agitation and upheaval, must be reshaped and remade.
How far there may be a new rule and vision, and how far a
mere re-shuffling of old tyranny, will be duly revealed.
Irish Labour, after a shattering and inhuman history, is
being called to come forth and work with mind and soul as
well as body. It is responding to the call, though a
goodly element of it yet is like a tired sleeper, suddenly
awakened, whose frame is still weary, whose mind is confused,
whose spirit is scarcely conscious: it does not seem
entirely sure for the moment that the Commonwealth may not
be a dream of the departing night rather than a fact of the
rising day. All the happier will be the discovery, with
growing consciousness and confidence, with experience of
scientific organisation inspired by an ideal, with training
in cooperation both social and mental, that Life to those who
will it can be allied with Beauty, and Work with Wonder.'

The 1919 Congress was attended by 220 delegates, somewhat less than the year before but still twice the number that attended in 1917. There was however no delegate with an English address and few enough from Belfast and Derry. The number of delegates from amalgamated unions had fallen substantially when compared with the previous year, the number of delegates from Irish-based unions had increased substantially, the Irish Transport sending an unprecedented 68 delegates. Furthermore there were now thirty trades councils represented where before there was only a handful, and these clearly were fostered by the high national sentiment of the time. This then was the Congress that fell to considering the major restructuring of the trade union movement.

It was the first substantial deeply-worked attempt at trade union reform, transcending the ideas of the previous conferences while at the same time attempting to meet the difficulties of the amalgamated unions. A memorandum was prepared for the conference by a subcommittee consisting of Johnson, O'Brien and O'Lehane of the Irish Drapers' Assistants Association; it went to the conference from the subcommittee, not from the national executive, and it was clearly drafted by Johnson, and to a great extent it was his answer to the drive for syndicalism, in particular the drive for a specifically Irish OBU, while taking account of the pluralism of the amalgamated unions, the posture of the trade unionists in the north, and of his own aversion to highly-centralised bureaucratic control. The memorandum, a motion from O'Lehane of the Irish Drapers and the discussion that followed are remarkable in that they raise very many of the problems regarding restructuring that were to trouble the trade union movement up to the present time.

The memorandum[45] began by recognising that there were nearly three-quarters of a million adult wage earners in Ireland, of whom approximately a quarter of a million were organised, but even here there were about seventy societies, some small and weak, with 'no good reason for their continued existence as separate organisations'. The objects

were then stated: the defence of what was won, the improving
of living standards, the influencing of public authorities,
and 'eventually taking over control of industry by the
organised working class.' Clarkson saw this as bringing
the syndicalist ideal concretely before the delegates [46]
but the position was more complex than that. The syndicalist
ideal derived its fervour, for many members, from the heady
nationalism of the time and was ultimately inconsistent
with both British-based unions and with northern Unionist
sympathies, and yet it carried the considerable authority
of the socialist international. This was the dilemma which
the memorandum attempted to overcome.

The memorandum therefore went on to recognise as an ultimate
objective 'a single all-inclusive Irish Workers Union - one
Union for all workers - one authority to be finally
responsible for financing and controlling all the larger
movements'. But throughout what followed there was much
insistence on the long-term nature of this objective. At
the outset as well there was a stand against excessive
centrality in administration: 'a considerable amount of
autonomy, local in a regional sense and sectional in an
industrial sense, is desirable, subject only to the central
control in matters which directly affect the whole', and
when the memorandum came later to the question of strike pay,
it was explicit in rejecting the idea of a central fund for
this purpose, insisting thereby that industrial action should
primarily be a matter for the unions themselves.

However, in the ideal state, it contemplated a highly
corporate solution, all workers being organised in industrial
sections, these sections being organised locally and also
nationally, the sections being composed of all workers
in that industry. The trades councils, or councils of
industrial sections, would provide the labour centre locally,
while the various national industrial sections would form
a national governing body, the OBU. The aim then was to
convert all horizontally organised, locally organised and
general unions into a number of large industry-based unions
since this in fact is what the industrial sections would

initially be. The memorandum went on to outline the broad
industrial sectors for the purposes of the reorganisation,
and in view of its later importance we set it out here.
It is obvious that the number of members one could command
in any industrial section and one's future prospects in
membership growth were in practice very influential factors
for the trade unions and the men who served them professionally:

1. Agriculture, Land, Quarries, Roads and Fisheries:
    General Agriculture, Dairying, and Cattle, Road Workers,
    Quarrymen and Fishermen.

2. Transport and Communications:
    Docks, Railway Services, Shipping and Carting, Motor
    Traction, Air Service.

3. Building and Construction:
    Navvying, Structure Workers, and Furnishing.

4. Food Supplies - Preparatory Processes:
    Flour Mills, Bakeries, Butchers, Pork Butchers,
    Confectionery Trades, Breweries and Distilleries.

5. Distributive Trades (including Catering and Personal Services):
    Shop Workers, Drapery Trades, Ironmongery Trades,
    Grocery Trades, Warehousing and Porters, Clerical
    Staffs, Hotel Workers, Hairdressers.

6. Engineering and Metal-Working Trades (including Ship-Building):

7. Clothing and Textiles:
    Spinners and Weavers, Cotton, Woollen and Flax, Tailors
    and Dressmakers, "Making-up" Trades, Cotton and Linen
    Goods, Bootmakers, Leather Workers.

8. Printing, Paper and Allied Trades:
    Printing Trades, Paper Trades, Bookbinding etc.

9. Public Services - Municipal and State:
    Post Office, Law Officers, Education, Excise and
    Customs, Land etc.

10. Miscellaneous.

Much of this would have favoured the Irish Transport. As
we have seen, it had already a substantial membership in
agriculture, and in the last three years membership had
leapt up in a number of the other categories, the first
industrial section accounting for a half of the 100,000
odd members.[47]

But all this was described as a rough outline of an organisation
to be aimed at, and it was recognised that amalgamation would
be a slow and doubtful process. And so the memorandum, frankly
conscious of the fact that nearly half the total organised
workers were enrolled in four or five general workers unions,
looked to those unions first,[48] urging that they create
industrial sections within themselves; and then in each
town or district, industrial committees or workers industrial
councils would be formed, made up of representatives from
the industrial sections of the general unions, and from the
craft unions in the industries concerned. These would be
linked nationally by means of national industrial councils
for each industry. This was a policy of gradualism; it
was also a policy of grassroots initiative, powerfully
fostered but essentially springing from the unions themselves.
The advantage was that it could be put into operation by any
single industrial group without waiting on general acceptance,
and (significantly, as we shall see in a moment) the distributive trade was mentioned as a case in point. But the
fostering of such initiative was indeed intended to be substantial. On current membership it was recommended that
subscriptions be collected for the purpose of voting £3,000
immediately to its administration, and either £500 or £1,000
a week thereafter (i.e. either a ½d or 1d per member).
However, the absence of any specific resolution on money
tended to make the whole thing a little hollow, although
we must recognise the diffidence in proposing radically new
ideas which always characterised the Congress, a tentativeness
which took the form of evolving discussions from conference
to conference on many important matters.

The standing orders committee had recommended that the resolution from the Irish Drapers' Assistants' Association should be taken with this report, which would imply that the two were at least consistent with one another. In fact this was not the case, although O'Lehane of the Drapers was one of the sub-committee responsible for the report. The substance of his resolution lay in the powers of the national executive '(which) should be very considerably increased so as to secure generally more co-ordinated effort in regard to Industrial and Political action.'[49] He wished to have a scheme worked out and a special conference called to adopt it. The nub of the whole thing however appeared in an extension of the resolution which made suggestions on the manner in which the national executive should be strengthened. The idea quite simply was that the national executive of Congress should have control of the strike funds, and that no strike could take place without its sanction. Furthermore, the national executive would have charge of all political and other propaganda. He contemplated a differently constituted executive, three and the secretary being resident in Dublin, three in Belfast and two in Cork. The arguments O'Lehane used to support his motion were ones which are still familiar today, the inequity of being involved in another's dispute without consultation; and on the other hand, the weakness of the trade union response when there was no concerted action. But the idea of a centralised strike fund, the idea of a centralised bureaucracy, indeed the idea of instant Irish OBU was foreign to the whole spirit of the sub-committee's report, despite O'Lehane's association with it.

Yet Johnson chose to disguise the conflict, making a little fun of ambitious unions which added 'allied trades' to their titles and set out to recruit all sorts of workers, and urging that they should keep larger and better planned possibilities in view. He recognised the weakness of leaving with the unions themselves the operation of strike funds, but he claimed that they could go a long way without changing the present arrangement. In any event - and this

was the key to his dilemma - many unions would be very
reluctant to agree to such a procedure, and apart from that
'they knew that the financial control of some unions was
across the water.'[50]   But he suggested that O'Lehane's
motion should be adopted as a guide. As far as the
suggestions in the resolution went, this was quite
appropriate, but O'Lehane had sought a decision quite
explicitly on the holding of a special congress on the
topic, a proposal very much at variance with the spirit
of gradualism in Johnson's memorandum. In the event no
such congress was held, although a great deal of other
reorganisation took place.

In the debate that followed there were three distinct
positions, but all seemed to accept the ultimate wisdom
of the OBU. Firstly there were the Irish National Painters,
who wanted 'a meeting of all purely Irish Trades Union
delegates to take into consideration the forming of a
purely Irish Confederation.'[51]   The crudeness of the view
caused some amusement and was not taken seriously in that
form. Secondly there was the view expressed by Foran of
the Irish Transport and by a large number of others who
recognised current inter-union inadequacies, a commitment
to OBU but a concern at the same time with the importance
of gradualism: the movement must come from the grass
roots, people were as yet reluctant, and whatever was done
should be done gradually. Thirdly there was the position
of the amalgamated unions, somewhat unsure of themselves,
seeking a footing in these confused jingoistic times, unable to deny the national impulse, unable to deny the
impulse to syndicalism which the OBU expressed, and yet
profoundly anxious to retain the essentially British and
kingdom-wide character of their organisations. Of course
the engineering unions were concerned about the north where
they had 6,500 of their 9,000 members, but the NUR on the
other hand, claiming a nationalist performance second to
none, took the same view. They pointed to the support
given by members of amalgamated unions during the anti-
conscription campaign and on Labour Day. What was needed was

more development along the lines already emerging, that is
more amalgamation such as those among engineering unions
and among the railway unions for example, allied with a
vigorous campaign for membership which had resulted already
in the astonishing performance of the Irish Transport.
(The NUR had itself grown very rapidly from 1916 onwards,
but with a powerful separatist feeling in its branches,
a feeling which was recognised in its own Irish publication
New Way.) To the amalgamated unions, then, the proposal
was inopportune, tending to further disruption in that it
would raise the possibility of a separate organisation
for amalgamated unions. Despite their opposition, the
resolution was adopted by 131 votes to 50.

We can see in the debate as well the early signs of the
conflict between the Irish Transport and those unions that
were to form the Amalgamated Transport and General Workers
Union in 1922, a conflict that was to persist into the
forties. The Irish Transport, in furtherance of a dispute,
had tied up the farmers in Co. Meath, but the cattle had
been driven to Belfast and the dockers there had not
helped. It was through the medium of the National Union of
Dock Labourers that the Amalgamated Transport was later
established in Ireland, and about it all still lay the
echoes of the two Liverpool Irishmen, Sexton and Larkin.

O'Lehane pushed busily ahead, particularly in his own
industry, and a sophisticated system of federation was
proposed for the unions engaged in distribution, a
sort of Clapham Junction of an arrangement where the
original unions would continue to operate for domestic
matters, the Federation for more important, and where only
the Federation, and not the unions, could accept new
members. But this never worked; instead the Irish members
of the National Amalgamated Union of Shop Assistants decided to

join with the Drapers' Assistants, a solution much in
keeping with the mood of the time. O'Lehane himself died
very soon after the 1919 congress, and the larger dynamic
role of Congress as an immediate OBU seemed to die as well.
Instead the stirabout of organisational development
continued, characterised by two things, the amalgamation
of like unions and the splintering of the amalgamateds, both
tendencies indeed summarised in the distributive workers'
experience.

Let us take first the more positive aspects of amalgamation
and growth. Clarkson[52] makes considerable play of the
'diminution in the number of trade unions, accompanied by
an increase in the number of trade unionists' from 1919
to 1922 or so, and while the growth in members was indeed
remarkable he exaggerates greatly the significance of the
fall in the number of unions, principally because his base
line is placed in a period of exceptional effervescence not
only in trade unions but in trades councils as well, and the
fall in the number, somewhat less in fact than he states,
was largely a drift back to the norm. Yet considerable
headway was made. Apart from the drapers, there were the
engineering workers, beginning in a splintering from the
great Amalgamated Society of Engineers. The Irish Engineering,
Shipbuilding and Foundry Trades Union, which had emerged by
1920, absorbed a number of the small Irish unions, and by
1921 had increased its membership from 1400 to 4,500.[53]
There was, as we have already seen, a considerable development
in the railways although the expansion of the National Union
of Railwaymen was accompanied by powerful separatist tendencies in the branches. But the great success story was
that of the Irish Transport, claiming in 1920 over 100,000
members in 400 branches, that is to say one half of all
trade union members in the country, north and south.[54]
In view of the small size of Irish unions generally, many
of them being still local and sectional in character, the
Irish Transport was doubly dominant in Irish affairs,
sending 102 delegates to the annual conferences of
Congress both in 1921 and 1922, that is almost one

half of the total number of delegates attending. In 1920-21,
the Irish Transport, for example, absorbed the Irish
Agricultural and General Workers Union, the Cork Brewery
Workers and the Tipperary Workingmen's Union.

But there was splintering as well, inevitably under the
nationalist impulse of the time. As Judge[55] remarks:
'a number of local branches, primarily in Dublin, broke away
from English societies and set up autonomous Irish unions.
They began to organise not only in the same industries but
in opposition to the English societies on a strictly nationalistic basis.' As early as 1917 the Irish National Union
of Vintners, Grocers and Allied Trades Assistants was founded,
partly in a breakaway from the National Amalgamated Union of
Shop Assistants, and the following year the sheetmetal workers
broke away from the amalgamated union to form the National
Union of Sheetmetal Makers and Gas Meter Makers. In 1920
the Irish Electrical Industrial Union sprang also from the
amalgamated engineering society, and the Cork Corporation,
under its influence, and the influence of the time, decided
that all their future engineering employees should join it.
A troubled trade union movement eventually got the decision
rescinded.[56] The Irish Engineering and Foundry Union was
also formed by breakaway from the amalgamated society and in
1921 the Irish National Union of Woodworkers splintered from
the Amalgamated Society of Woodworkers. The Irish Bookbinders
broke away from the amalgamated union in 1920; in 1922 were
formed, also by breakaways, the Irish National League of
the Blind and the Dublin and District Electrotypers; and in
1923 the Electrical Trade Union (Ireland). Inevitably of
course separate civil service unions and associations were
created on the establishment of the Free State, with,
however, their names and scope of activity largely unchanged.
It was a restless and difficult time. A row in the Dublin
Trade Union Council, which had been developing since 1919,
came to a head, when O'Brien and the Irish Transport pulled
out in 1921 and formed the rival Dublin Workers Council.

But there was much in this nationalist development which was
seen by all sides to be unhealthy. 'We have seen and heard
a lot about mushroom unions that have sprung up', said
J.T. O'Farrell[57] of the Railway Clerks at the 1922 Congress
in Dublin. 'We have seen the manner in which they have
bifurcated and split themselves up after they seceded from
the amalgamated unions. We talk a lot about internationalism,
and we practice parochialism.' He was speaking against a
motion from the Limerick trades council that all Irish
workers should be catered for by Irish unions, and the debate
took place not only against a background of industrial unrest but in the fearful opening months of the civil war
where the growing militarism which had been so vigorously
condemned by Congress eventually burst into open conflict.
'It is a green resolution from green people', said O'Farrell,
and more bitterly: 'If we are to believe one tenth of
what we heard within the last few days about the tyrannies of
Irishmen against Irishmen, one would imagine it would be
better to be in an amalgamated union than an Irish union.
The Limerick Trades Council had complained that the amalgamated unions were listening to two voices, and this was
hotly denied by O'Farrell: 'It is not a fact that the
members of the amalgamated unions are listening to two voices.
The amalgamated unions do not seek representation in the
British Trade Union Congress. No body or no set of bodies
in this Congress carries out the dictates of Congress better
than the amalgamated bodies. They have proved themselves
as good trade unionists as any body in the Congress, and
we are not going to start an era of freedom by imposing conscription or coercion on any workers affiliated to this
assembly.' Tom Foran of the Irish Transport was not impressed by the arguments in favour of the amalgamated unions,
as one might expect, but clearly as a one-union man he had
little time for a motion which contemplated a multiplicity
of Irish unions and the great weakness that to him it implied.
He consequently asked that the motion should be withdrawn,
and all support faded.[58] The fact of course was that there
were far more terrible things to trouble the delegates'
minds at this Congress of 1922. Let us glance briefly then
at the events which had taken place in the upheaval of the
last two or three years.

In September 1919, as we have seen, Dail Eireann was
suppressed as a dangerous association, and gradually there
developed throughout the country, with the exception of the
north, a guerilla warfare by the Irish Republican Army,
to which the British government responded with a special
auxiliary force, the Black and Tans. The IRA's success
depended to a considerable extent on a sympathetic population, but since this was not the case generally in the
north, the IRA could do little more than mount an occasional
attack on a police or military barracks. The result however
was that in Ulster a special armed constabulary was
established in November 1920, who in the event were almost
all protestants. In practice too the British government
began to recognise the six northern counties as a separate
administrative unit, deciding in September 1920 to set up
two regional governments, a move which was by now too little
and too late for the south, but which culminated in the
creation of the parliament of Northern Ireland in May
of the following year, and set the course of development
inevitably towards partition.

And what of the Congress? Inevitably a great number of
active trade unionists were also involved in the political
conflict. In the spring of 1920, 100 men were arrested,
and promptly went on hunger strike. The Congress called
an immediate general strike beginning on April 13, and the
Irish members of the amalgamated unions appealed to workers
in Britain for support. In Ireland, outside the Belfast
area, the strike was well supported, and by the evening of
April 14 the British government capitulated, the men were
released and work was immediately resumed. The trade unions
were proud both of their achievement and of their discipline;
not only were essential services exempted during the strike,
but the resumption was also immediate and universal. Of
course there was a good deal of socialist support in Britain
for Ireland's demand for self-determination. In 1920 the
Scottish TUC supported a motion on Irish self-determination
without a dissentient voice. The British Labour Party also
recognised that what would have satisfied Redmond was now no

longer adequate, and in a series of difficult debates
eventually proposed the withdrawal of all armed forces,
the placing of the maintenance of law and order under each
local authority, and the establishing of a constituent
assembly by proportional representation, which would implement whatever constitution was desired by the Irish
people, subject to justice for minorities and British
military and naval security.

But this goodnatured helplessness was sorely tried by the
events in Belfast in that summer of 1920. Belfast had
been essentially a protestant city up to the early part
of the 19th century, when in a reasonably brief period
of fifty years or so, the catholic population increased
from eight per cent of the total to thirty per cent or so.
The Reform Acts intensified the problem by extending the
franchise. Furthermore that catholic population which in
these years had immigrated to Belfast were largely from
rural areas and were markedly different in their language
and their life style from the urban dwellers, a difference
reinforced by their employment in menial work, in domestic
service and in unskilled industrial jobs. From there on,
we see a mounting ebb and flow of tension, reaching a
crisis of unparalleled viciousness in this period from 1920
to 1922, unparalleled that is to say, up to then. In the
decade before this, Belfast saw the signing of the Ulster
covenant, the formation of the Ulster Volunteer Force, the
gunrunning from Larne to Belfast, and the formation of the
provisional government under Carson's chairmanship. At the
celebrations of July 12, 1920, Carson, conscious of the
threat to the ancient constitution, violently attacked Sinn
Fein, which he saw working through all sorts of organisations,
in particular the church and the labour movement. Clarkson[59]
attributes much of what followed to the inflammatory
character of this address, although it is much more likely
to have been a reaction to the many catholics employed
during the war in the shipyards, compounded by a traditional
sectarian bitterness. Yet the specific origin of the
violence can be traced to the high feelings of that July 12

1920, and James Sexton[60] of the dockworkers, now a member
of parliament, could say passionately on July 26, within a
week of the outbreak of the pogrom: 'Only this afternoon
I had messages from Belfast to say that the situation
there is getting more intense every hour and the spirit that
has been raised by these incidents on 12th July is alone
responsible for the discussion (sic) and division amongst
the members of my own organisation. I now take the
opportunity of denouncing any attempt on the part of anyone inside or outside this House of raising that hatred
that exists between the two people, members of the one union
with different opinions...'Catholic workers were violently
expelled from the shipyards on July 21st, 'the gates were
smashed down with sledges, the vests and shirts of those
at work torn open to see were the men wearing any Catholic
emblems.'[61] The frightfulness spread rapidly to the docks
(with the exception of the deep sea docks, where the workers,
exclusively catholic, were members of the Irish Transport)
and to other employments, reaching the railways by September.
The NUR were vigorous in their condemnation and expressed
'surprise and disgust that any employer of labour should be
influenced by such methods.'[62] They demanded the immediate
reinstatement of the men with full pay for time lost.

The union which made the most considerable stand in all
this was, however, the Amalgamated Society of Carpenters and
Joiners, whose executive member for Ireland was a catholic
and who was himself driven from the shipyards in September.
The Carpenters' meeting, when the EC representatives visited
Belfast in August, was banned by Major General Bainbridge,
and on September 18 they decided on strike action to
begin on September 25, and to exclude from union membership
all those who remained at work after that date.[63] The
action was directed against the employers, because although
they claimed that they did not discriminate, the
Carpenters Society could say: 'We are convinced that the
Belfast employers could, if they so desired, have prevented
this disgraceful and vindictive boycott of sections of their
workmen'[64] and the largest shipyard firm, while announcing
that they had abolished the religious test, nonetheless

required that those seeking jobs at their yard must sign
the declaration compiled by the vigilance committee.[65]
But the union was bitter at the lack of support from other
unions; and indeed the British TUC, while its heart was
in the right place, found the whole situation distasteful,
intractable and bewildering. The Portsmouth conference in
September 1920 decided to call together the representatives
of the unions concerned, and a subcommittee of the Parliamentary
Committee visited Belfast in December. They reported
despairingly that the history and traditions of the people
in Ireland in relation to political and religious questions
found no parallel in this country. 'Moreover in any consideration of the situation in Belfast due regard must be
paid to the deplorable and chaotic condition of affairs in
Ireland at the present time.'[66]   In fact, if anything, the
uncompromising position taken up by the Carpenters Union was
seen as a major difficulty in the short term at least.
However the union held on, the tide swinging somewhat its
way because of a wage dispute that began to develop in this
time of economic difficulties but ultimately the problem
was not resolved for two years, the union reporting finally
that its bedrock principle had been maintained.[67]

In the meantime Belfast passed through a period of great
sectarian conflict. Clarkson described it as a period of
murder and arson, unparalleled in intensity and brutality
anywhere else in Ireland.[68] From the summer of 1920,
the rest of the south attempted a boycott of Belfast goods
and things got steadily worse. About this time as well,
there was a sharp downturn in the economy, particularly
in the south where the boom suddenly collapsed. In the
north this gave the sectarian question, which was so often
a matter of jobs and housing, a special urgency. As we have
seen, the Parliament of Northern Ireland came into being
in May 1921, and in view of the violence of the time, the
proportional representation system had little spreading
effect, the Unionists getting an unprecedented 40 seats,
while the IRA and the Nationalists returned only twelve,

and in any event refused to sit.   There quickly followed
the Special Powers Act, the establishment of the Royal
Ulster Constabulary and the abolition of proportional
representation in local elections, an essential move if
the Unionists were to regain control of Londonderry, Tyrone
and Fermanagh, which had opted to join the Irish Free State.
The newly-established Free State government agreed to call
off the Belfast boycott, and the Ulster government ruthlessly
put an end to the rioting in Belfast in the summer of 1922.
There was grievous suffering during the period.   Part of
the objective appears to have been to drive the catholics
into the Falls Road ghetto;   many houses were burnt therefore, and their occupants driven out, and the total number
of deaths was 544, of which 232 took place in 1922.[69]

In September 1920, while the NUR were engaging in a condemnation of sectarian discrimination, they were confronted
in all the areas outside Belfast with a strike of their
members against the carriage of munitions of war.   The
NUR refused point blank to support the Irish membership,
even though the TUC was sympathetic and the Irish Congress
gave overwhelming support.   But the war in the south was
intensifying, Cork city was set aflame, and the strike in
the railways was all the more alarming since it threatened
food supplies at this difficult time.   In these circumstances
the Irish Congress recommended settlement (which the Great
Northern Railway did nothing to help) and the matter was
resolved in early 1921.

Eventually a truce was effected in July 1921 between the
IRA and the British Army, and after protracted discussion
the fateful Anglo-Irish treaty was concluded in December
which conferred dominion status on the whole country, but
permitted the Northern Ireland parliament to opt out, which
of course they did.   It now remained for the Dail to
ratify what had been done.   In the meantime Congress had
become profoundly concerned at the level of unemployment
which they estimated to be 130,000[70] and at the widespread
hardship of the time.   They sought a meeting directly with

Dail Eireann and were received by the whole parliament on
January 10 1922, the very morning on which Arthur Griffith
had formed a new government. On the same day they
issued a manifesto to the workers of Ireland, asking them
to turn now to the struggle against capitalism. 'Henceforth
your fight shall be against conditions which make your
lives a perpetual struggle against sordid poverty, dirt and
ignorance; a fight against the soul-destroying grind of
wage slavery.'[71] The manifesto is full of a flabby rhetoric
directed principally against employers, much in contrast
to the political statements issued in the months that
followed. 'Royalist sycophants when kings were in the
ascendant, we now discover them seeking favours of the
Republic. Upholders of the old regime when it paid, they
are now suspiciously eager to make their peace with the new.
Always the enemies of the people's cause, they now claim
special favours from the people when their own champion
has retired from the fight.' It is probable that the
Labour Party and the trade unions were making a bid to
direct the intense feelings, which the Treaty was giving
rise to, into more manageable channels. They were insistent that they had not been consulted one way or the other
about the Treaty. Certainly the country was in a strange
and dangerous mood. Kevin O'Higgins later in the year[72]
estimated that in the opposition to the government there was
twenty per cent idealism, twenty per cent crime, 'and
between these two 20 per cents, there flows 60 per cent
of sheer futility that is neither one thing nor the other
but that will go on until some very definite reason is put
up to it why it should not go on.' Not only was there
growing militarism and violence, to which we shall refer in
a moment, but the headiness of the period resulted in a
sudden epidemic of soviets and workers councils which took
over both industrial and agricultural undertakings; they
were suppressed by the Provisional Government but they
embarrassed the trade union movement greatly, particularly
the Irish Transport which was sued for damages by irate
employers.[73]

Later in January 1922 Dail Eireann ratified the treaty by
64 votes to 57; but it was clear that the opponents of the
treaty would not accept it without at the very least a
further reference to the people. Over the Christmas
period of 1921 the Congress had become involved as well
in the complicated and rather grotesque wrangling about
formulae in which they tried to bring the two sides
together, and failed. Immediately after the Dail decision
to ratify the treaty, there was a split in the ranks of
the army, and a new army executive called for the allegiance
of all Republican volunteers. It seemed clear that an
election must soon take place, and in February a special
conference of Congress in Dublin decided overwhelmingly
to contest it. The election however was delayed, and in
the meantime arrests and acts of violence began to grow
in number throughout the country, under the alleged authority
of one force or the other. There was also what Congress[74]
described as mean and venomous propaganda, and 'the poverty,
unemployment and suffering which are thrust upon the civil
population by alleged military necessity.' In these
circumstances Congress issued a statement to the Dublin
newspapers on April 11   protesting against the rule of the
gun and the bomb 'when handled by Irish armies and irresponsible individuals.'[75] 'We deplore the growth of the idea
that the Army may be law unto itself; that the possession
of arms gives authority which may be exercised regardless
of the civil power. This criticism is not directed only
against one section of the Army - both forces have sometimes
shown that they have learned lessons in arrogance from
the British occupation.' A peace conference had been
arranged by the Archbishop of Dublin and the Congress urged
that the Army Executive in the Four Courts, that is the
Republican group, should be involved, but Collins and
Griffith would have none of it. However the Congress were
invited to send representatives to the conference with
proposals which might result in a settlement. The Dail
had been reconvened for April 25   and the Congress, in order
to strengthen their voice against the growth of militarist
power, decided on a general strike on the day before,
Monday April 24   from 6 in the morning until 9 at night,

and to this end they issued a manifesto on April 20
'It is important that the workers of Ireland whose spokesmen we are should have an opportunity to give expression
in an emphatic manner to their will in these matters so
vitally affecting their lives and liberties.'[76] They once
again condemned the rule of the gun, that military men could
commit acts of violence against civilians and be immune
from prosecution and punishment, and in this they claimed
that they had ample evidence that men in both forces were
guilty of many instances of inexcusable aggression;[77] and
they continued: 'The country demands of the Dail that it
should assert its authority and accept the responsibilities
of government, or confess its impotence and make way for
the people.'

The general strike on April 24 was apparently very successful.
According to the report to the August annual conference
of Congress, 'the call for a general strike was received
joyously and responded to universally. Immense demonstrations
were held in all the large towns and cities, and the people
clearly expressed their antipathy to being governed by men
who rule by the authority of the rifle and revolver.'[78]
Unfortunately however militarism continued unabated.

Eventually the general election took place in June. In
the Dail both sides in the treaty dispute decided by a pact
in May to continue as one party and candidates went forward
as panel candidates, the object being to test the
acceptability of the treaty. By reason of this 33 members were
elected unopposed, and a substantial number of persons
in fact had no opportunity of voting; as it was, however,
of the 93 panel candidates elected, 58 were supporters of
the treaty and 35 opponents. Congress would have nothing
to do with this arrangement and insisted on seeing it as
a straightforward election. Of their eighteen candidates
they triumphantly elected 17 and began their career as a
full parliamentary party. But in fact things got worse
and worse. The Four Courts, the headquarters of the Republican
army executive, was bombed on June 28 and the civil war was
on in earnest.

When the Congress met in August in Dublin, it was in this
bitter dangerous atmosphere. The press had been censored,
concealing in particular the restlessness of the people
because of the militarism and the growth in the number of
atrocities. The IRA had threatened to shoot railway workers,
and other workers in the public service, for collaborating
with the government. And over all there was the fear to
speak plainly about what was happening. R.S. Anthony,
a well-known Cork delegate,[79] said: 'In the South of Ireland,
I submit, as far as Cork City is concerned, there is a
tendency to hush everything. Under the present regime
there are people afraid really to speak out what is in the
back of their minds. Well, we are living under a most intolerable
militaristic system in Cork City to-day ... Let it be
Republican or Free State, there is militarism. I have
seen examples of Free State militarism in Dublin, and I
have seen examples of Republican militarism in Cork City,
which would be enough to make any Irishman blush.' Only a
short time before the labour movement in Cork had mounted
a very large demonstration against militarism, which had a
marked effect for at least a couple of weeks, and Anthony
urged that the labour movement should, at a given date,
demonstrate in every city, town, village and hamlet. But
Johnson was opposed to any further general strikes; they
could now have little effect. In the meantime of course
the Dail was not meeting and the Labour deputies threatened
to resign their seats if it did not meet by the end of August.
In the event it met on September 9.

Arthur Griffith died in the same month of August 1922, and
Collins was killed ten days later. Cosgrave succeeded as head
of the government, and eventually hostilities came to an
end in the spring of 1923, leaving scars that would remain
deep and unhealed for many years.

The Labour Party settled down immediately to a helpful and
fruitful opposition under Tom Johnson's leadership. The
draft constitution had been published on the morning of the
June 1922 general election, and the Labour Party looked

for an end to fustian language and sought a fresh and clear
approach, all without much success. In the election of the
following year (August 1923) the Labour Party lost a good
deal of support. Cumann na nGaedheal secured sixty seats,
and the Republicans forty, while Labour who had forty-three
candidates in the field elected only fourteen, two of the
unsuccessful outgoing deputies being William O'Brien of the
Transport Union and Cathal O'Shannon, the two who had
accompanied Johnson to the peace conference with de Valera,
Cathal Brugha, Griffith and Collins in the April of the
year before. Nevertheless, since de Valera and the
Republican party refused to take the oath and therefore
to sit in parliament, the Labour Party, although reduced
in numbers, provided the opposition, and contintued to do
so until 1927 when de Valera entered the Dail.

But in that same year began the squalid, personal, rather
trivial strife that was to characterise much of the
activities of the trade union movement for the next thirty
years. In April 1923 Jim Larkin returned from America
after an absence of nine years or so, but in terms of Irish
trade unionism after an absence of an aeon of time. There
was the foolish business of a 'food ship' which he wanted
to purchase from New York to relieve distress in Belfast,
which the Executive Committee of the Irish Transport
refused to sanction. This was patched up, but by June he
was in conflict with the Executive, and appealed over their
heads to the rank and file.[80] He tried to prevent the
Congress meeting in August 1923, to the point of invoking
the law, and when this failed, mounted protests outside
the Mansion House in Dublin where the Congress was meeting.
The complicated splurge of legal actions between Larkin
and the others in the Transport Union were heard by way
of consolidated actions in February 1924; Larkin failed
and in March was expelled; in July the Workers Union of
Ireland was registered. Larkin earned the undying hatred
of William O'Brien, now dominant in the Transport Union,
and for twenty years - indeed until Congress split in the

forties - Larkin and the Workers Union of Ireland were
excluded from the Irish Congress, essentially because of
O'Brien's opposition.

But if this decade during which Larkin was absent in the
US, this decade of 1914 to 1924, was of lasting and
extensive significance for Ireland, it was no less so
for other countries. The fever of 1914, although gross
and lunatic in modern eyes, had been seen as a destiny in
blood and battle; and Pearse was reflecting a common mood
when he spoke of the old land of Europe being renewed in
the blood of the battlefield. And if there was in these
islands an air of the euphoric about the terrible business
of war, there was an air of the euphoric as well in other
great social matters, in the breathless accomplishment of
nationalism, in the defence of the Ulster constitution and
way of life, and in the distant promise of the marxist
revolution. What followed was bitterness and disillusion
as men tried to find their way back in to a rational society,
accompanied by social unease widespread throughout Europe,
where the splurge of soviets in Ireland was quite a minor
phenomenon compared to the upheavals elsewhere. But the
millenarian feeling of the earlier years seems to have been
intensified rather than diminished by the horror of the war,
giving a special quality to the social movements of the time,
a quality that was heady and radical, and therefore somewhat alarming to conservative institutions such as trade
unions. We find the trade unions in Europe therefore, no
less than the trade unions in Ireland, although deeply stirred
by the Russian revolution, nonetheless preaching gradualism
as they always did, sympathetic to the ideal but hostile to
sudden radical change, as Rosa Luxemburg and the Sparticists
in Berlin found to their cost. And yet there was, during
this period in many parts of Europe, pathetic in view of
the barbarism that was to come, a brightness of youth, a
swiftness of philosophical thought, that increased the
sense of promise. All this was to die.

In Ireland, in view of the civil war, it died very quickly,
and with it died as well something of the idea of democracy,
or at least it was seriously damaged in the claim by violent
men to possess a validity which was anterior to democracy
and which ultimately did not require it. The democratic
form of government was, for much of the twenties, seriously
in question, until in fact de Valera decided to embrace it,
and bring, as a result, political stability to the country.
But the democratic spirit itself was blunted. Although
political forms became secure, there seemed to spread,
from the thirties onwards, a shadow of parochialism over
the south in particular, reflecting the exhaustion of the
unhappy time, when indeed much more terrible things were
happening in Europe - but it was all much in contrast with
the lively separatism of the past which was so attractive
to international socialism, and which Ireland had developed
in the context of the wider European theatre. Gradually the
north, which could not be accommodated in such an extended
parish, sank out of consciousness of the south except as the
basis for a slogan against British injustice, and the north
itself, cautious and suspicious, conscious not of millen-
arianism but only of the ugliness of sectarian conflict,
drew more and more into itself and into its Britishness.

In view of all the upheaval of the period, in view of the
gulf that grew between the Free State and Ulster, it
seemed curious at first sight that the Congress remained
united. Of course Johnson's influence was powerful here;
but the fact was that while some unions, and particularly
the Irish Transport, were significant, the Congress itself
had no great importance, although this does not diminish
the value of its contribution both to social thinking and
to peace. Even as a labour party it rested primarily
on its personalities, not on its policies. There was a
further reason why Congress held together. Even if a
division were logical, nobody had the energy to do much
about it.

While there was some economic recovery in the south in 1924,
the dismal decline continued substantially until 1926, until
indeed the rising level of economic activity abroad began
to have some effect. It was a situation made worse in the
Free State by the government's conviction - deeply held
at the time - that neither special measures to develop
industry nor the undertaking of the cost of the provision
of welfare should interfere with the promotion of agriculture
and as a consequence little was done to improve the appallingly
bad unemployment problem; and the extensive city slums
continued to fester. Emigration was unusually high,
particularly to the United States, which was in a flood of
prosperity. In the spring of 1924 Congress held a special
conference on the protection of Irish industry; and in the
following year a further special conference was held on the
employment conditions in Ardnacrusha where the great
electricity generating station was being built.

Lawlessness had continued right throughout 1923 and 1924
from August 1923 until February 1924 there were over 700
cases of arson and robbery under arms, and it was not until
July 1924 that de Valera, who had been imprisoned in the
August of the previous year, was released. In March the inevitable tension between the military and civil powers worked
its way to a crisis in the army mutiny; two ministers
resigned; generals were dismissed, and the state trembled
again on the brink; but O'Higgins and the civil power
prevailed and bloodshed was avoided.

And in such unsettled circumstances there was a growing
centralisation of power in administration - a growing
bureaucracy - already remarked on fearfully by Congress,
whose anxiety would continue to grow as the decade went by.
The Department of Local Government, newly established in 1924,
grew in power, often because the people themselves seemed
to have lost confidence in their own ability to govern

themselves locally. Not only did they acquiesce in the
elimination in 1924 of rural districts councils, but
when the Minister for Local Government took power in 1925
to inquire into the conduct of local bodies and dissolve
them if necessary, putting commissioners in their place,
the people generally welcomed the system with relief, and
even contrived ways by which the commissioners could be
reappointed. By 1929 Cork council had appointed a manager,
with considerable powers; the system spread rapidly until
it became the settled system of local government. But
it was from this point in 1925 that we see a despairing
rejection of government by popular local democracy.

In the north, the linen industry continued to boom, and would
continue to do so until 1927, collapsing, as the American
economy collapsed, in 1929. But for the shipyards it was a
different story, and in 1923, 18 per cent of the insured
population was unemployed. And indeed the north was more
vulnerable in matters of this kind, since, while in the
Free State over half the occupied population were in agriculture, in the north only one quarter or so were thus
engaged.[81] But on the other hand Belfast had now become a
capital city in its own right and on the Castlereagh Hills,
outside the city, a vasty parkland stretched up to the new
marble and alabaster parliament building which became known
as Stormont. This too confronted the Labour Party people
in the north with a new situation, and Congress at its
meeting in Cork in August 1924 was alarmed to find that the
Belfast Labour Party had declared itself to be the Northern
Ireland Labour Party. Cathal O'Shannon insisted that whatever
the difficulties, there should be no separation of any part
of the movement; but it was a difficult situation. The
Northern Ireland Labour Party was distinct from the British
Labour Party, but it was also independent of the Irish
Labour Party, although as Mortished pointed out 'many,
probably most, of the Unions and individuals affiliated to it,
are affiliated, directly or indirectly, to the Irish Labour
Party.'[82] And of course when Mortished wrote in 1926,

William McMullen of the Irish Transport, **who** was a
member of the national executive of Congress, was also
a member of Stormont parliament. The reality of political
events had ripped apart the idea of a single labour party
for the whole country north and south. It left intact -
as yet - the idea of a single trade union movement, but
only, one suspects, because the syndicalist commitment to a
united movement, politically and industrially, was now
shadow thin, even among those who had spoken most vehemently
in its favour; and we can mark too from this time the
gradual drift away of the political arm from the industrial
arm, so that when in 1930 the movement divided, and Ireland
lost its uniqueness in the socialist world, it was like an
old man dying quietly in his sleep, all the fret somehow
quite irrelevant now.

But there was an even more final breach. In December 1925
the London Agreement concerning the Boundary was concluded
in circumstances which did not give the Irish government
much choice, but which caused Congress to issue a vigorous
manifesto declaring the agreement to be a betrayal of the
indivisible Ireland, and deploring in particular the
abolition of the Council of Ireland. The partition of
Ireland was at last a fact.

The effervescence in the trade unions had now subsided,
both in stirabout of organisation and the level of involvement. This last was very evident from the attendance
at the annual conferences during the mid-twenties and for
a decade or more to come. But if the number of delegates
as a whole fell by a third or so when compared to the period
up to 1923, the number of delegates sent from the Irish
Transport plummeted **from over** 100 in 1922 **to** 42
in 1926 and 22 in 1930.[83] Nevertheless the Irish-based
unions maintained an overwhelming majority on the national
executive of Congress, sometimes as much as three to one,
a lead they were not to lose until the dramatic events of
1944 and the split in the movement.

In this more stable period of decline there was some
concern about the restructuring of the trade union movement and indeed a special conference for the purpose was held in
November 1927, but although wise things were said and
reasserted, somehow there was a certain absentminded air
about it, as busy men stole time from the engrossing
business of politics; an absence of conviction that was
particularly irritating to the powerful housekeeping
instincts of the Women Workers Union. It is to these
matters that we finally turn in this chapter.

On January 7 1926 R.J.P. Mortished, now assistant secretary
to Johnson, who was much engaged in political affairs,
addressed[84] the Statistical and Social Inquiry Society of
Ireland, a very venerable society which still meets in the
solemn Victorian library of the Royal Irish Academy. His
endeavour was to give some picture of the forms of organisation in the trade union movement in Ireland, which he
found difficult to do, not only because of the diversity of
structure that existed, but also because 'it is impossible
to secure, from any source, statistics of membership that
are even remotely satisfactory, and the figures that are
given in this paper must be regarded generally as the
roughest of indications.'[85] This is a point of some
significance, not only for this period but even today where
the figures are more often than not supplied by the unions
themselves, and may, for political or organisational reasons,
be somewhat augmented or diminished.

Mortished's first classification was between Irish-based
and British-based unions, reflecting no doubt the
sensitivity of the time.[86] He numbered 21 unions with
headquarters in Ireland (among which he included a small
local Belfast union) the total membership of which he
calculated at something over 100,000. In contrast, the
unions with headquarters in Great Britain had, in Ireland
as a whole, only 47,000 members, the number of unions
being 17. The Irish Transport was still the largest union by

far in the whole country, with over 60,000 members. In
the case of the Irish-based unions, only five others had
3,000 members or more, the Irish Union of Distributive
Workers and Clerks numbering 9,500, and the three
unions of teachers (whom Mortished, rather ironically
in view of the subsequent strife between them,
lumps together as one) numbering very nearly thirteen
thousand. Of the unions with headquarters in Great Britain,
only four had more than 3,000 members, the National Union
of Railwaymen, then the largest of such unions, numbering
11,700, the Amalgamated Transport and General Workers'
Union with 8,000 members, the Amalgamated Scoiety of Woodworkers 7,400, and the Tailor and Garment Workers Trade
Union 3,700. There were two other railway unions of
significance, the railway clerks with 2,700 and the drivers
and firemen with just over 2,000.

This distinction between Irish-based and British-based
unions absorbed much of Mortished's attention, but to him,
the settled position, the position that had existed for a
very long time, was the steady development of the British-
based unions, either by direct recruitment or by the
absorption of small local societies, and the recent period
of nationalist fervour he saw as already on the wane. 'There
was for a long period a very marked tendency for Irish
workers to become members of cross-Channel unions ... In
recent years, there has been a tendency in the opposite
direction, but except in the case of the Irish Transport
and General Workers' Union, the later tendency has been
much weaker. To some extent it has been inspired by national
feeling and by an entirely mistaken notion that cross-
Channel unions drained money from Ireland. But against
the promptings of national feeling may in many cases be
urged the practical economic advantages of membership of
a Union that caters for the same class of workers in Great
Britain, on the double ground that Irish workers not infrequently migrate across the water and that industrial
conditions in this country are in many cases dominated by
conditions in the more highly developed country. A greater

aggregate membership also offers considerable advantages
in administration and benefits; the attraction of size
has also shown in the case of the Irish Transport and
General Workers' Union, which has absorbed a number of small
local societies.'[87] The answer for many unions appeared to
be to give substantial autonomy to their Irish members,
thus attempting to gain the best of both worlds. 'Some
of these cross-Channel Unions', said Mortished[88] 'devolve
a substantial measure of autonomy upon their Irish membership. The Railway Clerks' Association has an Irish Office,
an Irish Secretary (Senator J.T. O'Farrell), and an Irish
Council. The National Union of Railwaymen also has an Irish
Office and Secretary, and for a short period had an Irish
Council. The Amalgamated Transport and General Workers'
Union, the National Sailors' and Firemen's Union, the
Typographical Association, and the National Amalgamated
Furnishing Trades' Association have Irish Offices and
Secretaries or Organisers. The Amalgamated Engineering
Union has two Organisers, one for the Free State and one
for Northern Ireland. In many cases Ireland is a separate
district for the election of a member or members of the
Union Executive; the Amalgamated Society of Woodworkers,
for example, has a full-time representative of Ireland on
its Executive.' A trade union official, in a situation
such as Mortished found himself, could be forgiven for
seizing an opportunity to promote as much as to inform,
because the fact was that despite this considerable play
on autonomy, there were many in the trade union movement,
as we shall see later, who did not understand it to be so.
Yet Mortished's profile of the trade union movement at the
time is still reasonably accurate today, despite the vast
increase in numbers and the great changes in our society.
The majority of building workers were in cross-Channel unions,
with the exception of some old or local unions; compositors
in the printing trade nad also a Dublin society, and the
Typographical Association organised the rest of the country.
In contrast with the building trade, the Irish-based unions
in the engineering trades were the young organisations,

formed by a break-away from the British unions and by
widening their scope; and there were the two great general
unions, the Irish Transport and the Amalgamated Transport.
Only in the railways do we see a marked difference; in
Mortished's time all the railway workers, with the exception of the railway shops, were in cross-Channel unions.
This is much changed now, and the changing of it was
associated with one of the major constitutional issues
in Irish trade union history. Consequently the efforts
at reorganisation, which were soon to be renewed, have still
a relevance to our time.

Despite the diversity in the political structures of the
country, despite the growing legal complications where
some unions had to deal with three distinct administrations,
Westminster, Stormont and Dublin, Mortished was still
insistent on the unity of the trade union movement. 'Not only
is there no partition of the Trade Unions but Congress after
Congress has declared that there is not going to be.'[89]
And this difficulty of being diverse politically yet united
as a trade union centre was yet another source of tension
within an organisation which was both a trade union and a
political party, and which expected its officers to act for
both at the same time and in the same way. There must
have been much discussion, even at that early date, of the
incongruity of a syndicalist structure in a society so
frankly impervious to the idea, causing Mortished to say:
'The Irish method of combining the two functions in one
organisation with a single Executive has its advantages,
but the experience which has been gained in the last few
years and which could not have been gained previously
owing to the political conditions has shown that there are
serious disadvantages. Henceforth there is likely to be
a tendency towards a more distinct form of organisation
on the political side, though a complete separation is not
to be expected, at any rate for a considerable time to come.'[90]
This in fact is reducing syndicalism to a technique for
dealing with a current society, and there is nothing in it

of the blazing revolutionary spirit which called on trade
unions to organise according to industry so that they
could eventually take over those industries and through
them the whole of society. The idea of organisation by
industry remained, but now one suspects more as an exercise
in trade union efficiency than anything else. Mortished
calls it the most interesting classification of unions,
although he does not discuss why this should be so. He
provides eight industrial groups[91] and allots to each the
unions concerned and occasionally the numbers involved.
The groups are transport, building and woodworking, engineering and metalworking, printing, clothing, distributive
trades, milling and baking, and the public services. There
is the astonishing omission of agriculture and fisheries
from this list (which in other respects is similar to but
less sophisticated than the 1919 reorganisation proposal)
and since membership numbers are attempted in each category,
we must assume that the agricultural membership was of much
less significance than it had been five years earlier. The
Irish Transport appears in no less than seven of the eight
categories, and the Amalgamated Transport in two, which
indicates perhaps more clearly than anything else how
much a general union the Irish Transport had become. A
large number of unions, a multiplicity of unions as we would now
call it, is seen in the areas of building and engineering, just
as it is today, and also of course in the public service, but
for different and less intractable reasons. But Mortished
makes no comment on any of this. He merely sets out the
categories and leaves it at that. Congress itself however
would take up the question later that August of 1926 at its
annual conference. But before considering the Congress
initiative let us turn to the rather revealing account which
Mortished gives of the trades councils.

We have already noticed how they rapidly increased in number
after 1917 from a handful of five or so, to fifteen in 1918,
and forty-six in 1921, falling back to fifteen or sixteen
during the period we now speak of. Mortished describes them
as trades councils or workers' councils; 'the latter name
is merely a new-fashioned variant of the former and dates

from 1917, reflecting the Councils of Workers, Soldiers
and Peasants, which the Russian Revolution of that year
made famous, and expressing also a growing desire to
emphasise a broad solidarity and to minimise distinctions
between the craftsman and the labourer, who had in some
cases shown a tendency to organise separately.'[92] The
councils seemed to be strong in the large urban areas, weak
in the smaller towns, and almost impossible to organise
in the rural areas. At the time they existed in Belfast,
Dublin, Derry, Cork, Limerick, Wexford, Drogheda, Mullingar,
Sligo, Newry, Navan and Athlone. Mortished mentions six
other areas where short-lived councils had existed. We
have already noted the splintering of the Dublin Council
under the impact of the Irish Transport, and at this period
the same union had refused to take part in the councils in
Cork and Limerick. On the other hand there were many smaller
councils which it completely dominated by reason of its
size. The councils had both political and industrial
functions; but their future was obscure, politically because,
being urban essentially, it was difficult for them to organise
for rural elections, and industrially because already there
was a tendency for agreements to be made on a national basis
with national employer organisations. The councils still
exist today, in much the same mood of uncertain purpose,
suffering of course as all local bodies in the south from
the heavy bureaucratisation of local government, which has
so blunted our instincts for local democracy.

Finally to round out the organisational structure of the
time, there were a number of federations, most of which
became insignificant in time, although the Shipbuilding and
Engineering Federation in Belfast has been outstandingly
effective and influential; and there was Congress itself
speaking for perhaps 160,000 members, and claiming from the
unions contributions of 3d. per member per annum.

Although Mortished in January 1926 said that he did not
expect a separation of the political side for a considerable
time to come, it was nonetheless the driving thought behind

the motion on reorganisation which was moved by the
national executive the following August in Galway. At
first sight the motion might be taken to concern itself only
with a more efficient structure but in fact it provided a
searching out of the ground on the question of a division
of the movement. It read: 'That in view of the growth
of Labour political activity and organisation, the situation
created by the establishment of two new Governments in Ireland,
the multiplicity of Unions, and the difficulties of Trade
Union organisation in small urban and rural areas, the
National Executive be instructed to arrange for a survey of
working class industrial organisation in Ireland and to submit as soon as practicable a report upon the possibilities
of securing greater simplicity and effectiveness in
organisation.'[93] Johnson in moving the motion dealt first
with the problems of the new political situation, and the
legal complexities; and then spoke of the overlapping and
wasteful union situation; and mentioned as one of the
matters which needed inquiry 'the big question of industrial
organisation, of what could be done to link up trade unions
associated with a particular industry or group of industries.'[94] Far from being a point in passing, however, this
idea of industrial unions was central to an amendment put
forward by the redoubtable Helena Molony of the Irish
Women Workers' Union. She sought a special committee to
consider reorganisation of the industrial side of the labour
movement along industrial lines, and even indicated the
industrial groupings which should be represented; these
were probably hastily devised since the list omits both
agriculture and the public services. But her amendment
fell on stony ground, probably not helped by her desire to
establish a body other than the Executive to do the task;
and the original motion of the Executive was carried un-
amended. Significantly a motion from Bray, seeking, in explicit
terms, a division between the Irish Labour Party and the
Irish Congress, was withdrawn.

But little enough was done about it all and the impatient
Women Workers the following August 1927 in Dublin urged by

resolution that the survey which was to be undertaken in
1926 should now be the first duty of the Executive. In
this time of tumbling membership, and low morale, they also
associated with their resolution what they called an 'Into
the Unions' campaign. Of course there was much inter-
union strife between the Irish Transport and Larkin, whose
resounding and inspiring calls for peace when he returned
from America in 1923, whose enthusiastic march through Dublin
the following year under a scarlet Russian banner,[95] had
gradually deteriorated into rows about union membership in
the Gas Company and the Docks, and into a vicious hostility
to the political aspirations of Congress. But above all there
was heavy unemployment and the pervasive depression. Both
Johnson and Mortished rather crossly spoke of the difficulties in making a survey, and the cost in staff which it
would require. Nor did they like the proposed idea of an
industrial committee although its only task, the Women
Workers pleaded, would be to advise the national executive.
But of course there was no doubt about the need for some
campaign of revival, a more immediate task than restructuring. Johnson[96] said 'that some of their recent troubles
arose out of getting unions into one union. They had come
into one union, but were beginning to disperse again, and
they must go easier this time. It was desirable that there
should be fewer unions and more unity, but the important thing
was to get the individual workers into the unions, no matter
what union they got into.' They therefore accepted the
idea of a conference to launch an 'Into the Unions' campaign,
and they secured a recasting of the Women Workers' resolution
so that while such a conference would be called, its object
would be to plan the campaign, not review the national
executive's work. This resulted in the conference of
November 1927, the last substantial review and discussion
on the movement before it divided into two, the political
party and the trade union body.

Before dealing with this conference however, let us glance
briefly at the development of events. Belfast, where morale was

also low, experienced a vast unemployment problem which in the
worst years of 1925 and 1931 caused about a quarter of
the insured population to be out of work. But this was
the time too when what has been gracefully called a
'politically homogeneous'[97] administration was created. 'The
Governor was a leading Unionist peer, the judges were also
Unionists; the civil servants were either Ulster-born of
Unionist leanings or new arrivals from Whitehall ready to
accept and work the system as best they could.'[98] We have
already noted the highly conservative economic policies in
the Free State, although there was some rise in per capita
income from 1926 to 1929. But everything was dominated by
the uncertain and violent political situation. In March 1926
de Valera had broken with Sinn Fein on the issue of
parliamentary democracy, and in May formed a new party,
Fianna Fail. In the June 1927 elections he did very well,
securing 44 seats as against the Government party's 47, and
Labour's 22.[99] No individual party had a majority in the
143 seat parliament, but de Valera dramatically refused to
take the oath of allegiance which was a condition of taking
one's seat; and Cosgrave once again formed a government.
The next month one of the most vigorous of the Government's
ministers, Kevin O'Higgins, was shot down in the street, and his
death caused the Government to introduce far-reaching public
safety legislation. Further legislation left de Valera
with no alternative but to take the oath and enter the Dail,
which he did, claiming that the oath in any event was an
empty formula. A further general election followed in the
Autumn of 1927. Labour suffered badly from its divisions.
Larkin stood and was elected but was unable to take his seat
since he was a bankrupt. His son Jim (whose later contribution to the labour movement was to be considerable)
stood in Johnson's constituency. Not only was he not
elected, but the divided vote resulted in Johnson losing
his seat. In all Labour lost nine seats, including that of
their leader. The two major parties gained, the government
party getting 67 seats and Fianna Fail 57. The smaller parties

suffered greatly, and Cosgrave continued in power with the support of the much diminished Farmers Party. In fact the future shape of Irish party politics had now been set, as violent men accepted democratic procedures, not as propaganda devices, but as the only validation of authority. Moreover, so overwhelming was the divide between pro-Treaty and anti-Treaty opinion that the two parties that represented these two views obscured the multi-party objective which proportional representation was designed to foster. Not only were the Labour Party and the Farmers Party much diminished, and Redmond's short-lived National League quite extinguished, but Larkin himself in a by-election in 1928, which Fianna Fail chose to contest, was badly defeated, and in effect politically emasculated. But violence began to increase once again from 1928 onwards, continuing until 1931, and as the number of shootings increased there was widespread intimidation of juries, and eventually a Public Safety Act and military tribunals.

Apart from the question of reorganisation, there were a number of other problems that were troubling the trade unions at the time. There was the legal question. Mortished, early in 1926, had been concerned about the matter of registration of trade unions and what it meant in the changed circumstances of the time. Registration was not compulsory, but since it conferred a number of ad-vantages, most unions in fact registered. Before 1920 if a union registered in London, Dublin or Edinburgh (according to the location of its head office) it could be automatically recorded in any of the other cities. Now however there were three governments with full authority over registration, Westminster, Stormont and Dublin. More than that, because of the British Trade Unions and Trade Disputes Act 1927, the Post Office Workers had to disaffiliate in respect of their Northern Ireland membership, and indeed at the time the full implications of this legislation were by no means clear to Congress. The British TUC were also concerned about the complex legal position, and wished to explore it with the Irish Congress. Because of this, the national executive

in 1928 sought from the annual conference authority to
adapt the Constitution of Congress and the standing orders
to meet 'the requirements of affiliated trade unions in
consequence of the changed legal position.'[100] The meeting
between the representatives of the two congresses took
place immediately after the annual conference, the object
being 'to discuss the legal position of Unions with members
in the Saorstat.'[101] The British unions were confronted
with a dilemma since the Irish Registrar had decided in
the event to refuse to register in future the rules of
British unions; but they decided to temporise, and a
meeting in October of British unions with members in the
Irish Free State decided not to contest the Registrar's
decision in the courts but rather to continue as before.

Secondly let us glance at the usual housekeeping stresses
of the time, as new unions joined or disputes broke out.
The Irish Engineering and Industrial Union delayed the
affiliation of the Electrical Trade Union (Ireland) for a
couple of years; and there was the embarrassing fact that
the Amalgamated Transport, because of its rules, was unable
to pay its appropriate contribution to Congress. A dispute
broke out in the labour movement in Kilkenny because of the
nomination of candidates, but on the other hand in 1929
the long standing row in Dublin was resolved and the Workers'
Council and the Trades Council merged. A number of disputes
between unions were dealt with, the Bakers and the Irish
Transport, the Distributive Workers and the Garment Workers;
but above all the dispute in the Belfast docks between the
Irish Transport and the Amalgamated Transport. The really
tearing row between the Irish Transport and the Workers
Union of Ireland receives no mention in the Congress reports,
because of course Larkin's union was not in affiliation.

The dispute between the Irish Transport and the Amalgamated
Transport is particularly interesting, resulting as it did
in the promise of a _modus vivendi_ between these two general

unions and leading as well to the adoption of explicit
procedures for dealing with inter-union disputes in the
future. In the highly sensitive area of the Belfast docks
the Amalgamated Transport had instructed a crane-driver
member not to work if members of the Irish Transport were
employed to unload the ship, and indeed arising from this
the amalgamated union accepted some Irish Transport members
into membership. The national executive shrewdly left the
matter to be resolved by two of its members in Belfast.
Fortunately the problem was largely a misunderstanding. The
Amalgamated Transport had not appreciated that although their
members had unloaded the ship before, it was now being
serviced by a different stevedore who employed Irish
Transport members, and custom had clearly indicated that
the stevedore and not the ship was the determining factor.
But the disputes committee of two went on to mark the
friendly relations between the two unions and recommended
that the unions should meet together for the purpose of
avoiding disputes in the future.

However the disputes committee of the national executive
had no clear function in disputes of this kind; and one of
the members of this disputes committee, M. Courtney of
Belfast, now very conscious of what needed to be done, put
forward to the Limerick annual conference in August 1929 a
comprehensive constitutional change which gave the national
executive and its disputes committee power to investigate
inter-union disputes, power to summon unions before it and
require evidence from them, certain powers regarding the
costs of the proceedings, and the right, if a union refused
to recognise its ruling, to report the fact to all unions,
and if it continued to refuse, to report the matter to
Congress. The delegates in 1929 seemed principally concerned
to have excluded from such a procedure any disputes on
demarcation, which made Johnson very impatient. However
Watters of the NUR argued cogently that there was as yet
no general agreement as to the right basis of organisation.
'There were adherents of the craft Union as against the
composite Union; there were two or three forms of industrial

unionism, and there were conflicting views as between Irish
and International Unions.' Courtney in replying pointed
out that almost all the opposition came from delegates of
unions who were actually working in Great Britain under the
scheme he proposed; but he wisely withdrew his motion in
order to give the unions twelve months to consider it. In
this he was successful and in 1930 the scheme was adopted
in the form in which he had originally proposed it.

Finally there is the question of reorganisation and renewal.
True to their word the National Executive called a
special conference on industrial organisation on November 22
and 23 in 1927. It was a consultative conference rather
than a decisive one, and to emphasise the point still further
the various resolutions were cast in the form of recommendations.
They were pallid and tentative, containing no teeth, and
full of gradualism. In the matter of improving membership
they recommended mass demonstrations, propaganda leaflets,
band parades and concerts; but the difficult questions were
all dodged although the conference was loud with good intent.
The amalgamation of unions was to be given early and serious
consideration, but the establishing of a special committee
to promote it was headed off. As for promoting industrial
based unions, and branches of unions, in the same industry
and 'preparation for the eventual amalgamation of constituent unions of where this is not practicable a permanent
close Federation of Unions ..',[102] Congress cautiously agreed
(because it was a sensitive area) to invite non-affiliated
unions to join; and unions with headquarters outside Ireland
were urged to appoint an Irish organiser, and in addition
'some form of representative body for the consideration of
matters of peculiar or special concern to the Irish membership'[103]
- which a number of unions claimed they had already done.
Finally 'the difficult problem of the future of Trades and
Workers' Councils was discussed by the conference but
remitted to the councils themselves and to the National
Executive for further study.'[104] It is not surprising then
that at the close of the conference the Women Workers once

again pressed, by way of amendment, for more urgency, their
device being the coopting of five members by the national
executive for the work of industrial organisation, and
while they disclaimed any lack of confidence in the
national executive, they made it clear that they thought
they were too occupied with other matters. The amendment
of course was defeated, but the point was central. The
national executive had made a great attempt at a show, at
the outset of the conference, and had prepared a manifesto
to the workers of Ireland which the conference had adopted
as its first business. It was rather a grand manifesto,
full of ringing phrases. 'In the name of the great body
of organised Irish workers this special Conference of
Trade Unions and Trades and Workers Councils .. sends to
all workers in the towns and in the countryside of Ireland
a message of greeting and a summons to action.'[105] There
was substantial emphasis on the gains of the last decade;
but economic conditions had made swift victories now
impossible; and there was the problem of unemployment,
draining the unions both of members and of funds. The
call was first to defend what had been won; but the
greater ideal was not forgotten. 'If the Ireland of the
future is to be the home of real freedom, it must have
more than democratic political institutions; it must have
democratic industrial organisations - and they must be
developed out of the trade union movement of to-day.'[106]
But gradualism was carefully emphasised. 'It will not
be easily or swiftly accomplished. But if we set ourselves
to work now, with enduring enthusiasm, we shall prove
ourselves worthy of our historic past and lay the foundations
of a glorious future.'[107] It all ended ringingly: 'In the
name of the pioneers, known and unknown, of the past, the
fruits of whose sacrifices we have inherited, and in the
name of your children, whose happiness depends on your
efforts, we call upon all of you, Workers of Ireland, to
rally to your Unions ..'[108] The emptiness of the whole
affair was demonstrated when the national executive reported
to the annual conference in August in Belfast. The results,

they said, were disappointing: no suggestions from unions,
no activity (with one exception) traceable to the conference,
no organised demonstrations, although leaflets had been
prepared and distributed; and as for the national executive
itself, it had at last begun the survey of industrial
organisation promised in 1926; and although question forms
had been issued, a great number of organisations had not
replied, and of those that did, no examination of the
returns had been made as yet because of pressure of work.
The following year, 1929, in Limerick, William Norton struck
at the heart of the matter when he proposed a committee
to consider the desirability of separating the industrial
and political organisations, and arising from this a
special Congress was held in Dublin in February 28 1930
where the decision was made in a brief and businesslike
way. From April 1 1930 the two separate bodies came into
existence, and although much claim was made for their
interdependence, they grew gradually apart. More than that,
many of the big names declared[109] for the political organisation, including Tom Johnson, and since Mortished at this
point went off to Geneva to undertake a successful career
with the ILO, the secretariat fell vacant, and Eamonn Lynch
was appointed. In the immediate aftermath of the division,
there was greater activity in the matter of restructuring,
or at least a greater urgency in the discussion, impelled
as well by the impact which the rationalising of industry
(as it was called) was having on employment; but while this
was so, the trade union movement was at a low ebb, in the
deepening gloom of the depression, conscious of some great
past, conscious too of a dreary present, and finding itself
shrugged off as being of lesser account by the men who
regarded themselves as leaders of the working class movement.
This is perhaps less than fair to them. They had recognised
that the syndicalist idea was not practicable in current
circumstances, nor, as far as they could see, was it likely
to be so in the future. Connolly's ideal - which had lived

in some form when it was associated with national
fervour - was now quite dead. Many now saw Russia as
a 'malignant and alien power'[110] and any ideas associated
with marxism were seen as malignant and alien as well.
Not surprisingly then, the Congress constitution of 1930
cautiously avoided a claim that the whole produce of the
labour of the workers should be under their ownership and
control. The great vision drifted away and within this
passionless framework, there grew up instead what appeared
to many to be the largely fruitless squabbling of bitter men.

Notes on Chapter Two

1.   ITUC & LP, 1916 p.22.

2.   ibid. pp.22,23.

3.   ibid. p.23.

4.   Lloyd George was unaware until then of the existence of
     an Irish Congress - an interesting insight into its
     significance at the time.

5.   ibid. p.14.

6.   ibid. pp. 14, 15.

7.   ITUC & LP, 1916 p.58

8.   see Ireland at Berne: ILP & TUC 1919 p.18.

9.   Op.cit. pp. 323,324.

10. Jerome J. Judge: "The Labour Movement in the Republic
     of Ireland" Ph.D. thesis NUI 1955 p.236. Emmet Larkin
     (op.cit. p.262) attributes the growth of the Irish
     Transport in 1918 mainly to the wage demand movement
     in Britain and Ireland, which seems hardly satisfactory.
     Of course increasing union membership was a phenomenon
     throughout Europe at the time (cf Walter Kendall:
     The Labour Movement in Europe 1975).

11. Ireland at Berne op.cit. p.5

12. ibid. p.18.

13. ITUC & LP, 1917 p.5.

14. ibid. p.7.

15. ITUC & LP, 1917 p.56.

16. ibid. p.56.

17. ibid.pp.56,57.

18. ibid. p.57.

19. ITUC & LP, 1918 p.19.

20. ibid. p.20.

21. ibid. p.20.

22. ibid. p.20.

23. Ireland at Berne op.cit. p.19.

24. ibid. p.19.

25. ITUC & LP, 1918 pp.8,9.

26. ITUC & LP, 1918 p.9.

27. ILP & TUC, p.16.

28. ILP & TUC, 1918 p.11.

29. ibid. p.104.

30. ibid. p.104.

31. See Arthur Mitchell: Labour in Irish History 1974
     which gives a very thorough account of the build-up of
     pressures on the Congress; it may not however be
     sufficiently sensitive to Congress's problem in
     regard to the north.

32. ILP & TUC 1918 p.104.

33. Corish, in Wexford, for example, refused to withdraw
     from the 1918 election and his personal following
     saw him safely elected.

34. Op.cit. p.171.

35. Cullen op.cit. p.172.

36. Clarkson op.cit. p.362.

37. ibid. p.362.

38. ILP & TUC, 1918 p.33.

39. ILP & TUC, 1919 p.42.

40. ibid. pp.42,43.

41. ibid. p.44. For the use of the strike weapon at this
     time, see Mitchell op.cit. pp.117-22.

42. ILP & TUC, 1919 p.18.

43. W.P. Ryan: The Irish Labour Movement: 1919
     p.262-3.

44. ibid. pp.264-65,

45. ILP & TUC, 1919 p.61.

46. Clarkson op.cit. p.321.

47. Clarkson op.cit. p.324.

48.   They were encouraged to organise even craft workers
       in the smaller towns where no craft unions existed.

49.   ILP & TUC, 1919 p.99.

50.   ibid. p.102.

51.   ibid. p.106.

52.   Clarkson op.cit. 320.

53.   In 1920-1921 the Irish Stationery Engine Drivers, the
       Whitesmiths and the Brass Finishers Unions were
       amalgamated with the IEU.

54.   Their membership in agriculture did not increase
       during this period but their membership in transport
       and communications doubled; and it more than doubled
       in the general industrial sector, giving a member-
       ship in early 1920 of 103,000 in round numbers as
       against 44,000 in mid-1918.

55.   Judge Ph.D. thesis op.cit. p.38.

56.   ILP & TUC, 1922 p.243.

57.   ibid. p.241.

58.   Judge (Ph.D. thesis op.cit. p.38) speaks of this
       debate as a final attempt to form one Irish union
       for all Irish workers. It was nothing of the kind.

59.   Clarkson op.cit. p.365.

60.   Quoted in Clarkson op.cit. p.369.

61.   ILP & TUC, 1920

62.   Clarkson op.cit. p.425.

63.   Clarkson op.cit. p.429; S. Higgenbottam: "Our
       Society's History" 1939 p.227. Only 600 obeyed the
       strike call and up to 2,000 were expelled as a result.

64.   Higgenbottom op.cit. p.228.

65.   ibid.

66.   Clarkson op.cit. p.427.

67.   Higgenbottam op.cit. p.229.

68.   Clarkson op.cit. p.372.

69.   Ian Budge & Cornelius O'Leary: Approach to Crisis:
       A Study of Belfast Politics 1613-1970:Macmillan,
       1973 p.143.

70.   ILP & TUC, 1922 p.15.

71.   ibid. p.19.

72.   Quoted in James Meenan: The Irish Economy since
       1922, Liverpool University Press, 1970 pp.31, 32.

73.   Cf. Arthur Mitchell op.cit. pp.139-43.

74.   ILP & TUC, 1922 p.23

75.   ibid. p.23.

76.   ibid. p.25.

77.   ibid. p.26.

78.   ILP & TUC, 1922 p.28

79.   ibid. p.141.

80.   He also toured the union branches, spoke at a number
       of public meetings, and called powerfully for peace.
       In all this he was enthusiastically received.

81.   Cullen op.cit. p.174.

82.   R.J.P. Mortished: Journal of the Statistical and Social
       Inquiry Society of Ireland Part C1 Vol.XV. October 1927
       p.228.

83.   The membership of the Irish Transport fell from 100,000
       in 1922 to 20,000 in 1929. See Ruaidhri Roberts Trade
       Union Organisation in Ireland: Journal of the
       Statistical and Social Inquiry Society of Ireland, Vol.
       XX: 1958-59: p.93.

84.   Mortished op.cit. p.213.

85.   op.cit. p.213.

86.   His figures are for 31.12.1924.

87.   Mortished op.cit.pp.217, 218.

88.   ibid. p.219.

89.   Mortished op.cit. p.228.

90.   Mortished op.cit. p.227.

91.   See appendix two.

92.   Mortished op.cit. p.224.

93.   ILP & TUC, 1926 p.152.

94.   ibid. p.153.

95.   Emmet Larkin: op.cit. p.276.

96.   ILP & TUC, p.69.

97.   Budge & O'Leary op.cit. p.144

98.   ibid.

99.   For an account of Labour's attempt to promote local
      parties, see Mitchell op.cit. p.220.

100. ILP & TUC 1928 p.103.

101. ILP & TUC, 1929 p.12.

102. ILP & TUC, 1928 p.17.

103. ibid. p.18.

104. ibid. p.19.

105. ILP & TUC, 1928 p.12.

106. ibid. p.14.

107. ibid.

108. ibid.

109. The special congress of 1930 decided that officers of
      Congress would be ineligible for office in the party
      and vice versa (Special Congress Report pp. 12,24).

110. Larkin op.cit. p.285 quoting from The Irish Times
      of August 14 1925.

Chapter Three

Stress

-i-

In the division of the labour movement in 1930, therefore,
the trade union organisation was the remnant. There is
little or no mention, in the report of the special
congress, of any advantage which the division might bring
to the trade unions; the object was to free the Labour
Party for political activity, to create 'a reorganised and
revivified Labour Party ... a new departure in the political
progress of the country.'[1] The trade union type organisation
was frankly too limiting. 'Our ranks must be as comprehensive as our policies', said the president of Congress,
T.J. O'Connell, 'uniting farmer and town-worker, wage-earner,
salary-earner, professional man, shopkeeper, industrialist,
housewife, in the bonds of genuine political conviction,
realist patriotism and patient enthusiasm for social progress
and reconstruction,'[2] a sentiment reinforced in more blunt
terms by William Norton, who was later to become leader of
the party: 'It is not possible, practically or efficiently
to have combined in one movement the trade unions and the
political organisations. That kind of machinery is not
suitable for the direction and control of the political
Labour Party and this fact is becoming increasingly obvious
in the country.'[3]

There was a belief of course that circumstances favoured a
Labour party. The idea of a Labour government was no longer
a curiosity in Europe; and in Ireland, the Congress leaders
believed that while dissatisfaction, and even hostility,
was growing with regard to Cumann na nGaedheal, the country
was not 'yet prepared to entrust its destinies to Fianna Fail.'[4]

Yet the Irish Labour Party and Trade Union Congress looked
a most unlikely starter. It had a grubby syndicalist look
about it which did not attract the middle class and the
intellectual left, and while this, under the banner of class
conflict, might be acceptable if the working class gave the
movement political support, the position in fact was quite
the contrary and quite deplorable. Dan Morrissey, a delegate
to the special congress of 1930, declared impatiently: 'Here
in the heart of the Trade Union movement with 40,000 trade
unionists affiliated to the United Trades and Labour Council
you could not return a single Labour man for any of the 26
Dublin City and County constituencies .. It is because we in
the Dail realise that things cannot go on with a miserable
little Labour Party, as at present, that we desire a change
in the organisation.'[5] The fact was that the Labour Party
did not appear to rely on any coherent political policy;
indeed, as we have already noted, the Labour deputies who had
secured election depended essentially on a personal following,
much more than on any political programme or, for that matter,
on any trade union support.

There seems to be a dilemma in attempting a syndicalist
solution in a parliamentary democracy. Trade unionists
are elected to represent not so much the person in his
full social role (and certainly not in his political role)
but rather in his role of dissent. A trade union is an anti-
establishment gesture (although trade union leaders might
be somewhat shocked at such an idea); but such a gesture can
be made only when the establishment is secure: otherwise
it is too perilous. In the present difficulties in Northern
Ireland we have seen, for example, radicals well supported
for trade union office, but hopelessly defeated at the
political polls; and equally in this critical period in
1930, the Congress leaders were aware that such a dilemma
existed, that while syndicalism might succeed by revolution,
it could never succeed by parliamentary democratic means
and consequently a bid had to be made for an independent
party of the left which would recommend itself to many in a
broadly based way as an alternative establishment.

If the new party were to be of the left, then, it should
not be embarrassingly so; and in the draft constitutions
both of the new Labour Party and the new trade union body,
socialist principles were prudently muted, as organisations
were shaped for different times. There were some quite
good reasons for this development, as we shall see in a
moment, although William Norton, to say the least of it,
was somewhat fanciful when he claimed that 'James Connolly,
were he alive today, would be the first to endorse the
proposals now being submitted to Congress.'[6]

Here we see clearly the political ambiguity which lies at
the heart of the Irish labour movement and which has continued to our own day. Connolly was regarded as the prophet
of the movement; in the introduction to the published reports
of the time, his motion at the 1912 Clonmel congress (seeking
independent representation for Labour on all public boards)
was presented as the great watershed in the political evolution
of Congress, a point that was referred to once again by
T.J. O'Connell at this special congress of 1930. This
exaggerates the significance of the Clonmel resolution but
not the significance of Connolly himself. He had been
virtually canonised by William O'Brien, and although Johnson
took a more measured view, we nevertheless find not only
socialism but echoes of syndicalism in the draft democratic
programme which Johnson submitted, at their request, to the
Sinn Fein leaders in January 1919.[7] 'It shall be the purpose
of the Government,' he wrote, 'to encourage the organisation
of the people citizens (sic) into Trade Unions and Cooperative Societies
with a view to the control and administration of the
industries by the workers engaged in those industries.'

But in the event, Connolly's ideas were virtually impossible
to implement. As far as socialism was concerned, the Labour
politicians themselves not only did not need a political
philosophy, but, worse than that, found this one to be
embarrassing; and as for the syndicalist structure of the
Labour movement, this had been found in practice to be a

serious liability. Connolly therefore continued to be
lauded as a prophet, while his teachings were gingerly put
aside. There was a good deal of this that came from sheer
political pragmatism and consequently it looked a little
shabby at times, and perhaps a little shamefaced, when confronted with the pure ringing voice of idealism. But
it seems clear that Johnson reached down for much deeper
and more compelling reasons for his reluctance to support
the socialism of Connolly; and in examining these reasons,
we must not underestimate Thomas Johnson's influence at
this most formative time. He was secretary of the Congress;
but more than that, for much of the twenties, he was not
only leader of the Labour party in Dail Eireann but leader
of the official opposition as well.

In July 1925, full of misgivings with regard to his own
adequacy as a leader,[8] Johnson had contemplated not
continuing as secretary of Congress, and wrote a lengthy
letter to the national executive.[9] '..I see', he said,
'how great is the opportunity and how insistent the need
that the workers should be wisely led and inspired by a
lofty purpose ..' and if he were to continue in office he
was anxious to know how far his own thinking was consistent
with that of the national executive. For that reason he set
down his views at some length. At no time did he mention
Connolly, although there was much in what he said that not
only departed from syndicalism but actually discounted it.
'...I have advocated', he said, 'the use by the workers of
political means and parliamentary institutions to further
their cause. I have opposed the proposition that the
workers should rely solely on their economic power to attain
their ends - the theory that only by organising their strength
in the field of industry and using it to bring the economic
machinery to a full stop can the workers' ideals be realised.
I have acted in the belief that a democratic government would
preserve the fundamental rights which have been won and would
not lightly cast aside those social obligations which they had
inherited from their predecessors - and in that faith I
have played a somewhat prominent part in helping to create

a public opinion favourable to the political institutions
through which the will of the people may be exercised.'
With regard to the current campaign on unemployment he asked:
'Shall the aim be honestly to remove poverty ... or are we
to agitate and organise with the object of waging the "class
war" more relentlessly, and use "the unemployed" and the
"poverty of the workers" as propogandist cries to justify
our actions?' For the truth was that he had little time
for the left wing of European Labour, for the class struggle
and notions of conflict for economic power. 'I do not think
this view of the mission of the Labour Movement has any
promise of ultimate usefulness in Ireland .. In this
connection I ask the Executive to walk warily when entering
upon an adult education policy. The Independent Working-Class
Education Movement is doing excellent work and the National
Council of Labour Colleges has succeeded in pushing that
work with tremendous vigour. But let us not overlook the
fact that the dominant ideas within the movement, as judged
by the text books in commonest use, are in direct conflict
with the religious faith of our people.[10] Nothing would I
dread more than to give occasion for a charge that I was
even partially responsible for entering upon a policy
which will inevitably, as I believe, mean the splitting up,
on doctrinal grounds, of the Labour Movement in Ireland ..'

These views I have set out at some length, because they
represent very fairly the settled position of many of the
trade union and Labour leaders that followed, although their
articulation was obscured at times by the need to pay public
tribute to James Connolly.[11] There were some of course who
continued to be uncompromisingly radical; and on the other
hand, there were many, especially in the forties and fifties,
who reflected the impatient dogmatism of the Catholic
Church of the time; but the substantive trade union opinion
was really that outlined by Johnson in 1925, a sensitive,
mild, parliamentary socialism.[12]

But there were quite a number at the 1930 special congress
who, while they were prepared to abandon the syndicalist
structure, nonetheless wanted fullblooded socialist
objectives both for the Congress and for the party. The
Women Workers[13] led the way; and where the draft constitution of Congress sought 'for all workers, subject to
the general interest, adequate control of the industries
or services in which they were engaged',[14] the Women
Workers moved the following instead: '(a) To win for the
workers of Ireland collectively the ownership and control
of the whole produce of their labour. (b) To secure the
management and control of all industries, and services,
by the whole body of workers, manual and mental, engaged
therein in the interests of the nation and subject to the
Authority of the National Government.'[15] There was a
good deal of pooh-poohing of this from the platform; it
was true that some such phrases had appeared in the 1918
constitution of Congress but that was because of the need
to find a formula at the time to express both trade union
and political aspirations, a formula which now seemed
rather in the clouds. The executive draft, the platform
claimed, was a straightforward statement that people could
understand. But although the women were defeated by 60 votes
to 31 they got a good deal of important support, not least
from William McMullen of the Irish Transport.[16] Later in
the conference the same question arose again, this time
in connection with the draft constitution of the Labour
Party, and having already had a run over the field, the
delegates showed more sharpness of position and more
impatience. Helena Molony in moving her amendment said
spiritedly that the objects in the constitution 'contained
all the vagueness and insincerity of an election speech'[17].
McMullen described them as pink, bourgeois and middle class
and Cathal O'Shannon urged the delegates to pitch their
banner a little nearer the skies; nevertheless the amendment
was defeated by 52 votes to 34. It appears however that there
was no attempt at any real debate, and the discussion that
did take place appeared to be short and somewhat perfunctory,
as if the substance of agreement had been reached at an

earlier stage by those who commanded the majority. Finally
there was much anxiety about relations politically with the
Northern Ireland Labour Party (which was represented at the
special congress by Sam Kyle and two others); in this
account of trade unions, however, it is a topic which,
regretfully, we cannot pursue.[18]

The Labour Party was now launched on its separate way, with
its separate leadership, full of hope that, stripped of its
constricting trade union shell, it would blossom as a full
socialist party with a broad general appeal. It was a hope
that was not fulfilled. The character of the Labour Party
continued   for many years to be intractably the same.

-ii-

The great watershed in trade union history - certainly up
to the reconciliation of the late fifties - was the commission
on trade union organisation which was established by
Congress in 1936 and which reported three years later. But
from the year 1930, when the trade union movement went its
separate way, until 1936, there were a number of major
developments, a number of shifts in the attitudes of some
of the leaders, which contributed greatly to the intractable
character of the commission's discussions.

First, however, let us review those eventful years of the
early thirties. Curiously, as far as the south was concerned, the great depression which began in 1929 did not
initially have any great effect. Terms of trade favoured
the Free State to begin with, since the price of grain and
animal feeding stuffs - which it imported - fell much more
rapidly than its great exports of livestock and livestock
products;[19]   furthermore industry in the south, being
essentially concerned with the domestic market, was not as
sensitive to world depression. Indeed one notices in Louie
Bennett's presidential address to Congress in 1932 that the

note of excited expectation because of the change in
government was in no way dimmed by economic gloom. But
a month or two later came the beginning of the economic
war with Britain, which resulted in a dramatic fall in the
export of agricultural produce, the low-point being reached
in 1934. The coal-cattle pact between the two countries
brought some recovery in 1935, gradually developing into the
Anglo-Irish Trade Agreement in 1938 which brought the
dispute to an end.[20]

This also was the time when notions of national self-
sufficiency were in the air. De Valera himself in 1931,
before he took office, declared his aim of making Ireland
as far as possible self-sufficient: 'the countries which
to-day are suffering most from the prevailing depression
are those which are most dependent on foreign trade ';
and as a consequence he proposed to protect every branch of
agriculture. The economic dispute with Britain intensified
this programme of self-sufficiency in agriculture, and
various financial subsidies and aids were given for wheat,
oats, barley, sugar beet, tobacco, fruit and vegetables.
Industrially too protectionism became inevitable; Ireland
in 1931 was one of the last countries which espoused free
trade[21] and de Valera, when he came to power, moved so
rapidly to protectionism and to the creation of radical
powers in the matter for government that the trade union
movement, despite its general support, expressed some
disquiet. There was therefore an acceleration of industrialisation and as a result a considerable increase in
industrial employment which rose from 110,000 to 166,000 between
1931 and 1938.[22]   But, as Cullen remarks, once the
more obvious possibilities of industrial expansion had been
exploited, new opportunities were likely to be few[23] and by
1936 the rate of industrial output began to decline. But
although employment in industry had risen, there was nevertheless, throughout the Free State as a whole, a considerable
increase in unemployment, standing in 1935 at 133,000 which
was double the level of 1926.[24] Because of the great

depression, emigration to the United States, so rich a flood
during the twenties, had dried up, and for the same reason
emigration to other countries also fell. As we shall see,
there was much complaint among the trade unions about the
effect of new industrial practices on employment in industry,
but it appears now that this was not the major cause of the
extensive, stagnant unemployment of the time.

The north in contrast suffered a devastating decline in
industrial employment during the period, experiencing in
fact the highest unemployment rate in the United Kingdom.
It was a story of unremitting difficulty, right throughout
the thirties. In 1932, one-quarter of the insured population
was unemployed[25], the figure rising to 60 per cent among shipbuilding and engineering workers. 'In 1933 Harland and Wolff
did not launch a single ship, and in 1934, Workman, Clark
and Company went out of business.'[26] In the further recession in 1938, nearly 30 per cent of the insured population
was unemployed, including half of all the workers in the
linen industry. On the other hand, agriculture did quite
well, gaining from the disputes between the Free State and
Britain.

This was the economic backdrop to an unstable and sometimes
violent political community. However, the political mix
was extraordinarily different north and south. In the
Free State, which we shall consider first, the repeal of
the Public Safety Act at the end of 1928 marked, as we have
already noted, an increase in violence and in particular an
increase in the intimidation of juries which made the containment of violence by normal judicial means less and less
effective. In 1931, the number of shootings became alarming,
illegal drilling was on the increase, and, worse than that,
those who hoped for a growth in parliamentary authority
were shocked to see Fianna Fail march with the IRA to
Bodenstown in June. By October things had reached such
a point that the government established military tribunals
with far-reaching and quite draconian powers, so draconian
in fact that public feeling swept the other way, and Fianna

Fail, who conducted a circumspect election campaign,
secured 72 seats in the general election of early 1932,
while Cumann na nGaedheal polled only 57. Labour dropped
disastrously again from 10 to 7, but its support of de
Valera gave him an overall 79 seats as against 74 for
all the others. On 9 March 1932 de Valera entered on
government. He immediately released the republican
prisoners, and discontinued the military tribunal.

But the thuggish behaviour of some republicans at Cumann
na ñGaedheal meetings brought its own response. August
1932 saw the Army Comrades Association, formed the year
before by T.F. O'Higgins, open its ranks to the public
generally, so that now there were two unofficial bodies,
polarised on the civil war issue, and prepared if necessary
to adopt violent means. De Valera's overwhelming success in
the general election of 1933, which made him independent
of the Labour Party, was followed by open IRA recruitment,
and also an intensification of the activities of the extreme
right. General Eoin O'Duffy, who had been Commissioner of
Police under Cumann na nGaedheal and who had been dismissed
by de Valera, now became leader of the reconstituted Army
Comrades Association, who, renamed the National Guard, began,
in imitation of continental models, to wear blue shirts.
In August 1933 there was the astonishing episode of the
proposed mass march to Glasnevin via Leinster House (with
echoes of Mussolini's march on Rome), which in the event
was banned by the government, and abandoned by O'Duffy.
But it brought into being a special armed auxiliary force,
the Broy Harriers, as they were known, recruited by the
government from old IRA men. Moreover, the government,
thoroughly alarmed, banned the National Guard and re-
surrected the military tribunal. At this point O'Duffy
moved powerfully into the political field, leaping into the
leadership in September 1933 of a fusion of three groups,
his own National Guard, Cosgrave's Cumann na nGaedheal
party, and the National Centre Party, a farmers' party,
which had sprung up vigorously in 1932. Cosgrave was pre-

pared to serve under him as one vice-president among three,
although O'Duffy himself was not a member of parliament,
indicating more clearly perhaps than anything else the
twilight into which parliamentary democracy had drifted.
But this was the climax of O'Duffy's career. His sheer
recklessness of speech - some called it hysteria - caused
prominent resignations from the new party, and by September
of the following year 1934, O'Duffy himself was obliged
to resign. After some time, Cosgrave emerged as leader
of the new united party which gradually became known
familiarly as Fine Gael. In 1935 O'Duffy attempted to form
the National Corporate Party, and in 1936 he went adventuring
to Spain with 700 of his blueshirts, to fight for Franco's
cause.[27] He was never a force again in Irish politics.

As we shall see, the opposition of trade unions to fascism,
and fascist ideas, built up steadily from 1932, culminating in an extensive public campaign in 1934. 'If anyone
should doubt that the Trade Union and Labour Movements
were not in peril,' said Michael Duffy in his presidential
address in 1934, 'then let me tell that person to go and
study the public pronouncements of the Fine Gael professors
and politicians, and he will find both movements were in
imminent danger.'[28] Professor James Hogan of University
College Cork was one of those professors; he was full of
alarm about communism, and indeed about a communist IRA,
and both he and Professor Michael Tierney of University
College Dublin were enthusiasts for the idea of the corporate
state in its Italian form, although they had not the same
enthusiasm for Mussolini; on the other hand Hogan at
an early stage rejected O'Duffy and his excesses. It is
not at all certain how much enthusiasm Cosgrave had for
the whole development.

It was clear enough that to the left lay communism and to
the right fascism, but what complicated the matter greatly
was the notion of vocational organisation, espoused by
Pius XI in Quadragessimo Anno, which was issued in May 1931

and which became the immensely popular guide of Muintir
na Tire[29] and other catholic social groups. In the case
of some European countries, it might be urged as a sort
of middle-of-the-road solution in a society whose chaotic
economies needed a strong organisational frame (and throughout the thirties many trade unionists who violently opposed
fascism seemed to regard some form of vocational organisation
as almost inevitable); but on the other hand, with its
notions of integrated corporate structuring, it opened the
way powerfully to fascist solutions. These problems we
shall discuss at a later stage.

During this period of 1933-1934, violence continued, and
there were several murders. De Valera was of course reluctant
to move against the IRA, and he attempted to woo them in
various ways; but when this failed, they too experienced
the Broy Harriers and the military tribunal. But a split
in the republican movement itself (a split which has its
echoes in the officials and provisionals of our own day)
weakened them greatly. The country was very shocked in 1936
by a number of brutal killings; on June 18 the IRA was
declared illegal, and its chief of staff sentenced to three
months imprisonment by the military tribunal. The IRA
too were caught up by the Spanish crusade, but in their
case on the Republican side, and two or three hundred left
to take up Spanish arms. Gradually, therefore, and very
unsteadily, parliamentary democracy began to reassert itself
in the Free State. But what of the north? 'What we have
now', said Craig in 1922, 'we hold', and this was achieved
by the overwhelming dominance of the Unionists in Stormont.
Northern Ireland began self-avowedly as a protestant state
for a protestant people, a view reinforced by the nationalists
and the republicans who refused to take their seats in
Stormont. It was an accurate enough reflection of the
feelings of the catholic population who, although they
amounted to approximately a third of the whole, saw little
future for themselves, and saw the new state itself as uncertain in any event. But after the debâcle of the Boundary

Commission, the state of Northern Ireland began to take
on a more permanent appearance, and Joe Devlin, the
nationalist leader, took up his seat in parliament, to be
followed very shortly by others of his party. Such
participation in public affairs was notoriously weak and
uncertain. However, by 1930 the vehement sectarian controversy with regard to primary schooling had been
resolved; and the dreary agony of unemployment became of
greater significance than the sectarian question. The riot
in Belfast in 1932 that led to two deaths and much destruction
of property was quite non-sectarian. A hunger march to
Stormont had been banned by the Minister for Home Affairs,
but crowds gathered nonetheless both in the Falls and Shankill.
The police baton-charged the crowds in the Falls and fired
over their heads; the Shankill crowd rioted in support.[30]
But the sectarian character soon returned to dominate Belfast
with its penury and its soup kitchens. Undoubtedly the
success of de Valera in the 1932 election in the Free State
re-awakened old fears which the Cosgrave administration had
somewhat lulled, particularly when, in the following year,
de Valera stood as an abstentionist candidate for South
Down and won. The Ulster Protestant League which was
founded in 1932 campaigned against any social or economic
intercourse with catholics[31] and as unemployment continued,
sectarian feelings began to increase, reaching their climax
on July 12 1935, when rioting broke out in the Falls-Shankill
area and lasted for three weeks. During this dreadful
time 12 people were killed and many were injured or made
homeless. But the catholic population were on the whole
apathetic and made little enough response. Nevertheless
sectarian and political tensions (and they tended now to
be almost identical) continued to intensify, as de Valera
drew away from Britain, and Northern Ireland drew ever
closer to it.

Both north and south the trade union movement was at its
lowest ebb. The number of delegates attending the annual
conference in 1929 was 121, the lowest figure since the
burgeoning in 1918, but from this on the tempo began to
quicken again, as industrial employment on the whole improved
under protection.

In considering the events which led up to the trade union
commission of inquiry in 1936 we can distinguish three
impulses towards trade union reform, and although we
identify them separately, they were deeply intertwined.
The first was the desire of the trade union movement to
attain its social objectives, in particular to combat the
worst effects of industrialisation and to combat the dangers
of fascism; this impulse was probably the weakest of the
three. Secondly there was the desire to coordinate trade
union activity, and in particular to avoid disputes which
both weakened the trade union movement and brought it into
disrepute; and thirdly - closely related to this - there
was the belief, not by any means confined to the Irish based
unions, that the days of the British unions in Ireland were
numbered, and that their demise in the national interest
should be hurried along. To many it appeared self-evident
that this should be so, and - in a manner which reveals only
too clearly the character of the society of the time - it was
by far the greatest impulse towards structural reform, far
more real and far more immediate than the achievement of
high-sounding socialist aims or even the promise of more
efficiency in getting things done. This belief in the
extinguishing of the British-based unions in the Free State
coincided with their actual increase in membership, perhaps
because, quite fortuitously, they happened to be well
organised in those industries which grew under protection. It
was this indeed which sharpened the conflict and gave a
certain inevitability to the split when it eventually came
in the following decade. But this was all much later.

It is important, before we begin to consider these three
strands bearing on trade union organisation, to remember
how weak the trade unions were at the time, and, in national
terms, how lacking they were in significance; and when we
come to consider the growing acrimony during the thirties,
it is important that we should not import into it the
wider national implications which such disputes might carry today.

Let us take first then the larger question of unemployment
and industrialisation. Although the Free State may have
been cushioned to some extent against the worst effects
of the depression, we must not lose sight of the grinding
poverty of the time and the personal disaster of disemployment. In Dublin in 1931, for example, thirty-five
per cent of the population was living at a density of more
than two persons to a room, and in one ward in the city,
Mountjoy, almost half the people were living at a density
of more than four to a room.[32]

At this time there was a popular view in many countries that
new machines, new processes and factory reorganisation were
contributing greatly to unemployment, and furthermore that
such increased production that came from these changes did
little to absorb those who were disemployed. In 1929 the
Women Workers had taken up this point at the annual conference to such good effect that the executive appointed
a committee to investigate and report. The committee's
remit also included works councils, which **they** merely
touched on, and the employment of women, which **they** were
unable to reach; but a substantial report was presented to
the 1930 annual conference on industrial rationalisation, as
it was called, and clearly a great deal of work had gone into
it.[33] However, it was adopted by the 1930 annual conference
without discussion; it was described as an interim report,
but the committee never made another, and the committee itself
did not appear to be particularly heavyweight - of the eight
members only three were members of the national executive,
and one of these attended no meeting of the committee. On the
other hand, two members, Louie Bennett and Denis Cullen,
became presidents of Congress in the years that immediately
followed. Few enough unions replied to the questionnaire
of the committee; among those who did not were some of the
large unions with widespread interests, and one suspects that
many saw in unemployment a far deeper and more pervasive

problem than could be atrributed to industrial rationalisation
alone.

Such replies as were received - from ten unions and from the
Belfast and Limerick trades councils - give a predictable
enough picture. The Limerick council estimated that in
the sweets industry and in condensed milk and in butter,
fifty per cent of the women workers were unemployed, and
in the tobacco trade girls under 16 were being employed
instead of women; and the Irish Women Workers reported
that new machinery in the laundries and in bottling plants
had caused much unemployment. The women had suffered also
in the printing trade, unlike the men who had benefited
from the increased volume of printing work; paper bag
machines and binding machines caused much redundancy. Matters
were made worse by amalgamations and the closure of old firms.
One can therefore understand only too well the anxiety of
Louie Bennett and the manner in which she connected unemployment and industrial change. There was unemployment
too among the men - just as pervasive as among the women -
although the limited number of replies does not help very
much. In Limerick the council estimated that in flour
milling, forty per cent of the men were unemployed, and in
the bacon trade thirty-three per cent. The Belfast council
was unable to provide an adequate picture, but the seamen
claimed that the introduction of oil-burning vessels had
reduced employment by fifty per cent. Clerks had suffered
substantially because of the introduction of comptometers;
in the case of the railways, reports were contradictory.
On the other hand, the bakers, the printers and the craftworkers
in the furniture trade were holding their own.

One of the most significant reports was that of the Amalgamated
Engineering Union which estimated that 'one out of every six
fully skilled men in a shop (was) displaced by semi-skilled
and boy labour owing to the simplified working of up-to-
date machines.' And they pointed out that the possibilities
of safeguards were nullified by the number of competing
unions in the trade. 'Only solid industrial organisation

can safeguard workers.' This was much in contrast with
the printers and the bricklayers who could resist lower-
skilled labour and maintain the level of their wages by
tight organisation.

There were of course many solutions proposed by the
committee: alternative employment, compensation, the
raising of the school leaving age, the extending of holidays,
the limiting of the number of apprentices, and so forth,
but the question of tight organisation came prominently
through in the conclusions. 'We have found', they said, 'that
all whom we have consulted agree that the one really reliable
defence force for the workers is solid and tight organisation.
We have also found a general conviction that the present
system of Trade Union organisation in Ireland is thoroughly
unsatisfactory and that the movement itself needs rationalisation. Our correspondents have urged that competing
Trade Unions in one industry should cease to compete; and
again, that all Trade Unions concerned in an industry should
amalgamate or form a Federation. A means by which this
desirable end may be achieved has not been suggested, and
we, as a special Committee, feel that it would be outside
our terms of reference to tackle the subject of Trade
Union organisation, but we suggest to the Congress that
it demands immediate and most serious attention.'[34]

The subject may have demanded immediate and most serious
attention, but in fact it did not get it, and perhaps we
should reflect for a moment on the possible reasons for
this. The unions that were able to defend themselves
against a lowering of skill and a reduction in wages were
tightly organised not on an industry basis but on the
basis of the skill itself. This in itself would hardly
have been enough, but the groups in addition were tribal
in character, each person giving a swift and unquestioned
loyalty to the other members, and forming thereby the
basis of the work-group's economic power. This the bricklayers had, and the printers, the furniture workers

and the seamen seemed to manifest it as well. It was the
tribalism of craft. It had nothing to do with a federal
structure or with industry-wide unions; the tribalism
would not extend so far. The Women Workers Union, who
saw their members suffering both in the printing industry
and in the furniture industry, no doubt hoped that this
loyalty could be extended to them if the same union or
federation were to cater for all, but it is not immediately
clear that this would follow. Furthermore the position
of the AEU might have been misunderstood; they were,
one imagines, referring to competing unions, not within an
industry, but within the skill itself, inhibiting the
development of a craft loyalty in a trade which did not have
as strong traditions as the others had. It would be very
wrong to discount - even in the circumstances of the thirties -
the possibilities that lay with industry-wide trade unionism,
but there is an ambiguity in using the loyalty within crafts
or skills as an analogue. While tribal loyalty can be
remarkable in defence of its own, it can be quite disruptive
to the larger comity, even when that comity is made up of
fellow workers and trade unionists. Larkin's cry that an
injury to one is the concern of all finds a response only
among those who are already tightly knit in a common fate.
No strong feelings of this kind existed at the broad level
of an industry, and consequently there was little impulse
to create industry-wide organisation which reflected a
commonly-shared fate. If they had been created then perhaps
such loyalties could have been fostered, but the creation
of such organisation in the first instance, without any
natural trend in that direction, would have been a formidable
task. This was a dilemma that occurred again and again in
the years that followed.

On the other hand one would expect that amalgamations should
occur within the same skill or among neighbouring skills,
and experience in Britain right down through the years bears
this out. There was something of the same development in
the Free State - and later in the Republic - but here there
is a central frustration which gives the Irish situation
its special character, because the multiplicity of unions

within certain skills sprang, as we have seen, from the
breaking off from amalgamated unions of nationalist-
inspired groups who, characteristically, were small and
intensely separatist, and who consequently would view a
merger not as amalgamation but as domination, both numerically
and politically. The complaint of the AEU, therefore,
concerning competing unions - even when it referred to workers
within the same skill - had a somewhat hollow ring to it.

Although the report of the committee was adopted without
discussion, there was some debate on trade union cooperation
on an industry basis when the National Amalgamated Furniture
Trades Association moved a resolution on the control of
industry.[35] But the resolution was most non-committal. It
directed that the Congress executive - as far as practicable -
should establish industrial committees in each industry,
to correlate the work of the unions, to strengthen organisation and to promote joint action. The debate which was
limp, brief and repetitive, dealt essentially with the
wrangles of unions within an industry. The role of trades
councils in promoting joint action was not discussed, nor
was the question of worker control. Let us however consider
briefly what the committee reported about both these
significant questions.

The committee did little more than 'point to the importance
of stimulating the activities of Trades and Workers'
Councils' largely, it would appear, under the stimulus of
Limerick.[36] In a trade union structure such as that which
exists in Ireland, where characteristically there are many
national, horizontally-organised unions (that is, spread
throughout a number of industries), there are usually three
major points of interunion contact; at the national level
(which was met by Congress for example), at the level of
an industry (which was the substance of the 1930 debate),
and at the level of the local community, that is to say the
trades council. Yet clearly the trades councils were not
regarded as a fruitful line of development. We have already
noted how events were moving against them. In the absence of

political stimulus they tumbled down in number from 46
in 1921 (the high point) to 10 in the year we now discuss.[37]
Industrially too, the trend towards national bargaining
tended to make them irrelevant. Some were unhappy organisations: the Dublin council, for one, had been wracked
with dissension, and apart from all that, the effective
rejection by the Irish people of real local government and
the centrality that followed diminished their significance
both in function and in the general regard of the members.
And yet there remains the uneasy feeling that as a unifying
agency among trade unions they are somewhat undervalued.
In any event, in the report of the special committee, they
ranked little more than a mention.

Towards the close of the committee's report, there were
some unclear passages concerning industrial councils and
works councils. Although the idea of worker control - an
idea very close to Connolly's syndicalism - seemed to be
always the objective in some form, and although the report
spoke explicitly of an equal share in the control of industry,
the report saw in the works councils merely a means of
getting 'a voice in industrial changes' and this in fact
was the full extent of what was discussed. Indeed R.M. Fox,
a member of the committee, fearing for the worker's independence, favoured separate workers' committees 'with possible
representation on joint committees.'[38] The larger thinking
had been much eroded by the practical difficulties of the
time, and was in considerable contrast to the fine rhetoric
of the constitution debate a few months earlier.

There was therefore considerable complexity in the relations
between the unions at the time, and this we shall explore
more fully when we come to discuss our two further topics,
the disputes between unions and the tensions between
amalgamated and Irish-based organisations, but before leaving
the wider social initiatives of the trade union movement,
let us consider their response to fascism and to the growth
of the power of the state.

Unemployment too is the backdrop against which we must set
our discussion on the rise of fascism in Ireland in the
early thirties and the reaction of the trade union movement
to it. The sheer scale of the unemployment problem in
some European countries - far worse indeed than the Irish
experience - began to be realised in the years that
immediately followed, dwarfing the concern about industrial
organisation, although this still was debated in the annual
conference of 1932.[39] Denis Cullen, who was president in
1931, spoke graphically of the rise in unemployment, particularly in Germany. 'The mind stands aghast, appalled, at
the figures indicated, and at the sum of human anguish, misery
and suffering represented by them.'[40] But when he spoke
about the danger of recurring economic crises, he recognised
that 'this may appear to have only a remote or indirect
interest for us ...' If such remoteness existed, it quickly
disappeared, and the following year, Luke Duffy, when moving
the major resolution on economic planning, was very conscious
of the immediacy and of the relevance of what was happening
in Germany: 'Somebody has said that the peace of Europe
today depends on the life of one old man who is 86 years of
age. It is suggested that if the President of the German
Republic dropped dead tomorrow there would be a revolution
in Germany which would sweep all Europe and sweep aside
what we call civilisation. It is a doubtful civilisation
where you find millions unemployed, millions hungry, and
millions goaded to desperation in the midst of a world of
plenty.'[41]

Of course in August 1932, when the Congress met in Cork,
they were well pleased with the vigorous policies of de
Valera's government. Louie Bennett was president, the
first woman to hold the office, and in an address of some
power she praised the policy of the new government which
'has brought a wave of hope and vitality into depressed and

apathetic ranks' but she was deeply concerned at the sudden
increase of the power of the state which she saw as a
fascist tendency:[42]   'I refer to differential tariffs, and
taxes, powers assumed to promote certain industries and
business enterprises and to place an embargo on others.
Many of these schemes may be excellent but they bring us
perilously near to a Dictatorship',[43]   a sentiment from
which William Norton gently tried to disengage the Congress
in his vote of thanks, pointing out that the tariff policy
followed the lines of other governments who had adopted
protection.

There was one major recommendation to the government which
was urged both by Louie Bennett in her address and by the
conference itself. It was that a national economic council
be established 'to plan and reorganise the industrial,
economic, social and financial organisations of the Nation,
and to secure that the economic programme of the First Dail
will be effectively applied as an essential element of
National Reconstruction.'[44]   Congress contemplated a considerable extension of state activity: the assuming
possession of unoccupied or unused land; the assuming
control of industrial and public utilities and their
democratic management (in which the workers would have a
voice).[45]   The national economic council itself, however,
was seen as essentially an advisory council in which the
trade unions would have an influential part to play.

There was considerable confidence that the council would
in fact be set up. 'This has been stated over and over
again by the head of state,' said Luke Duffy in his reply
to the debate, 'and I have no doubt that there will be
an Economic Council established ...'[46]   In the event it
never was. Instead the menace of fascism came to dominate
all the social thinking of the trade union movement.

'Socialism and Fascism are both on trial,' said Louie Bennett

in her presidential address in 1932. 'They are working
on the mind of Europe like an autumn wind in the trees.
And we are likely to see rapid revolutionary changes in the
economic structure of many countries, our own included, in
the course of the next few years.'[47] These changes were
intensified by widespread unemployment and economic decline.
But if Ireland now suffered under the effects of the economic
war, the trade unions were ready enough to recognise the
greater dangers elsewhere. 'Today,' said Sean P. Campbell[48]
in Killarney in 1933, 'the period of expansion seems to
have ended, and society is sick unto death, and unable to
shake off the advance of deadly economic coma which is over-
taking it, despite all the economic conferences of the
statesmen of the world, who foregather one day in Locarno,
another in Lausanne, and yet again in London.' It was the
consequence of all this that appalled them 'when we look at
the face of modern Europe with its catastrophic political
upheavals arising from economic depression and resulting
in the entire destruction of democratic principles of
Government, Trade Unions, and all other democratic organisations -
where even religious freedom is in peril, and race hatred
inculcated; and where war with all its fiendish abominations
of mass destruction trembles in the balance.'[49] At the
Congress of 1933 there had been vigorous attacks on the growth
of dictatorship in Germany; and Norton had very explicitly
nailed the growth of fascism in Ireland; it was still however
a matter of resolution and debate. Then in 1934 the trade
unions suddenly saw a threat to themselves, to their freedom
and indeed to their very existence, and their statesmanlike,
if sincere concern, suddenly developed into a fullblooded and
very extensive anti-fascist campaign. Fine Gael, under O'Duffy,
announced early in 1934 its intention to establish the
Corporate State, as it described it, and the implications
of this for the trade unions was spelt out by O'Duffy in a
speech in Kildare on February 25: 'The Corporative plan is
to organise all the employers in a federation with a joint
council, and give this federation statutory powers to
regulate the industry it represents ... In case the workers and

employers cannot agree the case will go to a labour court,
presided over by a judicial officer, which will have power
to deliver a binding decision.'[50] The trade unions were
profoundly alarmed, saw this as 'a facsimile of the ideology
of the Fascist dictators on the Continent,'[51] and saw
themselves in great peril. In conjunction with the Labour
Party they launched a campaign which began on May 6 ('the
Connolly Memorial Sunday' as they called it) and issued a
joint manifesto to the workers of Ireland. The national
executive reported to the annual conference in August 1934
that large demonstrations were held in all the principal
centres of population, 'the size of the demonstrations and
the enthusiasm expressed being indicative of the intense
feeling of hostility which had been aroused by Blueshirt
Fascism.'[52]

But the position was not at all as straightforward as it
might appear, for two reasons: first because of catholic
social teaching on vocational corporations, as they were
sometimes called, and secondly because syndicalist and
socialist solutions also contemplated some corporate notion
of the state. In the circumstances of 1934, the first reason
was the more telling, particularly when the leaders of
the Blueshirt movement, avowed catholics, had explicitly
dissociated the movement from fascism. Despite these
denials, Johnson, at the 1934 annual conference, went to
some lengths to trace the clear fascist character of the
Blueshirts, reflecting thereby the anxiety of some of the
delegates in the matter; on the other hand, he was not
prepared to condemn vocationalism. Earlier, in June, he
had tried to deal with both points in an article in The
Distributive Worker; Professor Alfred O'Rahilly, of
University College Cork, a highly influential catholic
apologist, had written an earlier article in the same magazine on
vocational corporations, and Johnson quickly agreed that
this was a timely warning against the indiscriminate de-
nunciation of the idea.[53] After all he had found it among

such divergent groups as the French and Italian syndicalists, the industrial unionists and Socialist Labour party of America, the Guild Socialists of England, and even, the Dail Commission on the Resources of Ireland (1920-21); but in particular he found it in Connolly's social democracy. 'These quotations show that the corporate plan for controlling industry is not <u>necessarily</u> an anti-democratic device. But it is easy to see that the corporate idea may be seized upon to consolidate the power of the capitalist class and perpetuate the dependent status of the workers as a class. To understand why Labour combats the Blue Shirt propaganda for a Corporate State one needs to see that they associate with it a denial of democracy and a reassertion of the principle of autocracy.'[54]

It was easy enough to discount full-blown fascism, to discount the violent antiliberalism of a man such as Mussolini who could claim: 'We were the first to state, in the face of demoliberal individualism, that the individual exists only in so far as he is within the State and subjected to the requirements of the State and that as civilisation assumes aspects which grow more and more complicated, individual freedom becomes more and more restricted.'[55] There were few in Ireland who would officially go along with such ideas. What troubled the trade unions was the idea of vocational organisation, and here one could sense an uneasy acceptance of its inevitability. The debate in Dail Eireann on the Constitution of 1937, and in particular the question of the second house of the Oireachtas, gave considerable prominence to the idea of vocational organisation, and following a resolution from the Senate in July 1938 the government established a commission to report on the matter which began its work in 1939 and sat until 1943. The Commission recommended a vast pervasive system of vocational organisation but were careful to avoid any interference with the free individually elected parliament. Louie Bennett and Sean Campbell, the two trade union representatives, were very unhappy.

They felt obliged to endorse the main thrust of the report towards vocationalism[56] (everything seemed to point that way) but the panoply of national assembly, governing body and director seemed to them premature and open to mis-conception.[57]

Mortished, now in the ILO, who submitted a memorandum on the question in 1939[58] - more of an informative than of a policy kind - saw merit in the idea in that it might provide a parish-pump type of group democracy which in his view was so appallingly lacking in the local government structure in Ireland, not indeed in substitution for democratic local government but rather as part of the same family of development. But it appears in all this that the point was to some extent missed. Organisations in a democracy - and we have made this point already with regard to trade unions - do not organise men and women, but rather certain roles they perform, whether the role be familial, political or economic. The citizen is free because it is his role that is organised and restricted, not him; he is somehow in-dependent of his various roles and therefore of the organ-isations that organise them. It is precisely this that vocational organisation, no less than fascism, challenges; it was this that made men and women in the trade union tradition uneasy; and ultimately it may well have in-fluenced the Fianna Fail government in its brusque dis-missal of the whole grand design as recommended by the commission.

Let us return however to the Irish Trade Union Congress, remarking on how the interest in fascism faded as that movement itself began to break up. Perhaps, however, before we close this section, we should note the efforts to affiliate to the International Federation of Trade Unions, proposed first in 1935, but failing for lack of a money resolution to support it, and which was taken up again in 1936. This time it got a full dress debate, and internationalism was strongly urged by many in order, in particular, that the Irish trade unions should play their part in combating

international fascism. The Irish National Teachers
Organisation was full of concern and feared a communist
connection. However, the conference, after some very high-
minded statements, adopted a recommendation both to affiliate
to the Federation and to raise the appropriate contribution
by change of rule. But in 1937,[59] despite the grand rhetoric
of the year before, the executive recommended that they
would not raise the contribution that year, and when Sam
Kyle protested, and INTO representative moved next business[60]
and the whole adventure sank without a trace.

All in all therefore, these major political and social
challenges of the time, although they influenced the
thinking within the trade unions, and influenced the
environment in which they worked, had no apparent effect
on the structure of the trade union movement. Fascism was
a philosophical challenge and perhaps did not require a
structural response, but wage-cuts and redundancy were quite
another matter, and here the organisational response that
actually did take place revealed only too clearly the
movement's more obvious defects - the weakness of the unions
and their multiplicity. But the underlying causes of
that weakness were by no means as clearly seen, and there
was a certain amount of bewilderment and frustration that
more was not attempted.

-v-

Let us now turn to the question of disputes between unions,
and within that context, the growing stress between Irish
unions and British unions; and as we do so we must note
as well the change in tone at the Congress meetings, the
growing acrimony and at times the nastiness that characterised the debates.

The tension developed essentially within the Free State.

Belfast at that time was not prominent in the affairs of
the Trade Union Congress. There were broadly two reasons
for this. The first was the weakness and apathy in trade union
organisation in the north;[61] and secondly, a number of
unions with large membership in the north were not
affiliated to the Irish Congress at all. In its final
report in 1939 the Trade Union Commission of Inquiry said
in Memorandum No.1: 'There is a large number of Trade
Unionists in Northern Ireland who, for many reasons, do
not cooperate in the work of the Irish Trade Union Congress,
though in many cases some Unions of these workers are
affiliated to the British and Scottish Trade Union Congresses.
Owing to this non-cooperation, these Trade Unionists of the
North do not, generally speaking, come into contact with the
Trade Union Movement as represented by the Irish Trade
Union Congress';[62] and William O'Brien in a memorandum to
the same commission in 1936[63] made a special point of this
and gave as examples 'the National Union of General and
Municipal Workers, the National Union of Distributive and
Allied Workers, the Amalgamated Engineering Union, Boiler-
makers', Shipwrights, and other unions having a considerable
membership in the Belfast shipyards.' On the other hand,
the conflict as it developed between British-based and Irish-
based unions within the Irish Congress was clearly seen
as disruptive of relations north and south. But the
relationship thus threatened with disruption was now quite
different from that of the early years when the Congress
was born. At that time, the trades councils in Dublin and
Belfast were two largely independent pillars, two distinct
groups, who, if they offended one another, might draw apart.
Now the emphasis had changed from trades council to trade
union and in particular to such great unions as the NUR,[64]
the ASW (who had in fact almost exactly the same number
of members north and south)[65] and the Amalgamated Transport[66]
whose long and bitter dispute with the Irish Transport[67]
was the centrepiece of all that took place. The question
essentially was whether such unions should continue in the
Free State and the notion of disruption was in the main concerned with the splintering away of the Free State members

from unions, some of which had traditionally represented all the workers appropriate to them throughout these islands, and the creation of two quite separate trade unions systems north and south.

In the British-Irish context then, the major dispute was that between the Irish Transport and the Amalgamated Transport; and in the exclusively Irish-based context, the major dispute turned on the long-standing row between Jim Larkin and William O'Brien, which boiled towards a climax as the decade went by. The other major disputes were in the craft area – carpenters, electricians and plasterers – and while they had a British-Irish dimension, they were also straightforward organisational conflicts turning on a specific trade union clash of interests. But the attitude of the Irish Transport to these disputes was also of great significance. It seems wiser therefore, in evaluating the events that followed, to put William O'Brien and the Irish Transport in the centre of our discussions, recognising how overwhelming their contribution was to the impulse for structural change.

There was a most inauspicious beginning to the relations between the Amalgamated Transport and the Irish Transport, quite apart from the earlier conflict between Larkin and Sexton. The Irish Transport and General Workers Union was formed, as we have seen, in 1909. In the year 1921, as a result of an amalgamation of a number of large unions with many members in transport, there was registered in England the Transport and General Workers Union, which, as Mr Justice Meredith[68] pointed out in 1935, 'was as accurately descriptive of the general character of the Union in England as the title "Irish Transport and General Workers Union" was of the union in Ireland.' This, however, was of little help to an anxious Irish Transport when the newly amalgamated union recorded its rules in Ireland in January 1922. The position was further confused when the new union opened its

Irish office in Parnell Square in Dublin where the
executive offices of the Irish Transport were also
situated; and this caused William O'Brien to write an
alarmed but courteous letter to Ernest Bevin in late
February 1922.[69] The reply a month later was hardly helpful;
Bevin dismissed the point quite cursorily, and indulgently
remarked: 'Surely the word "Irish" has some value in indicating the different society, at any rate if I were to
say it hadn't, you, I think, would be the first to re-
monstrate with me.'[70] The Irish Transport instituted proceedings in the Dail Eireann courts, and in June 1922 got an
order restraining the amalgamated union from using the name
Transport and General Workers Union. The amalgamated union
by rule decided that in Ireland it would be known as the
Amalgamated Transport and General Workers Union, and the
amended rule was recorded with the Registrar of Trade Unions
in Saorstat Eireann in August 1925. Later this was to
lead to a further action challenging the validity of such
recording, and this was the case that came to hearing in 1935
before Judge Meredith. Yet in the period we now speak of,
that is 1929-30, there had not yet developed that uncompromising sense of conflict which was ultimately to shatter
the trade union movement.

There had been a lengthy strike in the tram services in the
summer of 1929, an employment which was the cockpit of much
conflict, and in the summer of the following year there was
a threatened railway strike, which was averted by a last-
minute intervention by the Minister for Industry and Commerce.
It was suggested that the question of English and Irish
unions was involved, but this was sharply dismissed as an
irrelevancy by T.J. O'Connell in his 1930 presidential address
to Congress. The burden of his address was that there
should be a system of public inquiry into threatened industrial disputes - averting strikes, and securing equity
by a public airing in good time. Industrial peace was the
primary objective of course but also 'we should in such
circumstances have heard less about the activities of "foreign"

Unions and perhaps a great deal more about the attempts
of Railway and Bus Magnates to subordinate the transport
services of this country to the interests of foreign
companies in which they have a considerable financial
interest.'[71] And in such a context the foreign union
difficulty was 'a subterfuge (which) was adopted to cloud
the issue.'

Nor was this merely whitewashing. We have already noted
the settlement some years before of a dispute in the Belfast
docks between the Irish Transport and the Amalgamated
Transport, and this had resulted in a proposal in 1929 for
a system of adjudication by Congress of inter-union disputes,
a proposal which was adopted in 1930 on a motion by McMullen
of the Irish Transport, supported by Tom Kennedy of the same
union. (In the acrimonious debate at the 1934 Congress,
McMullen claimed that in this matter the Amalgamated Transport
had 'treated the sub-committee, the National Executive and
the Congress with absolute contempt'[72] but there was no
suggestion of that at the time). Indeed up to the outbreak
of its dispute with the Amalgamated Transport in 1933,
the Irish Transport appears to have adopted a helpful approach
generally to the growing problem of Irish and amalgamated
unions. This was quite evident in the significant debate
in 1930 on the admission to affiliation of the Irish National
Union of Woodworkers, a debate which gives an early insight
into the character of the problem and the various positions
which trade unions took up.

Apart from the ancient Dublin craft unions, the Irish-
based unions - even the Irish Transport - had, as we have
seen, their origins in break-away movements from the British
unions of earlier days; and in this the Irish National
Union of Woodworkers was no different, having broken away in
1921 from the Amalgamated Society of Woodworkers. Towards
the end of the twenties it had applied to Congress for
affiliation, which the ASW vigorously opposed, threatening
to resign if the national union were admitted. This was a

conundrum, since not only was the ASW a great traditional
union in Ireland, but it numbered 7,000 members in contrast
with five hundred or so in the case of the INUW. The
national executive temporised: 'Time was a great healer,
and perhaps in the course of time some settlement might be
reached.'[73] But in the meantime, the INUW remained unaffiliated, which greatly nettled nationalist-minded delegates.
The great argument put forward by the amalgamated unions
was that splintering weakened the trade union movement,
but this was impatiently dismissed by the nationalist
delegates, who claimed that the trouble lay not in the
number of unions but, as Helena Molony remarked[74] in the
fact that 'there were too many conflicting unions and too
many standards of trade unionism. 'As to breakaways,'
she continued, 'they might be justified or not. In this
case the break-away had justified itself. The whole history
of the country, as well as the history of the Labour movement,
justified the break-away policy.' Johnson, more soberly,
tended to think that time conferred legitimacy, and the union,
after all, had persisted for nine years; but in the event, the
view of the national executive prevailed, William O'Brien
emphasising that 'this was not an issue between Irish and
Cross-channel Unions, and had never been considered in that
spirit.'[75] His hope was that the national executive would
smooth the matter out. But this in the circumstances was
most unlikely; the ASW could not readily give way, and once
the nationalist bell was sounded the Irish-based union
could not be refused.

In normal trade union circumstances, it is doubtful if a
union such as the INUW would have ever been considered for
affiliation because of the settled policy against multiplicity. This policy was quite firm despite the remarks of
Helena Molony. Indeed in 1936, even when the Irish-
amalgamated rivalry was in full flood, the national executive,
reported, quite explicitly, that when several small unions
had applied for affiliation they had recommended that they

seek association instead with larger analogous unions, the
Cork Commercial Travellers and the Irish Union of Distributive
Workers and Clerks being a case in point. But where the
nationalist impulse dominated other considerations, as it
did with the INUW, the approach was quite different, and
was in marked contrast - as the amalgamated unions were
quick to point out - to the decisions in two other cases
in the years that followed, the ETU (England) and the
plasterers. When the ETU (England) applied in 1932 they
were offered affiliation on condition that they confined
their activities to the north - where they were well
represented - excluding the south where they were not. While
there was a bitter reaction from some of the northern
delegates, who saw it as a rejection of all northern unions,
the fact of the matter was that such a suggestion was
entirely sensible in the circumstances, and no doubt the
president of Congress, Louie Bennett, was quite sincere
when she declared herself to be deeply grieved at any
implication of prejudice. 'I am strongly opposed to any
conflict in this country in the Trade Union Movement between
British and Irish Trade Unions ... If I saw the slightest
trace of prejudice ... I would not have stood for it.'[76]
The feeling of conflict was much more intense in 1936 when
the affiliation of the British-based National Association
of Operative Plasterers was rejected. Again this was seen
by some of the northern delegates as a rejection of the
northern presence in Congress; but in purely trade union
terms the decision was an understandable one. The Dublin
plasterers union,[77] ancient and arrogant, were seething
with annoyance at a strike-breaking demarché by some members
of the British union, and even though their interest lay
only in Dublin, they had a considerable point. It was not
then that these decisions were necessarily wrong; rather
did they appear sinister in the light of the decision in
the case of the INUW.

When the national executive accepted the INUW into
affiliation in 1931, the ASW, as they had threatened to do,
disaffiliated. There was a considerable effort to woo them

back, O'Brien showing a good deal of anxiety in the matter.
By 1934 they had succeeded; but now the whole climate
changed, as the row between the Irish Transport and the
Amalgamated Transport came to dominate trade union affairs;
and it is not unlikely that if the ASW withdrawal had
occurred some years later, the same effort would not have
been made to bring them back. But of course the situation
began to change for the amalgamated unions as well. When
faced with the nationalist challenge, their desire to remain
stiffened, and consequently their interest in Congress
quickened as well. It was all seen by some trade unionists
as a shabby business, particularly as, in this year 1934,
the trade unions were confronted with the perilous challenge
of fascism.

On January 5 1934 the Amalgamated Transport and General
Workers Union wrote to the national executive of the Irish
Trade Union Congress stating that they wished to 'invoke
the machinery of Congress in connection with the effort
being made to take their members into the Irish Transport
and General Workers Union.'[78] The dispute arose on the
sensitive matter of the Dublin trams. The Amalgamated
Transport may have anticipated the establishing of a disputes
committee as occurred in the dispute in the Belfast docks
some years before, but the resident committee decided to
remit the case to a full meeting of the national executive
on February 2. In the meantime, the response of the Irish
Transport to the complaint was sought, and this response
converted what may have been a jurisdictional dispute into
a matter of major national principle, and, because the
two largest unions were concerned, polarised the whole trade
union movement on the same issue. 'To describe', they said,
'as "poaching" the revolt of the Dublin Tramwaymen ... is
a wanton misuse of a well-understood term; in fact, it is
a claim that Irishmen shall not be permitted to manage their
own affairs ... Neither can we admit that our action in
this case in any way violates the Constitution of Congress ...

Obviously there is nothing in the Constitution of Congress
which would prevent Irish workers from severing their
relations with foreign Unions whenever they desired to give
their allegiance to an Irish Union.'[79]   It was only too
clear, then, why the matter was referred to the whole
national executive;   right from the very outset it was seen
as being a far larger question than a jurisdictional dispute.
But before the national executive met at all an invitation
was issued in its name on January 30 to representatives
of 'unions with headquarters outside this country' to attend
a conference 'to discuss the question of their Irish
membership.'[80]

But what was the purpose in such a conference?   In their
annual report to the August conference the national executive
declared that the decision was in no way actuated by any
hostility to unions 'with headquarters outside the country;
in fact a tribute for the good work well done by English
Trade Unions in Ireland has been recorded by the National
Executive.'[81]   On the contrary they were actuated 'solely
by the desire that all those concerned would secure a full
appreciation of the changing circumstances of the country
and the changes that were taking place in the minds of
the members of the British-controlled Trade Unions.'   The
dispute between the two unions was seen as part of a general
movement threatening the integrity of the trade union movement,
which could be preserved only 'if there is a mutual
appreciation by those concerned of the economic and political
developments now taking place in Ireland ... As national
self-consciousness grows it will express itself in all phases
and activity of the national life of the country.'[82]   In a
word, the amalgamated unions were being asked to preside at
their own demise.

Not surprisingly, at their meeting of February 2, the
national executive found for the Irish Transport;   and, also
not surprisingly, the conference of the amalgamated unions

did not take place; these unions stated that they would
have to discuss the matter between themselves first. The
effect of this discussion was very quickly seen.[83]

For ten years or more the number of delegates from amalgamated unions attending annual conference had hovered
around the forty mark, rising to forty-five and dropping
to thirty-eight. Suddenly in 1934 the number leapt up to
seventy-two, and continued steadily to rise over the next
decade until the year of the split, 1945, when the number stood
at ninety-four. It was not until the following conference,
that of 1935, that the number of Irish union delegates
increased from their normal 90 (or a little less) to 105,
and it was two years later before their peak figure of 124
was reached. The same trend is even more clearly reflected
in the delegate numbers from the two transport unions.
The Amalgamated Transport in 1934 more than doubled the
number of its delegates from 12 to 25, which was almost
the same number as that fielded in that year by the Irish
Transport; it was the following year, 1935, before the Irish
Transport increased its number from 27 to 33. But the
national executive (which must have been full of stress
at the time)[84] remained during this period relatively
unchanged, the Irish unions outnumbering the amalgamated
unions by more than two to one, and although the majority
diminished in the years that followed it still remained
under the control of the Irish-based unions until the fateful
conference of 1945 when the position was dramatically
reversed. We must take care however not to see all this
in too stark terms; there were a number of Irish-based unions
who would strongly support the amalgamated position and some
amalgamated unions as well who were anxious to respond to
the nationalist impulse.

The national executive - whether they intended it or not -
had now called into being a grouping of amalgamated unions
with a clearly defined interest, and fortified by this and

by his substantial delegation, Sam Kyle of the Amalgamated
Transport threw down the gauntlet at the August conference
of 1934. It seemed clear from the manner in which Kyle
presented his case, that the Irish Transport had decided to
campaign for members in the tramway branch of the amalgamated
union. Kyle's motion deplored the decision of the national
executive to support the Irish Transport in this and declared
that all unions affiliated to the Congress were equally
entitled to the protection of the rules.[85] The railway
unions and the ASW were vigorous in support. Some, like
O'Carroll of the Railway Clerks,[86] would have wished to see
it all as merely a domestic squabble but to many it was
without doubt an amalgamated-Irish conflict, and here Barron
of the ASW, a Glasgow delegate, made the substance of the
amalgamated case: 'The moment this agitation started his
Society took steps to ascertain the opinion of every branch
in Ireland, and everyone of them, without exception stated
definitely that they had no desire to leave the Amalgamated
Society.'[87] This was reinforced by Campbell of the very
influential National Union of Railwaymen who was himself a
Dublin delegate. They had held a conference immediately
after independence and again in 1933 in order to put the
suggestion that the members form an Irish-based union and
on each occasion the opinion of the members was heavily
against it. The contrary view, the nationalist view, was
put by Helena Molony: national self-consciousness was
growing, and the current dispute was an incident in a
situation which was becoming widespread. In order to avoid
confusion and chaos she suggested again the venerable proposal
that the trade union movement should be reconstructed along
industrial lines. As we shall see, this as a device - as a
formula which had an acceptable ring about it - became the
keystone for later discussion. But the impetus behind the
formula was not one of efficiency and better service, but
rather of nationalism. More than that, it was a nationalism
which derived its power from principle, not from any observed
defects in the amalgamated unions. There was no evidence,

in the recorded material in any event, of trade union
colonialism.   The Irish members of the amalgamated unions
not only possessed a traditional loyalty to those unions,
but, in the manner of trade unions, in practice also
ran their own affairs.   The nationalist delegates did not
criticise the amalgamated unions as such;   their position
was more basic.   They believed that Irish members for
nationalistic reasons more and more wished to abandon
amalgamated unions, and they should be permitted to do so.
O'Brien summarised it well.   He claimed he had never taken
a prejudiced attitude towards the British unions but 'we are
a separate and distinct nationality.   We believe we know
what the Labour movement stands for in this country ...   If it
is the parting of the ways and there is no way of avoiding it,
we will have to part and you will have to make up your
minds as to whether we can do without you better than you
can do without us;   but the policy of this Congress, and of
the Irish Labour movement in the past has been that British
and Irish unions can work amicably together, and whether
sections of Irish workers should be in Irish Unions or in
English unions was a matter for the workers to decide for
themselves.'[88]   But O'Brien intended to do more than wait
and see how members would choose.   His object clearly was
to neutralise Congress and give some legitimacy to a campaign
which the Irish Transport wished to mount, a campaign no
doubt made more compelling in view of the growing strength
of the amalgamated unions.

These views were all predictable enough, but for the
amalgamated unions perhaps the most disturbing voice was
that of Johnson.   He had been sincerely impressed by the
quite different legislative development in the Free State
and Britain.   His view therefore was that the national
executive 'merely asked the amalgamated unions to do for
this country, long before any crisis arose, what was found
to be necessary in other countries.   He quite understood that
the great majority of the Irish members of the British Unions,
as they were called, did desire to remain with those Unions.

He quite recognised that, but the national executive might
have to take into consideration the fact that there was
growing up a different code of laws, a different legislative
atmosphere affecting Trades Unions in this country from
that which prevailed in Britain.'[89]   Johnson was a sincere
and thoughtful man, and reflected the feeling of the time
of inevitable separatism in all matters, a separatism so
profound that it would prevail over the trade union loyalties
of large numbers of people whose organisations had served
them well. As we shall see in a moment, these remarks
of Johnson's were to be given much greater significance
by the judgement of Judge Meredith in the October of the
following year.

The 1934 debate was a drawn battle, as alarmed delegates
sought a withdrawal of both the appropriate paragraph of the
report of the national executive, and also of Sam Kyle's
resolution. The question went back to the national executive,
who, on a general policy basis, set up a subcommittee to
suggest machinery which could be applied where members wished
to change from one union to another. Broadly they settled
for due notice and required that the transferring members
should be in-benefit, and they submitted their proposal
to both transport unions. This was of course all quite
beside the point. However, the Amalgamated Transport agreed
with the proposal (it accorded with their view of what
was appropriate) but the Irish Transport pleaded that they
were too busy because of a transport strike, and much later,
refused on some grounds of inadequate representation on the
subcommittee which devised the formula. Actually the strike -
a lengthy one of eleven weeks in the Dublin Tramways in the
spring of 1935 - took a good deal of steam out of the dispute
since both unions cooperated quite well in a common
cause. But the Congress of 1935 also noted other 'acrimonious
incidents' which they considered sprang from the same difficulty.
As one delegate remarked: 'By their quarrels with one another,
and not working in harmony, they were doing much to strengthen
the numbers of the unorganised.'[90]

It was a most contentious time. A local row between
carpenters in the midlands took on the aspect of an ASW-
INUW conflict, and in Cork a similar row between members
of the two unions led in 1937 to a Court of Inquiry under
the Industrial Courts Act 1919.[91] There was trouble between
the Irish unions themselves. The Irish Engineering and
Industrial Union, for example, had infuriated the Irish
Transport by welshing on their undertaking to support them
in their row with the Carlow Sugar Beet Factory on the
question of unionisation. But the other major row - the
row which had echoed right down through the years - was
that between the Irish Transport on the one hand and Larkin
and the Workers Union of Ireland on the other.

Larkin's union had been excluded not only from Congress
but from the Dublin Trade Union Council as well, and when
in that stormy year of 1934 he applied for membership of the
Dublin body there was a vehement reaction from William
O'Brien: 'So far as we are concerned we will not associate
with James Larkin either inside or outside the Council, and
if he is admitted this Union will have no option but to
withdraw from affiliation.'[92] The letter to the Dublin
council which contained this remark was bitterly uncompromising:
'For more than eleven years James Larkin has waged war on
the Labour movement, commencing with his attack upon the
Trade Union Congress in August 1923 and continued to the
present year when he attempted to disrupt the Connolly
Celebration held under the auspices of the Council. No
employer, or combination of employers, has ever inflicted
upon the Labour movement the damage which James Larkin is
directly responsible for ... To admit the arch-wrecker James
Larkin would mean the end of the Council, as his vanity and
egoism is such that he is incapable of working in any
movement in which he has not absolute control ...' The
conflict here then was of a different kind from that which
existed between the transport unions. In the case of the
Irish Transport and the Workers Union, there was a personal

antagonism so profound that no solution was found to it
until both O'Brien and Larkin had left the trade union
scene - and this did not take place until thirteen years
or more had elapsed. Larkin in fact was not without support
for all his impatience. He succeeded in being admitted
to the Dublin council and as a delegate from that body he
appeared at the annual conference to plead the case for
the admission of his own union, the Workers Union of Ireland,
into affiliation. The debate was largely a wrangle about
procedure, in which the Irish Transport took no part, but
the motion of next business, which was intended to suppress
Larkin, succeeded by a very slender majority. Larkin's
union was in fact never admitted - not in any event until
after the split in 1945, although Larkin himself attended
as a delegate from the Dublin Trades Council. It is
important to recognise the influence of this dispute in that
it effectively excluded the use of the trades or local
council as a device for restructuring Congress, and one can
see even in the preliminary proposals for reform in 1935 a
great chariness about their development.

-vi-

Let us now turn to the question of the legal status of the
amalgamated trade unions in the Free State, a question which,
from the point of view of these unions, grew steadily more
alarming. When the Free State was first established the
British offices became very concerned about their legal
status, but they decided on the whole to let sleeping dogs
lie. Now however the whole thing was pulled into the
courts of law as the Irish Transport in its conflict with
the Amalgamated Transport sought a declaration that the
recording of that union as a registered union in the Free
State was illegal and invalid.

It is necessary for the purposes of the discussion to sketch
in briefly the legal background to the problem. The Trade

Union Act of 1871[93] provided for the voluntary registration
of trade unions, and the Trade Union Act Amendment Act 1876[94]
provided that a registered trade union operating in more
than one of the three countries, England, Scotland and
Ireland, then constituting the United Kingdom, should be
registered in the country in which its registered offices
were situated, but that if it wished to operate in another
of the countries, it should send its rules to the registrar
there, who would record them. This was sufficient for it
to be regarded as a registered union in that country. The
point was that it did not have to seek registration there;
one registration was sufficient and would be effective for
the other countries, on the registrars of those countries
recording the rules. This naturally was the procedure
followed by the amalgamated unions in Ireland, and in
particular it was the procedure followed by the Amalgamated
Transport and General Workers Union. By virtue of section
three of the Adaptations of Enactments Act 1922 the name
Ireland came to mean Saorstat Eireann but this radically
altered the whole basis of the section which, as Judge
Meredith later pointed out,[95] was based on a legislative
union of the three countries. The fact was that the
British legislation never contemplated a situation where
a trade union, established and controlled outside the
United Kingdom, operated within the United Kingdom; and
when the same legal construct was imported automatically
into the law of the Free State a situation of mutual
exclusivity arose.

The government took the view that the system of recording was
no longer operative in the Free State, and trade unions registered
in Great Britain, even though recorded here in Ireland, must
be regarded as unregistered; and this they conveyed to the
Congress in a memorandum in 1928[96] with the comment that the
position required the serious attention of the members
affected.

It is important however that we should see the question of

registration in perspective. The essential character of a
trade union, under the 1871 Act and subsequent legislation,
depended on its being defined as such, not on whether it
was registered or not. Registration was not a necessary
condition to its existence but it conferred advantages in
regard to taxation, the control of property and legal proceedings. This of course was why the amalgamated unions
decided against any precipitate action in the matter. But
once the distinction was raised between registered and
unregistered unions, there was no reason why the significance
of registration should not be greatly augmented, simplifying
what many claimed was a chaotic trade union structure, and
perhaps as well cutting at the artery in the case of the
amalgamated unions. The legislative programme of the
government was in any event of a radical and separatist
character and they had already expressed impatience with
the trade union structure and a determination to achieve by
legislation what the trade unions had so far failed to achieve
by agreement. This is what gave great significance to the
judgement of Judge Meredith in the autumn of 1935 when he
declared that 'the recording in the Registry of Trade
Unions in Saorstat Eireann of the Rules of the Transport
and General Workers' Union or of the Amalgamated Transport
and General Workers' Union, or of any amendment of the said
Rules, is inoperative and of no legal effect.'[97] Sam Kyle
at the subsequent annual conference in 1936 pushed for a
statement from Congress regretting the action of the Irish
Transport in taking the case to court, and seeking protection
for the members now affected, but in view of the fact that
machinery for inquiry into such matters was now under
discussion, Congress took no action in the matter.

Perhaps before going on, it might be as well to glance at
the position of trade union law in Northern Ireland, noting
that in important respects it differed both from that in the
Free State and, later, from that in the rest of the United Kingdom.
Under the Trade Disputes and Trade Unions Act (Northern Ireland)
1927,[98] a strike or lock-out was declared illegal 'if it has

any object other than or in addition to the furtherance of
a trade dispute ... and is designed or calculated to coerce
the government ...' and there were some other important
differences as well, in particular concerning the political
levy. But as far as the trade unions' legal status was
concerned, the law was the same as that in the United Kingdom.

These then were the circumstances in which Congress established
its commission of inquiry in April 1936. Already in 1935 the
national executive in its report to the annual conference
had made rather far-reaching recommendations designed
to discourage house unions (that is, unions controlled by
employers) and splinter groups; the object was to prevent
'the rise of undisciplined so-called Trade Unions at the
instigation of every individual who considers he has a
grievance against an existing union.'[99] They declared that
Congress should not recognise such groups. Furthermore trades
councils should not accept branches of unions into membership without the sanction of the national executive. And
finally they recommended that national joint industrial
councils should be created, of representatives of each bona
fide trade union operating within each specific industry,
to which matters of joint concern must be submitted.[100]
But running through the recommendation was a great sense
of agitation. They spoke of warring competitive unions,
disintegrating new bodies and internecine union warfare,
which conveys an impression of a state of affairs more
extensive, more perilous and more fragmentary than we have
been able to establish here. Yet a resolution supporting
the executive recommendation which was moved by Scott of the
Dublin council (a body now apparently doing good work in
promoting groupings) resulted in little discussion. One
suspects that the substance of the difficulty lay in two
areas: on the one hand in the conflict between the two
transport unions, inflating and perhaps distorting other
Irish-amalgamated difficulties, and on the other hand in
the totally irresolvable conflict between Larkin and O'Brien.

This in no way diminishes the intractability of the problem.
However, it simplifies it and identifies its more powerful
causes. Within the normal bubble of unrest - normal in a
structure such as that of the Irish trade union movement -
the nationalist impulse both enlarged and inflamed the
stresses of the time. The unions sought some structural
solution, but opportunities were limited. Because of the
other great conflict, the personal conflict between O'Brien
and Larkin, no consideration could be given (as we have
noted) to integration at a local trades council level; such
councils at the time were probably inherently inadequate
in any event.

It was in these circumstances that the classical well-
regarded solution of industry-based unionism again became
significant. It emerged as the dominant theme in the
work of the trade union commission of inquiry that was
soon to be established. And waiting in the wings was a
government, separatist, nationalist and impatient for
good order.

Notes on Chapter Three

1. ILP & TUC: Special Congress Report 1930 p.5.

2. ibid. p.6.

3. ibid. p.7

4. ibid. p.5.

5. ibid. p.9.

6. ibid. p.7.

7. Johnson's papers: available in the National Library of
    Ireland: Ms. 17124.

8. Johnson about this time had taken a libel action against
    Larkin for vituperative attacks on him in The Irish
    Worker in which he was accused of being 'an English
    traitor' 'going over to capitalism.' Thomas Johnson
    had been born in Liverpool in 1872, but had taken a job
    in Kinsale as a clerk when he was nineteen years of
    age. He became a commercial traveller in Belfast,
    immediately began his trade union career in that city,
    rising to be president of Congress in 1916 and secretary
    in 1918. (Johnson papers: 17149(1).) (For a trans-
    cript of the hearing of the action Johnson v Larkin
    in April 1925 see Johnson papers 17149 (11).)

9. William O'Brien's papers: available in the National
    Library: Ms.13951.

10. Johnson's own family background was Church of England
    (Johnson papers 17149 (1).)

11. It is likely that William O'Brien himself never departed
    from his belief in Connolly's teachings, but Larkin
    had taken to him the banner of radicalism, and O'Brien's
    intractable dispute with him, which persisted from 1923
    (when Larkin returned from the US) for a full quarter
    of a century, obliged him to reserve.

12. In 1936 the Labour Party adopted a new constitution
    which was introduced by Johnson, pledging the party
    to the establishment of a Workers' Republic, but the
    Irish National Teachers Organisation, after consulting
    with the Catholic Hierarchy, challenged it, and in
    a new constitution in 1940 the objective became the
    establishment of a "Republican form of government."
    (See also J.H. Whyte: Church and State in Modern Ireland
    1923-1970 Gill and Macmillan Dublin 1971, pp. 81-84)
    For a Labour Party debate on Connolly's relevance, see

The Labour Party fifth annual conference: February
10 - 12, 1936 pp. 101-11. Unfortunately, the practice
of publishing a transcript of the annual conference
debates was discontinued in the early forties. Finally
see The Labour Party: Report 1937 where on page 14
there is an account of an article hostile to the
Labour Party which had been published in Osservatore
Romano and carried in the Irish Independent on February
18 1937; it had in fact been originally summarised
from an article in the Irish Catholic. Norton
immediately wrote to the Cardinal Secretary of State,
Cardinal Pacelli, denying that the trade unions and the
Labour Party 'tacitly support Communism' and stating
that their policies were 'based on Christian teaching.'

13.   Irish Women Workers' Union.

14.   Special Congress Report 1930, p.39.

15.   ibid. p.10.

16.   ibid. p.11.

17.   ibid. p.18.

18.   See Budge and O'Leary: Approach to Crisis: A Study of
      Belfast Politics 1613-1970 Macmillan 1973 p.151.

19.   Cullen op.cit. p.176.

20.   Meenan op.cit. p.97.

21.   Cullen op.cit. p.178.

22.   ibid. p.178.

23.   ibid. p.179

24.   ibid. p.178.

25.   ibid. p.180.

26.   ibid. p.180.

27.   F.S.L. Lyons: Ireland since the Famine, Weidenfeld and
      Nicolson   1971 pp.518-28.

28.   ITUC 1936 p.27.

29.   J.H. Whyte: Church and State in Modern Ireland 1923-1970, 1971.
                                                          p.68

30.   Budge and O'Leary op.cit. p.151.

31.   idem.

32.   See Cullen: op. cit. p.175

33. ITUC 1930 p.43

34. ITUC 1930 p.48

35. ITUC 1930 p.101 ff.

36. ibid. p.49.

37. Judge: Ph.D. thesis: op.cit. Appendix II.

38. ITUC 1930 p.50.

39. ITUC 1932 p.85.

40. ibid. p.21.

41. ibid. p.82.

42. ibid. p.25.

43. ibid. p.26.

44. ibid. p.79.

45. ibid. p.80.

46. ibid. p.87.

47. ibid. p.21.

48. ITUC 1933 p.21. He was president that year.

49. Senator Michael Duffy in his presidential address to the
    Irish Trade Union Congress 1934 ITUC 1934 p.24.

50. Quoted in ITUC 1934 pp.38, 39.

51. ibid. p.39.

52. ibid. p.39.

53. "The Corporate State and Fascism" in The Distributive
    Worker June 1934 p.137.

54. ibid.

55. Quoted in Report of Commission on Vocational Organisation
    op.cit. p.12.

56. Although Larkin and also Morrow from Belfast were wary,
    if uncertain, about vocationalism, Eamonn Lynch favoured
    it; and during the 1938 debate at the annual conference
    of Congress on the Senate he said: 'The Second House of
    the Oireachtas was created on the principle of vocational

or functional democracy. The National Executive looked
on a House created in such a manner with favour. The
Labour movement, so far as he knew it - and he had been
for many years associated with it - had always endorsed
the principle of vocationalism, in its application
to representative institutions. In my experience of the
Trade Union and Labour movement, I find that the further
people were to the left in politics the more they
appeared to endorse and approve of the principles of
vocationalism in Governmental institutions. You will
find that in all countries in the world. Therefore,
if the National Executive approved, as they did, of a
Second House, established on the basis of vocational
representation, they were naturally in harmony with
the best and most progressive thought in the whole
Labour movement.' (ITUC 1938 p.130). Furthermore
in 1939 Louie Bennett is reported as follows: 'After
a good deal of instruction in the last few months she
had come to the conclusion that vocational organisation
was just a polite way of speaking of "corporative
organisation." I do not think we, in the Trade Union
movement, have any reason for completely turning down
the corporative system. None of us is satisfied with
the present social system and we need something new.
I believe myself, rightly or wrongly, that it would be
possible to find the road to real democracy through
corporative organisation, but I am not at all sure
that this commission will arrive at the sort of
corporative organisation we would desire unless they are
very carefully watched and led by the Trade Union
movement.' (ITUC 1939, p.157).

57. Report of Commission on Vocational Organisation op.cit. p.480.

58. Johnson papers op.cit. manuscript 17265.

59. ITUC 1937 p.169.

60. In this regard footnote 12 is also significant.

61. 'In the North there was a total of 64,000 members of
     trade unions out of almost 300,000 persons engaged
     in industry' - R. Morrow ITUC 1937 p.155.

62. Trade Union Commission of Inquiry and Report of the
     Trade Union Conference 1939 ITUC p.6.

63. O'Brien papers op.cit. 13971.

64. National Union of Railwaymen.

65. Amalgamated Society of Woodworkers. For membership
     in Ireland branch by branch see also O'Brien papers 13971.

66. Amalgamated Transport and General Workers Union.

67. Irish Transport and General Workers Union.

68. Irish Transport and General Workers Union v. Amalgamated Transport and General Workers Union([1936] I.R. 471).

69. ITUC 1936 p.158.

70. ibid.

71. ITUC 1930 pp.25, 26.

72. ITUC 1934 p.129.

73. R. Tynan on behalf of the national executive: ITUC 1930 p.73.

74. ITUC 1930 p.75.

75. ibid. p.74.

76. ITUC 1932 p.99.

77. Operative Plasterers Trade Society of Dublin.

78. ITUC 1934 p.50.

79. ibid. p.51.

80. ibid. p.52.

81. ibid. p.52.

82. ibid. p.52.

83. Later, the Irish unions were highly critical of the amalgamated unions meeting together (CIU 1945).

84. The vote on the national executive in favour of the ITGWU action was nine to five (ITUC 1934 p.123).

85. ITUC 1934 p.122.

86. Railway Clerks' Association.

87. ITUC 1934 p.127.

88. ibid p.133.

89. ibid. p.133.

90. ITUC 1935 p.162.

91. O'Brien papers 13971.

92. O'Brien papers 15676 (1).

93. 34 & 35 Vict. c.31.

94. 39 & 40 Vict. c.22.

95.   op.cit.

96.   O'Brien papers 13971.

97.   op.cit.

98.   See below p. 344

99.   ITUC 1935 p.66.

100. The term national joint industrial council is a
      confusing one, because the term joint industrial council
      was of growing significance in indicating a joint
      employer-trade union negotiating body; the modern
      term for the purely trade union industry-based council
      is trade union group.

Chapter Four

The Trade Union Commission

-i-

The special conference of April 1936 directed the national
executive of the Irish Trade Union Congress to 'forthwith
set up a Commission to inquire into and report on the terms
of reference to the unions.' And the terms of reference,
which show only too clearly the marks of the tortured years
which went before, were as follows:[1]

(1)   The amalgamation or grouping of Unions analogous to
       or associated with one another within specific
       industries or occupation.

(2)   To set up machinery for
       (a)   coordinating the conduct of trade disputes,
              (i)   national or local,
              (ii)   single unit or multi-unit;

       (b)   to set up machinery of a permanent arbitral
              character to decide on industrial demarcation
              and other inter-Union disputes.

(3)   To advise on rules to govern applications for
       affiliation by organisations to

       (a)   the Irish Trade Union Congress
       (b)   Trades or Workers Councils.

(4)   To inquire into the legal position of the Trade Unions.

(5)   To make recommendations for general organisation.

The establishing of the commission was seen at the time as
a 'complete turning point in the life of the Trade Union
Movement.'[2] The twelve appointed, with Eamonn Lynch the

secretary, included all the major names in the trade union
movement at the time, with both Kyle and O'Brien serving.
The fact that such a commission was established seemed
somehow to fill the members of Congress with hope. 'We shall
have lightened our burden when we have left behind us those
corroding domestic quarrels which vitiate our energies and
dissipate our means ...'[3]   And when Eamonn Lynch as editor
came to write the introduction to the annual report for the
year 1936 he could conclude, perhaps rather sententiously:
'The Congress has by no means reached its fullest development,
and the future must witness further progress in its integrating
activities, as the Trade Union units organically solidify
themselves into less numerous, more clearly industrially
defined, and hence more financially and economically powerful
bodies. With these improvements in the growth and scientific
departmentalisation of the Movement, the Congress will
inevitably become more and more the general nerve centre,
giving point, direction and cohesion to the whole Trade
Union Movement.'[4] None of this came to pass. Instead the
establishing of the commission was a further major step
towards the cleavage that lay ahead.

William O'Brien's thinking dominated the commission. Before
the end of the year he had produced a draft reorganisation
plan under the first point of the terms of reference.
Early in 1937 it was submitted by a divided commission to
the national executive, where it failed to get agreement.
It was circulated to the unions for their comments and
eventually, virtually unchanged, formed memorandum I in the
highly ambiguous report to the special conference of
February 9 1939. There is no evidence of a proposal gradually
evolving over the period. On the contrary, O'Brien, at the
outset, confronted the trade union movement with a total
plan of reform, and the subsequent three years were spent
trying to cope with his challenge.

His proposal - as might be expected - was that all trade

union members should be grouped in ten or so industrial
unions. This idea, as we have seen, had a vast and
impressive pedigree. But in O'Brien's approach there was
none of the softness of gradualism - so much a part, for
example of the 1919 proposals.[5] He was dealing with an
immediate situation. The proposal suffered from all the
impracticalities of similar proposals in the past, which
O'Brien must have seen as clearly as anyone else; and
for that reason it has been suggested that he was motivated
more by a desire to see amalgamated unions expelled, and
the Irish Transport much augmented, than by a desire for
reform. This was no doubt partly true; but at the same
time, his dominant motive does appear to have been trade
union reform, and this was accepted by his colleagues on
the commission. Indeed Robert Morrow of the Belfast Trades
Council said at the special conference in February 1939: 'I
am aware as a member of the Commission - and I only missed
one meeting - that the motives behind the minds of those
people was not to try to terminate English unions in Ireland.
Of that I am firmly convinced. Their sole aim and object,
in putting that document forward,was that it was in the
interest of the Trade Unions and Workers in Ireland. I don't
believe one of the individual signatories to Memorandum I
had anything in the back of his mind in so far as the
Amalgamated Unions are concerned.'[6] It is only fair to say
that there were many who took quite a different view.

The memorandum[7] which O'Brien submitted to the commission
in November 1936 first analysed the fragmented nature of the
trade union movement, with its 49 unions, and 134,000 members;
only two unions had a membership exceeding 10,000 and as
many as 17 had a membership less than 500.[8] He visualised
ten groupings which in his early 1936 memorandum were as
follows:

Building and Furnishing	23,000
Engineering, Shipbuilding and Vehicle Building	6,000
Seamen and Port Workers	18,000
Rail and Road Workers	17,000
Printing and Paper Workers	6,000
Bakery Workers	2,000
Distributive, Clerical and Supervisory	9,000
Teachers	9,500
Civil Service	5,500
General Workers	38,000

In the final report of the commission, the order and titles remain much the same. The membership numbers are dropped and after each grouping there is inserted a list of unions which make up the group.[9] It is important to recognise that the proposed list of unions showed no duplication. Each remained exclusively within its appropriate category; and the implication therefore was that each union would shed any members it had in other categories. This is what caused much of the complaint on grounds of impracticality, particularly where a union such as a building union had members scattered throughout industry.

But O'Brien had no very strong views on how these groups might work out their salvation. He was quite flexible in the matter. His interest lay in the transport group, and in particular in the area of the general workers. In his memorandum to the commission in 1936 there is a highly significant paragraph which we do not meet again in the report:[10] 'There are three unions catering for transport and general workers with 59,000 members; three unions catering for rail and road workers with almost 12,000 members; and one union catering for seamen with 1,000, a total of approximately 72,000, or almost 55 per cent of the total affiliated member- ship. In addition, there are a number of other unions having about 11,000 members, the membership of which is catered for by one or other of the three general workers' unions, making a total of approximately 83,000, or more than 60 per cent of the entire affiliated membership.' He thought that a suggestion that they would be all organised in one transport and general workers union 'would probably not be regarded as an acceptable solution in present circumstances' and he therefore suggested 'three fairly compact separate unions of (a) seamen and port workers, (b) rail and road workers and (c) general workers ...' The other seven categories fell around this central stem. He may well have had in mind therefore the development of one union in this area. For a start, however, he was satisfied to fix his base among the general workers, shedding members in the other industrial groupings. It is illuminating to consider in full category 10, that of general workers, in memorandum I of the commission's report, and also the comment that follows it:

> 10. General Workers:
> Irish Municipal Employees' Trade Union; Limerick Corporation Employees' Society; Irish Transport and General Workers' Union; Amalgamated Transport and General Workers' Union; National Union of Boot and Shoe Operatives; National Union of Tailors and Garment Makers; Irish Women Workers' Union; Cork Operative Butchers' Society.
>
> To complete the above plan of industrial re-organisation, it will be necessary to take from the Unions of General Workers those sections of their membership where they are associated within the Industrial Union Group outlined above. This allocation of such general workers as, for instance, the Bread Van Drivers to the Bakery Group, the Drapery Porters to the Distributive Group, the Builders' Labourers to the Building Group, the Road Transport Workers to the Rail and Road Transport Group etc. will necessarily deplete the existing General Workers' Unions. The necessity for the separate existence

> of these General Workers' Unions will have
> disappeared; they will be merged in a new
> single General Workers' Union. This new union,
> will, however, receive a large accretion of
> strength from the general re-organisation of all
> workers throughout industry, which must follow
> from the adoption of the above plan in its
> entirety.[11]

The italics in the above passage are mine, but they
indicate the central point. The general workers group was
expected to increase greatly in size, as the more specialised groups shed members; and within that group there
was a place for one union only. This was the grand design.
This was also quite different from the earlier categorisations,
although there was a superficial similarity. In 1919[12]
the rather idealistic proposal of one big union with
industrial sections sprang from the chiliasm of the time
which enlarged and excited Connolly's syndicalist theories.
Mortished's classification[13] in 1926 was more an exercise
in taxonomy than in restructuring, and there was no
suggestion that multi-industry unions should shed members
and concentrate on one industry alone. But O'Brien was
concerned with restructuring, not with taxonomy; he was
concerned with one-industry unions and therefore with the
shedding of members, and while there was not the thrust of
idealism behind his proposals such as existed in 1919,
nonetheless the impulse was a powerful one, springing, as
he saw it, from the general workers group, perhaps moving
into the transport group as well, but one way or the other
bidding fair to dominate the whole trade union movement.
It is interesting to note that the general workers group
was not in fact specific to any industry (unlike all the
others) indicating quite clearly its flexibility and its
potential for growth.

There were two major problems in this approach; the first

concerned the north and the second concerned the other
unions which organised general workers, both problems being
fundamental and extensive. Let us consider the north first.
The proposal on the face of it purported to be concerned
with the reorganisation of the whole trade union movement,
north and south, but the notion of one general union would
make no sense in these circumstances; the Irish Transport
had little influence in the north, while in the south on
the other hand, a bid for hegemony was perfectly practicable.
Furthermore, the call for a recognition of the growth of
national feeling was of significance when it was seen in the
context of a Free State organisation, but made little more
than aspirational sense when applied to the island as a whole.
But if we recognise that O'Brien, despite the all-Ireland
character of the proposal, was in fact thinking of a
nationalist trade union movement for the Free State, then
everything is much more explicable; because, in such
circumstances, the objective of one general union would be
realised by the giving of dominance to the Irish Transport
in the south, and to the Amalgamated Transport in the north.
Such a plan would of course confirm still more explicitly
the partition of the country, which the trade union movement
as a whole had deplored, but it is one of the ironic
difficulties of the nationalist position that the more
intense its nationalist and anti-partition feeling the
more explicitly does it partition the country north and
south in social and economic matters.

But such a proposal for reorganisation - theoretically for
the whole country but in practice for the Free State -
would not have been possible if there had been a substantial
northern presence in Congress. In fact there was not. We
have remarked already on the weakness of the northern
movement,[14] and its disinterest in Congress, only too
clearly evidenced in memorandum I of the report of the
commission; and we noted a passage from O'Brien's 1936 submission[15] pointing out that Northern Ireland presented

considerable difficulty and indicating some of the prominent
unions not affiliated to Congress. The passage continued:
'If the great body of trade unionists in Northern Ireland
are to be associated with us it would be necessary to allow
the fullest measure of autonomy in that area. Otherwise it
is more than doubtful that they would consent to link up
with us.' This seems to convey clearly enough the notion of
separate but cooperative development. We gain the same
impression from the place of origin of the delegates. In
1937, 74% came from Dublin and the south generally while
only 17% came from the north; in 1938, when both the
Irish Transport and the Amalgamated Transport were very
sensitive to voting strength, the number of delegates from
Dublin and the south represented 77% of the total, and those
from the north still only 17%.[16] This contrasts with the
early character of Congress, much more evenly balanced north
and south; in 1901, for example, 68% of the delegates came
from Dublin and the south, and 32% from the north. At that
time the total number however was only 71, as against 210
both in 1937 and in 1938. Let us contrast this with a
current date, 1972, where the number of delegates is dramatically larger, over 470, in fact, and where the per-
centages lie at 75% with addresses in Dublin or the south,
and 25% in the north. This underrepresents the north at
present, where there are over 40% of all trade unionists
(263,000 out of 650,000)[17] but it also underlines the very
substantial underrepresentation of northern trade unionists
in the critical period of the mid-thirties.

What was of considerable significance in the mid-thirties,
however, was the presence of cross-channel delegates, as
they were described, delegates with addresses in England,
Wales or Scotland. There were no such delegates in 1901
(nor could there be in 1972[18]), but in 1937 they accounted for
9% of the delegates, and in 1938, 6%. When one remembers
that such delegates were necessarily senior officials and
very influential, their impact must have been far greater
even than the percentage indicates. The amalgamated-Irish
dispute, therefore, which took place essentially within the

Free State, caused the anxious involvement of British
officials, concerned - in fairness - not only with the
welfare of their unions but with the express desire of
many Irish members to continue a traditional loyalty to
amalgamated unions that had existed for many, many years.
As for the north, it became shadowy and of lesser account
as tension mounted between the amalgamated and the Irish
unions within the Free State.

The focus of the debate therefore was in the second problem
area, the response of the other general unions to O'Brien's
proposals, and the response of the amalgamated unions as
a whole. This is what polarised the discussion at the
special conference which considered the commission's report.
It is important to recognise however that the proposal
threatened the continuance not only of the amalgamated unions
but of Irish-based general unions as well. There were two
which require particular mention. The Workers' Union of
Ireland was not represented in Congress and since trades
councils were not admitted to the special conference in 1939,
Larkin could not use such a device to make his voice heard.[19]
Secondly there was the Women Workers Union. They were
obviously much torn by the recommendation. Helena Molony
supported O'Brien's memorandum I; indeed without her it
would have been a minority view on the commission. Her
union had been a vigorous supporter of industry-based unions
and separatism in national development, but when the theory
was given practical effect it spelled apparently the
elimination of a union consisting only of women. This was
the dilemma. In these circumstances she entered a reservation
to her acceptance of memorandum I, a reservation which held
that while organising women on sex lines was theoretically
wrong, nevertheless there still was temporary necessity for
a women's union 'owing to the fact that women are a separate
economic class.'[20] But her union in the debate in 1939
went further, and rejected memorandum I altogether in favour
of the alternative offered by Sam Kyle.[21]

This then was O'Brien's strategy. He availed of the
traditional and compelling idea of industrial organisation

of unions in order to dominate, if not expel, the amalgamated
unions in the Free State, to diminish further his ancient
enemy Larkin, and the Workers Union of Ireland, and to
establish a commanding position for his own union, the
Irish Transport, throughout the trade union movement of the
south. All this was abundantly clear from the outset, from
his initial memorandum of November 1936.

By the end of 1936 the commission had prepared, under its
second term of reference, a proposal to deal with inter-
union disputes, which contemplated the establishing of an
industrial court with a president and a registrar.[22] Its
suggested powers were considerable. Where there was a
demarcation dispute, where there was a dispute concerning
the terms of a joint claim and even in the area of poaching
of members, its decision was to be final. It was also given
the power to identify the union which should have sole
organising rights of new members in a particular industry,
although in this matter there was an appeal to the annual
conference of Congress whose decision would be final. This
proposal too, prepared at the end of 1936, continued virtually
unchanged into memorandum I of the commission's report, with,
however, the added point that 'the successful operation
of the above machinery depends on the acceptance of some
such principles as those put forward under Item 1 of the
terms of reference.'[23] This notion of the mutual dependence
of the two sets of proposals was later challenged at the
1939 special conference; but there is no doubt that they
hung together as part of the same plan. The industrial
court, with its power to identify a union with sole
organising rights in a particular industry (even though it
concerned only new members) was the instrument by which
the objectives under the first term of reference could be
secured. These ideas were of the first importance and were
later developed and legislated for in the 1941 act.[24]

All this material had been circulated to the unions in 1937

and a long period of gestation followed.[25] It was not until
early 1938 that a draft proposal under the third term of
reference was considered by the commission; it had been
prepared by J.T. O'Farrell of the Railway Clerks'
Association and dealt with the 'facility with which unnecessary, undesirable and superfluous unions can secure
official recognition, through affiliation to the Trade
Union Congress, and still more so, to the local Trades'
and Workers' Councils.'[26] The introductory material was
recast in the final report of the commission[27] but the
recommendation again remained virtually unchanged: no
trades council, under the penalty of itself being expelled,
would be permitted to accept an unaffiliated union into
membership without the consent of the national executive.
This helped amalgamated unions such as O'Farrell's which
were under pressure from nationalist breakaways or the
possibility of them; but of course it also helped O'Brien
who wished to see, as an alternative to the amalgamated
unions, not a fragmented trade union movement but an OBU.[28]

The recommendations under terms of reference four and five
need not delay us. Reference four merely summarised the
legal position of trade unions particularly in regard to
registration, and reference five, under general organisation,
recommended, in quite a draconian way, that after a date to
be stated 'all within the industry must be either in their
respective union or out of the job,'[29] and emphasised once
again the interdependent character of all that was
recommended. The proposals as a whole then, covering terms
of reference 1 to 5, were presented in August to the national
executive as the draft report of the commission. The
object apparently was to submit it to a special conference
in October. At this point the balloon went up.

On September 6 C.D. Watters[30] of the National Union of
Railwaymen, a member of the commission, submitted a memorandum which declared that he could not subscribe to the

recommendations under item 1. He recognised the unsatisfactory nature of trade union organisation, which he
believed came from the haphazard growth of the movement,
but he considered the proposal for reform quite impractical.
It was a confused memorandum, but it was followed by a far
clearer statement along the same lines by Sam Kyle later
in the month; and indeed it seems that Watters was much
influenced by Kyle, and, as a consequence apparently
suffered a change of heart. In any event, in a letter to
O'Brien on September 20, Eamonn Lynch, the secretary,
remarked:[31] 'It is hard to understand Watters' paragraphs
considering he sat with us on the last occasion and,
apparently, was in agreement with the Report, provided it
was signed by myself.' This remark is also an important
reminder that the proposals as a whole were apparently
regarded in quite a low-key way by many of the amalgamated
unions for much of the time.

Kyle's memorandum[32] of September 19 1938 formed the substance
later of the alternative memorandum, memorandum II, in the
commission's report. It made the same point that Watters
did, but more trenchantly. Kyle considered the proposals
under item 1 of the terms of reference much too grandiose.
'The suggestion that the entire Trade Union movement in
Ireland should be scrapped and that there should be substituted ten industrial groups is quite unworkable ...'
He considered that practical schemes should be drawn up for
merging the small unions, not breaking up the larger ones;
and the suggestion he made himself to that end was that the
unions should agree to respect and recognise each other's
union cards. He resisted the draconian recommendation under
item 5, fearing that it invited state intervention. Thus
were the battle lines drawn in one report; it now contained memorandum I, largely of O'Brien's devising and
supported by five members (one, Helena Molony, with a
substantial reservation); memorandum II, of Kyle's
devising, supported by five members all from amalgamated
unions; and to this was added a third memorandum from

William Norton, the leader of the Labour Party, and also
a member of the commission. His memorandum was in substance
the same as Kyle's but probably for reasons of political
prudence he did not wish to align himself with either group.
One member signified no view. Miss Molony's reservation
was so substantial that it is difficult not to regard it
as a contrary view; indeed Kyle himself was of such an
opinion at the 1939 special conference. If this is so,
then O'Brien relied on four members of the twelve for substantive support. Yet in the report which was placed before
the unions, memorandum I appeared to be the substantive report,
and memorandum II and III the lesser alternatives. It was
a most judicious piece of presentation.

But despite all this, it was clear from an early stage that
O'Brien's proposals were headed for disaster. In Eamonn Lynch's
letter to O'Brien on September 20 1938, to which we have
already referred, he confessed that any further work on the
proposals would be a sheer waste of time.[33] 'I have no hope
that the principles set forth under item 1 of our terms of
reference will find the least endorsement anywhere. Then, as
you agree, the rest of the Report depends on the acceptance
of item 1. Item 2 etc. will fall to the ground.' He
recommended that they should inform the national executive
that unanimity was impossible and that the whole thing should
be abandoned. Then in a very perceptive passage he argued
that if the report were to be sent to the unions with the
support of only some members of the commission, there should
be no question of calling a special conference to discuss
the matter unless a substantial number of unions desired it.
'On no account should the National Executive fix the
conference arbitrarily .... The onus for calling the special
conference should be put on the Unions. If they desire a
conference let them express their desire; that would at
least indicate that they desired the subject carried further.
If they do not, then we should not go further.' Clearly
Lynch feared for the unity and stability of the trade union
movement if the matter was pressed further without some
general consensus; but his fears ran even deeper, and, in the

event, were prophetic: 'Again, if the Government are now
about to introduce legislation, and as far as can be
learned, they will not delay long, would it not be undesirable to have a Conference which the Unions did not
desire and which could only be abortive? We might easily
leave ourselves open to a most unfair and unwarrantable
accusation of having inspired the Government by our Report.'
Desirable or not, the conference was held. It opened in the
Teacher's Hall, 36 Parnell Square Dublin on Thursday
February 9 1939 under the chairmanship of the president of
Congress P.T. Daly.

-ii-

It has since been suggested that the manner in which Daly
chaired the conference greatly influenced the result. The
Report of the Commission on Vocational Organisation[34]
described what occurred as follows: 'Owing to the form
of procedure followed, the proposal for regrouping was not
put directly to the meeting on its merits. A resolution
approving of the memorandum of the five other members was
carried. This was taken as a rejection of the proposal
for regrouping. The chairman refused to accept an amendment
to adopt this proposal on the ground that it was a direct
negative. Many of the delegates protested against his
ruling and withdrew from the hall.' And yet it is difficult
to see what alternative Daly had. At that time he was an
elderly man, nearing the end of a stormy trade union and
political career in which O'Brien had prominently figured.[35]
Apparently when Larkin decided to go to the US in 1914 he
wanted to leave P.T. Daly in charge of the union, but
Connolly objected so vigorously that Daly was given
responsibility for the insurance activities of the union
instead. He allied himself to Delia Larkin in the disputations
that followed, he was removed from the insurance post, but in

a direct conflict with O'Brien, he succeeded in becoming
secretary of the Dublin United Trades Council in 1919.
Uniquely, a slander issue in which he was involved (it
concerned IRB funds) was arbitrated on by Dail Eireann; but
O'Brien, bent on having the matter determined, was
deliberately vituperative about him in public, causing
Daly to take an action for slander in the courts which was
heard during 1924 and 1925. He failed; and more than that,
had been unable to meet the costs of the action. Yet now
at this point he was president of the Irish Trade Union
Congress, having defeated Sam Kyle the year before for the
position of vice-president and thereby succeeding to the
presidency; more than that, he appears to have been
supported in the vote by the Irish Transport. Whatever else
might be said, his trade union experience was considerable.

It is important too to bear in mind, before discussing this
difficult conference of February 1939, that there were still
many things that the unions had in common. A lengthy dispute
in the building industry in the spring of 1937, which lasted
seventeen weeks in all, brought the Dublin building unions
together under the chairmanship of Somerville of the ASW.
Apparently morale was very high despite the length of the
strike, and Michael Keyes of the NUR at the August 1937
conference said that the Dublin fight had marked the upsurge
of the labour movement in the metropolis.[36] Furthermore,
Dawson Gordon of the Belfast Trades Council offered 'not
only moral but material assistance; if help was sought he
was sure that the Northern workers would be prepared
readily to give it.'[37] On a more general political note, there
was the growing anxiety concerning the centralisation of
government and the influence of what was described as the
managerial system. Early in 1937 Congress had written to
the Department of Local Government in very strong terms
concerning 'the very dictatorial powers vested in managers
appointed to the several local authorities.'[38] 'My National
Executive,' wrote Eamonn Lynch, 'consider that it is highly
detrimental to the development of national political

responsibility and civic consciousness to deprive the
people of their popular functions. This incapacity must
inevitably lead to civic indolence, political morbidity
and decay.'[39] As might be expected, the Minister was un-
impressed. The system operated as yet in only three county
boroughs and one borough, and far from receiving complaints,
there were requests for its extension. But trade union
anxieties were in no way diminished: ' ...the workers
fought,' said John McCabe of the Irish Transport in 1938,[40]
'against the occupation of the country by a foreign power
and claimed that they had the brains and ability to manage
their own affairs, they should now, that they had some
measure of freedom, show that they were competent to do these
things. A man was put over us in the Dublin Corporation,
to keep us in order, as if we were unruly children. There
we have a manager, who consults us, but that is all. We are
merely rubber stamps, our only duty being to strike the rate.'
However, as we have already seen, the managerial system by
general public consent spread throughout the country, with
indeed much of the effect on local democracy which the trade
unions feared. It is of course a common occurrence that when
local societies feel threatened (as indeed they did during
these difficult times) they consent to, and perhaps urge,
more power at the centre, distrusting their own ability to
keep the peace, and trading as a result the quality of their
local democracy for the hope of a greater security which
the centre would assure.

But apart from all these matters of common cause among
the trade unions, there was the symbol of unity in the fact
that the Congress met in August 1938 in Bangor, Northern
Ireland, and among the platform party were H.H. Elvin,
President of the British TUC, and Baillie William Elger,
secretary of the Scottish TUC. The President Jerry Hurley
of Cork said that the location of the Congress that year in a
town in Northern Ireland was a 'striking indication of the
unity of the Trade Union movement in Ireland, and is, in my
opinion, a good augury for the future unity of our country.'[41]

It was in fact an augury neither for the unity of the
country nor of the trade union movement.

The meeting of February 9 1939 was a 'conference of trade
union representatives' who, it was hoped, would be armed
'with plenary powers so that the Conference may give
directions to (the) National Executive to take definitive
action.'[42] This was a confusing matter to begin with. As
the chairman P.T. Daly pointed out, in an early disagreement
with William O'Brien: 'Whatever is done here cannot be
final; it will have to be discussed by the Trade Union
Congress. This is not a Congress: it is a Conference.
There are Unions affiliated with Congress not here today,
because they did not think it wise ...' This O'Brien
was not prepared to accept. 'I don't see what authority
Congress would have', he said, 'if this Conference came to
a decision.'[43] This conclusion probably reflected the
uncertainty and unhappiness of a number of prominent
officials, including Eamonn Lynch. Usually special congresses
and special consultative conferences are quite distinct;
the latter are never decisive, while, on the other hand,
special congresses usually are. A special congress however
would include trades council representatives (and in this
case would probably have enabled Larkin to attend) and this
may have been a consideration. One way or the other then,
the conference of 1930 which was not a congress but which
had decision-making powers, was at best an ambivalent and
unprecedented organ. However, there was little substance
in the chairman's point about certain affiliated unions
not being represented. True, there were present representatives
from only 39 unions as against 49 at the annual congress
in August 1938, but the absent unions were small and
specialised, and could not really have affected the issue.

As a result of its somewhat uncertain character, the
conference was quite unstructured. There was no lead speaker
from the national executive; in the circumstances it is
difficult to see how there could have been. The various

memoranda were placed before the delegates as the national
executive report, with some neutral introductory remarks
from Eamonn Lynch. O'Brien had already achieved a great
deal by having memorandum I (which as we have seen was
supported by a minority only) presented as the main report,
to which the second and more acceptable memorandum had the
character of a minority report.[44] In such circumstances
O'Brien himself was probably slow to take a further
initiative, and wished to feel out the meeting. There was
some deliberateness about this since a conference of the
Irish-based unions had taken place the day before to discuss
a joint approach.[45]

Kyle therefore moved first, his substantive point being
that his memorandum, memorandum II, had in fact majority
support on the commission of inquiry and majority support
as well on the basis of the trade union membership represented
by the commission members who upheld it. There followed
some uncertain general discussion both on the merits of the
various proposals and the kind of procedure that the conference
might follow, and then John Marchbank of the NUR, who
eventually came to dominate the conference, proposed that
the conference approve the conclusions of memorandum II 'to
the extent that they refer to Item (1) of the Terms of
Reference.'[46] This was the key proposal. It reversed the
whole thrust and direction of the discussion, discounting
the advantage which O'Brien had gained in the manner in which
the report had been presented, and making the adoption of
Kyle's memorandum II the major topic of the conference.
Almost at once O'Brien began to express concern; but while
there had been an earlier decision to discuss the terms of
reference one by one, no one had moved the adoption of any
part of memorandum I; consequently, the chairman P.T.Daly
held crisply to due procedure: 'If the motion is proposed
I must either accept it or reject it. The motion is in order,
and can be discussed with the first Term of Reference.'[47]
Discussion continued on the merits of the various proposals,
and also on the merits of British-based and Irish-based unions;

and then John Swift of the Irish Bakers[48] tried to reverse
the thrust of the debate by proposing, as an amendment
to Marchbank's motion that the conference adhere to
'Memorandum I Item (1) of the Terms of Reference.'[49] The
chairman ruled the amendment out of order on the grounds
that it was a direct negative, which brought O'Brien, in
a confused way, into the discussion to claim that the
conference was entitled to adopt either memorandum. Later
in the debate Lawlor of the Irish Municipal Employees Trade
Union tried again: 'I understand if the motion is carried
on Memorandum No.2 it will nullify the first portion of the
report. Should it not be the other way round?' 'That',
said the chairman, 'is a hypothetical question.'[50]

We have noted that the debate on the general issues had been
continuing all this time, the tone being open, frank and
responsible, so much so that Gould of the National Boot and
Shoe Operatives declared: 'I think the tone of the debate
this morning was excellent. There were no backers of
sectional separation, and I shall hold the memory of the
morning's debate in very high appreciation, whatever the
future may determine,'[51] a sentiment which the delegates
applauded. Within a short time however the atmosphere
began to sour. Now Whelan of the DTPS[52] pushed forward
with a motion that memorandum I be adopted, which the
chairman again dismissed as a direct negative. O'Brien
came back a number of times, but failed to move him. In
those circumstances he eventually suggested that if a vote
was not permitted on memorandum I there should be no vote
taken at all. But the chairman was adamant: 'Let there
by no misapprehension about this. The vote will be on the
report of certain members of the Commission, namely
Messrs. Sam Kyle, J.T. O'Farrell, Michael Somerville,
R. Morrow and C.D. Watters.'[53]

A little later Drumgoole the chairman of the commission was
called upon to reply to the debate. He made quite a

compelling case for memorandum I on general organisational grounds. Nor did he see it as an issue between amalgamated and Irish unions: 'As Chairman of the Commission, I never thought that even if the conditions contained in Memorandum I were adopted, it would necessarily mean that any of the groups would be a wholly Irish group. What we wanted to get at was that the existing membership should be grouped in 10 Trade Unions, each Union having its own autonomous section, with its own benefits and scale of contributions, and one Executive responsible to each'.[54] It is extremely difficult to determine what precisely he meant by this; he may have had some picture of the various unions retaining their individuality within the industrial groupings; but it is likely enough that the general obscurity of the speech was a tribute more to his heart than his head. He concluded: 'We cannot present a united front as things are today. I have listened with great sorrow to the leaders of the movement telling the difficulty and the trouble they have had with other leaders owing to differences between them. No one denies that these things exist. The Commission, with the great experience and intimate knowledge of the movement in Ireland, put before you what we believed to be the only solution of the problem. You may say we are going too fast, and that what we propose could not be implemented at the present moment. That may be, but I assure you, no matter what your position, that the time will come when the suggestions contained in Memorandum I will be the actual position of Trade Unions in Ireland, whether it be ten, twenty or thirty unions. I oppose the motion put forward by Mr Marchbank.'[55] Some of this may ring strange at first sight, particularly the identification of memorandum I with the commission as a whole, and the emphasis on their intimate knowledge of Ireland; it helps to clarify matters however if we remember how conscious the delegates were that the signatories of Sam Kyle's memorandum II were uniformly from the British-based unions.

Now came the final contest between William O'Brien and the
chair. The chairman declared he was putting the vote,
O'Brien still protesting that both documents should be voted
on. The card vote resulted in 85,211 voting for the motion,
and 70,836 against, 21 unions being for the motion and 18
against.[56] The chairman declared the motion carried.
Whelan of the DTPS immediately moved that the principle of
amalgamation or grouping as set out in memorandum I should be
approved by the conference. The chairman refused to accept
the motion. O'Brien was infuriated: 'You gave me an undertaking that such a motion would be taken.' 'The vote', said
the chairman, 'was between Document No. 1 and 2.' 'No,' said
O'Brien. The chairman was insistent: 'I gave the assurance
that the vote would be between Memorandum I and II. The
vote we took was the substitution of one document for another.
The proposal was that we should approve of the proposals
set out in Memorandum II to the extent that they referred
to Item (1) of the terms of reference. My interpretation
is that Document No.2 is substituted for No.1 to the extent
set out in the resolution.' 'I want to state definitely,'
said O'Brien, 'that I only took part in the vote on the
distinct understanding that there would be a second vote on
Memorandum I.' The chairman replied: 'The motion substituting one document for another was voted on.' At this
point the break came. 'As a protest against your ruling,'
said O'Brien, 'I withdraw from this meeting.' O'Brien then
left, accompanied by some of the delegates.[57]

The chairman was badly shaken, and protested that if he had
said or done anything to hurt anyone he was very sorry.
What he had done had been done out of a sense of duty. He
suggested that there was little purpose in continuing; but
Marchbank would have none of it: 'I should say there is
every reason why we should go on and dispose of our business
in a business-like manner.'[58] And this in fact was done,
Marchbank proposing the adoption of the rest of the memorandum I, subject to a prudent number of savers, which

removed anything radical from their character. He was also
the one who proposed the vote of thanks to the chairman
for his 'tact, discretion and wisdom, and the greatest
patience in dealing with the many problems that came up
for discussion.' Thus the special 1939 conference ended[59]
and the split in the trade union movement began.

-iii-

The Trade Union Bill of 1941 sprang directly from all this.
More than that, the government now claimed that because of
the national importance of good trade union organisation,
they had prompted the establishing of the trade union commission
of inquiry in the first place. What was hinted at during
the various Congress debates was now made explicit: the
public interest required that if the trade union movement
could not provide good order in its affairs then the
government must do so by legislation. Sean McEntee, Lemass's
successor in Industry and Commerce, when he introduced the
second stage of his bill on June 4 1941[60] spoke of disputes,
strikes and general industrial unrest and went on: 'So
serious had the situation become in this regard that in 1936
the then Minister for Industry and Commerce decided that an
effort should be made to deal with the evil by executive
action within the trade union movement itself. He made
representations to the Irish Trade Union Congress, set the
position, as he saw it, before them and said that, if the
Congress was unable to deal with it the Government, in the
interests of the community as a whole, would be compelled to
act.'[61] He described the establishing of the commission and
then said: 'Unfortunately, notwithstanding the report of the
Commission of Inquiry set up by the Trade Union Congress,
notwithstanding subsequent further effort made in 1939 by the

Congress to secure a more rational work organisation of the
workers, the trade union movement appears of itself to be
unable to carry the matter further, and the evils which
all admit exist must remain to curse and plague Irish
industry unless some other power take action.   In these
circumstances the Government is bound to intervene by
making such changes in trade union law as may reduce the
incidence of trade union disputes generally and inter-trade
union disputes in particular.'[62]

This then was the justification for the legislation;   more
than that the terms of the legislation were given sanction
by reference to the proposals of memorandum I of the
commission's report.   For that reason the Minister referred
to the report again and again, tabled it for the benefit
of the deputies[63] and quoted long passages from it, including the exchange between the chairman and William O'Brien
which led to the walk-out.   However he presented the whole
business in a highly partisan manner - whether for political
advantage or because he really saw it that way, it is
difficult to say.   Memorandum I was seen as a progressive
attempt at reform by the 'Irish unions';   it was blocked
by the 'English unions' for reasons of self-interest;   and
Norton, the leader of the Labour Party (who had contributed
the third memorandum), could be dismissed as a wily politician
who wanted it both ways.   This view, as presented by the
Minister in Dail Eireann in 1941, had a considerable influence
in forming the public mind on what had taken place.

Memorandum I, the Minister declared, 'received the greatest
body of support inside the Commission'[64] although subsequently
rejected by Congress.   It was a memorandum 'which, I think,
was signed by five persons who were representatives of trade
unions having their headquarters in this country, trade
unions which might be concisely and popularly described as
Irish trade unions on the Commission of Inquiry. Those gentlemen,

all of them with national records of which any of us might
be proud, recommended ...' and he quoted the section from
memorandum I dealing with the industrial court, an idea of
course from which the Trade Union Bill had derived its
dynamic. These then were the progressive Irish representatives. On the other hand there were the harbingers of
darkness. 'But the Congress was jockeyed by the vested
interests which are concerned to thwart and defeat any
attempt to reorganise the Irish trade union movement into a
position where the memorandum was never submitted to a vote
of the special conference called to consider the report of
the Commission of Inquiry.'[65] Both Norton and Keyes loudly
protested that this was not true; but MacEntee claimed that
he was supported by the report of the commission, and he
selected John Marchbank as the principal culprit. 'At the
conference, a resolution was proposed by a certain Mr
John Marchbank, who does not live in this country; I think
he is general secretary of a union which has its headquarters in Great Britain. He came over specially for the
conference. I think Mr John Marchbank is very well known to
at least two deputies in the house.' 'And respected,' inter-
jected Michael Keyes.[66] 'That may be', replied MacEntee.
'He certainly did your work well. Whether he did a good
day's work for the country or not is another matter.'[67]
The Minister at this point quoted the final exchange between
O'Brien and the chairman, and went on: 'Mr Marchbank having
asserted the control of the English trade unions over the
special conference of the Irish trade union movement, then,
Sir, no less than four other resolutions from this conference
were adopted.'[68] 'With the support', said Norton, 'of the Irish
unions in some cases.' 'With the support', replied MacEntee,
'of all the vested interests that have been battening on the
Irish trade unionists, with the support of all those people
who have been concerned in their internecine strife, and who
have been the source of the baneful jealousies which, Deputy
Norton has admitted, do exist. The English trade unions with,

as I have said, the vested interests which have been
battening upon the Irish trade union movement, succeeded
in defeating this attempt on the part of the Irish trade
union movement to cure abuses.'[69]

The views that MacEntee expressed were not only the views
of the government but of a great number of others besides.
In the nationalist climate of the time they had an immense
plausibility.[70]   Furthermore there is no reason to believe
that MacEntee was not entirely sincere in his impatience
with those who opposed memorandum I, and since its proposals
seemed so practical and sensible, he could only conclude
that those who opposed it did so for the worst of reasons.
Norton during the Dail debate on more than one occasion protested that the Minister did not know what he was talking
about.   Norton's objection to the memorandum had been the
same as Kyle's - that ultimately the whole thing was impractical, and worse, would be divisive if pursued.   In
evaluating this, it is necessary to recognise that the trade
union movement is essentially a political society: in a
sense its leadership is more sensitive to the democratic
will of its members than a government needs be to its
electorate.   The system of party democracy, the notion of
the political leader and his personally selected team, as
well as the matters of great national importance that must be
dealt with-all tend to provide the government with a buffer
between settled policies and the pressures of the electorate,
and consequently provide for a greater measure of discretion.
In the smaller field of trade union democracy these buffers
do not exist.   It is unlikely that MacEntee and the government
recognised this.   Indeed it seems clear that they did not
see the political society as an analogue at all.   If there
was to be an analogy in judging a trade union's behaviour,
then it was the business firm or the administrative institution,
and there was an unspoken assumption that trade union leaders
should be able to act with the same decisiveness as the
managers of such undertakings, and if they did not it was
because of inadequacy or malice.   Indeed this view of the

nature of trade unions persisted in the minds of the
Fianna Fail government down to very recent times, long after
the amalgamated unions had been accepted as a useful and
proper part of the Irish trade union scene.

In the next chapter, we shall discuss more fully the Trade
Union Bill, its enactment, the conflicts it caused and its
eventual fate. Our concern here is to establish not only
what the trade union commission of inquiry actually did,
but what it was understood by many to have done, and in
regard to the latter the Dail debate in the summer of 1941
is most illuminating.

-iii-

An 'Irish union' group with a separately organised identity
now began to emerge in the Congress. Prior to the special
conference of February 9 1939, there was a meeting of 'Irish
Unions affiliated to the Trade Union Congress.'[71] The
convenors were Whelan of the DTPS, Owen Hynes and, curiously,
Michael Drumgoole the chairman of the commission, but
acting in his role as an official of the Irish Union of
Distributive Workers and Clerks. We must recognise as well
that the amalgamated unions had since 1934 been urged by
Congress itself to consult among one another about their
special position;[72] in this way the drift apart began to be
institutionalised. The meeting took place in the offices
of the DTPS on February 8, the day before the special conference began; and a further meeting was convened on March 2
to consider the results of the special conference. The
result was clear and dramatic.

It was decided to establish an advisory council of 'Irish
Trade Unions in affiliation to the Irish Trade Union Congress.'

It was further decided 'that a provisional Committee be
appointed to devise a National and Economic policy for
Irish Unions and report back to a further meeting within
three months.'[73] It was decided to seek the support of
other Irish-based unions, and while declaring their desire
to work in harmony with the Trade Union Congress, nevertheless
they considered that 'the Congress is in a difficult position
in regard to the question of trade union reorganisation as
it is composed of both Irish and British unions and is,
therefore, precluded from taking any action that might
be considered by the British unions to prejudice their position'.[74]
The work of the special commission had ended in deadlock.
'The British unions do not want any change, believing
apparently that any scheme of reorganisation would be detrimental to their status in the country, and the Irish Unions
hitherto have had no means of expressing an independent
point of view ...' They concluded that if the problem was
left as it now stood, they were inviting the government to
interfere. 'Surely the unions themselves ought to be able
to devise some scheme of reorganisation as a remedy for the
existing state of affairs.' The Council of Irish Unions was
the beginning of the remedy as they saw it; technically it
was advisory in character, but in its printed material the
word "advisory" was spelt in tiny lettering as befitted the
reality;[75] it was formally established on May 23 1939,
and although the final breach did not come until six years
later, effectively from that date the division within the
Congress had become institutionalised.

-iv-

All this time there were great constitutional changes taking
place in the south, as de Valera pursued his policy of

political separatism which greatly reinforced the view
that British-based unions were inappropriate in an independent Irish state.   In 1935 de Valera had confronted
Britain with the Irish Nationality and Citizenship Act
and the Aliens Act which declared not only that Irish
citizens were not British subjects but that British subjects
were aliens in the Free State, although exempt from the
consequences of their alien status by executive order.
Judicial appeal to the Privy Council was abolished (in
which, incidentally, the Privy Council itself later concurred)
and then, taking advantage of the constitutional crisis in
Britain on the abdication of Edward VIII in December 1936,
de Valera, in a matter of two days, rushed through
legislation the effect of which was to abolish the functions
of the Governor General and to confine the Crown to being
an instrument for external relations, thus clearing the
way for what was in effect a republican constitution in 1937.
To de Valera and to the government, Eire was now outside
the commonwealth;   Britain took a directly contrary view,
but decided not to rock the boat.

The claim in the Constitution to the national territory did
little to help relations with the north;   and the position
greatly worsened in January 1939 when the IRA, in pursuit
of the destruction of partition, opened a bombing campaign
in England.   De Valera responded, as he had to, with the
Treason Act and the Offences Against the State Act, and
eventually with the Emergency Powers Act from which came the
special internment camp in the Curragh.   All this put the
north-south trade union connection under considerable strain,
and in the minds of many people put seriously in question
the continuance of British-based unions in the south.   We
have already seen this hostility building up over the decade,
culminating in the debate in Dail Eireann in 1941;   and
indeed the mood was well caught by the Commission on
Vocational Organisation which was established in January 1939:
'National sovereignty', it stated (despite the disclaimer

of the trade union members) 'and national security require
that the control of trade unions in this country should be
in the hands of Irish nationals. We hold that it is
extremely dangerous that persons outside the jurisdiction of
the State should have ultimate control in such an important
matter as the trade disputes of its citizens.'[76]

In the domestic field of trade union law in the south,
the constitution had a fundamental, but at the outset an
obscure effect, since it carried forward the law that was
already there while at the same time changing the context
in which it operated in a number of important ways. Under
Article 40 (6) (iii), the state guaranteed, subject to public
order and morality, the right of the citizens to form
associations and unions, and went on to provide however that
laws could be enacted for the regulation and control in the
public interest of the exercise of the foregoing right.
Indeed all this was to become a cockpit of legal debate
both in the forties and in the fifties which reflected a
deep ambiguity in the law's attitude to trade unions, and
which Mortished summarised rather perceptively as follows:[77]
'It would seem therefore that we have taken over a body of
law which is still based, at least in part, on a presumption
that there is something dubiously lawful about trade unions
and superimposed on it is a constitutional guarantee of the
right to form trade unions.' We shall find this ambiguity
lying at the heart of the discussion in the chapters that
follow; for the moment it is necessary to remark on only
one other basic change, the shift of the debate, by reason
of the Constitution, from parliament to the courts of law.
Since the time of the great trade union campaign which resulted
in the Trade Disputes Act of 1906, and in which trade unions
in Ireland played a substantial part, the leaders of the
movement very clearly distinguished between decisions of
parliament on the one hand and what they called
'judge-made law' on the other, law which was evident
in the Taff Vale[78] case and in the Irish case Quinn v.
Leathem[79] which together in the early years of

the century seemed to strip the trade unions of the protection of earlier legislation. This judge-made law they
saw as being influenced by considerations of class and
privilege, and their electoral success in 1906 and the
change in the law that followed emphasised once again that
the remedy lay in the supremacy of parliament over the
encrusted precedents of the law courts. After the Constitution
of 1937 this in practice broadly continued to be the case
except where matters of constitutional rights arose, and
here the final function of interpretation lay with the
Supreme Court to which legislation to change the law was
also subject, the only democratic appeal lying above it
being the rather forbidding one of a referendum on constitutional change; and it was in fact in this area of
constitutional rights that trade unions found themselves
deeply entangled in the years that followed.[80]

A third distinctive characteristic in the state in the south,
one which reinforced the national impulse towards separatism
and the legal divide which the Constitution created, was the
growing influence of the Roman Catholic Church. This is
evident in the Constitution; while article 40 which dealt
with personal rights 'was very much in the liberal, almost
one might say the egalitarian, tradition',[81] it was followed
by a number of articles - 41 to 44 - concerning family,
education, private property and religion which 'take on a
specifically Catholic flavour, or, as has sometimes been
suggested a Thomist and scholastic flavour.'[82] And if
Article 44 stopped short at giving a special constitutional
position to the Catholic church this probably reflected
de Valera's personal tough-mindedness in these matters. It
was an unhealthy relationship, that which existed between
church and state. There was now no overt involvement by the
clergy in party political issues, much in contrast with their
love of the hustings in the early years of the century when
in the confusion after the fall of Parnell there was the
vigour of clerical support for men like Healy, the opposition
to others such as John Dillon, and archbishop countering
archbishop in conflicting support. Instead, at the time we

speak of, the Church seemed to have taken on more and more
a unitary character, speaking with one voice through certain
recognised leaders, avoiding the cut and thrust of political
debate as if they were in some respects members of an
alien state, silent in regard to matters that did not
affect their special position, but swift, unanimous and
authoritative in matters in which they saw their rights
involved. And as the pluralist character of Irish society
gradually disappeared, so also did their authority grow
so that where there were matters in which they had a special
concern, as for example education, the state silently
yielded to them, creating in turn a situation where major
matters of social policy could never be the subject of
open political debate. Of course it is true that in practice
questions of personal morality still ranked as the most
important topics on which the bishops spoke - even by the
end of the thirties dance-halls were still the most frequent
single topic for mention in episcopal pastorals[83] - yet
at the same time their influence in major political matters
was real and considerable. They appeared to be obsessive
in their fear of communism, although the number of communists
in Ireland was negligible[84]; they supported strongly ideas
of corporatism, and were clearly sympathetic to Franco's
cause.[85] It was a measure of de Valera's strength that he
refused to take part in an anti-communist crusade, refused
to withdraw recognition from the republican government in
Spain and eventually in 1937 forbade by law Irish citizens
to enlist on either side in the Spanish civil war.[86] His
successors in the forties showed far less capacity in these
matters and in the event found themselves plunged into disarray.

Nineteen thirty-eight brought an end to the economic war; not
only that but de Valera's personal relations with Britain, and in
particular with Chamberlain, had improved greatly; and in fact
the British government had supported de Valera's candidature
in 1938 when he became president of the Assembly of the

League of Nations. De Valera's major achievement at that time, however, was the agreement in 1938 under which the British government would evacuate military bases in the twenty-six counties, bases that had been guaranteed by the Treaty. This was what made possible an independent foreign policy. As a result, when war broke out in September 1939, Eire was able to remain neutral in circumstances where the United Kingdom (including Northern Ireland) was a belligerent. While the benefits of such a non-belligerent policy were incalculably great, nevertheless the southern state grew more and more isolationist in character, and the particular characteristics which we have noted here, nationalist, religious and juridical, intensified as well.

Notes on Chapter Four

1.   ITUC 1936 p.45

2.   ibid. p.46

3.   idem.

4.   ibid. Introduction.

5.   ILP & TUC, 1919 p.61.

6.   ibid. p.32.

7.   O'Brien papers 13971.

8.   See appendix three.

9.   See appendix four.

10.   O'Brien papers 13971.

11.   ibid. p.9.

12.   ILP & TUC, 1919 p.61.

13.   R.J.P. Mortished: op.cit. p.221.

14.   See p.119 above.

15.   O'Brien papers op.cit.

16.   Source: various annual reports of the Congress.

17.   Trade Union Information Irish Congress of Trade
        Unions February 1972.

18.   See later p.456.

19.   Larkin gained considerable personal prestige about this
        time, being elected in 1936 as an independent to the
        Dublin Municipal Council and to Dail Eireann the
        following year. (see Emmet Larkin: op.cit. p.298).

20.   Trade union commission of inquiry: op.cit. p.16.
        The Irish Women Workers Union was established by James
        Larkin in 1911, as a separate union, since he believed
        that 'person' in the rules of the Irish Transport
        meant 'male person'. (The union amended its rules to
        overcome the difficulty in 1918.) Larkin appointed
        his sister Delia as general secretary and himself as
        president. When Delia followed him to the US in 1915,
        James Connolly appointed Helena Molony as secretary.
        (O'Brien papers: 13970.)

21. ibid. p.45.

22. ibid. pp.11, 12. See also O'Brien papers 13971.

23. ibid. p.13.

24. Trade Union Act 1941 (No.22 of 1941).

25. But a radical division clearly existed by now. In
     December 1937 the national executive noted that
     agreement could not be reached under item I of the
     terms of reference. (See introduction to memorandum II ibid)

26. O'Brien papers 13971.

27. Trade union commission of inquiry and report of
     conference 1939 op.cit. pp.13, 14.

28. OBU, One Big Union, was a slogan deriving as we have
     already seen, directly from Connolly's syndicalism,
     and continues to be the legend on the badges of the
     Irish Transport.

29. O'Brien papers 13971.

30. idem.

31. idem.

32. idem.

33. idem.

34. op.cit. p.193.

35. O'Brien papers 15675.

36. ITUC 1937 p.160.

37. idem.

38. ibid. p.59.

39. idem.

40. ITUC 1938 p.106.

41. ibid. p.26.

42. Trade union commission of inquiry and report of
     conference 1939 op.cit. p.4.

43. ibid. p.25.

44. In any event it was very much shorter - almost a note when compared to memorandum I.

45. See below p.167

46. Trade union commission of inquiry and report of conference 1939 op.cit. p.29.

47. ibid. p.31.

48. Irish Bakers', Confectioners' and Allied Workers' Amalgamated Union.

49. Trade union commission of inquiry and report of conference 1939 op.cit. p.33.

50. ibid. p.34.

51. ibid. p.36.

52. Dublin Typographical Provident Society.

53. Trade union commission of inquiry and report of conference 1939 op.cit. p.44.

54. ibid. p.46.

55. ibid. p.46.

56. ibid. p.47.

57. ibid. p.47.

58. ibid. p.48.

59. We owe the rather comprehensive report of the special conference of 1939 in large part to P.T. Daly. Eamonn Lynch (clearly anxious to play the whole thing down) in the account which he submitted to the 1939 annual congress merely noted the decisions in as brief a way as possible, and gave none of the discussion. Although there were vehement protests from some Congress delegates, he was reluctant to give way, but P.T. Daly gave a swift and brusque assurance that the stenographer's report would be published. (ITUC 1939, pp.100-101, 153-155).

60. Dail Debates vol.85, col. 1535 ff.

61. Dail Debates vol.83, col. 1540.

62. ibid. 1542.

63. ibid. vol.84, col. 117.

64. ibid. 120.

65. ibid. 843.

66. Michael Keyes, a Labour deputy, was prominent in the NUR, the union of which Marchbank was general secretary.

67. Dail Debates vol.84, col. 845.

68. ibid. 846.

69. idem.

70. Sean MacEntee, away from the polemics of debate, put such a view succinctly and unwaveringly in a letter to J. Moran dated July 1 1941. (O'Brien papers 13974).

71. O'Brien papers 13974.

72. See above p.125

73. O'Brien papers 13974. It is interesting that this committee should have among its members Helena Molony of the Irish Women Workers and M. Leyden of the INTO, representatives of unions which in the split of 1945 remained with the Irish TUC.

74. O'Brien papers 13974.

75. idem.

76. Commission on Vocational Organisation op.cit. par. 583.

77. In a lecture given in November 1951 under the auspices of the Civics Institute. Johnson papers Ms. 17265.

78. Taff Vale Railway v Amalgamated Society of Railway Servants [1901] A.C. 426.

79. Quinn v Leathem [1901] A.C. 495.

80. See Chapter Twelve below.

81. Lyons op.cit. p.539.

82. Lyons op.cit. p.540.

83. Whyte op.cit. p.73.

84. Donal Nevin: "Radical Movements in the Twenties and Thirties": in Secret Societies in Ireland: ed. T. Desmond Williams: Gill and Macmillan, 1973 p.173

85. Whyte op.cit. p.91.

86. The Spanish Civil War (Non-Intervention) Act 1937.

Chapter Five

The Act of 1941

-i-

Irish neutrality during the second world war was a considerable achievement, which, although it owed a good deal
to fortune, owed a great deal more to the deft diplomacy of
de Valera. But at this terrible time in the history of the
world, the fact of Eire's neutrality imposed - in the words
of F.S.L. Lyons[1]-'a kind of screen, or glass, through which
they peered darkly at the storm outside.' In the south it
was a dreary time. True, there was considerable anxiety
after the fall of France in 1940; and the bombing of Belfast
brought the war terrifyingly close, but by the summer of
that year hostilities changed to the east with the outbreak
of war between Russia and Germany, and by the year's end
the United States had entered the war, and the conviction
had begun to grow that - however long postponed it might be -
victory would eventually lie with the Allies. In such
circumstances, Eire's external position appeared to be secure
enough, and the country became engrossed in the domestic
problems of the time.

Unlike the experience in the first world war, there was now
no bonanza for farmers; the agricultural industry had
been weakened by the depression and by the economic war,
and also by an unfortunate outbreak of foot-and-mouth
disease in 1941. But quite apart from that, Britain exercised
tight control on farm prices, and in 1944 'prices offered
by the British Ministry of Food were actually lower than
pre-war prices.'[2] On the other hand, imported raw materials
became ever scarcer, and employment fell heavily. Ordinary

goods became difficult to get: 'by 1943 the community had
25 per cent of its normal requirements of tea, 20 per cent
of its requirements of petrol, less than 15 per cent of its
paraffin, 16 per cent of its gas coal, no domestic coal
whatever and 22 per cent of its textiles.'[3] Inevitably the
price level leaped upwards. The cost of living indeed, which
in 1938 stood at 173,[4] had risen by 1943 to 284, and in
order to avoid catastrophic inflation, wages and salaries
were pinned by emergency legislation. These then were the
circumstances of great domestic difficulty in which the
trade unions found themselves, and in which they worked
out their own rather disedifying institutional conflict.
The split eventually came in 1945, the year of the war's end,
and one year after the celebration of the Golden Jubilee of
Congress, the fiftieth year of its foundation.

In the field of politics, in this period from 1939 to 1945,
Fianna Fail at first lost heavily in popularity, inevitably
because of the standstill on wages and the rapid rise in the
cost of living, and perhaps as well because of the Trade
Union Act of 1941. This last is somewhat speculative, but
to Dubliners in any event, the Trade Union Act, taken in
conjunction with the wages standstill order, looked uncomm-
only like union bashing - and this is always a little perilous politically. Labour's star began to rise (as also
did that of the farmers' party) culminating in a very cred-
itable performance in the general election of 1943. But
then the labour movement became wracked with dissension, and
in the general election which de Valera felt obliged to call
the following year, the Labour Party did very badly. Fine
Gael had also been tumbling in popularity, and they performed
badly both in 1943 and 1944; they won only 30 seats in 1944
as against 45 in 1938. Consequently, at the end of the war,
Fianna Fail found themselves in a stronger position than
even in their triumphant year of 1938, because although their
total tally of seats (76 from a total of 138) was one less

than in 1938, they faced, with their comfortable majority,
a fragmented and uncertain opposition.

All this was indeed domestic, and the cataclysm outside
obscured. But although the trade union movement, in common
with society as a whole in the south, faced inwards, it also
Janus-like had to face outwards at times to the surge of
these great international events. This was necessarily so
because of the substantial presence in the south of the
amalgamated unions with their close collegiate ties with
the British movement; but in particular it was so because
the Irish Trade Union Congress was still an all-Ireland
movement, incorporating Belfast and Derry, Newry and Portadown.
Admittedly the northern presence in Congress was weak at the
beginning of the decade, but it gradually began to grow in
strength and we note by 1945 not only the very vigorous contribution of Robert Getgood but the establishing as well
of a Northern Ireland advisory committee. This to some
extent reflected the sharply different experience of the
two parts of the island as the war developed, the south
stagnant, dark and dull, and the north, particularly after
the arrival of the American troops in early 1942, humming
with activity both because of the war effort and because
of the massive building programme needed to accommodate
over 120,000 US personnel.[5]

In what we have said so far, Eire's neutrality may appear
as something negative and parochial. There were quite a
number in the country - including some prominent Fine Gael
politicians - who took such a view. And indeed there was
a sense in which it was all that was said of it: a non-
involvement springing from a belief that the people of
Ireland had no real right to a view in a matter of such
importance, that they were best advised to keep out of it.
It was not that they were not concerned; of course they were.
Rather was it that, in their provincialism, they felt that
any view they might have on the conflict had little

legitimacy. But if Eire's neutrality had rested solely on
such grounds, it is doubtful if it would have been so
widely and so profoundly supported by the people generally
right throughout the war. In fact it was also an expression of very positive noncommitment. There was, as one
might have expected, a widespread and traditional concern
for the British position, although in the early years of
the war there was as well some sympathy with the German
cause; but in the ultimate, it was the immensity of the
tragedy that most influenced the mind of the south rather
than any partisanship. Neutrality then, insofar as it represented this feeling, was an important and positive policy.

Yet as the war began to enter its final phase, and when
the great work of postwar reconstruction came to be considered, those trade unionists in Ireland who were caught up
in the bright challenge of a new beginning saw in the neutrality of their colleagues something trivial, something
parochial and even something perverse, and there is no
doubt that these very different perceptions made their
contribution to the eventual fracturing of the trade union
movement.

-ii-

Let us consider then the events that led the government to
enact the Trade Union Act of 1941, the most radical attempt
that has so far been made to restructure, by legislative
means, the trade union movement. We have seen how the substance of the proposal was taken from memorandum I of the
trade union commission of inquiry, but there was a great
deal in the current situation which impelled the government
to take some step of this kind. 'War', remarked Senator
Douglas,[6] 'makes the chronic acute,' and the government,
facing the immense challenge of the time, became more and

more impatient with the tangle of trade union difficulties.
Furthermore when Sean Lemass moved to the Department of
Supplies - which had been established in December 1939 -
the Department of Industry and Commerce, and therefore
trade union affairs, came to be dealt with by Sean MacEntee,
a man who, as we have already seen, was disposed to take a
far more uncompromising line.

Even before the outbreak of war in 1939, the government's
policy of decentralising industry was causing a good deal
of sour feeling among trade unions and some industrial
unrest, a rather protracted and bitter dispute occurring
for example in the boot and shoe industry in Westport. The
government considered that an essential part of their industrial decentralisation policy was a differential in wages
between urban and rural workers. This was facilitated by
the fact that rural workers were poorly unionised and were
anxious for work; and in a number of cases - Donegal textiles
being a particular example - they joined with the employers
in a low wage policy. The trade unions on the other hand
sought a uniform rate throughout the country. It was
essential for them to do so. In the first place they feared
for the continuing employment of their urban members; and
in a more immediate sense they found that when they negotiated increases with substantial employers - under the various joint industrial councils and conciliation boards -
these employers soon began to complain bitterly of undercutting from others not only from outside the urban area
but from the 'back streets of Dublin.'[7] It was in these
circumstances that the trade unions looked to the Conditions
of Employment Act, section 50 of which provided for the
registration of agreements and the legal enforcement of
the wage terms throughout the appropriate industry. But
an act which appeared to promise so much when it was first
enacted in 1936 now seemed to evaporate. The government
was immensely reluctant to register agreements where a

uniform national wage was involved,[8] and said so much.
Cathal O'Shannon crossly pointed out that his union, the
Irish Transport, had concluded over 180 wage agreements
and had succeeded in having only one registered, the agreement in the hosiery industry[9] and that quite clearly because
'the employers in the big centres like Dublin and Cork
were affected in their trade by the undercutting of their
prices by the materials produced in Donegal...'[10]   So far
did the government go in this that they refused to sanction
a Trade Board increase in the shirt-making industry in order
to establish a differential between Donegal and the rest.[11]
All this was unlikely to make the unions particularly popular in the rural areas.   Indeed one delegate to the 1940
annual congress which discussed the matter, wryly said
that rural workers now opposed unionisation, saying for
example: 'Here is the Transport Union coming in to break
up the industry as they want it for the big centres.'[12]

These then were some of the difficulties of the time, difficulties which in themselves were predictable enough but
which were greatly exacerbated by war time conditions.
Prices, as we have seen, increased rapidly, causing the
workers, anxiously, to seek compensation.   The government,
giving a hint of the legislation to come, tried to damp back
increases, and a delegate to the 1940 Congress bitterly
complained '... we find that in every industry where the
Minister had direct or indirect control he had exercised
that control to prevent wages going up.   Where we have been
able to induce or convince in many cases reactionary local
bodies, that it was necessary to make some concession to the
workers to meet the increasing cost of living the responsible Minister has exercised his authority and withheld sanction for such increases.'[13]   Inevitably many workers saw
themselves as being selectively and unfairly treated: 'It
is evident that the Government has not prevented the employer class and the rentier class from making profits out
of the situation,'[14]   and this contributed to the unrest.

Unrest among the workers seemed to be the central issue of
the time, leading to the first overt parliamentary move in
the matter when Senator James Douglas proposed a motion in
Seanad Eireann on 14 March 1940: 'That Seanad Eireann would
welcome the introduction by the Government of a Bill generally amending the law in relation to trade disputes, and in
particular providing for the establishment of a permanent
industrial court for the examination of industrial disputes
and the promulgation of advisory judgements ' He declared
his motion to be a matter of urgency because 'one of my
principal reasons is that, for pretty obvious reasons, the
public mind has been much concerned with the question of
strikes and the possible methods of avoiding the loss sustained through labour disputes.'[15] He visualised one or
more permanent industrial courts, the president, having
the powers of a High Court judge, and being assisted by ass-
essors.[16] If on application, an employer was upheld by the
court or agreed with the court's ruling, then the union lost
the protection of the Trade Disputes Act. Although Douglas
protested that his proposal protected the right to strike,
it would have sharply limited it.

But how much effective industrial unrest existed at the time?
Douglas in the Senate quoted the 1939 Statistical Abstract[17]
to show that from 1931 to 1938 there were 805 disputes involving
87,426 workers and that 3,169,990 working days were
lost in the period, the average number per annum being 396,248.[18]
But on closer examination one finds that apart from 1937 where
the building strike resulted in a loss of a million and a
half working days, there is no great variation in the pattern,[19] the average was consistently since the beginning
of the decade around about 200,000, and 1939 standing at
106,476 was by no means too bad. But sometimes a mood of
industrial unease is not necessarily expressed in strike
statistics, and the memory seems to have been that 1939 was
a difficult year. Michael Colgan, when explaining to the

1945 Congress of Irish Unions, the need for a break from
the old congress said: 'In 1939 there were strikes all
over the place; there were pickets in every street in Dublin.
In the main the disputes were between Unions, not between
employers and employees. We realised then that such a position could not continue or the whole movement here would
go down in disaster.'[20] Colgan had been a member of the
Congress executive council at the time and in 1941 became
president. Furthermore when Sean MacEntee as Minister for
Industry and Commerce came to listen to the debate on the
Douglas motion in the Senate on April 24 1940, his concern
about strikes was very explicit, and he spoke of the view
that the government already had, 'that this evil of the undue prevalence of strikes, and so many cases of participation in unjustifiable strike action, is one that is arousing
public anger.'[21] In fact the number of disputes actually
begun in 1939 was substantially less than in the two previous years.[22] MacEntee was not at all sure that the problem could be met by juridicial means, and he directed the
Senate's attention to what he clearly regarded as the major
problem, setting the scene as well for the later legislation: 'Mention has been made of another fruitful cause of
labour disputes in the country - and it has been adverted
to elsewhere - that is, the rivalry which exists between the
trade union organisations ... We all can say that the workers
have a right to organise and withdraw their labour in order
to enforce what they regard as their claims to just remuneration. But it is quite a different matter to say that two
bodies of organised workers can go to war with each other
and to war with the community simply in order to decide which
of them is going to have the right to control employment in
any particular industry or in any particular concern. Yet
perhaps one of the most fruitful causes of strikes within
the past four or five years has been this trade union rivalry. This is a matter to which first attention should be
given by those who are concerned to maintain in the fullest
sense the rights of the workers to justly withdraw their
labour.'[23] The thrust of this - leading logically to the

legislation of the following year - was that the remedy for
industrial unrest lay primarily, not in legal penalties,
but in overcoming the defects in trade union organisation,
defects that sprang above all else from the rivalry between the amalgamated and the Irish unions.

But hostility to the unions lay much deeper than that. True,
Senator Douglas rested his case on the wholly proper argument that in these exceptional times there was a temptation
for trade unions to seek - and on occasion for employers
to agree to - quite excessive increases, which instead of
protecting the workers' interests ultimately would damage
them; and in these circumstances he was anxious to see established state machinery which would help to keep increases
at a reasonable level. But the organisation of which he
was vice-president, the Federation of Irish Manufacturers,
saw the problem lying firstly in the character of the
workers (and to some extent the employers) themselves. In
their submissions in the spring of 1940 to the Commission
on Vocational Organisation they said that many observers had
noted a lack of pride in his work on the part of the Irish
worker. Output was low, and production costs high. Despite
that, 'in many industries even the nominal wages are higher
than in Great Britain.'[24] They gave example after example
of the low response to incentives (although a large number
of these examples seemed to relate to rural female labour),
pointing out in passing that in the building industry, one
of the largest in Ireland, 'the effect of the great wage increase
of 1937 resulted in an expenditure of £2 million more
in 1938 but employed only 84 more workers out of a total of
28,000 - the supreme example of the fact that increased
wages do not affect output in many instances.'[25] And taking
the picture in the round 'the output in Irish industry is
definitely limited by the fact that in any industry in any
part of Ireland where piece work is engaged upon, a relatively high proportion of the workers are not willing or have
not the ambition, or do not possess the capacity to work
their machines at a rate which will enable the product to be
sold at the lowest possible price, as compared with workers
in English and foreign industries.'[26]

But this of course was not the case with Irish workers
abroad: 'It is a notorious fact that in the world outside
Ireland, Irishmen quickly distinguish themselves as hard
workers and when they enter and find permanent employment
in a country with a long tradition of nationality and
discipline, reveal very few of the weaknesses above mentioned.
The whole problem, therefore, is related in some way to the
actual fact of living in Ireland.'[27] And what did this fact
of living in Ireland constitute? 'During the nineteenth
century Industry was virtually destroyed by English Penal
legislation, there followed rapid emigration, often of the
best elements to the United States and British Colonies and
those who remained suffered through the rack renting system
which began to terminate only in 1890. The great National
revival beginning in 1905 did much to revive individual
initiative and enterprise. The improvement in agricultural
output and the growth in cattle farming brought much needed
financial improvement to the people. No sooner had these
influences made themselves felt, however, than the entire
country was plunged into a disturbed and irregular life through
the effects of the Great War: the rapid rise in cattle prices,
and with it, increases in prosperity, followed by the National
struggle for independence.'[28] These and the events that
followed from the civil war 'delayed the growth of National
and Social discipline, so urgently needed in a young State.'[29]
Then came the high protection movement in the nineteen thirties
with the further complication that 'during the last eight
years the people have been consistently taught the doctrine
that the State can provide their wherewithal at very little
return in the way of sacrifice and effort ... (To) bring
about rapid industrialisation among a rural population and
to accompany this with social legislation rapidly improving
their working conditions, accompanied by Unemployment Assistance
legislation of a very generous order - is not to invite
the best possible results as far as labour output is concerned.'[30]
The Federation felt that while the answer did not lie altogether with education, nonetheless it was the key to the
future, particularly education in the 'basic principles
regarding economic life.'[31] And they took some pains

to set out at length the characteristics 'of the worker in
the country with a long tradition of internal peace...'[32]
He recognises that he is only one part of the community,
he does not slack at work, he accepts the 'capital system'
until a better system is found, 'he does not live in an attitude
of perpetual resentment towards high salaried proprietors
and executives ... The worker will be taught from the
time he is a child that he has an obligation towards the State
and towards the other citizens, and that the more interest
he takes in the welfare of his industry the more he regards
himself as one of a family engaged in an enterprise for
the benefit of the citizens as a whole, the more likely is
that industry to progress.'[33] Industrial unrest as well
as low production came therefore from a most imperfect
grasp of Ireland's economic circumstances and the people's
social responsibility. 'Until education in the State includes
teaching both employers and workers the fundamental economic
law that 14% of the population is engaged in industrial
production, 53% are engaged in agricultural production (of
which one-third is exported) and that industry - unless
huge outlets for exports are discovered - must be regarded as
subsidiary to agriculture, output will never be sufficiently
high.'[34] The trade unions in the view of the Federation not
only reflected these inadequacies but made them very much
worse: 'It is significant that millions of days have been
lost in strikes since 1935, all of which reduced output and
raised costs. At least, half a million days were lost for
no good reason. Production was reduced by £1,200,000 in two
years. Since 1935 over one-third of the disputes have been
due to Union disputes, dismissal of workers, or the refusal
of Unions to sign a collective agreement.'[35] In the case
of the building industry they remarked on 'the existence of
a ridiculous number of rival Unions whose leaders are far
from responsible individuals in many instances.'[36] And in
fact the Federation submitted a memorandum to the Minister
for Industry and Commerce on trade unions in the course of
which they said: 'Owing to the former British connection
there were established here at the opening of the industrial

revival British and Irish Unions covering the same forms
of employment. Such duplication has created the most undesirable expansion in the total number of Unions. What
were intended to be protective societies for workers have
become quasi commercial organisations each attempting to
secure the largest volume of support through offering to
obtain better remuneration. The officers of these unions,
far from maintaining a co-operative attitude, frequently
denounce each others' mutual activities. The multiplication
of unions not only has continued to increase steadily but
has proceeded in two directions. There are rival unions of
exactly the same type but there are also so many varieties
of Trade Unions for any one industry, that any attempt at
employer-worker co-operation is utterly impossible. The
Trade Union Congress has been virtually powerless to prevent
this multiplication and has accepted the affiliations of
Trade Unions when the individual members were well aware of
the dangers arising.... In large and important industries,
strikes have occurred involving thousands of days work. No
settlement could be obtained because of the difficulty of
negotiating terms with so many and various unions. Frequently
the strike has been so long protracted that the workers would
gladly settle but are faced by intimidation and mass appeal
to hold out, and in every case the rival unions menace has
lengthened the dispute.'[37]

There were members of the Commission on Vocational Organisation to whom these memoranda were submitted who regarded
them as very exaggerated, a view which was sharply contradicted
by the secretary of the Federation Mr E.H. Childers[38]
in a letter to the Commission in July 1940.[39] But it seems
from the other information that is available that the Federation's view was somewhat highly-coloured. It does however
give something of the flavour of the attitude to workers and
trade unions held at that time by prominent business
people.

In the meantime egalitarian notions have become more widespread, and we are now more sensitive to the necessarily

subsidiary role which the worker was given in all this, and
more sensitive too perhaps to that lack of fundamental respect on which all tribalism is built, although in fairness
to the memoranda which we have quoted here, they contain a
number of attempts to join employers in the general sinful-
ness.

But trade union leaders saw themselves and their organisations in a very different light, far removed indeed from the
rather domestic and rather diminished view of the Federation
of Irish Manufacturers, whose experience seemed to be dominated by young rural girls with little economic sense, or
by laggardly tradesmen vigorous only in the pursuit of wage
increases. To them the outstanding fact was the rising tide
of unemployment, for which a solution had to be found, while
at the same time increasing wages to meet the rapid increase
in prices. Here were two legitimate demands, both imperative,
which could defeat one another, and of course the trade unions
were conscious of this and were very conscious too of their
responsibility to help in finding some way through. Consequently they were deeply stung by Lemass's remark in Dail
Eireann on March 29 1939: 'I think it is not unfair to our
Trade Union Movement as a whole to say that they have been
indifferent to the problem of unemployment.' They rejected
this statement as being 'flagrantly incorrect'[40] in a lengthy
pamphlet which they published widely throughout the country
and in which they reviewed all their policy statements since
1931.[41] And in this review we see something of their vision
of themselves and of their movement, particularly when they
come to discuss the more radical and long-term proposals for
the restructuring of society. Unemployment, poverty and all
the rest could be remedied only by organising the resources
of the country on a planned basis. They condemned what they
considered to be efforts 'to stabilise private ownership in
the vital industries, which is being done by bounties, tariffs and quotas.'[42] Public ownership was the answer, and
as early as 1932 at the dawn of the country's industrialisation, they urged the state to take possession of all

unoccupied and unused land, to vest in the state 'fundamental
industrial and political utility undertakings ...(and) to
secure the democratic management of fundamental Industries
and Services...'[43] There is nothing in this which is not
entirely plausible to modern commonsense. There were, however,
some who would say that it contained a deeper radicalism;
and to an extent this was no doubt true. The Workers' Union
of Ireland, in particular, officially espoused a policy which
had varied little from Connolly's syndicalism; the union
was a total expression of the working class: 'We recognise
no limit ... to our activities locally or nationally, and
our offices are a clearing house, hourly and daily, for
all the hardships, troubles and worries, that never cease
besetting the common people. We are an industrial organisation,
a cultural organisation, a welfare organisation, and a
social organisation...'[44] In their submission to the
Commission on Vocational Organisation they were much more
explicit than the other unions, stating their objective
to be the creation of an OBU, one general union 'composed
of industrial sections'[45] but - and here Connolly's syndicalism
comes through with great clarity - 'our ultimate object
is the realisation of our belief that wealth producers of the
nation, the wage earners in industry, commerce, and
agriculture, and the working farmer, should own, control,
and govern the nation, its wealth and resources, and its
economy in the interests of the common working people. We
strive to organise and educate the workers to the realisation
of that objective.' Although this was very much a
minority view, it is nonetheless of significance,
representing as it did not merely an intellectual view of
the role of the proletariat, but something felt in the heart
about the revolutionary role of the poor and the deprived,
a recognition perhaps that they had a surer understanding
of social reality than the wealthy and the privileged.
It is easy to dismiss this as a form of working-class
tribalism, mirroring the tribalism of the well-to-do; but
Christianity is full of the same kind of insight, and it
may well be explained - at least in part - by the fact that
the lowly see all men in their full humanity, including the
powerful in the land; while those to whom it is given to

command men are easily tempted to dehumanise them, and see
them as objects for their use. But if as the WUI did, one
sees in the working class the seeds of social revolution, one
also is reluctant to muddy the distinction between them
and those of privilege, and consequently one views with great
reserve joint institutions between employer and trade union,
working class and the wealthy, except where trade union activity
strictly requires it. And this was a view which seems to
have influenced at least to some extent the thinking of James
Larkin Junior who from the war's end onwards was the towering
figure in the Irish trade union movement, and who well may
have been the author of the submission which his union made
to the Commission on Vocational Organisation in 1940.

But of course the view of the vast majority in the trade
union movement was much closer to that of Tom Johnson, which
we have already described.[46] The reorganisation of society,
the domination of capitalism, was to be achieved by
parliamentary means - by close co-operation between the trade
union movement and the Labour Party; and frequently we find
trade union leaders denying any extremism in their policies,
claiming rather a progressive approach, which was gradually
gaining acceptance. P.T. Daly[47] in 1939, looking back over the
years, said: 'At the first Congress of this organisation
the resolutions proposed were but minor cycles in the programme
of world events. Our critics condemned them then. They were
"anti-Christian" and what was more to be condemned in the
views of our critics, they were "socialistic" and should not
be tolerated. Leaders were pointed out as inclining in that
direction, and the workers were taught to shun them as they
would his Satanic Majesty. With the passage of time some
of the minor demands have been conceded. We have now made
legal the position of the Trade Union picket: we have
had the Trade Union dispute recognised as a legal entity - but
still to be fought for in the court: we have got the terribly
socialistic old age pension: we have got a national system
of health insurance and unemployment insurances. All

these were amongst the things which were condemned close on
fifty years ago, for advocating which some of the younger men
of that period were sent out into the wilderness as unclean –
unfit for association with those to whom they looked for guidance.' True, Sam Kyle could say: 'We are born free, but
society has made us serfs. We can only regain our complete
freedom by changing society. Capitalism will not be destroyed
by coquetting with capitalism.'[48] But his remedy certainly
did not lie in revolution, and he distrusted the political
judgement of those who were grossly deprived: 'It
is a fallacy to assume that economic distress induces clear
thinking, that radicalism is the result of a hungry stomach,
that the growth of labour opinion is the outcome of crises.
Herein lies the value of Trade Union activity. Increased
remuneration, better conditions of working, more leisure to
study and play, an enlarged standard of life, greater economic
security, create the environment in which rebels against the
existing order of things develop. Poverty induces that psych-
ological instability, which will clutch desperately at a pan-
acea for the removal of immediate ills, instead of getting
down to the root causes of distress and their elimination.
The unemployed and the underfed are not free....We seek to
make possible informed, responsible, self-controlled men and
women...' While in this view, the Connolly ethic that the
working class must stand alone may have been approved in theory,
the fact was that Sam Kyle and the vast majority of trade
unionists wished to co-operate in full with the government
and indeed all others for the betterment of society. In the
thirties they had pressed for an Economic Planning Commission[49]
and, quite apart from proposals to give additional money assistance to unemployed, they proposed a considerable extension
of public works, and rather romantically, a scheme of co-operative farms where the unemployed could become self-sufficient,
remembering no doubt Connolly and his account of the Ralahine
experiment in 1832.[50] They had been greatly strengthened in
their view by what they saw the Labour government do in New
Zealand.[51] The report of the Banking Commission in 1938

whetted their appetite for further and more extensive surveys, and increased their belief in the need for a national economic council. At the outbreak of war, they were deeply disappointed that the government did not involve them formally in meeting the crisis. 'The Government, apart from the major item of national defence, have not thought fit to ask the Trade Union Congress as such, to assist', said Sam Kyle in 1940.[52] But this did not lessen their commitment. 'We deplore this, and hope that even yet they will endeavour to harness every available man and woman to serve the nation's interest to the best of their ability.' They joined with the Labour Party in publishing and publicising a pamphlet 'Planning for the Crisis'[53] and towards the end of July 1940 they met the Taoiseach and members of the government suggesting the establishment of an Economic Council which would be purely consultative, 'the membership of the Council to be some ten or twelve persons, including the Ministers for Industry and Commerce, Supplies and Agriculture, the Parliamentary Secretary to the Minister for Finance and representatives of Labour, Industry, and possibly, Agriculture who would be appointed by the Government after consultation with the interests concerned.'[54] But the government would have nothing to do with the idea, preferring to consult with the various groups separately when they thought it appropriate to do so.[55] Thus the trade unions, for whatever reason, were not seen by the government as economic partners at this difficult time; and inevitably relations were distant and distrustful, particularly because of the pressure which the government more and more in 1940 exercised on employers to refuse wage increases. In a word, to the government, trade unions were problem organisations, which, if the occasion demanded it, must be regulated in the public interest. It is not unlikely however, that while the government maintained this distance with the Irish Trade Union Congress, its relations with the Council of Irish Unions may have been closer and more co-operative. There is much in the events that followed that would support such a view.

But let us take up one further theme in our attempt to
catch the mood of the time: the feeling of the inadequacy
of ordinary people to handle responsibly diverse political
and social institutions. It lay heavily over all the
country, and nowhere was it clearer than in local government,
where the managerial system had become more and more a settled
feature of administration, although the labour representatives
continued to complain bitterly that they had been turned into
tailors' dummies and that the manager 'had control over the
destinies of every man, woman and child in his area -
socially, economically and in every other way.'[56] But the
inadequacy of the ordinary people was accepted nonetheless.
The constitutional trade unionist, firmly committed to
parliamentary democracy, looked to education as the remedy; as
also did bodies such as the Federation of Irish Manufacturers.
But there were others who questioned the whole idea of popular
parliamentary democracy and, while they would abhor the Italian
and the German experiments, they looked with sympathy to
Portugal; and as we have seen a Commission on Vocational
Organisation was appointed in March 1939. To some
influential people, then, it was not a question of more
education in order to work a popular democracy better; it
was much more profound, and in a sense it was a reaching back
by countries in the Roman Catholic tradition to a system
earlier than the Protestant economic and political individualism.[57]
This individualism had been a heady experience, providing the
dynamic for the industrial revolution and the flowering
of mass democracy that followed. It had its gross and dark
side in the capitalism of exploitation, and this was clear
enough. But in its emphasis on individualism it also had the
effect of blurring and dimming the reality of social
institutions, by which 'a link is made between the past
and the future. Instead of a moving point between something vanished and something yet to be, the present moment
for any society provides through its steady categories
a fixed centre which holds the past and draws the future
to itself.'[58] There were those then who saw men unsettled and bewildered, without the steady and continuous
institutions of which the Church was the great exemplar,
and they wished therefore to create the political

institutions which would counter such individualism, and
which would rescue men from the unrest and the anxieties of
the Heraclitean flux. Inevitably trade unions and similar
organisations, unless they were integrated in a stable system,
were objects of some suspicion. It must be emphasised, however,
that the Fianna Fail government of the time, although
prepared to centralise, were ultimately committed to an open
parliamentary system of government.

The trade unions recognised that they were vulnerable. Ireland
was of course committed to free democratic institutions, but
they were very conscious nonetheless that in the recent past
'the Trade Unions of Norway, Belgium, Czecho Slovakia, Austria,
Denmark, Holland (and France) have all been crushed ...'[59] And
this at least made it easier to contemplate some trade union
restrictions here. Indeed in Northern Ireland the war very
quickly brought about a situation where, for practical purposes,
strikes and lock-outs were debarred, and arbitration was the
only recourse.[60] And they recognised too that this
vulnerability was much increased by the internal defects in
the trade union movement. Liberty in some cases had become
licence. 'We see rather dangerous tendencies, now and again,
in the form of unofficial strikes,' said J.T. O'Farrell at
the 1940 Congress,[61] 'strikes that are entirely unjustified
and that set aside the Trade Union regulations concerned
and the Trade Union officials concerned with the negotiations
and that are at the same time, a form of blackmail on the
community ... The public will surrender a tremendous amount for
the sake of public order ... There is a trend here in our own
country to consider a restriction on Trade Union activities,
based, mainly, on the incidents to which I have referred. These
are given as an excuse, notwithstanding the fact that the
overwhelming majority of Trade Union members act in a perfectly
constitutional way and in a manner of which no reasonable
person can complain.' It is not surprising then that
they saw in Senator Douglas's Senate motion a threat to trade
unions, part of 'the campaign that had been conducted for some

time past in favour of legislative action designed to impair
the machinery of Trade Unionism, to deprive the Unions of
rights won in part struggles, and to prevent organised
workers from exercising full liberty of organisation and
combination.'[62]   And a motion was adopted by the 1940 annual
Congress calling on the unions to resist any such attack
upon their freedom. Interestingly enough, in the light of
what was to happen in a few short months, it was moved by
William McMullen of the Irish Transport and General
Workers Union.

Finally, we must bear in mind, when considering the government's
attempts to legislate in this area, that the trade union
movement in 1940 was far, far less significant in numbers
than it is today. Inevitably, at this time, there was
interest in the arithmetic of trade union membership, and
apart from the Congress annual reports[63] we find in particular
in William O'Brien's papers[64] a number of documents bearing
on the matter, the two principal being a list of organisations
of workers, their membership and affiliations as on November 1
1940, probably prepared by the Department of Industry and
Commerce, and secondly a written reply in Dail Eireann on
February 7 1945 setting out the unions which had been granted
negotiating licences under the 1941 act, with, inter alia,
their membership: the information is for 1943. There is
also in the memoranda submitted by the Department of Industry
and Commerce to the Commission on Vocational Organisation[65]
a list of trade unions registered under the Trade Union
Acts 1871-1935, the information being for 1937.

We have set out in appendix five a table showing in some
detail the Irish trade union membership for 1970. This
helps to contrast the present time with that of 30 years ago.
In 1940, it was calculated, there were 163,000 members
in the unions affiliated to the ITUC.[66] This compares
with a 1970 figure of 602,700. As far as the twenty-six county
area is concerned, the number in 1940 was 103,000 compared
with 371,500 in 1970. But in the north the contrast is even

greater; the 1940 members of unions affiliated to the ITUC
numbered 60,000 as compared with 231,200 in 1970. But how
accurate a picture is this of the number of organised workers, whether in unions affiliated to Congress or not? In
1970 we see from appendix five that the percentage for the
country as a whole of those affiliated to Congress is 93%,
and for the Republic it is also 93%. We must recognise however that unlike 1970[67] the earlier figures are derived from the
numbers declared by the unions for the purpose of affiliation to Congress and   contain some degree of underestimation.   In the analysis for 1940[68]   we see an attempt not
only to take. account of unions not affiliated to Congress
but union underestimates of members as well, the following
table being provided in the analysis for the twenty-six
counties of Eire:

Irish unions:

affiliated to ITUC	79,000	
underestimate (say)	25,000	
not affiliated (say)	16,000	120,000 (80%)

British unions:

affiliated to ITUC	24,000	
not affiliated (say)	6,000	30,000 (20%)
		150,000

The most important point is, of course, that the trade union
movement in 1940 was perhaps only one quarter the size in
membership of the trade union movement today; indeed the
largest union, the Irish Transport, now contains almost as
many members as did the whole trade union movement north and
south in 1940, and all this in a country the population of which
has not dramatically altered over the years.

There are some further points of interest. When we review
all the material that is available to us we find that the
Irish Transport returned for the period 1937 to 1943 figures

which varied from 32,000 to 36,000, probably for the country
as a whole. Today the number is over four times as large.
But from our point of view here, it is important to recognise
how close the Amalgamated Transport was to this figure: in
the early forties it returned a membership for the whole
country of 35,000, although its membership in Eire was a mere
3,000 or 4,000. (In 1941 it affiliated for 33,000, somewhat
less than its actual membership if we are to judge from the
other returns of the time. In more recent times, it has
adopted a policy of substantial under-affiliation; in 1970,
the ICTU calculated[69] that the Amalgamated Transport had a
membership of 101,300.)[70] But if the two unions, the
Irish Transport and the Amalgamated Transport, were very
close in membership and in voting power, they were very
different indeed in regard to their geographical distribution.

As for Larkin's union, the Workers Union of Ireland, there
is an extraordinary variation in the returns of the period;
the document submitted to the Commission on Vocational
Organisation showed a figure of 16,997 for 1937, while the
number shown for the purposes of making an application for a
licence in the early forties was 5,000. The other documents,
however, appear to establish a membership of 8,000 or 9,000.
In 1970 the union was affiliated to Congress for 30,000 and
Congress itself estimated its actual membership as marginally
more than that.[71] We have already noted the great increase
in numbers in the general unions over the years; one of the
consequences of this of course is that unions - strong in the
forties - that did not increase as rapidly, declined in
significance; the Irish Union of Distributive Workers and
Clerks and the Irish National Teachers Organisation are two such
examples, although both increased their membership by 50
per cent or so. The ASW declined in significance for the same
reason, but the other great amalgamated craft union, the
Amalgamated Engineering Union, has greatly increased its
membership over the years in the south - quite dramatically in
fact, probably reflecting growing industrialisation; in

Eire in 1940, its membership was given variously as 600 or
1,600; in 1970 it was 5,400 in the south and 32,700 in the
country as a whole. In the nineteen forties the National
Union of Railwaymen was a force, with a membership in the
country as a whole of 8,000 of whom 5,500 were in the south.
It has since disappeared, in circumstances, as we shall
see, of the greatest interest.

This then was the trade union movement in the early years
of the forties, small in numbers, fragmented in organisation,
much confused politically, and troublesome to impatient
and serious-minded men confronted with the problems of a
world at war.

-iii-

In July 1940 William O'Brien was elected president of Congress
in succession to Sam Kyle, to hold office until July 1941;
and it was during these months that the government confronted
the trade union movement not only with the trade union bill
but with the wages standstill order as well. The other two
elected officers, Michael Colgan, the vice-president and
Sean Campbell the treasurer, were later to join with O'Brien
as founder members of the Congress of Irish Unions.
Of the remaining twelve members of the national executive,
two, Kennedy and McMullen, were members of the Irish
Transport, and Drumgoole of the Distributive Workers was
also an O'Brien supporter. Six members of the executive
therefore were committed to the O'Brien policy; on the other
hand, six members were representatives of amalgamated unions,
and of the remaining three, one represented the Cork Trades
Council, one represented the Irish Bakers, and one the
Post Office Workers: these two latter unions, in the crisis
of 1945, remained with the Irish Trade Union Congress.

It has been represented that in this situation the Irish
unions had a majority over the amalgamated unions of nine to
six, but the position was more complex than that. As for the
secretary, Eamonn Lynch, he survived to write the annual
report, but not to present it to the 1941 Congress. By
then he had resigned (an event which O'Brien deliberately
glossed over)[72] and Campbell the treasurer acted as secretary until Cathal O'Shannon was appointed some time later.[73]

The news of the proposed trade union legislation broke on
October 30 1940. The secretary of the Department of Industry and Commerce invited the Congress national executive to
come to see him. He refused to give them anything in writing, but the purpose was made perfectly clear. A further
meeting took place on November 20, and in the absence of any
written communication from the Department, the national executive itself circulated the unions on December 17, setting
forth the proposals 'as they were orally given'.[74] The bill
was published on April 30 1941.

The official reaction of the ITUC was one of anxiety and hostility, but it was muted during this time. O'Brien and a
number of the national executive clearly took a different
view, although it is difficult to determine precisely the
nature of the relationship between them and the government.
Judge, who is reputed to have had numerous interviews with
O'Brien during the course of his study,[75] says: 'What actually happened was that previous to the passing of the Bill
the unofficial Council of Irish Unions within the TUC, headed
by William O'Brien and two other members of the NE collabor-
ated with representatives of the Fianna Fail government.'
But this may be putting the point too bluntly. Certainly
the Council of Irish Unions had a separate meeting with the
Department of Industry and Commerce about the same time, but
in his manuscript notes[76] O'Brien mentions this in a subsidiary way, noting first the Department's meeting with the
national executive. There is no reason to believe that

O'Brien had any special relationship with members of the
Fianna Fail government, apart from an old soldier form of
camaraderie;   for example he never reached first name terms
with Sean Lemass, although many of his colleagues did,[77]
and it seems likely enough that there was a mutuality of
purpose in the case of both O'Brien and the government
which required no conspiracy to support it.   It was probably
this more than any specific agreement which caused both de
Valera and MacEntee to speak later of support for the legislation among prominent trade unionists.[78]

Nevertheless, the real aim of the Trade Union Act 1941[79]
was precisely that which William O'Brien attempted in 1939:
to restructure the trade union movement.   It proposed to do so
by giving to a majority union the sole right to organise a
particular class of workers, and it established (under Part
III)a tribunal with powers to confer such a right.   It also
succeeded, as we shall see, in making life more difficult
for the amalgamated unions; so that O'Brien's two objectives
of rationalisation and national exclusivity were both provided for.   The other provisions in the act flowed from this,
and when eventually in 1946 the Supreme Court held that
Part III of the act (which established the tribunal) was
contrary to the Constitution of the country, we were left,
as a basis for our modern trade union law, with a piece of
legislation which has an odd half-finished look to it, like
the blank blind wall of a building whose twin has never been
constructed.

It is one thing to establish a tribunal which could confer
on a trade union sole rights of organisation; it is quite
another matter to ensure that its decisions are observed.
How, in a word, does one enforce such things?

First it was necessary to clear the ground and try to dominate the situation. With this in mind, the government began
by looking not so much at the character of trade unions as

at their activities; and they identified the activity of
negotiation – of bargaining – as the central one, distinguishing
it from all others. It was this activity, the activity
of negotiation, on which they decided to concentrate, reserving
it only to bodies specially licensed for the purpose. Any
body which attempted to negotiate wages and conditions and
which was not licensed for the purpose (with certain
stated exceptions) committed an offence; furthermore the
extensive protection of the Trade Disputes Act 1906 – so
essential to the conduct of a strike – was reserved to
licensed bodies. Without such a licence a trade union might
declare itself such in its rules, might engage in benevolent
activities, but in its essential activity it was emasculated.
This was a radical change. As we have seen[80] under the 1871
Act and subsequent legislation, the essential character of
a trade union depended not on its being registered as such
under an act of parliament, but on its being defined as such.
But now, whatever its definition, its central activity, the
activity which gave it effective existence, could be
exercised only if it were granted a negotiation licence
by the government.

This raised an intriguing question. A negotiation licence
might be issued at the government's discretion or it might
be issued automatically on the fulfilling of certain conditions.
The first sounds quite intolerable in a free democratic
society; but in fact a variation of such an idea was contemplated by Lemass in the sixties, when he offered the Irish
Congress of Trade Unions the right, at its discretion, to
block the issue of a licence, a right which the Congress
national executive hastily refused. The government in 1941
adopted the second course, the issuing of a negotiation licence
automatically on the fulfilling of certain conditions, but
of course there is considerable scope for using such general
conditions selectively, and indeed in the public interest.
There was a widespread desire at the time to discourage
small, frivolous and breakaway unions and to encourage

large and stable groupings, and consequently as a condition
to the issue of a negotiation licence the government required
the union to make a deposit in the High Court of a sum of
money, which, although it varied with the size of the union,
was very large, the minimum deposit being £1,000 and the
maximum £10,000. In view of the very small membership in
unions in Ireland these were very substantial sums indeed.
Furthermore the deposit could be attached on foot of a court
order, decree or judgement.

There was an interesting modification of this provision regarding
deposits, a modification which clearly discriminated against
the amalgamated unions. It came quite late in the proceedings in Dail Eireann, when the government, sensitive
to the anxieties of the small Irish unions, introduced a new
section which permitted the Minister to abate the deposit
by seventy-five per cent, but only in the case of Irish-based
unions.[81]

It is clear from this, and indeed from the whole thrust of
the legislation, that amalgamated unions must be capable of
being distinguished from Irish-based unions. With this object
in view, the act gracefully took note of the Meredith
judgement[82] and declared an authorised trade union to be
either a trade union registered under the Trade Union Acts
1871 to 1935, or, if it was not registered, a trade union
under the law of another country with its headquarters control
situated in that country. Both were authorised trade unions;
both were eligible to apply for negotiating licences, but if
one wished to identify the Irish-based union all one had to do
was to refer to a trade union registered under the trade
union acts 1871 to 1935. Having made the distinction, the act
went on to require the amalgamated unions to fulfil certain
quite proper conditions; they were obliged to have an
office within the state, they were obliged to have a
representative within the state who could be served with
official documents, and they were obliged to notify changes
in rules, committee members and principal officers. But when
the act came, in Part III, to consider the tribunal, a number
of marked disabilities began to arise.

Quite explicitly, the act provided that the tribunal 'shall
not grant a determination ... that a trade union registered
under the law of another country and having its headquarters
control in that country ... shall alone have the right to
organise workmen of any particular class.' Such unions could
of course defend themselves if another union made an application
which would exclude them, and there were statutory grounds
for defence, particularly with regard to the rights and
benefits of the members; but unlike the Irish-based unions
they could themselves take no initiative in the matter.
Furthermore they had a good deal to fear from the manner in
which the tribunal was constituted. The tribunal was to sit
as a board of three, an independent chairman appointed by
the minister, and two trade union representatives selected
by the minister from a panel to which the unions made
nomination.[83] This gave the minister considerable flexibility
in regard to choice, but there would have been an outcry
had he appointed the two trade union representatives from among
the unions associated with the caucus of the Council of Irish
Unions. Eventually when he came to set up the tribunal in
1943, he went as far as he reasonably could to provide a
balance, short of appointing a member of an amalgamated union,
and he chose Cairns of the Post Office Workers Union to sit
with Owen Hynes who was prominent in the Council of Irish
Unions. Even if the amalgamated unions could have anticipated
this in 1941, the apparent evenhandedness meant very
little, since the chairman, although independent in trade
union matters, could hardly be independent in a matter of
government policy such as the fostering of Irish-based
unions and the displacing of amalgamated ones. There was an
appeals system of course, but essentially its power lay in
reference back rather than reversal and there was little
to be gained from it.

The act went on to provide that after a determination by
the tribunal, a displaced union committed an offence if it
accepted as new members those in the class of worker concerned;
and if this appears to be a rather cumbersome and long-

drawn-out means of displacing the amalgamated unions, it
must be seen in the context of the act as a whole, the system of negotiating licences first stabilising and clarifying
the position, and then the other provisions coming into play:
the fact that an amalgamated union could not apply for a
determination, the fact that (under the committee stage amendment) it was to suffer substantial discrimination in the matter
of deposits, and finally the overwhelming fact that the 'public interest' which the tribunal was obliged to follow,could
mean at this time one thing merely, that subject to the protection of certain membership rights and benefits, the object
of the tribunal was to exclude progressively British-based
unions from organising workers in the state, until eventually
they were altogether extinguished. We must also recognise
how aptly the act met the other objects which were sought by
O'Brien's 1936 memorandum:[84] the organisation of unions into
exclusive industrial groups, but in a manner which gave considerable advantage to a great general union, which as an
OBU (diversified perhaps on an industrial basis) would come
to dominate the whole trade union movement.   There was a
vehement reaction just as there was in 1939, not only from
the amalgamated unions but from the Irish-based general unions
as well, none being more vigorous or more vocal in dissent
than the Workers Union of Ireland. Under the leadership of
Larkin, and in particular of his son Young Jim, it spear-
headed the campaign of protest by the Dublin Council of Action which dominated the months between the publication of
the bill at the end of April and the opening of the Annual
Congress on July 16 1941. To this we shall return in a moment.

A position already very difficult was suddenly much inflamed
when on May 7, a little over a week after the publication of
the trade union bill, the government, not surprisingly in
the circumstances, promulgated the wages standstill order.[85]
In effect it prohibited employers from giving any increase
in remuneration, even on the foot of a cost-of-living bonus

scheme, and, as for the trade unions, it removed from them
their legal immunity in the case of any industrial action
done in contravention of the order. Thus the very citadel
of trade union integrity was in peril.

The national executive of Congress had decided to call a
special conference on May 16 to protest against the trade
union bill; they extended the scope of the meeting in
order to protest against the wages standstill order as well,
and adopted two resolutions, predictably worded, which contemplated that the Labour Party, at that time at least, would
have the major task in opposing both measures. If this
rather measured response seems somehow out of key with
the considerable crisis which now beset the trade union movement,
we must look for an explanation to the policies of William
O'Brien and those who supported him. In his address to the
annual conference of Congress in July, he seemed to take the
view that while one could not approve of the trade union bill,
one had to accept it as inevitable, largely because the trade
union movement itself had failed to put matters right; 'as
a consequence of the failure to meet the situation we have
now governmental interference in our movement in a manner that
is quite naturally resented but for which we ourselves in our
affiliated unions are so largely responsible.'[86]

To O'Brien, a difficult situation was made worse by two great
problems, the first being endemic, that of the amalgamated
unions, and the second quite fortuitous, the wages standstill
order. With regard to the first, the words he used in his
address as president of the whole Irish trade union movement
were uncompromisingly partisan and vindictive: 'We all, of
course, can understand that no matter what the proposals in
the measure were there would be an outcry from the superfluous
unions which we all want to see eliminated - or, to use an
expression in fashion in some quarters "liquidated". These
were sure to protest no matter what form "the surgeon's
knife" took.' But it was the second, the wages

standstill order, which really did the damage. 'Order No.
83', he said, 'was entirely unnecessary, provocative, ill-
advised and a grave blunder on the part of the Government.
The Order was certain to arouse a storm among the workers.
And in the midst of the resentment, irritation and bad-feel-
ing created by the Order the Government chose to introduce
its Trade Union Bill. Its reception, as anybody with knowledge of the Labour position would know in advance, was
naturally hostile. In the circumstances and the atmosphere
created by Order 83 that was the reception it was bound to
get. For this the Government is solely responsible [87] In
view of the very high feeling that had developed during June
he was obliged to speak out as well against the principle of
government interference by legislation, recognising the 'widespread view that (the bill) is but the first of a series of
measures which will, step by step, deprive the unions of
their hard-won rights secured by generations of effort and
sacrifice.'[88] But although he recognised that this view
existed, he had no intention of allowing it to imperil a legislative development which suited his objectives so admir-
ably. He was therefore anxious that the wave of protest
should be kept diffuse and on as low a key as possible.

It was in these circumstances that he viewed with great
resentment the activities of his arch-enemy Larkin, particularly in the weeks leading up to the July Congress of
1941. The Dublin Council of Trade Unions (from which the
Irish Transport had withdrawn when it admitted Larkin's
union into affiliation) established a Council of Action to
fight both the bill and the wages standstill order, and on
Sunday June 28 1941, a few weeks before the annual congress
took place, there was a great demonstration in Dublin.
Larkin seemed to have recaptured something of his old magic.
A parade of trade unions ended with a mass meeting in College
Green, 'acclaimed', said John Swift[89] 'one of the biggest
held in Dublin, ending with a stirring speech by Larkin
senior, which he dramatically terminated by holding aloft a
copy of the Trade Union Bill and setting it alight with a

match. This had a great response from the crowd.' It also
had a considerable response from the Labour Party, the leader
of which, William Norton, had also spoken from the platform
at College Green. As a result the Labour Party decided not
to move any amendments to the bill in Dail Eireann, so that
its total opposition to the measure might in no way be com-
promised.[90] The success of the Council of Action owed a
great deal not only to Larkin senior, but also to the considerable organising ability of his son, young Jim as he
was called. It met with widespread approval from a great
number of trade union members, and was remembered particularly for its effectiveness. Leo Crawford, who was later
to become secretary of the breakaway Congress of Irish Unions
but whose hostility to the bill was beyond question, said in
October 1941[91] that the Labour Party in refusing to put down
amendments to the bill 'was actuated by a demonstration that
took place in Dublin against the Act, the like of which had
not been seen since 1913. The demonstration gave definite
instructions that there was to be uncompromising opposition
to the Act. When the history of this agitation comes to
be written at least the Council of Action can say that they
fought.' But the meeting in College Green on June 28 was
not so much a unique event as a climax to a period of rather
intense activity. The Council of Action took up the pallid
resolution which had been adopted by the special trade union
conference of May 16 and carried it far beyond the point
which O'Brien would have countenanced. In a lengthy circular
to all affiliated trade unions[92] (probably drafted by young
Jim Larkin) they not only condemned with great vehemence both
the bill and the wages standstill order but they warned in
quite extravagant terms about the future: 'The final step
will be the transformation of the Unions, or rather their
submersion, in corporative organisations made up of both
workers and employers and directly under the control of the
Government.... The perspective set out above is not without
foundation or recklessly or partisanly put forward.... An
Taoiseach only last week expressed his view that "corporative organisation" would come in this country by stages. A

Commission set up by the Government has been sitting for
some time making inquiries into corporative organisation
and many on that Commission are in favour of the Corporative
State - the present Bill is not merely a measure to shackle
the Trade Union Movement, it is a testing piece for the
movement...' They saw how the desire for national unity at
this critical time was being used against them and
resented it, particularly since they had co-operated in the
national effort to the fullest extent possible to them, and
they replied with some violence: 'This Bill is a crime against
national unity, against the best interests of the country and
the Irish people and it is a flagrant example of the employing
class taking advantage of the apparent docility of the Trade
Union Movement, taking advantage of the workers' ever present
willingness to serve the nation to rush through this piece of
class legislation. But the Trade Union Movement cannot and
will not permit this crime against the Irish workers and the
Irish people to be committed.' And then once again echoing
Connolly's syndicalism: 'The Irish Trade Union Movement will
not sacrifice its independence and the rights of its members
at the behest of any group, party or Government, outside the
working class, not even to preserve national unity, because
the Irish working class is the basis of the Irish nation...'

There was a sense in which this was a confrontation between
the tribalism of class **and the tribalism of nation**. It was not
perhaps very explicit since the Council of Action did not
reject national tribalism but claimed for the workers its
purest form; nevertheless since it stood for the preservat-
ion of British-based unions on working class grounds, it was
opposed to the xenophobia of the time. In the past, as we
have seen, nationalist sentiment, in the people at large,
rapidly overwhelmed international socialist ideals; but this
was not the case here. There was of course the remarkable
leadership offered by the Larkins; but there was also something intrinsic in what they offered: a strong sense of
working class identify and solidarity so central that the
other aspects of the socialist doctrine were not significant,
and powerful enough to challenge the nationalist position.

O'Brien tried to meet the problem in a number of ways. On
May 24 the national executive of Congress saw the Taoiseach
on the question of the wages standstill order, and on June
16, at a further meeting with the Minister for Industry and
Commerce, some minor amendments were secured, largely dealing
with the legitimising of claims that had been caught in mid-
flight. Furthermore, in early June during the second reading
of the trade union bill, there were introduced, as we have
already noted, some amendments that made the position substantially better for the Irish-based unions; and consequently
despite the vigour of the Council of Action, an impression
was given of divided counsels within the trade union movement -
or perhaps worse: 'A good deal of opposition,' said The Leader
of May 31 'is being voiced in official Labour circles to the
Trade Union Bill; but we happen to know that a considerable
proportion of it is hollow and insincere' - a point much
reinforced by the manner in which the Minister for Industry
and Commerce dealt with the matter in Dail Eireann the following week.[93] But on July 16, the Irish Independent carried
a letter from the venerable Tom Johnson, which in more measured
and temperate language supported much of the activity of the
Council of Action. He made two points which are central to
our understanding of the effect of the legislation. In the
first place it was essentially conservative in character:
'The Bill will render it difficult to introduce any new principle of organisation in trade unions. Trade Unions have not
all grown from a single root, nor are their constitutions
framed on identical lines. The Bill appears to have been
framed in the belief that the existing Unions are capable
of satisfying all needs, that no new Unions are required, and
that a "break-away" must be prevented by law.' There were a
substantial number of unorganised workers in the State and
these, because of the difficulty in getting enough money to
make the appropriate deposit, would be obliged to join existing unions rather than form their own. Here Johnson no doubt
had in mind O'Brien's ambitions for the Transport Union; but
in fairness, the amendments in June during the committee stage
of the bill largely met this particular point, although the

general thrust of the criticism had plausibility at the time.
His second point was more fundamental and more well-based.
It referred to the extraordinary powers which the proposed
tribunal could wield, far beyond anything in the 'recommendation presented to a Special Conference of Trade Unions....
The proposed Tribunal will have power to determine the form
and character of the Trade Union movement in this country for
the future.' He dealt at some length with the various types
of organisation that were possible - in fact a little fanci-
fully - and suggested that since the measure went farther than
anyone in the trade union movement had ever suggested, and
farther perhaps than the government really intended, the matter
should be postponed 'to give the unions another opportunity
to correct in their own way the faults and weaknesses that
are admitted to exist.' Johnson's letter appeared on the
opening day of the 1941 annual congress.

As if all this were not enough, there appears to have been a
predatory foray by the Irish Transport into the Dublin tramway membership of the amalgamated union, and Sam Kyle was
outraged and seeking a confrontation. Apparently in January
1940 a joint application by the two unions to the Dublin
United Tramway Company for a wage increase was refused; and
both unions gave notice of termination of an agreement they
had with the company which had been in existence since 1937.
This freed them to take further industrial action, but despite the Amalgamated Transport's wishes, the Irish Transport refused to take the matter further, and in the absence
of a united approach, the Amalgamated Transport also held its
hand. The Irish Transport now, however, entered into separate
negotiations with the company, secured a wage increase, and
in October had it promulgated in the garages as applying to
its members only, 'as an inducement', complained a furious
Sam Kyle,[94] 'to members of the Amalgamated Transport and
General Workers' Union to join their Union.' The Amalgamated
Transport asked Congress, in accordance with its rules, to
establish a disputes committee, and the national executive

on a vote of eight to seven refused, partly on the grounds
that the Dublin Trades Council was examining it. This complication was cleared out of the way but when the application for a disputes committee was renewed, O'Brien as chairman of the national executive ruled it out of order. To
Kyle, probably quite correctly,[95] this was an arrangement,
a conspiracy in fact, on the part of a large employer and
the Irish Transport to undermine an amalgamated union. In
making such an arrangement with an employer, the Irish Transport, he believed, was guilty of a 'wanton and deliberate
betrayal of all Trade Union practice'[96] but to O'Brien and
to many of the leaders in the Irish Transport there was
clearly a larger and different loyalty which quite overwhelmed the industrial divide. Kyle decided to appeal the
matter to the annual congress in July and for that reason he
submitted a resolution which not only asked Congress to establish a disputes committee but which by adroit phrasing
managed to include, within the confines of the resolution,
the whole history of the dispute. O'Brien refused to allow
it to be placed on the Congress agenda. A moderate and concerned resolution from the Belfast Trades Council was also
excluded from the agenda. It was therefore a highly frustrated Sam Kyle who led his substantial delegation into the
annual conference of Congress in the Whitworth Hall Drogheda
on July 16 1941.

It was quite an appalling Congress. William O'Brien might
have succeeded in securing an uneasy majority on the national
executive, but he was only too conscious of the fact that
trade union opinion generally was against him. It appears
therefore that he decided to use his position as chairman of
the conference to frustrate any attempt to reverse him. Nevertheless in his presidential address at the opening of Congress
he made a considerable bid for legitimacy. 'At the opening',
he declared, 'of this Forty-Seventh Annual Meeting of the
Irish Trade Union Congress - perhaps the most critical and,
in its consequences, the most momentous for Congress itself
in nearly half a century of history - I may be permitted to

strike something of a personal note.'[97] And he went on to outline quite a remarkable trade union career. He had been a delegate to every congress for over thirty years; he had been a member of the national executive continuously for nineteen years, and he had presided four times over Congress, including the great special congress of 1918 which decided on the national strike against conscription. 'For weal or woe, Congress last year again conferred on me the honour of Presidency for a year which is likely to see the complete transformation of the whole movement in this country.'[98] In his address, as we have already noted, he condemned the wages standstill order, recognised the opposition to the trade union bill, but stressed again and again the need to reorganise the trade union movement. And since obviously some positive response to the members' unrest was necessary, he directed the Congress in particular to the support of the political arm of the movement, the Labour Party. This he hoped would be both acceptable and safe. The really dangerous counter to the trade union bill would have been a refusal by the trade unions to work it, in a word by a united determination to refuse to take out negotiating licences, and this in fact became the major issue in the months that followed. It was a move which O'Brien anticipated would come, and which he was determined to prevent developing.

Right from the beginning there was dispute. Sam Kyle moved the reference back[99] of the report of the standing orders committee[100] on the grounds that the resolution on his row with the Irish Transport was not on the agenda. The national executive had decided to exclude it, and the standing orders committee had taken the view - quite wrongly in Kyle's opinion - that they should place on the conference agenda only those matters referred to them by the national executive. O'Brien put the motion of reference back immediately to the conference without discussion, and the motion was carried by voice alone; not even a show of hands was necessary. It showed instantly and crisply the feeling of the conference. And thus the first conflict - the conflict between the two transport unions - was exposed.

It was followed immediately by the second internal trade
union conflict, that between Larkin's union and O'Brien,
far more bitter and uncompromising in character, but somewhat muted on this occasion. In the applications for affiliation, the report of the national executive recorded that
three cases were as yet under consideration. One of these
was the Workers Union of Ireland. Gilbert Lynch of the Amalgamated Transport (but speaking for the Dublin Trades Union
Council) moved, in view of the needs of the time, that Congress
direct the incoming national executive to grant the affiliations. O'Brien as president refused to accept the motion, on
the grounds that the national executive and not the annual
conference had the final responsibility regarding affiliations. The delegates were indignant at this filching of powers
from them; they felt they were being made to look ridiculous
and there was much wrangling about the interpretation of the
rules. But O'Brien was adamant. J.T. O'Farrell explained
carefully to the conference that if they wished they could
refer back the section; but this too O'Brien ruthlessly ruled
out of order, on the grounds that no decision was contained
in the section concerned, and therefore there was nothing
to refer back. Feeling began to run very high, and at the
end of the debate Larkin, as a delegate from the Dublin Trades
Union Council, came in, quite gently in all the circumstances
and largely on the question of interpretation. The conference
adjourned for the day with his contribution still unfinished.
When it resumed the following morning, O'Brien had armed
himself with chapter and verse to support his interpretation; but Larkin was reluctant to pursue the matter much further. He was conscious of the fact that he had the 'overwhelming opinion of the delegates on our side'[101] and did
not wish to waste further time on rules. Instead he wanted
to get down as quickly as possible to the serious matters
that confronted the trade unions. But in fact, almost immediately afterwards, the conference was sucked into a morass
of difficulty in the matter of the standing orders commitee
report.

Cathal O'Shannon the chairman of the standing orders committee presented once again their original report unchanged, on the grounds that since the resolutions concerned did not appear on the agenda, 'Standing Orders Committee had neither the authority nor the obligation under the Constitution to report on them to Congress.'[102] Kyle was not prepared to tolerate this, and promptly read in full - and in all its historical detail - the resolution which the committee had excluded, and since he was not permitted to move it, he moved once again the reference back of the standing orders committee report. There was a great deal of argument both in regard to procedure and in regard to the issue itself, the dispute between the two transport unions. The procedural question was particularly difficult; not only was there the problem of the standing orders committee not placing the motions on the agenda, but there was the prior problem of the national executive excluding them in the first instance. O'Brien remained silent on this issue for a long period, and eventually, when he was challenged, offered as an explanation that the parties to the dispute had failed to submit the case to a disputes committee and consequently by rule it could not be raised at annual conference. This was particularly infuriating to the Amalgamated Transport delegates since they had requested such a disputes committee and the national executive had refused it; and once again, on the question being put, the matter was referred back to the standing orders committee.

The conference now moved to the very centrepiece of disputation, the wages standstill order and the trade union bill. Although the wages standstill order arose later in time than the trade union bill, it was dealt with first by the annual report and consequently came up for discussion first as well. It is likely enough that O'Brien arranged it in that way. He was not really vulnerable on the wages standstill order, nor was there a great deal that anyone could do about it except increase the vehemence of one's protest. A lengthy discussion

on the wages standstill order could be expected therefore
to release a good deal of the pent up anger and frustration,
before the more difficult trade union bill came to be considered. Quite fortuitously, the reference back of the standing orders committee report helped him further, since the
conference had also referred back, inter alia, the traditional recommendation that resolutions be taken with the appropriate paragraphs in the report. O'Brien therefore was
free to take the annual report first, paragraph by paragraph,
postponing all the resolutions until after this was done,
and greatly simplifying his control of the procedure.

The debate on the wages standstill order therefore was lengthy
and angry but to no great purpose. There was much talk about
the absence of a lead from the national executive, that there
should have been a more vigorous form of campaign and Larkin
in particular made an impressive appeal for unity of purpose,
and such vigour in their protest that the government would
be obliged to go to the country: '....No matter what diverse
views we have let us stand together... that when the next demonstration comes it will be under the direction of the Trades
Council and the Congress Executive.'[103] There were complaints
that the national executive had not given support to the Dublin
campaign, which delegates, who supported O'Brien, could
counter by declaring, quite correctly, their wholehearted
opposition to the wages standstill order. The debate therefore dragged on, the delegates conscious that they were somehow missing the point, yet so deeply involved that they felt
obliged to come forward and contribute to the debate, and it
was not until he was prompted by J.T. O'Farrell that O'Brien
decided to bring the discussion to a close with the formal
adoption of the section. This brought the conference to the
section dealing with the trade union bill.

If O'Brien had hoped that this protracted debate had dulled
the edge of anger, he was mistaken. Again the discussion began
with a procedural problem. The Dublin Trades Union Council

had submitted an emergency motion which had raised the basic
policy issue: that delegates be asked 'to pledge themselves
that they would not register unions if the Bill was passed
or forced through the Dail';[104] but this the national
executive had also excluded from the agenda. Just before the
debate on the trade union bill opened, the standing orders
committee came before the conference to report on a non-
contentious matter, and the Dublin delegates clearly intended
to take advantage of the occasion to challenge the exclusion
of their emergency motion; but the President, William O'Brien,
briskly disposed of the report before they had the opportunity
to do so and left P.T. Daly and the Dublin delegates fumbling
and annoyed. There was now however no motion to give the debate
direction, and consequently the delegates resorted once
again to the device of referring back the section of the
report. They made it abundantly clear why they were doing
this; again and again there were accusations that no lead
had been given, that the national executive had failed to
do its duty, and as Archie Jackson of the Dublin council put
it: 'By the reference back we mean to imply that we want
a more determined stand taken on the matter.'[105] It was
Jackson too who said, rather ominously as he rose to speak,
that they realised that the movement was at the parting of
the ways. Yet there were other voices, apart from O'Brien's
supporters, who were somewhat anxious about the course of
events; Keyes of the NUR, who had also been prominent in the
Dail debate, clearly felt that the trade union response was
quite adequate; perhaps he feared where the Dublin council
proposal might lead them; and in the recriminatory mood of
a defeated man, J.T. O'Farrell of the other amalgamated
railway union, the Railway Clerks' Association, was bitter about
the failure of the Labour Party to resist adequately at the
committee state in Dail Eireann the conferring of advantages
exclusively on Irish-based unions. 'We shall forgive anyone
who has acted with good will but it is not always easy to
forget.'[106] Yet the decision of the Labour Party not to move
any amendments - which he bitterly complained of - had been
influenced, probably more than anything else, by the vociferous
campaign of the Dublin council. There followed a highly

coloured contribution by William Norton, in which he spoke
of 'filthy attacks by the Minister on British trade union
officials' and 'most obnoxious' provisions of the bill.
But this was a minor thread in a debate that focussed overwhelmingly on the inadequacies of the national executive's
response. The day's proceedings were drawing to a close,
and P.T. Daly pressed that the national executive agree
that a resolution be formulated by the morning, but O'Brien
was noncommittal. Predictably, when the debate resumed on
Friday morning, no motion had been permitted. Again O'Brien
appeared to be reluctant to put the question until he was
obliged to do so; but the delegates saw little point in further discussion and,when the motion to refer back was put it
was carried. The delegates had succeeded in conveying their
dissatisfaction, but in the absence of a motion, it was all
very negative.

This was now the third and final day of the conference and
so far only four of the thirty sections of the annual report
had been dealt with and none of the resolutions. O'Brien
now, once the central discussion had been disposed of, began
to deal with the rest of the report at a breakneck speed
bringing protests from the delegates 'because of the indecent
and callous way in which the rest of the business was being
treated.'[107] The benighted standing orders committee appeared again with a non-contentious report but this was also
referred back because they had as yet made no report on the
question which had already been referred back to them twice.
The unhappy conference pushed on; and when eventually all
the sections were dealt with and O'Brien put the motion that
the report as a whole be adopted, this too was rejected by
the delegates. There followed however a reasonable discussion on unemployment, and some further stability was restored
by the addresses, formal and predictable, of the fraternal
delegates from the Scottish TUC and from the Irish Labour
Party. But then matters began to disintegrate again, as
O'Brien pushed through the business; there were loud

complaints about his dictatorial attitude, that he was in danger
of reducing the trade union movement to a farce; and some
unions, in protest, refused to propose the motions which stood
on the agenda in their names. But O'Brien was quite unmoved,
even when the badly mauled standing orders committee returned
finally to report that it had resigned in despair. There
was some satisfaction however for the amalgamated unions in
the result of the election of vice-president; this post leads
virtually automatically to that of president the following
year and normally only one nomination is made, the unions
deciding on a consensus basis. On this occasion however,
there could be no consensus and consequently a straightforward
contest took place. Getgood of the Amalgamated Transport
withdrew in order to leave the issue a clear one between
Keyes of the NUR and Kennedy of the Irish Transport; Keyes
won comfortably by 101 votes to 84.[108] Not only that, but
Larkin himself very nearly made the executive; Drumgoole,
the last man to be elected, got 98 votes to Larkin's 95.

And yet, after all this, when O'Brien rose to make his
valedictory address he was quite unperturbed - even jocose.
'There is one thing', he said, 'on which there will probably
be agreement: it has been a Congress in which there was life.
The most appalling thing in any movement is apathy and
indifference.'[109] And if there was a 'very strong burden
of criticism of the old Executive, and speaking quite impartially,
I think there was a fair amount of material upon which that
view could be founded, the new Executive, whether you like it
or not is very, very like the old Executive. Even the
Standing Orders Committee which at one stage seemed to me to
be almost more unpopular than the Chairman has by a remarkable
state of affairs been re-elected...' He joked about their
relief at having a new chairman, and confessed an ambition
to be present and alive at his own funeral to hear what they
would say of him. He told them that he was about to publish
his reminiscences, but not all of them. 'I will write
them all, but some chapters will be kept back for a few years
until things settle down. A few chapters will be under
lock and key for fifty years, not to be released until
then.[110] I doubt if any of you will be alive to

read them; but your children and grandchildren will be reading about it. Some of these documents will be carefully
preserved - they will be best sellers - and I will leave the
copywright (sic) to a small collection of my friends in the labour
movement. The revenue from these books will be a steady
income for the Labour movement; and as the years pass by
all my fights, faults and unpopular rulings will be forgotten and my virtue will ascend and ascend. That will be
a very nice position if any of you live to see it....'[111]
It was little wonder that the incoming president Michael
Colgan, in closing the conference, said: 'I want to say that
it has been a strange Congress. Some of us felt that it was
the strangest Congress we have attended....'[112]

Notes on Chapter Five

1.   F.S.L. Lyons in Ireland in the War Years and After
      1939-51 ed. Kevin B. Nowlan and T. Desmond Williams
      1969 p.67.

2.   James F. Meenan op.cit. p.33

3.   James F. Meenan op.cit. p.36

4.   On the basis of a price level in July 1914 being equal
      to 100.

5.   David Kennedy: in Ireland in the War Years and After,
      1939-51, op. cit. p.60.

6.   Senate Debates Vol.24, March 14 1940 col.1004.

7.   ITUC 1940 p.99.

8.   ibid. p.95.

9.   ibid. p.93.

10.   ibid. p.96.

11.   ibid. p.138.

12.   ITUC 1940 p.98.

13.   Gilbert Lynch of the Amalgamated Transport: ibid. p.100-101.

14.   ibid. p.100.

15.   Senate Debates Vol.24, March 14 1940 col.1004.

16.   ibid. col.1013.

17.   ibid. col.1006.

18.   See tables supplied by the Department of Industry and
      Commerce to the Commission on Vocational Organisation:
      Vol. 18 doc. 165;   available in the National Library.

19.   ibid. In 1931 there were 310,199 days lost through
      disputes;   in 1932, 42,152;   in 1933, 200,126;
      in 1934, 180,080;   in 1935, 288,077;   in 1936,
      185,623;   in 1937, 1,754,949 (1,492,107 in building
      and construction);   in 1938, 208,784;   in 1939, 106,476,
      and in the first four months of 1940, 90,628.

20.   CIU 1945 p.54.

21.   Senate Debates Vol.24, April 24 1940.

22.   Department of Industry and Commerce op.cit. where
      we find that the total number of disputes begun in
      1939 was 99, while in 1938 it was 137 and in 1937 it
      was 145.

23.   Senate Debates, Vol.24, April 24 1940.

24.   Submissions to the Commission, Vol.16 Doc.92 p.4.

25.   ibid. Doc. 92A p.4.

26.   Ibid. p.3. For a British union's view of the lack
      of sophistication in Irish workers at the time, see
      Alan Fox: A History of the National Union of Boot and
      Shoe Operatives 1894-1957; 1958, pp.482-83. But
      this applied essentially to newly-recruited industrial
      workers. In the craft trades, for example, Irish
      influence was often considerable in the British
      unions; cf. Clement J. Bundock, The National Union
      of Printing, Bookbinding and Paper Workers, 1959,
      pp.19-21, 56-57, 461.

27.   ibid. p.3.

28.   ibid. p.1.

29.   ibid.

30.   ibid.

31.   ibid p.2.

32.   ibid.

33.   ibid. pp.2-3.

34.   ibid. p.5.

35.   ibid. Doc. 92 p.5.

36.   ibid. Doc. 92A p.5.

37.   ibid. Doc 92A Extract from Memorandum ... p.1.

38.   After a distinguished political career Mr Childers
      became President of Ireland.

39.   Submissions, Doc. 92B.

40.   ITUC 1939 p.66.

41.   ibid. p.38.

42.   ibid. p.79.

43.   ibid. p.68.

44.   Submission to the Commission on Vocational Organisation
       op.cit. Vol.18 Doc. 136.

45.   ibid.

46.   p.95 above.

47.   ITUC 1939 p.30.

48.   ITUC 1940 p.31.

49.   ITUC 1939 p.74.

50.   ibid. p.81.

51.   ibid p.171.

52.   ibid. 1940 p.30.

53.   ibid. p.43.

54.   ibid. 1941 p.36.

55.   ibid. p.37.

56.   ITUC 1940 p.134.

57.   The Catholic Church - in Ireland as in France - is a
       societal church and is unhappy about individualism
       whether that individualism is sustained by religious
       feeling or not. It is therefore uneasy with political
       democracy, and the attempt to espouse fascism in the
       thirties might be seen as an effort to give a
       societal construct to a society which was seen as
       failing because of an excess of individualist notions
       (and this is what I have suggested here.) 'Individualism
       is of democratic origin,' says de Tocqueville in
       Democracy in America, 'and it threatens to spread in
       same ration as the equality of conditions ... Among
       aristocratic nations, as families remain for centuries
       in the same condition, often on the same spot, all
       generations become as it were contemporaneous. A man
       almost always knows his forefathers and respects them;
       he thinks he already sees his remote descendants and
       he loves them ... Amongst democratic nations new
       families are constantly springing up, others are con-
       stantly falling away, and all that remain change their
       condition; the woof of time is every instant broken,
       and the track of generations effaced. Those who went
       before are soon forgotten; of those who will come
       after no one has any idea; the interest of man is con-
       fined to those in close propinquity to himself. As
       each class approximates to other classes, and inter-
       mingles with them its members become indifferent and as
       strangers to one another. Aristocracy had made a chain
       of all the members of the community, from the peasant

to the king; democracy breaks that chain and severs
every link of it ... They owe nothing to any man,
they expect nothing from any man; they acquire the
habit of always considering themselves as standing
alone, and they are apt to imagine that their whole
destiny is in their own hands. Thus not only does
democracy make every man forget his ancestors, but it
hides his descendants and separates his contemporaries from
him; it throws him back for ever on himself alone, and
threatens in the end to confine him within the solitude
of his own heart. [Louis Dumont: Homo Hierarchicus
1972 pp. 52-53.]
See also Geoffrey Barraclough, An Introduction to
Contemporary History , Pelican 1974 edition, where
in discussing the characteristics of the world since
1880, Professor Barraclough speaks of the 'jettisoning
of the inherited baggage of European culture' (p.244)
and goes on: 'It was this sense of alienation, of
disinheritance, of the individual's incommunicable
solitude, that was the framework of art and writing
in the years before and after the First World War.'

In a word, man became atomised in a rapidly changing
present, his past irrelevant and his future uncertain, and one can see in socialism, in nationalism,
in the various fascist and neo-fascist solutions,
despite their radically conflicting character, a
common rejection of individualism and the atomising
of man.

58. cf. Louis Dumont: Homo Hierarchicus and in particular
the Introduction of Mary Douglas to Paladin Edition:
London 1972 p.21.

59. ITUC 1940 p.28.

60. ITUC 1940 p.92.

61. ibid. p.32.

62. ibid. p.119.

63. These faithfully set out each year the membership of
each union on which the sum payable in affiliation
fees was based. These figures may not always correspond
to actual membership. See later.

64. William O'Brien papers, Ms. 13974.

65. Vol.12. Doc.17A.

66. The 1941 ITUC report states that at the annual congress
259,012 members were represented, but it appears
that this figure included members of trades councils,
many of whom would already have been taken into account.
Judge (op.cit. M.Econ.Sc. thesis) calculates the 1940
figure at 162,384; and if one takes the total of members

for whom affiliation fees were paid at the 1941 Congress the number is 171,228.

67. The figure for 1970, 602,700, and the other figures in appendix five, are not merely the figures on which affiliation fees were based, but accurate accounts in so far as it was possible.

68. William O'Brien papers Ms.13974.

69. See appendix five.

70. ICTU 1970.

71. See appendix five.

72. ITUC 1941 p.136.

73. Lynch, clearly, was out of sympathy with the independent activities of O'Brien's Council of Irish Unions and referred in his annual report (p.30) - implicitly with disapproval - to the separate consultations between the Department of Industry and Commerce and 'Trade Unions outside the National Executive.'

74. ITUC 1941. p.30.

75. Judge Ph.D. thesis op.cit. p.56.

76. O'Brien papers Ms. 13974.

77. Information supplied by Fintan Kennedy, now President of the IT & GWU, whose father was Tom Kennedy.

78. See ICTU 1941 p.121 where Larkin is reported as follows during the debates: 'He spoke of a deputation to An Taoiseach and the Minister for Industry and Commerce when Mr MacEntee stated that this Bill did not come of his own initiative, and also that he was doing this with the knowledge of unions and union officials. I said to him: "If you are as truthful as you are alleged to be tell us the name of the union or the union official." Mr de Valera turned round and said: "I think you are entitled to an answer" and then he admitted that he could not give the names of the unions or officials.'

79. No.22 of 1941.

80. p.132 above.

81. O'Brien papers: Ms 13974. O'Brien received a letter from the Minister's office dated 21 June 1941 as follows: 'I beg to enclose copies of two amendments which the Minister is moving on the Committee stage of the above Bill. I think you will agree that these amendments will represent considerable easements to

Irish Unions.' The second amendment modified the schedule of deposits somewhat.

82. see p.133 above.

83. The act provided for a chairman and four ordinary members, two to sit with him on matters dealing with trade unions of masters and two with trade unions of workmen; in practice only the latter was significant.

84. See above pp. 145, 146

85. Emergency Powers (no.83) Order 1941 issued under the Emergency Powers Act 1939.

86. ITUC 1941 p.77.

87. ibid. p.76.

88. ibid. p.77.

89. See John Swift: History of the Dublin Bakers Dublin 1948 p.342. Swift was vice-president of the Dublin Council of Trade Unions at the time.

90. ITUC report of the Special Conference on the Trade Union Act, 1941, October 23 1941, p.20.
When the Bill came to the Senate however, the Parliamentary Labour Party was overruled in the matter by the National Executive. (ibid. p.39). We shall later see that the effect of adopting the resolution put to the October conference was that the labour movement excluded itself from proposing amendments to the act.

91. ibid. p.19.

92. William O'Brien papers Ms. 13974.

93. see p. 163 above.

94. ITUC 1941 p.99.

95. See William O'Brien papers Ms. 13974. Some rough notes had been prepared by O'Brien on the dispute, perhaps for some meeting or other. In them he relied a good deal on the fact that he did not wish to break their agreement with the Company. It also appears that the Company was pressing very strongly for an arrangement by which one union only would represent the men. On the other hand the general manager of the Company at the time A.P. Reynolds (O'Brien refers

to A.P.R.) was referred to by O'Brien as a
'Fianna Boy' (that is a one time member of the
republican youth movement) and this may well
explain a good deal.

96.   ITUC 1941 p.99.

97.   ibid. p.72.

98..   ibid. p.72.

99.   A motion to refer back a recommendation is in fact
        a proposal that that recommendation be rejected. In
        the case of a report, a reference back is usually
        intended to convey disapproval of what was done.

100.   A standing orders committee is appointed for the purpose
        of making recommendations which facilitate the business
        of Congress. They usually bring in a considered
        report at the beginning of conference, setting out a
        large number of procedural matters, and also make
        recommendations of a procedural kind during the
        conference as the business demands. The practice
        of Congress is to elect a standing orders committee
        at the annual conference prior to that in which they
        hold office, in order to permit them to consider
        their major initial recommendations at some length.

101.   ITUC 1941 p.95.

102.   ibid. p.97.

103.   1941 p.112.

104.   ibid. p.117.

105.   ibid. p.119.

106.   ibid. p.121.

107.   ibid. p.127.

108.   ibid. 163.

109.   ibid. 164.

110.   O'Brien apparently never kept his promise. He dictated
        his reminiscences to Edward MacLysaght under the
        title Forth the Banners Go (Dublin, The Three Candles
        1969) which contains nothing of any great significance,
        and the small number of autobiographical chapters in
        his papers in the National Library (vide Ms. 15704 (1))
        have little merit.

111.   ITUC 1941 pp.165-66.

112.   ibid. p.166.

Chapter Six

Schism

-i-

There was another reason for the strangeness of the 1941
Congress - apart from the rather ludicrous manner in which
it was conducted. In the minds of many there had now
grown a feeling of artificiality about the idea of an
all-Ireland Congress, and although the amalgamated unions
could field in 1941 84 of the 206 delegates[1] and although
O'Brien with 35,000 members appeared to represent only one
fifth of the total membership within Congress, the fact
remained that in the 26 counties Irish-based union membership outnumbered amalgamated union membership four to one,[2]
and this was the context in which O'Brien and his colleagues
saw the situation, and in which all these events had
significance. It was this feeling of artificiality which
contributed to the collapse of trade union unity which came
four years later, in 1945. Let us then, in considering
the years between, explore three themes, the first being
the trade union act and the gradual dying away of protest,
the second being the dominating effect of the wages standstill orders, and the third, the immensely disruptive
effect of the Larkin-O'Brien dispute.

-ii-

We have seen how intense the feeling was when the trade
union bill was introduced, but to O'Brien it was a protest
that was not securely grounded. He saw it as generated by

Larkin and the Dublin council, whose influence in any event
did not extend very much beyond the city.   It was significant
for example that Cork had remained quite calm;   P.J. O'Brien
of the Cork no.2 branch of the Irish Transport wrote to
William O'Brien on October 21 1941,[3] a few days before the
special conference, about the position in Cork generally:
'There is not much activity', he wrote, 're Trade Union act
here, although some branch meetings of Societies have been
held, but not resulting in any information ... Most unions
seem to be adopting a policy of wait and see. I would incline
to the view that while there would be a latent opposition,
that in the last analysis, they would not be a party to
refusing to take out a negotiating licence .....' O'Brien
clearly shared this view, and no doubt considered that the
best approach was to allow the protest to burn itself out,
which, in the event, it did, with surprising rapidity.

But the Labour Party saw things quite differently. Norton,
as we have seen, had been greatly impressed by the Council
of Action and particularly by the rally in College Green,[4]
and refused the request of the national executive of Congress
to put forward amendments to the bill in Dail Eireann
(although they later did so in the Senate) on the grounds that
it might imply some degree of consent to the principles in
the bill;[5] more than that, a joint meeting of the national
executive and the administrative council of the Labour Party
decided by majority 'to request the National Executive
to ask the unions not to take out licences under the Bill.'[6]
This was a call for leadership in a direct confrontation with
the government - which was precisely what O'Brien wished
to avoid. The national executive, not surprisingly therefore,
responded by deciding to call a conference 'at which the
unions would be asked to state their views towards the Bill,
particularly in relation to the question of taking out a
licence or not.'[7] This was the special conference that
was held on October 21 1941.

Let us consider first the implications of not taking out
a licence. Some unions seemed a little confused, despite
the clear explanation of Cathal O'Shannon, now secretary of
the Congress, and during the course of the debate quite
a number spoke of being opposed to registration which as we
have seen[8] is quite a separate matter and did not arise
here at all. However the issue was clearly the refusal to
take out a licence. With certain exceptions, a union that
attempted to negotiate without a licence committed an offence;
nor had it the protection of the trade union acts. Sam Kyle
seemed to be of the view that the business of wage determination could still be carried on[9] but this was most unlikely.
A union that refused to take out a licence - unless there was
absolute unanimity - in fact emasculated itself, and consequently with few exceptions, all the unions, Irish and
amalgamated alike, warily looked over their shoulder to see
what other unions in the same field proposed to do. Even
Sam Kyle, despite his forthright opposition, reserved the
right to reconsider the decision 'in the light of
eventualities that may occur.'[10] The only hope was vigorous
and united leadership from the top, and this the national
executive were not prepared to give; the conference had not
been called to decide policy; it had not been called to
hear the views of the national executive. The purpose was
to hear the views of the unions, which in the circumstances
of the case could be expected to be cautious and self-protective.

This became very clear right from the outset when Crawford -
who although a member of an Irish-based union was violently
opposed to the act in any form - was ruled out of order
when he proposed that no trade union should apply for a
negotiating licence.[11] The conference was a consultative
conference merely, although the point was established not
without some confusion. Two important points followed.
In the first place, the number of delegates was not in
proportion to the strength of the unions; the Irish Transport
sent only 11 delegates, and the Amalgamated Transport only 6.

(This incidentally is also the precise number they sent to
the second conference in the following March, which indicates
perhaps some arrangement between them.) The Women Workers
on the other hand sent eight delegates. Secondly, since it
was a trade union conference, no delegates from trades councils
were permitted to attend; Larkin therefore was excluded,
and so also was the fiery vehemence of the Council of Action,
although Crawford did his best. Nonetheless the October
conference had caused quite a lot of anxiety in the English
offices; no less than 23 delegates attended from outside
Ireland, 20 from England, 2 from Scotland and one from Wales,
and if one adds the 8 delegates from Northern Ireland
(the usual number was 4 or 5) the number from outside
Eire was 31 from a total of 143. However, interest in
Britain quickly waned; the special conference in March
1942 saw only 4 cross-Channel delegates. Indeed the normal
attendance from Britain at Irish conferences was very low;
at the annual conferences both in 1941 and in 1942 - which
spanned this difficult time - the delegates with cross-
Channel addresses represented little more than 2 per cent
and the Northern Ireland delegates marginally less.[12]
The agonising debates of the time, therefore, were in their
essentials Eire debates concerned with the deeply conflicting views
of Irish trade unionism held by the men and women of the south.

There were a number of other matters which strengthened
O'Brien's hand for the conference. Sean Lemass had resumed
the ministry of Industry and Commerce and had immediately
offered a much more conciliatory approach, indicating that
he was open to suggestions on how the act might be amended -
even though it had only just been enacted. The Council of
Irish Unions had met him early in October (without proper
authority, Crawford angrily claimed)[13] and arising from it,
three amendments were suggested;[14] the first, under section
6, reducing considerably the minister's discretion in
exempting organisations from the need to have a licence;
the second, also under section 6, clarifying mediation, and

the third, the most radical, covering appeal against exclusion from trade union membership;   this last referred
to section 35 which, in the case of a union with sole rights
of organisation, provided that an excluded worker could
appeal to the district court, and it was suggested instead
that each union, subject to the tribunal's approval, should
make its own arrangements for appeal. Lemass readily agreed
to all three - indeed they in no way affected the substance
of the act - and he quickly introduced a new act the following
year giving them effect.[15]   Sam Kyle made considerable
play at the October conference of the visit of the Council
of Irish Unions to Lemass[16] but it seems that some amalgamated unions visited him as well before the conference
began.[17]   One way or the other, all this conveyed very much
an impression that the question was largely settled before
the conference began.

Secondly it strengthened O'Brien's hand that there should
be such widespread concern about a confrontation with
the government over a measure which was now enacted. There
were some of course who made the point that there was
nothing improper in making the whole thing unworkable;
but these were difficult and dangerous times, and there was
a good deal to be said for the view that whether one disagreed with the act or not, it was now the law of the land,
and while one might seek its amendment one had nonetheless
to obey it while it stood. The representatives of the
English offices were chary about a confrontation as well;
after all they operated in Britain where the legislative
restrictions in war time were very much greater, and apart
from that, they were senior officials, very conscious of
the implications of fostering an approach in another country
which might be regarded as subversive. We must remember
as well that, quite apart from the exigencies of war,
this was a time when much of the democratic protest which is
commonplace today would have been regarded with considerable
alarm. In any event, all these trends emerged very clearly
in the conference debate.

Thirdly O'Brien's temperate and temporising approach was
strengthened by the fact that although the measure was
law it would not take effect at least until the following
March, that is to say for a period of five months. Fourthly
he was fortunate in that the president of Congress, and
therefore the chairman of the meeting, was Michael Colgan
of the Bookbinders, who was a strong supporter of the
Council of Irish Unions. Finally it must be remembered
that although we have made William O'Brien the centrepiece
of this discussion, he was in fact a spokesman for quite
widespread and deeply held opinion, and it is interesting
to remark that he himself took no part in the conference
debate.

Inevitably, the national executive suffered a good deal of
barracking for not offering leadership, but the chairman
insisted that the unions should declare themselves first -
that this after all was the purpose of the conference, and
eventually a roll call of unions was begun, which, once it
got under way, effectively took the steam out of the conference.
Eight unions, the core of the Council of Irish Unions, voted
for taking out a negotiating licence; and while some unions
opposed the whole thing root and branch, the majority
either temporised or, if they voted against seeking a licence,
did so on the clear understanding that if events required it,
they would mend their hand. The chairman therefore could say
with a good deal of truth: 'The discussion today has resulted
in a big number of Unions sitting on the fence, if I may say so.
They have not disclosed what the attitude of their unions is
and what it is likely to be. Others have stood up and said
openly that they are opposed to seeking a licence, while other
unions have got up and said that their unions have already
decided to seek licences. We have been criticised on not
giving a lead. What position would this Conference be in
if we had given a lead ....?'[18] In these circumstances he
would not entertain any proposal such as Crawford had
originally suggested:[19] 'I will not take a motion that will
bind people to a different course of action from that decided
on by their members.'[20]

This seemed to leave the trade union movement in considerable disarray, and Norton, anxious to secure some
common platform, proposed 'that this Congress instructs
the National Executive immediately to inaugurate a
national campaign to compel the Government to withdraw
the Trade Union Act 1941.' His argument was that while
some unions had decided to take out licences, in fact no
union had sought the bill, and in the five or six months
available before its implementation they should agitate
for its repeal 'which they were entitled, even constitut-
ionally',[21] to do. The debate that followed was
somewhat recriminatory, but the conference as a whole
supported the idea, Tom Kennedy on behalf of the Irish
Transport confessing that he saw little purpose in such
an agitation, but if they wanted it, the Irish Transport
would be with them. The motion was adopted by a show of
hands, and the chairman stated that he understood that,
in order to avoid a charge of insincerity, its adoption
'cut out any attempt in the meantime to amend the act.'
But when Swift went further and suggested that unions
should pledge themselves 'not to register pending a
further Congress early in the New Year'[22] the chairman
would have none of it. Despite the decision to agitate,
unions were free to take out licences under the act
if they wished.

The national campaign, however, was something of a disaster.
This was clear from the report to the second special
conference which was held in the Mansion House in
Dublin on March 26 1942. With a somewhat exquisite -
if unconscious irony - the government had fixed
May 1 as the date for the operation of section 6 of the act,
that is to say the section dealing with the necessity to

hold negotiating licences,[23] and since the national
campaign was also coming to a close, the national
executive had decided to call this second special
conference for the purpose of hearing a report. The
campaign had been carried out by a joint council of the
Congress and the Labour Party[24] who originally intended
to hold public meetings in seventeen centres during the
period from November 1941 to March 1942. In the event
only ten such meetings were held; 'in five centres ...
the local people found it impossible to arrange meetings
and in two others ... transport difficulties led to
abandonment of arrangements.'[25] Miss McDowell of the
Women Workers was inclined to the view that the programme
was badly designed, that a great number of the counties
had been left unvisited,[26] but the general view was that
the Joint Council had done all they could[27] - that in fact
the people were not interested and could not be roused.
'We found throughout the country', said Michael Colgan
the chairman, 'a certain amount of apathy. I feel I
would be correct in saying that, with the exception of the
City of Dublin, we found no evidence that there was much
enthusiasm among the rank and file of the working class
for having the Act withdrawn or its operation postponed.'[28]
'The campaign is buried,' said John Swift; 'this is the
funeral service.'[29] He, for one, was clearly of the view
that things would have been different if certain unions had
in fact not withheld their support. Perhaps this was so, but
the fact was that while O'Brien and other Irish-based
trade union leaders formally opposed the act, they in
practice supported it; in addition Kyle - and the
amalgamated unions generally - had no stomach for political
confrontation in war time. 'Our campaign', he said, 'has
not succeeded in getting the withdrawal of the Act, and

therefore we can do nothing further, in my opinion, than
to work for its repeal in a constitutional way.'[30]
Apart from all that, Lemass, who had no mean skill in
these matters, was doing a good deal to stiffen the reality
of the act. In the first place he announced a few weeks
before the conference began that he intended to amend the
wages standstill order and allow at least some increases,
but - and this was the key point - 'applications for
wage increases under the proposed order (could) not be
made by a Trade Union that has not taken out a licence
under the Trade Union Act 1941.' This is of the greatest
significance and we shall take it up later as our second
theme. On the other hand Lemass made it clear publicly
on numerous occasions 'that he was willing to meet representatives of the Unions on changes in the Act.'[31]
The national executive were unable to do anything about
this because of the decision of the October conference,
but when Ferguson, the secretary of the Department of
Industry and Commerce,wrote to them asking for their
views on the regulations which should govern the inspection
of registers of members, the national executive decided
at least to circulate the request and gather the opinions of
the unions. The Congress made some attempt to cast itself
in a more positive role by seeking a meeting with the
Taoiseach on the general undesirability of the legislation
but he refused to see them, much to their annoyance.

What then could this rather lame special conference do?
It unanimously adopted a resolution urging support for the
Labour Party in its efforts to secure repeal of the act
and it protested 'most emphatically'[32] against the Taoiseach's
refusal to meet the national executive; but on an
informal basis it was clear that the act had been accepted -
from which there were two consequences, trade unions were
free to apply for licences under the act, and the national

executive was free to suggest amendments. On this latter
point, it is true that at the March conference the chairman
refused to make a ruling[33] but at the 1942 annual conference
when Barry of Cork proposed that the national executive
take up with Lemass the amendments he had discussed with
the Council of Irish Unions, the motion was adopted without
debate.[34] Lemass responded by sending the national executive
a white paper setting out the proposed amending legislation,
discussed the provisions with them, and as we have seen[35]
rapidly enacted them as the Trade Union Act 1942. On the
former point, the applying by unions for negotiating licences,
the annual report stated in 1942[36] that 'numbers of Trade
Unions and other associations have taken out licences under
the Act'; eventually all did; the act had come to stay.[37]

But of course the real problem lay not in the business of
negotiating licences but in the idea of a tribunal which
would restructure the trade union movement in a manner
close to O'Brien's original plan and in a manner as well
highly prejudicial in the amalgamated unions. But that part
of the act (part III) was not yet in operation[38] and was not
to be implemented in fact until April 1943. Perhaps this
accounts - at least in part - for the rather low key acceptance
of the positions at the March conference in 1941. Perhaps
more significantly, there also appears to have been some
view that part III would not be availed of by trade unions.
Louie Bennett of the Women Workers may have been putting
explicitly what was behind many of the calls at the conference
for trade union unity, when she said: 'We are all aware
that there are many difficulties in our movement that ought
to be cleared up. We know that under this Act a Tribunal
will be appointed to tidy up our movement. We have an
opportunity in the next few months, if the proper steps
are taken, to do a good deal of tightening up ourselves.
There is an opportunity for the National Executive to give an
effective lead: by seeking unity and then finding what is

the best way to counteract the evils contained in the Act
and to prevent that Tribunal from ever having anything to
do with our movement. There is no need for us to go to
that Tribunal. We can settle these matters ourselves
without ever approaching the Tribunal. Let us, at least,
avoid the shame that any Trade Union will approach that
Tribunal to ask for any consideration.'[39] 'It is no use',
said John Swift, 'recriminating against those who thought it
wise not to give their support ... the dangers ahead are even
greater. The only just reason, in my opinion, for accepting
the Act would be that our movement would be better and have
greater unity by accepting it.'[40] Of course Swift had very
much in mind the wages standstill, the ESB Pensions Bill
and the prospect of further legislation, but it was also
abundantly clear that the only way in which the rigours of
the Tribunal could be avoided was by a united trade union
initiative to put things to rights themselves. There was a
third reason for the low key response. Nineteen forty·two saw the
beginning of a brief but significant honeymoon between the
Amalgamated Transport and the Irish Transport, a state
of affairs which affected not only the Congress attitude to
the Trade Union Act, but which contributed as well to the
isolation and exclusion of Larkin. The national executive
had appointed 'a Sub-Committee on Inter-Union Relations'[41]
to try to resolve the on-going row between the two general
unions. They were surprisingly successful, and included in
the eight-point agreement was a provision for joint machinery
to resolve problems of implementation and interpretation.
'Pride of place,' said the president, Michael Colgan,[42] in
his address to the July annual conference in 1942,'in the
achievements of the National Executive during the past
twelve months must be given to the Working Agreement concluded between the two Transport Unions - the Amalgamated
Transport Union and the Irish Transport and General Workers
Union. Congress is well aware that over a number of years

the differences between these two great Unions had an injurious effect on the whole Trade Union Movement in
Ireland. But with a cooperation that should be an inspiration
to everyone of us here, the respective Secretaries of the
two unions, Messrs. Sam Kyle and William O'Brien, made it
possible for a hard-working sub-committee of the National
Executive to have an agreement reached that will, I am sure,
have far-reaching effects. It will result in a better
understanding between the Unions and, with the machinery
provided for under the agreement, the causes that created
differences and ofttimes bitterness between the members of
the two Unions in the past will be removed. And the terms
of this Agreement are such that it could be signed by any
two or more Unions.'

It was this that gave hope that the Tribunal would in the
event be unnecessary. Indeed from Kyle's point of view,
this hope may well have been at least one of the reasons
for his coming to terms with O'Brien. In any event,
heartened by it all, Congress made a considerable effort
not merely to promote harmony among unions but to tackle
itself once again the old problem of reorganisation which,
as they said, the Trade Union Act had brought out in a new
light and in a new form.[43] They tried to foster amalgamation,
again with no success; and the following year, 1943, a
resolution of remarkable woolliness but big intent was proposed by Sean Campbell on behalf of the national executive
which concluded: '... this Congress urges upon all Unions
the urgent need of taking steps for the early unification
upon satisfactory lines of organisations for whose separate
existence and independent operation there is no industrial
justification, and authorises the National Executive to
take such steps as it may consider necessary to implement
this resolution.'[44] The motion was adopted readily enough
without much debate, Gerry Doyle of the Plasterers remarking[45]
'They all knew that a Tribunal had been set up under the
Trade Union Act, but no matter what differences and quarrels

there had been between Unions, he did not see any of them
tumbling over themselves to avail of that Tribunal.   He
believed that a lot of good work could be done by a
Committee set up by the National Executive without
utilising the Trade Union Act for the purpose.'

But whatever intentions they might have had not to avail
of the tribunal, the unions - and indeed the national
executive of Congress - had already taken steps to protect
themselves in the new situation: to make sure that they
would not be left out in the cold. The previous March,
the government, when announcing that part III of the act
would be brought into operation on April 5, had invited
each union licensed under the act to nominate a person to
the panel from which in turn the minister would select the
two workmen representatives.[46]   'From information supplied
by our affiliated Unions,' said Congress later[47],
'virtually all our Unions that are holders of licences have
made nominations to the Panel.' Indeed the national executive
itself nominated one of its own members, P.J. Cairns, who in
the event was appointed workmen member, the other being Owen
Hynes.[48] Nor was the national executive reluctant to offer
the Minister their views on who the chairman of the tribunal
might be[49]; and the following year 1944 we find them
drawing up, for the use of affiliated unions, a model appeal
machinery for the purposes of section 5 of the amending act
of 1942. But at the same time the national executive continued to make the point that as far as trade unions of
workers were concerned 'Congress is the central authority
in Trade Unionism'.[50] It is difficult to say how seriously
they viewed such a statement in the circumstances. Certainly
towards the end of 1943,[51] when they had some experience
of a number of tribunal applications[52] they circularised
the unions asking that they notify them of their intention to
make application and await their observations, and a sub-
committee of the national executive was appointed to examine

and report; but there is no indication here of any
intention of exercising Congress authority to deflect an
application or modify it.

It is against such a background then that we must evaluate
the national executive resolution in 1943 to reorganise
the trade union movement from within. The woolliness which
we noted in the terms of the resolution increased rather
than diminished. Indeed it is difficult to believe that
anything very serious was intended. Campbell in his speech
proposing the motion seemed to have been seeking some
sensible amalgamations to overcome waste of resources
without 'harking-back to the old discussion of the
respective merits of industrial unionism, and craft unionism
and general unionism' and without the 'reopening of the issue
debated in Special Conference of the regrouping of our
affiliated Unions.'[53] But this, in all the circumstances,
was a singularly naive view. Nor was what followed from it
in any way impressive. A subcommittee was established (in
fact of senior national executive members) which declared
as a principle, for example, that merger and not simply
absorption was the desirable course and then had 'frank,
full and helpful' discussions with unions in four industries.[54]
It was all somehow irrelevant; the reality clearly lay
elsewhere, and the unions knew it.

Applications to the tribunal therefore began to grow quietly
in significance. It was reported to the annual congress
in 1944 that a number had been made, but all had been refused.[55]
Three applications followed, from building workers, from
bookbinders, and thirdly, the application which led eventually
to the Supreme Court and to the total reversal of the trend of
the time, the application of the Irish Transport and General
Workers Union in respect of the road passenger and tramway
services of Coras Iompair Eireann.[56] The application had
been made on April 14 1945, and on April 27 the National
Union of Railwaymen 'issued a plenary summons claiming a

declaration that Part III of the Act of 1941 was invalid
as being repugnant to the Constitution.'[57] It is important to remember that when the case came before the
High Court in July 1945 Judge Gavan Duffy held against
the NUR and for the Tribunal. Consequently, when we
come to consider the destruction of the unity of Congress
over the years 1944 and 1945,[58] we must bear in mind that
as far as O'Brien, the Irish Transport and the other Irish
unions were concerned, the tribunal existed and was coming
into play.

This then was our first theme, the Trade Union Act and the
gradual dying away of protest in its regard. Let us now
consider our second theme, the dominating effect of the
wages standstill orders.

-iii-

We have seen that William O'Brien initially feared that the
wages standstill order had put in peril the trade union
bill. We have seen that the two became linked together
in the protests that followed, and whatever might be said
about the desirability of having some order in trade union
organisation, one could expect nothing but vigorous opposition
to a stop in wages. Yet, in fact the wages orders came to
strengthen rather than weaken the acceptability of the Trade
Union Acts, particularly in the matter of negotiating licences.
This came about because, in the nature of things, one cannot
maintain an absolute standstill on wages, and in this case
a new order made on April 9 1942[59] had the effect of con-
verting a standstill into a system of carefully supervised
wage increases, in the administration of which the trade
unions were inevitably involved. It was a logical enough

step for the government to insist - and for the trade
unions to agree - that only those unions which had taken
out negotiating licences could participate in the system.

But the situation was always one of stress. Even though
certain increases were given under these orders from April
1942 onwards, the general effect was very punishing. The
cost of living was increasing rapidly. The index had stood
at 173 in August 1939;[60] by May of the following year it
had become 204, continuing to rise very rapidly to 275 in
mid-May 1943. The pace thereafter slackened slightly,
but nevertheless in February 1944 it had reached 296 or
nearly 70 per cent above the prewar figures, before it began
to drop back a little. But of course the impact on certain
consumer items was far greater than on others. Keane of
the Post Office Workers' Union, commenting on the leap in the
index of 102 points (from 173, August 1939 to 275 in May 1943),
pointed out that 'the increase in relation to foodstuffs
dealt with in the compilation of the figure was from 158 to
237 points; clothing from 225 to 421 points; fuel and light
from 180 to 335 points.'[61] The contrast with wages was
very marked, inevitably so. 'In industry generally,'
said Keane in July 1943, 'the great majority of workers had
got an increase of 8/- a week.'[62] And by 1944 the trade
unions calculated[63] that average wages including bonus
'cannot have risen by more than 12 per cent.' The conferences
of the time were full of protest about the inadequacy of the
price control system; in addition to that there was the
problem of the blackmarket, as first sugar, tea and fuel
were rationed; and later bread, clothing and other items.
The government toughened up both on controls and penalties
but at the Congress of 1944 we find the part of the annual report
of the national executive dealing with such matters was
referred back on the grounds that it did not attack the
government's performance with sufficient vigour.

Trade union officials in the south were sourly conscious

as well that in Northern Ireland wages were higher and the
cost of living less oppressive.[64] But one can push the
feeling of stress too far. Everybody was well aware of the
great difficulty of the time, and on the whole they recognised
that the government was handling the supplies crisis with
a good deal of skill. Unemployment was biting hard as
raw materials dried up; many entered the army and vast
numbers emigrated, particularly from areas outside Dublin[65]
and it was obvious enough that excessive price control could
result in further disemployment.[66] It is against this
background then that we must view the wage orders and the
wage tribunals of the period; people were prepared to put
up with a great deal in order to survive in a world everywhere devastated by war.

Lemass had reason to believe therefore that the situation
was manageable, and immediately he resumed office as
Minister for Industry and Commerce, he began to take steps
to soften the rigours of the first wages standstill
order[67] which had been promulgated on May 7 1941, only a
short time before. His public offer of consultation resulted
in a meeting in November 1941 between him and the national
executive of Congress.[68] From this he managed to convey
publicly the impression that the trade union movement was a
partner in the new arrangements under the order, 166, which
was promulgated on April 9 1942,[69] causing the national
executive much embarrassment: 'It may be well to affirm
here, contrary to the impression given in later public
statements, including the Minister's, that on this the
Government's attitude and action did not meet with the
approval of the National Executive, and that the Government's
sequel to this Order was not based upon the representations
made by the National Executive.'[70] Furthermore the trade
unions, at first sight, found the new order immensely complex
and constricting. 'The machinery is of a particularly
cumbersome nature,' said Michael Colgan, the chairman of the

1942 annual conference,[71] 'and would appear to have been
framed for the purpose of making it difficult for
applicants for increases' and McMullen moved on behalf
of the national executive that the whole of the machinery
of the tribunals under the order should be scrapped.[72]
But although this motion was adopted as a matter of course,
there were clearly many who saw a good deal of sense in
the arrangements, particularly after a further meeting with
Lemass on June 29 1942. There was a substantial note of
acquiescence in the manner in which Cathal O'Shannon reported
to the 1942 annual conference: '...the Minister ... realised ...
that our whole objection was to the general basic principles
of Orders 83 and 166, but he said quite frankly, in
justice to him, in justice to you, and in justice to us,
that the Government has made up its mind that it was not
going to alter the basic principles of the Order, but that
he would do his best to make the machinery workable and
speedy.'[73] The fact was of course that the unions had
decided to work the system, and at the same Congress
Crawford caustically remarked on the 'unseemly scramble
among Unions, some of them affiliated, for seats on the
Tribunals.'[74] Furthermore Lemass, as he was often to do in
the future, managed to combine a warm, cooperative approach
to the trade union movement with a steely approach to the
Labour Party on the general grounds that his party, Fianna
Fail, was more representative politically of the bulk of
trade union members than was the Labour Party, which on a
headcount[75] was manifestly true. He was reported[76] as
saying that the most significant thing that had happened
in the emergency 'was the failure of the Labour Party to
rouse indignation amongst the workers against the stabilisation
of wages.' And this, although a political quip, had
sufficient truth in it to cut deep.

Let us consider the foundation order then, no.166, which
Congress believed was so cumbersome that it should be
scrapped.[77] The instrument provided for the establishment
of advisory tribunals of three members, a chairman (district

justices were a popular choice), one employer member and one
employee member, and, in regard to the latter two, they
were appointed by the Minister from the appropriate panels
established under section 22 of the 1941 Act, that is to
say the panels from which would be drawn the representatives
for the very different trade union tribunal to be established
under part III of the 1941 Act. The trade unions found
that when they nominated to the workmen's panel for the
purposes of wages, they, willy-nilly, nominated for the
purposes of the trade union tribunal as well. Not only that
but, as we have already recognised, only unions licensed under
the act could make application to the tribunals. No increases in wages of any kind could be given except in
accordance with the order.[78] Sam Kyle initially had some
small hope that the requirements of the 1941 act could be
ignored in practice; but now, by reason of the order 166,
trade unions had no alternative but to take out a
negotiating licence and, in most cases, to nominate as well
to the workmen's panel under section 22 of part III of the
act. Finally the order explicitly removed the protection
of the Trade Disputes Act 1906 where unions acted in contravention of the order.[79]

First a clear base had to be established on which a bonus
system was to be built, and for that reason the first
application to the advisory tribunal was for a standard
wage determination. Before making a recommendation to the
minister the tribunal had to publish its intention to
investigate and hear representations; it was only when
he was satisfied that all this had been done would the
minister issue a wages (standard rate) order. But in fact
all this looked much more complicated than it actually was,
since in a great many cases the standard rate was well-
known and the business could be disposed of in a few
minutes. The order then provided for certain maximum
bonuses that licensed trade unions might apply for, the
appropriate one at this stage being 2s. for 10 points above
the official cost of living index figure of 225. The

application was initially made to the minister, who, if
he was satisfied, referred it to the appropriate tribunal,
which, as before, had to give public notice of its intention
to investigate, hear interested parties, and provide, with
its recommendation, a comprehensive report of the effect of
a bonus increase. Where the minister confirmed a bonus
order, it was still permissive merely; but the union was
free to take its own steps to compel performance, and in
this sense industrial action became implicitly recognised
as at least one procedure.

In order to improve the machinery, and in his bid for
cooperation, Lemass issued almost immediately five
amending orders[80] but in 1942, there was still a great
deal of protest in the air and in October, parades and
public meetings were held in Dublin, Cork and Limerick
(the Dublin one leading to a rather idiotic row with Larkin's
union which we shall discuss later); Congress regarded them
as being remarkably successful[81] and Lemass, always sensitive
to these matters, invited the national executive back in
November to discuss further improvements. A new order was
issued on March 2 1943,[82] which went quite a distance to
meet the Congress. 'It will be seen', said O'Shannon,[83]
'that in this matter of wage increases and bonuses the labours
of the National Executive have not been altogether in vain.'
Of course the amounts were pitifully small and the procedure often protracted, but the national executive could
report - not without pride[84] - that nominees of the national
executive and nominees of the unions had served on the
tribunals all over the state 'and have had a big share
in securing such increases by way of bonus as have been
obtained by many thousands of workers. Between bonuses and
standard wage rates upwards of 800 Orders have been made,
most of them after hearings before Tribunals. For these
the greater credit is due to the Worker Members whose time -
often prolonged - experience, skill, patience and judgement
have been of invaluable benefit to the Unions and the wage-

earners on whose behalf they have been readily given.'[85]
The difficult demanding business of working the system
had come to prevail, and the principles underlying both
the Trade Union Acts and the wage control orders had
slipped into the background.

Before leaving our theme of wage control, perhaps a word
should be said about the public service. An agreement
had been reached in 1920[86] between the civil service staffs
and the government of the time that civil servants would
be paid by way of a basic salary and a bonus, the bonus to
be calculated on a sliding scale which was related to the
cost of living index. In October 1922 that index (the base
being 100 in 1914) stood at 189[87] but from then on it began
gradually to decline, and civil service wages and salaries
to decline with it. In 1929 it had fallen to 176 and by
1935 to 156. The civil service staffs put up with it,
hoping for better days and 'heartened by promises made by
Mr de Valera in 1933 when he said that the Government would
continue their obligations and honour the agreement.'[88]
Thereafter the position changed; in 1938 the index stood
at 173 and continued to rise. In 1940, in advance of the
general wages standstill order (and no doubt in order to
stiffen commitment by setting their own house in order first)
the government decided to call a halt to the upward sliding
scale of civil service bonuses, by means of the Civil
Service Stabilisation of Bonus Order. It was bad enough
to be the first to be selected for the standstill, but
what distressed the civil service employees almost more
than any other aspect was that the bonus had been stabilised
at a cost of living index level of 185 when in fact the
index stood at 192. This remained to irritate civil
service associations for many years to come. Nor was de
Valera at all happy to see Congress involving themselves
in this matter, although two unions with substantial civil
service membership were affiliates, the Post Office Workers
Union and the Civil Service Clerical Association. This he

believed was a matter for the Department of Finance and
the civil service associations and Congress should keep
out.[89]

-iv-

Let us turn to our third theme of this period of the early
forties, the disruptive effect of the Larkin-O'Brien dispute, so disruptive in fact that, to many who lived through
the time, it overshadowed all the other difficulties which
the trade union movement had to face.

Larkin, up to 1942, continued to attend Congress as a
delegate from the Dublin Council of Trade Unions (a body
from which the Irish Transport had withdrawn when it admitted Larkin's union into membership) and he continued
as well to seek the affiliation to Congress in its own right
of the Workers Union of Ireland. Once again in 1942 the
application from his union was refused, but this time,
the national executive stated the reason explicitly:
'Workers' Union of Ireland, because its record as a cause
of disruptive action within the Trade Union movement and a
promoter of libels against officers of affiliated Unions
and of Congress itself would make its admission a disintegrating instead of a harmonious element within Congress.'[90]
This was the first time that reasons had been offered by the
national executive for refusing affiliation,[91] but much in
contrast with the case of the Workers' Union, the three other
applications that the national executive rejected, were
refused on grounds of conflicts of jurisdiction or on
questions of possible merger. However, the condemnation
of Larkin and the Workers' Union did not spring only from
William O'Brien. Larkin had again been in the courts, this
time for libelling Denis Cullen of the Bakers' Union, a

member of the national executive. Perhaps this was at least one reason why Sam Kyle, of all people, undertook to speak on behalf of the national executive when the reference back of that part of the report was moved.[92] It must be remembered, however, that this 1942 Congress was the Congress of the honeymoon of the two transport unions, whose harmony had so impressed the president and the delegates.

Larkin was deeply hurt by Sam Kyle's support for the decision to refuse his union affiliation, and he was incensed by the reason given in the Congress report.[93] But worse was to come when the national executive moved a change in the constitution[94] which would require that a trades council could send as delegates to Congress only members of trade unions which were affiliated to Congress. This of course meant that Larkin would no longer be able to attend Congress as a delegate from the Dublin Council. Once again Kyle was prominent in proposing the change, although some years earlier he had helped to defeat a similar suggestion. Larkin was outraged at the implication that his was not a bona fide trade union. He called for honesty; he asked for help from the uncommitted unions, he blundered back over old disputes, calling William O'Brien an unmitigated liar,[95] but it was all to no avail. The motion was carried by 107 votes to 60, and Larkin was excluded.

The national executive resentment washed on to the Dublin Council which had supported Larkin. There was what appeared to be a somewhat manufactured row about representation on the wage tribunals, and then the national executive seized on an incident during the protest parade in October 1942 against the wages standstill.[96] Larkin's union (which had been judiciously placed near the centre of the parade) had, they claimed, broken away, threatening the parade with disorganisation. It appears that a third of the procession arrived when the meeting was half over. Larkin explained

that the breakaway in College Green was for the purpose
of checking on attendance, since his members were subject
to a fine if they did not take part; and the Dublin Council
were prepared to accept the explanation. But the national
executive was not, and there was a good deal of talk about
disaffiliating the council. In the event they settled for
recording formally that the 'action of the Council ... has
been reprehensible in the highest degree ... and that a
future offence of this kind can be met only with a decision
to disaffiliate the offending body.' The Dublin Council
however had no intention of being disaffiliated, and they
were not prepared to allow the row between Larkin and the
national executive to divide them. Crawford, at the
Congress of 1943, defended the position of the Council very
fully, but without vehemence, and with an evident desire to
rise above the quarrels of the past. 'I believe it would be
a tragedy if the Trades Council went out of affiliation.
We have performed work which would not otherwise have been
done. There were signs of disunity: that was not made in
our generation; we knew nothing about it and we want to get
away from it. We want to get away from the quarrels that
have obtained between individuals and personalities. We
want unity: it will have to be achieved some time.
Personalities did enter into the movement: you are asked
which side you are on, and if you are not on one side or
the other, you are told you are in the wilderness.'[97] But
there was no doubt which side Congress was on just then.
When Crawford moved the reference back of what the national
executive had done, he was overwhelmingly defeated. The
important point however was that the Dublin Council's
support for Larkin emerged as a limited one.

But Larkin could never be underestimated. His political
militancy was always simple, explicit and attractive to the
rank and file, and this was what most disturbed William O'Brien.
'I am Ishmael', said Larkin at an earlier stage in the 1942
Congress when the trade union act was under discussion,[98]

'possibly making my swansong today in this particular
assembly. I suggest that even now it is not too late to
test the government.' It might be done by taking an
industry or a section of an industry and making a stand there.
'If my Union was chosen to do it I would not hesitate for
a moment to tell them it was their duty to take the field.'
And if the trade unions had no heart for such militancy,
he urged that at least there was always the political arm
of the movement.

At this time Larkin's political star was in the ascendant.
In the flush of antagonism to the trade union bill and
the wages standstill order, he had been admitted to the
Labour Party in December 1941 with his son Jim.   There
was some opposition to his admission - not especially strong -
from the Irish Transport representatives, but their hostility
to him began to mount when he successfully contested the
local elections in August 1942,   and when his influence
increased.[99]

In May 1943 parliament was dissolved and a general election
called for the following month, with Labour convinced that
it was stronger now than it had been for a very long time.
Larkin of course was a candidate, but the Administrative
Council of the Labour Party by a very slender majority
(two members were absent) refused to ratify his candidature.
The fact was that the Irish Transport members, under
instructions from their union, voted for the refusal;   all
the other members of the Administrative Council voted in
favour of ratification.   But the political workers in the
field could see no sense in this, and despite the decision,
the Dublin candidates and the Dublin executive committee
of the Labour Party, anxious to win seats in Dublin, supported
his candidature and he was elected.   The Irish Transport,
unwaveringly vindictive when it came to Larkin, moved at
the Administrative Council that the chairman and the secretary
of the Dublin executive committee should be expelled from
the party (the former was young Jim Larkin);   but now, with

all members of the Administrative Council present they
were in a minority - although barely so - and their motion
was defeated.

In January 1944 the Irish Transport disaffiliated from the
Labour Party. The Parliamentary Labour Party - which had
almost doubled its representation[100] was also disrupted.
Five deputies seceded, forming a National Labour Party in
Dail Eireann.

This was a step of great importance, and even though the
Irish Transport leadership appears to have been empowered
to take such action by their July 1943 annual conference[101]
nevertheless it left them very exposed, not least in regard
to their own membership. They offered two reasons for
disaffiliation. Firstly there was the disruptive effect of
Larkin and to some extent his son.[102] The Labour Party
leaders had decided to play tough on this issue. The Irish
Transport had already divided the Dublin Council of Trade
Unions because of it, they had made the Congress come to
heel, and now they wished to dominate the Labour Party as
well. Larkin, on the other hand, in May 1943, during the
general election campaign, had swallowed his pride in the
cause of unity and on the urging of the Labour Party had
written '... if in the heat of past conflicts statements
were made by me, I regret having made such statements if those
statements today appear as obstacles in the way of a united
effort by all members of the Party at the present moment.'[103]
But, in the words of the Labour Party's official statement:
'... the (Irish Transport) Union officials would not abandon
the position they had taken up. So far as they were
concerned Larkin must be driven into the wilderness and kept
there ... they believed the (Irish Transport) officials were
unreasonable and dominated by a thirst for revenge.'[104]
There was a good deal of distaste, therefore, for the highly
personal flavour which the row exhibited, and furthermore,
despite the authorisation at the Irish Transport's July

conference, the Labour Party were of the view that the step
to disaffiliate had been taken 'without any reference to
their own members.'[105]

It was in these circumstances that the second reason for
disaffiliation - a reason placed first in their statements[106] -
became significant; it was to the effect that the administrative council had failed to abide by the Constitution
of the Labour Party; in fact it was an accusation that
communists had been permitted to join the party. And
here, because of the mood of the country at the time, the
fat was really in the fire.

The Labour Party were loud in their disclaimers. 'The
officers of the I.T. & G.W.U. are aware', they declared,[107]
'that the Constitution of the Labour Party was framed to
exclude the possibility of Communists or members of similar
organisations becoming members of the Party.' And three
years ago they had cancelled the membership of a person who
'had affiliation with a body closely akin to the Communist
Party.'[108] More than that, they were very angry at what they
considered to be the cynicism of some of the Irish Transport
leaders in starting such a scare. 'Indeed people acquainted
with the facts must be greatly amazed by the new-found
hostility to Communism in certain quarters.'[109] They went
on to claim that the Irish Transport itself was affiliated
to a marxian International. On this they were on very shaky
ground. It would have been far nearer the truth but much more
difficult to maintain that William O'Brien himself - in his
unwaveringly loyalty to Connolly's teachings - was still
fundamentally a marxist; and it is likely enough that
William McMullen would also have been sympathetic to such a
view. On the other hand, it must be recognised that the
reply of the Irish Transport[110] to the Labour Party official
statement - a reply which was issued under William O'Brien's
name - gives quite a contrary impression, and there is no
doubt that sounding the communist firebell was a good ploy in
the case of both Larkin senior and Larkin junior.

We have already seen how Larkin senior had attended the fifth
congress of the Comintern in 1924. He had been elected to
the executive committee as well as to the executive of the
Red International of Labour Unions, the Profintern.[111]
The Irish Transport now made highly coloured use of this.[112]
The early row between Larkin and the Irish Transport leaders
was not a personality vendetta but 'a deliberate attempt to
smash the union ... The really significant aspect of that
campaign of disruption was that Larkin was not alone in it.
He had the active and sinister backing of the Communist
Party. Then, and all through the conflict,' said the
Irish Transport, 'those apostles of chaos assailed the Union
and the Labour Party by almost every method of gangsterdom,
and in the height of the campaign Mr Larkin was lionised in
Moscow, where the Third International invested him with a
twenty-fifth share in the rulership of the earth when the
world revolution would take place.[113] The Communist hatred
of the Irish Transport and General Workers' Union has never
abated; while on the other hand their alignment with Larkin
is as close today as it was then. It was the Communists
in the Labour Party who sponsored the campaign to have
Larkin adopted as an official Labour Party candidate in the
last election. It was before them and their threats that
Mr Norton quailed. It was in deference to the intimidation
of the self-appointed Dublin Executive, the hub of the
Communist organisation inside the Party, that the Party
Constitution was violated ...' In his obsession with Larkin,
it was O'Brien's practice to keep notes of what Larkin said
or did[114] and in his circular letter[115] to the branches of
the Irish Transport on January 15 1944 he drew attention to
a report that Larkin, when addressing a labour summer school
in England in the summer of 1943, said that the Irish workers
intended to seize full power when the opportunity came.
'What the Bosheviks did in Russia, Socialist-led workers
would do in Ireland one day.'

James Larkin junior was just as vulnerable. Not only had

he spent some time in Moscow, but in June 1933 he had presided at a congress of workers' revolutionary groups for the purpose of forming a communist party.[116] In this present dispute, the fact that he had been chairman of the Dublin executive which had supported his father was seen by the Irish Transport as part of 'the gangster tactics of the Communist elements, led by James Larkin Junior, and John Ireland ...; both of whom had long and active connection with the Communist Party ...'[117] Furthermore the younger Larkin 'had already been trained in the technique of Communist propaganda in the Lenin College, Moscow ... and he had already stood as an official Communist candidate for the Dail.'[118] The case therefore was well made; and if William O'Brien himself was not necessarily hostile to marxist thinking, his union generally was most vehemently so, expressing indeed the widespread feeling of the time.

Most vigorous in its accusations of communist domination in the labour movement was the Catholic Standard, so much so that, in the special inquiry into communist activity which the Labour Party undertook in 1944, their request for facts was met with the statement from one witness 'that the mass of evidence adduced in the articles which have appeared in the Standard is so well documented that no further evidence from me or from anybody else appears to be necessary.'[119] And there is correspondence[120] during early 1944 between William O'Brien and P.J. O'Brien, a prominent Irish Transport official in Cork, during which the latter continued to report on his contacts with Alfred O'Rahilly, the Cork university professor who was the most prominent polemicist in the Standard and indeed dominated its policy.[121]

The Report of the Labour Party Committee of Inquiry[122] into communism in the party mentioned a number of persons by name, some by way of exoneration, and four for the purposes of expulsion (they had been in Belfast during the Belfast communist conference); but they made no mention of the Larkins. Instead they attempted to meet the point by saying,[123] 'there are in the Dublin Branches a few members who, at one time or other, were members of the Communist Party, but there are also in the Dublin branches many members

who, at one time or another, were members of the Fianna
Fail and of Fine Gael Parties. The Dublin membership also
includes a number of young men who were formerly identified
with the IRA. In the absence of evidence, we refuse to
believe these men have any affinity with atheistic Communism;
on the contrary we believe some of them, at least, are very
definitely anti-Communist. Apart from this aspect of the
campaign with which we are dealing, we consider that when
a person formally and publicly breaks off association with
a political party of which he has been a member, and, in an
equally public manner associates himself with another party,
it would be the height of folly on the part of the latter to
refuse him admission to its ranks.' The report concluded
by stating that its election programme was based 'on a set
of principles in keeping with Christian Doctrine and wholly
at variance with the principles of atheistic Communism.'
This no doubt was so, but it did not save them from disaster.
In the 1944 general election (called within a year by the
government because of the weakness of their position) only
8 of the 12 outgoing Labour Party deputies were returned, while
4 of the 5 deputies who had broken away to form the National
Party were elected. The combined Labour vote showed a drop
of 74,000, or a third, as compared with the election of
June 1943.[124]

On reflection, all this must be seen primarily as the disruptive effect of the enmity between William O'Brien and
some of his close colleagues on the one hand and James Larkin
senior on the other. There was little substance in the
communist scare. It would seem that both the numbers and
the influence of communists in the country were very much
exaggerated.[125] It had effect because it caught at the
hysteria of the time. What is interesting however is how
strong - even though a breach occurred - was the basic sense
of unity within the party, aided no doubt by an awareness
of the political reality. Most members were deeply troubled
by the disruption. Even the Irish Transport politicians

were divided about the whole matter; while five[126] sitting
deputies formed National Labour, three of their union
colleagues refused to break away,[127] and men like James
Hickey,[128] who went along with the union, did so while
explicitly expressing dissent.[129] There was no fundamental
rift in the party, and this was only too clear in the manner
in which they buried the hatchet in 1948 in order to join
in the first Inter-party government.[130]

Nevertheless O'Brien had not hesitated to rip the party
asunder at the point of its major opportunity, and having
taken such a step with the political arm of the labour
movement, it was much less difficult to contemplate ripping
the trade union movement asunder as well if this were necessary.
Of course Larkin had been ejected and no longer troubled him,
but there remained, as there always did, the activities of the
amalgamated unions and in particular the Amalgamated Transport,
which, although relations in 1943 were very good, nevertheless offended O'Brien nationally, affronted the growth
of the Irish Transport, and in particular frustrated the
development of an orderly Irish-based trade union movement
which he now firmly believed was necessary to the economic
and social development of the country. The Trade Union
Acts now held out some hope that in time the structure of the
movement would be improved, but it was not at all clear that
this in itself was adequate. When the disruption came in 1945
it shattered the trade union movement in a very fundamental
way, much more fundamental than in the case of the Labour
Party,[131] and yet, as we shall see, the trade union movement
too, despite its great diversity, had a strong sense of
unity, which right from the very outset attempted to reassert
itself.

-v-

Let us pause at this twilight time before the great breach
in the trade union movement, and attempt some evaluation,
just as the annual Congress itself did in what was both
its last meeting as a united body and the fiftieth year
of its foundation. This year of 1943-44, the year of the
golden jubilee of Congress, saw the presidency of Robert
Getgood, 'a man from the banks of the Lagan', whose election
was hailed as a manifestation of the unity of the trade
union movement north and south.[132] Indeed he was the first
Belfast president to be so elected since Tom Johnson in 1916.
It is fitting therefore that we should consider first the
position of the north.

In an effort to mark the occasion, Getgood, in his presidential address in 1944,[133] presented a historical review of
the trade union movement, in which he dealt no less with the
north than the south. The thirties had been a difficult
time, as we have noted earlier,[134] with wages falling and
unemployment rising until in July 1938 the number of unemployed exceeded 100,000;[135] but from then onwards, as
Britain moved to a war footing, the figure fell, until by
1944 there was full employment throughout the province.

The unions had agreed 'to allow trade practices to be set
aside for the duration (of the war). Strikes and lockouts
(were) outlawed',[136] and a system of compulsory arbitration
imposed.[137] Not only that but the Restrictions of Employment
Order, 1942, limited the movement of workers from one
industry to another. None of these matters incidentally
appear to have come before the national executive or the
annual conference of Congress for consideration. However,
there were compensations for the workers in the north.
The cost of living had been controlled to some extent by

subsidies, and wages had risen rapidly, in some cases quite
startlingly so. From August 1939 to February 1944, the
cost of living, much in contrast with the south, had
risen by only 29 per cent and wages had increased by
anything from 35 per cent to 70 per cent.[138]

Yet now, with the war's end in sight, there was much impatience with these restrictions and much anxiety as well
about employment prospects when demobilisation took place
and industry returned to peace time production. Strikes
began to occur despite their illegality, a dispute by
engineering workers involving, in February 1944, over
12,000 people.[139] Interest by the northern trade unionists
in Congress began to quicken - indeed from 1942 onwards.
During the twenties and thirties, the north had quite faded
from Congress, had become shadowy and remote, dealing with
its own affairs in its own context. The Congress had become
an essentially twenty-six county affair, so much so that
Michael Colgan in 1942 delivered the early part of his
presidential address in Irish.[140] Beattie of the INTO,[141]
a Northern Ireland MP, had been asked to move the vote of
thanks, and possibly to restore the balance made the point
that 'while Northern Ireland is a political entity it has
within it an industrial community. I have asked many times:
"Why is it that the Irish Trade Union Congress is not a
party to the activities of the movement in the North?" and
I have failed, up to the moment, to get an answer ...'[142]
Colgan, in his response, claimed that the lack of interest
lay with the north not with the national executive. To a
great extent this must have been true. Now, however, there
was a marked change. The national executive reported to the
1943 annual conference[143] that they had established a special
committee to look into the matter, and the following year the
annual conference was presented with a fully fledged 'Committee
on Congress Membership in Northern Ireland'[144] which, on
the recommendation of their special committee, had been
established by the national executive. It was very much a

subcommittee of the national executive, all members being
appointed by them; four were union members resident in
Northern Ireland, two were members of the national executive
and the chairman and secretary were <u>ex officio</u> the president
and general secretary of Congress. The committee was
advisory and consultative merely, although 'normally (its)
advice ... would be acted upon'[145] but even then the point
was repetitively made that the whole thing was tentative and
experimental. The national executive knew that they were
in troubled waters and were most cautious, presenting the
annual conference with a <u>fait accompli</u> rather than opening
the matter for debate. Nevertheless a motion of Jack
Macgougan's[146] that the committee should be democratically
elected was well debated, being defeated however when it
was opposed both by Kyle of the Amalgamated Transport and
McMullen of the Irish Transport. In the difficult
circumstances of 1945, the same motion, this time moved
by Harold Binks,[147] was withdrawn after a brief debate.
But in fact the point was largely won. A special conference
of affiliated organisations having members in Northern Ireland
was held in Belfast early the following November and they
recommended for appointment to a Northern Ireland Committee
ten Northern Ireland delegates who with the President, the
Vice-President and the Secretary (or Assistant Secretary)
of Congress constituted the first Northern Ireland Committee,
although it still possessed in the formal sense, merely
sub-committee status.[148] Let us consider then why this
committee was established, and why the national executive
approached the question so tentatively.

Some of the reasons for the growing interest in Congress
are obvious enough, the increase in trade union activity
as the end of wartime restrictions came in sight, the
influence perhaps of Bob Getgood in the national executive,
and indeed the greater number of delegates from the north
who attended the annual conferences.[149] Nor should we ever
underestimate what we have recognised on more than one
occasion, the instinctive sense of trade union unity, which
continuously surprises one by its persistence. But there

were two other influential reasons, both of the greatest
interest. The first was the understandable response of
the amalgamated unions to the parading nationalism of
William O'Brien and the Irish Transport. The Amalgamated
Transport, for example, while the vast majority of its
members were in Northern Ireland, nevertheless had substantial membership in the south, and other unions were
similarly placed.[150] It was natural therefore that they
should respond to a threat of an Irish-based trade union
movement - and the loss of their southern membership - by
emphasising the integral nature of northern membership.
But here the emphasis on the north reflected the southern
needs of the amalgamated unions; it did not of itself
reflect any grassroots interest by northern members in
Congress; certainly it could not be taken to mean that in
Northern Ireland there was any desire for Congress to become
involved in domestic industrial matters. And while this
was true in a general sense, nevertheless there was in fact
a reason for involving Congress in northern affairs, a reason
somewhat complex in its origin and constituting the second
basis for the growing interest in a united trade union
centre. There were two strands here. The first was the
heartfelt anxiety of a Belfast socialist like Billy McCullough
that the pressure for employment when the war ended would
result in sectarian strife particularly as even in 1943
'irresponsible people are repeatedly making statements which
tend to heap fuel on the fire of division that exists.'[151]
He hoped that a central trade union authority would 'bring
about the state of affairs we so desire - the brotherhood
of the workers North and South', which of course meant -
as it so often does - the brotherhood of catholic and
protestant workers. This objective, though laudable, was
hardly very influential; but there was a second strand,
a very practical desire to counter the practice of the
conservative northern administration to pick and choose
the trade unions they proposed to deal with, and to face
them instead with a united trade union centre. McCullough in

1943 put it well:[152]   'Despite the fact that they had a
large number of Unions there, Congress and the National
Executive, in relation to the situation in the North, had no
authority at all.   The British TUC for instance had a direct
approach to the British Cabinet, and during this emergency
the Cabinet could not have operated without that cooperation.
He took it that virtually a similar situation existed in
the Twenty-Six Counties;   that the Irish TUC was, on
occasions, in collaboration with the Government.   There was
no such contact in the north except through the individual
Trade Unions.'   If then, in the expansion which was expected
in the postwar world, the northern government could continue,
in McMullen's phrase,[153] to 'hand-pick the trade union
representatives on Committees', the prospect would be an
impossible one for independent-minded trade union leaders
whether nationalist or socialist.   There was always the
alternative of an Ulster TUC, but this would have been at
the expense of abandoning the southern membership of the
amalgamated unions - and perhaps the abandoning of something
even deeper.   Consequently the solution seemed to lie with
a judicious exploration of the idea of a northern committee,
not with any real independence (because this would raise
the threat of an Ulster TUC) but with sufficient identity
to be accepted by the Northern Ireland government as a
valid northern trade union centre.   In the event, as we shall
see in chapter 7, this strategy had a complex and difficult
history.   And as for William O'Brien and his colleagues,
the development of a northern centre would by no means have
been unwelcome.   After all it gave validity to the notion
of separateness, so essential to the objective of an Eire
organisation standing apart.   Certainly Cathal O'Shannon
gave much emphasis to the diverse (even fragmented) interests
of Congress and the need to reflect these interests in a
structure which might be equally diverse:[154] 'For over
twenty years (Congress) has been carrying on its activities
under two separate and unrelated State jurisdictions and

under three separate and distinct codes of legislation
of different origins and on different bases. In these
five years of war our Congress and many of its affiliated
Trade Unions have, consequently, been in the unique position
of working in both belligerent and non-belligerent States
and under vastly different orders and regulations ...'
O'Shannon went on to claim that Congress and its affiliated
Unions were coming through with unimpaired authority and
power. But this was the gilt on the gingerbread. O'Shannon
must have known that despite the calm of the jubilee year
the position was indeed a fragile one.

Let us turn from the north to southern matters. One gets
the impression of little trade union activity during this
time. There was continuous anxiety about unemployment,
in particular when the war would end; there was anxiety
about the growth of government bureaucracy. The Labour
Party, however, seemed to provide, before the debâcle of
1944, a prospect of real advance for the labour movement.
In the wake of its substantial success in the local elections[155]
its annual conference in April 1943 was the largest it had
held, up to then. Yet it is important to recognise once
again how underdeveloped politically the Labour Party in
fact was. Many unions remained unaffiliated, and we still
see it more as a gathering of politicians with their individual followings than a party with a coherent platform.
'I would rather see it more of a composite body,' said
Gilbert Lynch in 1943[156] 'rather than a Party of individuals.' Furthermore when political action was spoken of,
horizons were limited. There was little evidence of hard
thinking regarding the future, or regarding the north.
Instead there was some general and quite impractical notion
that if Labour secured a majority north and south, the
two administrations would together resolve the border
problem.[157] When the split came in the Labour Party in 1944
the prospect of an early political impact by Labour disappeared.

In all these circumstances, there was in the Congress debates
of the time a dominating domestic note, heavy with the

stresses of interunion rivalry and with the immediate
problems of wage adjustments and wage tribunals;   there
was little evidence of constructive thinking on the major
problems of the time. Mortished, who returned from Canada
to represent the International Labour Office at the 1942
annual conference, was shocked that things were so domestic.
'I doubt, if I may speak quite frankly', he said,[158] 'personally
I doubt whether people not only in this room but outside
realise the full gravity of the situation with which we
are faced ... a situation so critical that many of the things
we are discussing now will fade into comparative in-
significance ... We are faced with the necessity of deciding
what really is the kind of world we want to live in and how
we are going to make that kind of world ...' Yet the problems
were so strident that they were pushing their way into the
trade union movement, and if there was little evidence
of constructive thinking in their regard it was probably
because views on certain matters were so profoundly opposed
that constructive thinking was not possible. As the problems
of the time became even more insistent, so also did the
stresses within the trade union movement until eventually
they became intolerable.

The two opposing views - which could not be reconciled in
the circumstances of the time - have already emerged during
the course of this account; now, however, they became more
explicit, more pointed, more naked to our view. Let us
take first the attitude of mind, the disposition, which
informed those who broke away to establish the Congress of
Irish Unions. That inward-looking nationalism, much intensified by the isolation in which the south found itself,
grew more and more imperative. On two occasions during the
war years, resolutions from amalgamated unions, which were
intended to be rhetorical and confirmatory, ran into an
embarrassing quagmire. The first was in 1942 when a
resolution condemning fascism was actually defeated by 47
votes to 43[159] - granted, during a debate which was confused
by a number of issues, but during which one Irish Transport

delegate remarked that it was an attempt to get Congress
to express a point of view that would commit them to one set
of combatants. The following year a similar resolution was
submitted,[160] the speeches in favour being more judiciously
handled, and it was adopted by 50 votes to 28, but not
without some expression of anti-British sentiment. The
second occasion was in 1943 when a resolution from Sam Kyle
urging aid for refugees 'from the tyranny of the invaders
of their country'[161] received some rough handling, but was
eventually carried by a substantial majority, principally
because Kyle emphasised that the aid was to be given through
the Red Cross or the government.

But it was a nationalism too which greatly resented - as Irish
nationalism always did - British influence on Irish affairs;
and this, as we shall see, was precisely the role which the
amalgamated unions appeared to adopt on the issue of the
London conference. In the immediate aftermath of the split,
there was a good deal of insistence that 'alien control
in any shape or form must be resisted'[162] and there was much
insistence as well on the need for the Irish nation to fulfil
its destiny.[163] Although this last still had millenarian
echoes from earlier years, it referred essentially to the
idea of getting rid of constraints, in the expectation that
once this was done, the Irish people would realise their
potential; and to hardheaded people there was little of the
Rousseauesque in the idea that whatever opportunity there
was for social, economic and cultural development, these
could hardly be expected if there were constraints of an
alien kind which had no necessary identity of interest with
the Irish condition.

Of course in trade union terms it was difficult to fit the
north into such a nationalist concept; and the ITUC made
considerable play of this point when the split came.
The Congress of Irish Unions in response began by saying

that far from being partitionist, Ireland to them meant
the whole island[164] but that, for immediate purposes, they
had to recognise the reality as it stood; however, developing
behind it was some naive expectation that, following the
example of the south, Ulster would cast the crown aside and
become green, an expectation which was possible only
because many southern trade unionists were woefully ignorant
of the true dimensions of northern society. And if those
who themselves sprang from the north and knew it well - men
like O'Shannon and McMullen - appeared to make little effort
to inform their colleagues to the contrary, it was probably
because on all sides, the north (apart from its catholic
minority) was in truth never seen as part of the essential
Irish society. The notion of a pluralist society seemed
quite impractical and unlikely to the nationalist sentiment
of the time.

All this was greatly reinforced by the steady growth of
profound religious feeling among the catholic people of
the south. This was essentially a question of how the
people focussed on reality, how they perceived it; it raises
once again[165] the significance of stable institutions which
are seen as dominating the flux of events. So deep was
catholic sentiment - overwhelmingly demonstrated in 1932
in the Eucharistic Congress and reinforced by the isolation
of the years that followed - that the vast majority of
people were set in a solemn moral structure that remedied the
past and secured the future, immensely nourishing to the spirit,
but ruthless in its demand for submission. It would of
course, be wrong to suggest that all the nationalist labour
leaders were fully of this persuasion; indeed quite a
number had, in regard to the whole religious ethic, an independent if not a somewhat cynical cast of mind, but being
of the subculture, they were deeply sensitive to its demands,
much in contrast with their northern colleagues to whom the
whole business was incomprehensible and full of a somewhat
repellent medievalism. It was a climate of opinion that

was indeed compelling. It provided the Church leaders
with the unswerving loyalty which they commanded; in
official functions, the Cardinal took precedence over the
President, the Archbishop of Dublin over the Prime Minister.
The reality of life lay primarily in the structure of the
Church and the secular reality lay beneath and outside it.
We can see this influence in the sympathy extended to the
quasi-fascist notion of a corporate state[166] and in the
uncertainty in condemning fascism in general. But above all
we can see how it caused men to view communism - or any
form of atheism - with great hostility, so great indeed
that the suspicion of it devastated the Labour Party.

If nationalist sentiment distrusted a war alliance which
included British arms, catholic sentiment no less distrusted that which included communist Russia, and both
blended to reinforce the notion of neutrality - the desire
to hold the victors at some distance; it was a positive
policy of neutrality demanded by the sentiment of the time
and quite different from the neutrality of non-involvement
of the early war years.

This then was the first position. Opposing it was the
traditional, liberal, mildly socialist and reforming
disposition so attractive to modern opinion and so widespread, but, in the aftermath of the war, caught up in a
great detestation of fascism and in a great wave of
millenarian feeling that a new world could be created in
which incidentally the labour movement believed it had a
considerable part to play. Kyle, in proposing the critical
resolution on the London conference in 1944[167] stressed
that it was a reaching out to trade unionists in all lands
'whether they are in Germany, in France, in Italy or in
Australia',[168] and here we meet the central point of the
dilemma, because to Kyle and to many others, the war that
was drawing to a close was a war of ideologies more than
a war of nations: it was fascism rather than Germany which
had to be defeated, a fascism that had crushed the German

trade unions as well as all other free German institutions.
In such circumstances it was the task of the allies to
restore Germany to the German people, and in that context,
it was the task of the trade unions in the free world to
help the German workers to build their trade union movement once again (as indeed Bevin was later to do in a most
distinguished manner.) But to nationalist sentiment in 1944
the war was a conflict of nations far more than ideologies,
and the London conference not really a world trade union
gathering but rather one for representatives of 'Allied
Nations and representatives from the underground movements
of the suppressed countries.'[169] If one viewed the war -
as Kyle did, and the British trade union movement did - as
a means of defeating an evil and crippling ideology in which
no free institutions could survive, then victory meant
a great flowering of international socialist solidarity
so deeply valued by many trade union leaders; but if one saw
the war, as Irish nationalists did, as a further conflict
between Britain and Germany in which Britain (with the aid
of America and Russia) was triumphant, then there were far
more significant objectives to be secured - freedom from
British dominance, freedom from the snares of communism -
than the creation of some questionable trade union international. Inevitably when they were confronted with all
this, with this strange and powerful blend of nationalism
and religion, the leaders of the amalgamated unions were
impatient and angered. Certainly the northern representatives
found it perverse; and as for those in the south who understood nationalist sentiment but yet held to a wider international loyalty, they could cry out in some distress:
'(The Irish unions) have appealed to two of the most noble
feelings that beat within the human breast: love of God and
love of country. They have twisted that in order to spread
in the breasts of men, fear, suspicion and hatred of their
fellow men.'[170]

Tom Johnson who, after O'Shannon had left to go to the
Congress of Irish Unions, had acted as general secretary

for a brief period in 1945,[171] attempted to confront in an
objective and unemotional way the problem of nationalism
in trade unions.[172] He recognised the significance of
nationalism but urged that the interests of the working
class, in whatever country, should be placed higher, and
in view of the Connolly hagiography that had developed in
the Irish Transport he drew heavily on his writings for
support and also on the fact that the Irish Transport, when
it originally broke away in 1909 from the amalgamated union,
was activated by a desire to serve better the needs of the
Irish workingclass, not by any nationalist separatism.
However, there was a source of conflict here; there was no
gainsaying that. Johnson tried to meet it by urging that
it could be lived with; it was not the most serious
difference of view within the trade union movement, ranking
well below, for example, the difference of view between those
who accepted the current organisation of society and attempted
to improve the workers' lot within its terms, and those who
wished to change society itself, root and branch; if this
more basic difference could be lived with, so also could
nationalism.

But the point here was not so much the existence of a
difference of view or even how radical such a difference
could be, but rather whether a state of affairs existed
which brought such views into conflict. With regard to the
difference in trade union objectives, there was nothing to
make it significant in the circumstances of the time; there
was no fundamental decision which turned on whether one saw
a trade union as having a subsidiary or a radical role in
society. It remained a matter merely of debate. It was
quite other however in the case of the difference between
trade unions understood nationally and trade unions understood as part of an international workingclass movement.
Johnson's view that they could survive together was right
only if nothing threw them into conflict. However the whole
issue of the London conference threw them directly into
conflict. It is to this question of the London conference
that we now turn.

-vi-

In 1943 the British TUC decided to sponsor a world trade
union conference to be held in London on June 5 1944.   To
it were invited the national trade union centres in named
countries and states, that is to say representatives
from both allied and neutral countries and from some of
the suppressed trade union movements in German-occupied
Europe.[173]   It was intended to be exploratory and tentative
in character but the ultimate aim was to establish a world
trade union centre.   During the first week of the conference it was proposed to discuss the allied war effort
and related matters, and to this the trade unions of the
neutral countries were not invited.   The topics for the
second week were relief, rehabilitation and problems of
postwar reconstruction, including the reconstruction of the
trade union movement.   The Irish Trade Union Congress
(although representing belligerent as well as non-
belligerent areas) was, for these purposes, regarded as being
representative of a neutral country and was invited for
the second week only.

The national executive received the invitation in November
1943; it deeply divided them, but in January by majority
they decided that they were unable to accept.   They were
pressed for a reason by 'two affiliated unions and two
affiliated councils', reconsidered the matter and in April
1944 decided 'that in present circumstances it would not be
advisable to send a delegation.'[174]   In the meantime, the
Belfast Trades Union Council, because of the refusal of
Congress, had themselves sought from the British TUC an
invitation to the conference and had been issued with one.
(The national executive expressed annoyance but could do
little about it.)   Thus, that part of the country which was
involved in the war was, right from the outset, delegated
to the conference;   the issue was whether the Irish TUC -

seen essentially as a trade union centre from a neutral
country - should be represented. This, at first sight,
did not appear to be unmanageable, particularly since the
conference, because of travel difficulties, had been postponed indefinitely. But Sam Kyle felt deeply about the
issue and deliberately sought a confrontation.

He put down a motion for the 1944 conference which stressed
international workingclass solidarity and noted 'with
regret the decision of the national executive to decline
the invitation.' The motion after a lengthy debate was
carried by 96 votes to 75. During the debate, which was
conducted in a very proper and serious manner, William
O'Brien made it clear that so radical was this resolution,
so basic in its cleavage of policies, that if it were passed
it would be 'the first step in the break-up of this Congress.'[175]
Yet even its adoption did not necessarily mean disaster.
It merely directed the national executive 'to show the trade
unionists of other countries that (they) were with them in
their efforts for the restoration of their Trade Unions'[176]
but it did not explicitly reverse their decision. However,
the election for the national executive radically altered
the whole position. Up to then the Irish-based unions
had always had a majority on the national executive (at
least since the foundation of the two states in Ireland);[177]
now in 1944 the power swung the other way, giving the
majority to the amalgamated unions.

In these circumstances the new national executive rescinded
the decision of their predecessors, and appointed Michael
Keyes and Gilbert Lynch to attend the London conference which
took place the following February. The following month, on
March 21 1945, fifteen Irish-based unions[178] met and adopted
a resolution to the effect that 'the opinions and aspirations
of Irish Labour cannot be expressed by the Irish Trade Union
Conference, which is controlled by British Trade Unions and
that the Irish Unions affiliated to Congress occupy an

intolerable and humiliating position; that we recommend our
affiliated unions to withdraw from Congress and establish
an organisation composed of Trade Unions with headquarters
in Ireland; and that Conference reassembles on April 25
to consider replies from affiliated Unions.'[179] A report
of the meeting appeared in the evening newspapers, and there
was much talk[180] not only of unions being urged to disaffiliate from the Irish TUC, but also of trade union
members being urged to break away from the amalgamated unions.
Two days later, on March 23 1945, Sam Kyle at a meeting of
the national executive proposed a motion which 'deplored
and condemned ... this mischievous attempt at sabotage.'[181]
Tom Kennedy, who as president of Congress was in the chair,
declined to accept the motion; he was promptly voted out
of the chair, Gilbert Lynch installed instead and the motion
adopted. On April 25 the 15 Irish-based unions at their
resumed conference decided that 'as fourteen of the fifteen
Unions represented at the Conference of March 21st, have now
ratified the Recommendation adopted, this Conference decides
to establish a National Trade Union Organisation composed
of Unions with headquarters in Ireland and free from the
control of British Trade Unions; and that a Provisional
Committee be appointed to take the necessary steps to give
effect to this decision...'[182] Immediately thereafter the
ten unions that were members of the Irish Trade Union
Congress, including the Irish Transport, formally disaffiliated.[183]

But was this in fact a deliberate takeover by the amalgamated
unions? Certainly the unions that broke away were convinced of it. The amalgamated unions, using their northern
membership as well as their southern, were in a position.
to dominate domestic trade union matters in the 26 counties.[184]
As the Congress of Irish Unions pointed out,[185] the amalgamated
unions had 105,000 members affiliated to Congress as against
81,000 for the Irish-based unions; but only 29,000 of those
were registered for the purposes of the Trade Union Acts

(i.e. 29,000 were active members in the south), as against
77,000 in the case of the Irish unions. This was the
claim they made, and at first sight it was a compelling one.

Yet there appears on closer examination to have been no
conspiracy, no attempt to take over, although it is true
that on the basis of affiliated membership there could
have been. Kyle and others felt passionately about the issue
of postwar reconstruction, but it was a passion which sought
to convince by debate rather than to manipulate institutions
for the purposes of formal support. Certainly there is no
evidence of any attempt to flood the Congress of 1944 with
amalgamated delegates - quite the contrary. Although the
affiliated membership of the amalgamated unions had increased by 40,000 since 1937, the number of delegates they
had sent to the 1944 Congress had actually declined slightly.[186]
Indeed it had been their settled practice not to send their
full delegations, and 1944 was no exception. They had paid
affiliation fees to Congress on the basis of 108,000 members[187]
(as against 80,000 in the case of the Irish-based unions)
but they had sent only 88 delegates; the Irish-based unions
had sent 115.[188] The implication here was clear and they
hammered it home. The Irish-based unions at the 1944 conference
could have defeated Sam Kyle's motion if they wished.
In fact only 73 delegates voted against it, 51 being from
the Irish Transport.

And what of the dramatic changes in the balance of power
on the national executive? Again there is no evidence of any
attempt on the part of the amalgamated unions to dominate.
In the year 1940-41   when William O'Brien was president,
feeling, as we have seen, ran very high, and this was
reflected in the contest for the vice-presidency in 1941,[189]
when Getgood withdrew in order not to split the amalgamated
vote and Keyes defeated Kennedy. Following the détente
between the two transport unions, however, the vice-president

thereafter was chosen by consensus, only one name appearing
on the ballot sheet, and 1944 was no exception.[190] It
appears therefore that the change in the national executive
was quite fortuitous; indeed it is clear that this must
have been so, since the delegates were the electorate, and
the balance among the delegates had not changed. A number
of things contributed to it. Of the outgoing members of
the national executive, Sean Walsh, of the Limerick Trades
Council, who had polled strongly in 1943, did not stand;
Michael Colgan, who was the last to be elected in 1943, was
defeated on this occasion, and so also was Leo Crawford,
when they were confronted with a strong challenge from
J.T. O'Farrell of the Railway Clerks and Barry of the ASW,
both managing to edge into the last two seats. The amalgamated
unions were also aided by the fact that the outgoing president,
Bob Getgood, normally a weak candidate, was given a large
courtesy vote, and Gilbert Lynch, also weak in national
executive elections, was unopposed as vice-president. All
this was enough to tip the balance. The result was the
election of nine amalgamated members as against six from
Irish-based unions, the very contrary of the position in 1943.

On March 23 immediately after their defeat at the national
executive, the three members from the Irish Transport
(Kennedy, McMullen and O'Brien), Campbell of the DTPS,
Drumgoole of the Distributive Workers and Cathal O'Shannon,
the general secretary, all resigned.[191] The remaining members
of the national executive received the Workers Union of
Ireland into affiliation, and in filling the vacancies on the
national executive they coopted Jim Larkin junior, and four
others[192] all from Irish based-unions which had remained
with the ITUC.

In response to the foundation conference of the Congress of
Irish Unions on April 25, the Irish Trade Union Congress held
a stabilising conference on May 11. Manifestos were promulgated by both organisations, the substance of which we have
already discussed, the CIU relying heavily on the danger of
alien control and the ITUC deploring the destruction of trade
union unity, north and south.[193] The rift was now clear.

The Irish Transport and the Irish Union of Distributive
Workers and Clerks were the major unions in the breakaway
CIU,[194] the others being small craft unions (the National
Union of Vintners Grocers and Allied Trades Assistants
was to be admitted a little later). On the other hand,
a large number of Irish-based unions had remained with the
Irish TUC, the public service unions, the teachers, the
assurance workers and the women workers. When it came to
figures, the unions of the ITUC had in membership 72,000
of the trade unionists in the south (and approximately the
same number in the north) which, they claimed, compared
with 53,000 in the case of the unions affiliated to the CIU -
though by July 1945 Cathal O'Shannon, now CIU general secretary,
was claiming 77,500.[195] One way or the other, the southern
membership was effectively split in two. And in that July
of 1945 two trade union congresses met in conference, the
Irish TUC from 4th to 6th in Dublin, and the Congress of
Irish Unions from 25th to 27th in Killarney.

-vii-

The ageing William O'Brien was now nearer his ideal of an
Irish-based trade union movement than he had ever been.
The plan that he had proposed nearly ten years earlier was
not only still valid, but had more realism now than it ever
had. The days of conflicting loyalties, of uncertain trade
union brotherhood and ambiguous nationalist feeling were
gone, and everything was clear, everything was explicit
in the polarisation which had taken place. One could now
speak in plain words, demanding the loyalty of Irish workers
for Irish trade unions, demanding that British trade unions

should honourably withdraw and leave Irishmen to handle
their own affairs (such a request was issued by the
Congress of Irish Unions on June 15)[196], arranging for
Irish trade unionists to be compensated for any benefits
they might lose in leaving British unions, confident that
this was really the only tie that held them to alien
organisations.[197] O'Brien could look with some confidence
to Lemass and the government, who had immediately informed
the ITUC[198] that they must consider recognising the new
congress - even before it had been formally established.
True, Lemass had deplored the fact that there was a
divided organisation, particularly as this impeded the
discussions he had planned to have with the trade unions
on arrangements to meet the surge of postwar problems;[199]
but it was quite clear where he thought the solution should
lie. 'The trade union situation here', he said,[200] 'is, to
say the least of it, unusual. It is the result of the fact
that the achievement of national independence occurred after
the development of modern trade unions in Great Britain, and
by modern trade unions I mean national unions as distinct
from purely local organisations. It will, I feel sure, be
agreed that if national independence had been accomplished
earlier, the British trade unions would not have extended
their operations to this country, no more than they extended them to Denmark or Belgium or other adjacent independent states.' Because the government needed to discuss with
the trade union movement legislative and social problems,
they viewed the existing disunity with very grave anxiety.
'The government would welcome a development which would lead
to a reestablishment of one central organisation of Irish
trade unions, an organisation which it could consult, in the
confidence that the opinion received would be fully representative, free from political bias and derived from consideration
of the interests of the workers related only to national
circumstances. If that development should result from a
voluntary withdrawal of British unions from activity within
the State, the government would have no reason to deplore it
and every reason to welcome it.'

But the greatest strength of the Congress of Irish Unions
lay in the working of the Trade Union Tribunal under part III
of the 1941 Act.[201]   Lemass, when   challenged by James
Dillon in Dail Eireann[202] that 'certain types of trade unions
are to be eschewed and others approved; in fact that a trade
union to survive in this country must follow the design
approved by the Taoiseach', denied it heatedly, and claimed
that the government wished to proceed by agreement and did not
propose 'to take power to require conformity with any pre-
determined plan.'[203]   But in fact the Trade Union Acts, as
we have seen, gave the Irish-based unions -and indeed a
large general union such as the Irish Transport - a very
considerable advantage, so considerable that a number of the
amalgamated unions themselves began to feel that their days
were numbered. True, immediately after the split, the
Irish TUC still looked very strong; so many Irish-based
unions remained affiliated to it. But when one examined
the position more closely, one found that these Irish-
based unions were of little significance in the expansionary
plans of the Congress of Irish Unions, since they were largely
specialised unions in the public service area. If the
tribunal worked in the way anticipated, the postwar expansion
should benefit the general workers in the Irish Transport,
the distributive workers and the Dublin craft unions, all
well-represented in the CIU. And finally, even if there was
a challenge to O'Brien from his erstwhile trade union
colleagues that he had not brought the trade union movement
with him, that many of his own members deplored the split,
that trades councils still continued to remain affiliated
to the ITUC and continued at the same time to retain in
affiliation branches of CIU unions,[204] even if all that were
true (and there was much substance in it) O'Brien believed
that these men spoke only on behalf of the small labour
leadership in the country, but that he himself, with his
simple direct nationalist appeal was nearer the heart of the
people and that consequently he would ultimately prevail.

It is not surprising then that O'Brien, on April 14 1945 -
that is immediately the breach occurred - should have made
application to the trade union tribunal in respect of the
road passenger and tramway service of CIE.[205]   We have
seen how this was blocked by a High Court action instituted
by the National Union of Railwaymen, but when the Congress
of Irish Unions met in Killarney at the end of July 1945,
they had already won the first round when Gavan Duffy had
held for the tribunal earlier in the month. It was not
until a year later that the Supreme Court reversed the
decision, placed the amalgamated unions on an equal footing
with the Irish unions and effectively established the
principle that if men wanted a multiplicity of unions on
the job there should be nothing to inhibit it.

But although all this is so, we nevertheless find even in
1945 the unwavering instinct for trade union unity.
Almost immediately there was established an unofficial
unity committee[206] - which however could make little
headway. There were many who wished to build bridges,
particularly Louie Bennett,[207] and even in the dark days of
July 1945 the social evening which was arranged by the ITUC
for the delegates of its Congress was attended by members
of CIU unions, causing one delegate to say the following
day:[208]   'We must throw our minds back to the very fine
demonstration of unity that we had at the social function
last night when we had amongst us members of the Unions that
had disaffiliated, men who have given long service to the
movement and who have been loyal friends of those on the
platform and in Congress ... I am a rank and file worker
myself, and I know that every worker deplores the differences
that exist between the prominent men in the Movement.
Let us forget what O'Brien did or what any other man did,
let us bear that in mind and be big enough and strong
enough to consider, first, the interests of the rank and
file who will suffer most as a result of this split.'
There were many throughout the trade union movement who felt
the same.

Notes on Chapter Six

1.   Judge Ph.D. thesis Appendix II.

2.   See p.198 above,
        However, all Irish·based unions by no means supported
        the principle of an exclusively Irish trade union
        movement. See p.277 below.

3.   William O'Brien Ms. no. 13974.

4.   ITUC Special Conference October 23 1941.

5.   ibid. p.20.

6.   ibid. p.7.

7.   ibid. p.7.

8.   See p.203 above.

9.   ibid. p.20.

10.   ibid. p.25.

11.   ibid. p.11.

12.   The lack of involvement of Northern Ireland trade
        unionists during this time is particularly remarkable.
        In contrast to the 2% which they represented at
        this time, the percentage in 1901 was 32% of the
        total and even in 1937 and 1938 it was 17%. On the
        other hand there were no cross-Channel delegates
        in 1901 and even in the critical year of 1937 these
        delegates did not number more than 9%. The 20 cross-
        Channel delegates that attended the October 1941
        conference represented about 16% of the total.
        See p.148 above.

13.   ITUC Special Conference October 1941   p.19.

14.   ibid. pp. 25-27.

15.   Trade Union Act, 1942 no. 23 of 1942.

16.   ITUC Special Conference October 1941, pp.24-28.

17.   W.J. Whelan of the DTPS, who was secretary of the
        Council of Irish Unions, was stung by Kyle's remarks
        to reply: 'They would think it was a crime that they,
        as Irishmen, should go to see a Minister of the Irish
        Government. Mr Kyle had not told them that his Union
        had sent over representatives, and that the day before
        a queue had to be formed of representatives of cross-
        Channel Unions going to see the Minister about the Act.'
        (ITUC Special Conference, p.34).

18.   ITUC Special Conference October 1941 p.30.

19.   Crawford's proposal in its final form was: 'That
        this conference decides to advise affiliated Unions
        not to register under the Act.' (ibid. p.11).

20.   ibid. p.31.

21.   ibid. p.31.

22.   ibid. p.42.

23.   This also automatically brought into play section 11,
        which withdrew from all except holders of negotiating
        licences the protection of the Trade Disputes Act 1906.

24.   ITUC Special Conference: March Report p.6.

25.   ibid. p.7.

26.   O'Shannon's reply to this criticism incidentally
        throws light on the state of trade union organisation
        throughout the country at the time. 'There are',
        he said (ibid. p.19), 'counties like Donegal, Mayo,
        Longford, Monaghan and Leitrim in which there is
        practically no Trade Union movement of any kind at
        all and in which the movement - and, to some extent,
        the Labour Party - has no contact ... There were a
        number of counties like Kerry, Carlow, Tipperary,
        Galway, Waterford, Wexford and Cavan and some others
        in which we did make contact but found that it was
        impossible for the local people to get a meeting
        of the Trade Union Act at all ... Let me say quite
        frankly that even in some of the counties in which we
        had meetings it took me four or five times to write
        to local people to get them even to reply and some of
        them have not replied yet.'

27.   See O'Farrell ibid. p.17.

28.   ibid. pp. 14-15.

29.   ibid. p.19.

30.   ibid. p.16.

31.   ibid. p.9.

32.   ibid. p.32.

33.   ibid. p.32.

34.   ITUC Annual Congress 1942 p.111.

35.   See p.233 above.

36.   ibid. p.28.

37.   An ESB Pensions Bill of the time, which included an
        anti-strike clause,greatly contributed to the general
        concern. This too was quickly amended by Lemass.

38.   Indeed the whole act had been designed to come into
        operation on a gradual basis, section 6 being im-
        plemented by order 'not earlier than six months
        after the passing of the Act' (Section 6(9)) and Part III
        coming into operation not earlier than six months
        after that again (Section 18).

39.   ITUC Special Conference March 1942 pp.22-23.

40.   ibid. p.19.

41.   ITUC 1942 p.23.

42.   ibid. p.70.

43.   ibid. p.22.

44.   ITUC 1943 p.101. The amalgamated unions at this
        time may have been to some extent influenced by
        developments in Britain where the TUC
        Southport conference in 1943 instructed the general
        council to conduct an inquiry into trade union structure
        and closer unity. An interim report came before the
        Blackpool Congress in 1944 and a final report came
        before the Brighton Congress in October 1946. The
        report was published by the TUC in 1946 under the
        title   Trade Union Structure and Closer Unity.
        However, the report aimed more at the better
        organisation of the functions of trade unions than
        the better organisation of the unions themselves:
        while amalgamations and systems of common working
        were recommended, the unions were explicitly left in
        charge of their own specific areas, and their
        legitimacy in such areas was not challenged. This
        would tend to reinforce the line taken continuously
        by the amalgamated unions at the Irish TUC. It is
        probable that the British thinking became much more
        influential in Ireland some years later when the
        unity talks began and when a number of solutions were
        under consideration. (See p.467 below)

45.   ibid. p.102.

46.   Sections 22 and 23.

47.   ITUC Annual Congress 1943 p.28 But see also p.247.

48.   This in fact was a judicious balance: Hynes of the
        Bricklayers was an Irish union man; but Cairns of the
        Post Office Workers Union, while not from an amalgamated
        union,was from a union which had supported the
        amalgamated position in 1939. See p.154 above. See
        also p.205 above.

49. One suspects that they wished to avoid the appointment
     of a lawyer, a profession they distrusted. In fact,
     D. Sullivan, the chief conciliation officer of the
     Department of Industry and Commerce, was appointed.

50. ITUC 1944 p.29.

51. ITUC 1944 p.30.

52. Apparently proceedings at the Tribunal hearings were
     both legalistic and tedious, providing an additional
     reason for the Congress initiative. (See Louie
     Bennett ITUC 1945 p.108.)

53. ITUC 1943 p.101.

54. ITUC 1944 pp.25-26

55. ITUC 1944 p.30.

56. ITUC 1945 p.20.

57. NUR v. Sullivan [1947] I.R.77.

58. The court sittings were on 3, 4 and 6 July 1945;
     while Congress was held almost on the same days,
     4, 5 and 6 July.

59. Emergency Powers (no.166) Order 1942.

60. The base was 100 for July 1914.

61. ITUC 1943 p.71.

62. idem.

63. ITUC 1944 p.24.

64. ITUC 1943 p.24.

65. Meenan: The Irish Economy Since 1922, op.cit.p. 210.

66. See William Norton ITUC 1944 pp.91,92.

67. Emergency Powers (no.83) Order 1941.

68. ITUC 1942 p.30.

69. Emergency Powers (no.166) Order 1942.

70. ITUC 1942 p.30. See also p. 211 above.

71. ITUC 1942 p.76.

72. ITUC 1942 p.112.

73.   ITUC 1942 p.114.

74.   ibid. p.104.

75.   This is a complex matter; it does not necessarily mean that they supported Fianna Fail in the same sense as that in which they supported trade unions. See the discussion on the organisation of roles, p.117 above.

76.   ITUC 1942 p.117.

77.   SR & O 1942 No.121 is an alternative reference to Emergency Powers (no.166) Order 1942. See also ITUC 1942 pp. 30-32, 70, 113-114.

78.   i.e. normally they had to be referred to the advisory tribunals but exceptionally to the Railway Wages Board, the trade boards (under the Trade Boards Acts 1909-1918) or apprenticeship committees under the Act of 1931.

79.   It is interesting to see how this was done. First, strikes were defined under article 1, a notoriously difficult task: 'The word "strike" means the cessation of work by a body of employees acting in combination, or a concerted refusal or a refusal under a common understanding of any number of employees or persons who were employees to continue to work or to accept employment.' Then article 7 provided: 'The provisions of the Trade Disputes Act 1906 shall not apply to any act done in contemplation of a strike which is designed or calculated to cause an employer to contravene (whether by act or omission) Article 4 of this Order, and any such act shall be deemed, for the purpose of the Conspiracy and Protection of Property Act 1875 and the said Trade Disputes Act 1906, not to be done in contemplation or furtherance of a trade dispute.'

80.   ITUC 1943 p.25.

81.   ibid. p.26.

82.   Emergency Powers (no.260) Order 1943.

83.   ITUC 1943 p.26.

84.   ITUC 1943 p.25. The same procedure of consultation and amendment was repeated during 1943-1944.

85.   ibid. p.25.

86.   See W.J. Farrell ITUC 1944 p.117.

87.   Meenan op.cit. p.66.

88.   ITUC 1944 p.117.

89.   ITUC 1942 p.32.

90.   ITUC 1942 p.22.

91.   ibid.

92.   ibid.

93.   ITUC 1942 p.86.

94.   ITUC 1942 p.121: The text of the motion was:
        'Delegates to an Annual Congress or Special Congress
        must be bona fide members of a Trade Union affiliated
        to Congress and members or permanent officials of the
        organisation electing them to represent it at Congress.'
        Both the mover, Cairns, and the seconder, Kyle,
        urged, ingenuously, the need to exclude persons who
        were not trade unionists or organisations such as
        tenants associations, a point which could have been
        met by requiring that delegates be members of bona fide
        trade unions, whether affiliated to Congress or not;
        but of course the purpose was to exclude Larkin.

95.   ITUC 1942 p.126.

96.   ITUC 1943 pp.32, 89.

97.   ITUC 1943 p.91.

98.   ITUC 1942 p.119.

99.   See The Labour Party: Official statement relating
        to the disaffiliation of the Irish Transport and
        General Workers Union Dublin: February 1944. See
        also Labour Party: Report for the year 1944, p.2.

100.   From 9 seats in 1938 to 17 in 1943.

101.   William O'Brien: Circular letter to all branch
        secretaries January 15 1944. O'Brien papers 15676(1).

102.   The Labour Party official statement op.cit. p.3.

103.   ibid. p.5.

104.   ibid. p.5.

105.   ibid. p.4.

106.   ibid. p.3.

107.   ibid. p.7.

108.   ibid. p.7.

109.   ibid. pp. 7-8.

110.   Johnson papers Ms. 17197.

111.   Donal Nevin in Secret Societies in Ireland, ed.
        T. Desmond Williams p.171.

112.	Johnson papers op.cit. p.5.

113.	The italics are in the original.

114.	From an interview with Donal Nevin.

115.	William O'Brien papers: Ms 15676(1).

116.	Donal Nevin in Secret Societies in Ireland op.cit. p.173.

117.	Johnson papers op.cit. pp. 7-8.

118.	ibid. p.8.

119.	Labour Party Committee of Inquiry p.2. Johnson papers 17267.

120.	William O'Brien papers: Ms 13960.

121.	Whyte op.cit. p.71.

122.	Johnson papers 17267.

123.	ibid. p.4.

124.	In the election of January 1944 Fianna Fail improved its position from an uncertain 67 seats in 1943 to a comfortable 76. All the other parties disimproved but none as disastrously as Labour. The poll was a low one.

125.	Donal Nevin in Secret Societies in Ireland op.cit. p.173.

126.	James Everett, James P. Pattison, John O'Leary, Dan Spring and T.D. Looney.

127.	T.J. Murphy, Richard Corish and Patrick Hogan.

128.	Hickey was chairman of the Party (ITUC 1942 p.43).

129.	Labour Party: Official Statement op.cit. p.6.

130.	The formal reunion took place in 1950.

131.	For a description of the relations between the ITUC and the Labour Party see Labour Party: Annual Report 1944 p.2.

132.	ITUC 1943 p.140.

133.	It was later published as a pamphlet, Belfast 1944.

134.	See p.100 above.

135.	ITUC 1944 p.79.

136.	ITUC 1944 p.80.

137.	National Arbitration Order (58a).

138. ITUC 1944 p.75.

139. ibid. p.81.

140. ITUC 1942 p.69.

141. The Irish National Teachers Organisation, a union, which, while it had members north and south, relied heavily on primary teachers in catholic schools.

142. ITUC 1942 p.79.

143. ITUC 1943 p.38.

144. ITUC 1944 p.27. From the outset it was known as the Northern Ireland Committee.

145. ITUC 1944 p.27.

146. ITUC 1944 p.98. Macgougan at that time represented the Clerical and Administrative Workers Union, Belfast.

147. ITUC 1945 p.158; Binks represented the same union.

148. See later Chapter 8.

149. There were at the 1943 annual conference in Cork 49 delegates with addresses in Belfast or elsewhere in the north, or approximately 24% of the total. This compares with only 17% in 1937 and 1938 (see p.149), But Belfast was at war, and Cork was far distant from it, and this may have had its attractions.

150. See p.198.

151. ITUC 1943 p.109.

152. ibid. p.110.

153. ITUC 1944 p.101.

154. ITUC 1944 p.22.

155. ITUC 1943 p.43. There was an increase from 5 per cent to 16 per cent on the county councils 'making Labour the largest single party on many of the local authorities.'

156. ITUC 1943 p.97.

157. ITUC 1943 p.98.

158. ITUC 1942 p.109.

159. ibid. p.159

160.   ITUC 1943 p.130.

161.   ITUC 1943 p.117.

162.   Congress of Irish Unions: A History of the Foundation:
       Reports of proceedings of the first annual meeting ...
       and second annual meeting 1946 p.4.

163.   ibid. p.22.

164.   ibid. p.39.

165.   See p.195 above.

166.   Although the Commission on Vocational Organisation
       had not reported, we note in 1942 (ITUC 1942 p.164)
       a growing sympathy with the Portuguese form of
       corporatism even among such stalwarts as Louie
       Bennett, causing J.T. O'Farrell of the Railway Clerks'
       Association (an amalgamated union) to remark at the
       special conference in March 1942 (p.17): 'There is a
       tendency here for some time past to drive us in to a
       more insular and narrower atmosphere than had pre-
       vailed ... There is a very obvious admiration for
       what is known as the Corporate State. You are told
       to look to Portugal as the symbol of what can be
       the Ireland of the future.'

167.   ITUC 1944 p.104.

168.   ITUC 1944 p.105.

169.   ibid. p.106.

170.   Gilbert Lynch in his presidential address to the 1945
       annual conference of the ITUC. ITUC 1945 p.99.

171.   From May 1945 when O'Shannon resigned to October when
       Ruaidhri Roberts was appointed.

172.   ITUC 1945 p.32. The above passage is based on the
       report of the national executive to the 1945 annual
       conference of the ITUC which was drafted by Johnson.

173.   ITUC 1944 p.35.

174.   ibid.

175.   ibid. p.106.

176.   ibid. p.104.

177.   See Judge Ph.D. thesis Appendix II. 1918 was the
       last occasion, and then the relationship between Irish-
       based and amalgamated was not significant.

178.   Of these, ten were affiliated to Congress: the Irish
       Bookbinders and Allied Trades Union; Irish Society
       of Woodcutting Machinists; Electrical Trades Union

(Ireland); Electrotypers' and Stereotypers' Society,
Dublin and District; Building Workers' Trade Union;
Dublin Typographical Provident Society; Irish Union
of Distributive Workers and Clerks; Irish Transport
and General Workers Union; Irish Engineering
Industrial Union; Operative Plasterers' Trade Society.
The other five were: Irish National Painters' and
Decorators' Trade Union; Irish National Union of
Woodworkers; Irish Seamen and Port Workers' Union;
National Union of Sheet Metal Workers; United House
and Ship Painters Trade Union.

179.   CIU op.cit. 1946 p.16.

180.   ITUC 1945 p.30.

181.   ibid.

182.   CIU op.cit. 1946 pp. 17,18.

183.   ITUC 1945 p.41.

184.   This was impossible in the north: 'The Six-County
       Government refuses to recognise or negotiate with
       the Irish Trade Union Congress, but when our
       Government consults the Trade Union Congress it may be
       presented with a decision which represents not the
       views of purely Irish Unions, but of Unions and Union
       officials whose headquarters are outside Ireland.'
       (CIU op.cit. 1946 p.6.)

185.   ibid. p.7.

186.   ITUC 1945 p.60.

187.   Numbers vary slightly in the two accounts, that of the
       CIU and the ITUC, but the difference is not significant.

188.   ITUC 1945 p.60. Nor are there grounds for believing
       that either group had tried to strengthen its position
       by encouraging or blocking affiliations. Those that
       were blocked - apart from the WUI - were blocked
       for jurisdictional reasons (they were since 1941, Irish
       Engineering and Foundry Union, Irish Automobile
       Drivers' and Mechanics' Union and the Irish National
       Union of Vintners Grocers and Allied Trades Assistants);
       and those that were accepted (1941, the Amalgamated
       Engineering Union; 1942: National League of the Blind,
       Amalgamated Union of Upholsterers; 1943: Clerical and
       Administrative Workers Union, National Union of
       Printing Bookbinding and Paper Workers; 1944: National
       Union of Journalists and Building Workers Trade Union -
       an amalgam of some unions already affiliated) showed
       more the beginnings of a white-collar trend than
       anything else.

189. Traditionally there is no contest for the presidency, the vice-president automatically succeeding.

190. In 1942 Getgood was elected vice-president, in 1943 Tom Kennedy, and in 1944 Gilbert Lynch, all unopposed and clearly following an agreed alternation.

191. The other representative of an Irish-based union was P.J. Cairns of the Post Office Workers who would have strongly supported the ITUC position.

192. The four were Louie Bennett of the IWWU, Frank Foley of the Irish Municipal Employees Union, John Swift of the Bakers and James O'Keeffe of the National League of the Blind.

193. For the CIU manifesto CIU op.cit. pp. 19-25; for the ITUC manifesto, ITUC 1945 pp.58-61.

194. Initially the ITUC claimed that the breakaway CIU represented 53,000 workers, of whom 36,000 were in the Irish Transport and 10,000 in the IUDWC. (ITUC 1945 p.31).

195. CIU op.cit. p.45.

196. ibid. p.44 and for the resolution to the same effect ibid. p.46.

197. ibid. p.49.

198. ITUC 1945 p.31. Lemass wrote to the national executive of the ITUC on April 27 1945 and met them on May 7.

199. Dail Debates June 26 1945 col. 1561.

200. ibid. June 27 1945 col. 1658.

201. See p.204 above.

202. Dail Debates June 26 col. 1594.

203. ibid. June 26 col. 1561.

204. ITUC 1945 p.98; CIU op.cit. 1946 p.59.

205. See p. 242 above.

206. ITUC 1945 pp. 122-23.

207. ibid. pp. 123-25.

208. J. Byrne of the Irish Bakers ibid. 129.

Part Two

*From the End of the War
to 1960 and the Unification
of the Trade Union Movement*

Chapter Seven

Post-War Ireland

-i-

Despite the hopes that were expressed immediately after
the split in 1945, despite the recognition of old friend-
ships, despite a number of serious and practical steps to
bridge the divide, it was eight long years before that
fruitful initiative took place which led eventually to
unity, years in which, if anything, the Congresses drifted
further and further apart, causing Leo Crawford to remark
in his hardheaded way that they would not see reunification
in their lifetime.

Nor was it a matter of personal enmities persisting over
the years. William O'Brien had retired in 1946, and within
a year, in early 1947, Big Jim Larkin was dead. There is
no doubt that O'Brien in particular had done a great deal
to bring about the breach; but while he sharpened and increased the sense of conflict, the divide already existed,
profound and apparently irreconcilable, between catholic
nationalist sentiment on the one hand, and, on the other,
the more liberal, mildly socialist British form of trade
unionism.[1] It was a conflict, a dilemma, which, as we have
seen, was experienced in the twenty-six counties of Eire;
the problems in the north, though deeply interwoven with
those of the south, had quite a different dimension.
Furthermore it was a conflict which was intensified by some
remarkable political and social developments which the
south experienced during this period; and it is to these
that we first turn.

Broadly these developments turned on two major events, the
first being the declaration of the Republic in 1949 and
the second the crisis in 1951 concerning maternity welfare
proposals which came to be known as the mother and child
scheme, a crisis which, in Dr Lyons's phrase 'had been
resolved, apparently, by the abject capitulation of the
secular to the spiritual power.'[2] But the background to
these events is important too. This was a grim time for the
south, lying helplessly in its economic doldrums at the
edge of a booming Europe, its emigration at the rate of
40,000 a year or more, the highest indeed since the
eighteen eighties,[3] its external assets - hoarded during
the war - now wasting away, until by 1956 recurrent deficits
had wiped them out, and the number of its unemployed
depressingly great and - as far as anyone could judge -
intractably so. It was not until 1958, towards the very
end of our period, that the Irish society of the south,
uncertainly and with fragile hopes, began to move into the
years of its great economic expansion.

-ii-

Let us consider first the events which led to the declaration
of the Republic and its consequences. Politically, Fianna
Fail was in decline. Looking back now, it might appear
that two coalition governments briefly interrupted the long
reign of de Valera's party, but in fact from 1948 to 1957
Fianna Fail was woefully weak. True, the first inter-party
government - from 1948 to 1951 - ended in the debâcle of the
mother and child crisis, but the Fianna Fail government
that replaced it (and it might well have been otherwise) was
a minority government which in the 1954 election made its
worst showing since 1932, and an interparty government once
again took over and lasted until March 1957 when Fianna Fail

overwhelmed it in a dramatic change of fortune.

One can see immediately how the eclipse of Fianna Fail was
of the greatest importance to the trade union movement since
the Labour Party (quickly mending its differences) was
involved in government in a very immediate way right throughout the period; and the trade union movement naturally
reflected this. It is a matter which we shall discuss more
fully in a later paragraph. For the purposes of the present
discussion, the eclipse of Fianna Fail at the time had two
important consequences. In the first place it brought into
government not only the Labour Party and the farmers' party,
but under the conservative leadership of Fine Gael, the
government also included a radical Republican party, Clann
na Poblachta, which almost overnight had sprung into being.

There were great pressures involved in maintaining a balance
among such disparate interests, and no doubt this was a major
reason why the Taoiseach of the time, John A. Costello,
despite the conservative character of his own party, Fine
Gael, announced in September 1948 (in Canada of all places)
the intention of the Irish government to declare a republic;
and this in fact was done with overt symbolism on Easter
Monday 1949. The people of the new Republic took the
whole business phlegmatically enough; it did not appear to
them to have any great moment. But to Britain it was quite
otherwise; there could now be no ambiguity about the fact
that the Irish government had abandoned the Commonwealth[4]
much in contrast with India which also declared itself to
be a republic in the same year. True, in regard to citizenship and in regard to trade the Republic of Ireland did not
suffer in its relations with Britain, but there was a
devastating reaction in regard to Northern Ireland. Such
fragile constitutional links as existed between north and
south were shattered and in the Ireland Act of the same year,
1949, the Westminster government reinforced in a very explicit
manner the status of the northern province as an integral
part of the United Kingdom.[5]

If the object were the achievment of a twenty-six county
republic the matter could have ended there. But the object
of nationalist sentiment was never that; on the contrary
its object was the achievement of a thirty-two county
republic - in a word the inclusion of the north within the
republic - and this in fact was what made the whole problem
so intractable. The loyalist majority in the north were
of course vehemently and utterly opposed to any such idea
(and the Ireland Act was intended to give their opposition
statutory support)[6] but in the south, persistently and unwaveringly, the views of the majority in the north were
sidestepped and the whole problem was seen in terms of
British domination of a part of Ireland, sustained by
British imperial self-interest and capable of being remedied
by a British imperial capitulation. The two views of the
same set of circumstances were grotesquely out of phase.

We come now to the second consequence of the eclipse of
Fianna Fail in 1948. De Valera, now out of office, was
free to bend his energies to an international campaign
against the partition of Ireland, which he conducted in the
United States, in Australia and in Britain itself;   as an
idea it began to dominate Ireland's foreign relations
during the first half of the decade of the fifties. Ireland's
'sore thumb' policy regarding the north, its readiness to
raise the question abrasively on every international
occasion, gave to those outside these islands a good deal
of puzzlement and some tedium, but at home, it gave to
the northern loyalists a powerful sense of being beleaguered
and to the republican movement an equally powerful sense of
the rightness of their cause.

But then quite clearly the attempt to woo radical republicans
into the paths of parliamentary democracy failed. In the
election of 1951, MacBride's party was almost wiped out (the
mother and child controversy had a great deal to do with it
of course) and, even in 1954 when the interparty government
again took office, Clann na Poblachta was only a shadow,
with three deputies in Dail Eireann. MacBride agreed to

support the government but he refused a ministry, hoping
perhaps, by a stance of critical non-involvement, to recover
the support of those who drank from the pure republican
well. But the signs were ominous. It is doubtful if
many in the military wing of the republican movement were
ever tempted by parliamentary democracy; and in the more
indulgent days of the first interparty government, the IRA
were able to regroup. Soon after the eclipse of MacBride,
raids began for arms both in the north and in Britain,
particularly during 1954 and 1955. And then on December 12
1956 the IRA launched their campaign 'operation harvest,
to destroy(in the north) key installations, buildings,
custom posts, oil refineries, bridges and RUC barracks.'[7]
The government anxiously and somewhat uncertainly began to
move against them, and MacBride, on whose support it
depended for office, proposed in Dail Eireann a vote of
no confidence, both on the grounds of the government's
economic performance and on the grounds that it had failed
to unify the country. Fianna Fail's triumphant return in
the election that followed resulted in a vigorous attempt
to dominate the IRA, although its campaign of violence
against the north did not in fact come to an end until 1962.

The second major event which indicates the character of
the period was the mother and child crisis. We must
remember that in these years the great popular movement
which was Roman Catholicism in Ireland had entered its most
triumphalist phase. We must remember too that the Republic's
war-time isolation was ended not so much by the European
Recovery Programme, nor by the substantial sums received
in American aid; it was ended primarily by the magic of
the Holy Year when in 1950 thousands of Irish men and women
made the trip to Rome to visit as pilgrims the great
basilicas. It was a return not to the Anglo-American world
but to the ancient world of Christendom. The Congress of
Irish Unions decided formally at their annual conference
of that year to send two representatives to Rome 'to convey

to the Holy Father the loyalty and homage of the Irish
Working Class.'[8] This was much more than a formality.
The two representatives, Leo Crawford and Michael Colgan,
that is to say the secretary and the president of Congress,
could, in their written report to the following Congress
in 1951, say: 'It was a never-to-be-forgotten experience
when the Holy Father came out ... on the balcony of the
Castel and spoke to the crowds in the courtyard ... The
crowning moment of our experience was when we knelt for his
Apostolic Benediction as the shades of night were closing
in on the scene.'[9] Furthermore, from a very limited budget,
the Congress the following year sent two other representatives
to Rome 'to represent the workers of Ireland at the
celebrations' in connection with the diamond jubilee of
the publication of 'Rerum Novarum', the social encyclical of
Leo XIII. It is hardly surprising then to find at the same
Congress of 1951 explicit support for the recommendations
of the Commission on Vocational Organisation.[10]

It was in such a context, in such a climate of opinion,
that the bishops spoke. Their authority was unquestioned in
the field of education, and in many matters of social policy.
But it went further than that. For example they laid down
by episcopal instruction the precise hours within which
dancing should take place in their various dioceses[11] and this
was accepted without demur by the secular authority.
Consequently when they opposed Dr Browne's mother and child
scheme as being contrary to catholic teaching, the government
crumbled. In fact the high point of Catholic Church influence
had already been reached and during the late fifties it
began to wane; however this was not at all obvious at the time,
and when the bishops spoke, they spoke with considerable
legitimacy. The mother and child crisis, therefore, demonstrated
to the loyalist north in particular, the dominance of Rome
politically and socially.

But there were not two attitudes in the south, one catholic
and one nationalist; on the contrary the chemistry of popular

feeling, since they were both popular movements, blended them into one, giving the society of the time its unique character. The legitimacy of a bishop's ukase therefore sprang not from catholicism alone but from a special value system which incorporated nationalism as well. When the bishops strayed beyond this, even their legitimacy tended to evaporate. For example in January 1956, in most comprehensive terms, they had declared that it was a mortal sin not only to be a member of the IRA, but even to offer it approval.[12] Yet one year later, when two young men were killed in an attack on a police barracks in Northern Ireland, one of them, Sean South, 'an ardent Catholic (and) a former member of the Legion of Mary',[13] was given quite spontaneously a heroic funeral by the people of his native Limerick in which large numbers of clergy took part.

The point here is that within this catholic-nationalist value system we are confronted not merely with nationalist sentiment, but one which went further, which accepted, if it did not honour, a kind of romantic militarism, a romantic recourse to violence in political matters, to such an extent that the bishops' pleas for peace appeared theoretical and unreal. And equally unreal to those nationalists who were trade union members was the great tradition of peace within the trade union movement itself. Here the two trade union positions were sharply divergent, and divergent in a manner which discussion could not readily overcome, indeed in respect of which discussion was profoundly inhibited. There was for example the brief but remarkable debate at the Congress of Irish Unions 1957 annual conference when unity was already largely accomplished, which demonstrated how perilous the divide really was. On December 12 1956 the Provisional United Trade Union Organisation (the temporary umbrella committee of the two congresses) because of recent events in Hungary and the Middle East had issued a statement rejecting war and the use of violence and went on: 'We further declare our belief that in this critical hour of history, the workers of Ireland can most effectively declare their adherence to the ideals of Peace and Freedom

by adding to their generous sympathy for the present victims
of oppression a renunciation on the part of the Irish people
of the use of violence whether by the association of our
country with groupings of Powers for warlike aims, or by
a deliberate resort to repression or violence by any authority
or any group concerned with political differences and problems
affecting Ireland. We assert our confidence that although
our country is among the smallest of nations, our people
can be of assistance in the resolution of the conflicts
which beset the world if in our own affairs we resolutely
adhere to the principles of Charity upon which Peace and
Freedom depend.'[14] In accordance with agreed procedure,
the report containing this statement came before the
delegates of the Congress of Irish Unions at their annual
conference the following July. But by now the IRA had
launched their campaign against the north; the sentiment
in the statement was being put to the test. Two delegates
used the occasion to complain about internment without
trial under the Offences Against the State Act, but Sean
O'Murchu of Cork[15] came straight to the point: 'I feel
I am expressing', he said, 'not alone my own personal views
but ... the views of a large volume of the opinion of the
members of my union[16] ... Insofar as this Section of the
Report implies in any way a repudiation of what James
Connolly did in 1916, then it is repugnant to every feeling
I have and to every feeling which I hold dear. I suggest
that if you ... make a subscription to the principles of
Charity ... the best thing that this Congress could do
would be to agree to a proposition - that you mark this as
read, pass it in silence and let it rest in peace with the
spirit of James Connolly a great Labour leader who was
also a great soldier.' What is interesting here is not so
much the remarks of an IRA sympathiser but rather the
reaction of the Congress to them. Only two other persons
contributed. The president, Larry Hudson, said that the
PUO statement referred to Hungary and the Middle East; he

also suspected that the delegates who raised the question
were speaking for themselves and not for their unions.
But the healing remarks were made by P.J. O'Brien,[17] also
of Cork; they are significant since they clearly summarised
the feeling of the conference. '(He) said that there were
obviously people there identified with another section of
the national movement who felt it was their duty to adopt
a certain stand ... They could get into aspects of that
particular matter which would bring a large division of
opinion amongst their members, and consequently, he thought
the best thing they could do was to move "next business".'
On a show of hands this was agreed.

Throughout our period therefore, we can see the Congress
of Irish Unions struggling with this terrible dilemma, its
insistent demand for Irish-based and Irish controlled unions
on the one hand, but at the same time an equal insistence
that the north must be included in the solution. And what
could be said of the north? To the loyalists, southern
Ireland had become more, not less, alien, alien in its
vehement republicanism and anti-British sentiment and alien
also in the strange and (in their eyes) superstitious dominance
of the Roman church. And yet despite all this, reconciliation
did take place and a solution was found. In the south, as
we shall see, there was the fact of the united Labour Party
participating in government, the fact of common problems
of an imperative kind, the fact of Irish-based unions within
the Irish Trade Union Congress, uneasy themselves with
British influence, but above all there was the simple
fact of a growing goodwill among a number of trade union
leaders on each side.

More than that, throughout the whole period the trade unions
in the north remained faithful to the idea of a united all-
Ireland trade union movement, when many felt that the logic
of their position was to abandon the Republic altogether
and form an Ulster TUC. Before tracing the difficult path
of reconciliation in the south, therefore, we shall first

consider the north, and the efforts of the trade unions there
to maintain and develop common institutions with such a
troublesome south and at the same time secure recognition
from an intensely conservative and deeply suspicious
northern administration.

It is necessary, however, as a preliminary to our discussion
both of the north and of the south, to review briefly the
picture of the trade union movement in Ireland as it appears
from the figures for trade union membership.

-iii-

We are fortunate that the research department of the Irish
Trade Union Congress undertook in 1952-53 a survey of all
trade union membership in the country. The results of the
survey were published in two issues of Trade Union Information
in early 1953;[18] they were taken up subsequently by the
joint committee of the two congresses, which had been
established soon after to promote trade union unity, and
were published in summary form as an appendix to the committee's
Joint Memorandum on Trade Union Unity in April 1954. The
important point was that the survey did not rely merely
on the returns of the unions themselves, not merely on the
figures officially returned to the registrars or other
official bodies. The efforts to secure accuracy and comprehensiveness are evident from the account given in the
first article on March 1953, which we have set out in full
in appendix six.

This however was a very sensitive area, and it is not
surprising that the Congress of Irish Unions did not
explicitly support their accuracy. Indeed each congress
also published appendices to the same Joint Memorandum on
Trade Union Unity setting out the returns which they themselves

had received from their affiliated unions; and a footnote
went on to say[19] in a markedly neutral fashion that the
figures from the survey were 'regarded by the Irish Trade
Union Congress as presenting a more comprehensive picture
of trade union membership in Ireland than can be gained
from affiliation figures alone and of course (significantly)
the analysis of membership between Northern Ireland and
the Republic etc. which are relevant to the present discussion
cannot be based upon affiliation figures.' Nonetheless
the very fact that they were published in the Joint
Memorandum gives them considerable authority.

One of the difficulties was that the survey figures departed
substantially from the figures supplied by the two great
transport unions. We can see (appendix eight) that, judging
from the survey, the Irish Transport and General Workers
Union had overestimated its membership by 20,000. The
survey report says:[20] 'According to the return made to the
Registrar of Friendly Societies, the membership of the
Irish Transport and General Workers' Union at the end of
1950 was 116,257. The membership returned to the Department
of Industry and Commerce as at April 1951, was 140,439.
The membership given in the seventh annual report of the
Congress of Irish Unions for 1951 was 130,000.' The ITUC
survey estimated the figure to be 128,000, and although
the point is referred to in some detail in the summary
which appears with the Joint Memorandum, it is not
challenged by the Irish Transport. It is true of course
that everybody recognised how difficult it was to be
accurate in these matters, particularly in the case of a
large general union with some fluctuation in membership.
The Amalgamated Transport and General Workers' Union is
also remarkable, but in its case, for underestimation.
In the return it made itself to the ITUC (see appendix eight)
it had declared only 40,000 members while the ITUC survey
calculated its membership to be 90,000. If we contrast the
two congresses, we find that in the case of the CIU there is

reasonable correspondence between the affiliated membership
of the unions and the membership estimated by the survey
(188,929 as against 172,454); but there is remarkable
underaffiliation apparent in the case of the ITUC which
could not be accounted for by the underaffiliation of the
Amalgamated Transport alone. The full membership of the
unions affiliated to the Irish Trade Union Congress was
calculated from the survey to be 297,866 while the declared
membership (see appendix eight) amounted to a mere 210,663.
It is likely that this reflected a growing uncertainty on
the part of the amalgamated unions with regard to their
future in the Republic and with regard to their relations
with the Irish Trade Union Congress.

As far as the Republic was concerned, the second article
in Trade Union Information[21] provided a chart, which is
reproduced in appendix seven. It will be seen that at
the time, the unions with chief offices in the Republic
represented an overwhelming 86% of the 319,343 organised
workers. One is also struck by the large number of very
small unions; but on the other hand even if one estimates
the Irish Transport at 128,000, it represents two-fifths
of the total trade union membership. Here we speak of
all unions based in the Republic, whether they were
affiliated to the Irish Trade Union Congress or the Congress
of Irish Unions. When we view the Irish Transport in the
context of the Congress of Irish Unions alone, we find that
it represented fully three-quarters of all the affiliated
membership; and we shall notice from time to time an unease among the smaller unions at the sheer dominating
advantage in numbers which the Irish Transport possessed,
despite its judicious reserve in matters of office.

Let us turn to the difficult and uncertain topic of
classification of trade unions in the Republic at this
time. Trade Union Information in its second article[22]
attempted a classification, which we have reproduced in
appendix seven. It is interesting to compare this to a

chart which Judge[23] (see appendix nine) prepared in which
he followed the classification which William O'Brien had
introduced as memorandum I in the 1939 Commission of
Inquiry (see appendix four) but recast to take account of
the membership and the types of trade unions as they
existed in 1950. Judge himself remarks on the difficulty
of classifying in the first instance, and also on the
difficulty of avoiding duplication. One must exercise
great caution therefore in basing any conclusions on the
figures. For example when we compare Judge's table with
O'Brien's (see above p.145) we find an astonishing fall
in rail and road transport and also in printing and
publishing, which, one suspects, is a problem principally
of classification.

What is noteworthy and of great importance, however, is
the growth of general unions from O'Brien's 1939 figure of
38,000 to a 1950 figure of something approaching 200,000.
The ITUC survey estimated the figure for general unions
to be 170,000, somewhat less than Judge's figure; but it
classifies the other unions quite differently, and it is
difficult therefore to be sure that one is comparing like
with like. The fact remains however that the figure is
significantly large.[23A] The astonishing growth of the general
unions during this time is further borne out in a recent
study by Hillery and Kelly of University College Dublin,[24]
remarkable even for a period when trade union membership
generally was growing rapidly. We set out some of their
findings in appendix eleven, where we see that between 1945
and 1950, membership of general unions more than doubled,
from 80,335 to 163,038 (which is much nearer the ITUC survey
figure than Judge's) while they estimate that trade union
membership as a whole increased from 172,000 to 285,000.[25]
To appreciate fully, however, the extent of the increase
in general union membership[26] we should note that they
estimate the increase in membership in the other union

categories, white-collar and craft, as merely 17% and 9%
respectively during the period. But of course they also
warn about the difficulties of classification; certainly
some increase in general union membership must be accounted
for by an increase in white-collar membership, for example.[27]

According to Hillery and Kelly, the percentage of members
in British-based unions declined substantially during
the period (see appendix twelve)which, after an initial
absolute increase from 1945 to 1950, experienced not only
a percentage decline in relation to total trade union
membership but an actual decline in numbers during the whole
period of the fifties, not picking up again until the early
years of the following decade.

In the Republic therefore there was in the years immediately
after the war's end a very rapid increase in trade union
membership, an increase which was experienced principally
by the general unions which were Irish-based; the British-
based unions on the whole failed to sustain the increase,
and throughout the period they appeared to be in decline.[28]

In the case of Northern Ireland, the survey reported in
Trade Union Information (see appendix seven) also set out
a summary membership chart. The contrast with the Republic
could not be clearer; ninety per cent of the 194,000
organised workers were in British-based unions, and, of the
number that remained, more than half were in unions with
chief offices in Northern Ireland, leaving a figure of
8,000 or so as members of five unions with chief offices
in the Republic. But there is a strong similarity of
structure with the Republic; we note the very large number
of very small unions, while the Amalgamated Transport Union,
mirroring the Irish Transport in the south, represented
two-fifths of the total membership. In contrast with the
Irish Transport and the CIU, however, the Amalgamated Transport
had not anything like the same dominance in number in relation
to the ITUC.

In the north as well there was a rapid increase in trade
union membership immediately after the war. D.W. Bleakley[29]
in 1954 estimated that membership rose from 142,000 in 1945
to 200,000 in 1953. We set out in appendix thirteen the
various tables of trade union membership which he derived
largely from official sources.

There is a further contrast with the south. In the north
there are a number of trade union federations, particularly
in engineering, building and printing, the most important
being the Confederation of Shipbuilding and Engineering Unions.
This is a national federation, with at the time forty-eight
district committees, of which one was in Belfast. Affiliated
to it were twenty-five national unions.[30] In the case of the
building industry the National Federation of Building Trade
Operatives was founded in 1918, and indeed, as far as the
amalgamated unions were concerned, extended its activities
to the south.[31] These federations were not merely consultative bodies; they had the power to negotiate wages
and working conditions, and according to Bleakley the
National Federation of Building Trade Operatives 'had a
great deal of authority in regard to strike action.'[32]
Bleakley goes on: 'Since a good many delegates to the
District Committees of these bodies are trade union
officials, the decisions arrived at exert a considerable
influence on local industry.'[33] It is clear of course that
the existence of these federations greatly simplified trade
union representation at a provincial level; their number
was small and in conjunction with the Amalgamated Transport
they could be urged as a non-contentious alternative to
the ITUC Northern Committee. Once again, the point of
greatest interest was the continued support for the Northern
Ireland Committee, despite the pressure of the government
and the readiness of the alternative.

One would have imagined that under the influence of Connolly's
syndicalism there should have grown up in the south a stronger

federalist movement, particularly on an industry basis, than existed generally in the United Kingdom. The fact that the contrary was the case probably reflects the difficulty of accommodating the nationalist impulse. When, many years before, in 1906 a federation had been suggested[34] it was seen by many at the time as a Sinn Fein ploy to exclude the amalgamated or British-based unions, and after the splintering in the period from 1917 to 1922[35] when a number of parallel Irish-based unions were established, federation was made extremely difficult. In the north, therefore, despite a similar complexity of structure, the trade union movement presented a more orderly appearance than it did in the south, where it was not only riven between two congresses but was undeveloped as well in federal or industrial terms.[36]

Notes on Chapter Seven

1.   See above pp. 266-71.

2.   F.S.L. Lyons: Ireland Since the Famine op.cit. p.569.
        For an excellent and detailed account of the con-
        troversy, see J.H. Whyte Church and State in Modern Ireland
        op.cit. Chapters VII and VIII.

3.   cf. James Meenan: The Irish Economy Since 1922 p.205.

4.   Lyons op.cit. p.402.

5.   ibid. p.728.

6.   The Ireland Act declared inter alia, that 'in no
        event will Northern Ireland or any part thereof cease
        to be part of His Majesty's dominions and of the
        United Kingdom, without the consent of the parliament
        of Northern Ireland.'

7.   Seamus Breathnach: The Irish Police Anvil Books
        Dublin 1974 p.102.

8.   Congress of Irish Unions 1950 p.132.

9.   Congress of Irish Unions 1951 p.17.

10.   ibid. p.145.

11.   Whyte op.cit. p.304.

12.   Whyte op.cit. p.321.

13.   ibid.

14.   Provisional United Trade Union Organisation: Second
        Report p.36.

15.   CIU 1957 p.151.

16.   O Murchu was a delegate from the Irish Engineering,
        Industrial and Electrical Trade Union.

17.   CIU 1957 p.155.

18.   Trade Union Information Vol.VIII No.43 for March 1953;
        Vol. VIII No.44 for April 1953.

19.   Joint Memorandum on Trade Union Unity (published as an
        appendix to the 1954 Annual Report of the Congress
        of Irish Unions) p.3.

20.   op.cit. March 1953 pp.2-3.

309

21.   op.cit. April 1953.

22.   idem.

23.   Judge op.cit. M.Econ.Sc. thesis 1951.

23A.   Judge also provides figures indicating trade union
       membership at the time, and while, for a number of
       reasons, they are difficult to reconcile precisely
       with the figures here, they do not depart in any
       major way from the affiliated membership reported
       by the ITUC in 1954 (Annual Report p.27) which we
       set out as appendix ten.

24.   B. Hillery and A. Kelly: 'Aspects of Trade Union
       Membership' in Management XXI, 4, April 1974, pp.26-27.

25.   These figures are somewhat less than those estimated
       at the time by the ITUC survey, which gave the total
       figure at the end of 1952 in the Republic as 319,343
       while Hillery and Kelly give it as 304,318 for 1951.
       They do not give information on their sources but
       the general indication is no doubt reliable. However
       all this gives us a further insight into the problem
       of accurately determining trade union membership,
       a problem we have already met in the last chapter
       (p. 197 above).   In its annual report in 1955
       the ITUC state that their affiliated membership (for
       the whole country) appeared to double from 1944 to 1954
       but they go on to say (p.27): 'In 1944 however there
       is little doubt that the affiliated membership of some
       affiliated unions was seriously understated. Also
       a number of unions which were not affiliated in 1944
       have subsequently affiliated in one or other of the
       Congresses. Membership probably did not double between
       1944 and 1954 but there is little doubt that the increase
       was substantial.'

26.   It is difficult to escape the conclusion that what
       was really witnessed was a dramatic increase in the
       membership of the IT & GWU and, to a somewhat lesser
       extent, the WUI. In 1944, the IT had affiliated for
       36,000 members; in 1952 for four times that number,
       148,442. The WUI in 1945 affiliated for 8,000
       members, in 1952 for three times that number, 25,000.
       The Amalgamated Transport on the other hand increased
       during the period from 35,000 to 40,000 (granted, an
       unreliable figure) and the Irish Union of Distributive
       Workers and Clerks from 10,172 to 14,697.

27.   Ruaidhri Roberts in his address to the Statistical
       and Social Inquiry Society in 1959 presented a very
       useful and comprehensive table of trade union membership
       as affiliated to the congresses (see appendix seventeen).
       It is derived essentially from the trade union returns,
       the ITUC figures approximating closely enough to Judge
       (M.Econ.Sc. op.cit.) and the CIU figures corresponding
       exactly. It confirms in a very dramatic way the increase

in membership even during the war years; ('workers
found', said Roberts, 'that increases in wages permitted
under the Emergency Powers Orders could be obtained
almost automatically through a trade union, and there
is no doubt that at this time many groups of workers
joined unions with this purpose in mind') and
particularly in the years immediately after the war
when 'employment in industry expanded rapidly while,
at the same time, the establishment of the Labour
Court, and the pattern of post war wage negotiations
were conducive to trade union membership.' Roberts
goes on in the same address to consider membership
figures as compiled by the Department of Industry and
Commerce (Journal of Statistical and Social Inquiry
Society of Ireland (1958-59) XX: 2 : p.96)) to whom
'returns are made by each union only once in each
period of three years, but these returns include
both British and Irish unions and are probably the
most complete available statements of trade union
membership.' He uses them 'with supplementary
information from other sources' to estimate membership
(probably over the period 1955 to 1958) in the Republic
at 327,185 and in Northern Ireland at 198,000 giving
a total of 525,185 including unions unaffiliated to
Congress which numbered in membership approximately
23,000. These seem a little high. For the Republic,
Hillery estimated the membership in trade unions in
1955 to have been 310,456 and in 1960 318,572 and in
Trade Union Information for March 1957 (Vol.XIII, no.74)
reference is made to the Report of the Registrar for
Friendly Societies for 1955 where the aggregate Northern
Ireland membership at the end of 1954 was given as
189,962. Yet Bleakley, also working from official
sources (see appendix thirteen), gives the Northern
Ireland figure for 1953 as 200,000. All this underlines the difficulty of precision in the matter, but
obviously Bleakley included unions which either were
not registered or if registered had not made returns.

28. A further insight into trade union organisation in the
     Republic in these years is given in a survey on trade
     union finance for the years 1939 to 1951 which was
     published in Trade Union Information Vol.IX, No.52 for
     February-March 1954. The survey was based on the
     returns made to the Registrar of Friendly Societies,
     but at the outset it is recognised that this in itself
     is limiting; there were only '53 trade unions
     registered with the Registrar out of approximately
     115 known to be operating in the twenty six counties.'
     The fact was that the British-based unions did not
     register at all; and of course the myriad civil
     service associations had no reason to. 'Of the un-
     registered unions 30 have their chief offices outside
     the state. Practically all of the 32 other unregistered
     unions are civil service associations.' We have
     already seen that the British-based unions would have

had considerable difficulty in effecting registration
(perhaps they might have registered their Irish office
separately) but of course this did not affect their
eligibility for a negotiating licence. The same
difficulty still exists. In the 1972 Report of the
Registrar for Friendly Societies, the number of
workers' trade unions registered for 1970 was 61
(104 in total, less 43 employers trade unions) while
the number of unions identified by Congress in the
Republic was 95 (see appendix five). There are however,
some interesting figures which emerge. In 1951 as reported in
Trade Union Information (op.cit.), the 115 unions in
the Republic represented 320,000 members, while the
53 registered unions represented only 240,834, according
to their returns to the Registrar. In 1970 the 95
unions in the Republic represented 386,000 members
(see appendix five) while the 61 registered unions
returned a membership of 326,644 (Report of Registrar
of Friendly Societies 1972: i.e. a gross figure of
338,058 less employers number 11,414). This means
that while in 1951 the registered unions represented
75 per cent of all trade unionists in the Republic,
in 1970 they represented 85% - probably indicating as
much as anything else the tendency for public service
unions to register formally.

The article in Trade Union Information February/March
1954 concerned itself of course with finance, and
perhaps before leaving the period it is interesting
to remark that in 1951 members contributed, in the
case of the registered trade unions a total of
£447,092 which represented an average annual contribution of £1.17.2 per annum, or 8½d. per week
(which Trade Union Information stated was a little
more than a third of what a member contributed
prewar) the members' contributions amounting to 88 per
cent of total income. Brian J. Hillery (The Economic
and Social Review V,3, April 1974 pp.345-52) also
basing his figures on the returns to the Registrar
of Friendly Societies, calculated that in 1970 members
contributed in the case of registered trade unions
a total of £1,817,488 which represented an annual
contribution of £5.56 or less than 11p. a week (the
1951 8½d would correspond to 3.57p.), the members'
contributions amounting to 86% of total income.
Finally as an indication of financial strength, Trade
Union Information calculated that in 1951 (the figures
are translated into the new currency) average funds per
member were £4.75 compared to £2.25 in 1939 and
compared to £8.05 in Britain in 1952, while Hillery
calculated that in 1953 average funds per member stood
at £5.69 while in 1970 they stood at £12.14, which
at 1953 prices represents £6.52. 1953 is probably a
more typical year to take as a base; 1951 was particularly

strike-ridden. It is clear then that the financial strength of the trade union movement as a whole has not increased greatly, relatively speaking, in the last twenty years.

29. D.W. Bleakley 'The Northern Ireland Trade Union Movement' in the Journal of the Statistical and Social Inquiry Society of Ireland: XIX, 1953-54 p.158.

30. ibid. p.162.

31. See also Charles McCarthy The Decade of Upheaval Dublin 1973 p.80. In the building trade Irish-based unions were concentrated in Dublin, while the amalgamated unions were strong elsewhere in the south. This geographic difference of emphasis served to avoid conflict, particularly since the Dublin unions were normally the wage leaders.

32. Bleakley op.cit. p.162.

33. ibid.

34. see above p.12.

35. see above pp.54.

36. For a somewhat later study of trade union organisation, structure and scope in the Republic, see David O'Mahony: Industrial Relations in Ireland: ESRI Dublin 1964; and also Economic Aspects of Industrial Relations ESRI Dublin 1965.

Chapter Eight

The North

-i-

It is important to remember how much the north diverged
from the south during the decade immediately after the
war. Here we find no economic doldrums. On the contrary,
as Dr Lyons remarks, 'within a decade Northern Ireland
passed from the status of an exceptionally backward area
to full membership of the welfare state.'[1] In social
benefits and in educational provision Northern Ireland
leaped ahead of the Republic. Industry was encouraged,
aided and renewed by a substantial legislative programme,
first the Industries Development Acts, and later in the
fifties the Capital Grants to Industries Acts.[2] Yet despite
all this, two major characteristics of the society in
Northern Ireland continued to persist, one reinforcing the
other. The first was unemployment and the threat of unemployment, endemic in the traditional industries, despite
the considerable programme of industrial investment. The
second, the most difficult and disruptive element of all,
was the division of society on the basis of bitter sectarian
privilege. Catholics may have represented a third of the
population of the province but the province itself was a
determined protestant theocracy. When we look at the north
at the end of our period, in 1959, we find Basil Brooke
still Prime Minister, we find a unique system of pluralist
property voting, we find the gerrymandering of local constituencies particularly in Derry, all designed to reinforce
the protestant majority; and so vehement was the commitment
to protestant supremicist policies that a Minister of
Education who attempted to increase the financial support
for Roman Catholic schools was obliged to resign.[3] Since

religion - understood in a social and not a metaphysical
sense - profoundly affected the kind of job that was
available to one, and since trade unions in turn frequently
reflected an occupational emphasis, it followed that some
unions were overwhelmingly Protestant in membership. It
is difficult to get figures, but the present position is
at least a guide to the past; the general understanding
now is that in the unions representing engineering workers
perhaps one-eighth to one-tenth are catholic; in the case
of carpenters and joiners perhaps one-quarter; while
catholics are quite strong in number among bricklayers and
plasterers. However, in the case of the great general union,
the Amalgamated Transport, we are not surprised to find
that approximately half are catholic, a number which may
have grown in recent years as employment opportunities
developed.[4] The Northern Ireland committee spoke for all
trade unions in the north and all trade unionists, and since
the sectarian problem was - in the actual sense of that word -
unspeakable, it is not surprising that references to it at
the Northern Ireland Committee conferences should be somewhat
muted and obscure.[5] But it was always present in one form
or another, in the housing problem (where discrimination
could readily be exercised), in the strategies used to promote
employment, but above all it could be seen in the reluctance
of the Northern Ireland government to recognise the Northern
Ireland Committee, as the representative trade union centre
in the north. Trade union spokesmen[6] attributed this
reluctance to anti-workingclass bias on the part of the
Stormont government. There may have been something of that
in it, but the substance of the reason lay without doubt
in Stormont's contemptuous but at the same time uneasy
hostility to the south and also to the catholic minority
within its own borders who appeared to owe a stronger fealty
to the south than to the constitution of the state in which
they lived (although in truth the nationalist position in
the north and the nationalist position in the south were
markedly different, the first being a realistic cry from a
deprived people, the second a romantic myth concerning
imperial aggression.)

The dilemma for Northern Ireland trade unionists was considerable. In the flush of developments after the war, it was essential that they evolve a trade union centre in Northern Ireland;[7] but it had to be a centre which at one and the same time would do nothing to fracture the all-Ireland character of the trade union movement, and would also be acceptable to a Northern Ireland government which regarded the notion of a popular all-Ireland body as either fanciful or disloyal. A further problem was that the Northern Ireland government, despite what was said of it from time to time, did, after a fashion, recognise trade unions,[8] and they had consultations where appropriate with the federations in Northern Ireland and with the larger unions. The difficulty for the trade unions really lay in the manner of the consultation, in the fact that the Northern Ireland government could pick and choose whom they wished to consult,[9] and whom they wished to appoint to various government bodies; and this would continue to be the case unless a central trade union body was established. The solution could of course lie with the establishing of an Ulster TUC, independent of the Irish TUC, and, as we shall see, this was explicitly urged by the Northern Ireland government. But it was a solution which was never entertained seriously by the trade union movement, perhaps because unions such as the Amalgamated Transport, the AEU and the ASW had no wish to abandon their southern membership, but also, it must be added, because of the basic solidarity within these large amalgamated unions, which had been manifested in the south, in the years of stress up to 1945, in a number of ballots of support. Although the views of unions in the south were of much less significance than those in the north, it is as well to note in passing that in the south as well, nothing was done to promote the idea of an Ulster TUC. This was so, even though government pressure for trade union reform continuously raised the question in an awkward way. Louie Bennett, commenting on Lemass's suggestion of November 1945,[10] made the point that 'Mr Lemass places no confidence in Trade Union association between

North and South as a possible force in the elimination of
the Border. Or more probably, such association may not fit
in with his plans for industrial development. Northern
Ireland Trade Unionism controlled from a British Labour
Government, coupled with a Left Wing section here, may travel
too fast for the Eire Government's outlook.' And in the
later debates on the development of Irish-based unions she
was one who urged that 'if unity was achieved in the South,
leaving the Northern unions to their fate ...', it would
mean a protestant dominated Northern trade union movement
and catholic workers in the North would be victimised. [11]
An independent northern trade union movement might well have
been the consequence of William O'Brien's proposals, but
his successor William McMullen, who had worked in his early
days with Belfast dockers, feared the loss of northern
membership if an independent trade union movement developed
in the north although in some respects he appeared to
accept it as inevitable; [12] nevertheless he explicitly
resisted Lemass's proposals for reform by legislation, which,
since they could by definition apply to only one part of the
country, would by their very nature be divisive. The
preoccupations of the south we shall discuss later; for the
moment it is sufficient to note that throughout the trade
union movement, north and south, there was little support for
the idea of an Ulster TUC.

In these circumstances, it was decided to establish a
committee of the Irish Trade Union Congress to act as a
centre. The dilemma was how much authority it should have.
If too much were given to it, there was a danger that it
might develop into an Ulster TUC; but on the other hand
there was pressure among many trade unionists in the north,
particularly those who had no members in the south, for a
substantial degree of autonomy within the Congress structure.
The early years were in fact marked by a considerable
timidity with regard to the degree of freedom which the
Northern Ireland committee should be given; however, as time
went on, and as the Northern Minister of Labour in particular
became more and more hostile to what he regarded as a
southern Congress, the pressure grew for much greater autonomy

in practice if not juridically, and the status of the
Northern Ireland committee increased. But it was, for the
Northern Ireland trade union leadership, always a difficult
and ambiguous business.

Initially the Northern Ireland Committee was established
as a subcommittee of the National Executive, 'empowered
to act for the National Executive in matters peculiar to
the Six County area',[13] in pursuance of a recommendation
from a consultative conference of affiliated unions with
members in Northern Ireland which had met in Belfast on
November 3 1945. Its formal character as a subcommittee
remained largely unchanged until 1964,[14] but in practice
it became very much more than that. Let us look at a
number of indications of its growing autonomy. Perhaps
the most interesting indication is the manner in which its
meetings were chaired. In this matter, one can distinguish
between meetings of the committee itself, and the annual
conferences for unions with membership in Northern Ireland,
held under the committee's auspices. With regard to the
first, it was clearly intended that the president of
Congress (or in his absence the vice-president) would take
the chair, just as he did in the case of the national executive,
but because of the difficulties of travel, the committee
decided to appoint a chairman from among its members to
act when both the president and the vice-president were
unable to be present.[15] More and more, in the absence of
the national officers, the local man took the chair until,
by 1954, the reports of the meetings record that even when
Bob Smith, the president of Congress, was present, the locally
elected chairman, Harold Binks, took the chair.[16] We note
the same change of emphasis at the annual conferences, but here
of course it had far greater public significance, particularly
since the conferences gradually took on the character of
Northern Ireland congresses. Up to 1953 the president of
Congress took the chair at the conferences and also delivered
a key-note address. At this point however, the change

took place, partly for reasons that were fortuitous.
Harold Binks, to whom much of this development must be
credited, had been elected chairman in 1949, and in
February 1951 he had chaired a conference of trade unions
and educational bodies as part of the campaign mounted
by the Northern Ireland Committee concerning the Employment
and Training Act; however, a specific trade union
conference in Belfast on the same topic later in the month
was chaired by Miss Chenevix as president of Congress. In
1953, circumstances were somewhat unusual; the president
of Congress, Con Connolly, of the Cork Workers Council,[17]
was remote from Belfast and the affairs of the north; the
vice-president of Congress was John McAteer, who also held
the office of honorary secretary of the Northern Ireland
Committee, and could not very well chair its meetings.
Binks therefore presided. Much the same situation applied
in 1954, during McAteer's presidency of Congress. Moreover,
the annual conference met in Ballymena that June, and its
special northern and representative character was reinforced
when a formal welcome was extended by the Mayor of Ballymena,
Councillor T. Wilson, and also by Councillor Bell of the
Ballymena and District Trades and Labour Council. At this
point Binks became vice-president of Congress, and in 1955-56,
president, putting beyond question his right to preside
at Northern Ireland conferences. After his year of office
as president, his chairmanship of the Northern Ireland
Committee was much enhanced, and he continued thereafter to
chair the annual conferences, with the exception of 1958,
when Jack Macgougan as president took the chair.

A second interesting indication of the growing autonomy of
the Northern Ireland committee was the status accorded
to the local secretary, and his relations to the ITUC head
office in Dublin. In the first place Ruaidhri Roberts,
as secretary of Congress, was ex officio, a member of the
Northern Ireland committee, and indeed he attended most
meetings of the committee itself, and all the annual conferences.

However, apart from one or two matters (notably the major
debate on the non-recognition issue, which we shall deal
with later) he kept a low profile. Donal Nevin, the
research officer, attended occasionally, although in the
early days he provided a good deal of economic and statistical
material on northern affairs, material which later was
provided by the secretary of the committee himself. This
relationship with the head office of Congress did not itself
change; rather did the secretaryship of the Northern
Ireland committee grow within its context. Initially the
post was an honorary one, but from an early stage, from
1948 in fact,[18] the Northern Ireland committee sought a
full-time northern officer and a Northern Ireland office.
It must be emphasised, however, that they never questioned
the fact that this would be a national executive appointment,
not one proper to the Northern Ireland committee. A good
deal of delay attended the making of the decision, largely,
it appears, because of the additional cost involved. When
the decision was eventually taken in 1956, the person
appointed was W.J. Leeburn, a retired trade union official,
and on that score, and also on the grounds of lack of
consultation on the part of the national executive, there
was some concern expressed at the 1956 annual conference of
the Northern Ireland committee. However, on Leeburn's
retirement in 1960, William Blease was appointed, a vigorous
man who gave strength and direction to the committee in the
years that followed.

There is no doubt as well that a substantial degree of
autonomy was implied in the public resolutions adopted
by the Northern Ireland committee when making its claim
for recognition - resolutions, it must be noted, which were
approved in advance by the national executive and adopted
formally by subsequent congresses. At the annual Northern
Ireland conference, for example, which took place in Belfast
on October 9 1948, it was resolved 'that this conference as
representative of organised workers in Northern Ireland

re-affirms that the Northern Ireland committee of the Irish
Trade Union Congress is the appropriate authority to
nominate for positions on Government bodies ...[19] There
are three phrases of significance here; firstly the
resolution derived its legitimacy from 'the representative(s)
of organised workers in Northern Ireland'; secondly, the
right to nominate was sought not for the ITUC as a whole,
but for its Northern Ireland committee; and thirdly, the
Northern Ireland committee itself was described as an
'authority'.

But whatever about its public face, despite the flexibility
and the discretion which the committee occasionally exercised,
Congress itself had no doubt whatever that the Northern
Ireland committee was an essentially subsidiary body. At
the 1948 conference, which we have just discussed, James
Larkin, who that year was president of Congress, emphasised,
despite his other very encouraging remarks, that the
conference which adopted this impressive resolution was in
fact a consultative conference, that is to say, it was in
no sense authoritative or autonomous.[20] Indeed two years
later Sam Kyle, addressing a similar conference as the
current president of Congress, was even more explicit: 'The
conference is held', he said, 'solely to bring before the
representatives the work of the Northern Ireland committee
during the year, and being an ad hoc body is not policy
making, which function is held by the Annual Congress of the
ITUC.'[21] And the procedure regarding the agenda for the
Northern Ireland conference amply bears this out. Resolutions,
as we have already indicated, were controlled by the national
executive. They were devised, in the first place, not by
the unions but by the Northern Ireland committee; and the
resolutions thus prepared, before they could be placed on the
conference agenda, had to be ratified by the national
executive. On one occasion,[22] delegates to a Northern
Ireland conference, gained the approval of the meeting to
discuss an emergency resolution, that is to say, a resolution
that was not on the approved agenda, but the national executive

was not prepared to tolerate such a practice, and this
was made clear on their behalf by Leeburn in 1953, when
he went on to urge that they must 'recognise that this is
only a subsidiary conference.'[23]   On the other hand, it
would be wrong to conclude from this that Dublin dominated
Belfast.   The fact was that the control of the agenda by
the national executive had a good deal of sense to it.   The
annual conference of Congress was the policy-making body,
and all unions were free to place resolutions on its order
paper.   It would be odd, to say the least, if another policy
making body were created within the same   organisation;
therefore if policy was to be discussed in Northern Ireland,
it had to fall within the overall policy already decided
by the annual conferences of Congress, of which the national
executive was guardian.   Secondly, when one considers
the role of the national executive in all this it is
necessary to bear in mind that in northern matters it was
in practice guided by its northern members.   If there was
tension therefore between the national executive and the
Northern Ireland committee, it was much more a question of
different groupings and different interests within Northern
Ireland expressing themselves through the Congress structure,
rather than a conflict between Dublin and Belfast.   This
was well understood to be the case;   as we shall see, if
there was the slightest hint that strategy for Northern
Ireland might be determined by persons outside the province,
the rejection was immediate and overwhelming.   The formal
position therefore was one of considerable subsidiarity;
the actual position was probably much nearer the evaluation
urged by Harry Diamond during the debate in Stormont on
the Employment and Training Bill in October 1950:[24] 'It
(the ITUC) has a distinct and autonomous Northern Ireland
Committee ... the fact is that the mass of the workers
whose delegates are members of the Northern Committee of the
Irish Congress of Trade Unions are living and working here ...
The Minister (is) concerned with a mass of people of probably
every political opinion who are industrial workers ...'

This then was the somewhat ambiguous committee that sought
to be regarded as legitimately representative both in the
eyes of Northern Ireland trade union members and also in
the eyes of a highly suspicious Northern Ireland government.
How it fared can best be seen in the manner in which it
exercised the three 'functions' which were decided on at
its first meeting in November 1945.[25]   These were as follows:

> That the activities of the Committee should be
> confined to industrial and economic questions and
> matters which affect trade unions and workers,
> as such, leaving aside political issues except in
> so far as they are bound up with Trade Union
> interests.

> To promote the organisation of trades councils
> in Northern Ireland.

> To obtain formal recognition by the Government
> or its several Ministries by approaches on
> specific questions rather than by a general
> application for recognition.

All three required that the committee should be supported
by the Northern Ireland trade unionists; but it was
obviously the case that the achievement of the first and
third objectives required an adequate recognition of
legitimacy by the Northern Ireland government.

In the discussion that follows, we shall begin with the
initial steps taken by the Northern committee to secure
support from the trade unions of Northern Ireland, and
particularly the representative groupings of unions that
already existed; we shall then develop this notion of

trade union legitimacy further in a discussion on the
second function, that is the organisation of trades councils.
At this point - when we come to consider the first and third
objectives - we shall broaden the discussion, as we
necessarily must, in order to keep in view not only the
status of the Northern Ireland committee as seen by
trade union members, but as seen by the Northern Ireland
government as well, examining how the views of each of
these two contrasted more and more sharply, until by May
Day 1959, the Northern Ireland committee was stronger than
ever before among its trade union constituents, and never
less acceptable to the Northern Ireland administration.

Let us review the careful steps taken to establish the
committee.[26] First there were some early experiments,
specifically, in 1943, the Committee on Congress membership
in Northern Ireland;[27] then the basic proposals to establish
the committee, incorporating its terms of reference, were
made at a special conference of Northern Ireland trade
union delegates in Belfast on November 3 1945. These
proposals were circulated to all affiliated unions; they
were endorsed by the national executive and also
by the 1946 annual conference of Congress. A general
conference of Northern Ireland trade unions in Bangor in
September 1946[28] gave them a further endorsement; but
despite this impressive build-up, there was still some
concern about 'the various other bodies in Northern Ireland.'[29]
This of course referred to the federations and the Belfast
Trades Council; and it was decided to convene a meeting
of representatives of these bodies 'to ensure that agreement
be reached on representations on economical and industrial
questions affecting Northern Ireland trade unionists.'[30]
This was successful; and the following year's conference
welcomed the fact that 'the Belfast and District Trades
Union Council, the Belfast District Committee of the
Confederation of Shipbuilding and Engineering Unions and
the AEU had agreed that the Northern Ireland Committee should

be authorised to deal and to conduct representations to
the government relating to matters of common concern.'[31]
The fact that the committee had such an impressive pedigree
was referred to on more than one occasion in the difficult
years that followed.

Let us now turn to the question of trades councils. There
was much concern expressed at the time[32] that the number
of organised workers in Northern Ireland was so small,
140,000, it was claimed, from a possible 380,000 in employment
(a somewhat smaller estimate, incidentally, than Bleakley's).[33]
This was a problem for Northern Ireland as a whole. The
trade union groupings that already existed, particularly
the Belfast Trades Council and the Confederation of Shipbuilding and Engineering Unions, were not only concentrated
largely in Belfast but had an essentially Belfast character.
Therefore,when it came to the question of promoting trade
union activity elsewhere in the province, it was natural
that they should see such work as one of the functions of
the Northern Ireland committee, particularly when it took
the form of fostering trades councils.

There was in fact general and continuous pressure for their
development throughout the period. In 1946 it was reported[34]
that trades councils had been established in Newtownards,
Bangor, Coleraine, Enniskillen, Newry and Lisburn, which
with Belfast and Derry, came to eight in all. By 1955[35]
this impressive number had been further increased to eleven,
and had been restructured somewhat. Belfast, Derry, Bangor
and Newry still remained; but now in addition there was
Mid-Ulster, Holywood and District, Omagh, Strabane, Larne
and Coleraine. There was also a trades council in Ballymena
which courteously refused to affiliate to the Irish Trade
Union Congress, despite the fact that they welcomed the
Northern Ireland conference there in June 1954. Derry from
1952 onwards was a problem area because of the breakaway of a
large number of members of the National Union of Tailors
and Garment Workers, who went over to the Irish Transport.[36]

But there was a hardheaded recognition as well of the limits
of trades council activity.   Betty Sinclair, of the Belfast
Trades Council, urged on more than one occasion[37] that
annual conferences of trades councils should be organised;
but the Northern Ireland committee were most reluctant to
have anything to do with the idea.   Democratic authority
lay essentially with the trade unions, not with any
geographic horizontal grouping, and they did not wish to
have that position confused; but apart from that they possibly
feared as well that a conference of trades councils might
grow to be a dangerous and somewhat random alternative
to the Northern Ireland committee.

But this was a reasonable limitation in a situation in
which trades councils as a whole were warmly fostered.
It was quite contrary in the south, to which we briefly turn
before bringing our discussion on trades councils to a close.
Of course it is not at all surprising that the experience
there should be so very different.   Even in the 1920s there
had been some uncertainty regarding their role;[38]   later,
during the early forties, trade union unease regarding trades
councils - and in particular, Irish Transport unease - grew,
as Larkin, excluded from Congress, availed more and more of
the Dublin council as both a platform and an organisation
for popular protest.[39]   The split, when it came, complicated
things even more.[40]   In Dublin and in Cork, the CIU established
rival trades councils, but, as Walter Beirne said in 1946,
there was 'a good deal of confusion throughout the country
regarding the position of local councils.   In fact some of
the branches of Unions affiliated to the Congress of Irish
Unions were members of local Councils that were affiliated
to the Irish Trade Union Congress.'[41]   We shall take up
this topic more fully when we come to consider developments
in the south.

Let us now turn to the first function of the Northern Ireland
committee, remarking in particular not so much on what it

wished to achieve, but on what it wished to avoid, in other
words, its desire to '(leave) aside political issues except
in so far as they are bound up with Trade Union interests.'
In view of the condition of Northern Ireland politics,
this was in fact necessary for the committee's survival.
Since Northern Ireland was part of the United Kingdom, there
was always some expectation that the political poles would
lie with the middle classes on the one hand, and the working
class on the other. But in Northern Ireland the working
class people voted overwhelmingly for a unionist conservative
government, even when their own trade union leadership was
explicitly socialist, because the reality lay not in a
polarisation between working class and middle class but
between protestant and catholic, between loyalist and
republican; and the Labour candidates in turn, in the
years immediately after the war, reflected that reality by
adopting such qualifying descriptions as Commonwealth Labour
or Republican Labour.[42] But the Labour Party itself was
impatient for the more civilised British model, and when in
1949 the south declared itself a Republic, it resolved at its
April conference: 'That the Northern Ireland Labour Party
believes that the best interests of Northern Ireland lie in
maintaining the Constitutional links with the United Kingdom.'[43]
The result was disastrous. In the general election that soon
followed all nine Labour candidates were defeated; and it
was nearly ten years before they succeeded in gaining some
representation in Stormont once again.[44] They had failed to
impress the protestant working class and they had alienated
the catholics.

But of course some political involvement was inevitable.
Trade union leaders were frequently political leaders as well,
and,apart from that, the Labour political leaders and the
trade union leaders formed one community despite the profound divisions among the working class. There was always
some hope then that from a united trade union movement, a
united political movement would grow, not perhaps a very
practical hope, but no less necessary on that account.

At least it emphasised the virtues of such unity as existed,
and the need to preserve it. Harold Binks, for example,
in his address to the 1953 Northern Ireland conference,
atrributed the fragmented state of political Labour in
Northern Ireland to the division, north and south, in the
nineteen twenties, and urged that the same fate must not
overtake the trade unions: 'The link between the Labour
Party in each area was broken ... Now we have two labour
parties in Northern Ireland, sometimes opposed to one
another for the same seats, and we have several independent
labour groups as well. We also have many socialists now in
membership of no party or group ...'[45] It must be said in
passing that such a notion is somewhat fanciful. It is
difficult to see how the Irish Labour Party and Trade Union
Congress (as it was at the time) could have maintained a
common political organisation north and south, as well as a
trade union centre. Indeed the Northern Ireland Labour Party,
freed from organisational involvement with the south, had a
better chance of providing working class leadership in the
north. Yet fanciful or not, the notion of some overreaching
political and trade union organisation was always present.
In consequence there was a good deal of practical communication,
particularly in the north. A joint committee was established
between the Northern Ireland Labour Party and the Northern
Ireland committee to pursue the repeal of the 1927 Trades
Disputes Act[46] which had already been repealed in the United
Kingdom generally; and the Northern Ireland committee's
campaign for the abolition of plural voting and the granting
of univeral suffrage was clearly carried on in the context
of mutual cooperation. And what of the south? The shared
socialist tradition of the leaders resulted in some formal
links. The ITUC (and not merely its Northern Ireland
committee) received fraternal delegates from the Northern
Ireland Labour Party;[47] the national executive contributed
£50 to the Northern Ireland Labour Party to help in the
appointment of a parliamentary officer (it was in fact
Bob Getgood);[48] and in the specifically southern context,

a joint council was established between the Northern Ireland
Labour Party and the Irish Labour Party.[49] But the
relationship did not extend any further than this formal --
rather fragile- connection. This is clear from the embarrassing
incident which occurred at the ITUC annual conference in
Galway in 1950. Sam Napier had come to address the conference
as fraternal delegate from the Northern Ireland Labour Party;
but it was in the aftermath of the party's declaration for
the United Kingdom, and an outraged Sean Dunne - who was
both a TD and secretary of the Federation of Rural Workers -
moved the reference back of a section of the standing orders
committee report in order to deny Napier the opportunity of
speaking. 'We cannot accept', he said,[50] 'the proposition
put forward by the Northern Ireland Labour Party that they
accept the partition of Ireland ...' and his seconder,
J.D. Heery of the Municipal Employees,[51] was even more
explicit: 'I say that while these people proclaim that
they give allegiance to a country and king who divides the
workers of this country this Congress cannot recognise the
Party as a Labour Party.'[52] An embarrassed Sam Kyle, who was
in the chair, tried to smother the issue, by ruling it out
of order, but when he put the standing orders committee
report as a whole to the meeting, it was adopted by quite
a slender majority in the circumstances, 78 to 57.[53]
Sam Napier, when he came to address the conference, put his
party's dilemma very clearly.[54] They were a 'completely
independent and autonomous body without sectarian bias ...
making our fight within the frontiers of Northern Ireland
a struggle and choice between two entirely different
economic conceptions.' But the Unionist Party, in pursuit of
their objective of a 'one-Party state', were not concerned
with economic conceptions. 'In their attempts to destroy
all opposition the Unionist Party have cheapened loyalty -
one of the noblest qualities men can ever know - by making
it the emblem of political strife. Their smear campaigns -
backed up by a powerful Press - have used such labels as
"disloyal" and "rebels" to brand their opponents so that
the electors dread a bloody revolution at even the municipal

elections. By continually fanning the flames of fanatical
sectarian bitterness and hatred they have built and are
consolidating their rule. In the face of such policies
the Northern Ireland Labour Movement requires greater courage
and determination.'[55] This may have been quite admirable
but it did not take adequate account of the reality of a
profoundly divided working class; and to the trade unions it
was the reality that was all important if they were not to
fragment unutterably. In the United Kingdom generally,
the Labour Party and the trade unions could be regarded
as two aspects of the one movement; this was not the case
in Northern Ireland where the possibility of agreement lay
not in the substance of a common ideology but rather in
the seeking of common objectives.

But this may make too little of a real trade union ideology
which existed in its own right. Perhaps the problem may
best be understood by taking up a point which we made earlier,[56]
that is, that trade unions, political parties and similar
organisations are best understood as organising not men
but rather their roles - their roles as workers, or as
citizens - and that men themselves sharply distinguish between
these roles which may at times be accommodated within one
organisation, but at other times most certainly may not. In
the special circumstances of the north, therefore, there
were always many who would ensure politically the election
of those on whom they could rely to defend the political
union with the United Kingdom (and socialist trade union
leaders might be suspect here), but having done so, they
would then support those who represented a badly-needed
anti-establishment role. In these circumstances popular
trade union leaders were not infrequently catastrophic failures
in politics; and were very sensitive in practice to the
limits of their legitimacy. The desire therefore on the part
of the Northern Ireland committee to eschew political issues
was not only sensible but to a considerable extent inevitable as well. It required the practice of great restraint,

however, not only in their dealings with the Northern
Ireland government, which is the topic which we shall now
develop, but also in relation to the restless south,
roughly intruding into northern affairs first with the
declaration of the Republic in 1949, and later, in 1957,
with the IRA campaign of destruction.[57]

When we turn to the third objective of the Northern Ireland
committee, we find that the manner in which it is couched
is itself very revealing; 'to obtain formal recognition
by the Government or its several Ministries by approaches
on specific questions rather than by a general application
for recognition.' There are two interesting points we can
note here at the outset. The first is the cast of mind of
the northern trade unionist, cautious, patient, determined,
highly pragmatic - much in contrast with the south, and its
tendency to swift impulsive confrontations; as a result
when a confrontation develops in the north, it is rarely
because of impulsive mistakes and is all the more intractable
on that account. Secondly, there is a strong implication
in the manner in which the object is stated that, while the
Northern Ireland government would not formally recognise
the Northern Ireland committee, it could be expected by and
large to work along with it; and it is not unlikely that
this position was explored with representatives of the
Northern Ireland government beforehand.

-iii-

Let us look briefly at the narrative of events as they
developed. At the outset, practical recognition seemed to
come readily enough. Early in 1946, a direct approach
was made by the committee to the Minister of Commerce in
regard to the proposed merger of transport services, and a

deputation was received by him on March 12 1946.[58] The
committee took care not to overplay its hand, but towards
the end of the year they approached the Minister of Labour
on the question of wage council procedures. This was a
more central matter, but the Minister received their
representatives on November 18.[59] It was indeed a successful
beginning. In September of the following year, 1947,
however, they began to become entangled in the difficulties
that were to beset them for the following seventeen years,
that is, until formal recognition came in 1964. The
committee now raised the key issue: their right to consultation before the government made trade union appointments
to official bodies. The case in point was the Joint
Production Council, and at a meeting with the Minister of
Labour and his officials they asked that they should be
consulted before the trade union appointments to the
council were made.[60] But the Minister and his officials
were full of reservations, saying that if they were to
consult with trade unions about the appointments, it should
be with unions in Northern Ireland, and they went on quite
explicitly to urge on the Northern Ireland committee
representatives the advantages of an Ulster TUC. But at this
point, the committee's representatives were by no means down-
cast, and when they reported back to the Northern Ireland
conference later in the month,[61] they were hopeful that,
despite what was said, the committee would be given greater
not less acceptance, in the future. And there were reasonable
grounds for that hope. The Minister of Commerce continued
to be helpful. Following representations from the Northern
Ireland committee, he enlarged the Northern Ireland Tourist
Board in order to appoint a labour representative[62] and, from
the persons whose names were nominated to him, he chose
J. McAteer who was secretary of the committee. A cooperative attitude generally appeared to prevail. In
November 1947 senior advisory officers from the Board of
Trade[63] attended a special Northern Ireland committee meeting
to discuss production councils and production committees;

and in the following January the Minister of Commerce received
a deputation from the committee to discuss their suggestion
that the Industrial Organisation and Development Act be extended to Northern Ireland.[64] 'Since the establishment of
the Northern Ireland Committee,' said James Larkin in his
presidential address to the Northern Ireland annual conference
in Belfast in October 9 1948, 'it has staked its claim to be
recognised and consulted as the only representative body of
organised workers in Northern Ireland, and insists upon the
right to speak on behalf of organised workers. The claim has
been accepted not only by those bodies in the Movement who
have endeavoured to fill this need in the past but by those
in Government seats who did not in the beginning view the claim
with friendliness, but gradually, bit by bit we have established
the claim.'[65] But this may have been overstating it, even for
this honeymoon period. Ruaidhri Roberts was to say later that
there had been no consistent policy on the part of the government[66],
one minister giving recognition and another refusing it; and
even where there was a degree of acceptance, there was always
a tendency to play down its significance, as for example when
the Northern Ireland Labour Party, not the Northern Ireland
committee, had been invited to submit nominations for the
Statistics of Trade Advisory Committee (an invitation which,
in the event the party passed to the committee.) 'The reason',
said Roberts[67] 'they (the nominations) did not come to the
Northern Ireland Committee seems obvious enough. If the
Northern Ireland Committee could be placed in the position of
being just one of a number of Labour organisations competing
for the right to undertake the same functions, clearly it would
lose the authority of the movement to act as a trade union centre
should.' It was only too clear therefore that the legitimacy
of the Northern Ireland committee in the eyes of the unions
had to be fostered with no less vigour; and when Binks
proposed a resolution at the Northern Ireland conference in
October 1948 reaffirming the Northern Ireland committee as the
appropriate trade union authority for the purpose of nominations
to official bodies, he went on to appeal to individual trade
unions to forbid members to serve if they were approached by
the government, unless the Northern Ireland committee had been
consulted.[68] But there was a limit to the distance one could go
in these matters, as we shall see in a moment.

In following up Binks's resolution, the Committee requested
the Minister of Commerce,[69] to appoint a labour representative
to the Northern Ireland Electricity Board.[70] But now the
whole climate began to change. In March 1949 the Minister
replied by 'questioning the status of the Northern Ireland
Committee'.[71] Moreover, he did not regard the replies he
received from the committee as satisfactory. And then came the
crisis of the Employment and Training Act, and the gauntlet
was thrown down by Ivan Neill, the Minister of Labour.[72]

It had been decided by the Northern Ireland government to
introduce an Employment and Training Bill on precisely the
same lines as the British Act, with the exception of that part
of the act which provided for the establishment of a Youth
Employment Service. The omission was the cause of some controversy. Furthermore the Northern Ireland committee had not
been consulted before the measure was introduced. When the
Minister was challenged on this latter point by Mrs Lilian Calvert
during the second reading, his reply was diplomatically hazy:
'This is an enabling measure,' he said, 'and because of that,
the necessity for consultation as suggested by the honorable
lady member does not arise.' But when he was pressed to agree
to consultation before the committee stage was taken, he would
not give any undertaking to do so; he felt it would open doors
and 'prolong the passing of this legislation for an unduly long
time.'[73] Nor did he in fact do so, and when the committee stage
was reached some weeks later on October 17 he was berated by a
number of members, Mrs Calvert calling it absolutely scandalous,
and Harry Diamond 'a shameless performance.'[74] Whether stung
by this or not, the Minister decided to make what he described
as a considered reply to the question of consultation with the
northern committee. 'Now as regards this question of consultation,'
he said,[75] 'it has been the practice of the Ministry, when considering schemes of vocational training, to consult joint bodies
of employers or workers or to approach separately any responsible
body of employers or workers concerned ... In no instance has
a trade union been refused consultation in regard to training
scheme arrangements for occupations followed by its members.
Our representations to employers and trade unions in favour

of training have been made mostly on behalf of ex-Service men,
and I am happy to acknowledge that up to a point we have
received full and effective cooperation from the following
trade union organisations, the Federation of Building Trade
Operatives comprising amongst others ...' and he named ten
trade unions. 'Our more important unions', he said, 'are
grouped under the Confederation and the NFBTO which have their
headquarters in the United Kingdom. We are glad to consult
them, or indeed invividual trade unions on any of these matters,
at any time, but we do not particularly favour consultation
with an alternative self-constituted body whose head office
is in a foreign country ... more especially where the welfare
and interests of our own ex-Service men are at stake. I do
not propose to entertain suggested amendments to this Bill which
I received by post this morning from the Northern Ireland
Committee of the Irish Trade Union Congress and I think it
well to make my position in regard to this matter clear to
the House.' The Minister was unmoved by the vigorous protests
from Mrs Calvert and Harry Diamond, and in his reply to the
debate he did not bother to refer to the matter again. Binks,
when he came to review events in 1952,[76] attributed the blame
for non-recognition particularly to Major Neill. 'Over the
years' he claimed, 'they had had some form of recognition
from the various Ministries in the Northern Ireland government.
The present Minister of Health had not refused to meet them.
The Minister of Commerce had accorded them a certain degree
of recognition - each time the Tourist Board was being appointed
this Ministry had asked them for nominations. The Minister of
Education had also corresponded with them on certain matters.
The Ministers of Labour, however, and particularly the present
Minister, had absolutely refused to recognise them.'

To the trade unions then, the challenge appeared to come from
Major Neill, the Minister of Labour, rather than from
the government, and perhaps in the hope of quickly discounting it, they responded vigorously. On October 13,
that is even before the committee stage of the bill was
taken, 'a conference of trade union officials'[77] declared

that if the Minister did not consult, then they would 'refuse
to give any support to the measures introduced' and on
October 30, in response to the Minister's outright rejection
of the Northern Ireland committee, a considerable effort
was made to reinforce its legitimacy. At a conference
summoned by the ITUC and attended by the Confederation of
Building and Engineering Unions, the Building Federation,
the Printing Federation and the Belfast Trades Council, it
was agreed that each body separately should adopt a resolution
to be forwarded to the Minister of Labour that the Northern
Ireland committee be recognised as the central trade union
authority, and if it was not consulted, then they would
'refuse to consider any cooperation with the government in
the operation of the training scheme.'[78] But in fact the
Minister had more cabinet support than the unions believed,
and more than Binks would later concede. Early in 1951
the Committee organised a conference to which were invited
educational and other bodies concerned with the Employment
and Training Act, and arising from it they sought a meeting
with the Prime Minister Basil Brooke. He referred them to
the Minister of Labour, and when Neill refused to receive
them, his decision was endorsed by the Prime Minister.[79]
Neill's support was clear. Furthermore, the Committee was
now out of favour with other ministries. The Minister of
Health and Local Government proved quite unhelpful;[80] and
it was remarkable that, although nominations were accepted
for their management committees by the Northern Ireland
Hospital Authority, only 3 of the Committee's 104 nominations
were appointed.[81] Both sides then began to move to a
confrontation, the issue lying at the heart of the confrontation
being the Employment and Training Act, and in particular the
right of the Northern Ireland committee to be consulted when
trade union appointments were being made to the employment
and training committees established under the act.

McAteer at the conference of February 10 1951[82] identified
the basic policy issue for the trade unions. 'If they were

asked to serve individually', he said, 'on advisory committees
under the Act ... (they) must say no.' Of course this was
difficult because, if it was to work, it was essential that
nobody should break rank (and this was a great deal to ask);
and dangerous because, in an unemployment-ridden north,
these advisory committees were of considerable significance,
and trade union members could be expected to question rather
sharply any decision not to participate. This was the
dilemma that faced the policy conference that took place
in Belfast a week later on February 17 1951. It was not a
Northern Ireland committee conference; instead it was
declared to be 'a conference of representatives of national
executives of unions affiliated to the Irish Trade Union
Congress with membership in Northern Ireland.'[83] Furthermore
Ruaidhri Roberts, the general secretary, stated at the
outset that it was the national executive who had summoned
the conference emphasising thereby that it was not seen
as merely a local or provincial one. This may not have been
a wise decision in the event, although it was clearly
intended to be supportive merely, and in fact the object of
the conference was stated to be 'Government recognition of
the Northern Ireland Committee ...' not, it must be noted,
recognition of the Congress itself. The tension, however,
that sprang from this well-meaning attempt at support, in
itself provided a very informative insight into the
character of Northern Ireland trade unionism.

Roberts, who led the discussion (an unusual occurrence in
Northern Ireland conferences) gave a succinct history of
the development of the Northern Ireland committee and of its
evolving relations with the Northern Ireland government.
He then went on to outline a number of strategies which the
conference might debate. The first strategy contemplated
a 'quick fight' with the government[84] where unions would
agree that no member of theirs would accept any position
on a government sponsored body unless the Northern
Ireland committee were first consulted. Roberts recognised
himself that this was an extreme position to take up,
raising implications far wider than the Employment and

Training Act, but he offered it at least for debate. The
other strategies consisted of suggestions successively less
extreme; these were that there should be a schedule of
approved appointments to which unions could nominate without
reference to the Northern Ireland committee; or that a
committee of investigation should be established to examine
appointments post hoc; or, finally, that panels might be
established for nomination purposes. The first strategy
created the trouble. It was not intended to be a firm
proposal, but this did not diminish the force of the backlash.
One of the delegates, D. Madden of the AEU (who himself
had been a member of the Northern Ireland committee), declared
that the delegates had been dumbfounded by Roberts's statement[85]
and others followed up to say that such a proposal could
'drive a wedge between individual unions and the Northern
Ireland Committee.'[86]   Roberts was disposed to argue that
he had merely outlined the parameters of policy and both
Binks and McAteer attempted to come to the rescue by
domesticating the issue somewhat, but Porter of the National
Society of Painters summarised the feelings of at least
some of the delegates with a dangerous explicitness:[87]
'It does appear to me', he said, 'that they (the Northern
Ireland government) are not going to recognise you on
account of your headquarters being in Eire. Any action that
we may take as individual unions here today would have the
tendency to disenfranchise your members. You will definitely
disenfranchise your members if you take any action to force
the position. I think the whole kernal of your trouble
is that your headquarters are in Dublin, so when you go
to the Northern Ireland government you know what their minds
are in regard to a 'foreign' country. They will not have
anything to do with you.' The choice of personal pronouns
here, the use of 'you' instead of 'us' in speaking of the
Northern Ireland committee, is particularly significant. A
contribution by Betty Sinclair, however, appeared to change
the direction of the debate. She could speak with some
legitimacy since the organisation she served, the Belfast
Trades Council suffered a major displacement when the

Northern Ireland committee was established; yet it was a position which they 'had gladly given up.'[88] 'The Northern Ireland government', she went on, 'should not get away with talk of headquarters in a "foreign" country. The Church of Ireland has its headquarters in Dublin (and also) the Bank of Ireland and the GNR, and the government does not say that they are foreign concerns ... On general questions the Northern Ireland Committee is the only committee that can speak for us ...' Ruaidhri Roberts, at the close of the debate, proposed a motion to the effect that the Northern Ireland government should recognise the Northern Ireland committee on all _general_ matters[89] - about which there could be no disagreement; but when he pressed the matter further and attempted by way of a second motion to spell out in more detail what might be done, he found the proposal referred to the national executives of the various constituent unions. In fact it was not heard of again.

We have spent some time describing this debate, since it sheds considerable light on the character of Northern Ireland trade unionism. In the first place we can see a clear and unequivocal desire to hold together as a Northern Ireland trade union centre as against the government. But this objective was pursued by different groups for somewhat different reasons, and not without some tension. In the case of those who were communists or who were sympathetic to the more radical forms of socialism, they were far less likely to be courted by the Northern Ireland government and therefore had a great deal to gain from a Northern Ireland committee type structure. But there was always some distrust between those trade union leaders who were communist and those who were socialist. The communist voice was subdued at the level of the national executive of Congress, but in Northern Ireland, and particularly at the Northern Ireland annual conferences, the radical voice was far stronger.[90]

The objective of a Northern Ireland committee therefore,[91] united as against the government, was allied with a substantial concern for independence of action. In the case of the less radical trade union leadership, we find them influential not only in the national executive of Congress because of their large union membership, but for the same reason influential in political circles in Northern Ireland as well, and therefore less vigorous in uniting against the government. When they opted for a Northern Ireland committee therefore, and not an Ulster TUC, they were motivated not only by a desire for a wider trade union unity but, in the case of some, by the desire to retain their not unsubstantial membership in the south.[92] It followed then that while emphasising the authority of the national executive of Congress to their more radical brethren, they also in practice fostered independence of action within Congress for the Northern Ireland committee, in order to demonstrate to the government its essentially Northern Ireland character.

This desire for independence within the Congress reinforced the traditional sensitivity of the trade unions to any incursion by Congress into their freedom of action, a sensitivity no less marked in the south than in the north. And the sudden vigorous reaction to Roberts's speech can be seen as coming, in some measure, from this traditional stance. It was immediately recognised by both Roberts and Betty Sinclair in the manner in which they emphasised that the Northern Ireland committee would be concerned only with general matters. But this was only a small part of the story. The fact was that despite the insistence on the all-Ireland dimension, only the Northern Ireland committee was seen as legitimate by the trade unionists in the north, and when the full implications of a congress were presented to them, when Dublin really appeared to be raising its voice in northern affairs, there was a powerful rejection. This I believe is how we must interpret the reaction to Roberts's speech which, after all, was delivered in the context of a conference organised not from within

Northern Ireland but from Dublin. In the troubled,
divided circumstances of the north, when so much that
was fundamental was also unspeakable, there was a resentful
fear, on the part of members of both northern communities,
of remarks by outsiders either from the south or from Britain
which might upset the delicate balance, particularly if
it appeared that such remarks were being delivered in a
representative capacity. Normally of course there was little
danger of this. Congress presidents from the south not only
felt themselves to be walking on eggshells but on occasion
confessed to an inadequate understanding of the north and
its problems[93] which suited the Northern Ireland trade union
leadership very well. To them, Congress in its wider
dimension, was a necessary instrument in developing trade
union policy in the north, but it was essential that the
instrument should be wholly tame and malleable.

There is one further point in the debate to which we might
refer. It concerns the Dublin headquarters of Congress
and Betty Sinclair's claim that the northern government's
opposition on that account was a sham, since organisations
such as the Church of Ireland and the Great Northern Railways
had their headquarters in Dublin. This argument was
frequently used by trade union leaders, particularly in support
of the view that government opposition to Congress was
based not on any problem concerning headquarters but sprang
instead from its essentially anti-working class character.[94]
While of course the Stormont administration was a highly
conservative one, yet this argument was itself much too
facile. The United Kingdom had its roots in a theocratic
constitution, and while this in practice was of little
significance in Britain, it was still very much a constitutional reality in the north. The southern government
in these circumstances was certainly foreign and so also
was a catholic dominated trade union movement based in the
south; while on the other hand the Church of Ireland and the
Masons were patently not foreign, irrespective of where their
headquarters were sited.

When we return to the narrative, we find a situation
becoming more and more intractable. Rising unemployment[95]
caused the unions great alarm, and in February 1952 a
conference of trade union officials (not, it might be noted,
the Northern Ireland committee) sought a meeting with the
Prime Minister which was refused.[96] At the same time the
Minister of Labour, taking advantage of this growing anxiety,
renewed his invitation to individual trade unions to serve
on the County and County Borough Employment Advisory Committees.[97]
He may have taken some encouragement from the fact that the
trade unions and not the Northern Ireland committee had
approached the Prime Minister, but despite this, and despite
the misgivings expressed at the special conference in 1951,
the unions in the north demonstrated remarkable solidarity,
holding very firmly to the policy of non-cooperation. As
Brendan Harkin remarked[97A] at the 1952 annual conference
of Congress: 'With two ignoble exceptions Trade Union
officials had refused to have anything to do with these
Committees and that was the proper attitude.' But it was
a very difficult time for the trade union leadership
particularly for those with no membership in the south.
H.J. Curlis of the National Union of General and Municipal
Workers confessed that among his members there was a
feeling for a Northern Ireland TUC[98] although he declared
his union's loyalty to the Irish TUC. Fundamentally, however,
the commitment to a Congress Northern Ireland committee
strengthened rather than weakened; Madden of the AEU proposed
the key resolution of support for the Northern Ireland
committee at the Northern Ireland conference in 1952, and in
order to demonstrate the quality and the extent of the
commitment, the individual unions themselves sent messages
of protest to the Northern Ireland government on the issue
of non-recognition.[99]

With unemployment a continuous problem, the Northern Ireland
trade union leadership ran a not inconsiderable risk in
following the course they did. They met the risk in a

number of ways, and this is particularly noticeable from
1953 onwards. They increased the legitimacy of the Northern
Ireland committee in the eyes of the membership, in the
manner which we have already described; they met British
Labour MPs on their visit to Northern Ireland in 1955 and
explained their predicament[100] and they engaged in publicity
in a manner which gave the Northern Ireland committee leadership status despite the government's refusal to recognise them.[101]
The government on the other hand continued to exercise
pressure on the unions to join the advisory committees, not
without some effect; and there was some support for Cecil
Vance of the Amalgamated Transport in 1954 when he suggested
a review of the policy of non-cooperation. Fortunately
for the trade unions the Northern Ireland administration,
being a highly conservative one, had in any event certain
philosophical difficulties in the matter of protecting
and creating employment, and this became clear in particular
in the crisis in 1954 in Short Brothers and Harland when 800
jobs were threatened.[102] If the government had been more
vigorous in that regard the trade union posture of non-
cooperation in the matter of the Employment and Training
Act would have been far more difficult to sustain. As it
was, the Northern Ireland committee, with the assistance
of Congress, mounted a convincing and well-documented case
for economic development in Northern Ireland, in a manner
which was calculated to emphasise the conservatism of the
government approach. The government was determined to keep
the committee at arm's length, all the more explicitly so as
time went by. In the early summer of 1955, the government
had announced their intention to establish a National
Industrial Development Council; the membership of the council
was not published until November, six months later, and
although two trade unionists were appointed, there had been
no consultation with the Northern Ireland committee, who were
vigorous in their protests.[103] The committee, however,
decided to establish a continuous system of contact with the
members who had been appointed; and in November 1956, they

mounted a major consultative conference on the economy
of Northern Ireland.[104]   Now Harland and Wolff's were
faced with the threat of considerable redundancy as well[105]
giving a great deal of point to the campaign of the trade
unions for a programme of planned investment. By 1959
therefore, the possibility of one side wooing support away
from the other had quite disappeared, and both sides to
the dispute were fixed and intransigent in their views.

-iv-

Let us look finally on two considerations operating on the
trade unions in Northern Ireland, one drawing them towards
Britain, and the other towards the south, and probably on
the whole reinforcing the form of balanced institution which
the Northern Ireland committee represented. The first
consideration, that which drew the trade unions towards
Britain, rested on the need to be practical in all things.
And there were two areas above all where it was necessary
to be practical, the area of pay and the area of trade union
legislation. 'It must not be overlooked', said Binks on
one occasion,[106] 'that many workers in Northern Ireland are
governed by negotiations conducted in Great Britain by the
unions and employers' associations there.' That this was
manifestly the case was demonstrated in 1950 when workers
in Northern Ireland accepted so readily the wage freeze
which the Northern Ireland government without consultation
imposed on them.[107]   It embarrassed the northern trade union
leadership of course, but the reality was that the national
executives of the various unions in Britain had accepted
the freeze there, and that really disposed of the matter.
Furthermore it was always the settled policy in Northern
Ireland to seek pay parity with Britain where it did not

exist. In 1946 for example, in the matter of the Wages
Councils Act, the Northern Ireland committee recommended
that 'where differential rates of remuneration are
established under the Act as between Northern Ireland and
Great Britain to the disadvantage of Northern Ireland,
Labour members of the Council should endeavour to level
up the rates to the British standard.'[108] And this matter
of wage disparity was a widespread problem. 'Wage rates
in Northern Ireland', said Binks in 1953,[109] 'are 13 per
cent lower for males and 20 per cent lower for females
than in Great Britain.'

But if Northern Ireland workers looked to Britain for
wage leadership, they no less looked to Britain for parity
in other matters as well. 'As far as the working class
are concerned,' said Binks on the same occasion,[110] 'there
has never been "step by step" with Great Britain ... the
school leaving age is a year lower in Northern Ireland;
we have not got a Youth Employment Service; the Trades
Disputes Act (1927) had not been repealed; only householders
and their spouses in Northern Ireland have the vote in local
government elections, while for these elections and elections
for the Northern Ireland Parliament, there is still plural
voting for the property owning class ...' These were
legislative matters which had been remedied in Great Britain
but not in Northern Ireland. The fact that Northern Ireland
was an integral part of the United Kingdom and yet had
not kept abreast with Britain was the major argument advanced
for change. And to the trade unions the outstanding
difficulty, without question, was the Trade Disputes and
Trade Unions Act 1927.

When the act was adopted in Britain in July 1927, it
was condemned by trade unions as vindictive anti-working
class legislation. It appeared to spring from the general
strike of 1926, and a number of provisions were directed

explicitly against the notion of sympathetic strikes, reflecting no doubt the dread of syndicalism and the grève générale. It had set out to make such strikes illegal, and indeed all general strikes, and had run into immense drafting problems.[111] It also prohibited civil servants and their unions from associating with trade union groupings outside the civil service.[112] But while all this was alarming enough, the trade unions in particular were concerned about the provision concerning the political levy. The 1913 Act[113] reversing the judgement in Osborne's case[114] permitted trade unions to levy their members for political purposes but provided for individual members the right to contract out of the arrangement. The 1927 Act, however, reversed the arrangement, requiring each trade union member who wished to pay a political levy to contract in. This of course changed the whole situation radically; and the trade unions believed that this in fact was the real intention of the act, that relating it to the general strike was a pretence, and they were strengthened in their view by reason of the fact that in the years before the general strike there had been a great deal of pressure in the Conservative Party for an amendment of the 1913 Act.[115]

Although Northern Ireland had not been involved at all in the general strike, nevertheless the government there enacted a virtually identical measure in December 1927,[116] but while Westminster repealed the 1927 act in 1947, the Northern Ireland government continued the legislation in being, claiming that they should not slavishly follow Britain in all things.[117] They declared some anxiety about public order, but the Emergency Powers Act (Northern Ireland) of 1926 seemed to provide all that was necessary in the circumstances. It is probable therefore that the question of the political levy was ultimately the most significant consideration. However, the fact that the legislation continued

to run in Northern Ireland was not without its problems
for the Westminster government. Northern Ireland had to
be excluded for example from the United Kingdom's
ratification of Convention 87 of the International Labour
Organisation which concerned freedom of association and the
protection of the right to organise.[118]

Here then was an issue which greatly preoccupied Northern
Ireland trade unions, but which made sense only in the
United Kingdom context, which derived its vigour from a
continuous comparison with Britain, and which ultimately
could be resolved only by pressure from the Westminster
government, since it was most unlikely that the overwhelmingly conservative Northern Ireland administration
would experience a change of heart.

These then were some practical matters which drew the
trade unions in the north towards Britain. The contrary
consideration, the consideration which drew them towards
the south, sprang from developments within the trade union
movement itself, the gradual emergence of a united congress
for the whole country. In the following chapters, we shall
consider the interplay of north and south in regard to these
matters in some detail; all that is necessary at the moment
therefore is that we should indicate in outline how the
north was affected. The developments in the south which
eventually led to unity had not only promise for the north,
but in the early days of negotiation a considerable amount
of risk as well. Indeed at one stage it appeared that
the whole careful strategy of a Northern Ireland committee
was threatened. In 1953 the ice was broken, realistic talks
began between the congresses, and it appeared that there
would be major structural change. Therefore, views which
before were a matter merely for debate became in the
circumstances much more significant. William McMullen,
president of the Irish Transport and General Workers Union,
(whose leadership had become prominent on William O'Brien's

retirement) had of course no illusions whatever about the
real nature of the divided north, much in contrast with the
sentimental obtuseness of southern thinking in general.
To him the idea of loyalist workers in the north joining
Irish-based trade unions was ludicrous, and therefore
while he was committed to the policy of Irish-based and
Irish-controlled unions, he was prepared to settle for
such an arrangement within the Republic itself.[119]   To
him the problem was 'whether those Trade Unions in the
Republic who have been in organic association with the
Northern Trade Unionists in the Irish Trade Union Congress
prefer to remain in such association with them and leave the
movement in this state divided, or whether they will coalesce
with the Irish-based Unions here with the possibility of some
satisfactory arrangement being made with the Six County Trade
Unionists ...'[120]   But although McMullen did not propose it
here, this would have created a situation where an Ulster TUC
would have been unavoidable, and consequently it caused great
alarm among the trade union leadership in the north.   Binks
in addressing the 1953 Northern Ireland conference in
Coleraine[121] recognised that trade union unity was an urgent
necessity, 'but', he continued, 'a proposal which has found
favour in certain quarters gives cause for alarm here ...
A solution for unity ... would be the creation of two
separate administrative areas on the basis of the six and
twenty-six counties with provision for an all-Ireland
council of the two congresses ... with a view to
reunification ... on a thirty-two county basis at some
indefinable date in the future. I fail to see what good
purpose would be served by terminating one division on the
basis that a greater one is created ... (it) may very well lead
to further and more serious divisions ... People here who
have no love for our movement have been trying to sell us the
idea for a long time but we have resisted it and condemned
it ... (We) hope', said Binks in conclusion, 'that unity can
be achieved without endangering the present form of unity
which has existed for 59 years.' These remarks made in

June 1953 received a rather caustic reply from McMullen
when he addressed the CIU annual conference the following
month. The Irish TUC valued the link with the north in the
hope of securing a 'united Irish-based Trade Union movement
for the entire country.'[122] But he dismissed the notion
out of hand. 'This we could consider sound policy and wise
statesmanship if we could point to one fact or even one
gesture since the establishment of this state over 30 years
ago on the part of the Six County Trade Unionists in favour
of a reintegrated Irish Trade Union movement. The Northern
Trade Unionists, both politically and industrially, have
repeatedly declared in favour of the maintenance of the
present territorial status of the Six Counties area and have
no intention to either modify or abandon that attitude, and
while they may pay lip service privately to this ideal for
the purpose of maintaining the pretence of eventual Irish
Trade Union unity, there is nothing further from their
innermost thoughts than to abandon an atom of their present
partitionist attitude in this matter.' To McMullen then
a united trade union movement throughout the whole country
was impossible if one required - as the CIU did - that the
unions be Irish-based and Irish controlled. Furthermore
unity in the south could only be achieved by breaking up the
transborder character of the amalgamated unions within the
Irish TUC. Perhaps the most effective statement of the
contrary view was made by Bob Smith in his presidential
address to the ITUC in 1955, when a solution to the problem
was already in sight: 'No one can doubt', he said,[123] 'that
workers in the Republic do almost unanimously desire a
united Ireland. But they have been sedulously schooled to
accept an utterly false notion of the meaning of national
unity. In workers' organisations, in the Trade Union Movement,
we have a fine tradition of recognising the brotherhood of
man, and of accepting the principle that workers' interests
and workers' unity transcends national boundaries. In
Ireland we give those principles practical expression by
freely and of our own accord joining together in trade union
organisations constituted without reference to the border ...'

This desire to ground unity on the notion of an international workingclass brotherhood and to dominate thereby great social divisions was already of course a familiar and well-practiced policy among trade union leaders in the north, who had to face day in and day out the reality of 'sectarianism disgracefully represented as "religious" differences.'[124] 'We would be deaf and blind,' said Bob Smith,[125] 'if we did not know that these considerations are the primary considerations affecting the political decisions of large numbers of workers, trade unionists, in Belfast and Derry and Northern Ireland generally.'

It is not surprising therefore that the northern leadership were much concerned with developments in the south from 1953 onwards and much relieved when the solution proposed permitted them to retain the fullness of the amalgamated connection, requiring by way of Irish autonomy those things which in practice were conceded in any event. But despite this, the consent of their own northern membership was not by any means secure. Government representatives had not been slow to point out that even within the ITUC the Irish-based unions explicitly envisaged not only one congress for the whole country but the disappearance of the British-based unions, and the reunification of the congresses appeared to be the first step on the way. Consequently, immediately following the establishment of the umbrella body, the Provisional United Organisation, a number of careful consultative meetings took place in Northern Ireland; first of all Northern Ireland full-time officials on February 3 1956, and then, later the same month, a meeting of the PUO with the Northern Ireland Committee, the Belfast Trades Council and the confederations.[126] Of course they were immensely helped in this critical year of 1956 by reason of the fact that Harold Binks, the chairman of the Northern Ireland committee, was not alone the president of the ITUC but the first chairman of the Provisional United Organisation. They needed such institutional help when at the year's end IRA violence flared along the border.

Nevertheless when the draft constitution of the new congress
was published in 1957, Jack Macgougan, a prominent northern
leader, and that year's president of the ITUC, could welcome
it as 'a landmark in the evolution of trade union structures
in this country (because) it seeks to provide the basis of
unity between two different conceptions of trade union
organisation.'[127]   And this, quite successfully, was in
fact what it did.

Notes on Chapter Eight

1.   Lyons op.cit. p.731.

2.   ibid. p.735.

3.   Lyons op.cit. p.732.

4.   See also Charles McCarthy: 'Civil Strife and the Growth
      of Trade Union Unity: the case of Ireland' in Government
      and Opposition VIII, 4, 1973, p.410.

5.   Cf. Betty Sinclair, speaking at the Northern Ireland
      Conference 1956; this was perhaps the only mention
      of religion in any Northern Ireland Annual Conference
      report during the period, where in support of Leeburn's
      appointment as Northern Ireland officer, she said:
      'Mr Leeburn, in all the years I have been in the trade
      union movement, has never asked you what religion
      you are. It has never troubled him, and I think he is
      the best man for the job.'

6.   See Harold Binks ITUC 1952 p.158.

7.   See p.261 above.

8.   See p.264 above.

9.   The point was made explicitly by Billy McCullough at
      the ITUC Congress of 1950, p.74. 'I know', he said,
      'that it has been a bone of contention in Northern
      Ireland Trade Union circles in the past that the
      Northern Ireland Government hand-picks people for
      membership of these boards ...'

10.   William O'Brien papers Ms.13974.

11.   ITUC 1950 p.147.

12.   He recognised that since the loyalists would never
      join Irish-based unions, pressure for an exclusively
      Irish-based trade union movement in the south (and
      this he continuously urged but in a manner other than
      by statute) would mean a drift towards division north
      and south, in regard to which he hoped for 'some
      satisfactory arrangement.' See earlier p.347.

13.   ITUC 1946 p.23. Its members were appointed by the
      national executive, but in practice ten were elected
      by the Northern Ireland Conferences and nominated
      for appointment to the national executive. The other
      three were ex officio the President, the Vice-
      President and the Secretary or Assistant Secretary
      of Congress. See p.262 above.

14.   There was some development in the new ICTU constitution
      of 1959.   See p.457   below.

15.   Northern Ireland Committee Minutes November 30 1945.

16.   ibid.   August 13 1954.

17.   Con Connolly was the first rank-and-file member to be
      elected President, and since he was not a full-time
      official he would probably have found difficulty in
      travelling regularly to Belfast (see ITUC 1953 p.82).

18.   Minutes Northern Ireland Committee August 27 1948.

19.   1949 p.50.

20.   Report: Northern Ireland Conference 1948.

21.   ibid. 1950.

22.   ibid. 1950.   The resolution was non-contentious and
      concerned trade union unity.

23.   ibid. 1953.

24.   Parliamentary Debates: House of Commons Northern
      Ireland October 17 1950, cols. 1578/9.

25.   Northern Ireland Committee report to Second Annual
      Conference 21 Sept. 1946.

26.   See in particular Ruaidhri Roberts' address to the
      conference of February 17 1951:   Annual Report NI
      Conference 1950-51.

27.   See p. 261 above.   An early proposal by Tom Johnson
      c.1933, remarkably similar to what was eventually
      decided, is among the William O'Brien papers, Ms.   15676 (1).

28.   Second Annual Conference of the Northern Ireland
      Committee September 21 1946 - the first annual conference
      being taken to be the inaugural meeting on November 3
      1945 in Belfast.

29.   ibid. 1946.

30.   Roberts: Conference of February 17 1951.

31.   Annual Conference Newry September 27 1947.

32.   Annual Conference Belfast October 9 1948.

33.   see p. 306.

34. NI Annual Conference September 21 1946.

35. NI Annual Conference June 1955.

36. NI Annual Conference June 19 1953.

37. NI Annual Conference May 2 1958.

38. See above p. 75.

39. See also the Report of the Commission on Vocational Organisation pars. 301-302 where some background to trade councils is given.

40. The protest by the Dublin Council at the exclusive recognition of the CIU at the ILO in Geneva in 1945 did not help. See later p.364.

41. CIU 1946 p.180.

42. Lyons op.cit. p.738.

43. ibid. p.738.

44. ibid. p.738.

45. NI Annual conference June 19 1953.

46. ITUC 1946 p.177.

47. idem.

48. ITUC 1947 p.66.

49. ITUC 1946 p.177

50. ITUC 1950 p.89.

51. Irish Municipal Employees' Trade Union.

52. ITUC 1950 p.89.

53. idem. p.90.

54. idem p.92.

55. idem pp.93-94. Sean Dunne was not impressed and very soon after he proposed the suspension of standing orders in order to 'protest against the reception of a delegate from the Northern Ireland Labour Party, and directs the Executive to extend no such invitation in future.' He was supported by Keane of the INTO. Although Sam Kyle refused to permit speeches of support, the suspension of standing orders was agreed by the conference by 71 votes to 30. The debate on the

resolution that followed was remarkable for the
sincerity of the northern delegates who appealed
for its withdrawal. 'I have had my home raided in
the North of Ireland,' said Kerr of the Belfast
Trades Council, 'for my political beliefs and I am
a Protestant. I have spoken on behalf of Anti-
Partition candidates in the North; I have assisted
Jack Beattie in his campaign. Our friends ... have
made their protest. Is that not sufficient without
giving the Tory Press the ammunition they want? At
the moment we are faced with very heavy pressure
from the Northern Government to split from the
Irish T.U.C. We were told we would be consulted on
every occasion if only we would not be in association
with anybody in Dublin. We want to maintain our
allegiance to the T.U.C. We have fought for it
and will continue to fight for it ... If you continue
with this discussion you will split Congress wide
open'. In view of all this Sean Dunne, while declaring
himself an Irish Republican, withdrew the resolution
on the grounds that he had 'no desire to engender
bitterness or cause any split.' (ITUC 1950 pp.100-04)

56. See p. 117 above; see also McCarthy, Government and
Opposition VIII, 4, op.cit. p.430.

57. cf. Norman Kennedy ITUC 1957 p.190 where in contrast
with the normal low profile in these matters, he
roundly condemned violence, but also questioned whether
it should be answered by repressive measures merely.
'However necessary these steps may have been, they
represent the old story of force being met with force ...
If this is all that is done, I, for one, have the
unhappy feeling that we may see, after a further lapse
of time, another instalment, a new chapter of violence.'
And he went on to suggest a council appointed jointly
by the parliaments north and south, to deal both with
violence and discrimination.

58. NIC Report 1946.

59. ITUC 1947 p.65.

60. NIC Report 1947.

61. ibid.

62. ITUC special conference February 17 1951.

63. ITUC 1948 p.49.

64. ibid.

65. NI Conference October 9 1948.

66. Special Conference Belfast February 17 1951.

67. idem.

68. NI Conference October 9 1948.

69. At this time the Minister of Commerce was Sir Roland Thomas Nugent; he was succeeded by W.J. McCleery on November 4 1949.

70. NI Conference October 21 1949.

71. NI Conference October 21 1949.

72. Ivan Neill succeeded William Brian Maginness as Minister of Labour and National Insurance on January 12 1950.

73. Parliamentary Debates House of Commons Northern Ireland October 5 1950 col.1507.

74. ibid. October 17 cols. 1569-72.

75. ibid. cols. 1576-77.

76. ITUC 1952 p.154.

77. ITUC Special Conference Belfast February 17 1951.

78. ibid.

79. NIC Annual Report for conference June 15 1951.

80. idem.

81. idem.

82. idem.

83. idem.

84. idem.

85. ITUC Special Conference Belfast February 17 1951.

86. idem.

87. idem.

88. idem.

89. idem.

90. See p. 321 above.

91. There were some radicals who, unlike Betty Sinclair, were tempted by the idea of an Ulster TUC.

92. See p.315 above.

93. Louie Bennett said for example at this special conference in Belfast on February 17 1951: 'I always hesitate to speak before a Northern Ireland room as I feel I do not know enough about how you live and work ...'; and even Vic Feather of the British TUC, when he addressed the annual conference in Coleraine in 1953 on the question of national insurance, was not quite at ease.

94. See also p.314 above.

95. ITUC 1952 p.79.

96. NIC Report 1952;   ITUC 1952 p.79.

97. NIC 1952.

97A. ITUC 1952 p.153.

98. NIC Report 1952.

99. NIC 1952.

100. NIC 1955.

101. For example the Northern Ireland committee wrote to the Prime Minister in September 1952 seeking a meeting on a matter concerning wages councils, and published their letter at the same time. Thus their letter seeking a meeting got publicity rather than the later refusal of the Prime Minister to meet them.

102. NIC 1954.

103. NIC 1956.

104. NIC 1957.

105. ITUC 1956 p.278.

106. NIC 1953.

107. NI Committee 1950.

108. ITUC 1946 p.25.

109. NIC 1953. Even where the same minimum wage as in Britain was agreed, there was frequently a difference in take-home pay.

110. idem. There was also the difficulty that Northern
     Ireland was administratively and in cast of mind
     a province, unlike the south, which, despite its
     parochialism, was nonetheless the author of its own
     administrative and social development.

111. A very full account of the background to the legislation
     appears in Trade Union Information, X,60 February 1955
     where Lord Reading, a former Lord Chief Justice, is
     quoted as saying that the act was 'more vague, more
     indefinite, more lacking in precision ... than any Bill
     that I have ever seen or any Act of Parliament I have
     ever had to construe.'

112. Later when the act was repealed in Britain but not
     in Northern Ireland, the disability was removed from
     the Imperial civil servants employed in the North, but
     not from those employed by the Northern Ireland government.

113. Trade Union Act 1913.

114. Osborne v. A.S.R.S. [1910] A.C.87.

115. See Harold Binks ITUC 1955 p.163.

116. Trade Union Information op.cit.

117. ITUC 1955 p.163. Bob Getgood, who in 1947 was a
     member of parliament for Northern Ireland, had joined
     in introducing a private members' bill to repeal the
     act, which was defeated, and Getgood sadly reported
     to Congress: 'The Government took the line that we
     could not claim any monopoly of support from trade
     unionists. They claim, I think with a measure of
     truth, that otherwise good trade unionists had voted
     for a Government which, in this case, had imposed
     this shameful Act upon them.' (ITUC 1947 p.174).

118. Trade Union Information op.cit.

119. cf. CIU 1953 p.56 where he said: '...whatever
     concessions we may be prepared to make to meet the
     difficulties of the Northern situation in the eventual
     hope of a reintegrated Trade Union movement for the
     entire country, we must insist as a minimum that
     the Trade Unions operating in this state shall be Irish-
     based and controlled and freed from all outside
     interference.' See p.316 above.

120. CIU 1953 p.54.

121. NIC 1953.

122. CIU 1953 p.55.

123. ITUC 1955 p.137.

124. idem.

125. idem.

126. NIC 1956.

127. NIC 1958.

Chapter Nine

Division

-i-

We have seen how, in the north, the difficult relations
between the trade unions and the government were given
urgency and a sense of stress by the fact of unemployment.
In the south, unemployment imported no less a feeling of
tension into the situation there. This was particularly
so from 1952 onwards when a giddy and unbalanced post-war
boom collapsed into the stagnation of the fifties[1] and in
Dublin there were protest parades and demonstrations
organised by the Dublin Unemployed Association to which
the ITUC gave support.[2] But of course it was not only the
depressing figures in the live register that were significant;[3]
there was the flood of emigration during the whole decade
of the fifties, at least 400,000 - that is a figure higher
than in any other decade of the twentieth century.[4] The
rate of growth was averaging about two per cent per annum,
distressingly and substantially lower than any member of the
OEEC to which Ireland was now tending to look for comparison,
and there was an alarming feeling of a nation ageing and dying.

Fianna Fail were in government from June 1951 to May 1954 -
with, as we have seen, a fragile and uncertain mandate -
and therefore they, and not the coalition, met first the
intractable problem of stagnation, emigration and unrest.
Any attempt to resolve it inevitably involved the trade unions.
While de Valera could never really see the trade unions as
economic partners,[5] Lemass in Industry and Commerce had no
such difficulty; indeed as early as 1946, when he was

confronted with the great post-war pressure on wages
and later on prices, he sought their positive cooperation,
and again, in 1951, when he returned to office he attempted
to involve them in a joint enterprise, not only in regard
to wage management but also in regard to training and
apprenticeship legislation which he saw as a basic strategy
in the long-term development of a heavy and sluggish economy.
But the trade union movement was in considerable disarray,
not only divided between two congresses, but immensely
fragmented apart from that division. But the existence
of the two congresses was without doubt the greatest
difficulty; other structural problems could not really
be tackled until that was resolved, and in this chapter
and the next we shall trace the major efforts which were
made to restore such unity.

The trade unions of course were embarrassingly conscious
of the problem themselves. Later, in April 1954, when unity
was in the making, and when the drawbacks of disunity could
be more readily detailed, the joint committee of the two
congresses agreed 'that the existence of disunity creates
an undesirable and dangerous situation.'[6] They spoke of
the difficulties experienced in national wage bargaining, the
deferment of important and beneficial legislation, the
obstructing of trade union cooperation within an industry
and the impossibility of dealing with some interunion
disputes. 'Campaigns for the organisation of unorganised
workers cannot be planned or carried out on a national
level. Not only is the orderly growth and development of
the movement stultified and improvements in general
organisation made difficult, if not impossible, but a
situation is created in which the existing fabric of the
movement is imperilled by the absence of any of the normal
checks against "poaching", breakaways, and disruptive
competition.'[7] Of course this was written at a time
when the leadership of both congresses were disposed to
promote the idea of unity; nevertheless there is little doubt

that the problems were considerable - problems which became
more and more demanding as the years went by, so that by the
Autumn of 1953 there were powerful pressures which impelled
the congresses, despite their own difficulties, to find
some solution. Indeed we can mark two stages in our period,
the first being from 1945 to 1953, (which we deal with in
the present chapter) when the barriers to unity seemed
indeed unsurmountable, and the second stage from 1953 to
1959, when determinedly and carefully, unity was worked out.

We come therefore to examine the first stage, from 1945 to 1953,
in some detail, and it is helpful to see it in the context
of the various government administrations of the time. The
Fianna Fail administration, unlike that of the interparty
government, was always prepared to use legislation as an
instrument of reform, both to facilitate negotiation, as
under the Industrial Relations Act of 1946 (which the trade
unions welcomed) but also for the purpose of restructuring
the trade union movement, which of course was quite another
matter.

Up to 1948, Fianna Fail was in power and when the Supreme
Court held that 'Part III of the Trade Union Act , 1941
(was) in its main principles repugnant to the Constitution,'[8]
Lemass, despite his earlier disavowals[9] about the use of
legislation for trade union reform, immediately began
devising ways by which the objectives of the 1941 act could
still be achieved, causing the ITUC, in particular,
considerable anxiety. In contrast, during the interparty
administration from 1948 to 1951, the emphasis, under
Norton's influence, was altogether on voluntary endeavour.
Again the emphasis changed in 1951, when Fianna Fail
returned to power, and Lemass's obvious impatience, despite the
weak state of his party, gave urgency to the desire of both
congresses (neither of which at this stage favoured legislation)
to find a voluntary solution.

-ii-

The period up to 1948 is full of incident. It began in a
rather embarrassing way, since the first overt dispute between
the two congresses was argued out not in Ireland but in the
solemn multilingual councils of the ILO, a dispute in which
the Irish government was involved up to the hilt. It took
place at the 27th session of the conference of the International
Labour Organisation which was held in Paris in October-
November 1945. The point at issue was no trivial one,
raising as it did the basic question whether the CIU or the
ITUC was the more representative organisation. Article 3
of the constitution of the International Labour Organisation[10]
provides that non-government delegates and advisers must be
chosen 'in agreement with the industrial organisations, if
such organisations exist, which are most representative
of employers or work-people as the case may be in their
respective countries.' No non-government delegates had
been nominated by the Irish government during the war years,
but now when normality had returned, the government found
not one representative body of work-people in Ireland but two.
They invited both congresses to make nominations and since
there were two appointments to be made, one workers' delegate
and one workers' adviser, they may have had some distant
hope of arranging a compromise. In the event they decided
that they had to choose between one congress and the other.
This they did without further consultation with the ITUC,
who were infuriated to read in the newspapers that the two
appointees were from the CIU. It amounted to a recognition
by the government that CIU and not ITUC was the recognised
trade union centre. Tom Johnson, the acting secretary
of the ITUC, issued on behalf of the national executive
a strongly worded circular letter protesting against 'the
action of the Minister for Industry and Commerce in
selecting ... two nominees of a break-away minority
organisation calling itself the "Congress of Irish Unions."

The Irish Trade Union Congress represents a majority of
the organised workers of Ireland whether calculated on the
basis of Ireland as a whole, or of the Twenty-six counties
of Eire separately and from its nominees the workers' delegate
and adviser to the ILO Conference have hitherto been
selected ... (They regarded) the action of the Minister
as being in conflict with the democratic principles upon
which the International Labour Office is founded and a
direct challenge to the constitutional right of the workers
of Ireland to freedom of association.'[11]   The Irish TUC
rested its case on a simple mathematical calculation.
They represented '76,400 organised workers in Eire (while)
the twelve unions which seceded from the TUC had between
them 54,000 members ... based upon their affiliation to the
TUC in 1944';[12]   Johnson contrasted this in the year of
their disaffiliation with the figure they now claimed of
74,500.

To the Congress of Irish Unions, these were 'impudent and
misleading declarations.'[13]   No British-based union, in its
opinion,could be taken as representative of Irish workers;
and in any event such unions were already represented at
the ILO by the British TUC; this left, for purposes of
comparison, only those Irish-based unions which were in
affiliation with the Irish TUC, and the total membership
here was far less than the CIU represented. The difference
in fact lay not in arithmetic but in principle.

What is noteworthy here is that both ITUC and CIU had
deeply-felt commitments to what they regarded as the
natural and self-evident legitimacy of their position,
the ITUC relying on its long tradition of acceptance, the
reality of its own Irishness which arithmetic could not
upset; and the CIU relying on the overwhelming legitimacy
of national feeling. Both sides therefore felt some sense of
outrage, as a man does when his instinctive sense of the
legitimacy of things is challenged.

It was clear however that the view of the Congress of
Irish Unions was the one which the Irish government supported.
J. Williams, the Irish government delegate in a submission
to the ILO credentials committee[14] said that it was 'the
considered view of the Irish government that a delegate
and adviser from the Congress of Irish Unions could more
appropriately present the point of view of Irish workers
than nominees of a group who, because of external affiliations
could be influenced by the interests of workers' organisations
outside the country.'

In the event, while the credentials committee found for the
Irish government they nonetheless - very interestingly -
took the view that the two organisations appeared to be of
equal strength[15] and consequently expressed the hope that
'in all the circumstances in accordance with the provisions
of the Constitution of the International Labour Organisation
the Irish government should endeavour to secure accord between
these two organisations ...' It was a decision not to upset
the choice of the Irish government.[16] It could hardly be
regarded as an endorsement, although it was represented
as such by the triumphant CIU delegates.[17] It is interesting
to remark, however, that even during the two periods of
administration of the interparty government that followed,
in the next decade, and even though in the second
administration Norton, as Minister for Industry and Commerce,
was responsible for trade union affairs, the practice of
appointing exclusively the nominees of the Congress of
Irish Unions was not disturbed.

And yet the CIU representatives had much more reason to
be pleased than the rather careful opinion of the
credentials committee would indicate. In a conference of
nations, it seemed odd, and hardly worthy of support, that
trade unions based in one nation should attempt to dominate
in another. More than that, the ITUC had taken the rather
curious step of asking the British TUC to raise the objection
regarding the CIU credentials,[18] although - in the opinion
of the Irish government delegate in any event - the Irish

TUC could themselves have done so.[19]   True, the Dublin
Trades Union Council also registered an objection, but it
carried little additional weight.   The British representatives
were in a quandary, obviously not wishing in any way to be
identified with notions of trade union domination in another
country;   and consequently they took the greatest care to
emphasise that they were merely performing a formal function
on behalf of the ITUC in raising the matter.   Presumably,
the ITUC had hoped that the influence of the British TUC
would have carried weight (one of its representatives,
Joseph Hallsworth, was chairman of the workers' group at the
conference)[20] but the British TUC had its own reputation to
guard, and the very neutrality of its approach (admitted by
the CIU representatives at the time, although forgotten in
the myth-making that followed)[21] did little to help the
ITUC cause.   William O'Brien and Cathal O'Shannon could
afford to adopt a low profile since clearly the mood of the
conference lay with them.

-iii-

It was a very sobering experience for the ITUC.   In fact
their appeal at the ILO was the first and last burst of
righteous and unreflective indignation.   They began to move
towards the idea of some form of compromise, a compromise
sought particularly by the Irish-based unions within the
Irish TUC, and also to quite an extent by the Eire-based
officials of the amalgamated unions.   The essence of the
compromise was an attempt to come to terms with nationalism.
Larkin, junior, put it with great clarity in the debate   at
the ITUC annual conference in the summer of 1946.[22]   'Do we
not realise', he said,'that we have around us a developing
nationalism and that we have contributed to that?   You

cannot allow this to grow into existence and then ignore
it ... We have inculcated into the minds of our people
the idea of nationalism. We cannot turn round at the
nineteenth hour and tell people that everything we fought
for meant nothing and that they are not entitled to
travel further along that road, that they must come to a
full stop. I am quite sure that delegates from the
Amalgamated Unions realise to the full and appreciate our
difficulties ...' In fact in the period between the
ending of the ILO conference in November 1945, and the
summer trade union conferences in 1946, three important
steps towards compromise had been made by the leadership
of the ITUC, represented perhaps by three confrontations -
the word is hardly too strong - the first with Lemass,
the second with the CIU and the third with the British TUC,
each confrontation being a further step away from the
traditional trade union legitimacy which the ITUC believed
it possessed and towards a recognition of the greater and
more insistent legitimacy of nationalist sentiment. And
through it all - indeed most clearly in the first nine
years of disunity - the ITUC was the wooer and the CIU the wooed.

A copy of the ITUC's rather scorching resolution of September
1945[23] when the CIU nominees were chosen for the ILO had been
sent to Lemass and in the course of his reply he had charged
the ITUC that it was 'within the power of your National
Executive to make a substantial contribution to unity.'[24]
This was sufficient for the shaken ITUC to build on; they
sought an explanation and had in reply a lengthy letter from
Lemass on November 8 1945,[25] in which he first declared
his belief that 'in a democratic State, the Trade Union
Movement must play an increasingly important part in the
national life, not merely as a guardian of the workers'
interests, but as an essential part of the machinery of
industrial organisation, accepting the responsibilities
which relate to its real power, and proceeding from the
stage of negotiating particular agreements with private

employers to the stage of formulating and carrying into
effect a general policy for the furtherance of the long-
term interests of the workers as a class.' Having established
his <u>bona fides</u> in a manner which must have gratified the
ITUC Lemass then went on to identify the 'main matter in
issue (as) the continued operation of the British Trade
Unions here.' To achieve reunification, he contemplated
three steps, the first being 'a declaration of long-term
policy favouring the orderly withdrawal of such Unions'
which he thought the British unions themselves, in the
interests of all should not oppose; the second being 'a
joint approach to the British Trade Union Congress by both
the Irish Trade Union Congress and the Congress of Irish
Unions to discuss the voluntary withdrawal', including the
possible establishment here of new trade unions; and the
third being a meeting between the two Irish congresses to
restore unity and to supervise and facilitate the withdrawal.
The proposal was taken most seriously by the ITUC. When
their head office circulated copies of the Minister's
letter to the national executive, a note which accompanied
it (unsigned but possibly from Johnson) suggested that 'it
should be considered without regard to any prejudices
members may have regarding the Government, or suspicions
as to its motives. Our response to the letter may determine
the future of Trade Unionism in this country and a long
distance view should be taken as well as the present position.'[26]
It was clear from subsequent events that this too became
the view of the national executive as a whole, and in
taking such a view they made the first amd most significant
step on the road to compromise - since they were now
prepared to consider, as objectively as they could, that
the Irish trade union congress should be not merely a
national congress but a nationalist one.

A meeting with Lemass subsequently on November 22[27]
established that in all this he was speaking personally,
further that the government had no present intention of

taking any action 'detrimental to the amalgamated unions'
and finally that he was speaking in the context only of
the twentysix counties. Of course he could do little else,
but, apart from that, Lemass obviously expected that in time
the trade unions, no less than other groupings and associations,
would inevitably divide on the basis of the border, however
profoundly the unions might hold to the all-Ireland principle.
Nevertheless his whole approach had considerable skill,
even to the suggestion that trade union membership might
be made compulsory.

To wish to woo is one thing;   to find an opportunity is
another. In this case it was provided within a few days of
the Lemass meeting by William Norton whose union, significantly,
was a prominent affiliate of the ITUC but whose political
stature gave him some degree of independence. He proposed[28]
formally that three representatives from each congress should
meet under an agreed chairman 'to explore the possibility
of reuniting the movement',[29] and this they agreed to do, the
talks being launched on December 10 1945 in what Crawford
described as a blaze of publicity.[30]   In the discussions that
followed - under alternating chairmen - the CIU ruthlessly
required recognition of what they regarded as a natural
consequence of independent nationhood, the principle that
trade unions operating in Ireland must have their headquarters
in Ireland, and their executives must be elected by and
responsible to the members in Ireland.[31]   They based this
approach on the existence of the 'independent Irish state
operating through the Government of Ireland.'[32]   But to
the ITUC the 'acceptance of the principle underlying the CIU
formula would commit them to approval of the separation of
the members of a Union who live in one part of Ireland from
their fellow-members in another part of Ireland',[33] which the
CIU, with quite an astonishing disregard for the realities,
dismissed: 'On the contrary', they said,[34] 'if the
principle in the formula were applied as drafted the present
members of any particular British Union in any part of Ireland,
by their own act, would be joined in an Irish Union with their
fellow-workers of that Irish Union in all other parts of Ireland.

Although the ITUC could not swallow the CIU formula nevertheless
they decided that they would consult the British TUC, and in
the meantime they suggested that the conference should continue
for the purpose of discussing other matters. (We must
remember that at that time the Industrial Relations Bill
was under discussion with Lemass, both Congresses being engaged
in separate and independent discussions.) But as far as the
CIU were concerned, the ITUC had failed to agree with the first
and fundamental condition of cooperation, and they refused to
have further talks until this problem was solved. Once again,
however, we can see how significant was the move of the ITUC;
they had now undertaken the difficult and rather uncomfortable
task of exploring all these ideas with the British Trade
Union Congress.

And it was indeed somewhat difficult and uncomfortable. The
British TUC had no real function in the matter, despite the
ready assumption on Lemass's part - and indeed on the part of
others as well - that it manifestly had. In these islands, a
congress, British or Irish, ITUC or CIU, is not an authority as
much as a standing conference, representative of essentially
independent units. It can speak on matters of mutual concern,
it can, when explicitly empowered to do so, adjudicate between
one union and another, but it cannot, without creating great
resentment, concern itself with the internal affairs of any
one union. And this problem of the Irish membership of
certain affiliated unions was seen as an internal one
essentially, although common to a number of unions. Of course
this was well understood by the ITUC who declared that their
object was to consult with the national executives of the
amalgamated unions concerned, the British TUC being asked
merely to facilitate this.[35] The general council called a
conference in London on May 15 1946 as they were requested
to do[36] but the chairman of the meeting, Arthur Deakin, took
pains to point out that 'the General Council were acting as
a convening body and he felt that it was not within their
purview to come to any decision on the matter or to make
recommendations to their affiliated organisations because the

problems associated with the Irish membership were clearly
problems to be resolved by the Executive Councils and their
membership in Ireland.'[37] But the CIU did not apparently
appreciate the nature of this relationship; they expected
that there would have been some response from the British TUC,
and when there was no immediate sign, they assumed a
negative.[38] This added to the awkwardness of the move.
Secondly, those Irish officers and lay Irish officials of
the amalgamated unions who were on the national executive
of the ITUC - and they numbered eight of the total of fifteen -
were also in some subsidiary relationship to the general
officers of their unions, and these in turn, or at least the
prominent ones, were members of the general council of the
British TUC. Certainly, too much should not be made of this
point; even those Irish officials who were appointed and not
elected carried a substantial degree of democratic independence.
Nevertheless, subsidiarity is subsidiarity, creating its
own tensions; and it may have been the reason why the ITUC
sent as its two representatives to the British TUC conference,
Tom Johnson and Jim Larkin junior, neither having any connection
with amalgamated unions.

The statement that Johnson made to the conference was
balanced and sensitive. The CIU now represented a considerable
number of Irish trade unionists. Some of the remaining
Irish unions were also in danger of breaking away from the
ITUC, which already was made up largely of amalgamated unions.
Furthermore the campaign of the CIU unions to attract away
amalgamated members was likely to impress the younger men in
particular, and the outlook was bleak. Falling numbers
in the ITUC would result in a falling prestige in the eyes of
the government. Johnson had also been much impressed by Lemass's
view of the wider social and economic role of the trade union
movement, the fulfilling of which would require that the
presiding authority be within the country. Of course he
recognised that the Irish membership was loyal to the
amalgamated unions; and the Irish government, despite its

belief that they should withdraw, was unlikely to take
any overt step to that end, since they did not wish to
offend the Labour government in the United Kingdom with
which the British trade unions were closely associated.
Because of this there were some who believed that they might
postpone doing anything very much about the problem, that
it would be time enough to consider it when the Irish
government made a move. But to Johnson's mind the time
was now ripe for consideration; and he suggested a formula,
which had been hinted at in the talks with Lemass[39] in
November: 'It was that in the direction of Union policy
the Irish Trade Unionists would be masters of their own
decisions in matters affecting public affairs in general.
This could be secured by rule and practice and the method
of re-organisation might be framed so that the amalgamated
Unions' connection with Eire could be retained by some
system of federation.'[40] It is difficult to judge at this
remove how much precise thinking Johnson had given to this
formula. It seemed on the face of it to contain two quite
different ideas; the first provided procedural independence
in certain matters for the Irish membership of the amalgamated
unions, secured by internally arranged 'rule and practice' but,
on the other hand, the notion of federation, which was also
raised, conveyed quite a different idea; it implied
structural, not procedural, independence for the Irish
membership subject to joint federal control with the
United Kingdom organisation. The conference in London spent
some time questioning and discussing Johnson's statement[41]
but since we have no record of this, it is not possible to
say whether the matter was further explored. When the
report of the conference came before the ITUC July meetings,
there were some accusations of defeatism in regard to Johnson's
approach (which Larkin hotly denied) and much emphasis on
the loyalty of the Irish members to amalgamated unions.

But now the whole legal environment had suddenly changed
by reason of the Supreme Court judgement in the NUR case,
creating a dramatic and unexpected reversal in the course
of events. Its significance may not have been fully grasped
at the time of the trade union conferences. The judgement
was delivered on July 4, the day after the CIU congress had
opened, and five days before that of the ITUC began. Yet at
the ITUC conference, quite a number of delegates sensed
in the decision a great and fundamental change in fortune.
It is therefore tempting to see in this judgement the great
turning point in all these proceedings, the steps towards
compromise having been taken by the ITUC in the context of
the earlier unhelpful decision of the High Court, but now
these steps losing impetus once the threat of the administrative extinguishing of amalgamated unions had largely
disappeared. Yet the position was somewhat more complex
than that. Nationalist sentiment was continuing to grow
in confidence, indeed in stridency, giving a substantive
legitimacy to the CIU position, and making the Supreme
Court decision appear essentially as an escape hatch for
the amalgamated unions, based on a legal quibble. Certainly
it carried little positive moral force. The Catholic Bishop
of Galway, Dr Michael Browne (who had also been chairman of
the Commission on Vocational Organisation) both summarised
and further legitimated what many trade unionists must have
felt at the time, when he addressed the CIU conference in
Galway:[42] 'Trade unions exercise very great power in the
economic life of a people, and it is very important that the
men who govern them, the men who make decisions, should
accept loyally the industrial and financial obligations
of the nation and that there should be no conflict of
allegiance if a conflict of interests between countries
should arise. And it is also right and proper that we
should have a Congress of our own Irish Unions. Congress
is the national organisation - the instrument for securing
the unity, discipline and development of trade unions according
to our own needs and under our own laws. It is moreover the

instrument for representing and expressing the will of the
Irish workers and their outlook ... it is most important
that they should have a Congress to express their own
distinctive and independent views - a Congress which will
be unmistakably Irish and not subject to any alliances or
extraneous influences.' It was this vigorous sentiment
which Larkin junior recognised, dominating the personality
clashes of the past despite their bitterness.[43] Indeed he
remarked on how Arthur Deakin, the chairman of the London
conference had recognised the force of it as well:[44] '...
(putting) his finger on what to my mind, is the kernel of the
whole situation. He said it was not wise to regard this
situation as being merely one of conflict between Trade
Union Congresses or between Unions or between individuals.
They must realise that it had its background in the historical
process that across the water they had witnessed over a
number of years a struggle on the part of a small nation
to assert and develop its own nationality politically, and
therefore, as a consequence industrially, economically and
socially ...'

So clamorous was nationalist sentiment that the problem
of the trade union north, at this time, became quite obscured.
The vast majority of the organised workers there could in no
sense be regarded as supporters of a small nation engaged
in a historical struggle for independence; the very thought
of it filled them with the greatest foreboding. The solution
which saw nationality as the overwhelming fact was a solution
which, if stated explicitly, would have to exclude the
protestant north, and this would fill the nationalists with
equal foreboding and dismay. Beneath the surface in all this,
therefore, were ideological positions which were totally
irreconcilable. Solutions were in practice sought by
obscuring these positions, misunderstanding them, or by
partly stating them. There was much of this at the ITUC
conference, no less than at that of the CIU, the Irish members
of the amalgamated unions accommodating nationalist demands

by distinguishing between trade union activity and political
activity, moving somewhat to the position taken up by the
Northern Ireland committee. 'To my mind,' said Walter
Carpenter,[45] 'as a member of an Amalgamated Society -
Amalgamated Society of Woodworkers - and as a delegate to
the Dublin Trades Union Council there is no such thing as
a split operating in Dublin as far as the rank and file are
concerned ... The split really exists between people who
for their own aggrandisement are using the Trade Union and
Labour Movements to get positions. These people do not
want unity in the Movement ... Deputy Norton has paid a
compliment to the Amalgamated Societies that during the
national struggle and the fight for Independence in this
country they never interfered with men who were members of
their Unions. I am Secretary of the Irish Citizen Army
Comrades' Association and I have been a member of that Army
since its inception. I have always been a member of an
Amalgamated Society. I know men like myself who have been
interned in internment camps and when they came out they
found the Amalgamated Societies standing by them. They
gave me a clear card and continued my membership. We of
the Amalgamated Societies are international in our outlook ...
There is here a ring of the old socialist idea of separatism
which had a distinctly international character, and it
permitted one to see trade unions[46] in their capacity as
serving one range of social interests or roles but by no
means all, and certainly not their members' political roles,
except in some broadly understood socialist context.
This view also tended to throw emphasis on the basic unity
of the workers despite the split, which continued to be true
in an important way, and to discount the disunity between
the congresses as largely a matter of personalities, about
which Larkin, equally correctly, was so impatient. Because
Larkin not only recognised the emergent thrust of nationalism,
but recognised as well the great significance of Lemass's
offer of economic and industrial partnership. Certainly in
the case of the Industrial Relations Bill (the significance

of which we shall   discuss later) Lemass had been remarkably
and unprecedentedly open in his consultation, sending the
ITUC (and also the CIU) a draft of the bill in March,
and meeting them for consultation not only before the bill
was discussed in Dail Eireann, but also after the second
reading and again after the committee stage.[47]   Not that
the whole thing was not viewed with great suspicion by dyed-
in-the-wool trade unionists like Larkin senior[48] despite his
son's involvement in the discussions. But to Larkin junior
and to the ITUC leadership there was considerable promise
here. 'In our movement,' said the younger Larkin,[49] 'we
can no longer say that we can confine ourselves to Trade
Unionism. We are changing on that because we claim the
right to be consulted by Governments and to express our
viewpoint on legislation and policy and to comment to a
certain degree on political activities. If we make claims
then we have got to realise that we have to face the
possible consequences...' The first of the consequences was
the facing up to facts: the ITUC could not, as it now stood,
hope to fulfil such a role, firstly because it was one of
two divided voices, and secondly because even if it could
sit down with the CIU and the government, its legitimacy
as a representative of Irish workers in matters relating to
the Irish state was under challenge.

Despite the radical effect of the Supreme Court judgement
in the NUR case therefore, there were many in the Irish trade
union movement who felt keenly the need to resolve the dilemma.
What the Supreme Court judgement in fact did was to permit
the leadership of the amalgamated unions - particularly
the British leadership - to remain firm, confident that since
they could not now be extinguished administratively, they
could rely on the normal inertia of membership (almost more
than positive loyalty) to sustain them. It helped them
greatly therefore to play down the significance of the
congresses and their differences,[50] and to give the overwhelming
emphasis to the union itself, seeing all the problems in this

straightforward way, and maintaining a highly traditional,
conservative trade union approach. The right to hold to
this view in spite of moral and patriotic pressure to the
contrary was what was guaranteed by the Supreme Court to
the amalgamated unions, and it was this that gave the
decision its radical significance.[51]

-iv-

In the period from the summer of 1946 to the early months
of 1948 (when the new government was formed) there were
four major developments bearing on trade union structures
and how they might be understood, the first of course being
the Supreme Court decision in the NUR case, the second the
Industrial Relations Act which was enacted on August 27 1946,
the third Lemass's proposals of April 1947 for new trade
union legislation, prompted by his disappointment with the
NUR judgement but going well beyond what would be required
to reestablish the position as it was under the 1941 act,
and fourthly, in the autumn of 1947, the first essay by an
Irish government into the thorny business of a prices and
incomes policy, in which, deeply troubled by a sudden rush
of inflation,[52] they sought first the cooperation of the
trade unions, but held behind it the steely glove of
threatened legislation. These four matters go far beyond the
theme of our present discussion, the growth, in these years,
of trade union unity; they bear essentially on the
relationship between the trade unions and the state (whether
these relations are with the courts, the executive or the
legislature); and since we propose to take up this topic
of trade union-state relations in a later chapter, we shall
deal with these events here only insofar as they bear on
our theme of trade union unity.

After the Supreme Court decision in the NUR case, there was

little prospect of any major step towards voluntary withdrawal on the part of the amalgamated unions either acting
individually or in association with the British TUC; in
a word, Lemass's hopes of a rapprochement there had
evaporated. Nevertheless he was not prepared to let it go
at that. Indeed he had little alternative. The Emergency
Powers (260) Order was to lapse in September 1946, and with
it war-time wage controls. The Industrial Relations Act
was designed to meet, by means of the Labour Court, the
onrush of wage claims that was then expected, and a great
deal turned on the acceptability of the new machinery to
trade unions. Two worker members had to be appointed by the
government to the court on trade union nomination[53]; the
ITUC would accept that each Congress should nominate one[54]
but CIU would have none of it.[55] Lemass had an alternative
under the act, but it was a bad augury. He had invited both
congresses to meet under his chairmanship at the end of
August 1946[56] to discuss the nominations of the worker
members and also the question of trade union unity. But the
CIU refused to consider the question of nominations until
agreement was reached on the future of trade unions in
Ireland, and in that regard, they continued to insist that
as a precondition to any discussions the ITUC should accept
that the solution lay in 'the effective transfer of executive
control and authority over the branches of British Unions here
from British executives to Irish executives, and to a united
Trade Union Congress elected by and responsible only to the
trade unionists of this country.'[57] An alternative ITUC
formula spoke of recognising the problem for amalgamated
unions of an Irish state, and of consequential adjustments
in trade union administration and control; they could not
'make a declaration of principle which in effect endorsed
the demand of the CIU for the withdrawal of the Amalgamated
Unions from Ireland without any prior decision on the part of
the Irish members of such Unions.'[58] Lemass, always the
pragmatist, recognised their difficulty, and no doubt had

sympathy with the Irish-based unions within the ITUC, whose
point of view received such compelling expression from the
younger Larkin, but who, in the aftermath of the NUR case,
had to live with a situation where the future of the
amalgamated unions was virtually guaranteed. Lemass from
this time on became convinced that the ITUC, despite their
structural difficulties, were anxious to play a full part
in the development of Irish society and to cooperate with
the government to that end.[59] Consequently he took the
initiative at these talks of suggesting a formula himself,
very similar indeed to that of the ITUC but strengthened
somewhat. The CIU however insisted on having its precondition restored. In the breakdown that followed on
September 7, the CIU blamed the 'hardness' of the ITUC in not
accepting 'a slight change - the restoration of just two
lines',[60] but the two lines were crucial; and Lemass had
no alternative but to confess failure. He was later to
say that 'the gap left unbridged was very narrow',[61]
and to a practical man it no doubt appeared as such. But
once national intransigence is vehemently expressed,
pragmatism has no answer, and Lemass could not be seen as
questioning such a sentiment. It must have been clear to
him therefore that despite the goodwill of the ITUC leadership, an orderly trade union movement could be secured
only by extinguishing the British-based unions; yet, perhaps
because he felt constrained by the Supreme Court judgement
in the NUR case, or perhaps because of some growth of
appreciation of the ITUC position, when he came to consider
legislative measures once again the following year, he concentrated much more on the question of general trade union
reform than on the extinguishing of those British-based
unions that were then established in the country.

There was much at this time to compel Lemass to consider
legislative reform. True, the problem of appointing worker
members to the Labour Court was readily enough overcome by
inviting the major Irish-based industrial unions to nominate

under the alternative provision of the act; but the
awkwardness - indeed the peril - of having rival congresses,
one of which would have nothing whatever to do with the
other, remained to trouble both the government and industry
generally.Even where commonsense and the pressure of the
rank and file would seem to require some flexibility, the
CIU remained obdurate. For example, in November 1946[62] the
ITUC unions in the Electricity Supply Board (Larkin junior
was their group chairman) approached the CIU group of unions
in the same employment in order to suggest a joint negotiating
team, irrespective of congress affiliation, to process the
major claim then under way. Not only did CIU refuse this,
but they refused as well to sit with the ITUC at the same
table, lest it might imply joint negotiation; and when the
matter went before the Labour Court, they made separate
submissions. At a later stage of the proceedings in the
Labour Court, both groups did sit down at the same
conference table,[63] largely because the rank and file members
could see no sense in making an issue of it, but the CIU
never wavered in principle. Furthermore, during this time
we find expressed in CIU debates a good deal of concern
about subversive communist influence, and occasionally
some enthusiasm for vocationalism, all tending to raise
the level of xenophobia and with it the barrier to
communication with the ITUC unions.

On January 30 1947 Big Jim Larkin died, and it seemed as
if an era had come to a close. The Archbishop of Dublin
presided at his requiem mass which was attended by the
President of Ireland, by the Taoiseach and by the senior
members of the government. Thousands thronged to his
funeral in the snow-filled Dublin streets. On the same day young
Jim published a deeply moving letter[64] in which he called
for unity in the movement; he had been struck by the fact
that 'Jim Larkin had been mourned and his passing deeply
regretted by persons and organisations in every section and
division of the Irish Labour movement';[65] the CIU had

been formally represented at the obsequies, and his appeal was
primarily to them, to find at least the 'simplest common
denominator in policy and agree upon that as an immediate
objective ... If the greater measure of devotion is not
expressed by those of us who by chance are playing leading
roles, then let the real and living body of Labour – the
rank and file – show us and compel us to do our duty, but
let it be quick and decisive whoever takes the first step.'[66]
But an attempt by the ITUC to take such a step, to follow
up Larkin's personal appeal, was sharply rebuffed by the
CIU.[67]

Not surprisingly then, Lemass once again began to explore
the possibility of using legislation to resolve the trade
union dilemma in the public interest, and availing of the
fact that the statutory power to reduce deposits in the
case of Irish unions was running out,[68] he had discussions
with both congresses separately during May 1947. His new
proposals were quite radical.[69] Since he could not, in
the light of the Supreme Court decision 'deprive the citizen
of a free choice of the persons with whom he shall associate'
he turned away from the idea of regulating the formation of
such associations (which under the 1941 act could mean in
certain circumstances their extinction) and turned instead to
the regulation of their activities once they had emerged,
suggesting that only those that conformed with certain
statutory conditions could negotiate or could enjoy the
protection and privileges of the act of 1906. He suggested
the establishment of 'a competent and independent authority'[70]
which would not only register the trade unions, after inquiry,
but could also, it would appear, discontinue registration
(which in this case meant exclusion from trade union activity)
on the grounds that a union had not conformed with its own
rules or had been guilty of disruptive behaviour in regard
to other unions. He introduced the notion of an appeal
generally by a worker against a union on the grounds of
inequity, expulsion or refusal of membership, and also the

question of a union's contractual obligations. New
unions could be established only if the competent independent
authority approved and all new unions had to have their
headquarters within the state. This attacked the problem
of British-based unions in a rather oblique way; it said
nothing whatever about the amalgamated unions already in the
country, and the risk of being disestablished for some kind
of malfeasance applied no less to Irish-based unions.
Furthermore the craft unions within the CIU were deeply
uneasy about appeals by individual workers against their
traditional rights of admission to their craft. Lemass
gently wooed them on the whole matter, agreeing to introduce
a short bill to overcome the urgency of the deposits question
and urging them to come back to him with their own suggestions.
The going here on the part of both congresses was very
cautious. Lemass could hardly expect support from the ITUC -
although their reaction was surprisingly mild[71] - and in the
case of the CIU the real position was that they opposed any
further trade union legislation unless it was 'aimed at the
restriction or abolition of the operations of Foreign Unions.'[72]
However, the change in government the following February
brought this particular adventure to an end - at least for
the time being.

But during the course of the discussions on all this within
the councils of the CIU, there emerged a proposal for
statutory reform[73] which reflected very much the views of the
Commission on Vocational Organisation.[74] As a proposal
it appears to have been still-born, but there are two reasons
for examining it here; firstly, it appears to have been the
only proposal to apply in practice the Commission's
recommendations on trade union and industrial reform; and
secondly, while the proposal was still-born, it was put
forward by Owen Hynes of the Building Workers' Trade Union.
Hynes, although representing a craft union of about 2,000
members,was president of the CIU in 1948-49, and even more

important, was very close to Leo Crawford, who had been
appointed secretary of Congress in succession to O'Shannon.[75]
More than that, other craft union representatives were wont
to speak so highly of the solution offered by the Commission
on Vocational Organisation that one must conclude that Hynes's
view had some support among the Irish craft unions in general.[76]

Hynes had in mind the building industry in particular, where
he found a group system among trade unions which 'has
done very useful work, but has many weaknesses ...' since
they were dependent on the voluntary efforts of one of their
number to service the group, and because they 'had to
include the Cross Channel Unions amongst those taking part in
our deliberations.'[77] His remedy was to establish firstly
industrial groups within each industry (corresponding to
the Commission's workers' associations)[78] made up of
delegates from sections of workers - or in the case of
employer groups, of sections of employers - each section
to be designated by craft or occupation.[79] 'Where more
than one trade union caters for a particular Craft or
Occupation they shall be regarded as being members of the
one section for the purpose of the Act.'[80] The workers'
industrial group and the employers' industrial group would
send delegates to a joint industrial council (corresponding
to the Commission's joint industrial board)[81] where, inter
alia, they would discharge the function of negotiating on
wages and conditions. One must assume that the designation
of each section would be a statutory designation, and this
was the key to the exclusion of the British-based unions,
since willy-nilly they would be assumed into sections in the
appropriate industry, and secondly (and here Hynes took up
explicitly what the Commission urged as desirable) only
delegates from Irish-based unions could be elected to the
joint industrial council. In this way all effective functions
would be removed from the British-based unions. Hynes did not
follow the Commission on their idea of a national industrial
conference; but he did recognise the possibility of a

national joint industrial council which would meet the
needs of the building industry well enough.

The central strategy, then, lay in substituting 'sections' -
based on craft or occupation within each industry - for
trade unions; the unions would in practice be displaced
when their effective right to negotiate was removed - since
this was the logic of the proposal. And these sections
in turn would themselves exercise the negotiating function
only through the workers' industrial group which would in
fact constitute an industry-level unitary trade union.

There were perhaps two reasons why Hynes promoted such an
idea. Firstly, Catholicism as a powerful, pervading popular
sentiment was particularly strong among members of the
craft unions at the time, and this report of the Commission
on Vocational Organisation seemed to import into the
difficult tangled business of industrial relations the timeless
and solemn wisdom of the Roman church, particularly since the
report both offered such a clear and total answer to the
muddle that confronted the country, and did so with a ringing
sense of authority based on papal teaching. But secondly,
we must recognise that Hynes promoted it because the building
industry was probably one of the very few industries where
the wrongheadedness of the Commission's report was not
manifest, since there it could be assumed[82] that the unions
being industrial unions, could themselves form the sections
without any great change in their character or scope (that is,
as long as they were Irish-based.) The proposal however
would have created the most inordinate difficulties in many
other industries, and this no doubt was why it was never
pursued despite the solemnity of its provenance.

When we attempt to assess Hynes's proposal therefore we must
look behind it to the report of the Commission; and here
the real wrongheadedness lay in the assumption that one
resolved difficulties by means of a mechanical classification.

The Commission actually made much of the fact that one
should recognise 'the needs of organic life' in the trade
union movement[83] but in practice they appeared to be quite
insensitive to the essentially biological approach which
such a phrase implies and which is a far more sensible
way of seeking a solution. Once a tidy and pleasing symmetry
was devised, the rest was assumed to follow; indeed they
considered that their recommendations should be accepted
voluntarily on the basis of their intrinsic and self-
evident merit, rather than be imposed by statute. 'If at
present,' one passage runs[84] 'there are general or industrial
unions which overlap any scheme of classification found
necessary for the purpose of scheduling the industries
we are of opinion that it would be possible for such unions
to develop ad hoc organisations until experience has been
gained and the system has had time to grow. The existing
trade union organisations may prefer to retain their present
structure and form ad hoc bodies to fulfil the conditions of
vocational organisation. We are of opinion that in such
cases trade unions should not lose any of their present
privileges with the exception that the registered association
(if desired, ad hoc association) for each industry should
represent that industry and act as a negotiating body.'
But this is the very heartland of the problem for Irish-
based no less than British-based unions, since here the
report asks, without any apparent awareness of the enormity
of the question, that unions forego their fundamental,
individual and independent right to negotiate, in favour of
a group; it could be interpreted in no other way.
Furthermore, in its criticism of the 1941 Trade Union Act,[85]
particularly in relation to the extinguishing of British-
based unions, the Commission showed little appreciation of how
institutional change in practice is encompassed, how one
might use institutional catalysts to shape, change and
develop. Classification of itself, as we have already seen,
no matter how sophisticated and logical, is an intellectual
construct which may have very little relevance in the real world.

The determination of the CIU leadership to 'have nothing
to do with the TUC',[86] the recriminations when circumstances
obliged some contact at industry level,[87] the desire to 'use
all their influence on the rank and file of the Irish unions
still adhering to the TUC to get them to break the connection'[88]
caused the government and the Labour Party considerable
difficulty during the autumn of 1947 and in the early part
of 1948 during Ireland's first attempt to introduce a prices
and incomes policy. The ITUC greatly alarmed by rapidly
increasing prices saw Lemass on August 26 1947[89] and urged
the introduction of some new type of prices machinery which
would take the place of that provided by the Control of
Prices Act 1937.[90] But Lemass was unhelpful, seeing many
difficulties in the way of more extensive price control,
and he asked instead that the trade unions should defer wage
claims. Early in September an anxious and rather angry ITUC
wrote to the CIU suggesting an urgent meeting between the
congresses, but the request was brushed aside.[91] The CIU
themselves met Lemass on the question of prices, and intended
to deal with the matter independently.[92] Later in the month
when the situation had been confused and exacerbated by a press
leak,[93] the ITUC threatened a protest strike, and again
sought the cooperation of the CIU, meeting precisely the
same blank refusal.[94] Lemass now moved in the matter of
prices and productivity - and quite dramatically at that -
publishing, at the end of September, the Industrial Efficiency
and Prices Bill[95] which would establish a prices commission
with wide ranging powers not only with regard to prices but
also with regard to restrictive practices, and which would
establish as well joint development councils in industry.
Associated with this machinery he proposed the establishment
of a prices advisory committee consisting essentially of trade
union representatives;[96] but here he ran into difficulties
again. It became clear that he would have to establish not
one but two such prices advisory committees, one for the ITUC
and one for the CIU.[97]

In October, Lemass began to tackle the wages problem, the
attempt here being to stabilise at the current rates and to
index from there onwards, that is, to permit increases only
as the cost of living figure rose.[98]   But once again his
discussions were held with each congress separately, and
when the announcement of the government's intention to hold
a general election caused him to break off the negotiations,
he publicly regretted their protracted nature which he
attributed to the fact that he had to meet each congress in
separate discussions.[99]   The chairman of the Labour Court,
formally at the request of the FUE, invited the parties to
continue to meet in the court.   This was taken up, but each
congress went its own way, meeting the other parties
separately, deliberating separately by way of special conference,
and separately conveying their final assent to the general
wage agreement.[100]   Perhaps the only hopeful note was that
the agreement itself was imaginative and far-reaching, and
required acceptance of certain principles which could provide
stability despite CIU's unwavering hostility to the ITUC.

When the general election result became known, a result which
took the trade unions, no less than others, by surprise,[101]
it changed the environment dramatically.   Lemass's Industrial
Efficiency and Prices Bill (which had thoroughly alarmed
some employers)[102] fell, never to be reintroduced;   but the
most significant event, in this account of the development
of trade union unity, was the decision of the National Labour
Party deputies, who were within the CIU camp, to join with
the Irish Labour Party in the formation of the inter-party
government.   It was a flash-point;   and it welded a connection
-which grew steadily in importance - between the ITUC on the
one hand, and the unbending CIU, so determined to establish
and maintain an exclusive trade union system.

-v-

The period from February 1948 to June 1951, the period of
the coalition government, is normally regarded as one in
which, eschewing the idea of legislation, men bent their
efforts instead to the achievement of unity by discussion
and good will. But it was also a period of unrelieved failure,
because the fact is that conciliation is possible only when
both parties, and not merely one, desire it. And the CIU
had no interest whatever in conciliation. Apart from a
moment of disquiet when the new government took over - a
government which, despite the presence of the National
Labour Party, was so clearly influenced by the thinking of
the ITUC in trade union matters - the CIU found that its
policy of obdurate noncooperation was working quite well, and
indeed by 1951 had turned the endeavour of the ITUC to find
a settlement back on itself, bringing that organisation to
its lowest point since the whole difficult business began.
Because the objective of the CIU was to encompass the
destruction of the ITUC and what it stood for, to encompass
the destruction of the rather international, socialist
concept of trade union organisation, which could tolerate
British-based unions strong in the councils of the Irish
state; and with this object in mind, they had attempted
to attract away from the ITUC their Irish-based affiliates,
and had as well attempted to attract away from the British-
based unions their rank and file Irish membership. In the
event, while they made little headway in regard to the second,
their policies very nearly accomplished the first. They
were immensely aided by the fact that 1949, with its vehement
reaction to the Ireland Act, was in these years the high
point of nationalist fervour, and 1950, the Holy Year, was
equally the high point of Catholic fervour, making socialist
and internationalist ideas shabby and suspect.

At the outset in any event, the <u>rapprochement</u> between the
Labour Party and the National Labour Party did not result
in any initiatives which might bring the congresses together.
The Labour Party was very suspect in CIU eyes, not least
because of the substantial access of support which it
received from the amalgamated unions after the split in 1945.
But apart from that, the manner in which the <u>rapprochement</u>
arose caused a great deal of stress within the CIU and left
its leadership very aggrieved. In November 1947, when the
government announced its intention to hold a general election,
the National Labour Party had approached the CIU to establish
a common front, a proposal which the CIU embraced enthusiastically, and at a special conference of affiliated unions on
November 28 it was decided to 'give full support, moral and
financial, to the National Labour Party nominees';[103] more
than that, it was decided to set up a joint committee to
give effect to the decision. The dominant objective of the
CIU was of course the expulsion of the amalgamated unions,
and they had written to Fine Gael, Clann na Poblachta and
Fianna Fail seeking a pre-election statement of policy;
of the three, only Fianna Fail had come out in favour of
'an Irish self-contained trade union movement.'[104] This
then was the pre-election setting. When five National
Labour Party candidates were elected to Dail Eireann, they
found themselves, with a profound irony, holding the balance
of power between de Valera's government and an alliance of
the other parties. To the CIU the question was not in doubt;
because of Fianna Fail's clear position on Irish-based trade
unionism, the National Labour Party members should support
de Valera for Taoiseach, either joining with Fianna Fail in
government, if NLP policies could be accommodated, or
offering independent support in parliament.[105] But the
five men had somewhat diffent views; they believed that
they owed responsibility to the people who had elected them;
and these had scant concern with the problem of British-
based unions. They wanted to put Fianna Fail out of government
for a variety of reasons concerned with rural workers, with

old age pensioners, and generally with the inadequacy of
Fianna Fail in the social field. The joint committee of the
CIU and the NLP formally advised the deputies to support
Mr de Valera and not Mr Costello. The deputies decided
otherwise; and one of them, Mr Everett, received
ministerial office.

Feeling was still very high the following summer, at the time
of the CIU annual conference; Billy Whelan, the President,
in his formal address to the delegates actually spoke of
'the betrayal of the Trade Unions by politicians.'[106] It
was all greatly exacerbated by the fact that Dan Morrissey,
the new Minister for Industry and Commerce, had decided not
to send any delegates that year to the ILO in circumstances
which to the CIU were highly questionable. The minister had
held that the expenditure would not be justified, since the
conference was being held that year in Montreal, and dollars
were in short supply. But the CIU as a whole were quite
satisfied that Morrissey was merely dodging the issue -
that since he did not wish to nominate only CIU delegates
to the conference, he had decided not to send anyone. This
rankled as a practical weakening of the CIU position as the
nationally representative congress, particularly on the part
of Everett,   a member of the government. Yet there was a
limit beyond which all this could not be pushed. In the
first place, despite the strong feelings among the leadership
of the CIU, the five deputies were nevertheless nominated
by the Irish Transport as delegates to the CIU annual
conference, and there they spoke out in their defence. Everett
as minister even attempted to justify the decision regarding
the ILO, and was severely barracked for his pains.[107] But
despite this, and despite McMullen's own obvious annoyance,
McMullen himself, as leader of the Irish Transport delegation
insisted on the withdrawal by the chairman of the remark
concerning betrayal, and this - sourly enough - was done.[108]
If it had not been withdrawn, the five deputies might well
have reconsidered their continued relationship to the CIU,

on whom - when all was said and done - they did not
depend politically in any significant way.

Despite political pressure, despite some pressure from rank
and file membership, and despite at times considerable
public awkwardness, the CIU continued to hold to their position
of total non-cooperation[109] with an organisation which in
their view had no legitimacy. Relations between the Irish
trade unions and the European Recovery Programme brought
matters to a head once more. An invitation from Vincent
Tewson[110] to the CIU to attend a conference of the ERP trade
union advisory committee could be deflected somewhat since
there was a problem of inadequate notice - although CIU made
it clear in the correspondence that they would not have
attended had they to share representation with the ITUC.[111]
But in October 1948 the uncompromising nature of the CIU
position became even more manifest. George C. Marshall,
the US Secretary of State, expressed a desire to meet over
lunch in Paris the trade union leaders of the countries
participating in the programme. Time was very short, and
the Irish Minister for External Affairs, Sean MacBride,
decided to ask the CIU and the ITUC each to send one
representative. Norton, the deputy prime minister, rang
Crawford, who consulted his central council. There was
an instant refusal. Furthermore, the CIU approached both
the ERP chief in Ireland and the American chargé d'affaires
to explain that the sole right of the CIU to represent the
workers of Ireland could not be jeopardised by a division
of representation with the ITUC, and indeed that the American
delegation to the ILO in 1945 had supported the CIU position.
They also wrote to George Marshall himself[112] disavowing any
discourtesy, expressing great respect, but holding firm to
their right of sole representation 'more especially as the
majority of workers affiliated to the Irish Trade Union
Congress who are members of British Unions and who reside
in the partitioned Six Counties of Ireland are represented

internationally at all conferences by the British Delegations.'[113]
Nothing could have been more explicit, more public or more
indifferent to any notion of compromise.

-vi-

The two strands of the weave of popular Irish sentiment,
the two powerful dominating strands of nationalism and
religion, which gave so much strength and plausibility to
the CIU position, can be seen, in these years, in two
topics of debate at the congresses, the question of trade
union education and the question of international affiliation.
Of the two, the education topic was by far the more important,
having something of the character of a battle for the
soul of the trade union movement.

Immediately after the war, Professor Alfred O'Rahilly of
University College Cork, whose powerful anti-communist
polemics had dominated the columns of the Standard, began
a two-year diploma course in social and economic science
in his university college for trade unionists, twenty-four
of whom qualified in 1948.[114]   It was very highly regarded
by trade union leaders in Cork, whether they supported the
ITUC or the CIU, and both congresses reflected this approval.
Furthermore, the course was run in association with the
Cork School of Commerce, the principal of which, A.(Gus) Weldon,
was a prominent member of the ITUC-affiliated Vocational
Education Officers' Organisation. The picture was not at
all as clear in Dublin. Professor George O'Brien, of
University College Dublin, in response to an approach by a
joint committee of the Labour Party and the ITUC provided
an experimental course in economics and social science in
October 1945, which began very promisingly[115] but which

collapsed in the following year.[116]   Confronted with this,
the ITUC decided to call a special conference on adult
education in January 1948 which was attended by Ernest Green
the secretary of the Workers Educational Association, an
international university-linked body, which could be expected
to have some respectability in Ireland because of the
hostility shown it by the marxist inclined Labour Colleges.[117]
It was decided to launch a series of lectures and film shows,
and to enter into discussion with Mr Green, with the object of
establishing a branch of the WEA in the south of Ireland,
paralleling the branch in the north which had existed since
1907.[118]   The idea was to link the courses closely with the
universities, and the teachers' trade unions in addition were
involved in the initial planning. But the proposal ran into
some heavy weather at the ITUC annual conference in 1948.
Firstly, there was the accusation that the ITUC had to go to
England for guidance,[119] and secondly - and this point we shall
take up for discussion in a moment - there was the accusation
that while the WEA,was not tainted with communism, nevertheless
it was 'not positive in its outlook; its very weakness lies
in the freedom by which it allows the individual to choose
for himself the type of course he needs'[120] - a criticism
in which we see the powerful influence of the Cork
development. Although the idea of establishing a
branch of the WEA was agreed by the conference, an independent organisation, the People's College, Adult
Education Association, was in the event established in
October 1948[121] which, while it had good relations with
the WEA,was not structurally connected with it. Nor indeed -
and here it also differed from the WEA - was there any marked
connection with the universities. The committee had
approached UCD for a course in economic history; but this
came to nothing because the universities had already decided
'to provide extension courses in Economic and Social Science.'[122]
What actually happened was that in November 1948, Father
E.J. Coyne of UCD decided to follow O'Rahilly's lead
and approached the CIU with a proposal for a diploma course
in political and economic science especially designed for
young trade unionists.[123]   Father Coyne was understood to
be the person who drafted in substantial measure the

Report of the Commission on Vocational Organisation.[124]
The CIU responded enthusiastically and a class of over 250
was enrolled. As for the People's College, the initial
support from among the ITUC unions was very disappointing[125]
although the college itself has succeeded in surviving down
to the present day.[126] It suffered only too clearly from
the rather damaging charges that it was under British - or
in any event external - influences, and also that it did not
carry on its face the stamp of catholic orthodoxy.[127]

Let us try to see from this what objectives in worker
education lay behind the various proposals and courses.
There is no doubt that the original O'Rahilly experiment
in Cork set out to provide a form of worker education based
on 'tenets of faith and nationality',[128] and implicitly was
designed to combat the dreaded influence of marxism. It
was however expressed to be non-sectarian[129] and this claim
requires some examination. First of all the course, both in
the case of Coyne and of O'Rahilly, followed explicitly
catholic social teaching, and consequently if it was non-
sectarian it was so in some sort of secondary way. It was
non-sectarian, perhaps, in the sense that the moral
principles upon which it was based were common to all christian
churches, and christians other than catholics could follow
the course without conscientious difficulty; it was non-
sectarian in that its emphasis was a broad, not a narrow,
one, taking its stand on the spiritual rather than the
material (the latter having overtones of dialectical
materialism, and the former of christianity) and here its
approach found approval and support in the debates of the
ITUC no less than the CIU.[130] And thirdly, the course,
although a catholic one, was seen as non-sectarian since the
church had the plenitude of truth, and charges of sectarianism,
with some implication of a variety of acceptable positions,
made, in such circumstances, no sense whatever.

Those who espoused the cause of the WEA, and later the People's

College, found it difficult to be so explicit. They urged
that, in the WEA tradition, the students should decide
themselves what course they were to follow[131] causing
Patrick Crowley of the Assurance Representatives Organisation,
a Cork official who had himself qualified on the UCC course
to question the whole approach as not being positive enough.[132]
Roberts, in his clear analytical way, suggested that there
could be three approaches to worker education[133] the
propagandist approach, the vocational approach and the liberal
studies approach; they had chosen the last, attempting
to follow the best traditions which the universities had
established, and consequently they intended to provide a
wide variety of courses, not merely studies in economics
and sociology. But lurking behind a lot that was said on
behalf of the ITUC official position was some idea that
working class education must be the business of working
class organisations, reflecting the almost tribal divisions
in Britain between working class and middle class. Consequently,
to the CIU, claims that in the ITUC proposals a worker
could choose what subjects he wished looked extremely suspect.
In fact, to both groups, to the ITUC leadership no less than
to Coyne and O'Rahilly, education was not a neutral matter,
but while in the ITUC proposal the emphasis was on the
working class within society generally as against the
privileged classes, the emphasis, in the case of Coyne and
O'Rahilly, was on the catholic nation, as against other
nations, within which class had a minor meaning. The ITUC
path, with its implication of a conflict within Irish society
itself, was an ambiguous and uneasy one; while, on the
contrary, the catholic-nationalist path, enthusiastically
followed, seemed within the horizons of southern society,
to be calm, unifying and immensely plausible. Furthermore,
in the climate of the time, it was inconceivable to many that
education should be a matter of students picking and choosing
subjects in such a random way, particularly when the church
in all such matters was not only the obvious but the essential

guide, deriving from an assumption which pervaded as well
the report of the Commission on Vocational Organisation[134]
that men without strong and clear guidance are likely to
fall into social disarray and perhaps worse.

In the case of the catholic courses, all this could readily
enough mean education for a fortress, bent on defending
itself against alien influences from outside. And
certainly there was much to support such a view in the debates
on the question of international affiliation. The CIU, in this
period of post-war reorganisation, began to discuss affiliation
with the International Federation of Christian Trade Unions,
but the ITUC had been members of the World Federation of
Trade Unions since its establishment in Paris in 1945, Gilbert
Lynch, the Irish delegate being elected to the first general
council. Despite this obvious fact, Con Connolly of the
Cork Workers Council proposed at the 1948 ITUC annual
conference that the ITUC should seek affiliation with the
christians.[135] The fact that such a proposal, contradictory
on its face, led to anxious debate, is indicative of the
strength of feeling at grass roots. J.T O'Farrell,[136] on
behalf of the national executive, made a long and careful
speech in defence of the affiliation to the WFTU, dealing
in particular with its widely representative character.
But he defended the position by offering an alternative but
equally christian view of the ITUC role in such matters:
'I, as a Christian and a Catholic', he said, 'see nothing
whatever inconsistent with Christianity in playing our part
in the world trade union movement. If Ireland has a mission
in the world, as so many of us believe, I think the message
should not be delivered to the converted but to the un-
converted. The Christian missionaries of old when they went
forth to the Continent did not go into the monasteries or the
houses of rest. They went into the highways and byways to
try and bring the pagan into the Christian fold. We, by
running away from this great global international trade union

organisation, are running away from our responsibility and
merely going to the converted who do not need our advice
or our assistance at all. Are we so weak in faith and in
spirit that today we have to enter the protective umbrella
of a tiny organisation like the Christian Trade Union
International?' It was on this basis that the Cork proposal
was defeated. But O'Farrell's arguments must have seemed to
many to be largely debating points, a neat defence for a
position that was essentially indifferentist. The catholic-
nationalist mind at that time was, it would appear, a ghetto
mind to which such arguments were quite unconvincing. And
yet there is a further subtlety in the situation; it
was a mind which was not wholly xenophobic; rather was it
a mind which was hostile to the Anglo-Saxon socialist view
of the world while offering a certain warmth to continental
Europe which somehow was associated with ancient christendom,
and perhaps it was this view that flowered in the early
seventies to provide such a great popular response to the
European Community. In any case, events made this argument
on international affiliation pointless. The WFTU broke as
the cold war began, the west forming its own world
organisation, the International Confederation of Free Trade
Unions, to which the ITUC sought consequential affiliation.
But both the ITUC in this case, and the CIU in the case of
the christian federation, found the affiliation fees impossibly
high, and neither congress pursued the matter.

This powerful nationalist and catholic sentiment not only
strengthened the toughminded and unbending policy of the
CIU; it also made the Irish-based unions within the ITUC
very sensitive about implications of non-national and non-
catholic activities, creating the strong disruptive tendencies
within the ITUC itself. It was against such a background,
of a growing fragility in the ITUC, that the various voluntary
efforts were made to bridge the divide between the congresses.

There were three initiatives in all this period of the
interparty government, the first coming once again from
Larkin, and the second and third from the political arm
of the movement. Each had the full backing of the ITUC,
each met even a stiffer response from the CIU, and
each caused the position of the ITUC to deteriorate further.

Although Larkin was quite out of sympathy with the catholic
sentiment of the time, he was sensitive, as we have seen,[137]
to the powerful nationalist impulse in the people. When in
May 1949 the British Labour government published the Ireland
Bill with its guarantees to the north, feeling throughout
the south was very high - even thunderous. There had been
a mass meeting of the main political parties in O'Connell
Street on May 13[138] and at the Connolly Commemoration
celebration in Dublin the following day Larkin as president
of the ITUC declared that his national executive 'had
pledged themselves as Irishmen "to a resolution warning
the British labour movement of the crime they were perpetrating
and calling them to stop before they made an irretrievable
mistake. They had also expressed their desire to sit down
in friendship and brotherhood with the other side of the
Irish trade union movement - the CIU - to find a solution
to the problem ..."'[139] The outright condemnation of the
British labour government by the national executive of the
ITUC was quite remarkable in view of the northern dimension
of congress, and in view of the presence of the amalgamated
unions, although it was always discounted by the CIU as
being insincere and without substance.[140] Two days later
Larkin published a copy of a personal letter which he had
sent to Hynes, as president of the CIU, to Norton as leader
of the Labour Party, and to Everett as leader of the National
Labour Party, a move which was greeted, as Crawford caustically
remarked once again, with a blaze of publicity.[141] In

combating the Ireland Bill, Larkin recognised the
significance of the Irish vote in Britain. 'If the great
mass of Irish people in Great Britain and Northern Ireland',
he wrote,[142] 'are to be approached to understand partition ...
the Labour movement is the best organisation to do it (since)
... no group is so unequivocal in its opposition to partition ...
but if we are to speak of unity in our country ... how are
we to explain that similar unity has not been found possible
in our own labour movement.' He urged them to join with him as
president of the ITUC in summoning a joint conference.

No conference in fact took place, but in the correspondence
that followed Larkin's invitation and in the debates at
the two annual conferences in July, we can distinguish
four steps in the development of the argument. Firstly
Crawford even more sharply restated the CIU 'prerequisites
to any discussion, i.e. (1) that all Trade Unions operating
in the country should be Irish-based and controlled, and
(2) that a date be fixed for the implementation of this
principle.'[143] Secondly, the dilemma of the north was made
even more formidable. In the discussions that followed the
Norton initiative of November 1945[144] the CIU, when pushed,
had claimed that the principle of Irish-based unions applied
to the north as well; the issue had not been prominent in
the Lemass discussions in the late summer of 1946[145] since
the emphasis then was on the consequences for trade unions
of the existence of an independent Irish state, but now,
once again, the north became a critical issue, the CIU
reasserting its view that 'all Unions, operating in Ireland,
eligible for affiliation to an Irish Congress of Unions,
whether their headquarters are situated in the occupied
portion of Ireland or in the Republic of Ireland, should
be completely controlled by Irishmen, without any connection
with foreign Trade Unions, except the normal international
contacts enjoyed by Trade Unions in other free countries.'[146]
The Irish TUC protested at the utter irrationality of this;

there were in all only four Irish-based unions affiliated
to the congresses with members in Northern Ireland, one in
the CIU and three in the ITUC, numbering in all perhaps
10,000 members[147] from a total of 150,000; and it was
nonsense to see this as a base. They could only conclude
therefore that the CIU were prepared to partition the trade
union movement just as the country had been partitioned
politically. This greatly disturbed McMullen of the Irish
Transport who claimed that he was facing up to a twenty-
six county situation, and that the Northern Ireland labour
movement were in fact the partitionists.[148] One could
certainly build no bridge from such foundations. Thirdly
there was the CIU's view of the shape of the trade union
movement if the amalgamated unions withdrew or broke.
McMullen at the annual conference of the Irish Transport
in Mosney on June 22[149] had declared that in creating a
wholly Irish-based and Irish controlled movement it would
not be permissible 'to convert British unions into Irish
unions to form rival unions to the existing Irish ones, and
thus carry over the spirit of rivalry and rancour which the
split in the movement had to some extent engendered.' This
looked remarkably like a bid by the Irish Transport for
domination, for a great OBU. The view however was rejected
by McMullen, and this brings us to the fourth development
in the argument. McMullen stated again that what he aimed
at was not an OBU but a rationalised trade union movement
based on ten or twelve industrial organisations in accordance
with the 'Trade Union Report of 1939.'[150] This too, if one
accepted it at its current debating level, had strong
similarities with Hynes's vocationalism[151] to which
McMullen also declared himself to be pledged.[152] In the
event when the NUR and the National Union of Boot and Shoe
Operatives withdrew a couple of years later, there were
established instead independent Irish-based unions affiliated
to the ITUC. The circumstances in which this occurred
we shall discuss in a later paragraph.

At the CIU annual conference in Cork in July 1949 there
was quite a warm response from a number of delegates to
Larkin's initiative; but Crawford in particular was cynical
and suspicious. He looked to their actions and not to
their words. In the first place there was the question of
the ILO. The government had capitulated to CIU pressure
and had appointed two nominees to the ILO conference that
year, and the ITUC had again protested to the ILO
credentials committee.[153] This, in the opinion of the CIU,
raised great doubts about the ITUC's sincerity. Secondly
Crawford saw Larkin's initiative merely as a pretext to
offset public indignation at the Ireland Bill;[154] it was
a pretext he claimed, because in Northern Ireland the
amalgamated unions had supported the bill, and because
it could not have been enacted in Westminster without
their consent. But the fact seems to be that the CIU were
conscious of the growing success of their policy of total
non-cooperation.[155] Indeed some were of the view that
were it not for Larkin's move[156] the Ireland Bill would
have had the result of sweeping the Irish-based unions of
the ITUC into the CIU camp, damaging the ITUC irretrievably.
Whether this was so or not, McMullen himself seemed confident
that this was how things would develop in the future. It was
because of this that we notice a major shift in Irish
Transport policy. There was now no question of 'legislating
British unions out of this country.'[157] In fact they were
now opposed to such a policy. '... There has been a
profound change', he said, 'in the Trade Union situation
and the opinion of Trade Unionists, and the public, generally,
has undergone a violent change. The Irish forms of Trade
Union Organisations affiliated to the TUC have recently
been discussing the question of leaving that Congress and
joining the Congress of Irish Unions. I, therefore,
suggested in a recent speech that the Government should keep
their hands off this problem altogether, because I am rather
afraid that if the politicians get their hands on it, they

will mess the problem up. I think it should be left to the good sense of the Trade Unionists of the country to solve the problem themselves.'

When a week later the ITUC annual conference opened in Belfast, Roberts had had no final reply to the Larkin initiative, although the correspondence looked unpromising. Larkin made a presidential address of remarkable scope during which, despite the setting of the congress, he was caustic and uncompromising on the question of the Ireland Act. He himself had grown greatly in stature causing old Sam Kyle sincerely to remark 'great father, greater son ...'[158] Much of Larkin's address dealt with the great social and economic problems of the postwar world, but when he came to the question of trade union unity, he was testy about the absence of goodwill on the part of the CIU.[159] But in fact the Irish-based unions within the ITUC were very uneasy, the post office workers and the municipal workers urging the amalgamated unions to establish independent Irish-based unions.[160] Immediately after the conference, Roberts received a letter from Crawford, breaking off the correspondence. In August the ITUC attempted to revive the discussion with yet a further proposal[161] but this sank without trace.

It was now the turn of the politicians. The fact that the National Labour Party and the Labour Party sat together in government, and were soon to reunite, undoubtedly fostered the common community of the labour leadership, whether trade union or political; nevertheless the two formal attempts that were made, in the months that followed, by the political leadership to bridge the divide between the congresses were not very impressive, the first soon foundering, and the second evaporating before it had really begun. The second initiative in particular, led as it was by Norton, who was then Tanaiste, or deputy prime minister, raises the question of labour ministers acting in such matters, whether they can in fact doff their governmental role and adopt, in a matter of public concern merely that of familial brokers.

One suspects that Norton and his fellow ministers
quickly enough lost interest in pursuing such an uncomfortable role, despite the fact that they were profoundly
concerned for trade union unity, not least because of the
imminence of the local elections.

The events themselves add little to our understanding of the
attitudes of the parties and can be quickly recounted. It
appeared at first sight, however, that an important break-
through had been achieved. In November 1949 Jim Hickey
and Brendan Corish[162] of the National Labour Party offered
a formula which managed to get a joint conference of the
congresses under way. The formula, which both sides
accepted, recognised that the trade union movement in Ireland
should be Irish-based and controlled, but (it was somewhat
hedged around but clear enough) the changes necessary to
achieve this would be subject to a ballot of the members
concerned.[163] The extent of the concession, however, worried
the amalgamated unions, and despite the agreement that there
should be six a side, all the national executive of the
ITUC attended the first meeting in the Mansion House on
February 2 1950.[164] Sam Kyle of the Amalgamated Transport
claimed that, as things stood, his union was in fact Irish-
based and Irish controlled, causing the CIU to round on the
ITUC, with the charge that they had given merely nominal
acceptance to the principle. When the conference reconvened
on March 2 it perished on a dispute in the Clontarf (Dublin
city transport) garages, where the Irish Transport accused
the NUR, in somewhat obscure circumstances, of poaching
two of its members, and the CIU refused to attend any
further conferences until the dispute was resolved to the
satisfaction of the Irish Transport.[165]

Early the following June the Labour Party and the National
Labour Party reunited, and within a week[166] established

a high-level subcommittee consisting of Norton, Everett,
Corish, Hickey and Kyne, who approached both sides once
again. The CIU met the political leaders in October, and
having been assured that the ITUC had accepted the principle
of Irish-based and Irish controlled unions[167] agreed to a
joint conference. But the initiative appeared to fade
completely. Instead we find a changed arena, the problem
developing within the domestic confines of the ITUC rather
than across the divide of the two congresses - which, of
course, greatly vindicated the tough-line policy of the CIU.
Twelve Irish-based unions within the ITUC formed a distinct
group, met the national executive in October and later submitted a memorandum to them, to which the amalgamated union
members of the national executive replied the following
spring.[168] But, very significantly, in October 1950 as
well, a query was received by the CIU[169] asking whether, if
the Irish-based ITUC unions applied, they would be accepted
en bloc by the CIU (the fear of course here was that, on
the grounds of multiplicity, some might not be permitted
to retain their separate identity), to which the answer
was yes. From there on there was silence, however most
of the protagonists being caught up in the strange disturbing events that led to the resignation of Dr Browne,
the fall of the government and the general election of
June 1951 which brought Fianna Fail back into power.

But while these somewhat leisurely explorations were taking
place, the CIU never wavered in its policy of total non-
cooperation. During 1950 both congresses, because of the
great pressure of prices, brought the 1948 agreement to a
close, the ITUC in the summer,[170] and the CIU some months
later,[171] and both congresses attempted to hammer out a
policy to govern the negotiations which took place in the
autumn and winter of that year; but they did so in isolation
from one another, although dealing with the same parties
in the FUE and the Labour Court. The CIU, about this time,
began to have great misgivings about the operation of the

Labour Court[172] (a matter which came to crisis in May 1952)
but it did not share the problem with the ITUC, who, on
the whole, appeared to have little enough complaint, certainly
at that time. And once again, in April 1951, when under
the ECA programme, a joint visit of representatives of the
two congresses to the US was mooted the CIU curtly
refused[173] to entertain it.

-viii-

The June elections had brought Lemass back to Industry
and Commerce, and by the autumn he was again pushing the
legislative ideas which he had proposed in 1947.[174] In
March 1952 the ITUC held a special conference on the
proposals[175] and fell back for shelter on the extraordinarily negative convention 87 of the ILO[176] rejecting
any legal restriction of whatever kind on workers joining
or forming organisations, temporary or permanent, even to
the point of proposing that the idea of negotiating licences
should be abandoned. A comparable conference was held by
the CIU[177] which, while it was more positive, was somewhat
cynically so; it remained diplomatically silent on matters
with which it clearly disagreed: the removal of a union
from the register for malfeasance, the creation of personal
rights as against unions, and the rendering of agreements
subject to legal redress. But it proposed on the other hand –
and this was the substance of its view – that a condition
of registration of current unions, not merely new ones as
Lemass had suggested, should be that their headquarters
would be in Ireland. In a word, they aimed once more at
the exclusion of the British-based unions by means of
legislation, despite McMullen's disavowals.

In the meantime the economic scene had darkened greatly.
March 1952 brought a harsh hair-shirt budget. Strikes were
beginning to build up, the long intractable strikes that
were later to become so much a feature of Irish industrial
life. There was a strike of seamen for six weeks in the
autumn of 1951,[178] a hotel strike lasting for nine months,[179]
and a strike of electricians in CIE which began in April
1951 and pushed well into the summer of 1952;[180] and
mandays lost because of strikes began to mount in number.[181]
Once more, in the early months of 1952, a wage stttlement
was hammered out, each congress going its own way, the CIU
settling for a national figure of 12/6d but the ITUC
remaining openended.[182] In March the Irish-based unions
in the ITUC[183] had taken the initiative in asking the CIU
and the ITUC to meet in joint conference on the problems
facing them, but again the suggestion was rebuffed by the CIU.

By the summer of 1952, unemployment was again becoming a
grinding problem, but, as is often the case in an underdeveloped economy, it was accompanied by vacancies in
certain skilled occupations; and Lemass therefore turned,
at this time of serious recession, to the strategy of
increasing skills by improving a very ramshackle apprenticeship
system. He needed the cooperation of the trade unions on
two matters in particular, firstly on a joint approach to
the restructuring of apprenticeship generally, and secondly,
on a more liberal approach to the admission of persons into
the craft trades - which in practice raised the question of
free admission to union membership generally.[184] But in the
case of the first, the CIU refused in February 1953[185] to
attend a joint meeting with the ITUC on apprenticeship
matters, and the ITUC refused to continue on its own to
discuss the matter with the government on the grounds of
impracticality; and with regard to the second, union
admission, the CIU unions confessed great and abiding unease,
despite some impatient pressure from the government.[186]

It was in such circumstances that Lemass once again stated
publicly that legislation might be the only alternative.
In a speech in Dundalk in April 1953[187] he said that concern
about the disorganised state of the trade union movement was
not confined to members of trade unions, unity was desirable,
trade unions essential, and legislation could not be long
delayed. He was prepared to wait however in the hope that a
joint body would be created, or at least a joint committee
of the two congresses to discuss the matter. From this on,
we notice a marked change in the CIU approach, perhaps because
of Lemass's imperative statements (since no one really
wanted legislation) but also, one suspects, because in the
summer of 1953 John Conroy succeeded William McMullen
as General President of the Irish Transport, and James Larkin
at last found someone who wished not to reject but to respond
to his offers of a **rapprochement**.[188] Correspondence between
the two congresses opened - with some appropriateness -
on May 1 1953, survived the two annual conferences, to
flower into the unity conference in the Mansion House in the
autumn of the year.

-ix-

Lemass had made his critical April speech at the opening of
the headquarters in Dundalk of the Irish Shoe and Leather
Workers Union, an Irish-based union which that year had
replaced a traditional British-based one. There were in
fact two such developments at that time, the other being
in the National Union of Railwaymen, and therefore before
completing this chapter, before moving on to the fruitful
initiative of the late summer of 1953, let us examine these
two experiments, in which Irish unions were carved out of
amalgamated ones, giving thereby one final insight into the
attitudes of various parties of the period to the business
of trade union reorganisation.

The National Union of Boot and Shoe Operatives, which we
consider first, had a long history in this country,
organising their first members in Cork in 1885.[189]   It
entered its period of expansion in the early thirties,
when native industry was protected, and by the early forties
its return of affiliated membership to the ITUC was a
steady 3,500 (which however, as with many such returns,
must be taken to some extent as a book figure yet adequately
indicative).[190]   The Trade Union Act of 1941 appears to
have distressèd the executive council of the union greatly,
and rather than attempt to continue in Ireland in these
circumstances they decided that 'a separate Irish Boot and
Shoe Union should be created.'[191]   Furthermore negotiations
on pay became highly frustrating;   an incentive-based
industry was not helped by the strict requirements of the
Emergency Powers (No. 166) Order of 1942.[192]   (Incidentally,
we notice here how in the Boot and Shoe union - and the
same would seem to have applied at the time to the smaller
amalgamated unions - Ireland was seen as an integrated
district of the union as a whole, and the senior union
officers from Britain involved themselves personally in
major Irish negotiations.)   The Irish membership were
alarmed at the executive council's decision;   this was a time
of war and the industry was threatened with unemployment.
It was certainly no time, in their view, to cast loose from
the warmth and support of a large 'benefit' union.   The
executive council appreciated the point but they did not
reverse their decision.   They merely put it in abeyance[193].
The matter was not raised again until 1949.   The biennial
conference of the union took place that year in Margate.
The Ireland Bill had been published, feeling in the south
was very high, and the Irish delegates who met at the
conference decided to explore with the Irish membership of
the union the idea of establishing an Irish-based union.
About the same time, some of the Dundalk shopstewards (who,
interestingly, also appear to have been Fianna Fail
supporters) attempted, as an alternative solution, the

facilitating of an en bloc transfer to the Irish Transport
and General Workers Union, but although some discussion took
place, the idea came to nothing. This, however, was
interesting in two respects, in demonstrating the pressures
exercised by the Irish Transport, and in demonstrating as
well something of the hostility to what some saw as Irish
Transport ambitions, not unmixed, in the case of Labour
Party members, with memories of disruptions in the past.

The three Irish area officers of the union submitted a
memorandum to the executive council which proposed an
independent, but thirty-two county, Irish boot and shoe
union,[194] and discussion on the proposal took place with
the executive council during the winter of 1950 and the
early months of 1951. It was clear that the executive
council were still quite anxious to get out of Ireland.
For example, while there was, it was calculated, about
£16,000 to the credit of the Irish membership in the union
funds, they were prepared to give £35,000 towards the
establishment of the new union.[195] Meetings on the proposal
took place throughout the whole country, and in April 1951
a ballot was held. In the case of the Republic the vote
was two to one in favour (1,990 to 932)[196] although the
vote in Cork and in Kilkenny was negative.[197] The issue
was much clearer in the north: overwhelmingly - by 217 votes
to 45 - it was decided to reject the proposal. When in May
1951, it all came for ratification before the biennial
conference in Eastbourne, the union, as might be expected,
found itself in something of a quandary about the northern
vote, and in the hope of resolving the dilemma, the general
president of the union undertook to see the members in
Northern Ireland to try to persuade them to throw in their
lot with the Irish-based union. He met with an uncompromising
refusal, the members threatening that if they were pressurised,
they would either become non-union or join a local union
which was sectarian in character.[198] In such circumstances,
the executive council decided to retain the northern members

in the national union, and establish an Irish-based union
for the members in the Republic only. A conference of Irish
delegates, meeting in Limerick on December 1 and 2 1951
under the chairmanship of Paul Alexander, one of the Irish
area officers, established the new union, the Irish Shoe
and Leather Workers' Union. It had been intended to name
the union the National Shoe and Leather Workers' Union, but
the decision of the northern members to opt out caused the
change to be made[198A] - a change, which, when one reflects
on it, has no little significance. However a real bridge
was retained. The executive council intended to ask Paul
Alexander to continue as an official of their union, serving
northern Ireland, inter alia; but Alexander was also asked by
the new Irish union to become their first general president,
and when he decided to accept the office, the executive
council of the national union asked him to continue personally
to serve the northern members of their union as well; and
this he did for many years. But this was very far from
what was originally hoped, and Alexander expressed no little
regret[199] - a regret that was shared by the executive
council of the national union - that 'a barrier (now)
existed in the trade union movement as far as boot and
shoe workers were concerned.'

The National Union of Railwaymen had also had a very long
history in the country being established here first in 1885,
but really flowering from 1890.[200] But within the union
in Ireland there was always a powerful nationalist impulse.
Indeed as early as 1890 an effort had been made, having its
origins in Cork, to establish an Irish-based union for
railwaymen, which, while it did not develop, had as a
consequence the appointment of a full-time organiser for
Ireland and the establishment of a central hall in Dublin.
Nationalist feeling became critical in 1920. By that time -
and for a number of reasons - the union had expanded greatly,
now numbering 20,000 in Ireland, and it was a considerable
force.[201] The point of crisis arose because railwaymen

were expected to handle munitions, intended for the Black
and Tans which came through the port of Dublin. 'In May
1920 400 members of the NUR, belonging to the Dublin (North
Wall) branch, without asking for, or receiving the sanction
of the EC, refused to unload munitions'[202] which in turn
led to the closing of the port of Holyhead and the threat
of dismissals there. The NUR, although it did not sanction
the strike (it is difficult to see how it could) nevertheless
felt that it behaved very honourably, even courageously,
in the matter, using considerable pressure on the Westminster
government to abandon its 'purely regressive policy'[203]
in Ireland. At a specially convened conference of the British
TUC in July 1920 there was adopted, although by a tiny
majority, an NUR motion calling for 'a truce, the withdrawal of the British army of occupation and the summoning
of a special Irish Parliament with full Dominion Powers
in all Irish affairs.'[204] And when the North Wall strikers
eventually returned to work at the end of December (with an
undertaking that they would not suffer any penalty) the union
followed up with a resolution which declared that the 'murders
and outrages' then occurring in Ireland 'were the inevitable
result of the Government's failure to govern Ireland in
accordance with the wishes of the people.'[205] Indeed the
union was satisfied that their further meetings personally
with Lloyd George, led by their influential general
secretary, J.H. Thomas, played some part in bringing about
the treaty that eventually emerged.[206]

The creation of the Irish Free State in 1922 and the access
of nationalist feeling that followed found the NUR losing
members to the Irish Transport. The union at this time
considered leaving Ireland altogether, but it was decided
by the Irish membership in 1922 to continue as members
of the NUR but with much more local autonomy. This was
done, and the structures in Ireland strengthened, although
by 1924 membership had fallen to less than 14,000.[207]

Nationalist pressure continued, and through the years
membership drifted downwards; but from the early 1940s
in particular the NUR, conscious both of democratic equity
and of its own prestige found itself in a position of
growing embarrassment. The 1941 Trade Union Act was a
serious blow; but what particularly disturbed them was the
decision of CIE - under Irish Transport pressure - to
withdraw from the wages board.[208] They would have withdrawn altogether at that stage but the Supreme Court decision
in their favour on the issue of part III of the 1941 act,
which followed soon after, gave them a further lease of life.
They set about strengthening further the autonomy of the
Irish membership within the union, and although this did
not reach a level that satisfied them, nevertheless the Irish
membership were overwhelmingly in favour of remaining within
the NUR.[209] However, the NUR itself had had enough, and
despite the views of the Irish members they decided at their
annual conference in Hastings on July 11 1951 to withdraw
from the whole of Ireland by the end of 1952.[210] Even more
strongly and clearly than in the case of the boot and shoe
union, the NUR themselves pressed for withdrawal - in a
manner quite out of accord with the desires of the Irish
membership. Furthermore, they were not very much interested
in what arrangements were made after they had left; as far
as they were concerned the members could join another union,
more than one if they wished, they could split off north
and south or they could form a union of their own.[211] And
indeed so anxious were they to wash their hands of the whole
affair that they were prepared to offer the new Irish-based
union when it emerged a very substantial sum to get it under
way, far more than any capitation arrangement would indicate.[212]

The Irish membership, north and south, however, managed to
hold together to form a new union to take over from the NUR,
the National Association of Transport Employees. This was
largely a decision of the leadership in the three district
councils, in Cork, in Dublin and in Belfast, which they

carried with the membership generally. Perhaps there were
two reasons why the path was somewhat easier here, why the
north remained integrated with the rest. In the first place,
the number of members in the north was small, perhaps 2,000
in all; their employment was independent of that in Britain,
they never had had parity with British workers, and consequently they did not feel very strongly the need for an
amalgamated union. Secondly Chapman, who became the first
general secretary of the new union, himself bridged the
divide in that, although he was from Cork in the deep south,
he was a protestant.

How successful was all this? According to the affiliation
figures returned to the ITUC, the membership of the new
union declined further to about 6,000 but in regard to all
this Chapman strikes a note of caution. The decline in
the late forties and early fifties could be attributed in
part to the weeding out of names of persons who had ceased
to be members; and from 1952 onwards it was the practice
of the new union to understate its membership for affiliation
purposes, its total membership north and south being
between eight and nine thousand rather than the six
thousand returned.[213]

All this fell to be discussed at the annual conferences of
the two congresses, to some extent in 1951 but more
particularly in 1952. The CIU had been confronted with some
practical consequences of its policy, at least in part, and
of course there was much welcome for the move. As the 1952
president, Walter Beirne, remarked of the 'English
Executives': '...so sure as night follows day, their
reign in Ireland is coming to a close.'[214] But the Irish
Transport confessed to some unease. If more amalgamated
unions were to follow the same path, it was likely enough
that the boot and shoe pattern, and not that of the NUR, would
prevail, causing a partition north and south throughout the

trade union movement, and McMullen, with members in the
north, was particularly sensitive on this point.[215] Apart
from that the best efforts of the Irish Transport in the
case of the boot and shoe leadership and in the case of the
membership of the NUR had not prevented the establishment
of additional Irish-based unions, adding to the already
onerous number.

As far as the ITUC was concerned, Miss Chenevix, the
president of the 1951 conference congratulated both the
NUR and the boot and shoe union on their initiative[216] but
the matter was referred rather crossly to the private
session of the conference, one of the grounds being that in
the case of the NUR the matter was not finally decided.[217]
In the following year, Denis Larkin, on behalf of the
Workers Union of Ireland, proposed a motion approving of the
action of the National Union of Boot and Shoe Operatives
and of the NUR[218] and urged the ITUC to discuss the
possibility of a similar step with the other amalgamated
unions. This called a great deal of fire down on his head,
a string of delegates from the amalgamated unions going to
the rostrum, led by Norman Kennedy of the Amalgamated
Transport. Kennedy claimed[219] that internal union matters
were not appropriate for discussion at the congress, and
that in any event his members had already full autonomy in
Ireland; but in the debate that followed the greatest
anxiety was that such experiments would result rather in
the partition solution of the boot and shoe union
than in the all-Ireland solution of the NUR, echoing
McMullen's concern. It was seen as virtually inevitable
since the northern members could not allow themselves to be
divorced 'from British working classes; ... (it) would be
the death knell of first class agreements governing wages
and conditions.'[220] And a partitioned trade union movement
would mean a Northern Ireland TUC. Denis Larkin's
resolution was defeated quite substantially, by 99 votes to
66, and even an attempt to convert it into a simple vote of
approval - without urging any follow up - was cast aside

in order that the real issue should be debated. In fact,
neither Chapman nor Alexander was ever approached by any
other amalgamated union on their experiences in creating
these unions (nor, if it comes to that, did they at any
time consult with one another).

There is one final point to be made. Once again one is
impressed by the fact that all this was essentially an
Irish problem. It is clear from our account that the
NUR and the boot and shoe union both felt that they were
well out of Ireland, that the desire for them to remain
(vigorous in the case of the NUR) came from the Irish
membership. But apart from that there is also some indication
of the attitude of the London offices generally in that
neither at the 1951 annual conference of the ITUC nor at that
of 1952 was there any increase in the very small number of
delegates with cross-channel addresses.[221] It was an Irish
problem, of which the north was the most difficult and
worrying aspect.

And so we leave the barren years, and come to the difficult
but committed task of genuine reconciliation.

Notes on Chapter Nine

1. The government apparently saw the boom and the depression
    as phenomena associated with the Korean war and not
    essentially domestic; see the statement of de
    Valera as Taoiseach of July 25 1953 (CIU 1954 p.6).

2. ITUC 1954 p.55. However, in the autumn of 1953, some
    members of the Association were charged with obstruction
    and were jailed when they refused to give assurances
    regarding the future. Appeals by the ITUC and others
    failed to move the government and the protests died
    away. No corresponding support was given to the
    Unemployed Association by the CIU, some of whose leaders
    said of it that 'no organisation (was) more dangerous
    to the progress of this nation than the extraordinary
    organisation with the title Unemployed Men's Association.'
    (cf. M. Mervyn CIU 1953 p.130).

3. See also Trade Union Information Vol.9, no.52,
    February-March 1954.

4. Lyons op.cit. p.615.

5. The ITUC suggested in July 1953 an ad hoc interim
    committee representing government departments and the
    two congresses to review employment schemes; de
    Valera refused to entertain it. (ITUC 1954 p.53).

6. CIU 1954 appendix p.5.

7. ibid. p.6.

8. National Union of Railwaymen v. Sullivan and Ors [1947]
    I.R. 77 p.102.

9. See p.366 below.

10. Quoted in CIU 1945-46 p.96.

11. CIU 1945-46 p.97.

12. ibid. p.98.

13. ibid. p.84.

14. CIU 1945-46 p.99.

15. ibid. p.96.

16. This reflected settled practice. The ITUC annual
    report 1946 quotes in an appendix, p.57, an excerpt
    from the International Labour Office published for
    ILO by Allen and Unwin 1931, pp.58-60 as follows:

'The Conference has never yet refused to accept
credentials. It has sometimes concluded that the
conditions of Article 389 had not been complied with,
but it was always of the opinion that the
Government in question had acted with sufficient good
faith for its choice to be accepted, and it confined
itself to making recommendations as to the procedure
to be followed in future in order to avoid fresh disputes.'

17. Cathal O'Shannon in his report, spoke highly of the
members of the credentials committee, particularly
the chairman, of whom he said, with a journalist's
sense of colour: '... and the chairman was Mr Paul
Berg, Norwegian jurist, President of the Supreme Court,
a leader of the Norwegian resistance movement during
the war and the judge who passed sentence of death
on Quisling. Certainly an eminently competent,
impartial and experienced international jury on
credentials.' CIU 1945-46 p.94.

18. This is perfectly clear from the credentials committee
report (produced by the CIU as an appendix to their
1945-46 annual report p.95) but somewhat obscured
in the ITUC annual report, 1946 p.31.

19. CIU 1945-46 p.99.

20. ibid. p.93.

21. cf. CIU debate 1946 p.126.

22. ITUC 1946 pp. 165-66.

23. ITUC 1946 p.30.

24. William O'Brien papers: Ms. 13974. See also CIU 1945-
1946 p.99 for text.

25. ITUC 1946 p.41.

26. O'Brien papers Ms. 13974.

27. ITUC 1946 p.44.

28. CIU 1945-46 p.85.

29. ibid.

30. CIU 1945-46 p.126.

31. CIU 1945-46 p.127.

32. ibid.

33. ITUC 1946 p.34.

34. ibid. p.35.

35. ITUC 1946 p.37.

36. ibid. p.28.

37. idem.

38. CIU 1945-46 p.128.

39. ITUC 1946 p.46.

40. ibid. p.40.

41. ITUC 1946 p.163.

42. CIU 1945-46 p.115.

43. 'The fact', he said, 'that certain individuals because of their own selfish lust for power have taken advantage of that situation does not invalidate the statement that there is a problem.' (p.165). This was to counter a rather facile argument which dismissed anything more radical than personal enmities.

44. ITUC 1946 p.164.

45. ITUC 1946 p.161.

46. see above p. 329.

47. ITUC 1946 p.113.

48. ibid. p.104.

49. ibid. p.165.

50. One could perhaps claim that even in this account the congresses have had more than their due share of attention, and (following Sam Kyle) that the unions were really the significant bodies. But the idea is not really a starter. As we shall see congress and congresses became even more significant as the need for centrally determined policies became more and more clear.

51. The number of cross-channel delegates at this 1946 ITUC conference was 7, not indeed a large number, not at all as large as in October 1941 for example (see p.232 above) but they were prominent officials and influential. On the other hand in the special circumstances of the reduced ITUC the number of delegates with addresses in the north was large, but not unusually so, 45 from a listed total of 160 or 28%. (cf. p.262 & n.149 above).

52. From August 1946 to August 1947 the cost of living index rose by 10.8% (see the Taoiseach's statement in Dail Eireann, Dail Debates October 15 1947 384 ff.).

53. Subsection (4) of Section 10 of the Industrial
Relations Act provided that 'The Minister shall, in
respect of each workers' member, designate an
organisation representative of trade unions of workers
to nominate a person for appointment ... and the
Minister shall appoint the person so nominated.' An
alternative, however, was provided under subsection (5)
of Section 10 as follows: 'If ... (a) more than one
organisation representative of trade unions of workers
is in being, and (b) the Minister is of opinion that
it is undesirable that the appointment should be made
under subsection (4) of this section, he may by
regulations declare (that ...) the following provisions
shall have effect (i) the Minister shall invite trade
unions ... to nominate persons ... and (ii) he shall
make the appointment from amongst the persons so
nominated.' (ITUC 1946 p.27). In the event when
he adopted the second alternative he limited his
invitation 'to licensed Irish industrial unions with
3,000 members or over, the British Unions were not included, and the Irish service or non-industrial unions
such as Teachers, Post Office Workers and Bank Officials
were likewise excluded ...' The two congresses were
included. (Cathal O'Shannon report: Sept. 4 1946
O'Brien papers Ms. 13974). Despite all this Cathal
O'Shannon and Tom Johnson were the only two nominees
and were appointed.

54. ITUC 1947 p.27.

55. Cathal O'Shannon report Sept. 4 1946 op.cit.

56. They met on August 22, 26, 30 and finally on Sept. 7.

57. CIU 1947 p.12.

58. ITUC 1947 p.37.

59. Ruaidhri Roberts who had been appointed secretary from
October 1 1945 marks a change in Lemass's approach
from this time onwards.

60. CIU 1947 p.8.

61. The Irish Press April 9 1953.

62. ITUC 1947 p.84.

63. ITUC 1947 p.134.

64. ITUC 1947 p.23.

65. idem.

66. idem.

67. ITUC 1947 p.136.

68. Trade Union Act, Section 8.

69. See appendix fourteen.

70. ITUC 1947 p.75.

71. ITUC 1947 p.184.

72. Sub-committee on Revision of Trade Union Act 8 May 1947,William O'Brien papers op.cit.

73. Appendix fifteen.

74. op.cit.

75. Crawford was confirmed in the appointment on October 18 1946 (CIU 1947 p.18). Hynes appeared to be somewhat dominated by Crawford at the annual conference of the CIU in 1949 of which he was chairman. This at least is my personal recollection as a delegate.

76. There were, however, uncertain voices even within the Building Workers' Trade Union. For the flavour of the debate see CIU 1947 pp.110-112.

77. See appendix fifteen.

78. op.cit. pars. 568-571.

79. The Commission saw a section of workers as representing often very specific interests. They suggested, for example, in the clothing industry that piece workers and time workers should be separately represented. (par. 573). They wished, in a word, to substitute economic and occupational interest for class interest and to avoid having 'workers and employers in two opposing armies.' par.581.

80. See appendix fifteen.

81. op.cit. pars. 572-574.

82. It did not however meet the problem of craftsmen employed as maintenance workers in industries other than the building industry.

83. op.cit. par. 568.

84. op.cit. par. 569.

85. op.cit. pars. 581-584.

86. CIU 1948 p.77.

87. See for example the row in the printing trade group which was raised at the annual conference of the CIU 1948 pp.77-78. The group later disintegrated (CIU 1949 p.88).

88. ibid.

89. ITUC 1948 p.34.

90. This also was the view of the CIU; see CIU 1948 p.56.

91. CIU 1948 p.17.

92. CIU 1948 p.9.

93. ITUC 1948 p.36.

94. CIU 1948 p.17.

95. ITUC 1948 p.39; also CIU 1948 p.56.

96. ITUC 1948 p.37; also CIU 1948 p.10.

97. ITUC 1948 p.38.

98. ITUC 1948 p.23; also Dail Debates October 16 1948.

99. ITUC 1948 p.26

100. ITUC 1948 p.27.

101. ITUC 1948 p.100.

102. CIU 1948 p.56; also ITUC 1948 p.128.

103. CIU 1948 p.15.

104. idem.

105. idem.

106. CIU 1948 p.43.

107. CIU 1948 p.51.

108. CIU 1948 p.68.

109. There is an isolated instance of cooperation in the joint meeting with the Labour Court in May 1948 to review the work of joint labour committees; but this was untypical. (ITUC 1948 p.46.)

110. CIU 1949 p.11. Tewson wrote as secretary of the ERP Trade Union Advisory Committee; he also succeeded Citrine as secretary of the British TUC.

111. CIU 1949 p.11.

112. CIU 1949 p.14.

113. idem.

114. CIU 1948 p.112.

115.   ITUC 1946 p.47.

116.   ITUC 1947 p.74.

117.   Henry Pelling: A History of British Trade Unionism 1971
        p.147.

118.   ITUC 1948 p.143. The WEA had been established first in
        1903. (Pelling op.cit.)

119.   ITUC 1948 p.155.

120.   ITUC 1948 p.156.

121.   ITUC 1949 p.55.

122.   idem.

123.   CIU 1949 p.18.

124.   op.cit.

125.   ITUC 1949 p.150.

126.   This was largely because of the determination of
        Ruaidhri Roberts. As an association it tended to
        avoid emphasis on social and economic matters and
        aimed instead at a broader more 'liberal' approach,
        by which it might also distinguish itself from the
        social and economic extension courses of the
        universities. In the case of the catholic courses,
        the Jesuit fathers under Father E. Kent established
        within a few years the Catholic Workers College in
        Dublin. Leo Crawford reported them as saying that
        they established their course as a preliminary course
        to that in UCD which they believed could not be
        assimilated by the workers concerned. (CIU 1956, p.196).
        In the event it became immensely popular covering
        economics and sociology as well as explicitly trade
        union subjects. It continues to the present day (1975)
        now, however, under the title College of Industrial
        Relations. Both the UCD and the UCC courses ceased
        to exist in their original form.

127.   One could also refer to M. Hill at the ITUC debate
        on the People's College in 1954 (ITUC 1954 p.143)
        when he said: 'I am afraid that the Irish worker is
        frightened of the trade union movement's educational
        schemes unless they are assured beforehand that the
        education has Christian as well as trade union principles.'

128.   CIU 1948 p.113.

129.   CIU 1949 p.77.

130. See Louie Bennett's remarks ITUC 1948 p.191.

131. ITUC 1948 p.143.

132. ITUC 1948 p.156.

133. ITUC 1948 p.157.

134. Op.cit.

135. ITUC 1948 p.189.

136. idem.

137. p.364 above.

138. The Irish Times May 14 1949.

139. The Irish Times May 16 1949.

140. There is no record of the resolution in the 1949 annual
     report of the ITUC although there is warm support
     for Larkin's unity proposal (ITUC 1949 p.46). Neither
     is there any record of Larkin's initiating letter in
     the ITUC annual report, understandable perhaps since
     it was declared to be personal.

141. CIU 1949 p.93.

142. Irish Independent May 17 1949

143. ITUC 1949 p.46.

144. p.367 above.

145. p.375 above.

146. ITUC 1949 p.47.

147. ITUC 1949 p.48; p.84; see also p. 305.

148. CIU 1949 p.89.

149. The Irish Press June 23 1949.

150. CIU 1949 p.90. The CIU as a whole endorsed this view.

151. See p.380 above.

152. CIU 1951 p.98.

153. CIU 1949 p.94.

154. idem.

155. Frequently, there was mention at this time of a great flow of members into the Irish-based unions. This was discounted by the ITUC, but certainly in the period immediately after the war, numbers in the Irish Transport greatly increased (see p.304 above).

156. CIU 1949 p.94.

157. CIU 1949 p.89.

158. ITUC 1949 p.88. Yet, although a Dail deputy, he never received a ministry. He was an aloof man, but apart from that he was distrusted by his own party leadership because of his radicalism.

159. ITUC 1949 p.86.

160. ibid. p.131.

161. The proposal was to the effect that there should be one trade union movement, north and south, under Irish control, but that the changes necessary to achieve this should be subject to the democratic vote of the members concerned; it was also proposed that each congress should appoint representatives to recommend what structural alterations would be necessary or desirable. (ITUC 1950 p.31.)

162. Brendan Corish was then Parliamentary Secretary to the Minister for Local Government. He later became leader of the party and is Tanaiste in the government that presently holds office (1975).

163. CIU 1950 p.10.

164. ibid. p.11.

165. ibid. pp.13-18.

166. ibid. p.68.

167. CIU 1951 p.13.

168. ITUC 1951 pp.13, 51, 132, 133. It was decided to take the matter in private session and consequently we have no record of the debate. Neither were the memoranda reproduced in the annual report although they were circulated to the affiliated unions in November 1951 for information merely (ITUC 1952 p.27).

169. CIU 1951 pp.14, 77.

170. It was decided at a special wages conference on May 18 1950 and was endorsed by the annual conference (ITUC pp.26, 113).

171. At a special conference on October 13 1950; discussion had been taking place with the FUE since May.

172. CIU 1950 p.8.

173. CIU 1951 p.20.

174. p.378 above.

175. ITUC 1952 pp.27-31.

176. Convention on Freedom of Association and Protection
of the Right to Organise of the International Labour
Conference (No. 87 of 1948) ITUC 1952 p.91. See appendix 18.

177. CIU 1952 p.20.

178. CIU 1952 p.9.

179. CIU 1952, pp.21, 26.

180. CIU 1952 pp.21, 26, 100.

181. In 1950-51, there was a strike in banking, and in 1952
a particularly extensive strike in the printing industry.
The furniture trade was also affected. Mandays lost
were 217,000 in 1950, 545,000 in 1951 and 529,000 in 1952.
(ITUC 1953 p.32). The average lost during the thirties
was 200,000 per annum. cf. p.184 above.

182. CIU 1952 p.15; ITUC 1952 p.61.

183. ITUC 1952 p.27.

184. CIU 1953, pp.8, 17, 79.

185. ITUC 1953, p.36.

186. CIU 1953 p.16.

187. The Irish Press April 10 1953.

188. It is clear too that, despite their public positions,
a gradual softening of attitudes had been taking place
for some time.

189. National Union of Boot and Shoe Operatives: Official
Report of the Irish Union Delegate Conference:
December 1 and 2 1951. p.2.

190. From an interview with Paul Alexander, first General
President of the Irish Shoe and Leather Workers Union:
June 18 1975. See also Alan Fox: A History of the
National Union of Boot and Shoe Operatives 1874-1957,
pp.528-29.

191. NUBSO op.cit. p.3. The 1941 Act had a crushing effect
on a number of unions apart from the NUBSO and the NUR.
See for example Clement J. Bundock: The Story of the
National Union of Printing, Bookbinding and Paper
Workers, 1959, pp.475-76.

192. See above p. 246.

193. NUBSO op.cit. p.4.

194. ibid. p.1.

195. ibid. p.4.

196. ibid. p.7.

197. Paul Alexander interview.

198. idem.

198[A]. NUBSO op.cit. p.9.

199. ibid. p.42. See also the account in Alan Fox op.cit.
      pp.620-622 where with some justification the union
      took pride in the fact that 'the whole process (was)
      unmarred by bitterness or recrimination.' There is
      a further point. In the ballot papers prepared by the
      National Union of Boot and Shoe Operatives, the members
      do not in fact appear to have been invited to give
      a view on an all-Ireland union. The members in the
      south were invited to declare for or against 'the
      establishment of a separate Union in Eire' and the
      members in the north were invited to declare for or
      against 'attachment to a separate Union in Ireland.'
      Perhaps to the members in the north, the issue was
      clear enough, although the word 'attachment' is not
      without significance as implying some subsidiary role.
      The members in the south however may not have been
      in a position to indicate a choice between an all-
      Ireland union and a southern union; for example an all-
      Ireland union might well have its headquarters in
      Belfast, as John Conroy had taken some pains to point out.
      Mr Paul Alexander believes however that the issue was
      clear enough. In a letter to me on August 21 1975 he
      stated: 'I can understand that it might appear con-
      fusing to anybody outside the industry as to what was
      meant when reading the wording of the Ballot Papers.
      At the time it was fully explained to all members in
      each branch as to what we had in mind and was clearly
      understood by them. The location of the Central Office
      was much discussed and was not determined for some
      months after the voting. Dundalk was ultimately
      decided upon because the bulk of the membership resided
      there. The cost of servicing them would therefore
      be less costly. In regard to the meetings held either
      in the North or South we spoke in terms of an Irish
      union, not in terms of a union based in Eire or the
      26 Counties. Naturally we were very disappointed with
      the N. Ireland result as were the Executive Council of
      the English Union and as a result, J. Crawford G.P.
      and myself were advised to consult the membership in
      the North again. We held meetings in all the northern

branches and endeavoured to get them to change their
minds. These meetings were well attended but our
efforts proved fruitless.' The voting in the various
areas is of considerable interest, and I am very much
in the debt of Mr Paul Alexander both for copies of
the ballot papers and for the following voting analysis.

EIRE

	FOR	AGAINST		FOR	AGAINST
Drogheda	183	34	Edenderry	71	17
Ballinsloe	82	23	Dublin	148	37
Westport	38	23	Birr	46	4
Cork	122	133	Killarney	58	12
Waterford	25	18	Kilkenny	29	85
Clonmel	146	64	Tralee	78	5
Carlow	66	53	Dundalk	578	298
Carrickmacross	170	75	Castleblayney	84	10
Bailieborough	66	41			

Totals: FOR - 1990:   AGAINST - 932

NORTHERN IRELAND

	FOR	AGAINST		FOR	AGAINST
Armagh	32	26	Banbridge	4	91
Belfast	9	100			

Totals: FOR - 45:   AGAINST - 217.

Full membership (Financial) of Ireland 4,990
Total poll   3,184
Percentage poll   60 approx ...

The manner in which the questions were put may well
have affected the vote in certain areas, and may have
contributed as well to the relatively low poll.

200. Philip S. Bagwell: The Railwaymen: The History of
      the National Union of Railwaymen London 1963 p.133.

201. ibid. p.445.

202. idem.

203. ibid. p.446.

204. idem.

205. idem.

206. ibid. p.447

207. ibid. p.449.

208. ibid. 628. In a submission to the Commission on
Vocational Organisation in the early forties, the NUR
stated in evidence that it was not opposed to the idea
of an independent Irish organisation and was prepared
to transfer funds to such an organisation, if it
were established, in proportion to membership.
(Report: op.cit. p.367 par.584).

209. From an interview with W.T. Chapman March 25 1975.

210. Bagwell op.cit. p.629.

211. Chapman interview.

212. idem.

213. Chapman interview; cf. ITUC 1954.

214. CIU 1952 p.50.

215. CIU 1951 p.77.

216. ITUC 1951 p.75.

217. ITUC 1951 p.132.

218. ITUC 1952 p.195.

219. ITUC 1952 p.198.

220. ITUC 1952 p.200.

221. Percentage of delegates for selected years attending
ITUC annual conferences with addresses in Dublin (and
south): Belfast (and north): cross-channel

	Dublin (& south)	Belfast (& north)	Cross-channel
1901	68%	32%	–
1937	74%	17%	9%
1938	77%	17%	6%
1943		24%	
1951	59%	36%	5%
1952	54%	40%	6%
1972	75%	25%	–

(continued ...)

See above pp.149, 198, 232, 262,275.1937 was the period
of the William O'Brien putsch; in 1938 the British
offices relaxed. 1943 was the high point in the
dispute between the Irish Transport and the Amalgamated
Transport. The dramatic change in 1951 shows the
consequences of the split. The 1951 meeting was in
Killarney and in judging the all-Ireland balance
would be a fairer picture than Derry in 1952. The
balance in 1951 does not differ greatly from that in 1901.

Chapter Ten

Reconciliation

-i-

In the long perspective of the years there were, in the
trade union movement in Ireland, three great episodes of
integrative leadership. The first, accomplished by the
Dublin and Belfast trades councils, was the careful stitching
together in 1894 of the Irish Trades Union Congress. The
second is the one we shall now discuss, the creation of a
single trade union centre, the Irish Congress of Trade Unions,
after many years of division, and the third was the
development in the early 1970s of the great national pay
agreements with their attendant institutions. It is true
that the trade union movement saw at least two other
remarkable episodes in trade union leadership, Larkin's
from 1907 to 1914, and William O'Brien's from the mid-
thirties to the mid-forties when he very nearly succeeded
in altering radically the whole structure of the trade union
movement; but the first was personal and charismatic, and
the second, for all its power, was essentially disruptive.
Here, since we are focussing on the development of
institutions, we are concerned with integrative leadership,
the kind that builds and consolidates structures.

Much has been said, particularly in recent years, about
the inadequacies of trade union leadership, a great deal no
doubt stemming from a misunderstanding of the nature of
democratic leadership in the first place; and this outstanding episode in integrative leadership in the fifties
provides us at least with an opportunity of examining the
manner in which it is exercised. The men who provided the
leadership - in particular John Conroy of the Irish Transport,
Jim Larkin of the Workers Union of Ireland and Norman
Kennedy of the Amalgamated Transport - were not, for all their

diverse abilities, men of outstanding charismatic character.
With the exception perhaps of Larkin,[1] their power to
exhort was not exceptional. Rather did they take skilful
advantage of the power which democratic leadership confers.
It is not the power of the centurion, who says to a man,
come and he cometh, and go and he goeth; and yet there
are certain commanding heights[2] which are available to a
democratic leader which are of great significance. There is,
for example, the power to initiate, and - equally importantly -
the power to neglect to respond when a response would do
harm; there is the considerable power to determine the nature
and the form of the question which should be put for
democratic decision; there is the power to determine the
scope of the voting group when the question is being put;[3]
and - for our purposes probably the most interesting of all -
there is the power to promote structural change in advance
of agreement in principle, that is to say in the absence of it;
and in promoting such structural changes to foster joint
working arrangements. With much of this is associated
the notion of using time constructively, allowing irresolvable
situations to rest, waiting for the chemistry of time to change
their character and in this way to develop a solution.
Some of these points have already been exemplified in the case
of the boot and shoe union[4] and as we proceed through this
account we shall mark their exercise from time to time.

It is axiomatic that all these devices of democratic
leadership must be exercised within the democratic consensus,
but this consensus is a complex matter, which cannot be
understood fully by speaking merely of parameters, emphasising
as they do the constraints on action; it is better perhaps
to see the consensus as a mood or a spirit in society, its
aspirations liable to frustration when leaders fail to respond
to it, or even fail to articulate it; but on the other
hand capable of developing and growing, finding in articulation and action, new insights and deeper aspirations.
This then is what creative democratic leadership can provide,
and such leadership is particularly significant when a
general aspiration is subject to many anxieties and

hostilities within a society, many confusions
dictions.

And thus it was with the trade union movement in 1953. True,
again and again we are told that the workers ardently desired
unity[5] but for many rank and file members the pressing need
for unity was by no means as clear as it was for the leadership, since their horizon was dominated more often than not
by the affairs of their own union rather than those of the
congresses. On the contrary, there was much to make the
influential second-string leadership - the leadership in
executives and in branches - fear a movement towards unity:
in the amalgamated unions because it might mean their
destruction in the south, in Northern Ireland because it
might hopelessly compromise them in their delicate relationship
with the government and with each other, and even among the
Irish-based unions of the CIU because it might dilute the
fundamental nationalist position which they had sacrificed
so much to achieve and which they thought of as their
ultimate security. Furthermore nearly a decade had passed
during which men had lived with a divided movement, longer
indeed if one counts from the stresses which had arisen as
long ago as 1939, and there was some acceptance now of that
position as a natural and normal one, which, despite
declarations to the contrary, was unlikely to change.
Nevertheless the trade union leadership was now intent upon
achieving unity in spite of the many difficulties - some
apparently quite insurmountable - in their path.

-ii-

The beginning was inauspicious. The initiative of May 1
1953 could easily have fallen into a barren wrangle on

formulae without resulting in any meeting at all, and indeed
it began with the imposition by CIU of what was described
as a condition precedent, that unity should be 'on the basis
of the Irish trade union movement being wholly Irish based
and controlled'[6] and furthermore that joint discussions would
be premature unless this were accepted. But although it
might appear to have been a tough-minded beginning on the
part of the CIU, in fact they were asking no more than the
ITUC had already conceded. The question had been put with
some care. Let us consider the background a little. In
1949 the difficulty had not been the principle but its
application to Northern Ireland.[7] Later in the year Hickey
and Corish seemed, in quite inauspicious circumstances, to
have hammered out agreement to a formula to give the principle
expression.[8] Consequently the ITUC could reply that this
was something which the conference 'should have in view ...'
and they continued: 'it is accepted without question that
the proposed discussions must be very largely concerned with
questions relating to the interpretation and application
of this principle.'[9] But this made the CIU fear that once
again they would be presented with Sam Kyle's formula that
even as things stood, amalgamated unions were in practice
Irish-based and controlled, and the atmosphere began to
grow a little murky. But in great contrast with the past,
neither side was prepared to allow the negotiations to slide
into a wrangle on paper before they had really begun. The
ITUC suggested a meeting to explore the difficulties, or, as
an alternative, an exchange of memoranda. The latter was
agreed by the CIU[10] and despite their initial aggressiveness
they now, in Bottom's memorable phrase, roared them as
gently as a sucking-dove, declaring themselves to 'be fully
conscious of the difficulties confronting the ITUC' and
being 'anxious to give all the assistance possible.' Once
the memorandum was received from the ITUC a date for the
conference could be arranged; in other words there was now
no question of the memorandum satisfying the condition
precedent; it was sufficient merely that it should be submitted. And here we mark the careful confusion which permitted

the CIU to neglect to push the point home.[11] This brought
the correspondence to June 1953 and when the annual
conferences of the two congresses took place in July, there
was much reinforcement from the delegates of the trend of
events, a marked atmosphere of optimism and goodwill[12] and a
diplomatic withdrawal from the CIU conference of a hardline
and divisive resolution.[13]

The ITUC memorandum of July 1953[14] while it contained nothing
new was a succinct and very competent assessment of the
notion of Irish control. It did not anticipate what the
eventual outcome might be, but the thrust of the memorandum
was clear enough. Irish control in the sense in which it was
used by the CIU would repel Northern Ireland members and
consolidate partition. But Irish control could be understood in a number of ways. If one were to view it in terms
of a central congress, it could mean majority control (not
exclusive control) by those unions which had headquarters
within the state - and this could be readily achieved.
If one were to view it in terms of an amalgamated union,
it could mean more explicit autonomy for Irish members in
Irish matters - and this too could be readily achieved.
And there was a strong implication as well that under a congress
united in these circumstances there would be a working towards
a solution of the problem of amalgamated unions along the lines
of the NUR solution - although here one notices in the
memorandum an uncertain voice, an anxiety for the principle
'that workers' interests transcend national boundaries.'[15]

Here we notice the dimension of time introduced into the
strategy, closely similar to Johnson's gradualism in the
early years of the movement.[16] It is a key idea in the
reforming of organisations. Reform here depends on
identifying the maximum which is agreed at any one time and
developing structural change at least up to that level.
The future, as we have already said, must lie in the hope
that elements now altogether incompatible will, in the
passage of time, alter and find a resolution. It has the

considerable advantage of permitting progress to be continuous
if slow; it has the considerable disadvantage of committing
all the parties to some extent to a road which is at the
very least obscure and which may be perilous. It is
therefore only possible as a strategy when the leadership
on both sides have a powerful commitment to a common
objective even if the manner of its achievement is uncertain;
and because this aptly enough describes the state of affairs
in the Irish trade union leadership at the time, it was
adopted by them.

The CIU memorandum, which was submitted on November 19 1954[17]
when the discussions on trade union unity were already
well under way, reiterated the point with some considerable
force that 'no body, group or individual outside Ireland
should have any power, influence or opportunity to in any
way impede or interfere ...'[18] But the strategy of
gradualism appeared to be accepted, at least in part, since
it spoke of 'the eventual elimination'[19] of British unions in
Ireland, and pointed to the way of solving the problem,
the way of the NUR, the National Boot and Shoe Operatives
and the woodcutting machinists (who in fact transferred to
an Irish-based union). The problem of the north was not
mentioned although there was a recognition that separate
statistical and research services might have to be provided
on a regional basis. But the memorandum is of great
significance in that it once more sought to involve the
British TUC and the executives of the amalgamated unions -
because the CIU was convinced that if the consent of the
British offices could be secured a solution along the lines
of the NUR and the others would readily emerge. This desire
to secure a commitment from the British TUC and the British
offices resulted in the second crisis in the negotiations,
a crisis that would have, in previous circumstances, wrecked
them utterly.

Before moving on, it is necessary to note another theme which

is present in the CIU memorandum, a theme which is basic
to our study and which we shall take up in the
next chapter. It concerns the ever-recurrent objective of
industry-based trade unions. Not only, it was considered,
would a united trade union movement provide better services
for the members and better representation, but it would
foster as well 'the reorganisation of the movement on
industrial lines.'[20] The same objective was more vigorously
stated by the ITUC; in its memorandum one of the strong
arguments advanced in favour of gradualism was that under
a united congress 'a natural consequence of the establishment
of machinery for the development of industrial coordination
would be a further development in importance of purely Irish
trade union institutions, responsible solely to the Irish
trade union movement.'[21] In fact before the unity talks
had become a reality, and in response to Lemass's impatience
regarding trade union structures, the ITUC had held a
special conference in Dublin on July 11 1953 where the idea
of a permanent trade union commission was explored, the object
being to promote structural reform on industrial lines and to
deal with internal disputes, an idea which was taken up again
in the sixties by the united congress.[22] Furthermore, the
following year, 1954, Roberts, in a very extensive and rather
radical memorandum[23] which he submitted to the unity
committee, took up the notion of restructuring on an industrial
basis not merely as an objective of a united congress but as
a very catalyst by which the movement could be united in
the first place, proposing dual membership of a number of
industrial federations which in turn would generate a general
confederation corresponding to the united congress. The idea,
as we shall see, although it created unease and little
enough discussion,[24] appeared again during the reorganisation
discussion in the sixties and also in the course of the
memorandum submitted by Johannes Schregle of the ILO in 1975.
A joint committee of the two congresses began discussions
in September 1953 in the Mansion House Dublin under the
chairmanship of Professor John Busteed of University College Cork

(although in truth there appeared to be little enough need
for an independent conciliator at this stage)[24A] and by April
1954 they were in a position to present, to separate
consultative conferences of the two congresses, a joint
memorandum on trade union unity[25] which in its appendices
(to these we have already referred) not only detailed the
events leading up to the conference and the memoranda
submitted by both sides, but gave details as well of current
trade union membership and organisation.

The joint memorandum on trade union unity (which was well
received by both congresses)[26] provided a good example
of the third strategic power which is vested in democratic
leadership, the power to influence the scope of the electorate.
The memorandum recorded approval and acceptance of the
principle of the Irish trade union movement being wholly Irish
based and controlled[27] and further of the principle of 'an
all Ireland (thirty-two county) trade union movement with
one Central Trade Union Authority.' With regard to
validating the final decision, paragraph (c), reflecting
CIU policy, declared that 'any final proposals ... shall
be submitted to a general ballot of the trade union members
in Ireland in the unions affiliated to both Congresses in
Ireland' which, on its face, could have meant only that
Irish-based members could outvote amalgamated members
(particularly in the north) and commit them to a majority
all-Ireland view. But this had to be read in the light of
the subsequent paragraph (d) which gave the ITUC precisely
the protection it sought: 'that this joint conference re-
affirms the duty and responsibility of both Congresses to
protect and uphold the democratic principles cf the trade
union movement, and recognises as a fundamental principle
to be observed in any proposal for the reorganisation of
the trade union movement that such reorganisation shall be
subject to the consent of the trade union members concerned,
determined democratically by ballot.'[28] Members of

amalgamated unions therefore could not be required to leave
their union and join another unless they consented by an
internal majority; a majority among trade union members
generally on the question would not prevail over their
internal vote. It appears in fact that the requirement
of a ballot of all the members in the country was introduced
by the CIU as a counter to the ITUC claim that the proposals
should be subject to the consent of the unions affected[29] -
although one suspects that the CIU might have been concerned
here more with consistency in its own policy than anything
else, since its proposals, coming in the final document
before and not after the more restrictive ITUC proposal,
would clearly be governed by it.

As we have seen, the mythology of the Irish-based unions
assumed that since the normal and natural organisations
for Irishmen were Irish unions, it followed that one need
only identify and remove certain barriers, and the problem
would be resolved. The barriers, in their opinion, had
to lie in practical matters such as the jobs of the Irish
officials and the continuation of benefits, barriers which
had to be removed before a fair vote could be taken. It was
for this reason that the CIU pressed a reluctant ITUC
to open discussions with the executives of the amalgamated unions
and with the British TUC to secure, in Crawford's words,
'that assurances should be given before the ballot that benefits
built up in British unions should be protected.'[30] But the
ITUC would not agree to anything so explicit. In the joint
unity memorandum they had committed themselves not only to
a meeting with the British TUC and the executives of the
amalgamated unions, but also to the preparation of a
memorandum for the purpose; in fact no such memorandum was
prepared and in the event the joint conference merely asked
the British TUC 'whether they would be kind enough to act as
a convenor of the proposed conference of representatives
of unions with headquarters in Britain and members in Ireland'
enclosing the joint unity memorandum for information.[31]

Vincent Tewson of the British TUC initially reacted
sympathetically and positively[32] but when the general council
had an opportunity of looking at the proposal in May they
became alarmed, because it appeared that their support
was being sought 'in devising ways and means by which control
of the unions in Ireland would be transferred to the Irish
members.'[33] They refused therefore to act as convenors.[34]
The unity committee declared that they had quite misunderstood the position, that they were being asked merely
to convene the conference; but Tewson was adamant, although
as a conciliatory gesture he suggested a meeting to deal
with any misunderstandings,[35] an invitation which the unity
committee accepted. In fact the meeting did not take place
until December 1954, it was conducted on behalf of the British
TUC by George Woodcock, then assistant secretary,[36] it was
absolutely unfruitful, and by March the unity committee
had reached deadlock.

Much of this frustration was in fact anticipated at the
July 1954 conferences of both congresses, Crawford of the
CIU falling back on his traditional pessimism regarding the
whole exercise, and in the case of the ITUC a tendency for
the delegates from the amalgamated unions to become anxious
and recriminatory. 'If the movement is to progress,' said
J.P. Forristal of the Typographical Association,[37] 'it must
be a natural growth and it must not be subject to either
regimentation or dictatorial control from within or without ...
it must not become the plaything of any political party.
Stop playing "Chase me Charlie" with Kathleen ni Houlihan,
take your heads out of the clouds and get down to the practical
problems of benefiting the workers.' And Jim Larkin, not
without some sadness, remarked: 'Not all the CIU representatives
seemed to have a complete knowledge of that large centre
of trade union strength in Belfast and the six northern
counties. At many of our meetings endless hours were spent
trying to get them to appreciate what the position was in
the North-East corner. We made very considerable progress.
The practical difficulties have now come. It is agreed that

there has been a complete lack of understanding of what it
is that keeps tens of thousands of Irishmen within British
unions. There has been a point of view put forward that
if certain assurances were given about benefits and the
maintenance of industrial strength and if the increasing
ability shown over the past twenty-five years of Irish-based
unions to serve their members efficiently and well was
pointed out, then there would be an almost automatic acceptance
of the viewpoint of the CIU. Many of us were convinced
that that viewpoint was not well founded.'[38]

Indeed to a great extent all this procedure was in the nature
of an odyssey of understanding for the Irish-based unions,
an odyssey which was as yet far from the Graecian shore.
Even in the discussions with Woodcock in December Crawford
had stressed, despite the different view held by the ITUC,
that the reluctance of some Irish members of amalgamated
unions to join Irish-based unions was merely a matter of
benefits, and because this was so, the amalgamated unions
should give a guarantee regarding such benefits before a
ballot took place. And when the British TUC refused to
convene a meeting for the purpose, the CIU pressed, in
pursuit of the same objective, for individual meetings with
the executives of the amalgamated unions, which the ITUC
refused initially to have anything to do with. It was all
rather embarrassing for them. As we have already seen,[39] the
Irish officers of the amalgamated unions - those who served
on the ITUC national executive - were regional officers by
definition, frequently being officers appointed by the British
offices and not elected by the members; they were now being
pressed - against their better judgement and against what
they firmly believed to be the overwhelming opinion of their
members - to take up with their own national executives
the question of Irish separatism.

But in quite an unexpected manner, this most unpromising
situation was turned to good account, again underlying the

immense strength of the commitment among the leadership.
The ITUC national executive undertook to reconsider their
decision not to approach the executives of the amalgamated
unions; but they went further. They convinced the CIU
that 'to approach the British unions individually without
the frame work of some new central organisation that would
induce them to change over to Irish-based unions would be
futile.' Consequently it was decided to consider the
possibility of a 'provisional unity committee' and a
drafting subcommittee was established on June 2 1955 with
this end in view.[40] This of course meant that the idea of
securing in advance certain assurances from the British
offices was abandoned. At best they might be secured
when general agreement between the congresses had been
achieved (assuming that such assurances would be still relevant)
in which case they could not be expected to influence the
development of that agreement. The manner of the decision
decently obscured this point, and again the CIU prudently
neglected to pursue it.

The subcommittee worked rapidly and well. On January 5 of
the following year, 1956, separate special delegate conferences of the two congresses endorsed the constitution
of the Provisional United Organisation, and on January 12
its first formal meeting took place.

-iii-

The Provisional United Organisation was established at a time
when the trade union movement was profoundly in need of a
common centre and a united leadership, and moreover was
conscious of its need. These were the dark days of economic
recession, of widespread unemployment and unprecedented
levels of emigration. It was a period of social and political

unrest; the unemployed association had disappeared, but
radicalism had not; the IRA were already raiding for arms,
to be followed at the year's end with restless violence along
the border. The major problem for the trade unions, which
all these events intensified, was the impact of a large
disorganised wage movement, which by early 1956 had left
them somewhat shaken. This was the fifth round of wage
increases since the war, and the first great free-for-all
round that the country had experienced. True, the first
round of wage increases after the war[41] was not centrally
negotiated and, in that sense, could be described as a free
for all, as also was the third, but although they showed
some diversity, neither had the tear-away character of the
fifth round. Perhaps a word on its background therefore
would not be out of place.

The fourth round had been centrally negotiated on the part
of the CIU in May 1952, being 12/6 for male workers and
although the ITUC remained independent of the agreement
they followed broadly the same pattern.[42] A long period
followed in which there was very little movement; in fact
the fifth round did not begin until the spring of 1955.
The economic indicators at the time were hardly favourable.
The number of unemployed which had reached 76,000 in 1953[43]
remained unabated in 1954[44] while the consumer price index
had risen during the period from May 1952 to early 1955
by eight or nine percent.[45] In the past this figure would
probably have been the target for wage increases, but there
was every sign that this round would be an ambitious one,
certainly aiming at a figure higher than that indicated
by the consumer price index. On February 28 1955 the CIU
gave three months notice of their intention to terminate
the fourth round agreement[46] but the significant move,
setting the tone for the round, came a little over a month
later in early April. The ITUC which did not require to
give notice since they had not been parties to any fourth
round agreement, issued a statement that pushed aspirations

alarmingly high.   The justification for increases, they
claimed, lay not merely in cost of living increases, but
in the restoration of 1939 living standards and recompense
for increased productivity.[47]   There was a mood of
frustration and anxiety, which the Federated Union of Employers
did not help when they refused unequivocally to meet the
CIU on the question of renegotiating the agreement, and
nailed their colours to the mast by publishing the correspondence
which included a long apologia.   'The Consumer Price Index',
they claimed, '... shows an increase since the beginning
of 1952 of 10.5% whereas over the same period ... the rise
in the Index of Wage Rates is shown to be 9.5%'.[48]   About
the same time the ITUC formally invited the CIU[49] to join
with them - quite apart from the unity talks - in a discussion on the economy and on the wage situation, which
the CIU, unchanging in this matter, refused to do, becoming
not a little irate when this correspondence was published
as well.   We must remember that this too was the low point
in the unity talks, the discussions tangled in the British
TUC bureaucracy and gradually heading for deadlock.   Matters
were at a low ebb, there was a good deal of distrust in
the air, and unions began to look principally to their
individual advantage.

The interparty[50] government had come to power a year earlier
in May 1954 but Norton, who was now in the key ministry of
Industry and Commerce, appeared to be reluctant to interfere
with the course of events.   As the round developed, there
emerged a great diversity in the increases gained, from
eleven shillings to sixteen shillings and six pence;
moreover, the gains were made in an atmosphere of 'strikes,
bitterness, loss of man-hours, and inconvenience to industry
and the community',[51] and left behind 'glaring anomalies
which still remain to be adjusted.'[52]   The trade union
movement could claim that they had not favoured such a
free for all;   they had sought an orderly increase, centrally
negotiated;   and their experience in the fifth round reinforced

their conviction that 'a wage increase claimed on a cost
of living basis should be made at top level and (on) a
formula principle.'[53]

This statement was made by Mervyn in his presidential address
to the 1956 CIU annual conference, and we should note in
passing that it contains in it the seeds of a problem
which was to develop mightily in the years that followed;
because it appeared to distinguish cost of living
claims from all others, seeing such claims as the
proper material for national agreements, which, when concluded, left the parties free to pursue at their absolute
discretion, claims of a sectional character (status claims
or grade claims as they came to be known) irrespective
of their impact on the economy as a whole and on its
capacity to absorb them without further increases in living
costs. At least this was how the idea was to develop, to
trouble greatly the sixties, although Mervyn and his
colleagues at the time could not have been expected to
anticipate it.

Immediately after, the country plunged into economic doldrums,
from which it was not to recover until 1958 and this crisis
in the economic affairs of the society, combined with the
border campaign of the IRA, was eventually too much for the
fragile interparty government which was swept out of office
in the spring of 1957. But in early 1956, with the fifth
round not fully spent, the trade union movement, now very
wary about unstructured wage movements, was confronted with
a rising pressure for a further adjustment to cope with the
increased cost of living in circumstances that were highly
unfavourable. The PUO however had now been created and the
problem was passed to them.

We enter therefore into the last phase in this progress
towards trade union unity, a progress which was greatly helped
by the joint endeavour to dominate the wages problem. But

before dealing with that development let us mark one or two
other matters. This is a stage where we find in particular
the courageous device of building common structures before
agreement on common principles is secured - or at least
before their structural principles are worked out. Three
months after the establishment of the Provisional United
Organisation, the two congresses abandoned their headquarters (neither of which of course was elaborate) and set
up in twin offices in Merrion Street, giving the provisional
organisation as well a single home. The division on principle
can of course be somewhat exaggerated. There was during
all this time a growing consensus, despite the difficulty
of its expression. In May, for example, the two Dublin trades
councils, so long apart, jointly organised the commemorations
for James Connolly,[54] the first for eleven years; and Harold
Binks of Belfast,first chairman of the PUO,[55] president of the
ITUC and chairman of its northern committee,delivered the
oration outside the General Post Office in Dublin,
saturated as it was with the memories of 1916, where the
trade union formula - of a transnational and transreligious
workers' socialism - stood up quite well.

There is a further minor point - certainly too much should
not be made of it - which tended to bring together those who
were conservative. This was the rather strident character
of the radical left, particularly those who came from the
north to the annual conferences of the ITUC. There was a
certain rather grotesque gamesmanship which this radical
communist left engaged in, attaching powerful political
implications to motions on unemployment and peace, which
normally would be accepted without question; the catholic
nationalist group, frequently wrongfooted, felt profoundly
resentful, and the socialist groups would seek hurriedly for
amendments that would exclude communist overtones from the
proposals. This kind of gamesmanship, which was taken with
enormous seriousness, grew in intensity during the sixties,
dying away during the seventies as the fear of an East-West
confrontation died away as well. But as early as 1952,

Denis Larkin, after a long discussion on disarmament during
the annual conference, said - obliquely perhaps, but the
message was clear enough - 'this was the Irish Trade Union
Congress but listening to some of the speeches made there
one would imagine it was not taking place in Ireland at all
but in the heart of London, because instead of dealing
with matters affecting the workers of Ireland they had to
listen to the case for and against British Imperialistic
policy.'[56]   To the catholic nationalist south in particular,
the communist delegates from the north appeared to be devious,
disruptive and wholly unreliable, without indeed a redeeming
feature;   and in this regard they were certainly less than
fair.[57]   On the other hand, the solid commonsense of the
socialists from the north they found helpful and reassuring.
This point demonstrates as well the pressure of countervailing
sympathies among unions and among officials which spanned
the divide between the congresses, and, in the years of unity
that followed, effectively obscured it.

Having built a common structure then the two congresses,
somewhat fortuitously as we have seen, were presented, in the
crisis of rising living costs, with the opportunity of
engaging in a joint endeavour which to all in the trade
union movement at the time was of overriding interest.   The
idea of joint endeavour in such matters, in advance of unity,
had, as we have seen, been continuously urged by Jim Larkin,
and indeed in the strategy of the time it was a necessary
corollary to the idea of joint institutions and joint
office accommodation.   In fact in the months from January
to the July annual conferences, the PUO appeared to devote
their energies in particular to economic matters although
their explicit function was to draft a constitution for a
permanent organisation, and any other functions virtually
crept in under a general omnibus clause.[58]   Indeed so
dominant was the economic question that Mervyn expressed some
concern in his presidential address to the CIU 1956 Congress:
'The Provisional Committee ... has done much good work since
its formation, but the vital job is to draft a framework

of a Constitution for the new unified Centre. Little
progress has been made in that direction ...';[59]   indeed
Walter Beirne, who was secretary of the PUO, confessed that
they were still poles apart.[60]   However, probably reassured
by the congresses in July, a drafting committee on the
constitution met weekly from October 9 onwards and a draft
document was available by the following summer.[61]

The very complexity of the prices problem served to consolidate still more the joint endeavour of the PUO.   It
was certainly not a simple matter of seeking a compensatory
wage increase.   There was widespread anxiety about the
state of the economy and the high level of unemployment,
and in entering, in May 1956, into discussions with the
employers and the government, the trade unions sought -
apart from trying to remedy some of the anomalies of the
fifth round - to promote some stabilising of prices much
more than any increase in wages.[62]   This also was the reason
for the two economic conferences and the various planning
proposals which we shall later discuss.   Indeed it was not
until the following May (1957), when a particularly dismal
budget abolished food subsidies and pushed the cost of living
still higher, that the PUO sought authority to negotiate
some recompense, returning to another joint conference in
September 1957 with a national agreement setting increases
at 0.50p. a week.

The agreement represented a considerable constraint, and
although the economy was soon to swing into a long upward
phase, the arrangement held until 1959.   It was not without
cost, however, as is the nature of all such minimum settlements.
In the first place, the flat increase for all of 10 shillings
(or 50p.) a week caused much uneasiness among salaried
people, contributing substantially to their restlessness
in the decade that followed; but, perhaps even more important, we notice that the distinction between cost of living
claims and status claims, hinted at by Mervyn the year before,[63]
had now developed into a full-blown policy.   It arose on a
question of interpretation of the agreement.   The Irish

National Teachers Organisation, which in the south
represented primary teachers essentially, in seeking parity
of salary with secondary teachers, were informed by the
Minister for Finance that they were precluded from any
increase by the PUO-FUE agreement on the grounds that it
would have an influence on prices;[64] and this brought a
vigorous response from the PUO who stated, inter alia, that
'... the PUO-FUE agreement relates solely to wage claims
based on the increased cost of living and has no bearing
on or relevance to grade claims, claims of a status nature
or value of work claims.'[65] This principle was to be used
to considerable effect by the salaried groups in the years
that followed, becoming the key concept in their salary
policies.

But these were by no means the only matters referred by the
congresses to the PUO. Both the second (1956-57) and the
third (1957-58) reports became quite substantial documents
because of this transfer of business, more significant
indeed by far than the individual reports of the two
congresses and causing more significant discussion at the
annual conferences of the congresses than their individual
domestic reports did.

Here then was demonstrated the usefulness and practicality
of a single central trade union organisation, but at the
same time one must conclude that, despite the practical
reasons for unity, the potential for national wage bargaining,
the service and the protection of the members, the fact
still remained that the instinct for unity, the motivation
that succeeded in dominating the immense difficulties of
the time did not spring essentially from such practical
reasons at all but rather - to use a somewhat unfashionable
phrase - from a certain nobility of purpose in the leadership;
and if we offer two examples of it, it is for the purpose
of demonstrating something that was quite widely held.
John Conroy in 1954,[65A] although appealing at the time for
Irish-based unions, pointed out (perhaps unrealistically) that

an 'Irish based and controlled union (could have) its
head office in Belfast, Derry, Cork, Portadown or
elsewhere.' But, much more significantly, he went on:
'We want them (the trade union members in the north) to
realise that they will come in of their own free choice,
that they will be as free as they are now to decide how
their unions will operate with their consent and approval.
They must be free to be guided by their own consciences,
not by anybody else's wishes or desires. What we are doing
is endeavouring to bring about Trade union unity based on
the right of Irishmen, North and South, to control their
own destiny. I think we should be able to make some progress
but if we reach the stage where there is even the fear
that we are attempting to impose our religious or political
beliefs on some other section, then we shall reach the stage
of breaking point again ... While it is possible, as has
been indicated, that this job cannot be done this year, next
year or possibly for a number of years, at least let us sow
the seed of appreciation of the other person's point of view.
Even if we do not succeed, let us hope that those who come
after us will find it possible to complete the task that
we have given some aid to during our time.'

And Bob Smith[66] who was president of the ITUC in 1955
delivered a highly important address to the annual conference in the course of which he was remarkably outspoken:
'... We in the Labour movement, who should have a Labour
view point to express, tend to accept views from outside
the movement and to classify ourselves politically as
unionists or as anti-partitionists. Worse still, we in
Northern Ireland have so far forgotten the lessons of
Labour history as to expose ourselves to that very same
propaganda that was used to split and divide the united
front of the Trade Union Movement in 1907, and to allow
sectarianism, disgracefully represented as 'religious' differences,
to determine which of the two non-Labour lines of thought
we accept. I am not saying that this is universal or that it

would apply to the delegates to this conference - but we
would be deaf and blind if we did not know that these
considerations are the primary considerations affecting
the political decisions of large numbers of workers, trade
unionists, in Belfast and Derry and Northern Ireland generally.
But if we have been weak in combating these influences
in Northern Ireland, we have, if anything, been weaker in
the Republic. There we have allowed the mind and vision
of our members to be clouded and overcast by false propaganda on partition ... In workers' organisations, in the
Trade Union Movement, we have a fine tradition of recognising
the brotherhood of man, and of accepting the principle
that workers' interests and workers' unity transcend
national boundaries ... The existence of the Irish Trade
Union Congress and of its constituent unions on a thirty-
two county basis is made possible by the free consent of its
members and their recognition of their common interests.
This kind of unity has meaning because it is the unity
of people freely joining together to act together in their
common interest. This is what unification should and does
mean within the Labour movement. But the prevailing idea of
National Unity in the Republic has little in common with that
concept. The reality of common consent and common purpose so
representative of the Trade Union approach is submerged in
the flood of anti-partition propaganda. So bent and
distorted is this propaganda that in the name of unity we
are asked to accept not a policy of seeking common consent,
not a policy of **agreement** on common objectives, not any
positive policy at all, but an anti-partitionism which
condemns and does not seek to understand the majority of
the people in Northern Ireland, and would override their
objections and force their consent ...'

A draft constitution had been prepared by the summer of 1957;
but it was not circulated for discussion at the July conference -
a final and rather intriguing incident in democratic leadership;
instead the PUO waited until September and then circulated
it to the unions, releasing it at the same time to the press.[67]

This avoided the danger - remote but possible - of some
flashpoint of emotional and public hostility which might
unduly influence union opinion in advance. Early in 1958,
a meeting was held for northern members in Belfast and comments
were received from other unions. As a result of these,
some changes were made in the draft (not of substance, however)
and the constitution thus amended was adopted by separate
delegate conferences of the two congresses on February 10
1959. On February 11 1959, the Provisional United Trade
Union Organisation was dissolved and the Irish Congress of
Trade Unions was established.[68]

Notes on Chapter Ten

1. As a delegate I experienced personally his per-
    suasive powers for the first time at the special PUO
    conference in September 1957 to agree the 10/- a week
    national agreement, for which my union at the time,
    the Vocational Teachers Association, had little
    enough enthusiasm.

2. I am grateful to my colleague Geoffrey MacKechnie of
    the Department of Business Studies, TCD, for this
    idea of commanding heights. Furthermore he has
    identified, for management purposes, the significance
    of what he calls strategic neglect, a strategy which
    also has significance here. (See Geoffrey MacKechnie:
    Labour relations policies within the firm: Irish
    Productivity Centre 1975).

3. The question of scope is critical if one proposes
    to make a decision on the basis of a majority, and
    in political terms it has always been a matter of
    considerable ambiguity in Ireland. There are those
    who would claim that the people of Northern Ireland
    have no right to reject the views of the majority
    in the island as a whole, while there are those
    in the United Kingdom who would take the view that the
    people in Ireland as a whole had in earlier years no
    right to reject the majority view of the United
    Kingdom as a whole (a view that for other reasons
    would not be shared by the Protestant north). All in
    all this demonstrates the limitations of the majority
    rule system of decision making which is valid only
    in so far as it is accepted by general consensus as
    the appropriate way by which the general will may be
    determined. It is not a means by which substantial
    minorities can willy-nilly be overruled.

4. See above p.405.

5. ITUC 1953 p.92.

6. ITUC 1953 p.57.

7. See page 396 above.

8. See p.400 above.

9. ITUC 1953 p.58.

10. ITUC 1953 pp.59, 60.

11. The ITUC too showed considerable reserve particularly
    in the matter of nominating the representatives to
    attend the annual conferences of the ILO which the CIU
    insisted on retaining right up to the very end, refusing
    to pass the nominations even to the PUO in its final year.

12. CIU 1953 p.122.

13. idem.

14. Joint Memorandum on Trade Union Unity 1954: published with CIU 1954: Appendix III p.15.

15. ibid. p.19.

16. See p.46 above.

17. Joint Memorandum on Trade Union Unity op.cit. Appendix IV p.21.

18. ibid. p.22.

19. ibid. p.23.

20. ibid. p.22.

21. ibid. Appendix III p.17.

22. ITUC 1953 p.26.

23. The memorandum is on the files of the ICTU but was never published in full. An annex which set out a sample constitution was published by Schregle in his memorandum on Restructuring of the Irish Trade Union Movement (Geneva) 1975. It is mentioned in the Report of the Drafting Sub-Committee of the Joint Committee on Trade Union Unity (p.4) where it is referred to the PUO.

24. See the comment of W.J. Fitzpatrick of the IUDW & C, (CIU 1956 p.35) although curiously there were echoes in it of O'Lehane's proposal for the distributive trade in 1919 (see above p. 52). Roberts himself in later years saw his memorandum as a midwife for the solution that followed.

24[A]. The importance given to Professor Busteed's role by M.H. Browne seems somewhat exaggerated. See M.H. Browne: "Industrial Labour & Incomes Policy in the Republic of Ireland",in British Journal of Industrial Relations 1965 Vol.III p.51.

25. Joint Memorandum on Trade Union Unity op.cit.

26. Since, in view of what was proposed, CIU approval was more significant, see Conroy CIU 1954, p.41, which we later summarise (p. 444 below).

27. Joint Memorandum ... op.cit. p.4.

28. ibid. p.5.

29. See Crawford CIU 1954 p.34.

30. CIU 1954 p.34.

31. ITUC 1954 p.29.

32. idem.

33. idem.

34. They were even more reserved in their attitude than they were in 1946 - very possibly because of their experience then (see p.368 above).

35. CIU 1954 p.60.

36. CIU 1955 p.34. There was also some resentment that the Irish representatives were met only by an assistant secretary. (ibid. p.101.)

37. ITUC 1954 p.125.

38. ITUC 1954 p.126.

39. p.369 above.

40. CIU 1955 p.96; the ITUC report on the same matter is circumspectly skimpy,ITUC 1955 pp.40, 166.

41. For details of the rounds see appendix 16.

42. ITUC 1954 p.52.

43. ITUC 1953 p.42.

44. Trade Union Information Vol.11 Nos. 55-56 November-December 1955.

45. ibid. Vol.9. Nos. 53-54 June-July 1954 and Vol. 13 Nos. 78-79 September-October 1957.

46. CIU 1955 p.45.

47. ITUC 1955 p.69.

48. CIU 1955 p.47.

49. CIU 1955 pp.51, 52.

50. The word interparty was, at the time, used usually by supporters and the word coalition by opponents, a practice which was not followed when the national coalition government took office in March 1973.

51. CIU 1956 p.88.

52. CIU 1956 p.87.

53. CIU 1956 p.88.

54. ITUC 1956 p.115.

55. He became first chairman with of course the explicit consent of the CIU.

56.   ITUC 1952 p.197.

57.   William McMullen, writing in earlier days when
        Connolly first came to Belfast, made the point 'that
        in the main in those days the members of the socialist
        movement in (Belfast) were Protestants as the Catholics
        were in the main followers of the Irish Parliamentary
        Party. ... A few at the time embraced republicanism
        as well and twelve months later (1912) they paid the
        inevitable price ... during the fierce sectarian
        troubles that broke out in the Belfast shipyards when
        practically every known socialist found it impossible
        to continue at work, and were subjected to physical
        violence or exposed to the threat of it, as also was
        every Catholic employed there ...' (William McMullen
        in the introduction to James Connolly: The Workers'
        Republic 1951 p.4.)

58.   Clause 3 of the constitution of the Provisional United
        Organisation (see Report of the Drafting Sub-Committee
        1955) required that the Organisation should 'produce
        a constitution ...' and went on to give at length
        some indication of scope and procedure. Then in a
        final subparagraph (d) it states: 'The Provisional
        Committee shall in addition undertake such other
        functions as they may at any time be authorised to
        undertake by resolution adopted by both the Central
        Council of the Congress of Irish Unions and the
        National Executive of the Irish Trade Union Congress.'
        Yet we must remember that the PUO was not a joint
        committee; it was an organisation consisting of 'the
        Irish membership of unions affiliated to both
        Congresses' (4(b)) governed by an executive jointly
        appointed by the two congresses; and being in
        character therefore nearer a congress than an ad hoc
        committee it was not surprising that many general trade
        union matters pushed their way on to its agenda.

59.   CIU 1956 p.92.

60.   ibid. p.194.

61.   PUO Second Report 1957 p.7.

62.   See Roberts's account: ITUC 1956 p.221.

63.   See pp. 439-40 above.

64.   PUO: Third Report 1958 p.11.

65.   ibid. p.12. Indeed Roberts was of the view at
the time that national agreements would tend to
disappear as living costs ceased to be the only
consideration and factors such as increased
productivity became significant (Ruaidhri Roberts:
"Trade Union Organisation in Ireland", <u>Journal of
the Statistical and Social Inquiry Society of
Ireland,</u> Vol.XX,part II,p.106).

65[A].   CIU 1954 p.41.

66.   ITUC 1955 p.137.

67.   Third Report of the Provisional United Organisation p.7.

68.   The two congresses however continued in existence
until July 1959 when they both held their final
conference on the same dates, the CIU in Galway
and the ITUC in Cork.

Chapter Eleven

The New Congress

-i-

The final form of the constitution of the united congress
was without doubt a justification of the position taken up
by the Irish-based unions within the Irish TUC, and in
particular of the position taken up by Jim Larkin. But
justification or no, it must be seen as a tribute more to
the tolerance and perceptiveness of John Conroy and the CIU
leadership than anything else; but this in itself would
hardly have been enough were it not accompanied by a
considerable growth in understanding. That understanding
had grown substantially was clear from the rather remarkable
introduction by the PUO to the draft constitution.

There are five points which indicate the breadth of judgement
which was brought to the task. Firstly - and this indeed
we have accepted in this present work as basic to any study
of trade unions - the PUO in its introduction took note not
merely of the trade union structures but 'of the economic,
social and political conditions under which the trade unions
carry on their work, conditions which will continue to confront the Trade Union Movement for many years regardless of
what changes may take place within the movement.'[1] Secondly,
and this is a distinct point although associated with the first,
'trade unions consist of men and women who hold not only trade
union views, but also political, religious, economic and social
views. Because they hold such views, they are subject to
pressures and influences from outside the Trade Union
Movement and from sources which are at times antagonistic
to the workers and to the whole conception of a strong, national
trade union centre.'[2] And in this regard 'recent activities
in relation to Partition have made the situation even more
difficult and greatly intensified the problems ...' Thirdly,
they took note of the great variety of forms within the

trade union movement;   'the trade unions (making it up)
present a most complex pattern, with hardly two trade unions,
whether Irish-based or not, being exactly similar and in a
position to adopt the same proposals with the same ease.'[3]
Fourthly, there was a great variety in the manner of approach
in regard to finance and staffing and, in particular, there
were 'problems of industrial and trade agreements common
to, and negotiated in respect of, workers in northern and
southern Ireland and in the United Kingdom.'[4] These as we
have already seen were of great importance in the north,
and could bring benefits to relatively small numbers who of
themselves would have been unlikely to achieve them. And
finally, there was the need not only for recognition of this
complexity, but of the need for gradualism as well. The
objective was 'that the single trade union centre must be
Irish based and controlled, but equally that it must represent
the whole of Ireland.' But now it was explicitly recognised
and agreed between the executives that 'an enforced, overnight change can give either one or the other, it cannot
give both' and would indeed cause 'greater disunity in the
movement than has ever previously been experienced ... (being)
... rent and torn by bitter political, religious and social
divisions.'[5] Therefore while the draft constitution embodied
principles which were fully and sincerely agreed - namely,
'a trade union centre for the whole of Ireland which shall be
representative of, responsible to, and democratically controlled by Irish trade unionists'[6] - 'the full, complete and
final working out of such principles will be through steady,
gradual adaptation and change.'[7] In fact, despite the promises
of gradualism, the trade union movement has never, in the
years since then, progressed beyond the point substantially
established by this constitution, although the committee
on trade union organisation in the sixties probably
represented a determined effort to do so. It is fair to
say however that the draft constitution did embody the
principle of a 'trade union centre for the whole of Ireland ...

representative of, responsible to and democratically
controlled by Irish trade unionists.' Let us examine how
in fact this was achieved.

-ii-

We must bear in mind at the outset that unity was not the
only objective in the new constitution. There was also the
insistent desire to restructure the trade union movement,
a desire obscured by the more immediate objective of unity,
but nonetheless continuously present, and we shall find this
theme burgeoning out particularly in those sections of the
constitution which dealt with the provision of services
and the resolution of disputes. We are also fortunate
in having an authoritative commentary on the constitution
and other trade union matters in a paper[8] read by Ruaidhri
Roberts before the Statistical and Social Inquiry Society
of Ireland on April 17 1959 that is, very shortly after
the establishment of the Irish Congress of Trade Unions.

In securing the objective of Irish control, the new constitution did not require the amalgamated unions to break
with the English offices. In a word, unity was found
substantially within the current trade union structure.
The point was made with considerable emphasis at the special
ITUC conference of February 10 1959.[9] There had been a
newspaper report to the effect that they 'must break their
branch and office links with Britain' and in scotching it,
Roberts said with some force: 'As most of you know, this
is completely and absolutely untrue. There is no clause
requiring that British branch and office links must be
broken. From the point of view of the unions with headquarters in Britain the most important and most significant

feature of the Constitution of the ICTU is the fact that
it recognises the position of British unions in Ireland,
recognises the desire of the Irish membership of British
unions to retain their branch and other links with British
headquarters, and provides accordingly that these unions
shall have the right of affiliation to the Irish Congress
of Trade Unions. They have that right without any condition
concerning breaking with Britain either now or at any future
date. The only conditions they are subject to are conditions
with which most British unions with members in Ireland
already conform.'[10] The constitution in fact concerned
itself strictly with the control of Congress, the object
being to give Irish-based unions democratic dominance (that
is, majority dominance) and Irish members - whether
amalgamated or Irish-based - exclusive participation at the
two levels of decision-making in the organisation, the delegate
conference and the executive council. In the case of the
delegate conference, amalgamated unions could affiliate
only in respect of their Irish membership (clause 3), only
members resident in Ireland could be delegates or candidates
for election (clause 2 (b)), and the amalgamated unions
had to undertake to leave purely Irish matters to their
Irish membership (with an obligation to create structures
for the purpose (clause 2 (b)) and also, as far as possible
financial control of local funds. In the case of the
executive council, no less than ten seats in an executive
of nineteen - including officers - were reserved for
representatives of Irish based unions (clause 27). In these
respects, the constitution finally adopted[11] despite some
hedging and tidying departed little from the draft issued by
the PUO.

True, as Roberts later remarked,[12] the undertakings required
of the amalgamated unions were largely in operation already,
but this did not assuage the considerable unease of a number
of the British offices, and while we have not a published
record of the names of the cross-channel delegates who
attended the special ITUC conference on February 10 1959

their presence was emphatic - the conference being presented,
immediately the question of the constitution was put to the
floor, with delegate after delegate from Britain urging
reservation and opposition.[13]   But it was remarkable
that - with one exception - where an amalgamated union
opposed the constitution a cross-channel delegate spoke,
while on the other hand, where an amalgamated union supported
the constitution, the speaker more often than not was Irish.
More than that, the support of the prominent Northern Ireland
delegates was forceful and **near-unanimous**. In sum then, the
objections appeared to be technical and even vexatious, a
goodly number of the amalgamated unions in any event
supported unity, and when the vote was taken the constitution
was adopted by 148 votes to 81.[14]   Perhaps in regard to the
north, there are some quaint echoes of earlier years[15] when
the Belfast trades council, in that complex society of
religious and political divisions, found the Dublin trade
unionists less indelicate than their colleagues in the British
trade unions. In fact in 1959 the northern members had
secured a substantial change in the original PUO draft.
As we have seen, the Northern Ireland committee of the ITUC
had up to then been a subcommittee of the national executive,
and did not rank separately in the ITUC constitution. In
the PUO draft (clause 39) the executive council was obliged
to appoint a Northern Ireland committee from among its own
members with the addition of an unspecified number elected
by a Northern Ireland conference; but the practice already
established[16] gave the Northern Ireland members the right
of nomination, and this practice was in fact reaffirmed in
the final document which provided that the executive council
must appoint ten members nominated by a Northern Ireland
Conference (also clause 39.) Nevertheless - not surprisingly
in view of the difficult evolution of the committee in
the north[17] - its functions were held firmly within the congress
structure, its task being to 'implement the decisions of
Annual and Special Delegate Conference and of the Executive

Council on matters of concern to affiliated organisations
having members in Northern Ireland ...'[18] not, it must be
noted, to implement decisions of a Northern Ireland
conference, which would have raised the dangerous notion
of an Ulster TUC. The amended clause therefore represented
much better the actual situation as it existed in Northern
Ireland, and Roberts later rightly remarked that 'the ICTU
provisions ... do not materially affect the position in
Northern Ireland except insofar as they impose an obligation
to continue the existing arrangements.'[19] But the winning
of consent in the north for unity had not been easy,[20]
making the Northern Ireland members all the more determined
to hold what had been achieved. Terry Farrell, the president
of the CIU in 1958, had travelled north to the special
conference in Belfast on February 6 1958[21] and found the
experience something of a revelation.[22] 'Our visit showed
those of us from this Congress who were present, how great
are the differences and how deep the fears that confront
our Northern fellow trade unionists when they contemplate
a united Trade Union Movement. As a result of this
Conference, it is my own personal opinion, that the only
way to achieve unity within our ranks is for those of us
on both sides of the Border to face up to the difficulties
and to seek solutions mutually acceptable, and by frequent
meetings to allay fears, which have little foundation in fact.'

-iii-

Having dealt then with the problem of the control of the new
congress, let us pass to the second area of discussion,
the area of congress functions, and here we shall see coming
through, the insistent concern with improved organisation.
There were of course the normal, unsurprising functions: to

foster the interests of workers, to safeguard their living
standards, to represent their collective will; and these
need not delay us. On the question of trade union organisation,
clause 7(c) provided (unchanged from the PUO draft) that one
of the Congress functions should be 'to encourage the
effective organisation of workers in appropriate unions; to
assist in promoting closer cooperation between unions and
organic unity within the movement; to endeavour to reconcile
the views and relationships of unions organising similar
classes of workers and by the encouragement of amalgamation
to reduce the number of such unions; to provide for the
transfer of members from one union to another and generally,
to help to strengthen trade union organisation and cooperation
between unions.'[23] The objectives here have a wide span,
at one pole of which are very positive objectives such as
the promotion of organic unity and amalgamations, and at the
other pole, objectives merely designed to conserve what had
been achieved, for example provisions for the transfer of
members and for cooperation generally. But it is important
to remember that the drive **towards** a better trade union
structure was not confined to this clause; its echoes are
found throughout the constitution and consequently it is
helpful to take as a guide for our discussion in conjunction
with clause 7(c) the paper which Roberts delivered in 1959
to the Statistical and Social Inquiry Society of Ireland,[24]
and also that other memorandum[25] which he submitted to the
unity committee in 1954 and to which we have already referred.[26]

Firstly, in regard to the motive power behind restructuring,
there was in 1959 little trace left of the fervour of
syndicalism so vigorous in 1919[27] and none of the nationalism
that dominated O'Brien's thinking in 1939.[28] The new congress
had apparently taken over the pale pragmatism of the British
TUC. True, Roberts quoted in both his memorandum and his
1959 address Connolly's explicitly syndicalist expectations
for industrial unionism, to which if one would 'add the
concept of one Big Union embracing all, you have not only the

outline of the most effective form of combination for
industrial warfare today, but also for Social Administration
of the Cooperative Commonwealth of the future';[29] but
quickly went on to describe the British alternative where they
concluded 'that closer unity could most effectively be
achieved by following rules designed to avoid friction (the
Bridlington Agreement) and by the encouragement of a federal
structure, where possible leading to amalgamation.'[30] Of course
within this approach much could be done, as we shall see;
but the fact remained that the motivation was a practical
representational one, no greater than that. Moreover, the
objects of the new congress reflected it, the key phrase -
apart from very proper democratic aspirations - being: '... to
work for such fundamental changes in the social and economic
system as will secure for the workers of Ireland adequate
and effective participation in the control of the industries
and services in which they are employed.' (6(d)). This
represented a compromise between the constitutions of the CIU
and the ITUC. The CIU constitution[31] had spoken of workers'
'proper share in the wealth of the community, their rightful
position in the State, and their natural place in the control
of the industries and services in which their labour is
employed' - all relative terms that judiciously made no explicit
claims; and the ITUC was no different when all was said and
done, setting as a first objective the interests of the
community as a whole and then 'to secure for all workers,
subject to the general interest, adequate control of the
industries and services in which they are engaged.'[32] As it
was, whatever echoes of syndicalism may have been left in the
word control were now eliminated. Nor was the matter ever
debated. There were now no members from the Women Workers
Union to urge the ancient dream as they did in 1930,[33] to
demand 'for the workers of Ireland the ownership and control
of the whole produce of their labour' for all its heroic
irrelevance. Syndicalism had perhaps a spark of life in
1930; in 1959 it was quite dead.

The only motivation therefore for restructuring the trade
union movement was efficiency, efficiency in service and in
representation. It was of course a highly important objective
in its own right, and in order to enhance its importance
much was made of the current state of disorder - perhaps
in a somewhat exaggerated way. 'We have', said Roberts,
'153 unions organised as craft unions, industrial unions,
mixed unions, general unions, and service and professional
unions. Some are national, others are local. Each presumably
advocates its own form of organisation.'[34] In such circumstances reform was essential. Broadly speaking there were
two paths one could follow. The first was the way of the OBU,
the one big union; this was an essential first step to
Connolly's syndicalism (and perhaps to Hynes's vocationalism
as well)[35] but of course it was also capable, in a quite
non-political way, of providing a streamlined, unitary trade
union structure. The second way of reform was the way of the
British TUC pragmatists, the promotion of good order, and of
federations where they were appropriate. In the 1959 constitution of the Irish Congress of Trade Unions there is no
hint whatever of an OBU. Moreover Roberts in his 1959
address to the Statistical and Social Inquiry Society of
Ireland, although he referred to the OBU idea, decried the
notion of any 'rigid preconceived pattern'[36] in the evolution
of trade union organisation in the future. But the idea was
by no means forgotten. Roberts had himself, in 1954, made
a radical proposal for the establishment of a highly integrated
structure when the unity talks had fallen into a perilous
impasse.[37] Despite the coolness of its reception at the
time, and its lack of general support since, it is a document
of some significance.

When Roberts in 1954 came to consider the question of a
unified structure he was confronted at the outset with an
obvious and quite fundamental dilemma, how one could, in
such circumstances, maintain and protect in a real sense
the principle of freedom of association. This principle of

freedom of association had been carried to very considerable
lengths by the ITUC, largely in an effort to discount
Lemass's legislative proposals, and it is necessary to
examine its implications before proceeding. When the
ITUC was confronted by Lemass in 1947 with a very far-reaching
proposal for legislative reform[38] - much more important,
in Roberts' opinion,[39] than the issues disputed in the 1941
act - the national executive could do little more than urge
its unwisdom; 'whether we like it or not,' said Larkin,
'we cannot say to a government that they cannot introduce
legislation.'[40]   But when Lemass revived the question again
in 1952[41] the ITUC now found to hand a far-reaching convention
on freedom of association adopted by the International Labour
Organisation[42] which although not ratified by the Irish
government[43] now armed them with righteousness, and with a
blistering contempt[44] for the CIU who had not held the line.[45]
They could now oppose the government's legislative proposals
with a campaign for the ratification of the ILO conventions,
and this in fact was what they did. A special conference
of the ITUC on March 14 1952[46] nailed their colours to the
mast and created the policy in an extreme and unshakeable
manner. Very soon thereafter, Lemass in order not to
compromise the unity talks drew back from legislation; and
when Norton, on the change of government, became Minister
for Industry and Commerce in 1954, he yielded readily enough to
ITUC pressure and in 1955 lodged the instruments of
ratification with the International Labour Office.[47]

The two ILO conventions[48] had brought the principle of
freedom of association (insofar as it applied to trade unions
of employers or workers) an astonishing distance, particularly
in denying any role to the government in regulating the
principle in the public interest; and it probably should
be seen in the context of the immediate postwar period where
any hint of governmental interference with free democratic
institutions had an aftertaste of fascist intolerance.
When the Irish constitution had come to deal with such

fundamental rights, it guaranteed them 'subject to public
order and morality'[49] and provided, specifically in relation
to the right to form associations and unions that 'laws ...
may be enacted for the regulation and control in the
public interest of the exercise of the foregoing right.'[50]
The original draft of the ILO convention had also provided
in 1927 for the 'observance of legal formalities'[51] -
a provision which had been rejected by the workers' side
at the time. The 1947 conventions however now took the
guarantee well beyond the Irish constitutional position,
specifically as far as trade unions were concerned. In
particular it would if adopted defeat any plan by Lemass
to remain within the Irish constitution by permitting full
freedom of association but by limiting the exercise by
such associations of trade union functions. Any legislation
with such an object would be contrary to the conventions.

Fortified by this, the ITUC went right back to bedrock.
They declared[52] that there should be no restriction on
workers' freedom to join or to form trade unions. Any such
union should have the full protection of the law, and the
absence of a negotiating licence should be neither here
nor there. Any group that conformed to the definition of
a trade union should be entitled to have legal personality
conferred on it. In a word, they went behind the 1941
Act[53] to the notion that a union had the plenitude of rights
because it was defined as such not because it had a licence
conferred on it.[54] Did this mean then that the ITUC sought to
provide the full protection of the law for every passing
combination of workers who happened to seek a change in their
working conditions? Apparently this was the case. 'The
Irish TUC may condemn an organisation either on grounds of
disruptive tactics or because it is desirable that the workers
should join an existing organisation instead of forming a
new one. It has the right to advise its affiliated unions
not to offer their cooperation to an organisation which it
has condemned. But the Irish TUC has not, and does not,

claim the right for itself, nor does it admit the right of
any other body to terminate the existence or alter the legal
status of an organisation whose policy it has condemned.'
But we need to pause here and assess the position. The
ITUC had no intention whatever of tolerating breakaways
or disruptive groups. Throughout 1952, and 1953, they
had experienced disruptive breakaways both among the
Derry clothing workers and among the vocational education
officers in the south.[55] Not only that, but there had been
as well 'a great deal of indiscriminate transfers.'[56]
'Unless this rot is stopped,' said Roberts at the time, 'the
movement itself will rot like a piece of timber eaten by
woodworm.'[57] There was therefore no weakening on the idea
of regulating the right of free association. The point at
issue was whether the government should be the regulating
body or the congress.[58] Roberts reaffirmed the Congress
claim, the trade union claim, to be the sole regulating
body, in his address to the Statistical and Social Inquiry
Society of Ireland:[59] 'It is incorrect to interpret the
principle as if it meant that any worker should have the
right to join any union he chooses. Such an interpretation
would be destructive of the whole basis of trade union
organisation. It is the responsibility of unions and of
the Congress to determine the limitations on the scope of
organisation which individual unions should impose.'

There were some of course who said that the Congress
position did not differ in any substantial way from that
of the state, that while they were defending the right of
freedom of association they were circumscribing its exercise
to a point where in certain circumstances it could, for
practical purposes, be said to be extinguished; and
consequently there were some who would assert the principle
of freedom of association in as full a way as possible both
as against the union and as against the government. And
this in fact as we shall see later was the position taken
up by the Supreme Court[60] in the Educational Company case.

However, if one concedes the need for some regulation to
avoid the collapse of the trade union movement into
fragments, then no doubt the ITUC had a point about self-
regulation rather than state regulation, a debateable
point of course, but a substantial one nonetheless. But
once Roberts came to consider the idea of an OBU as
against a concourse of orderly but independent unions
then it was very difficult to see how one could speak of
freedom of association, since in fact there would be only
one association, the OBU.

This was the first dilemma that he met, but by no means the
only one. There were those who held that primarily one
organised on the basis of an industry, and the OBU was too
exaggerated a notion; on the other hand there were those
who saw a craft as the unifying principle of organisation
irrespective of the craftman's place of employment, con-
tradicting not only the OBU but industrial unionism
as well. And in any event, cementing the existing structure,
however illogical, was the persistent loyalty of rank and
file members to their traditional union; and this made
any suggestion that in the name of logic members should
transfer to other unions or types of union seem highly
artificial. 'On the surface,' said Roberts,[61] 'these
different theories - freedom of association, "O.B.U.",
industrial unionism, craft unionism, etc. - are contradictory, and in practice when pushed to their ultimate
conclusions regardless of other factors, they do in fact
result in contradictions and in sometimes bitter inter-
union disputes' and he went on in a note to say that 'it is
my impression that the bitterest arguments were those
cases in which genuinely held exaggerations of principle
were the basis of the case on each side.' Now, in order
to overcome all these problems he suggested that the OBU
idea should be better stated as 'the principle of unified
representation.'[62] But what did this mean? It meant
apparently that a central organisation would exercise, in the
name of all, only one trade union function, that is the

function of representation - not all trade union functions,
as an OBU would. Since no union would be disestablished
therefore, it would permit both the continuance of the
principle of freedom of association, and the continuance of
loyalty to craft union or industrial union. It was in the
following manner that Roberts presented his solution:[63]
'The picture therefore is this; a unified representative
body called the General Confederation, of which each union
member is a direct member.' He would also remain a member
of his own union; in other words what was suggested was
dual membership, not a federation of unions. The General
Confederation's functions 'are the functions of unified
representation and nothing more or less, therefore on the
one hand it does not interfere in the internal affairs
of unions except with their consent, and on the other hand it
supplies unions with the tools of unified representation.
It is divided into industrial segments for negotiation and
other such purposes, and into branches. The branches
are synonymous with the individual unions of which its
members are dual members. Its industrial segments are
directed by the branches belonging to each segment and
supported, financed and supplied with the information and
other necessary services by the central organisation of the
General Confederation.'[64] With a devastating neatness it
also resolved the current disunity between the congresses,
which having transferred to the General Confederation their
functions as national centres could 'revert to the simple
functions of arranging a representative annual gathering
of trade unionists giving expression to their views and
discussing the problems of the movement.'[65] More than that,
within the structure of the confederation, it promoted the
idea of a Northern Ireland TUC which would be acceptable
to the Northern Ireland government, an idea which must
have greatly alarmed the Northern Ireland representatives.
'The position then', said Roberts in summary,[66] 'would be

as follows: the General Confederation would be the National
Centre, constituted of Federations covering the entire membership of the trade union movement in Ireland. The Irish
TUC, the CIU, and the Northern Ireland TUC would exist
for the time being as separate entities. Their function
would be to convene an annual meeting of delegates of
their constituent unions and convey to the General Confederation such resolutions as they might adopt. The
Northern Ireland TUC would have an additional function insofar
as and for so long as the Confederation saw fit to delegate
to it, as an autonomous Northern Ireland organisation,
the right to make representations on behalf of Northern
Ireland trade unionists to the Northern Ireland Government.'

This then was Roberts's proposal in 1954; but everyone
apparently backed away from it. Most unions would not be
prepared to accept an OBU in any circumstances, and this
was particularly so in the case of the amalgamated unions.
And the fact was that despite the notion of unified
representation an OBU in some form was contemplated. In the
first place members could join the confederation directly
without joining any union, and secondly, resources of man-
power and money would be concentrated in the confederation's
hands. Apart from all that, there was the perilous
suggestion of a Northern Ireland TUC; and finally, the whole
thing had quite an alarming symmetry about it which looked
most odd in the real world. Yet, at the same time, we
must recognise the importance of Roberts's basic idea, the
idea of identifying a function and organising for its
efficient discharge rather than pursuing a new structure
as such. In Roberts's case he had used it virtually to build an
OBU but much could be done without creating any structural
change at all. This indeed was the central idea in the 1946
report of the British TUC.[67] Vincent Tewson described it
as a new approach to an old problem. 'Rather than pursuing
the idea of structure, the Report (deals) with the functions
that are performed by trade unions, irrespective of their

basic theory of organisation.' They therefore made no
radical recommendations on structure at all, and the PUO,
in following them as we shall see, made none either.
Secondly the function chosen by Roberts, the function of
unified representation, had an omniverous quality about it,
absorbing into itself all really significant trade union
functions. But one could always select a primary function,
without its being an omnibus one, such as was done much
later by the ICTU in 1970, when the negotiating function was
centralised under the executive council, as was also the
supervision of the agreements thus negotiated. However in
the work of Congress within the Employer-Labour Conference,
from 1970 onwards, and in the impact of the national wage
agreements, we recognise a powerful unifying thrust not in
trade union structure but in trade union performance.[68]

-iv-

The heady prospect of an OBU and similar adventures being
set aside, the PUO turned to the second path of trade union
reform, the path of the British pragmatists.[69] This is
what we see reflected in the new constitution of the ICTU
and in Roberts's 1959 address.[70] It is a path of no great
inspiration, pragmatic almost to the point of ideological
indifference, where certain arrangements were made to
regulate rows between unions particularly in regard to the
recruitment of members, and where certain urgings were made
towards federation and amalgamation. But the fact was that the
Irish trade union impetus towards restructure was always
stronger than the British one making the proposals more fibrous
despite their similarity to Bridlington.[71] In order to
demonstrate this a little more clearly, it is desirable to
reach back to 1953, when the ITUC, under the threat of

legislation, put forward its plan for restructuring.[72]
There were two things that the national executive wanted
to do: firstly, to make a determined attempt to restructure
the trade union movement, and secondly, to make more
sensible arrangements in regard to disputes between unions
and within unions. And in their proposals, being practical
men of affairs, they tried to provide for a specific agent
of change.

We have already noted, in the matter of creating new
structures in a democratic society, how significant the idea
of a catalyst is, and how irrelevant even the most logical
and compelling proposal is without it.[73] We saw how in 1919,
Johnson's proposal[74] had little catalysis built into it,
little of the machine of change, much in contrast with
Lemass's legislation of 1941[75] which, were it not for the
judgement in the NUR case, would have radically altered the
trade union movement. However, the very substance of the
ITUC proposal in 1953 was the creation of a catalyst for
change, for evolution, rather than any specific recommendation
on structure. A permanent commission was proposed - only
four of the sixteen members being appointed by the national
executive, the rest being elected by the unions. Its
functions were to study and report on structure and to foster
amalgamations, federations and the rest.[76] This then was the
agent of change, not a very remarkable one, but at least
specific to the task. It was given further status and
strength by the device of packaging[77] - where one can
cluster quite disparate functions in one institution, so
that those functions of **immediate significance can confer**
on the institution the status it requires to discharge
functions of a less significant or less acceptable kind.
We have already seen this device used in the functions
exercised by the PUO, the function of negotiation and
representation[78] giving added weight to the PUO's efforts to
unite the congresses, creating a helpful mood of solving
problems jointly, within which even physical integration,
such as joint offices, could be undertaken in advance of unity.

Something of this then was attempted by the ITUC in 1953,
in giving to the permanent commission, in addition to
fostering structural change, the task of investigating and
adjudicating on disputes both between unions and within a
union (that is to say the whole field of breakaways, poaching
and disruptive activities) and further 'where necessary to
recommend to the National Executive the condemnation of any
union or group of persons whom they adjudge guilty of acts
or practices harmful to the trade union movement.'[79]   These
judicial functions, clearly reminiscent of the 1939 proposal
for an industrial court,[80] would have made the commission a
body of some significance.[81]

The trade unions were uneasy. They were prepared to accept
the idea of adjudication in a dispute between one union and
another, but they found it difficult to accept the idea of
an adjudication by congress, or a committee of congress,
in an internal matter arising between the trade union
executive and some of its members. Yet this was precisely
the point that Lemass had pressed them on. Furthermore,
they also feared that a congress, enhanced in this way,
might be tempted to intervene in industrial disputes, that
is disputes between unions and employers, which the CIU in
any event was wont to do. Conscious of this, the national
executive approached it all very gingerly, suggesting not
a specific proposal but a first discussion, a green paper
as it were, and in that context it was adopted - to die, as
we have seen, the following year when the unity talks began.

The matter came to be revived again in 1955[82] under the
continuous pressure for better order. But now all that
was suggested was the 'main principles' of Bridlington[83]
and the proposals of the national executive were closely
modelled on them. These principles were concerned essentially
with disputes between unions, not disputes within unions -
and certainly not industrial disputes. They set out explicitly what in Roberts's view[84] was in any event settled

practice, the circumstances where a union may and where a
union may not recruit members of another union. But
Bridlington also included an urging towards a better
structure, put in rather a low key way, and the ITUC
decision of 1955 followed it in this as well. But now there
was no question of a permanent commission. The national
executive was charged with doing what it could. There was
built into it very little of the catalysis of 1953.

Finally, let us come to the new constitution of 1959 which
established the ICTU. Firstly, we find that the principles
of Bridlington remain; but now there is specific and quite
vigorous provision for their observance. Where a union was
disruptive, or where it rejected a disputes committee
finding, the executive council could investigate and
recommend expulsion.[85] This indeed was a contribution to
keeping the peace, but what of the idea of a better structure,
the idea of a fundamental reform which would make Bridlington
irrelevant and disputes between unions a thing of the past?
The new constitution, in spite of all that had been said,
seemed at first sight to provide little prospect of such an
improvement. But this may be looking at it with hindsight
rather than in the mood of expectation of the time. Certainly
very little was spelt out specifically, but to those who
drafted it and agreed it, that did not mean any lack of
commitment to reform but rather a belief in gradualism in
its attainment. And in that regard the catalyst, the
hope for change, lay principally in the fact that, despite
considerable difficulties, a united congress had been
created, stronger than any centre which had hitherto existed.
'The stronger centre', said Roberts,[86] 'will encourage, rather
than direct, a reduction in the number of unions and will
assist in the evolution of a more logical form of organisation
by encouraging the transfer of membership and the establishment
of machinery for closer working together of unions.' The
new congress was stronger because it was unified, but it
could be strengthened further, 'a strengthening ...' said Roberts[87]

'which will depend not only upon the fact that there will
be only one centre, but on the provisions of improved
services by that centre.' In fact the range of services
which the executive council could provide - assuming it was
given the resources to do so - was rather startling:
secretaries, information officers and advisers to industrial
committees, a legal department within congress and an
international department; research and information services;
health, safety and welfare advisory services; publicity
services and educational and training services.[88] For many
years, nothing like this was provided, and even today, with
some public funds at their back, Congress by no means provides
such a range, not surprisingly indeed in view of the fact
that large unions would wish to provide many of these services
for themselves. Yet at the time the commitment to
Congress was considerable, and it looked as if it could
exercise a great deal of influence.

Gradualism rested on the assumption that good relations and
joint working arrangements would build towards federation,
amalgamation and a more rational system; and there was much
in this regard that Congress could do, following Bridlington.
It could promote agreements on spheres of influence such as
already existed between the Irish Transport and the Amalgamated
Transport;[89] and in particular it could promote the
creation of industrial groups, that is the formation by
unions within an industry of a single group for negotiating
purposes. In the north there were the large confederations,
which had no parallel in the south, but at least there were
modest groups emerging, the outstanding example being the
Electricity Supply Board[90] - but there were others as well,
in the building industry for example, and in the national
transport authority Coras Iompair Eireann.[91] There was much
that could be said in criticism of them as Roberts made
clear in his memorandum of 1954: 'The nearest approximations
(to the Northern Ireland confederations) are the Building
Trades Groups and the Electricity Supply Board Conference.

Even in these cases the secretarial work is left to one of
the members and is done on a voluntary basis. No attempt is
made to develop these organisations as federations. They
have no funds, no office, no staff, and they have no rules.
As might be expected in a concern of such magnitude, problems
requiring the attention of all unions or many unions frequently
arise in CIE. There however the tendency has been to
establish ad hoc committees to meet each situation after it
had arisen.'[92] While in the years between a number of
additional industrial groups have come into being, they
have all by and large retained their primitive character,
principally because of union self-interest, but in 1959 it was
reasonable at least to hope that the new congress with its
vigorous services could cause them to develop perhaps into
federations, perhaps into the beginnings of an industry-
based structure.

And what of industrial disputes, that is disputes with
employers? The CIU from its traditions brought forward
into the new congress a readiness to become involved in
industrial disputes in a manner which the ITUC had always
avoided. The original CIU constitution provided[93] at
4(9) 'that unions should notify Congress before serving
strike notice where assistance will be requested from the
Central Council or where other unions will be involved, with
the object of having a round-table conference of all those
about to be involved or who are liable to be involved ... the
Central Council will select a panel of names, who will preside
if possible by rotation, at the conferences ... Any union
not conforming to the above will not be accorded service
of Congress in furtherance of such trade dispute.' The
provisions tended to be honoured at least as much in the
breach as the observance;[94] nevertheless we can see here a
congress much more involved in the cut and thrust of
industrial disputation than the ITUC.[95] In fact the
provisions were lost in some generalities in the new constitution and were not revived until the nineteen seventies;

yet the CIU unions, and in particular Crawford, brought to
the ICTU a tradition of involvement which became a substantial part of its character. There was another trend
as well emerging about this time to reinforce the CIU
tradition. Both the government and the employers tended
to involve Congress in industrial disputes in times of crisis,
the employers in particular regarding one union's breach
of a general agreement for example as a breach by the trade
union movement as a whole.[96]

There was one casualty in all this, if casualty it was.
Trades councils (which in Britain were refused affiliation)[97]
found that while they could still affiliate to the new
congress, their delegation to conference was limited to two,
the object being to avoid a danger that 'council delegates,
without the same responsibility as union delegates, could
dominate or unduly influence Congress policy.'[98] In fact
the congresses had now in these times of centralised
institutions and, despite the ambitions of the trades councils[99]
themselves, taken over the substance of their functions.[100]
Furthermore, congresses were controlled by the executives
of the unions, trades councils usually by the branches,
which sometimes threw up a kind of local leadership which
executive councils might wish to disavow.

But all in all, the picture of a congress united in purpose
and rich in services gave considerable hope for the future,
considerable hope for a much more rational structure. It
was one thing however to achieve a unity of congresses; it
was quite another to change unions heavy with tradition[101]
and Mortished, at least for one, recognised that unity of
itself could not be relied on to do it. Indeed the unity of
the congresses appeared to him to be more the expression of
an idea than a radical change of structure. 'We have got to
recognise', he said[102] to the ITUC conference in 1956 when he
addressed them as ILO representative, 'that social thinking
did not begin and end with Marx's Communist Manifesto in

1848 nor with Rerum Novarum more than forty years later,
nor with Quadragessimo Anno forty years after that, nor with
the writings of Connolly and the Proclamation of 1916. Things
did not stop with the establishment of the Northern Ireland
Government in 1920 or with the Constitution of 1937 nor will
it have stopped with the eventual formation of a no longer
provisional united trade union organisation in this country.
Things move because we have got to make them move. I feel
myself that there is no topic of greater importance to the
movement in this country than that it should sit down,
examine its own structure, examine the way in which it does
its work, examine the resources it is prepared to apply to
get the work done ...'

Nevertheless the united congress was - even of itself - a
vast step forward and began to play a greater and more
influential part in the management of industrial relations,
and therefore in society at large. And with this as a
prompt to the discussion, we come to deal with the relations
between trade unions and the three great organs of state,
the judiciary, the legislature and the government, and the
manner in which these relations in turn affect the
development and shape of the trade union movement.

Notes on Chapter Eleven

1.   Draft Constitution: PUO: p.4.

2.   ibid. p.5.

3.   ibid. p.4.

4.   ibid. p.5.

5.   ibid. p.5.

6.   ibid. p.6.

7.   ibid. p.6.

8.   Ruaidhri Roberts: "Trade Union Organisation in Ireland:"
        Journal of the Statistical and Social Inquiry Society
        of Ireland Vol.XX, part II.

9.   ITUC 1959 p.60 ff.

10.   ibid. p.63.

11.   See the final constitution as set out in the first
        report of the ICTU 1959 p.233.

12.   Roberts: Journal of the Statistical and Social
        Inquiry Society of Ireland, op.cit. p.98.

13.   The adoption of the constitution meant of course that
        cross channel members could no longer act as delegates
        and their names appear for the last time at the winding
        up congress of the ITUC in July 1959.

14.   Their opposition did not however impede them from
        affiliating to the newly established Irish Congress
        of Trade Unions. We have incidentally no detailed
        record of the CIU debate on the constitution; a brief
        note appears in CIU 1959 p.15. Reservations had been
        expressed by some delegates at the 1958 annual conference
        but the response to the draft constitution had been
        lethargic on the whole (pp. 135, 136, CIU 1958).
        It appears that the very solid leadership of Conroy and
        the Irish Transport was accepted in the matter.

15.   p. 7 above.

16.   See p.317 above.

17.   See Chapter 8.

18.   ICTU 1959 p.241.

19.   Roberts op.cit. p.102.

20.   See p.349 above.

21.   PUO Third Report 1958 p.7.

22.   CIU 1958   p.58.

23.   CIU 1959 p.235.

24.   op.cit.

25.   Memorandum on Trade Union Structure in Ireland.

26.   p.432 above.

27.   See above p.46.

28.   See above p.147.

29.   Roberts op.cit. p.103.

30.   idem. The policy document to which Roberts referred
        was Trade Union Structure and Closer Unity Trades
        Union Congress 1946, a report of a study which was
        initiated by the British TUC in 1943 and approved
        by their Brighton conference in 1946. It became
        of course effective policy for Northern Ireland, by
        reason of the fact that amalgamated unions were in
        overwhelming majority there and greatly influenced
        the ITUC generally.

31.   CIU 1958 p.218.

32.   ITUC 1959 p.140.

33.   See above p.97.

34.   Roberts: Memorandum on Trade Union Structure in
        Ireland: 1954 p.9.

35.   See p.379 above.

36.   Roberts op.cit. p.106.

37.   p.432 above.

38.   p.378 above.

39.   ITUC 1952 p.124.

40.   ITUC 1947 p.184.

41.   p.402 above.

42. ITUC 1955 p.114 where in appendix III to the annual
report the texts of the ILO Conventions are set out
in full; they are Convention 87: Freedom of
Association and Protection of the Right to Organise,
and Convention 98 concerning the Application of the
Principles of the Right to Organise and to Bargain
Collectively. The text is reproduced in appendix 18 below.

43. Nor by the British government in the case of Northern
Ireland because of the 1927 act.

44. See Roberts: ITUC 1952 p.119.

45. For the CIU position see p.402 above.

46. ITUC 1952 p.29.

47. ITUC 1955 p.37.

48. See appendix 18.

49. Article 40: 6: 1°.

50. Article 40: 6: 1°: iii.

51. ITUC 1955 p.35.

52. Two memoranda were sent to the government about this time,
the first immediately after the ITUC special conference
of March 15 1952 (ITUC 1952 p.27) and the second in
1953 (ITUC 1953 p.29); the second clarified the
definition of a trade union and dealt with negotiating
licences in particular.

53. See above p.133 and p.202.

54. Their definition, the classical early definition was
that as set out in s.23 of the Trade Union Act of
1871, as amended by s.16 of the Trade Union Act 1876
and as further amended by s.2(1) of the Trade Union
Act 1913, and in that amended form could be usefully
quoted in full here: 'The expression "trade union"
means any combination, whether temporary or permanent,
the principal objects of which are under its constitution,
the regulation of the relations between workmen and masters,
or between workmen and workmen or between masters and
masters, or the imposing of restrictive conditions
on the conduct of any trade or business, and also the
provision of benefits to members, whether such combination would or would not, if the Trade Union Act
1871 had not been passed, have been deemed to have been
an unlawful combination by reason of some one or more
of its purposes being in restraint of trade:

Provided that the Acts shall not affect:
(1) Any agreement between partners as to their own
business;

> (2) Any agreement between an employer and those employed by him as to such employment;
>
> (3) Any agreement in consideration of the sale of the goodwill of a business or of instruction in any profession, trade, or handicraft.
>
> Provided that any combination which is for the time being registered as a trade union shall be deemed to be a trade union as defined by the Act as long as it continues to be so registered.' (See ITUC 1953 p.29).

55. ITUC 1953 pp.30-31.

56. ITUC 1953 p.84.

57. idem.

58. Some unions, particularly the amalgamated unions (see ITUC 1953 p.88) were unhappy about giving any function to congress which would involve the internal affairs of a union; and of course whether a breakaway were justified or not would depend on an evaluation of just those internal affairs. It was not until 1963 that consent was given to the establishment of a congress appeals board with just this function. Therefore, at this point at least, while Congress claimed for the trade union movement the right to regulate freedom of association, and while it stated explicitly that some breakaways might be justified it had no authority to investigate or adjudicate.

59. Roberts: Journal of the Statistical and Social Inquiry Society of Ireland op.cit. p.105.

60. The Educational Company of Ireland v. Fitzpatrick [1961] I.R. 345.

61. Roberts Memorandum on Trade Union Structure in Ireland op.cit. pp. 19-20.

62. ibid. p.24.

63. ibid. p.36.

64. ibid. p.36.

65. ibid. p.45.

66. ibid. p.53.

67. Trade Union Structure and Closer Unity op.cit. p.3.

68. Before concluding our discussion on Roberts's plan we could recall O'Lehane's variation on the same theme in 1919 (p.52 above); he proposed a federation where the original union would continue to operate for domestic matters, the federation for more important, and where only

the federation, and not the unions, could accept
new members.

69.   See p.461 above.

70.   op.cit.

71.   This refers to the principles adopted at the Bridlington
        1939 Congress of the BTUC; Trade Union Structure
        and Closer Unity op.cit. pp. 8 and 30.

72.   ITUC 1953 p.26; also p.432 above.

73.   See p.381 above where the proposals of the Commission
        on Vocational Organisation in particular are discussed.
74.   p. 46   above.
        O'Lehane (see p.52 above) had a firm grip on the idea
        of a catalyst in proposing that in restructuring the
        trade union movement the national executive of the
        ITUC should have control of strike funds and no strike
        could take place without its sanction. Roberts raised
        the same idea in his memorandum of 1954 but he was
        somewhat ambiguous about it.

75.   p.202 above.

76.   ITUC 1953 p.26.

77.   See Berger, Berger and Kellner: The Homeless Mind:
        Penguin 1974 p.22, where a somewhat similar idea is
        discussed.

78.   p. 441 above.

79.   ITUC 1953 p.27.

80.   p.151 above.

81.   It is interesting to note that, in the nineteen sixties,
        these functions were discharged within congress not by
        one body but by four separate bodies: the promotion of
        a better structure by the Committee on Trade Union
        Organisation, disputes between unions by the disputes
        committee and by the demarcation tribunal, and disputes
        within unions by the appeals board. Here it was
        proposed that the permanent commission should dis-
        charge them all.

82.   ITUC 1955 p.146.

83.   Trade Union Structure and Closer Unity op.cit. p.30.
        There is also an excellent memorandum setting out the
        background to reorganisation in ITUC 1955 p.29.

84.   Roberts: Journal of the Statistical and Social Inquiry
        Society of Ireland op.cit. p.102.

85. Section 44.

86. op.cit. Journal of the Statistical and Social Inquiry
    Society of Ireland p.106.

87. idem.

88. Section 42.

89. Roberts: Memorandum 1954 where he says (p.10)
    '...the two largest unions, the Irish Transport ...
    and the Amalgamated Transport ... have for many years
    operated an agreement on spheres of organisation and ...
    this particular agreement has survived the split between
    the congresses. Such agreements are ... by no means
    universal...'

90. CIU 1954 p.17 & ITUC 1954 p.44.

91. CIU 1957 p.16.

92. op.cit. p.9.

93. CIU 1958 p.219.

94. CIU 1956 p.16; p.123.

95. As we have seen above (p.277) industrial unions
    were strongly organised in the CIU while in the ITUC
    there were many public service unions.

96. See for example the complaint of the FUE against the
    Irish Transport and the CIU in the case of the strike
    in the ironmongery trade (CIU 1955 pp.45-40).

97. Roberts: Journal of the Statistical and Social Inquiry
    Society of Ireland op.cit. p.99.

98. idem.

99. See for example the proposals of the Bray trades council
    ITUC 1956 p.173; ITUC 1957 p.33; and also the proposals
    of the Cork council CIU 1957 p.157.

100. Roberts op.cit. p.99.

101. Mortished ITUC p.247: 'We do, I think ... allow
     tradition to impose too heavy a hand on our organisation
     and our activities. Most of our present unions exist
     in their present form because that was the form appropriate
     to them a generation, or two generations ago, or, in some
     cases, even a hundred years ago.'

102. ITUC 1956 p.241.

Chapter Twelve

The Courts

-i-

In our discussion on the relations between the trade unions
and the state we shall take the study only as far as 1960
(or rather 1961 so that we can encompass the leading
case of the Educational Company v. Fitzpatrick)[1] which is
the scope of the present work. We shall approach it in the
manner which we have already indicated, taking first the law
courts and their decisions in regard to trade unions, moving
on to the legislature and finally the government.

Furthermore, our focus in this account will be on the Irish
Free State and later the Republic; this is not to exclude
the north but rather to recognise it as falling wholly
within the English system. In any case since the English
legal system is the ground and root of the law in the south,
a discussion of the south (despite some radical differences
that have since arisen) will serve to illuminate it to some
degree as well.

Let us turn then to our first area of discussion, the trade
unions and the courts. It is not our intention to rehearse
the development of judicial decisions from one case to
another[2] but rather to attempt to identify the broad thrust
of case law as it affected trade unions. Trade unions down
through the years have been suspicious of the courts, seeing
in them at times institutions that were class-ridden,
prejudiced and hostile. This view must be moderated of course;
otherwise it would suggest that our legal system is seriously
lacking in legitimacy in the eyes of a substantial number
of people. But a trade union member is also a citizen; a

trade union after all organises merely one of his social
roles[3] and as a citizen (that is to say, a member of the
political society) he might take a more benign view.
Nonetheless when he sat in trade union councils this wariness
of the courts – this defensiveness – was strongly and deeply
felt. It was evident at an early stage in the triumphant
achievement of the 1906 act[4] which was seen as democracy
defeating judge-made (that is to say, class-orientated) law,
the product, in Bentham's contemptuous phrase, of Judge & Co.[5]
It was evident in this country in the refusal of the trade
unions to have a lawyer as chairman of the Labour Court and
their resistance as well to the employment of professionally
qualified advocates in that body.[6] Nor, perhaps with
two major exceptions (the Rathmines case[7] which ended
disastrously for the union and the NUR case[8] which tended
in any case to reinforce the traditional common law position)
did the trade unions avail of the courts for the purposes of
justification; rather were they cast in the role of
defendants, of malefactors, of the rogue partners in the
enterprise of industry, and this intensified their feeling
that justice in the courts tended to be a one-sided justice
from which they had little to gain and a great deal to fear.
But of course every association or group at one time or
another feels itself ill-used by the organs of the state;
the trade unions believe that it was very much more than that –
that they suffered a special and consistent prejudice.
We can therefore quite properly and usefully discuss the
development of case law in Ireland by considering to what
extent such a trade union view had substance in fact.

There are those who would say that if the trade unions have
a point it is because of the great conservatism of the legal
system. Irish industrial society has experienced remarkable
development even since the war, and is an aeon distant from
the world of the nineteenth century. Trade unions have
developed with it, both in power and in status. But the law
on the other hand is, of its nature, most laggardly to change.

'The idea of law', as Lord Lloyd has remarked[9] 'is
notoriously a conservative one, and in a progressive and
rapidly developing society such as a social democracy the
reformulation of this idea tends to lag behind the actual
movements that are gradually emerging in society itself.'
A striking example of this conservatism was, as we shall see,
the influence of a tract on trade unions published by
Sir William Erle[10] in 1868 when he was chairman of the Royal
Commission and which continued to be quoted with approval
right down to our own time, to the judgement indeed of Mr
Justice Budd in the Educational Company case[11] nearly 100
years later. All this is hardly surprising since precedent
is at the heart of the administration of the common law
(unlike the civil law); it must perforce be heavily
traditionalist in character. The question that arises therefore is not so much the reason for this traditionalism
(which is indeed self-evident) but how, in such a precedent-
ridden system there is built in the necessary mechanism for
change, the response of the system to a rapidly changing
world, which common sense so obviously requires.

At first sight the answer might be regarded as simple enough.
If the courts are traditional then the legislature is
innovatory; new law is made by parliament - as indeed is
its exclusive right - and the 1906 Trade Disputes Act stands
as both a great example and a vindication of this relationship.
Mr Justice Gavan Duffy had an undoubted sympathy with this
point of view. In dealing with a conflict of interests
between an individual and a trade union in Cooper v. Millea[12]
he said it was 'regrettable that conflicting rights in this
sphere of law are not more extensively regulated by statute;
the inevitable result under the jurisprudence of this country
and of England has often been that important questions as
to how far organised labour may go have had to be decided
by the conceptions of individual Judges as to what may or may
not be lawful in the milky way of the common law, and some
such judgements are by no means a certain guide.' But the

question is not so easily answered; for legislation has a
certain ad hoc character, while judicial decisions address
themselves to precepts and principles. 'In the common law,'
says Roscoe Pound, the American jurist,[13] 'the system of law
of the English-speaking world, a statute furnishes a rule
for the cases within its purview but not a principle, a
starting point for reasoning as to cases outside its purview,
not a basis for analogical reasoning. For that, in the
common law system, we look to experience of the administration
of justice as shown in the reported decisions of the courts.'
That this is so is amply borne out once again in the
Educational Company case[14] where Mr Justice Budd, in restating
the great principle of individualism as enunciated by Sir
William Erle, in 1868, went on: 'As these were common law
rights they were, of course, subject to interference or
curtailment by the legislature in England or by the Constitution here or, indeed, by Acts of the Oireachtas passed
in conformity with the Constitution. In so far as they have
not been curtailed in such fashion they still exist.' It
is reasonable to conclude from this that while the 1906 Trade
Disputes Act excluded certain actions from consideration by
the courts, the principles underlying the law, despite the
enactment, remained unchanged. Perhaps in one sense this makes
far too much of the ineffectiveness of legislation to dominate
the course of events, and one can point to considerable
progress and effectiveness in matters of inheritance,
succession, property interests in general, and indeed in
much of the field of commercial law. 'But', as Pound has
pointed out,[15] 'where the questions are not of interests of
substance, where they do not immediately affect the economic
order, but are questions of weighing of human conduct and
passing upon its moral aspects, legislation has accomplished
little. No codification of the law of torts (wrongs) has
achieved any notable measure of success. Indeed modern codes
on this subject are content with significantly broad
generalisations.' Yet this is precisely the area into which
many trade union cases fall.

The principles of the law governing trade unions fell therefore
to be determined not so much by parliament as by the courts.
And how were the courts seen by the trade unions in the
exercise of this responsibility? Firstly there was a profound
ambiguity; while the Irish courts appeared at various times
to engage in law-making, at least implicitly, they usually
insisted that far from evolving precepts, they were merely
declaring the law as already determined. The second point
flows from this: because of the traditionalism of the law,
this meant judging current trade union activity on the
basis of nineteenth-century prejudice. And the third point
- the heart of the problem - was that when judges followed
nineteenth-century thinking on the grounds that their
function was essentially declaratory, they were in fact -
whether they were conscious of it or not - expressing their
own class-determined prejudice. Let us take these points
one by one.

-ii-

Montesquieu's principle of the division of powers, while
uncertain in its application to the legislature as against
the executive, expressed a deeply held view that the judiciary
should be a specialised and independent arm of the constitution of the state. A judge in the English system of
law is guaranteed independence by an appointment which is
virtually impregnable, but his very independence from any
influence, whether improper or benign, must confine him to
the exercise of an interpretative role. The law-making role
should be exercised only by those who are continuously
sensitive to the democratic will, in other words, the
regularly elected legislature. It was believed therefore
that if a judge were to exceed his interpretative role he
would damage the whole concept of an independent judiciary.

This traditional distinction between the roles of the
legislature and the judiciary found some expression in the
judgement of Mr Justice Gavan Duffy in the NUR case:[16]
'I think', he said, 'the attack on the statute by the N.U.R. is
really intended to defeat a legislative policy which it
mislikes, but this Court is concerned exclusively with the
legal objections raised. Policy is emphatically within the
legislative, as distinct from the judicial, domain. The
ingenious method adopted by the Oireachtas for strengthening
the power of workmen ... seems in fact well calculated to
achieve its purpose, but if that method looked most unpromising,
a Court of law would have no right to express any disapproval
of the policy behind the plan. I am not concerned with
the wisdom of the measure.'[17] And the Supreme Court in
reversing Mr Justice Gavan Duffy did so, among other things,
not in the context of denying the principle he had enunciated
but rather in pushing it still farther. Mr Justice Murnaghan
recognised 'that in the opinion of the Legislature, the
provisions of the Trade Union Act 1941 if put into operation
might confer certain advantages upon the workmen concerned
and the public generally; and it is apparent that if any
disadvantages should ensue the Legislature considered that
any such disadvantages were out-balanced by the advantages
to be derived from the measure. This Court cannot however
enter into any such consideration, but is concerned solely
with the question whether Part III of the Act is repugnant
to the Constitution.' The question of an evolving social
policy was therefore quite set aside; the wishes of the
legislature, no less than the wishes of quite a number of
trade unions and employers, were given little weight, and
the question was seen essentially as a dilemma of conflicting law, in a word as a question of interpretation.
In fact the principle was pressed to quite an extraordinary
length in the remarkable case in 1959 of Roundabout Ltd
v. Beirne,[18] a case where the employer appointed his barmen
directors of a company created for the purpose in order to
remove a dispute from the definition in the 1906 act, and

where Mr Justice Dixon, in holding for the employer said
that while the formation of the company may have been a
subterfuge 'the question which I must determine is whether
it is a successful subterfuge.' 'A very net point,' he
conceded, 'a technical one perhaps, but the whole subject
is itself rather technical.'

This approach of the courts, both here and in England, despite
its constitutional propriety, caused among some commentators
a vast impatience particularly when it was compared with
the more progressive performance of the courts in the United
States. '...The archaic belief in the separation of powers,'
wrote Michael Beloff rather fiercely,[19] 'the persistence of
the view that the judicial process is declaratory rather
than creative, that the judge is archaeologist rather than
architect has promoted analysis of what the principles of
law are at the expense of analysis of what they should be.'
It is all very well to state a principle; the practice
is quite another matter. And this approach, as Lord Lloyd
has pointed out,[20] 'although not without its influence, even
at the present day, has never been effectively adhered to for
the simple reason that it is not only unrealistic and im-
practicable but is based upon a fallacy ... Choices involving values form an essential feature of a good deal of
decision making. Judges, like other human beings, cannot
divorce themselves from the pattern of values which is
implicit in the society or the group to which they belong,
and no amount of consciously applied impartiality or judicial
lack of passion will succeed in eliminating the influence
of factors of this kind.' And the Irish judges did of course
recognise such influences. 'A case of this kind', said
Judge Lavery, in his judgement in the Educational Company
case,[21] 'raises many issues of a very serious kind. The Court
must confine itself to legal issues, though the other issues
may of course have to be considered as necessary to decide
the questions of law.' This, while conceding an influence,
does so in a bleak and negative way, and on this occasion
Judge Lavery went on to say that he proposed to follow a

decision of the Court of Appeal in England 'though the
decision does not express my own view. It has been
accepted and acted on for forty years and has become part
of the industrial law.' The first point made by the trade
unions therefore, that the courts emphasise their
declaratory role, has considerable substance.

-iii-

What now of the second point, that, as a consequence, current
trade union activity is judged on the basis of nineteenth-
century prejudice? But this argues that a good deal of
the thinking found its origin in the nineteenth century;
and if the law was largely developed at that time, then it
follows that the courts then took a far more innovatory and
creative approach to their role than they do today. Such
a view would be taken by Loren P. Beth who sees 'a tradition
of great creativity by judges' collapse into 'judicial
eunuchism'[22] though he would take a span of some two
hundred years. For our purposes however, all we need do
is mark the extraordinary contrast in this matter between
the views expressed by Judge Lavery and those of Sir
William Erle, whose statement on the law regarding trade unions
has echoed down through the years. 'There are', he wrote,[23]
'some relations between man and man which do not change, such
as birth; and the rules of law relating thereto do not
change. There are other relations which are perpetually
changing as society progresses, and the conflicts of rights
caused by this perpetual process of change is the subject
of a perpetual process of adjustment, according to principles
contained in the common law. The serfs and copyholders of
the middle ages passed through many variations of rights,
as well at common law as by statute, before they became

enfranchised electors. Rights in respect of contracts,
restraint of trade, combination, the relation between
employer and employed, and some kind of nuisances, afford
examples of perpetual change. An attempt to adjust them
by statute may succeed, if the authors and interpreters of
the statute understand the principles of the common law, and
in some degree incorporate them. Without that process the
interpretation of the words of the statute merely by a
dictionary leads often to unsatisfactory results. Even if
the statute is well drawn, society soon progresses beyond it, and
the need of the principles of the common law is constantly
renewed.' Let us pause at this point for the purpose of
contrasting the position thus stated by Erle with that of the
Irish courts a hundred years later. Firstly Erle asserted
the special position of the courts as against legislation in
the evolving of precepts and principles; but, secondly,
he saw these principles in a remarkably creative way, leading
apparently from serf to citizen, a view he repeats when he
deals with the triumph of equity in the development of the
English legal system, 'the Chancellors originating equitable
rules overruling law ...'[24] The contrast with Judge
Lavery in 1961 in his Supreme Court judgement in the
Educational Company case is considerable. The occasion is
the same as that we have already mentioned, his following of
the decision in White v. Riley:[25] 'The point decided', he
said,[26] 'was that if members of a trade union refused to work
with non-members of a trade union, or even with non-members
of their particular union, the withdrawal of their labour
constituted a trade dispute ..."connected with the employment
or non-employment ...of a person".' 'I should have thought',
he said,'that the phrase "the employment or non-employment"
referred directly or indirectly to the working conditions of
the person concerned - as an unskilled or unqualified person,
as an apprentice not having served his time, as working for
lower wages than trade union wages, and many other considerations
of the like kind. It would not have occurred to me that his

colour, his race, his religion, his not being a member of
a trade union or his membership of a particular trade union
would make his employment a proper subject for a trade dispute,
but the case of White v. Riley decided otherwise and has
been accepted in this Court in many instances.' Profound
questions of principle were raised here, linking trade union
membership or non-membership with conditions as basic as
race and religion and of course while in the eyes of Judge
Lavery all these were vindicated by having recourse to the
constitution (which made the decision in White v. Riley
irrelevant in the event) nonetheless for the purposes of
this part of the judgement, the judge appeared to favour
following an analogous case rather than apply what he perceived
to be a fundamental principle. These two statements, that of
Sir William Erle and that of Judge Lavery, may define the
contrast somewhat too sharply; but our purpose is to establish
a general difference in emphasis and this they do very well.

This emphasis certainly reveals how in the nineteenth century
Erle saw the law as developing, while in the twentieth Judge
Lavery saw it as received, giving substance to the suggestion
that nineteenth-century principles predominated - but
does it reveal class prejudice, the charge which lies at
the heart of the trade union case? Erle himself would
have denied it vigorously both in regard to the courts
and in regard to parliament. It seemed to him wrong to
'contradistinguish labourers or working men from capitalists
or employers, as if they were separate classes; for both
classes labour ...'[27] and he dismissed the topic at an early
stage 'because the law is concerned directly with the rights
of individuals, and only indirectly with the interests of
classes, and because the free course of trade secured by law
is a free course for each individual to dispose of his
labour or his capital according to his own choice.'[28] And in
regard to legislation he looked, with the complacent optimism
of his time, to the numerous statutes since the Reform Act
of 1832 'of enlightened wisdom and grand beneficent results,
both to society in general and to the less rich part of it
in particular; wherefrom an ever rising tide of improvement

has been continuously flowing abroad upon the whole body of
the people, without a suspicion of partiality for any class.'[29]
Nevertheless there is a suspect ring about the manner in
which he justifies the setting of fees by an association of
physicians or an association of barristers, in a manner
which he would forbid to an association of workmen.[30]

Let us pursue this suspicion by raising the fundamental
dilemma in Erle's approach; if there is not a mechanical
following of decided cases, if there exists a creative
innovatory principle, who guides it, on whose values does it
rely for growth? Erle answers the question readily enough.
While the principles 'originate practically from the people'[31]
nevertheless 'if the origin of the principles of the common
law is to be traced beyond their practical existence, they
seem to originate from conscience – that is, from the same
power which has made the majority of all free men of all ages
and languages to have a perception of that which they feel
to be just, and which they admire for itself, and assume to
be useful till the contrary be proved. And among free men
some are pre-eminently gifted with this perception of the
just.'[32] This then was the central point. The conscience
of the jurist was the guide, the jurist who relies on his own
sense of right, 'where an opinion is adopted because "aequum
esse mihi videtur."'[33] But these were not light or transient
views. 'The words of these men would not have been handed
down if they had merely expressed their intuitions before
their highest faculties had been trained by long and painful
effort ...'[34] Moreover 'they have their eminence because
their intuitions have accorded with those of the strong men
in the generations that have succeeded.'[35] In our modern
times, it is doubtful if we would find such a view so
explicitly stated. Perhaps today when our society relies
heavily on behaviourist and mechanical models to explain
itself, the courts might find themselves stripped of
legitimacy if they offered their personal 'quia aequum est'
although expressed in the context of a known tradition, and

perhaps for that reason they fall back heavily on a rule
already determined; or perhaps in the fashion of the time
they lack the moral vigour which makes such statements
legitimate on their face. But Erle saw no difficulty in this.

But if one concedes to a body of judicious and learned men
the task of guiding - although granted within a common
tradition - the evolution of the law, do they not import
into this the value system of the class from which they
spring? The contemporary American jurist Roscoe Pound
(who recognised fully the developmental role of the courts)
answered this by pointing to the widely different social origins
of those judges who dominated the formative years of American
law.[36] But Erle could point to no such diversity. Instead
he relied on the judge's capacity for dealing equitably with
people of all classes; and in any event, in his opinion,
the principles that were evolved were self-evidently right
and were supported by the people as a whole, and this applied
to trade unions no less than to any other group. Whether
this is a fair point or not requires a brief review - as far
as trade unions were concerned - of what these principles were.

The passage written by Sir William Erle in 1868 and quoted
by Judge Budd in 1960[37] ran as follows: 'Every person has
a right under the law as between himself and his fellow
subjects to full freedom in disposing of his own labour
or his own capital according to his will. It follows that
every person is subject to the correlative duty arising
therefrom and is prohibited from any obstruction to the
fullest exercise of this right which can be made compatible
with the exercise of similar rights by others.' This was
a phrase that at the time rang with great moral vigour. In
the nineteenth century the idea of an ethical society was of
enormous importance to a world profoundly conscious of
barbarism in everyday life. Hobhouse remarks on the
'severity, or rather barbarity, of the criminal law in Europe
down to the nineteenth century';[38] and despite the clear

vision of a central and impartial authority, distinguishing
between criminal and civil matters, adhering strictly to the
principle of individual responsibility, deciding exclusively
on evidence and testimony and relying on a public force for
the execution of its decision,[39] despite all this there was much
that was tribal or merely vindictive in the conduct of everyday
life; and many men far from reacting instantly to an ethical
challenge without reference to family or local ties saw
themselves like Hobhouse's Andoman Islanders[40] as spectators,
as neutral, quite unmoved themselves in the matter. Of
course to a great extent this must always be the case but the
notion of an overarching ethic was less widespread throughout
society than it is today.

But there was a considerable sense of the progressive evolution
of things and the powerhouse lay in the idea of individualism,
to which was already attributed the vast driving force behind
the development of industry. It was seen as the impetus behind
the development of law as well, and was formulated most in-
fluentially by Sir Henry Maine, with a sort of Darwinian
splendour: 'The word Status may be usefully employed to
construct a formula expressing the law of progress thus
indicated, which, whatever be its value, seems to me to be
sufficiently ascertained. All the forms of Status taken notice
of in the Law of Persons were derived from, and to some extent
are still coloured by, the powers and privileges anciently
residing in the Family. If then we employ Status, agreeably
with the usage of the best writers, to signify these personal
conditions only, and avoid applying the term to such conditions
as are the immediate or remote result of agreement, we may say
that the movement of the progressive societies has hitherto
been a movement <u>from Status to Contract</u>.'[41] One can appreciate
therefore how moral and how self-evident was Erle's statement.
In his tract, in accordance with these ideas, he established
first the right 'to a free Course for Trade in general'[42] and
then went on to establish the right 'to a free course for
trade in labour.'[43] Therefore 'a stop in the supply of
labour is obviously a damage in every trade; the causing of

stop is a restraint of trade; and all restraint of trade is, as above stated, presumed to be unlawful until the contrary be shown.' Despite this, under the same principle of individualism, a worker may freely choose to stop work[44] but what if he is induced to do so? Clearly another employer may cause this effect by offering the worker a higher wage; but where the object is to do damage 'to the party whose supply (of labour) is thus stopped',[45] where the motive is found to be malicious, then according to Erle a person who induces a worker to stop work 'should be found guilty of a wrong and made liable to damages. If two or more combine for the purpose of so causing damage, the combination would, I believe, be a crime.' We now approach directly the problem of trade union activity. While a man may freely stop work himself if he so desires, what if a number agree together to stop work, and what if they follow this up by urging others to do the same? What, in a word, of combinations? 'As to combinations,' said Erle,[46] 'each person has a right to choose whether he will labour or not, and also to choose the terms on which he will consent to labour, if labour be his choice. The power of choice in respect of labour and terms, which one person may exercise and declare singly, many after consultation may exercise jointly, and they may make a simultaneous declaration of their choice, and may lawfully act thereon for the immediate purpose of obtaining the required terms; but they cannot create any mutual obligation having the legal effect of binding each other not to work or not to employ unless upon terms allowed by the combination. Any arrangement for that purpose, whatever may be its purport or form, does not bind as an agreement, but is illegal, though not unlawful, on account of restraint of trade, and therefore void. Every party to it, who chooses to put an end to it, is thenceforward as free to claim his own terms for his own labour as if such arrangement had never been made; and any attempt to enforce, by unlawful coercion, performance of any such supposed agreement, against a party who chooses to break from it and labour or contract to labour upon different terms, is an attempt to obstruct him in the lawful exercise of his right to freedom to trade; and is thus a private wrong. It is also a violation of a duty towards the public - that is to say, of the duty to abstain from obstructing the exercise of the right to the free course of trade. A person can neither alienate for a time his freedom to dispose of his own labour or his own capital according to his own will ... nor alienate such freedom generally and make himself a slave ...; it follows that he cannot transfer it to the governing body of a union.' Coercive trade union activity therefore was profoundly wrong not only as offending against the great principle of individual liberty but as offending as well against the principle of progress, the principle of the evolution of society, on which the welfare of all depended. The majority report of the Royal Commission[47] chaired by Sir William Erle, following these principles, recommended that only those unions should have the protection of the law which in their rules declared explicitly against picketing, much strike action, closed shop arrangements, limiting apprentices and the like; and while in the event the much more liberal minority report was followed in the legislation of 1871[48] we must remember that the thrust of the common law remained unchanged - what was changed was merely its application in the circumstances stated by the statute.

How then does this help us in our consideration of class prejudice? In many respects this statement of the common law was a charter for the exploitation of the weak. On the other hand we must remember that the nineteenth century saw as well a powerful surge of social concern. Erle therefore and those that followed him would not have countenanced class exploitation as such; rather were they dominated by the notion of individualism and its central role in human progress. But it was difficult for them to avoid a distaste, and at times a hostility, for trade unions and their activities. There is the early example of Leathem v. Craig[49] where the union - indeed provocatively - not only sought to have non-members dismissed from their employment but would itself accept them in membership only after the severest penalty.

The judges had to distinguish Allen v. Flood[50] where the
House of Lords the year before asserted the right of a
person to do what would not otherwise be legally wrong, even
with a malicious object; and this they did by distinguishing
between the act of a single person and of a number who have
combined for the purpose. 'In pronouncing ... judgement',
said Judge O'Brien[51] in the Queen's Bench Division, 'we
shall have reason for confidence that, through the mass of
arguments, the conflicts of minds, and the array of authority,
we have reached the broad, open, solid ground of natural law,
of moral law, and the law of England alike - the law of
a nation that works, assuring to men an indefeasible liberty
to work without let or hindrance ... and we shall, not
least, maintain the ultimate authority of law, in declining
to join in the rush down the inclined plane to the level
at which are found the passions, the interests, the ignorance
and error of a class, prone to dangerous means, conscious
of political power, arrogant from past concession, and
confident in further aggression.' And if Chief Baron Palles
dissented he did so with regret, because he felt himself
'coerced by the judgement of the House of Lords in Allen v.
Flood to hold that the law is powerless to protect, from
that which the jury has found to be the tyranny of a trades union,
the sacred right of a workman to save himself and his family
from starvation by the work of his hands.'[52] Perhaps there
is more than a question of trade union prejudice here; there
is also some revolutionary fear of an alternative class
seeking an alternative society; and if this sounds somewhat
exaggerated, there is at the very least a profound dislike
of an alternative authority exercising public coercion within
a free society.

-iv-

We have therefore available to us from all this, certain

signposts when we come to discuss the third question, the
third charge of the trade unions, that when the judges
followed nineteenth-century thinking on the grounds that
their function was essentially declaratory, they were expressing, whether consciously or not, their own class-
determined prejudice. We shall expect in the first place,
our first signpost as it were, a deep instinctive attachment
by the Irish judges to the notion of individualism as expressed by Sir William Erle. Secondly, even if respect for
trade unions as such grows, we shall expect a strong distaste
for certain of their activities, to some extent when they
interfere with trade or when they picket on the streets, but
to a very considerable extent (because this raises the dread
of an alternative authority) when they exercise coercion in
regard to membership. It is important to appreciate how
differently this last problem can be viewed. To a trade union
it is usually intensely domestic, and of no great social
or political moment. Unless they have full membership, workers
in a hostile employment can be rendered more and not less
vulnerable by joining a union, and although union members
may themselves differ in theory on the propriety of compelling membership, the fact remains that when men in an
employment feel themselves in peril they instinctively
attempt to defend themselves against the danger of an alliance
between their employers and other workers who are not members
of the trade union. But the courts may not have this view of
the problem; instead there is frequently the appearance of
a union - perhaps for sinister reasons - compelling a worker
to join as a member against his will at the price of his
continuing in employment. Thirdly, and finally, we shall
expect as a further signpost to our study, a tight legalism
of interpretation, a concern with lex and not with ius; while
this had begun in an endeavour to limit strictly the
effect of statute - Lord Parker[53] in 1915 held for example
that the Trade Disputes Act, 1906, was not to be given a
wider meaning than was necessary, so as to unduly extend its
immunity, lest the common law rights of other persons be
unreasonably curtailed - it becomes much more than that;

rather it takes the form of the elevation of legalism into
a principle for the sake of the legitimacy it confers.
Professor Heuston[54] who has much sympathy for such an approach
in dealing with industrial disputes wrote in 1969:   'In my
view this is an area in which the lawyer can only obtain
and retain the confidence of all the parties if he emphasises
his traditional skills and virtues, especially those of
impartiality and rationality;' and he goes on to quote
Sir Owen Dixon, the former Chief Justice of the High Court
of Australia, apparently the outstanding common law judge of
our time, 'that close adherence to legal reasoning is the only
way to maintain the confidence of all parties in federal
conflicts. It may be that the court is thought to be
excessively legalistic. I should be sorry to think that it is
anything else. There is no other safe guide to judicial
decisions in great conflicts than a strict and complete
legalism.' Professor Heuston concludes the passage:
'Substitute "industrial" for "federal" and my point is made.'
We shall therefore expect to find that when this legalism is
directed in particular towards the 1906 Trade Disputes Act,
it will result in such complexities of legal reasoning as to
make the principles lying behind the law and their development
peculiarly difficult to discern.

This is very much an overview touching on a small number of
important cases, in order to trace the course of the law's
development. We begin to notice at an early stage the
increasing status of the trade unions in the eyes of the court.
It is a development, however, which is often shaky and uncertain. We have already seen how much the trade unions were
discouraged from availing of the courts in their own cause
in the 1928 case of R(I.U.D.W.&C.) v. Rathmines Urban
District Council.[55]   But the remarks of the judges are
revealing in this early case on a trade union's status in
the eyes of the law. The case concerned an endeavour
by the Irish Union of Distributive Workers and Clerks to
compel by writ of mandamus the Rathmines Urban District Council

to enforce the legal closing hours in the district. Judge
Hanna in the High Court[56] had held that although the trade
union, because of its uncertain legal status, had not any right
in itself, it had been made a proper prosecutor as representing
by implication from the statute the persons whose rights
had been invaded; but for other reasons he had refused to
make the order absolute, to which the court as a whole had
assented. But the Supreme Court took the view that since
the objects of the union did not cover the institution of
legal proceedings for this particular purpose, the conditional
order must be discharged;[57] more than that, even if the
registered objects of the union did include a power to
institute proceedings for such a purpose, this would not give
the union a sufficient interest to support an application
for mandamus. It appeared therefore that while the Taff
Vale case[58] was an authority for suing a trade union, 'no
authority (was) given for making such a body a plaintiff or
a prosecutor.'[59] 'These unions have a well-recognised position
in modern life,' said Judge Murnaghan, in delivering the
judgement of the court, 'and have established themselves
as necessary factors in determining the relations of employers
and workmen.' But he pointed out that while the Constitution
guaranteed the right to form associations or unions, it was
equally assertive of the principle of individual liberty.
'I can find no authority for the view that the individual
or his rights are merged in any association or union.'
Indeed he considered that once a trade union was recognised
as a legal entity it was quite as distinct from its members
as an incorporated company was from its shareholders. 'In
the field of politics a trade union may claim a right to act
on behalf of the majority of its members with a view to the
adoption of particular legislation, but in the field of law
the rights both of trade unions and individuals must be
defined in accordance with the law existing at the time. In
my view the doctrine of representation of individuals cannot
be applied so as to enable a trade union, which itself has no
legal standing, to represent individuals who have.' This of

course was disappointing for a trade union, but hardly
indicative of prejudice or hostility. Indeed the dissenting
judgement of the Chief Justice struck quite a warm note:[60]
'Trade unions have acquired so distinctive a type of personality in the world today that it is difficult to realise
the hesitant steps which legislation has followed after
their progress and growth - from the stage at which they
were regarded as anti-social and criminal, to the position at
which they stood at the parting of the legislative ways of
the Saorstat and Great Britain.' He rehearsed the decision
in the Taff Vale case, emphasised (as we have had occasion
to note already) that the 1906 act simply provided that
certain actions should not be entertained by any court,
without however affecting the status of trade unions as
litigant persons as declared by the House of Lords, and
therefore concluded that 'taking trade unions as we find them,
and examining their status in the light of the statutes and
of the judicial opinions ... a trade union which has been
registered ... is a legal person at least analogous to a
statutory corporation ... In my opinion a trade union is
as such capable of suing in its registered name in pursuance
of its defined objects.' While this opinion was set aside
by the majority of the court, the attitude expressed towards
trade unions was not.

In the thirties we find, as we anticipated, the question
of principle most sharply raised where a union attempted
to enforce membership, or, as an alternative, dismissal.
In the two leading cases of that period Ryan v. Cooke and
Quinn[61] (the Monument Creamery case, which incidentally
concerned membership but not dismissal) and Cooper v.
Millea[62] (to which we have already referred) the court held
against the union concerned; but it did so with some care,
anxious to discount any appearance of trade union prejudice.
'I may say', said Judge Johnson in the Monument Creamery
case, 'that I am in entire agreement ... as to the principles
of trade unionism and as to the necessity for the continued
existence of trade unions; but ... I am of opinion that the
provisions of the Trade Disputes Act 1906 afford no protection
to the defendants for what they did.' And Judge Gavan Duffy

in Cooper v. Millea (a confused and difficult case where
NUR members had reacted vehemently to the dread of a break-
away) emphasised the point as follows: 'It is the duty of
the Courts firmly to uphold the legal rights of workingmen
to combine; the right of combination, recognised by statute
in 1824 (when a repressive code, elaborated through three
centuries in England, was repealed), has now been securely
established, but only after a very severe struggle during
the 19th century and through the indomitable courage and
perseverance of workingmen against heavy odds; and the
right to form unions, subject to control in the public
interest,is expressly recognised by the Constitution.'
At this point at least, far from hostility or distaste these
judgements show considerable sympathy for trade unions as such.

But even if there was sympathy for trade unions, did the
very conservative administration of law in the Irish courts
import nineteenth-century prejudice into the proceedings?
Certainly, as we have already noted in our discussion on the
division of powers[63] the Irish courts were reluctant to
innovate and gave considerable emphasis to their declaratory
role. But now we must make a further distinction. This
declaratory role was not necessarily a conservative one in
every instance. If it were traditional as well as declaratory -
treating legislation, as far as it was possible to do so, as
ad hoc and not bearing on principle - then of course it would
be; but if while declaring the law it was particularly
sensitive to the national will as expressed in legislation,
and consciously looked to parliament for such guidance, that
was quite another matter. And this latter appeared
to be the view of Judge Gavan Duffy in his judgement in the
case of Cooper v. Millea when he held against the union on
the great issue of personal rights. The judges in the past
would have relied on the common law exclusively for this
purpose. In the event, Judge Gavan Duffy did this as well,
finding 'solid ground in the common law' for the 'governing
principle ... that trade unionists may lawfully combine for
lawful common purposes, even though their actions inflict

irreparable harm upon an individual, so long, and so long
only, as they confine their activities to lawful methods.'
The great common law judges of the nineteenth century would
not have expressed it in quite that way - and the reason
was perhaps that in this judgement the common law did not
rank as compellingly as it had in judgements in the past.
Judge Gavan Duffy followed it in the absence of a better guide,
in the absence of a statute. But he appeared to ground the
right he vindicated more on national policy than on the
common law, stating at an earlier stage, after he had declared
the rights of trade unions: 'At the same time, as a
matter of national social policy, every citizen is declared
to have the right to adequate means of livelihood, and, as
a matter of law, every man is entitled to be protected against
unlawful interference with his means of living, and that
protection he is entitled to seek and obtain from the Courts.'
And he went on to emphasise that it was indeed a matter of
law in which sympathy was an uncertain guide. 'The interests
of the individual and of organised labour must frequently
collide; if the union wins the victim may be crushed; yet
his ruin may be as irrelevant in a Court of law as the
failure or success of a trade union's policy; for the
injured man must prove that the law has been broken before
the Courts can give him redress.' The judgement therefore
while without doubt giving emphasis to the declaratory function
of the court was in no sense conservative; rather was there
an explicit expectation that parliament would play its
appropriate role in evolving new law, and in such circumstances
the fear of the dead hand of the past would be set aside.

But how influential was Mr Justice Gavan Duffy in the evolution
of this idea? In 1941 the government took a considerable step
in the direction he had indicated, enacting the Trade Union
Act of that year, and in a manner which we have already
explained in some detail[64] they provided for a system of sole
union organisation which appeared to some to invade the
liberty of the individual in his right to associate with whom
he wished. Judge Gavan Duffy was invited in 1945 to consider

the matter in the case of NUR v. Sullivan.[65]   When we examined
the judgements in this case earlier[66] we were concerned merely
with the emphasis by the court on its declaratory function;
but now we are digging somewhat deeper into this
declaratory principle recognising that in its application
it can be either progressive or conservative.   Judge Gavan
Duffy could, in ordinary circumstances, have been expected to
remain consistent in the matter; but now the Constitution
was pleaded for the first time (indeed almost as an after-
thought)[67] and he was asked to consider the statute not in
the light of the common law (which could not in his opinion
have prevailed against it), not in the context of national
policy (which in any event he would have seen the statute as
embodying), but in the context of fundamental written constitutional rights.   The Constitution did, as we have seen,
guarantee the liberty for the exercise, subject to public
order and morality, of the right of the citizens, inter alia,
'to form associations and unions.'   There was a modification,
however.   'Laws may be enacted for the regulation and control
in the public interest of the exercise of the foregoing right.'[68]
The problem was how this was to be construed.   The judge found
no difficulty in the matter.   'Let us see', he said,[69]
'what the Oireachtas has done.   The Constitution declares
that laws may be enacted for the regulation and control in
the public interest of the exercise of the citizen's right
to form associations and unions.   In passing the Act of 1941
Parliament therefore had to consider the public interest
and it proceeded in relation to trade unions to pass an Act
to confer an organising privilege on the stronger union or
unions, representing classes of workers, and to create, ad
hoc, a body qualified to adjudicate the monopoly to those
who ought to have it; that is the regulation and control that
commended itself to the Oireachtas in the public interest.'
There was the argument that the act invaded the right of the
citizens to form unions and associations because it created
a veto, and 'though the activity in question might be
regulated, it cannot lawfully be forbidden.'   But in the
judge's view 'an organic law is emphatically not to be parsed
as if it were an Income Tax Act' and furthermore, 'that the
text of a Constitution ought to attempt no more than to mark
its great outlines.'   He therefore held against the NUR

and for the statute.

But when the question was appealed to the Supreme Court the order of the High Court was reversed.[70] It all turned on how one viewed the Constitution. One could see it, as Judge Gavan Duffy did, as a broad framework of rights within which the Oireachtas is free 'to enforce the will of the People (which) is represented by the statutes passed in the interest of the common weal, as the Oireachtas for the time being understands that interest.' On the other hand one could take a much stricter and more legalistic interpretation; and this in fact was what the Supreme Court did in a judgement which shed little light on the great principles which had been raised in the High Court judgement. 'The Trade Union Act, 1941', they said,[71] '... purports to limit the right of the citizen to join one or more prescribed associations, i.e. the Union or Unions in respect of which a determination has been made. Any such limitation does undoubtedly deprive the citizen of a free choice of the persons with whom he shall associate. Both logically and practically, to **deprive a** person of the choice of the persons with whom he will associate, is not a control of the exercise of the right of association, but a denial of the right altogether.' There are those who would say that this imported into the Constitution the traditions of nineteenth-century individualism which had so profoundly influenced the common law; and let us therefore, particularly because of the High Court judgement, try to appreciate why such a tradition was seen as wrong in a **modern society.** The nineteenth-century jurists sought justice as devotedly as those of the twentieth century, but because they accepted as axiomatic the notion of progress, the notion of a beneficent, evolutionary force in society, it followed that they regarded the exercise of individual freedom in all things, the exercise of individual discretion, even of an individual whim, as a matter of the greatest importance, confident that it would, if given free rein, foster the character of a progressive society, and that the

progressive society in turn would be, by its nature, a
guarantee of justice. They were conscious of course,
distressingly so, of the manifest inequities that surrounded
them, but they were confident too that they would progressively disappear, and in the meantime they did what they
could to ameliorate them. The later twentieth century is far
more uncertain about progress, or any such unifying force in
society, and because of the highly integrated, mutually-
dependent, character of modern society, there are many who
would fear that individualism, pursued foolishly as a principle
which overrides almost everything else, could lead to chaos.
Justice is no less their concern, but it is justice based
on regulation rather than individual interest independently
pursued, a regulation which is the concern ultimately of
a just state; and a just state in turn must necessarily, in
their view, be democratic in its government and participative
in its institutions. One can see in Judge Gavan Duffy's
judgement therefore an instinct for such a development, while
in the Supreme Court, there are quite clearly the marks
of an earlier tradition.

And what of the trade unions? As we have already seen their
judgement was distorted by the schism within their ranks.
The NUR, who could have been regarded as the champions of
the right of free association in this latter case, had been
the defendants in the case of Cooper v. Millea where Judge
Gavan Duffy had found against them for denying this very
right. This was not a case of conversion; the NUR had
remained consistent throughout. But their focus was not a
focus on personal rights; they were concerned in a struggle
for survival, in which the enemy above all others was the
Irish Transport and General Workers Union. It was the
Irish Transport that had fostered the breakaway Federation
of Road and Rail Workers of which John Cooper was an un-
repentant member. It was the Irish Transport that stood to
gain from part III of the 1941 act, under which the NUR
was in peril of being extinguished in much of Ireland.

Perhaps to them, at the time, the courts, with their concern
for personal rights, had as random an appearance as a lottery.

And if the ITUC welcomed the Supreme Court judgement in the
NUR case it was not because they supported individualism
in the nineteenth century sense with all its dread overtones of a ruthless laissez-faire. On the contrary while
they declared a right of free association[72] it was a right
which had to be exercised under regulation - a regulation
which if necessary did not balk at prohibition; they
differed from the government in that they took the view
that the trade union movement itself and not the state should
be the regulatory power (this point we shall discuss further
in a later paragraph). In the special circumstances of the
NUR case they found the Supreme Court supporting their
objectives, but for reasons perilously at variance with their
own; and this would become only too clear when the Supreme
Court had recourse to the same principles in the Educational
Company case.

But is there evidence of class prejudice on the part of the
Supreme Court in this? It is difficult to say, so dominant
is the instinct for legalism - for rendering a declaratory
answer. One would suspect that freedom of association -
if not individualism - would have strong instinctive support;
and one would suspect as well that while trade unions would
be given due recognition, their welfare and growth in
society would not be seen as being of any great significance,
certainly not of sufficient significance to outweigh the full
exercise of such a fundamental right.

At this point we enter a period of very considerable
legalism indeed. The cases have been well recounted, in
particular by Heuston, Abrahamson and Delany.[73] Moreover,
with the possible exception of the Carlingford Lough case[74]
these were straightforward industrial disputes, uncomplicated
by aspirations of trade union hegemony. The Courts followed Lord
Parker[75] in tightly construing the immunities conferred by the 1906
act. There was the question of when a workman was not a workman

in three outstanding cases during the fifties, Smith v. Beirne,[76] British and Irish Steampacket Co. v. Branigan[77] (the Carlingford Lough case) and Roundabout Ltd. v. Beirne,[78] in the first of which the definition of a workman was construed almost to the point of the metaphysical. There was the case of Sherriff v. McMullen,[79] which limited the immunity for procurement of a breach of contract to one of employment; there was the Esplanade Pharmacy case[80] where it was held that a dispute on trading hours was not a dispute on working hours and was not protected; and there was the case of Brendan Dunne v. Fitzpatrick[81] which limited the extent to which picketing could be given immunity. No one could deny that in a number of these cases, the courts had common sense as well as legal grounds for deciding as they did; but the general effect was one of impregnable legalism, more strongly marked than in England,[82] which was also in the legalist tradition. Why this legalism developed so very strongly is not clear. A number of cases could be traced to one judge perhaps, Mr Justice Dixon, and his personal disposition; or one might speculate that the inward-looking society of the fifties was peculiarly subject to such conservatism. Nor did the courts themselves venture any basis for their legalism; they approached it all quite axiomatically, causing one commentator[83] to ask: 'In adjudicating on a matter of sweep and importance in a legalistic way, precisely what functions are the courts fulfilling?'

And what of the trade unions? When they expressed their concern at these decisions, they did so not on the grounds of class prejudice or of trade union prejudice, but rather because of this legalism in the approach of courts and the inadequacies of the statute. Thus Walter Beirne of the Irish National Union of Vintners', Grocers' and Allied Trades' Assistants, who had been so heavily involved in these disputes, said at the CIU conference in 1954,[84] soon after the Supreme Court decision in the case of Smith v. Beirne[85]: 'This (1906) Act is outmoded and outdated for nigh on fifty years. Trade Unions over the last fifteen

years have spent hundreds of thousands of pounds in trying
to find out what the provisions of this Act are, and we
are no wiser today, or very little wiser, than when the Act
was first introduced.' And later in the same debate, he said
on the question of legalism:[86] 'For the past fifty years
the lawyers in the lower Courts, the High Court and the
Supreme Court have been playing pitch-and-toss with this Act
and the problems are still only left in a position of being
ruled on from day to day as to whether a trade dispute is
legal within the meaning of the Act or not ... No judge
either in the High Court or the Supreme Court will give a
general direction in any matter relating to a trade dispute.
It is taken piece-meal and what appears to be a precedent
or a direction today is found tomorrow to be the exact
opposite and contradicted by the decision of some other court.'
While this may be somewhat exaggerated it expresses something
of the union's frustration. 'In the last nineteen years,'
said Beirne, 'my union has been in the courts on fifteen
occasions and our figure of expenditure has been about
£30,000.'

Walter Beirne, on this occasion, saw legislation as the means
of overcoming both the statute's inadequacies and the court's
legalism, at least in these specific instances; and he
was fortified in this because the decision in the case of
Smith v. Beirne[87] appeared to have the most alarming
consequences. Judge Dixon, whose decision was later approved
by the Supreme Court, had held that it was 'clear from the
provisions of the Trade Union Acts, as well as the Trade
Disputes Act of 1906, that the primary if not the sole concern
of trade unions was regarded as being with persons engaged
in trade or business and that the disputes contemplated were
those that might arise in trade or industry. To concede the
claim of a trade union to regulate the relations of employers
and employees, not engaged in any branch of trade or industry,
solely because the employee happened to be doing work of a
similar character to that of workers in a particular branch of
trade or industry would give a very wide and extended scope

to the Act of 1906, and give a trade union a broader field
of legalised intervention and activity than could reasonably
be supposed to have been contemplated by the Act of 1906.
It has been pointed out more than once that the Act should
receive a strict construction and the scope of its provisions
should not be unduly extended.' And what did this mean?
'It means in effect', said Walter Beirne,[88] 'that any worker
in the employment of Dublin Corporation, Cork Corporation,
Waterford Corporation, County Councils, Urban Councils, and
a number of other workers are no longer "workers" under the
definition of the Trade Disputes Act of 1906, and are not
entitled to take strike action in future in trade disputes ...
Workers building roads ... men mending paths in Dublin are
not entitled to be called building workers, and .. those
who are employed on direct labour schemes by Dublin
Corporation and the County Councils throughout the country
cannot be protected because their employers are not engaged
in trade or industry.' What seemed to be particularly
lunatic to Beirne was that there was a perfectly acceptable
definition of 'worker' in the Industrial Relations Act;
and he was therefore anxious to have this imported into the
1906 legislation.

His motion was adopted, but in a cautious way; and in the
event did not come to anything. John Conroy of the Irish
Transport, the only person apart from the seconder to
speak to it, while not directly opposing, thought it
perilous to open the door to amendments from employers and
others as well. After all, in recent years when strikes
took place affecting the public service 'there was an outcry
by the public, particularly by those who were opposed ...
to the trade union and labour movement to bring about
some restrictions ...', requirements regarding due process
in negotiation, balloting before strike, and the conduct
of pickets. Conroy was not a man who questioned good order
in industrial relations; quite the contrary. His point
lay deeper than that. He was perceptive in these matters,
and he sensed that there was a limit to what the courts should
do in industrial disputes; in certain circumstances there

might be a rejection of a court order with all the dangerous
implications (however unintended) of a revolt against society.

This raises the question of the legitimacy of a decision -
or an institution - in contrast with its legality.   It is
a theme which will become more and more significant to our
discussion, although here we shall merely open the topic.
Legality, in the context in which we use it here, has
an objective element in it;   legitimacy on the other hand is
concerned with the subjective characteristic of assent.
No doubt many give assent to court judgements in circumstances
where the court finds for the other party;   but the important
thing is that as long as there is broad public support for
the manner in which the courts administer justice, the views
of a participant in a particular case are irrelevant.
However when a group is large, or if small, economically
powerful, a judgement, despite its support by general assent,
may not be able to prevail against them, and in these
circumstances their view of the legitimacy of the judgement
becomes significant.   Beirne in 1954 said rather poignantly:[89]
'I find it very difficult to understand a decision of this
kind, but it is now the law and we have to accept it ...'
And trade unions as such would continue to take that view.
But things could be very different when emotions ran high
among the workers themselves.   Beirne of the Irish National
Union of Vintners', Grocers' and Allied Trades Assistants
(a union of barmen) and Fitzpatrick of the Irish Union of
Distributive Workers and Clerks, but in particular the former,
were engaged in the distributive trade, where numbers in
any one employment were usually small;   and a head of steam
among them was neither here nor there.   One might speculate
on whether this influenced employers or not;   certainly
these two unions were involved during this period in quite
a remarkable number of legal actions.[90]   But craft workers
for example are notoriously toughminded in disputes;   and
craft or not, when men feel profoundly aggrieved they may
wish to discount any court order - almost with a sense of
martyrdom - as occurred during the stormy events of 1968

when the Electricity (Special Provisions) Act 1966 was
implemented.

This raises an alarming prospect of inequity, in very truth
of one law for the strong and one for the weak; it could
indeed be the case, but trade unions, at least, do not
intend it. We shall discuss at a later stage the problems
of maintaining a general equity in such circumstances,
recognising with Roscoe Pound[91] 'that in labor disputes
some tolerance of disorder is a practical necessity even
where logic would call for strict application of settled rules
of law' and recognising as well that there may be a limit to
the scope of the court's activities in such matters - a
limit to its legitimacy. Nonetheless we see at this point
in our discussion a substantial number of important cases
coming quite properly before the courts, and we see as well
that the legalism of the court, far from increasing its
legitimacy, its acceptability as an institution - as
Professor Heuston rather expected[92] - created instead
a sense of profound frustration and distrust.

And so we come finally to a case which we have mentioned
on a number of occasions, the case of the Educational Company
of Ireland v. Fitzpatrick.[93] In the month of September
1959, twelve members of the clerical staff of the companies
concerned (there were two inter-connected firms) joined the
Irish Union of Distributive Workers and Clerks. The union
official sought a meeting with the employers to discuss
conditions of employment, which was refused initially,
but on the threat of a strike was conceded, and a new
salary scale was negotiated. The union members then began
to bring pressure on their clerical colleagues to join the
union - some of whom did. Nine however refused to do so,
and early in February 1960 the union members by vote
decided to refuse to remain at work with non-members. The
employers took the view that while their employees could join
a union if they wished, they had no intention of compelling

them to do so. On February 29 pickets were placed, and
were quickly restrained by an interim injunction, followed
by an interlocutory injunction a week later. When the
case came before the High Court in May the employers sought
a continuing injunction on the grounds that the picketing
was unlawful and contrary to the Constitution.

At the best this was a hazardous case for the union.
Firstly, it concerned the sensitive matter of compelling
trade union membership on the pain of dismissal from
employment, where one could expect, to judge from the past,
little instinctive sympathy from the court. And secondly
it concerned picketing, not merely strike action; this is
a radical distinction, because while strike action might
have justification as resting ultimately on the individual
freedom to withdraw one's labour if one wishes, picketing
on the other hand, being, under the common law, watching and
besetting, was inherently unlawful and would in ordinary
circumstances be actionable if the courts had not been
inhibited by statute. It followed therefore that the
application of the statute in this case would be most
carefully scrutinised.

But curiously, the tendency of the courts towards legalism
and tight construction appeared at the outset to support
the union's position. The question was whether this, being
a dispute concerning trade union membership, was a dispute
within the meaning of the 1906 Act. There had been at least
two leading cases in England, Valentine v. Hyde[94] in 1919
which held that it was not covered and White v. Riley[95] which
held that it was. But for forty years or more, the latter
case had been accepted as stating the law in the matter and
consequently both the High Court and the Supreme Court held,
though with some personal reservations, that the Educational
Company dispute was in fact a dispute within the meaning of
the Act. Immunity therefore would have been conferred on
picketing in this case were it not for the Constitution.
As we have seen, the role of the courts in regard to personal
rights under the Constitution can be interpreted in a number
of ways, and Mr Justice Budd in the High Court - in great

contrast to Judge Gavan Duffy in the NUR case[96] - chose
to be highly traditional. He held that Article 40 also
meant by implication 'that a citizen has the correlative
right not to form or join associations or unions if he does
not wish to do so..' and he felt greatly fortified in this
view by the NUR case.[97] 'From a practical point of view,
I am therefore driven to the conclusion that pressure of a
very potent nature is being brought on these men to compel
them to do that which they cannot be compelled to do having
regard to their constitutional rights, namely to join a
union ...'[98] But then he went on to ground his interpretation
of these rights in the traditional common law position,
not merely on the principle of freedom of association, but on
Erle's much more laissez-faire 'free course for trade in
general.'[99] 'Long before the present Constitution came into
force,' he said, 'there had been some impressive declarations
in various cases of the rights of the individual citizen...'
and he quoted a number: 'Prima facie, it is the privilege
of a trader in a free country in all matters not contrary
to law to regulate his own mode of carrying it on according
to his own discretion and choice', furthermore: 'all are
free to trade on what terms they will'; and again: 'The
liberty of a man's mind and will to say how he should bestow
himself and his means, his talents, and his industry, was
as much a subject of the law's protection as was that of his
body.' And then he went on to quote the famous passage
from the tract of Sir William Erle. The interesting point is
that in every case these statements were made before the turn
of the century. While the quotations were from English
case law and an English treatise, he saw nothing in them
'incompatible with Irish pre-Constitution law, and ... they
would be readily acceptable as pronouncements on the legal
rights of a citizen in this country ... in so far as they
have not been curtailed' by legislation in England or the
Constitution here. 'So far from being cut down or interfered
with these principles are to a great extent enshrined in
somewhat different language in the Constitution'; and he

went on to indicate how this was so. In this manner
Mr Justice Budd imported into the Constitution the nineteenth-
century principles of individualism, causing as a result,
legislation of very long standing to be set aside in favour
of a traditional common law position. The Supreme Court
were very divided on the issue, the Chief Justice taking the
view that the immunities conferred by the 1906 act were
well known to citizens when the Constitution was enacted,
and if it were intended to impose further constraints on
trade unions, it would have been done in clear and unambiguous
language. [100] But the majority upheld the decision of the
High Court, although it is difficult to be sure to what
extent they would have followed Judge Budd in his wholehearted reliance on individualism. Judge Kingsmill Moore,
who in this three-two decision could be taken as being the
most definitive, was very circumspect about the whole business
of coercion, pointing out that even in Constitutional matters
'..certain forms of pressure do not come within the province
of law to restrain. Unpopularity or social ostracism may
be coercive to prevent me from exercising a right guaranteed
to me, but the law has no concern with them, nor will it in
general interfere with economic pressure exercised by another
person in pursuance of his own legitimate interests.'[101]
The problem arose when the legislature intervened 'to authorise
or facilitate coercion by attempting to legalise acts,
directed to that end which previously were illegal and
restrainable.' This too was the justification in the
decision in the NUR case; and now 'if the Trade Disputes
Act had not been passed, but an identical Act were to be put
on the statute book tomorrow I conceive that it would be
unconstitutional to the extent that it purported to legalise
the use of picketing (an act previously illegal) for the
purpose of interfering with the exercise of my guaranteed
constitutional right of association or disassociation.'
The problem therefore lay in the act of picketing, not
in the strike as such.

-v-

Can we detect class prejudice in all this? It is difficult
to do so; indeed at the time most Irish people who were
educated and affluent believed the Republic of Ireland was
virtually a classless society - a view which was hardly
shared by wage earners in general and in particular by
urban workers. Nevertheless, the courts, being made up
of the educated and the affluent, would have found the question
of class prejudice, as we have raised it here, a somewhat
irrelevant and perhaps mildly offensive one. Furthermore,
we can detect little evidence of trade union prejudice, and
if the judges from time to time feel distaste for a certain
trade union activity, they identify that distaste, and
consciously attempt to discount it, relying as objectively
as they can on the law in the matter.

What we can clearly identify is a considerable and continuous
emphasis on the declaratory role of the courts. And this
in turn raised two profoundly contrasting approaches, the
progressive approach as indicated by Judge Gavan Duffy,
which looked to legislation to innovate, to state new law,
to express the changing and developing nature of the national
interest; and the conservative approach as indicated by
Judge Budd in the Educational Company case. This conservative
approach had two important aspects. Firstly, in its extreme
form, as presented by Judge Budd, it would see itself bound
in trade union matters to carry forward the exaggerated
individualism of the nineteenth century in a surprisingly
resolute manner; and secondly, it had, in great contrast
to the English legal system, a special instrument in the
Irish Constitution by which this could be done.

The Irish Constitution had introduced a radical difference
in the role of the courts in constitutional matters.
While in England, parliament, in such questions, could still
bid fair to dominate the courts, to dominate judge-made law -

although subsequent interpretation might greatly limit
its intent - the position was now quite other in the
Republic, where in constitutional issues, the views of
the court prevailed over parliament, since the Supreme Court
was the ultimate authority in declaring the meaning of the
Constitution and whether its provisions had been infringed.
If one tightly construed the Constitution therefore, and
if one did so on the basis of nineteenth-century principles,
one effectively negated, as Judge Gavan Duffy was quick to
see, certain progressive legislation, whether such legislation
expressed the will of the people or not.

The fact that the Irish courts, in such fundamental matters,
were placed above parliament imposed on them a far greater
responsibility for the care of basic constitutional rights
and their development than did the English constitution,
where the responsibility for such matters was spread among
the various organs of state. Yet we find - certainly up
to this point in 1961 - a great deal of uncertainty. The
problem that faces us is this. These contrasting views which
we have just examined were expressed at the level of the
High Court. The position of the Supreme Court on the same
issues is immensely difficult to determine. The fundamental
concepts which troubled the High Court judges were dealt
with by the Supreme Court inadequately if at all, with little
enough evidence of a deeper and more rigorous reflection.

Erle and the nineteenth-century jurists were right in this,
that in emphasising the principles behind the law, they
gave it a sense of coherence and predictability. When this
approach was modified in favour of an essentially declaratory
role understood in a legalistic way, and when the principles
behind the declarations were not adequately explored, then
the courts conveyed an impression of randomness and un-
predictability; and the whole purpose of legalism, the
attainment of objective equity, was turned on its head by the
very operation of legalism itself, which left cases to be
construed almost in the manner of a lottery.

Because of this, the legislature found great difficulty
in the years that followed in drafting legislation in this
area which, although expressing the general wishes of all,
ran the risk of being negated by the courts. A special
working party was established by the government[102] in
April 1962 on which the ICTU was represented to consider
inter alia 'legislative action which might be taken with a
view to protecting a union's right to take action to regulate
membership questions', but up to the present time, no
statute to this effect has been enacted, despite continuous
trade union pressure and a good deal of government good will.

This then is a picture of the relationship between the trade
unions and the courts up to 1960.

Notes on Chapter Twelve

1.   [1961] I.R. 345.

2.   Some work has been done in this field; see
Bernard Shillman: Trade Unionism and Trade Disputes
in Ireland 1960; J.B. McCartney: "Strike Law and
the Constitution" in The Irish Jurist 1964 Vol. XXX p.54.
R.F.V. Heuston: "Trade Unions and the Law" in The Irish
Jurist 1969, Vol. IV p.10. Max Abrahamson: "Trade
Disputes Act: Strict Interpretation in Ireland" in
Modern Law Review 1961 Vol. 24 p.596; V.T.H. Delany:
"Immunity in Tort and the Trade Disputes Act - A New
Limitation" in Modern Law Review 1955, Vol.18 p.338 and
also 1956 Vol. 19 p.310.

3.   p. 348 above and p.650.

4.   p. 11 above.

5.   Dennis Lloyd: The Idea of Law: Penguin 1974 p.260.

6.   p. 545 below.

7.   R. (I.U.D.W.&C.) v. Rathmines U.D.C. [1928] I.R. p.260.

8.   NUR v. Sullivan [1947] I.R. p.77.

9.   Dennis Lloyd op.cit. p.327.

10. Sir William Erle: The Law Relating to Trade Unions
in Tracts on Trade and Trade Unions: Macmillan 1868;
separately published Macmillan 1869; see also the
eleventh and final report of the Royal Commission on
Trade Unions 1869: Sessional Papers Vol.XXI
1868-69 (20) p.235.

11. [1961] I.R. 367. McCarthy and Ellis in Management By
Agreement Hutchinson 1973 find the roots of the 1971
Industrial Relations Act in Britain in the majority
report of the Erle Commission on Trade Unions of 1869
(see p.10).

12. [1938] I.R. 367.

13. Roscoe Pound: Justice According to Law: 1951 p.51.

14. [1961] I.R. 367.

15. Pound op.cit. p.41.

16. I.R. [1947] p.87.

17. I.R. [1947] p.99.

18. [1959] I.R. 423: in particular 426.

19. Michael Beloff: "Legal Education and the New Universities" in The Irish Jurist 1959 p.63. Incidentally the use of the word declaratory here must be distinguished from its use when a contrast is drawn between declaratory and executory judgements, a highly important procedural matter but one with which we are not concerned here.

20. Dennis Lloyd op.cit. p.262.

21. [1961] I.R. 383.

22. Loren P. Beth The Development of Judicial Review in Ireland 1937-1966 Dublin: Institute of Public Administration, 1967, p.6.

23. Sir William Erle: The Law Relating to Trade Unions: London 1869 p.47.

24. Erle op.cit. p.52.

25. [1921] I Ch.1.

26. [1961] I.R. 384.

27. Erle op.cit. p.18.

28. ibid. p.19.

29. ibid. p.54.

30. ibid. p.44.

31. ibid. p.50.

32. ibid. p.51.

33. ibid. p.51.

34. op.cit. p.51.

35. op.cit. p.52.

36. Pound op.cit. p.37.

37. [1961] I.R. 367 where Judge Budd although quoting the passage accurately attributes it to Sir J. Earle; also Erle op.cit. p.12.

38. L.T. Hobhouse: Morals in Evolution p.123.

39. ibid. p.71.

40. ibid. p.71.

41. Sir Henry Sumner Maine: Ancient Law 1878 ed. p.170.

42. Erle op.cit. p.5.

43. ibid. p.11.

44. Erle op.cit. p.21.

45. ibid. p.22.

46. ibid. p.23.

47. op.cit. Eleventh and final report.

48. Trade Union Act 1871.

49. [1899] I.R. 667.

50. [1898] A.C. 1

51. [1899] I.R. 701. He also quotes the passage of Erle's which is repeated later by Mr Justice Budd (see p.493 above.)

52. 1899 I.R. 701.

53. Larkin v. Long [1915] A.C. 814.

54. R.F.V. Heuston op.cit. p.12.

55. [1928] I.R. 260.

56. [1928] I.R. 260.

57. idem.

58. [1901] A.C. 426.

59. [1928] I.R. 282. We must emphasise that we are concerned here only with a trade union suing in its registered name, and only with the law at the time.

60. [1928] I.R. 299.

61. [1938] I.R. 512.

62. [1938] I.R. 749.

63. p.487 above.

64. See p.202 above.

65. [1947] I.R. 77.

66. See above p.487.

67. [1947] I.R. 85.

68. Article 40.6.1° iii.

69. [1947] I.R. 90. For a somwhat different evaluation see Beth op.cit. p.57. See also Kelly: Fundamental Rights in the Irish Law and Constitution Dublin: Allen Figgis 1961 p.117.

70.   [1947] I.R. 77.

71.   [1947] I.R. 102.

72.   See p.464 above.

73.   op.cit.

74.   British & Irish Steampacket Co. v. Brannigan [1958] I.R. 128.

75.   Larkin v. Long [1915] A.C. 814.

76.   [1955] 89 I.L.T.R. 24.

77.   [1958] I.R. 128.

78.   [1959] I.R. 423.

79.   [1952] I.R. 236.

80.   Esplanade Pharmacy Ltd. v. Larkin 1957 I.R. 285.

81.   [1958] I.R. 29.

82.   Heuston op.cit. p.14.

83.   Abrahamson op.cit. p.603.

84.   CIU 1954 p.117.

85.   [1955] 89 I.L.T.R. 24.

86.   CIU 1954 p.121.

87.   [1955] 89 I.L.T.R. 24.

88.   CIU 1954 p.116.

89.   CIU 1954 p.117.

90.   McCartney op.cit. p.55.

91.   Roscoe Pound op.cit. p.30.

92.   Heuston op.cit. p.12.

93.   [1961] I.R. 345.

94.   [1919] 2 Ch. 129.

95.   [1921] I.Ch. 1.

96.   [1947] I.R. 77.

97.   idem.

98.   [1961] I.R. 366.

99.   Erle op.cit. p.5.

100.   [1961] I.R. 379.

101.   [1961] I.R. 396.

102.   ICTU 1962 p.75.

Chapter Thirteen

Parliament and Government

-i-

The two other areas of discussion, the relations between
the trade unions and, on one hand, the legislature and, on
the other, the government, can be dealt with more briefly.
We shall discuss them separately, but it is necessary to
remember that we are dealing with a continuum - a single
weave of relationship between the government and the trade
unions, where the government may at one time act by way
of legislation through the Oireachtas, and at another through
the cultivation of non-statutory relationships, joint
institutions such as consultative committees and planning
committees being the most obvious. It is inevitable therefore
that we shall find one topic merge into the other, and even
when we are dealing with them separately we shall be conscious
of a continuous interplay between them.

We saw that the Supreme Court as a whole, while strictly
interpreting the given law, did not give any clear answer
to the problem of the nature of law itself. They regarded
themselves in an ultimate way as the protectors and interpreters of fundamental law, not because of any jural or
political concepts in particular, but because a strict
interpretation of the Constitution would have it so. And if
they appeared to take a very strict view of the manner in which
certain fundamental rights were expressed - a view which
seemed to take little enough account of the need to evolve
and reinterpret - this also reflected not so much a special
jural position regarding the origin of the law and the
sanctity of its expression but again the tendency to strict
interpretation of the given law as it stood without taking
much account of its deeper nature. The argument ultimately

as Lord Lloyd pointed out in another context[1] is a
circular one; the law was strictly interpreted because it
was the law, and it was the law because it was strictly
interpreted.

When we turn to a discussion on the legislature, however,
we must recognise that those governments which in trade
union matters were innovatory and reforming - that is the
Fianna Fail governments of the time - had a very clear belief
in the dominant role of the Oireachtas, quite remarkably
close to that expressed by Judge Gavan Duffy. De Valera,
who is credited with having drafted the 1937 Constitution,
was wary of having the Supreme Court as its interpreters,
and would, if he could, have adopted some other device.[2]
For he saw the Irish society of the south as a revolutionary
society, and the Constitution as a revolutionary constitution,
not in any violent sense but rather in the sense of giving
the Irish people the opportunity of evolving their own
society and their own institutions away from those of the
United Kingdom. He saw the fundamental rights in the
Constitution as guides to the legislature, not instruments
of restraint by which courts, very much in the English
tradition, might hamper the development of the nation; he
had, in Professor Kelly's words,[3] 'the sovereignty of the
People (and thus of their elected representatives) in the
central position of his constitutional plans, and naturally
this notion did not harmonise with the idea of judicial
review of legislation in the light of constitutional
declarations; indeed, the latter seemed downright unreal to
him.' He saw therefore not so much the law in evolution -
this would have been the care of the jurists as Erle had
indicated[4] - but rather society in evolution, which was the
care of the elected representatives of the people. The law
was a touchstone, a guide, a frame of right; if it had its
roots in the spirit of the people, this had to be understood
not in a metaphysical way, as the German jurists were often
prone to understand it, but more in the very concrete way in
which Ehrlich conceived the 'living law'.[5] There were some

who would say, grounding their view on the cultural inter-
mingling of nationalism and catholicism, that we were concerned not so much with the spirit of the people - whatever
that might mean - but with the natural law understood in a
clear-edged Thomistic sense; and that this natural law
was the frame of reference for the interpretation of all
positive law, the Constitution included;[6] but while a case
might intellectually be made for this, the reality lay much
more with the concrete experience of a steady moral frame, not
perhaps as mobile as Ehrlich's living law, more traditional
perhaps, more firm in its structure, on which a people
began to develop their own precepts and practices.

De Valera's government, therefore, in representing through
parliament the will of the people, saw legislation as an
instrument for the development of that will. Insofar as
trade unions did not impede this development, all was well;
where they did, then legislation could be availed of in the
national interest. It is clear however that in this matter,
one can view trade unions in two quite different ways.
Firstly one can see them as seeking to present, in an
alternative institution, the will of at least a section of
the people, seeking to provide a machinery of representation
which is extra-parliamentary. Daniel O'Connell's hostility
to trade unions[7] for example rested on just such a view.
In de Valera himself one is conscious from time to time
of a certain constraint regarding trade unions, a sharp
limit to what he regarded as their legitimate activities.
This applied both to their influence on national policy
and to the scope of their representation. With regard to
national policy we have for example - in advance of any
consultation with the trade unions - his bleak statement in
the Dail during the economic crisis in the autumn of 1947:[8]
'... if the trade unions cannot undertake such an agreement
(a temporary limitation of wage increases) ... either
because there is not unanimity amongst them or because their
rules prevent the union executives entering into firm
commitments of this nature, then the Government will produce

proposals for legislation to the same effect.' And with
regard to the scope of trade union activities there are
two indications we might note: he steadfastly refused to
meet the ITUC representatives when they endeavoured to give
aid to an affiliated civil service union;[9] and despite
great pressure to the contrary, the original Industrial
Relations Act of 1946 excluded from the consideration of the
Labour Court not only disputes in the civil service but
disputes in the local authority service as well, which since
they made claim on the 'taxpayer's purse'[10] were in the
government's view disputes with the community, not with the
employers as such.

In contrast with this we can sense in the approach of
Lemass, although he went along with his leader in principle,
a far greater recognition of trade union legitimacy in a
society that was more pluralist, much less simply structured -
where the government was engaged more in the business of
creative management than in the expressing of an evolutionary
will. In the war years and immediately thereafter, plans
that were designed with a quite rigorous control in mind
became converted into administrative systems essentially
accommodatory in character. Emergency Powers Order 83, which
had imposed an absolute standstill on wage increases, became
under Emergency Powers Order 166[11] a means by which was
established a highly participative system for giving limited
but equitable wage increases; and the threat of legislation
in 1947 grew into the first great voluntary national
agreement on pay.

The prevailing attitude of the Fianna Fail governments to
trade unions, therefore, and the settled attitude of the
interparty governments of the time both emphasised a
degree of active cooperation, and this meant winning the
support of trade unions for government policies. It
followed readily enough from this that the government, when it

created new institutions or embarked on new proposals in
the field of industrial relations was anxious to ensure
their legitimacy, primarily in the eyes of trade unions, but
if that could not be altogether achieved, then most
certainly in the eyes of the citizens at large. Consequently,
throughout the remainder of this discussion, we shall find
emerging as a dominant theme this notion of legitimacy which
we have already opened up in a preliminary way.[12]

Let us first, however, set out in a briefly schematic way
the manner in which trade union and industrial relations
legislation was seen in the Republic at the time. Trade
union legislation[13] (as distinct from industrial relations
legislation) set out broadly to do two things: firstly to
restructure the trade union movement (the 1941 act is the
outstanding example, and in particular part III) and secondly
to regulate the functions performed by trade unions. The
regulation of functions sprang from a system of legitimation
(the granting of a negotiating licence under the 1941 act.)
It was in the event exercised on the basis of objective
minimum criteria, which could still be made to benefit large
unions as against small, and Irish-based as against British-
based; but it could have been exercised in a discretionary
manner, either by a special independent authority, as Lemass
suggested in 1947,[14] or by the trade union centre, as he
suggested in the nineteen sixties. If it were to be exercised
in a discretionary manner, legitimation could be withdrawn
from, as well as conferred on, a trade union if it were
judged appropriate to do so. Penalties, therefore, which are
of the essence in regulation, arose in the following manner.
Where one had discretion to withdraw legitimation - to
withdraw a negotiating licence - and did so, then a union
committed an offence if it negotiated, and any industrial
action pursued by it would not attract the immunities conferred by the 1906 act. Even where no such discretion
existed - the practice in fact up to now - the protection
of the 1906 act could be withdrawn in certain stated

circumstances, for example in the case of strikes in
essential services (as de Valera threatened to do in the
flour milling strike);[15] in the case of picketing certain
establishments (as with the Electricity Supply Board in the
later sixties);[16] and where a trade union contravened a
statutory wage policy. The object here of course was to
make such trade union activities justiciable matters in the
ordinary courts. We have already recognised however that
there can be a serious limit to the legitimacy of the courts
in dealing with such matters, in particular in dealing with
disputes about which large numbers of people feel very strongly.
Professor Kahn-Freund in 1970,[17] in recalling the majority view
of the Donovan Commission[18] and also recent experience in
West Germany and Sweden, wrote: 'Certain aspects of labour
relations cannot be controlled by law. The law is likely
to be a failure whenever it seeks to counteract habits of
action or of inaction adopted by large numbers of men and
women in pursuance of established social customs, norms
of conduct or ethical or religious convictions. Policies
to control spontaneous strike movements by threats of
penalties or civil liabilities are doomed to failure ...'
This also, broadly speaking, was the view which Lemass
apparently had in the post-war years in Ireland, and not
surprisingly therefore, we do not find any great development
in trade union law from there on, in the law which attempted
to regulate trade union functions. Rather do we find the
major development taking place in the law which attempted
not to regulate but to facilitate, not to make disputes
justiciable in the law courts, but to seek to resolve
them by consensus; in a word the major development took place
in the field of industrial relations legislation rather than
in the field of trade union legislation, a development which
relied heavily on the legitimacy in the eyes of all concerned
of the institutions thus created rather than on any legal
sanctions.

Before dealing with industrial relations legislation however,

there are some reflections which can usefully be made concerning trade union law and our theme of legitimacy.

Firstly, it appears now that when the Trade Union Act of 1941
set out to restructure the trade union movement by fostering
large Irish-based unions, each enjoying sole representation,
it offered an idea which had considerable legitimacy in the
eyes of the people at large despite the vigorous campaign of
the ITUC; and it appears as well that the tribunal established
under the act could have had a like legitimacy. It was all
upended not by popular feeling but by a juridical view in
the Supreme Court of somewhat obscure construction. We have
seen that this legitimacy was conferred on the statute[19] not
only because of the nationalist and somewhat xenophobic climate
of the time, but also probably because during war years (or
indeed during any period of political peril) there is a
stronger presumption of government legitimacy in all its actions
than during the more argumentative days of peace. We shall
see this particularly strongly when we come to discuss the
emergency powers orders dealing with wages during the same period.

But there were other matters that Lemass would have wished to
include in a trade union bill.[20] In the first place, there
were matters concerning personal citizenship rights, entry
into a union for example when it meant entry into apprenticeship
or employment, or exclusion from a union without adequate
appeal, or the regularising of contracts between trade unions
and other persons; and secondly there were questions where
the public welfare was involved; entry into apprenticeship
was also one of these since it had an influence on the level
of skill in the community and its capacity to grow; but
there were also such matters as demarcation disputes which
damaged production (that is to say, disputes between unions
on the division of work between various skills) and picketing
in certain circumstances. Any legislative move in this area
was successfully resisted by trade unions (the Apprenticeship
Act of 1959 was highly participative); but they nevertheless

felt the threat quite keenly, and this contributed,
particularly in the sixties, to the development in addition
to a disputes committee, of such institutions within the ICTU
as an appeals board, a demarcation tribunal and in recent
times an industrial relations committee to consult on
prospective disputes and the possibility of pickets. The
intriguing question now is whether, if Lemass had pressed
ahead with legislation on some or all of these, they would
have been accepted as legitimate. True, such legislation
implied justiciability, but Lord Lloyd[21] has remarked that
in England (and the same applies to Ireland) we are
'bedevilled by a restricted idea of law, according to which
industrial disputes are not justiciable issues in the full
sense, but involve matters of policy which can best be left
to negotiation or voluntary arbitration. The fact that many
other developed countries, such as Australia, Sweden and
Germany, find it perfectly possible to regulate these disputes
by judicial or quasi-judicial machinery, and are satisfied
that objective criteria exist by which they might be
adequately resolved, is surely a sufficient indication that
a good deal of rethinking is called for in England on matters
of this kind.' In a word, if the ordinary courts did not
appear to be appropriate, then separate industrial courts
could be established with due regard for such centrality in
the overall administration of justice as to assure a general
equity. There is much to indicate that there was in the
forties in Ireland a substantial awareness of the labour
court systems in other countries, particularly New Zealand,
with its largely compulsory court of arbitration;[22] but
although the term labour court was used in the 1946 Industrial
Relations Act, it was not empowered generally to act in the
manner of those in many countries in continental Europe or
in Australasia; the concept behind it, as we shall see, was
quite different.

On the whole, it appeared that Lemass was wise in not pressing
the matter. Entry into apprenticeship was always most jealously

guarded by the powerful craft unions as the very basis of
their job security; and demarcation disputes are closely
associated with the pressure of developing techniques and
the obsolescence of skills, matters which again the unions
would see as essentially non-justiciable since they bore
primarily on security and survival. As for disputes between
members of a trade union and the trade union executive,
there would have been the most vigorous resistance to an
investigation of a trade union's internal affairs by an
outside authority. This at least is how it would be seen;
it would appear to many to contradict the essentially
democratic character of the trade union itself which should,
as a democratic institution, have in these matters a built-in
self-correcting process. This of course was often far from
the case, but the view was nonetheless strongly held. It
would seem then, that despite the promise of legitimacy for
trade union legislation implied in the acceptance of the 1941
act, it is doubtful if such legislation could have been pressed
much further, even if the government had been really
determined on doing so.

The forerunner of the Industrial Relations Act of 1946, the
Emergency Powers (no.166) Order, 1942, would, in normal
times, have, in all probability, been neither proposed by the
government nor accepted by the unions. Its comparative
ease in working, and its considerable equity, were at the
outset by no means apparent, and we have seen[23] how it was
resisted as being inordinately complex and therefore unworkable. It carried little legitimacy on its face, and
such acceptance as it received derived largely from that
presumption of legitimacy which all government action enjoys
in war time. But it did work - and it paved the way for
the Industrial Relations Act[24] that followed immediately
after the war, promoting the idea - in the unsophisticated
society of the time - of orderly submissions presented
with some care, and evaluated on the basis of objective
and generally accepted criteria.

When Lemass presented the Industrial Relations Bill to
parliament in the summer of 1946 he made a considerable
bid for legitimacy, for the general acceptability of the
institution he proposed to create, that is to say the Labour
Court. He did not wish the bill to be seen as a government
measure merely - that is, a party measure - but rather as
a reflection of industry's needs, in respect of which he
was an instrument: 'I do not', he said, 'regard this Bill
as a Government measure in the ordinary sense. It is a
measure designed to facilitate workers and employers
in adjusting their difficulties concerning wages and conditions
of employment, and I can say that within very wide limits
it will be framed as they want it framed subject to the
willingness of the Dail as a whole to accept what is proposed.
I regard myself merely as an instrument for bringing the Bill
before the Dail, steering it through its various stages and
bringing it into operation when enacted ...'[25] The measure
was to be essentially voluntary in character; this was the
central point: '(It) is not proposed to make its provisions
compulsory except to the extent that parties voluntarily and
knowingly submit themselves to it in their own interests.'[26]
In this regard a cursory reading of the act can be quite
misleading. It provides for the establishment of the Labour
Court in section 10 but then it goes on to consider quite
a large range of powers and institutions (joint labour
committees, employment regulation orders, area standard wages,
the registration of joint industrial councils and so forth)
before we meet the heart of the matter, the court's essentially
voluntary role. But Lemass left no one under any doubt that
this was indeed the heart of the matter:[27] 'In effect the
whole scheme of the Bill is that the Court will function
and will have powers only in relation to parties which
voluntarily decided to use it.' It could perhaps be urged
that even in New Zealand this also was the position since
compulsion arose only when workers had registered themselves
as an industrial union, and such registration was voluntary;

but Lemass had decided against any compulsory dimension:
'It is not intended to provide for compulsory arbitration.
I do not believe in compulsory arbitration imposed by law.
Compulsory arbitration involves, in the last resort, state
regulation of wages. It is meaningless if it does not include
as a logical consequence compulsory enforcement of decisions
and the prohibition of strikes and lock-outs contrary to
such decisions. In practice, compulsory arbitration decisions
are not in fact enforceable against a body of workers who
are opposed to their terms, at any rate in a free society.
Under this Bill, it will be open to any trade union of workers
or employers to refuse to use the Court and to rely solely
on its powers of negotiation or on the old-time weapons of
lock-outs and strikes. I am proposing the creation of this
Court however in the firm conviction that the great majority
of the workers and employers, the rank and file members and
the elected leaders, will welcome the prospect of securing
an adjustment of industrial differences in a rational and
commonsense manner, and will readily and generally use the
Court established by the Bill provided that their freedom
to take other action is not thereby impaired.'[28] And even
in purely inter-union disputes, and in demarcation disputes,
he thought the Labour Court might be able to help where the
trade union centre might find its authority damaged if it
attempted to do so.[29]

All this argued a very considerable inherent legitimacy, since
the court's decisions would not be supported by legal
sanctions. How then was this legitimacy to be achieved?
First, and probably most important, was the performance
of the court itself. Although decisions would not be
binding '...it is hoped that in the course of time, the
growth of confidence in the fairness of the Court, and in
the practical and commonsense basis of its awards will
create a situation in which its awards will ordinarily be
accepted.'[30] But some practical institutional steps could be
taken as well. The most significant was probably the conciliation service[31] which would resolve many disputes in its

own right but which would also have the effect of clarifying
the issues before the dispute went to the court. Secondly
there was the question of procedure. The court as we have
seen is drawn from the two sides of industry with an independent chairman, but only one opinion can be given on an
issue, and no other view may be disclosed.[32] Furthermore
the act gave procedural status to the court by conferring on
it the powers of the High Court in summoning witnesses and
examining them under oath. But this climate of legality
(intended no doubt to increase the status of the court) was
resisted, and while Lemass himself had an open mind in the
matter he yielded to trade union pressure and refused to
appoint a lawyer as chairman, and refused as well to make
any special provision for the representation of parties to
a dispute by counsel or by a solicitor.[33] The legal
profession confessed to be somewhat scandalised by this
decision, but no doubt the decision contributed to the
legitimacy of the court in the eyes of trade unions, not
surprisingly in view of their distrust of the courts of law.
In the event the Labour Court never took evidence under
oath, and on the one occasion on which an employer was
represented by counsel, the experience was a singularly unhappy one.[34] Finally, in this determination not to make
the court judicially remote but continuously relevant, it was
decided that the chairman should not be given the security
of tenure appropriate to a High Court judge[35] but rather that
the appointment should be on the basis of five year terms, since
he must show himself continuously to be acceptable to industry.
And Lemass's first appointee to the chair, R.J.P. Mortished,
an outstanding figure, nationally and internationally, would,
it was hoped, reinforce this idea of personal acceptability.

However, when we look at these provisions now, at a distance
from Lemass's persuasive urgings, they seem somewhat uncertain ground on which to build the degree of legitimacy
which the institution required. But we must remember here
that this was to Lemass only a part of a larger strategy,
the first step, in this country, towards a voluntary, integrated

prices and incomes policy, supported by statutory institutions. This larger idea, fascinating in its possibilities,
was still-born in the election of 1948 and we were left with
the Labour Court alone; we shall continue for the moment
with our consideration of the Labour Court and its legitimacy
but we shall take up later this wider issue of policy.

Between September 1946, when war-time controls had come to
an end, and the spring of 1947, wages had risen by about a
quarter; but then prices began to rise rapidly. The cost
of living figure which had remained stable from 1943 to
early 1947[36] showed an increase by August 1947 of no less
than 10.8 per cent[37] which in turn brought great pressure for
a further wave of wage increases. The emergency steps
announced by the Taoiseach on October 15 1947[38] contemplated
subsidies, price moderation and a policy of wage containment.
Lemass had invited the congresses to meet him and had
developed further on the government's wage proposals; these
suggested taking a base line for current wages, and indexing
from there onwards, that is to say linking the increases
in wages directly with the cost of living index. The
alternative, in this critical time, was the temporary control
of wages by legislation - legislation which would be
introduced after consultation, but legislation nonetheless.
The congresses - which had to be consulted separately[39] -
responded in a positive way, the CIU accepting Lemass's
voluntary approach,[40] and the ITUC, while accepting it in
principle, recommending an alternative system by which
increases might be calculated. But then on November 18 1947[41]
Lemass wrote to the congresses, postponing discussions in
view of the impending general election (which in the event
did not take place until the following February) and pleading
in the interim for moderation.

Since the government could now offer no leadership in this
critical matter until after the general election in the new
year, the Federated Union of Employers took the initiative

and asked the Labour Court to arrange conferences between
it and the two congresses - an invitation which permitted
Mortished to grasp the situation in a rather positive way;
and the Labour Court was presented with its first substantial
opportunity for influencing the development of a national
wage policy. By the end of January the terms of the 1948
national wage agreement had been hammered out, terms which
were finally cleared by both sides in early March.[42]

The agreement which was released by the Labour Court was
headed National Wages Policy, which in effect was what it
was, an agreed policy under which trade unions and
employers would negotiate increases. The policy agreement
was of indefinite duration; it would continue until it was
either amended or terminated, the latter requiring three
months notice to the Labour Court. It contemplated that,
save in exceptional circumstances, no claims should be
made for more than 11/- a week for adult male workers - and
others in accordance with practice - the onus for proving the
exception lying with the employer if less was offered or with
the union if more was sought; but this provision was seen
as being subject to 'further revision from time to time to
meet changes in the cost of living.' The principles set out
in the agreement recognised the close relationship between a
policy on wages and a policy on prices; the parties resolved
to make every effort to avoid unjustifiable price increases,
to avoid inflationary wage increases, to avoid stoppages in
work, and to promote efficiency and productivity. And most
significantly it was agreed that 'no stoppage of work should
take place until all the available procedures for settlement
by negotiation, including reference to the Labour Court or
other established machinery, have been exhausted.'
Interestingly, each trade union and each employer organisation
was asked separately to subscribe to this agreement of
principles; only a very small and unimportant minority
refused to do so.[43]

Here then we see the central strategy by which the Labour Court

hoped to introduce legitimacy into the system; and in order
to explain the thinking behind it, it is necessary to make
some remarks regarding the nature of disputes. One frequently
finds distinguished disputes about interests and disputes
about rights. It is at best a difficult distinction, but
broadly speaking, disputes about rights are seen as disputes
stemming from the interpretation or application of agreements;
there is no philosophical connotation. On the other hand,
where the parties fail to make a bargain, where there is
a direct clash between them, and where no explicit criteria
can be relied on to resolve the problem, then the dispute
is seen as a dispute about interests. The American practice,
as described by McCarthy and Ellis,[44] is quite explicitly
along these lines: 'By (disputes of right) is meant disputes
over the interpretation and application of a given agreement
that arise during the period of its operation. By (disputes
of interest) is meant disputes over the re-negotiation of
such an agreement, at a time when it is due for renewal.'
And then they add significantly: 'American unions usually
accept that "disputes of right" ought not to be settled by
the use of industrial action of any kind. They are prepared
to accept mediation, leading if necessary to a form of
mutually binding arbitration as a final means of settlement.
Strikes and other forms of industrial action are supposed
to be kept in reserve, for use in "disputes of interest"
which only tend to arise when a collective contract is up for
renewal.' Disputes about rights, then, can be distinguished
from disputes about interests in that they are essentially
justiciable. And Mortished was fully aware of such a
possibility in 1947. During the course of his address that
year to the Statistical and Social Inquiry Society of Ireland
he referred to the system in Sweden and said:[45] 'An Act
of 1928 set up a special Labour Court to deal with "disputes
over rights" as they are called, that is to say, disputes
concerning the validity, existence or interpretation of a
collective agreement. So long as an agreement is in force,
no strike or lock-out may take place in connection with a
dispute over rights under the agreement. The dispute must be

referred to the Court and the decision of the Court is legally enforceable. The Swedish Labour Court, like the corresponding bodies in Denmark and Norway, is thus strictly a court ...'

Mortished's objective appears then to have been to convert, by means of this 1948 national agreement, an industrial relations system based almost wholly on conflicting interests to one based on the concept of agreed rights and their orderly resolution. True, he could not compel acceptance of Labour Court decisions, as the Scandinavian courts could; but he had available to him a national framework agreement, containing agreed rights and obligations which were both substantive and procedural, and which carried substantial inherent legitimacy since both parties had solemnly entered into a commitment in their regard.

But all this was doomed to failure, partly because of the somewhat peremptory manner in which Mortished handled the court's procedure, and partly because of the great economic stress in the 1951-1952 period. Let us take the latter first. During 1950 pressure for a further wage increase began to mount and negotiations opened under the Labour Court once again. But the FUE on this occasion - in the light of the economic circumstances as they saw them - would have nothing to do with any further agreement. The Labour Court in the autumn seeing no possibility of an agreement, brought the discussions to a close, but in doing so greatly irritated the trade unions by saying in a public statement that 'the Court does not regard the case for a general increase in wages as proved and therefore cannot pronounce in favour of such an increase.'[46] In frustration both congresses terminated their commitment to the 1948 national agreement, although the CIU, in view of the serious economic situation, attempted to secure from its members unilateral acceptance of a 12/- ceiling.[47] The increases in the event in this third general round of wage increases ranged from 10/- to 18/- for men. But almost immediately pressure mounted again, and in February 1952 the CIU sought a meeting with Lemass, now returned to power, and arranged through him a joint conference

with the FUE which resulted in May in a national agreement,
rather hedged about with economic constraints, but providing for a maximum increase of 12/6 a week.[48] The ITUC
unions, although not parties to the agreement, broadly
followed the pattern thus established. This became known
as the fourth round.

It was during this period that criticism of the court became
particularly vehement, certainly on the part of the CIU.
It boiled up first in 1950 at the CIU annual conference.
Apparently dissatisfaction had been growing for some time,
but in September 1949 a dispute in the Road Freight Department
of CIE brought matters to a head.[49] The court appeared
to have been rather inflexible and juridical in its approach
and regarded some protests made by the CIU as bringing improper
pressure to bear on it. This was the occasion when CIE
was represented by counsel, and the hearing dragged on for
eleven or twelve days. The recommendation, when it issued,
was described by Walter Beirne as 'the most ill-considered
abuse of the officials of the Union concerned in the dispute.
There was no doubt', he said, 'that the language used by
the court was absolutely unrestrained and was completely
unworthy of an organisation established to bring about
conciliation.' The whole episode caused the CIU to take the
matter to the minister, and it appeared that as a consequence
the court adopted a more conciliatory approach. McMullen,
while reinforcing the criticism of the past, went on to say
that in two subsequent disputes 'the court followed the
procedure which the Act suggested it should follow and there
had been conciliation. They had not had the procedure based
on High Court procedure. They had no Senior or Junior Counsel;
in fact they had no sitting of the court at all. The parties
were interviewed separately and the Labour Court, by that
means, got a knowledge of the facts from every point of
view concerning the disputes, and the Court made recommendations.
Serious strikes were averted. He was very pleased that the
Court was now acting on the basis of conciliation. He had
decried it with full justification at a certain stage as
being a discredited body. He did not think he need withdraw

or apologise for that observation, because up to that stage,
it could not fairly be described as anything else. He was
very pleased that the Court had changed its technique.
He thought the Court could perform useful work and if continued
on its present basis would serve all the purposes intended
by the Act.'[50]   But Mortished clearly had no intention of
having the court cast in such a role, and in the September
of the following year, the CIU once again went to the
minister - now Lemass - with rather bitter criticisms.
To them, it appeared that the court was more concerned with
preserving its dignity than bringing a dispute to an end;
but its major criticism - significant in the climate of
the time - was that the court was excessively concerned
with the public interest, that is to say with national
economic policy, presumably as enunciated by the government,
but perhaps as understood independently by the court, and
this had done much to damage its legitimacy in the eyes of
the trade unions.[51] As a result the court had experienced
in its recommendations in recent time 'a large proportion
of rejections, especially in major cases.' Eventually in
May 1952, Mortished, who had been reappointed only the previous
year, resigned the post of chairman. 'We disagreed with
his approach to disputes,' said Walter Beirne in his presidential
address to the 1952 annual conference of the CIU,[52] 'and felt
that the effectiveness of the court was impaired by the
manner in which many serious cases were handled. Nevertheless
it must be admitted that although in its experimental
stage, the court performed some very useful work, and if
there were failures there were also successes ...' It was
admitted without question that Mortished was quite independent
of government. Was this then the failure of an irascible
man who saw himself as having a responsibility not merely
for the case in hand, but in a primary way, for the whole
economic community, or was there a deeper failure relating
to the institution itself? Before attempting a view, let us
move on to 1956, when, in response to a request from Norton
as Minister for Industry and Commerce, both congresses submitted

considered views on the performance of the court. Under
Mortished, the court had been accused of standing on its
dignity, partly because it had refused to reopen cases on
which it had already recommended (and in subsequent voluntary
settlements had been occasionally made to look foolish for
its pains); it had also been accused of concerning itself
unduly with constraints which the public interest imposed.
Now under the less colourful handling of Martin Keady and
the dullness of economic decline these considerations
evaporated. The CIU saw the court as having a fair measure
of success;[53] and while it continued to emphasise that its
role must be a conciliatory one, at the same time - rather
in a contradictory manner - it criticised the court for
not taking the initiative in national wage talks, and
particularly in following trends already established
rather than making fair decisions in its own right - a
criticism which would urge on the court a very explicit judicial
rather than conciliatory role. But this latter idea of the
court's deciding itself what was right rather than following
trends which had already emerged was repeated independently
by the ITUC[54] and to that end they recommended that the court
should publish an analysis of the claims and the reasons on
which their recommendations were based. It seems clear that
the conciliation recommendation in the CIU document was largely
an echo of the past, and both congresses seemed anxious
that the court should pursue an independent judicial role.
This was in accordance with the act - at least to the extent
that the function should be a judicial one - since it distinguished very clearly between the judicial role of the court
(albeit its recommendations were not enforceable) and the
conciliation service under its auspices. However there are
extremes in this; Mortished, in order to give the court
status, made it too remote, too reliant on impressive procedure borrowed from the courts of law. This attempt at
legitimacy was clearly a failure. But what of the temptation
offered by the congresses - that the court should plough an

independent furrow - since in the view of the congresses,
clearly, the court had now slipped too far the other way?
We have no way of judging. Under the change of government
the recommendations evaporated, and the court continued on
its way. It is unlikely in any event that such legitimacy as
it had could extend to the initiating of new wage
relationships of a major kind, and we have seen in recent
times that this function is best fulfilled by a joint national
bargaining body (not a judicial one) such as the mployer-
Labour Conference. Equally of course, Mortished's dream of
a system of justiciable rights based on joint agreements
was clearly unacceptable at the time, and was not to be
revived until the present decade.

Thus was formed the character of the Labour Court as the
sixties knew it, a court that was modest in what it attempted
to do, helping where it could, deciding on cases in the light
of clearly developing events, and cautiously providing,
in these circumstances, only the briefest of reports. It is
possible that institutionally it did not possess any greater
legitimacy than that, however forceful its officers might
wish to be, and this, as much as anything else, may have
been the reason for Mortished's failure.

As a footnote to our discussion on bargaining institutions,
let us look at the scheme of conciliation and arbitration
within the civil service. This was a system which turned on
the acceptance by both parties of the decision of an independent chairman; further the scheme was a procedural rather
than a substantive one, the disputes arising within it therefore
being more disputes that represented a conflict of interests
than any vindication of rights. In such circumstances one
would have expected to find an institution of fragile
acceptability. In fact the contrary was the case; the
decisions of this one man - this independent chairman - were
given, during the period we speak of, a considerable sense
of finality, even of sanctity, much in contrast with the
Labour Court. It is interesting to explore why this should

have been so. In the first place the civil service scheme
of conciliation and arbitration was not so much offered to
the civil servants as won by them from the government after
much pressure and much anxiety. Civil servants had always
accepted as axiomatic that they could not use trade union
pressure and their claims had been treated down through the
years with a casual indifference. Further, as we have
seen, they were excluded from the ambit of the Labour Court,
by section 4 of the 1946 act. A scheme such as was introduced in 1950 therefore represented not an alternative
bargaining system but a devastating change of fortune to
which they responded wholeheartedly. Secondly, reflecting
civil service traditions, submissions were made, certainly
at arbitration level, in a most extensive, indeed almost
in a baroque, manner, the employees taking a number of days
to make their initial presentation with a wealth of supporting
appendices, and the state side (or the official side as it
was called) replying in a like manner. There was little
of the exploration of the situation which would be common
under a conciliator and which would normally help in
arriving at an acceptable solution; instead the chairman
was expected to come to a conclusion on the basis of the
evidence submitted, which some considered, by reason of its
sheer weight and comprehensiveness, almost to oblige a
correct decision; otherwise of course, the vast amount of
cooperative work that went into the preparation of a claim
would have been all quite irrelevant. Thirdly, unlike the
chairman of the Labour Court, the civil service arbitration
board chairman was appointed for one year only, on the joint
nomination of the staff and the state, and if a chairman
showed himself to be unsympathetic to staff views
it was possible to wait for better days. Finally, however,
there was one event which seemed to seal the legitimacy of
the scheme in the eyes of the staff.[55] The first general
award of the civil service arbitration board was made in
January 1951, in accordance with the general third round
movement, but as we have seen the cost of living rose
alarmingly in the months that followed, and in November 1952,

the arbitration board on the application of the staff
associations made a further award which they conveyed to
the government. It was not until February 1953 that the
Minister for Finance published its terms, and in the meantime,
the civil servants who knew that an award had been made,
who did not know what it was but who now feared the worst,
seethed with impatience. The government, in accordance
with the conciliation and arbitration agreement, could vary
or reject an arbitration award in the public interest by
seeking parliament's approval, and in February they said
that they would give their view on what should be done when
the Budget came to be considered. The civil servants were
outraged, claiming that the whole substance of independent
arbitration had been put in question, and there were marches
and demonstrations of a quite unparalleled kind. In the
event the government decided to implement the increase from
April 1953 rather than the recommended November 1952, a
decision that was remedied when the second interparty
government took office in 1954. This of course was very
satisfactory for the civil service associations, but there
was a consequence: since they had insisted so powerfully
on the sanctity of arbitration awards, they committed themselves to the principle as well in a very considerable way.

The two systems therefore, that of the Labour Court and that
of the civil service, were greatly contrasting in character,
deriving from two quite different cultural traditions; in
the years that followed, and particularly in the nineteen
seventies, there were in some large state companies a
mingling of the two systems, in an attempt to gain some of
the legitimacy of both.

We should remark in passing on this dilemma of the government's
in the matter of public service pay, where it is, at one and
the same time, a guardian of the public interest and a
substantial employer of labour. This was the problem that
troubled de Valera in 1947 and probably can be met only by
the government distinguishing explicitly and institutionally

between its two roles. But this is easier said than done.
It too was a dilemma which became prominent in the nineteen
seventies, where while the government, as an employer merely,
could be represented on the Employer-Labour Conference, its
role as the ultimate guardian of the public interest became
somewhat uncertain.

There is one final point to be made, a point of considerable
importance in the development of trade union structures.
The civil servants found themselves represented by a vast
number of associations, some quite tiny and specialised,
which at first sight presented a difficult and complex
negotiating picture. In fact as things turned out, there
was little need for any restructuring. The bargaining
system, the scheme of conciliation and arbitration, by
providing staff side councils at departmental level and at
the level of the civil service as a whole, made the multiplicity of associations of little real significance.

-ii-

Let us come then to the third and last aspect of our discussion on the state and trade unions, the relationship
to them of the government, the executive. It is a relationship
which, as we anticipated, we have explored to a considerable
extent already. We consider first the objectives of the
trade unions in such a relationship, and certainly in the
years after the war these objectives were indeed modest,
and sprang essentially from the pressures of the time, rather
than from any doctrinaire view of society. Inflation brought
claims for increased wages of course, but when the trade
unions saw the government in the crisis of the late forties[56]
they looked as much to a control of prices as to an increase

in wages to meet the problem. They recognised that rapidly
increasing prices led not only to inequity and unrest,
but to unemployment as well; and later, during the fifties
in particular, they were to add to their programme a pressure
for economic development and increased productivity,
recognising that such increased productivity was a condition
of increased wages, and that therefore prices, wages and
productivity were all linked.

As for the implementation of such policies, trade union
imagination, in the years immediately after the war, did not
extend to the idea of worker participation in management as
it is now envisaged, although a motion to this effect was
proposed at the 1949 annual conference of the ITUC by the
redoubtable John Swift.[57]   Instead, as far as private industry
was concerned, they had a practical interest at three levels.
Firstly, they wanted to be consulted at works level where
the fashionable and somewhat mechanical systems of work
study were being introduced - a development to which they
were vulnerable because of their espousing of increased
production;[58]   secondly they wanted to be involved in consultative committees at industry level in order to promote
economic development;[59] and thirdly they wanted to participate
in the various councils which they considered the government
should establish with the same end in view, bodies such as
the Industrial Development Authority for example.[60]   None of
this was very radical and by the end of the fifties there
were prominent trade union leaders on such bodies as the
Irish Tourist Board,[61] the Income Tax Commission and the
Capital Investment Advisory Committee.[62]   In the case of the
public sector, the state companies in particular, they
sought as a matter of policy that 'a person with active
trade union experience' should be appointed to the boards;[63]
and the government found no difficulty in this. For example,
Roberts was appointed to the Board of the Sugar Company,
and Gerry Doyle to the board of Aer Rianta.

There was no question however of the trade unions nominating
directly to such boards, and the election of an employee
would have struck most people at the time as being very
implausible. The Minister retained his discretion in the
matter.

Such then were the objectives of the trade unions. As far
as the government was concerned, trade unions at best
were always something of a headache, but both Fianna Fail
and the interparty governments were, as we have seen,
determined on a programme of cooperation. Lemass, however,
seemed to have something more ambitious in mind. In setting
up the Labour Court in 1946, he envisaged a situation where
a national wage policy would spring naturally from the trade
unions' own awareness of the economic realities - and this
of course was a considerable legitimating factor in the
case of the Labour Court: 'I expressed the view', he said
in Dail Eireann,[64] 'that a national wages policy must emerge
as a result of agreement and cannot possibly be established
by means of compulsion. The Government will not be powerless.
As I pointed out, through its tariff policy, through its
price control measures, and by various devices including
exhortation and criticism, it will be able to influence
the views of others and the general trend of wage policy. But
in the long run that must come as a result of a wider
understanding of the national interest, and in particular
of the interests of the workers in relation to economic
development.' But if trade unions were to grow in economic
awareness, it could only be by their being involved in the
plans for economic development; and it was these ideas
that he developed further in the difficult autumn of 1947. He
was always wary of the impracticality of price control and
instead he envisaged a system of price surveillance; but
this he linked with the idea of industrial development and
the role of the trade unions in it. As we have seen,[65]
the Industrial Efficiency and Prices Bill,[66] which was introduced
in September 1947, proposed to establish a prices commission,

with powers much wider than its name might imply. The
commission would, after inquiry, recommend price control
orders and similar constraints; but also it could inquire
into restrictive practices and into the state of efficiency
of protected industries. The key point however was part VI
of the bill where, in a manner similar to the Industrial
Organisation and Development Act in the United Kingdom, it
provided for the establishment of development councils for
industry to consist of manufacturers and workers together
with independent persons. All this died with the government
when they went out of office in 1948; and Morrissey of
the interparty government was unmoved by trade union pleas
to revive it. Even when Lemass returned to office in 1951,
he chose not to continue with the idea in view of its
unpopularity among employers. Nevertheless, we can see in
all this the seeds of Lemass's approach to economic planning
by means of participative institutions which was so
characteristic of the sixties.

And what impact had all this on trade union structures? When
we consider the relationship between the trade unions and
the state in all its aspects, we recognise the great
significance of the Supreme Court decisions, both in the
NUR case and also in the case of the Educational Company v.
Fitzpatrick. These inhibited greatly any structural reform
of a radical kind not only by way of statute but even by way of
vigorous action on the part of the trade union itself in
building large integrated units. There were some who would
see in this a guarantee of the virtue of democracy; but
there is little doubt that it preserved the ICTU as an all-
Ireland centre when effective reform would almost certainly
have threatened it with partition.

The structure of the trade union movement therefore, as the
sixties opened, was a fragile and complex one, quite
unfitted to the task ahead, despite the sincerity and

goodwill of the leadership. In the years of great stress
that followed, it looked at times to be weak and inadequate;
and Lemass who had hoped, perhaps a little idealistically,
for some form of fruitful partnership, asked eventually,
not without bitterness, if there was any real prospect of
national agreements being fulfilled and national expansion
made possible.[67]

Notes on Chapter Thirteen

1. Lloyd op.cit. p.32:'laws are legitimate ... if they
    are enacted, and an enactment is legitimate if it
    conforms to those rules which prescribe procedures
    to be followed ...' He does not go as far as Weber
    who 'says that this circularity is intentional in
    order to allow for a belief in legitimacy divorced
    from any particular ideals or value judgements.'

2. Kelly op.cit. p.16.

3. idem. p.19.

4. op.cit. p.47.

5. Eugen Ehrlich: Fundamental Principles of the Sociology
    of Law: tr. Walter L. Moll: 1936: chapter XXI.

6. Such a view was expressed by Vincent Grogan, then
    parliamentary draftsman to the government, and quoted
    by Professor Kelly op.cit. p.41. But if Vincent
    Grogan's formulation is somewhat too theoretical, it
    is true on the other hand that the law, regarded as a
    matter of traditional and concrete consensus without
    any more objective validity, would not have been generally
    acceptable. Bishop Michael Browne, who had been chairman
    of the Commission on Vocational Organisation, speaking
    at the 1951 CIU Annual Conference (p.37.) said in
    regard to free trade unions: 'While the state may claim
    the right to regulate and control unions, if it be
    necessary in the public interest... the state cannot
    claim the right to create and to annul Unions or other
    Associations. It is this doctrine of natural rights
    that is very fundamental in our philosophy and in our
    outlook, particularly at the present day when the whole
    concept of liberty is so much attacked ... it is a
    strange thing that even in this country we can still
    find Acts coming on our Statute Book which reveal
    the totalitarian outlook ... that all rights are
    derived from the state, that what the state gives
    it can withdraw ... Some people think that nowadays
    liberty has a value of a secondary order, that liberty
    without well-being is of no use, and that if there be
    a choice between liberty and well-being, then well-being
    and security should be preferred...' Dr Browne saw -
    perceptively, of course - that a tendency to totalitarianism
    exists in bureaucracies in any event, almost by their
    nature, and that quite apart from day-to-day political
    influences on any government, the practice of
    administration itself made de Valera's notion of the
    government through parliament always expressing the
    will of the people a highly suspect one. He therefore

looked to a natural law which validated associations
in their own right, so that they did not ground their
existence on some positive law, creating no doubt
a strong presumption regarding their legal personality
as well (cf. Lloyd op.cit. p.302.) This has a
significance for the general idea of a consensus (see
p.427 above) which must operate within a frame of right
which is independent of it; and a just state regulating
trade unions such as we discussed earlier (see p.506
above) must be seen as not merely a consensual state
which de Valera's expression of the national will
might lead to. Perhaps this is bringing de Valera's
constitutional position too far. The Constitution is
dedicated - with intent - to the Most Holy Trinity,
which implies an objective morality; and the national
will must be seen within that context. Equally a
desire to devise systéms that are sensitive to the
consensus can also be seen within the same objective
framework of morality. There is a final point.
Perhaps this very pluralist approach by Bishop Browne
might appear odd in view of the tendencies towards
corporatism in the Report of the Commission on
Vocational Organisation; but we must remember that
there was, in these reforming years in social security,
a general desire on the part of the Church to limit
state ambitions in the interests of Church institutions.

7.   He considered combinations injurious but not local
       trades associations: cf. Clarkson op.cit.

8.   Dail Debates October 15 1947 cols. 389-390.

9.   ITUC 1952 p.35.

10.   Dail Debates July 9 1946 col.420. De Valera's concern
       extended even to the private sector when it provided
       essential services. He informed the Congress of Irish
       unions in the summer of 1947 that 'a stoppage of work
       in the flour-milling industry would be considered a
       national emergency and that the Government would take
       steps to declare such a strike illegal.' (CIU 1947 p.23).

11.   See p.246 above.

12.   p.511 above.

13.   The trade union acts of the period are: the act of 1935
       which concerned trade unions and land holding; the
       acts of 1941 and 1942 (see p.202 above); the act of
       1947 concerning deposits and the act of 1952 which
       also concerned deposits. For a discussion on the acts
       of 1871 and 1876 see p.131 above. See also among
       Johnson papers a paper by R.J.P. Mortished entitled
       'Irish Trade Union Law', being based on a lecture he
       delivered to a course organised by the Civics Institute
       in November 1951.

14. p.378 above.

15. CIU 1947 p.53.

16. McCarthy: The Decade of Upheaval 1973 pp.90, 113.

17. O. Kahn-Freund: "Trade Unions, the Law and Society"
     in Modern Law Review Vol.XXXIII, no.3, May 1970, p.241.

18. Royal Commission on Trade Unions and Employers'
     Associations 1965-1968 Cmnd.3623 1968.

19. p.233 above.

20. p.378 above.

21. Lloyd op.cit. p.333.

22. See Mortished: "The Industrial Relations Act 1946 Journal
     of the Statistical and Social Inquiry Society of
     Ireland 1947 Vol.XVII p.681. The Labour Court as it
     eventually emerged in 1946 was anticipated to quite
     an extent in a resolution moved in the 1945 CIU
     Annual Conference by Tom Kennedy (CIU 1945 p.62).

23. p.245 above.

24. cf. Mortished: Journal of the Statistical and Social
     Inquiry Society of Ireland op.cit; see also
     Commission on Vocational Organisation 1943 p.368,
     par. 586 ff. The principal act of 1946 was followed
     by an act of 1955 (which incidentally dealt with local
     government employees) and an act of 1959; but these
     are not substantive. We deal here of course only
     with legislation enacted up to 1960.

25. Dail Debates June 25 1946 col. 2282.

26. idem.

27. ibid. col. 2286.

28. idem.

29. ibid. 2288.

30. ibid.2289.

31. idem.

32. Industrial Relations Act: Section 20(4).

33. Dail Debates 16 July 1946: cols. 878, 922.

34. CIU 1950 p.62.

35. Dail Debates 16 July 1946 col. 863.

36. Dail Debates October 15 1947 col. 386.

37. ibid. col. 387.

38. ibid. 384 ff.

39. See p.383 above.

40. CIU 1948 p.12; ITUC 1948 p.25.

41. ITUC 1948 p.25.

42. ITUC 1948 p.30. For text see ITUC 1948 p.64.

43. ITUC 1948 p.30; p.67.

44. McCarthy and Ellis: Management by Agreement 1973 p.41.

45. Mortished op.cit. p.683.

46. ITUC 1951 p.59.

47. ITUC 1951 p.25; CIU 1951 p.10.

48. For the text see CIU 1952 p.18.

49. CIU 1950 p.61.

50. CIU 1950 p.66.

51. CIU 1952 p.11.

52. CIU 1952 p.47.

53. CIU 1956 p.14.

54. ITUC 1956 p.36.

55. ITUC 1953 p.33; p.95.

56. e.g. CIU 1948 p.56.

57. ITUC 1949 p.97.

58. CIU 1949 p.94; ITUC 1949 p.57 where is set out the text of a very comprehensive submission.

59. ITUC 1949 p.57.

60. CIU 1949 p.17.

61. ITUC 1957 p.39.

62. idem.

63. PUO Third Report p.18.

64. Dail Debates June 25 1946 Col.2366.

65. p.383 above.

66. ITUC 1948 p.39.

67. McCarthy: The Decade of Upheaval op.cit. p.86.

Chapter Fourteen

Linking Ahead

-i-

One can rest on the year 1960 as if it were a platform,
viewing on the one hand the manner in which our institutions were shaped in the years that had passed up to then,
but conscious at the same time of the great upheaval in the
decade and a half that followed, where in the north, after
a period of early promise under O'Neill's premiership, there
developed the demonic violence of recent times; and where
in the south there was the upsurge of the years of development,
striking at the crusted ways of the past, reaching their
climax of industrial turmoil in the maintenance dispute of
1969[1] and moving to the calmer but more complex problems of
the early seventies.

In the year 1960 as well, the trade union movement had
developed the structural shape, broadly speaking, that it
possesses today. The marks of its history lay heavy upon it,
its birth in a political society quite different from our
own, its development through years of great political change,
where the forces of nationalism, religion and political
tribalism all obliged it to different forms, its concern
throughout with its view of itself as, somehow or other, a
single integrated movement, which even in the darkest years
dominated trade union thinking. But when we try to evaluate
all this in the great watershed year of 1960 there is a
danger that we may be tempted to view it all as insiders,

as those who have journeyed with the trade unions throughout
the long years, and consequently less likely to see it all
with sufficient objectivity. And because of that, I have
chosen as an aid to such objectivity a view of trade unions
and society which was set out in the very last article[2]
written before his death by the grand old man of nascent
and dying civilisations, Arnold Toynbee. It is not a
particularly good article as such articles go, but it has
breadth and a sense of history - as indeed one should expect -
and by following it briefly as a guide, some of our concern
for objectivity may be achieved. The article was written
in October 1975 when the British government and the TUC were
struggling to formulate some general consensus on wage
increases which they ambitiously - and of course quite in-
accurately - described as a social contract. Toynbee saw it
as a bargaining between two sovereign powers in the community,
the government and the trade unions - because once the
government conceded the right to bargain at this level to
the trade unions, in Toynbee's opinion they also conceded
their sovereignty - with the implication of a radical
challenge to the supremacy of parliament within a democratic
state. Taking this as his theme, he drew two parallels with
time past, the first - a rather strained one perhaps - was
that of the Russian naval ratings, soldiers and peasants,
who, under Lenin's leadership, 'overthrew the Tsardom and
then challenged Lenin himself' only to be savagely suppressed.
'The same arts that did gain,' said Toynbee quoting Andrew
Marvell, 'a power, must it maintain.' The second parallel
he suggested was that of the plebs and patricians of post-
Tarquinian Rome, where the society of the time, ruled as it
was by an oligarchy, developed a state within a state -
imperium in imperio - which Toynbee saw as the counterpart
of the TUC, and the tribunes of the plebs as the Len Murrays
and Jack Joneses of their day. The plebs however worked
within a constitutional framework, engaged in secessions
(which corresponded to general strikes), and then saw their

leaders - because, although they represented manual workers, they were not themselves manual workers but rather men of professional negotiating skill - merge into the establishment, not only resolving the conflict of sovereign powers, but becoming the establishment's 'most effective constitutional agents for keeping the mass of the plebs under control.'

In summary then Toynbee's proposition would seem to be that the trade unions - organisations of manual workers as he understood it - form a separate imperium which can bargain with the government, thereby threatening its sovereignty, a threat which can be resolved either in the Russian manner, by a revolution leading to a destruction of the forces of the revolution by a new oligarchy, or by the domesticating of the revolutionary leadership within the establishment. Modestly, he suggested that there might be a third - unforseeable - way in which the problem could be resolved, which 'might be either less unpleasant or more unpleasant than either the Roman way or the Russian way...' The first way could conceivably have been the manner in which Connolly's syndicalism might have developed, although one must recognise that the violent suppression of the popular will by the revolutionary oligarchy in the aftermath of an autocratic Tsardom, would not necessarily occur in other societies. But this for our time and for our country is probably too speculative to be pursued seriously; and we must turn instead to Toynbee's other parallel of the plebs and the patricians, and the manner in which their crisis found resolution.

Let us explore first the notion of the imperium in imperio; and at the outset we must ask to what extent a government is sovereign within its own state in the sense in which Toynbee understood it. Power and authority - as we have come to recognise only too clearly - take many forms and are by no means confined, in an open society, to those who can physically coerce as a government ultimately is entitled to do. In

Ireland, in the society of the south, there was always the
Roman Catholic Church, whose view on matters within its
province was devastatingly powerful, bringing a government
to its knees as late as the nineteen fifties. And it is not
good enough to dismiss this as evidence of archaism in an
undeveloped democracy. The church was influential not
because it functioned as an oligarchy or the comforter and
supporter of an oligarchy (as it has done in many countries
in the past) but because its views and opinions were sanctioned
as legitimate by the democratic will.

There are circumstances then in which the democratic will can
express itself in political matters other than through
parliament and government; and perhaps it is necessary that
it should be so because of the role of parliament, certainly
in this country, where the ideal of decision-making on the
basis of open parliamentary debate no longer exists (if it
ever did), and where, on the contrary, the government determines
what should be done, largely in accordance with a general
programme which has been endorsed by the people by way of
general election, availing of parliament for the debate and
explication of the issues but in general quite confident
of the decision because of the system of tied or party voting.[3]
Nor is the party's general programme generated primarily within
the parliamentary structure, but rather by political feel,
by numerous grass-roots meetings and by the fruitful inter-
action of the public media, all of which is tested by the
occasional by-election and ultimately by a general election.
Modern democracy in this country therefore, despite certain
procedural expectations, is much more a popular democracy
than a parliamentary one. That of course is not necessarily
a bad thing, but it requires in turn that the people at large
should have a wide acquaintanceship with the issues involved.
At the same time, the business of government is in many
respects becoming both more centralised and more expert,
which makes popular decision-making doubly difficult, Indeed
when one takes account of the range of technical expertise

necessary to make policy decisions in a modern society, one
must recognise that the danger really lies, more than anything
else, in the undue sovereignty of the expert bureaucracy.
Modern democratic societies such as ours, with a tradition
of open government, have attempted to meet the problem –
not without great heart-searching and at times doubtful
commitment – by establishing expert bodies of considerable
influence, who, while not invading the right of the government
ultimately to decide, can challenge their judgements in public.

An early example of this was the Central Bank which, while
exercising more the role of a conservative guardian of the
currency than that of a political pathfinder, nevertheless
hung on grimly in the early fifties to its function of
independent and public comment despite maledictions flung
at its head by prominent public representatives such as
Sean MacBride and James Dillon[4] and survived[4A] to consolidate
such a role and see it respected, although frequently dis-
liked, in modern times. The outstanding example of such a
body in the sixties was the National Industrial Economic
Council, and its successor in the seventies, the more broadly-
based National Economic and Social Council. Some may urge
that this too is what trade unions and other similar
representative organisations do, providing a means by which
the consensus can be better understood and the sovereignty
of the bureaucrat circumscribed. But it is likely enough
that Toynbee would have drawn a distinction here between a
body which, by reason of its wisdom and expertise, is persuasive –
but leaving the government the ultimate decisive role – and
one which, by its economic or social power, can, whether it
is wise or not, coerce a government to its point of view.
Such a body, he might claim, is a trade union, and it is in
that sense an _imperium_. What can we say of this?

There are some who see modern political societies in any event
in such a pluralist fashion that they would challenge the
very notion of sovereignty, seeing the task of government
instead as primarily an attempt to hold some reasonable balance

between a number of stakeholders, some of national and
continuing significance in the economic field such as
representatives of industry, trade unions and agriculture,
and some of influence in certain specialised areas, such as
the church in the fields of education and health. In such
a view, Toynbee's account would seem to give an exaggerated
importance to the trade unions, who would be seen as merely
one stakeholder, albeit a powerful one, among a number of
others, within a political system designed to permit them all
to engage in a bargaining process. But this view, while
containing much that is valuable, is somehow unsatisfactory,
because on the one hand there is inadequate recognition of the
fact that while the government does in a pluralist way bargain
with the economic and social stakeholders, there is also an
important sense in which in certain circumstances it is
ultimately sovereign; and, on the other hand, because this
view would appear to understate the importance of trade unions
in the special economic dilemmas that have confronted these
islands in the post-war years.

Let us, at this stage, attempt to distinguish between at
least three kinds of government-trade union conflicts so
that we can clarify the issue a little more. In the first
place there are direct conflicts between the government and
its own employees; and here we can see, certainly in the
case of de Valera during the forties and fifties, a very
sharp reluctance to concede to civil service unions or Congress,
on their behalf, any equality of bargaining power,[5]
excluding them from the Labour Court and regarding them as
being in dispute not with the government as an employer but
rather with the community as a whole. The interparty
governments of the period were not prepared to take such an
extreme view, but it is significant that even they - when
they did provide for civil servants in 1950[6] a scheme of
conciliation and arbitration - were careful to hedge it round
with parliamentary safeguards in the public interest. In the

years since 1960, people have come to distinguish more
clearly the role of the government as an employer and the
role of the government as the political sovereign, and even
if a strike of civil servants were now to take place, it
would not necessarily be regarded as a strike against the
community, but even today this is not a major problem and
is clearly not what Toynbee had in mind.

Secondly, there are those strikes which arise from straightforward classical disputes about wages and conditions but
which occur in an area of public significance. Such a strike
was threatened in the flour milling industry in 1947 when
de Valera warned that in the public interest he would declare
it illegal.[7] When a government became involved in such
disputes it was very much as a guardian of the public
interest by reason of the locus of the strike or the manner
of its conduct. The government itself was not primarily
under challenge; and it is significant that when solutions
were sought it was largely in the field of putting to rights
the conditions within the industry that led to the strike,
as for example in the case of Irish shipping in 1957 where
'a wave of disreputable and disgraceful incidents' brought
the Irish flag 'into utter disrepute in various parts of the
world';[8] or in a number of instances in the nineteen sixties
where commissions of inquiry were set up to report on disputes
in, for example, the Electricity Supply Board, Bord na Mona
and the banks.[9] It is true that some could speak of these
strikes in the sense in which Toynbee did, of a sovereign
imperium exercising its will, but it was very much more a
blundering about, an upsurge of protest which struck at the
public interest either in a subsidiary way, or in order to
force a decision which however was essentially domestic
in character, despite the public impact of the strike itself.

There is a third area of disputation; it occurs when a
national wage bargain is being struck, and this is no doubt
the area which Toynbee had in mind. In the Republic at least,
national wage bargaining is essentially a post-war phenomenon.

We meet it first in the economic crisis in the autumn of
1947[10] when, in a rather primitive and negative fashion,
the government asked the unions to limit their wage claims;
and if they failed to do so the government itself would
'produce proposals for legislation to the same effect.'
This at least was de Valera's position, but as we have seen[11]
Lemass attempted to convert this bleak ultimatum into an
imaginative prices and incomes proposal, in which trade
unions were to be offered virtual economic partnership both
at national level, and at the level of industry by means
of the Industrial Efficiency and Prices Bill.[12] While,
in the event, a wage bargain was made, the larger strategy
came to nothing, and when Lemass was pressed by the unions
to revive the idea in 1958 he refused to do so because of
employer resistance.

Here then lies the origin of the arrangement which is at the
centre of Toynbee's concern, but before attempting to identify
all its elements, let us bear in mind two further
considerations. Firstly, in the national agreements of those
early years, the trade union congresses held faithfully
to their obligations, giving notice of cesser when it was
required, and not moving until this was done; and secondly,
and in contrast to this concern for due process, the national
agreements were themselves often put under threat when individual unions or groups of union members attempted to break
out of the arrangement because of some domestic pressure -
for which, as we have seen, the trade union movement as a whole
would tend to be blamed.[13]

All this developed considerably, firstly in the sixties, and
later in a more sophisticated form in the seventies; but
the elements that were to make up the national pay arrangement
of 1964[14] had already appeared in the 1947-1948 endeavours.
Indeed it is arguable that the collapse of the 1964 agreement
two years later sprang from a misunderstanding, a misperception,
of what these elements really were; and further, that the

success of the national pay agreements from 1970 to 1975
was greatly aided by a clearer view of what was actually
involved. Let us consider what these elements were.

The paradigm broadly is as follows. We find a government
anxious for some form of order in the matter of wages, either
restraint in a period of recession or an equitable distribution
of the increment in a period of expansion. We find trade
unions somewhat ambiguous about such proposals, recognising
on the one hand the good sense of protecting and promoting
employment and fostering good order in industrial relations,
and conscious on the other hand of the perils to a free
system of bargaining which national settlements imply.

Nor is this reluctance where it occurs mere perversity; there
is an instinctive awareness that national bargains, although
providing equity, can also at times defeat equity, because
being centralised and simplified solutions they are by their
nature insensitive to the horde of domestic problems which
arise throughout employment. Trade union feeling therefore
regarding the propriety of a national bargain will tend to
sway a good deal from support to hostility. We find the
employers also somewhat ambiguous in their approach, happy
enough if, during a period of recession, restraint is secured,
but unhappy, during a period of expansion, about offering
substantial national increases and perhaps later finding
individual unions clamouring for more.

These then are the typical attitudes of the parties. We
next come to consider how the parties relate to one another
in the making of a national wage settlement. Wages and
salaries are negotiated not with the government but between
employers and trade unions. This is the basis of the
arrangement. The government, except in the case of its own
employees, is involved only indirectly. It is not an
immediate party to the settlement despite its prominence
as a guardian of the public interest. It is important to
recognise this while not discounting the significance of the

government's contribution. Furthermore, we must again
distinguish, for these purposes, between a period of economic
expansion and a period of recession. In the former case,
when good order is the major objective, the government's role
is much more obviously a subsidiary one. It can provide
machinery to facilitate bargaining as it did in 1946;[15] it
can indicate the kind of bargain that might be secured,
as it did in 1947,[16] before the prospect of a general election
removed it from the proceedings; it can powerfully foster
a national agreement as it was to do in 1963[17] and again in
March 1974; but ultimately it has to wait on the employers
and the trade unions to accommodate one another. This
remained the case in the seventies even though the government
took part, as an employer, in the negotiations which brought
the national agreements into being. In a period of recession,
however, the government's role as a party to the settlement
becomes more prominent, since now there is no detailed bargain
to be made as a rule, but merely an undertaking to exercise
restraint, which employers can do little to buy, but which
the government may be in a position to attract. We have
already seen an example of this in 1950.[18]

In November of that year the Congress of Irish Unions,[19]
having failed with the employers to secure a wage formula,
discussed with the government the general state of the
economy, ranging over prices, profits, taxes and social
benefits, and in the light of the difficulties of the time,
they decided to request their members to limit their wage
claims to 12/- a week. The present (1975) arrangement in the
United Kingdom,where a maximum of £6 a week has been set,
is a more developed form of the same idea, since the
arrangement with the government there is more explicit; in
the case of the CIU in 1950 there was no explicit approval or
disapproval by the government of the arrangement, although
it is clear enough that there was some understanding
regarding a tighter surveillance of price increases. Perhaps
the most developed form of this kind of arrangement occurred

here in the Republic in 1975, when on September 24 the
national pay agreement, which had been concluded the previous
April, was formally converted into an indexation arrangement[20]
without maxima or minima, in response to the government's
containment of prices by means of substantial subsidies.

It appears that it is in this area that Toynbee's remarks
are most relevant, that is to say, in the setting of
parameters of restraint in a period of recession. Perhaps
one can describe this kind of arrangement as a bargain;
although it could be more accurately described as some form
of general understanding; but if it is to be regarded as a
bargain, what is the nature of the offer which the trade
unions make? And when we discuss the nature of such an offer,
we can discuss it in the context of the broader theme,
recognising that it will not differ in character whether it
is made more directly to the government in a period of
recession, or more generally to the employers as part of a
national wage bargain.

In considering what a trade union offer means in such
circumstances, we can begin by distinguishing the national
bargaining situation from one that occurs directly between
an employer and the trade union representing his employees.
In such a case, the bargain is made in circumstances where
the trade union can support its claim ultimately with the
threat of industrial action, that is to say, of a strike
or some other act of a coercive kind. The first and most
important offer of a trade union official to an employer
therefore is one of agreement rather than dispute. But
this does not occur in the national bargaining context, and
here lies an essential difference. If national negotiations
fail, it is left to the unions to bargain each in its own
way; there is never a question of the congress urging the
sanction of industrial action, except in the negative sense
that the unions, left to themselves, might perforce engage in it.
There is some implication in Toynbee's article that the
unions can force a national bargain on a government by

threatening some form of nationally devised industrial
action - the parallel being the secessions of the plebs. This
has never been contemplated in this country, and is in fact
alien to the whole system.

Secondly, in a direct bargain between employer and trade
union, the trade union representative can, because of the
explicit nature of the bargain, offer to commit his members
to some quid pro quo, such as increased productivity, once
the proposal is clear and has been the subject of general
consent; and he can do so with quite considerable confidence
that the arrangement will be honoured. There is a similar
kind of commitment in a national bargain; indeed it is the
substance of the trade union offer, although it normally
takes the form of an undertaking of restraint, either in
regard to all claims, except those nationally agreed, or in
regard to certain types of claim. But we must be careful to
recognise that such a national commitment is by its nature
more fragile and more general in character. It is not of
course agreed by the representatives of the congress; rather
is it recommended by them to a special delegate conference
of all the unions in affiliation, and this is the body that
makes the decision. The early agreements, the 1948 agreement
for example, provided for either adherence or rejection by
each of the individual trade unions and employer groups,
the effect of recording a rejection being not quite clear.
In recent years however, it was clear that a majority decision
at the ICTU special delegate conference was deemed to bind all,
both dissenting members within consenting unions, and
dissenting unions within congress. And it could be taken
that dissent would always be substantial, since the bargains
had to be made tightly, often uncertainly balanced for long
periods between acceptance and rejection. Despite this,
apart from the débâcle of the 1964 agreement, agreements
on the whole survived well, both during the forties and
fifties, and in recent times. Nevertheless, it is important
to mark the characteristics of a breakdown when it does occur.
It is never initiated at national level, although events

may drive it there. It is more likely than not caused by
the onset of a turbulent problem of a domestic kind, such
as we have already discussed. We saw much of this during
the currency of the 1964 national agreement. It usually
found the trade union leadership as dismayed as the employers.
Already we have noticed in the national agreements up to
1960 the growth of a somewhat simplistic view by the employers
and sometimes by the government of the role of trade union
leaders in the matter of national agreements, as if in some
way they could command the commitment of their members.
This was to burgeon in the nineteen sixties, causing the
employers in times of stress to upbraid the trade union
leaders for their lack of control of their members, or,
in the alternative, of their downright bad faith, seeing a
national bargain in much the same way as one would see the
purchase and sale of a house. But it is clear that what we
are concerned with here after all is not a contract of
personal penalty and obligation, but rather a series of mutual
commitments of a quasi-political nature; and in such
circumstances some flexibility must be permitted, as the
agreements in the seventies were quick to recognise. It is
true that if one is confronted with a group of workers hell-
bent for personal reasons on some claim,irrespective
of any national agreement, one could conclude, as Toynbee
might, that the trade union movement is holding the nation up
to ransom and is bargaining as a sovereign. But those who
are hell-bent on breaking the arrangement are not those who
concluded it in the first place; nor would the national trade
union leaders ever use coercive power to bring it to an end,
any more than they would use it to bring it about.[21]

On two occasions now we have made the point that the trade
union representatives engaged in the making of a national
bargain would not coerce in the manner in which they would
at the level of a firm. Needless to say,this does not
spring from any virtue acquired by sitting on the executive
council of the congress, but springs from the nature of things.

Let us explore why this must be so.

We again attempt a distinction between a direct employer-
trade union bargain and a national agreement. The first
is essentially sectional in character, sectional in that
there is an interest distinguished and maintained almost
as against everyone else, and therefore in a dispute situation
this sectional interest can dominate quite readily most other
considerations. In order to appreciate this a little more
fully, let us return to the idea that we have already explored[22] —
that trade unions, political parties, mothers' meetings and
indeed the state itself are best understood as organising
not people but rather their roles in society, so that a trade
union, for example, will tend to organise men not in their
political role but in their role as employees. Almost by
definition, the different organisation of these roles implies
differences of attitude, as the same persons cast themselves
into one organisational frame or another; and these attitudes,
within the same person, may be in conflict, just as a man
employed in the Electricity Supply Board may, objectively
speaking, find his political role as a citizen in conflict
with his trade union role as a striker for higher pay. The
problem is usually resolved in a situational way, and in
particular, the intensity and immediacy of the problem
determines readily enough which role should be prominent.
In a vigorous dispute between an employer and his employees
therefore, it is not surprising to find the trade union role
the dominant one. Once however a national bargain is under
consideration, the sense of immediacy is much diminished
and so also is the vigorous sense of sectional defence. One
is almost speaking of a political act in which the whole
nation - or at least a very substantial part of it - is
involved; and consequently,while attitudes appropriate
to an employee role are still prominent, there is now a much
greater place for the moderating effect of the political
role, that is to say the attitudes appropriate to a citizen.

And this really is the heart of the matter, because it bears
on the nature of the trade union mandate. There is a
powerful suggestion at times that trade unions speak
unequivocally for a class of people which socially and
economically must be regarded as being quite apart from
the rest of society. Toynbee, in likening modern trade
unions to the plebs and in emphasising their character as
organisations of manual workers, saw their mandate in much
these terms. In fact we have seen in this study - certainly
in the case of the Republic, although the United Kingdom may
be somewhat different - a steady development away from such
a notion of class-separateness. E.L. Richardson in the very
early years of the century could validly speak for the trades
of Dublin; and later Larkin could speak for the labourer
and the socially bereft. Connolly always saw trade unions in
class terms, and this view we find still strongly expressed
in the nineteen forties in the WUI submission to the
Commission on Vocational Organisation.[23] It is still a
traditional trade union stance, and for certain unions at
certain times it has still its old validity, but there were
a number of powerful forces in the south which tended to
fragment such a view of society. Firstly, there was the
influence of Labour's political aspirations, causing the
congress in the nineteen twenties to aspire as well to being
not only a political party but a national one, and therefore
reluctant to be locked within a class. The division of the
labour movement in the nineteen thirties, the decision that
the political wing and the trade union wing should each go
its own way, did something to resolve the ambiguity[24] but
there remained the strong emphasis that the key to
acceptability was a good trade union disposition rather than
membership of the working class. Secondly the powerful
chauvinist impulse of the forties and fifties, which, in the
south, put the nation first and the working class in a
subsidiary role within it, also diminished the significance
of class representation as such. Indeed there are those who
would say, perhaps with some truth, that the revolution in
Ireland in the years 1919 to 1921 was not merely a nationalist

revolution, but, in the nature of things, a proletarian
revolution as well. Thirdly, and in recent years most
importantly, there was the growth in number and influence of
white-collar unions within the trade union movement. We
can see readily enough the popularity of congress for white-
collar unions, particularly when, by the early sixties, the
Irish Conference of Professional and Service Associations[25]
had failed to establish an alternative white-collar trade
union centre. It is difficult to estimate the extent of the
growth of white-collar membership. One can say that by 1970
white-collar unions represented almost 23 per cent of
total union membership[26] but, as Aidan Kelly remarked,[27]
'there are many white-collar workers who are members of general
and other unions, and taking account of these, it is estimated
that total white-collar membership as a percentage of total
union membership is approximately 33 per cent.'[28] Toynbee's
parallel of a manual class is therefore quite inappropriate.
We have recognised of course that some unions do speak
for their members in a vigorous sectional way which has
strong overtones of class, but usually in regard to certain
issues at certain times. But it would be somewhat difficult
to claim that they normally speak in a settled and continuous
way as representative, for a variety of political and social
purposes, of a particular class or group; rather do they
speak in response to some deeply-felt but transitory issue.
But the subject is a difficult one, and we shall return to it
in a later paragraph. The real point in the present
discussion however is not the nature of the mandate given
to a trade union but the mandate possessed by the central trade
union organisation, by the congress, when it comes to the
national bargaining table. The fact is - and it knows it
very well - that it represents not so much a special group
or class within society but rather one important aspect of
a complex pattern of interests. This is why it has no real
mandate for industrial action - even if it wished to use it.
Having said that however, we must recognise as well that trade
union leaders, engaged in national bargaining, exercise

considerable influence, but it is the influence not of coercion but of democratic leadership largely in the manner which we have earlier attempted to describe.[29]

This then is our paradigm in the matter of national bargaining, quite distant from Toynbee's it must be said, and close enough in all conscience to the idea of an influential and independent expert body, which can challenge the judgement of the government but never invade its right to decide.

-ii-

Having, however, limited the concept in this way, we must nonetheless accept that trade unions are a significant force in certain highly important areas of government. Let us consider Toynbee's second point therefore, his expectation that in a manner similar to that of the tribunes of the plebs, the leaders would become domesticated as members of the establishment.

There is little doubt that Lemass had such an idea in mind when as early as 1945 he had urged that 'in a democratic State, the Trade Union Movement must play an increasingly important part in the national life, not merely as a guardian of the workers' interests, but as an essential part of the machinery of industrial organisation, accepting the responsibilities which relate to its real power, and proceeding from the stage of negotiating particular agreements with private employers to the stage of formulating and carrying into effect a general policy for the furtherance of the long-term interests of the workers as a class.'[30] He wished to view the unions not as adversaries to be bargained with but rather, in the national context, as partners in an economic and social enterprise. He attempted something of this, as we have seen, in 1947[31] but it was to become abundantly

clear as a policy when Lemass, in June 1959, entered on his
seven heady expansionary years as Taoiseach, and when he
attempted to catch the whole nation into a vast cooperative
endeavour.

The employers too - although hostile to the 1947 proposals
for development councils - nevertheless by 1959 had
cautiously joined in the formation of the Irish National
Productivity Committee[32] which, usually in the late autumn
of the year, promoted joint economic discussions in the
drafty acres of a deserted holiday camp. Even more
significantly they were to join with the trade unions in a
bipartite council, in 1961, the first Employer-Labour
Conference (which soon came to grief) and also in the tri-
partite Committee on Industrial Organisation, established
because of the challenge of the Common Market which was then
in the air.[33] All this was to lead up to the National Industrial
Economic Council which came into being two years later.

The trade unions took part fully in all this. Indeed in
large measure they had sought it. But they had misgivings.
There was a fundamental dilemma here. As long as a trade
union performed the role of an adversary (a civilised one,
let us concede for the purposes of the discussion) its members
could be confident that their views would be adequately
expressed. This was the function of the trade union and the
function was clear. However, the more a trade union
entered into a partnership with management, with the employer
(and let us take it at this level first, and discuss the
government level in a moment) the more confused would its
role be to its members, the more questionable would be its
legitimacy to speak on their behalf, and the more likely
would its members be to reject it, perhaps to the extreme
of unofficial action.[34] Indeed this is part of the difficulty
that lies currently behind certain juridical proposals for
the introduction of worker participation in the management
of industry. The dilemma might find a resolution in the kind

of institutions which were created for the purpose;
one could contemplate for example institutions that were
essentially consultative in character and which in no sense
could impose joint responsibility for strategic decisions.
What haunted trade unions was the fear of being trapped
into some agreement with management on wage restraint
or, worse, on redundancy.   Productivity committees met their
requirements well enough and were fostered by them, but the
proposals for development councils in the sixties (despite
the earlier support) foundered, although the failure there
must be attributed to other reasons as well.[35]

And what can we say of partnership at the national level,
where the employers are represented in a nationally
organised economic interest and where the government is
involved as well?   The situation is certainly quite
different, being much more broadly political in character;
furthermore, the trade unions are strongly impelled towards
such arrangements because of their concern with a policy
of secure and expanding employment no less than with higher
incomes.   But the dilemma, while not being as acute, still
remains to trouble one, particularly in the field of
national bargaining on pay, where the legitimacy of the trade
union centre in the eyes of the movement as a whole is of
the first importance.   The problem really lies in how far
such developments should be permitted to grow if they are
not to endanger the trade unions' legitimacy as representative
of quite distinct and at times quite contrary interests.

It is here that the nature of the trade union interest again
becomes significant, that is to say, whether it is seen
primarily as a question of class, or primarily as a question
of the special economic concern of those who happen to be
organised employees, irrespective of the nature of their
background or their employment.

We have already spoken of the steady development within the
trade union movement away from the notion of class-separateness,

at least in this country. We must now examine this phenomenon
a little more closely. One is very conscious of how
difficult the topic is, since the notion of class differs
so much from one society to another in its quality as an
idea and in the manner in which it is understood. But since
we must make some attempt - however difficult it may be -
to describe the manner in which such ideas had evolved by
1960, we shall venture a view on how two prominent trade
union officials saw the problem, two trade union leaders
who dominated the movement of the south during the fifties -
and also during the sixties - John Conroy and Jim Larkin, junior.

Both men saw themselves as class leaders essentially, and
only in that context as representatives of an economic
interest. They welcomed the advent of white-collar
unionism, and they welcomed the officials from such unions
who became prominent in the movement, but they welcomed them
as allies of the working class, and (certainly as far as
Conroy was concerned) not as harbingers of change within the
movement itself. Conroy also continuously sought the
recruitment to the Transport Union of well-educated and able
men, but he had no doubt that his union was necessarily an
expression of the working class, and this remained the case,
despite the substantial recruitment of white-collar workers.
Larkin's position was somewhat more complex. His union had,
in the fifties and sixties, developed strongly in certain
public employments, some of which were quite advanced
technologically, and he must have been very conscious of the
class shift. Perhaps his political hope in an ultimate
socialist solution in society made this development acceptable.
In any event, he carefully cultivated the professional,
technical and clerical workers within his union. But on the
other hand - and he was noteworthy in this - he showed a
marked reluctance to becoming too involved in Lemass's
adventures in partnership, distinguishing carefully, at
national level now, between consultative or bargaining
institutions which he welcomed, and on the other hand, those

institutions which implied co-responsibility, at which he
demurred. It was he who proposed and had carried the
withdrawal of Congress from the Employer-Labour Conference
in 1962.[36] He attended NIEC meetings in the sixties only
occasionally, and in a rather defensive way, and he showed
little enthusiasm for the experiments in national incomes
planning which so preoccupied the thinking of those years.
He was condemnatory of the Irish Conference of Professional
and Service Associations, refusing to agree to any
relationship between it and the ICTU,[37] but his opposition
appeared to be based not so much on class considerations as
on the awkward fact that the ICPSA included among its members
the County and City Managers' Association who technically
of course were employees but who in practice were the real
employers of staff under the local authorities. In a word,
he was extremely sensitive to the need for the trade unions
to continue to express an adversary role. But it is a
complex matter. His deeply-felt socialism could also have
led him on the same path - to a reluctance to cooperate in
a system which basically he saw as corrupt. Conroy on the
other hand - characteristically a much more open and cooperative man - was willing to bring the idea of joint
endeavour as far as he reasonably could, and spent a great
deal of time at NIEC and similar meetings. But he did so as
a working-class leader, and when in the dark days of 1968[38]
he found his members restless and rebellious of his leadership, he responded with a speech of great vituperation
against the capitalist and against the establishment in
Irish society.

We have still not come fully to terms with the nature of
trade unions, and one suspects that notions of class and
notions of economic interest while helpful are somewhat
crude for our purpose. Before exploring these ideas further
however, we should perhaps make use of them in venturing
some generalisations. In the first place, both those who
see the trade unions as primarily representing an economic

interest, (and this we must also understand in the warm
collegiate context of protection in the job), and those
who see them as primarily class-centred, instinctively take
care that they should not lose their legitimacy by
abandoning their adversary role in favour of one of joint
economic management. But it appears that those who are
most confident of their class role may also be more likely,
because of this confidence, to cooperate positively in
national matters. Certainly this was the case with the
Congress of Irish Unions in the years from 1946 to 1959;
and in contrast with the ITUC, with its penumbra of public
service unions, it might be argued that it was on the whole
a more working-class congress - but the point is at best
a fragile one, and cannot be pushed too far, since account
must be taken as well of the strongly nationalist character
of the CIU at this time. On the other hand, when we come
to those who see trade unions as representing primarily an
economic interest we find that when they do cooperate, they
tend, on the whole, to be sophisticated, watchful and negative,
reflecting the expectations of members who have joined
unions for very specific economic purposes, and who, if they
wished to cooperate in some national plan, would seek to do
so through other organisations.

How then should we evaluate what Toynbee has said? In the
Republic of Ireland[39] at least, the trade union leaders,
the tribunes of the plebs, could not be said to have been
domesticated in advance of their cohorts. If one were to
view them as representing merely an economic interest, then
their members were if anything more imperative in their
demands for a clear adversary role[40] and if one were to view
them as class leaders then it would appear that certainly
up to 1960 (and to quite an extent since then) they were
slower than their members to abandon the notion of class
representation; it was as if the trade union movement were
changing around them more rapidly than they themselves were
prepared to change, so that the vocabulary of class
differentiation, the talk of workers' rights and workers'

tribulations, the talk of capitalism and its evils, fell
more readily from their lips than it did from those who
made up the membership of their unions. Toynbee's dilemma
arose because he saw trade unions not only as essentially
class phenomena, but as essentially opposed to the
establishment in society and perhaps to society as a whole,
so that one was ultimately confronted either with the
destruction of their leadership or its domestication.
We can now see that this is a somewhat crude and superficial view. Nevertheless, we are still left with a question
regarding the nature of the trade union movement, a question
which so far we have failed to answer adequately - because
it is difficult to accept that perceptive men such as
Conroy and Larkin, when they spoke in the idiom of class,
were merely trapped by a kind of social archaism. We have
recognised, it is true, a movement away from the notion of
class-separateness, but not a movement away from trade
unionism, and a trade unionism at that which is manifestly
more significant than an organised economic interest. Class
is indeed an important part of it, its genesis in fact,
but it has implications which are greater than class, just
as socialism has, and these we shall attempt to explore
a little.

-iii-

What, firstly, can we say of the nature of the trade union
movement in the light of all that has been recounted here?
We have seen it as a powerful expression of a working-class
tradition which persisted despite the political upheavals
in the south, and the sectarian riots in the north, a
tradition which was described by the trade union leaders
themselves as international, but which to others[41] was better
understood as a common working-class tradition throughout
these islands. On the other hand we have seen it as a vehicle

of a chiliastic nationalism, and later as an expression of
the catholic-nationalist subculture, from which the Commission
on Vocational Organisation[42] would have wished to extirpate
any alternative working-class loyalties. We have seen these
traditions conflict and then attempt to accommodate one
another, finding a common frame in the Irish Congress of
Trade Unions of 1959, which in Jack Macgougan's phrase[43]
provided 'the basis of unity between two different conceptions
of trade union organisation.'[44] But we have also seen trade
unions as an expression of impatient and at times quite
predatory economic interest, and we have seen a conviction
among a substantial number of their members that this in
fact was their only legitimate role. There is no doubt that
the notion of class lies at the centre of the explanation,
as does the notion of economic interest, but if we ask ourselves why some, irrespective of class or economic interest,
are instinctive supporters of trade unionism and some equally
vigorous in their opposition, we may, in seeking an
explanation, find a parallel in the councils of the United
Nations, as described by Conor Cruise O'Brien in the early
chapters of To Katanga and Back where he distinguished
between those nations that were instinctively imperial and
those that instinctively identified with the oppressed -
the gloaters and the brooders, as he described them, but then
went on felicitously to say of the brooder that he was one
who could 'feel and vibrate with the sense of the great
revolutionary movements which shook the world and shake it
today, instead of contemplating these movements, as the
best-equipped of gloaters must do, from the remote and
critical eminence of historical success.'[45] In a word,
there is an attitude of mind that is trade unionism, much more
than any specific organisation. And what is the nature of
that attitude of mind that informs trade unions? It might
be seen, following Conor Cruise O'Brien, as having a
revolutionary cast, whether in the syndicalism of Connolly,
in the nationalism of William O'Brien or P.T. Daly, or in
the gradual evolution of Fabian socialism which Tom Johnson

would espouse. There is no doubt that the trade union
movement is strongly influenced by notions of secular
salvation[46] and in that sense is revolutionary, but it is
not revolutionary in any violent or vigorous way, despite
its occasional hagiography to the contrary. In these
pages we have seen it again and again counsel gradualism
in all things. It is indeed true that it does 'vibrate'
with the great social movements of our time, but much more
important to it is the notion of stability, and the civilised
intimacy of tradition by which men reach across the
generations, and by which 'a link is made between the past
and the future.'[47] It is not a means by which society as a
whole is opposed, but a means by which society as a whole is
understood. If one believes oneself to be a catholic, or a
Corkman, or a member of the working class, this is an expression
of one's relationship to society, not of one's opposition to it;
it is the house that one inhabits, the reference point that
gives meaning to one's larger social experience. This also
is what the trade union movement provides, to some in a
subsidiary and trivial way, but to others in a manner which
is quite considerable, dominating their other organisational
roles in society and influencing their attitudes accordingly.
One can find in such loyalties a secure point of reference,
something which counteracts, in Barraclough's phrase,[48] the
'sense of alienation, of disinheritance ...' which resulted
from 'the jettisoning of the inherited baggage of European
culture.' And if all this sounds a little fanciful in a
trade union context, it is no more than Sam Kyle himself
expressed when as president he addressed the 1950 annual
conference of the ITUC:[49] 'There surely is a force, a
reality at the very heart of things, which offers to man
the gift of stability and satisfaction in his daily life.
It is the search for and the application of this force that
should be the guiding principle of all our activities as
trade unionists and as men.'

It is important then to bear in mind that while trade unions by

their nature will pursue an economic interest, sometimes
to quite extreme lengths, and while at times such activity
may place them in opposition not only to their employers
but to society as a whole, the substance of the trade union
position does not lie in such opposition, but rather in an
attitude of mind by which society in all its complexity
is given some sense and purpose.

-iv-

And what finally can be said of the form of organisation
that would clothe all this? It would appear that the
spirit of trade unionism - the attitude of mind that
characterises it - can express itself through small
fragmented organisations no less than large general ones,
through many diverse local bodies as well as through a
highly unitary structure. If one can venture any general
proposition, it is that one is more likely to find the
genuinely independent, genuinely representative trade union
tradition better expressed in a complex and diverse structure
such as exists here and in Britain than in an elegant unitary
one such as exists in many European countries and which is more
a reflection of national political positions than grass-root
worker representation.[50] Connolly's syndicalism would have
required a far more logical structure than exists today,
and the leaders of the trade union movement themselves were,
as we have seen, always very conscious of the benefits of
large and sensible groupings. But Connolly's dream sprang
from political objectives which lay, strictly speaking,
outside the trade union movement itself, and the desires
of the trade union leaders from time to time, and in
particular those expressed in 1959, sprang also from something
not essential to the movement - the objective of greater

efficiency and **service**. Questions of efficiency and
service are matters which a leadership is conscious of, but
which a general membership is not. As long as the union is
clearly their union, as long as it continues to function,
they are reluctant to see changes, and indeed reluctant
to pay additional contributions for a promise of better
things to come. The fact is that trade union instincts
are often adequately met at quite an elementary level of
organisation, not perhaps as much if the union is one which
frankly pursues economic interests only, but, even there,
no great sophistication is sought by the membership.

Let us consider for a moment then those things that promote, not
so much trade unionism, as a more efficient trade union
structure, which is quite a different matter. We shall set
aside in this discussion the complex problem of legislation,
and consider the prospects of voluntary endeavour - largely
because we are unlikely to see in our time any experiment
comparable to the 1941 act. Let us set aside as well - for
a similar reason - the tearaway effect of a vast nationalist
impulse such as impelled the swift growth in number from
1917 onwards, dangerously fractured unions in the twenties
and in William O'Brien's time split the national movement,
but not to any marked degree the unions themselves. Indeed
the absence of such an impulse means on the whole the
absence as well of a disruptive force within the trade union
structure. What then can promote a more logical and
integrated form? Clearly national bargaining has a considerable
impact, with its demand for a wider understanding; but
much more important for a union's survival is the need for
adequate finance. The significant thing however is that
neither of these problems was really experienced in any
imperative way by the trade unions during the sixties.

But the trade union leaders in 1960 had hopes that rested on
other things, hopes, as we have seen, that a united congress
would promote by its vigour and its services a much more

rational structure in the trade union movement. In 1962
Congress established a committee on trade union organisation
which was given considerable status[51] and numerous
conferences took place during the decade. All has so far
ended disappointingly. The unions had enough money to
carry on, national bargaining fell into some disrepute
until the end of the decade, and in those turbulent years,
small, tightly organised unions did quite as well as another.
Indeed it is only in very recent times - at a conference in
fact in November 1975 which was called to consider a report
on structures commissioned from the ILO[52] - that we find some
indication that there might be a widespread change, and then
quite clearly because of the alarming effect of escalating
running costs on trade unions, traditionally sluggish in the
matter of increasing contributions, so much so that large
unions were manifestly feeling the pinch and some small
unions were virtually faced with extinction.

There is therefore no necessary reason why a strong trade
union tradition should cast up an elegant and unitary
structure. Indeed a movement by its very definition cannot
be identified with a single-structured organisation, but
rather is something of a consensus, something of a common
aim and a common tradition, which might manifest itself in
many different forms. Mortished was right to warn the
1956 ITUC conference against undue expectations when a united
congress would be created;[53] but because there are so many
practical organisational reasons for a better structure,
the problem will continue to beset the trade union leaders,
conscious, because of their wider horizons, of so much that
is necessary and so much that is left undone.

Notes on Chapter Fourteen

1.   McCarthy: _The Decade of Upheaval_ 1973 op.cit. p.150.

2.   _The Observer_ 26 October 1975 p.13.

3.   See also Basil Chubb: _Cabinet Government in Ireland_,
      Dublin 1974, pp.64 and 92.

4.   Maurice Moynihan: _Currency and Central Banking in
      Ireland 1922-1960_ pp.378-79.

4[A]. Although its governor, Joseph Brennan, felt obliged
      personally to resign in 1953 (Moynihan op.cit.
      pp.396-97), nevertheless the independent-mindedness
      of the Bank did not apparently falter. It is
      interesting to see here a parallel with the resignation
      of Mortished from the Labour Court in 1952 (see p.551 above).

5.   See p.537 above.

6.   See p.555 above.

7.   See p.537 and n.10 above.

8.   Extract from a letter from Irish Shipping to the
      Marine Port and General Workers Union May 1957:
      CIU 1958 p.13.

9.   Charles McCarthy: _The Decade of Upheaval_ op.cit.

10.   See p.536 above.

11.   See p.537 above.

12.   See p.383 above.

13.   See p.474 above.

14.   cf: McCarthy: _The Decade of Upheaval_ op.cit. p.73

15.   See p.543 above.

16.   See p.546 above.

17.   McCarthy: _The Decade of Upheaval_ op.cit. pp.74-75.

18.   See p.549 above.

19.   CIU 1951 p.9.

20.   That is to say, a direct linking of wage and salary
      increases with increases in the consumer price index.

21.   We have not dealt here with a situation in which the
      government might impose restraint by legislation.
      Apart from the standstill of the war years we have not -
      at least as yet - had such an experience in the Republic.

But of course the trade union movement in the United
Kingdom in recent years experienced a direct conflict
with a Conservative government there, not merely
in the matter of pay restraint but in the whole field
of legitimate trade union activity. Again it is quite
instructive to consider the role played by the trade
union centre in these events. The TUC launched
a successful campaign of non-registration and de-
registration for the purposes of the 1971 Industrial
Relations Act, culminating in the expulsion of twenty
unions in September 1973; but although at times it
appeared as if the Conservative government of the time
had taken leave of its senses, both in regard to the
recasting of a traditional industrial relations system
into a highly juridical one, and in regard to the
Counter-Inflation Act of 1972 and the standstills and
controls effected under it, nevertheless the TUC
appeared at all times to be moderate in its approach.
True, they called a one-day strike for July 31
1972 in support of the imprisoned dockers, who were
in the event released on July 25 through the intervention of the Official Solicitor, but it was
reasonable to anticipate such intervention at that stage.
On the other hand, they refused to extend their campaign
against the Industrial Relations Act beyond non-
registration, they left it to each union to make its own
protest against pay restraint in its own way on May 1
1973, and they engaged in quite substantial discussions
with the government and the CBI on stage III of the
prices and incomes proposals. All this was either
authorised or approved by delegate conference. More
directly relevant to our discussion here however,
was their approach to the miners' strike during the crisis
in the early months of 1974. They attempted to have
the miners' case treated as an exception, which other
unions would not follow; they asked the miners to postpone
their industrial action at one stage, in order to permit
certain formulae to be discussed, and only when the
general election was announced did they abandon their
public attempts at some form of mediation, to cast
their weight wholly behind the miners' cause. (see
Chronicle in British Journal of Industrial Relations
various issues March 1972 to July 1974.)

22.   p.329 above.

23.   p.191 above.

24.   Paul Johnson: "A Brotherhood of National Misery"in
      Management Vol.XXII Number 6/7 June-July 1975
      reprinted from New Statesman 1975; and Barry Desmond
      commenting on the article in the same issue of Management.

25.   McCarthy: The Decade of Upheaval op.cit. p.101-02.

26.   p.305 above.

27.   Aidan Kelly: "Changes in Occupational Structure and
       Industrial Relations in Ireland": Management Vol. XXII
       Number 6/7 June/July 1975 p.37.

28.   Van Beinum speaks of a different mentality among
       workers as a result of the rise in their economic
       position. 'The new mentality is characterised by a
       decreasing feeling of a collectively shared fate,
       and an increasing focus on individually and situationally
       determined problems. Class consciousness is changing
       into self consciousness.' And he goes on to discuss
       the new demands made on trade unions by reason of this,
       the new demands of a more complex welfare-type state,
       and the decreasing role of the union in the matter of
       members' personal welfare when sick or unemployed.
       (see Hans Van Beinum: The Morale of the Dublin
       Busmen Irish National Productivity Committee Dublin 1966
       pp.79-81.)

29.   p.427 above.

30.   ITUC 1946 p.41. It is already quoted at pp.672-73 above.

31.   p. 806 above.

32.   cf. Charles McCarthy: "Trade Unions and Economic
       Planning in Ireland": International Labour Review
       Vol. 94 No.1 Geneva July 1966.

33.   ibid.

34.   For recent experience in a number of European countries
       see Walter Kendall: The Labour Movement in Europe
       op.cit. and also Johannes Schregle"Labour Relations
       in Western Europe: Some Topical Issue"in International
       Labour Review Vol. 109 No.1. January 1974. See also
       the developments among the busmen in CIE in 1962
       (McCarthy, The Decade of Upheaval, op.cit. p.36).

35.   Ruaidhri Roberts for example saw the development councils
       as a threat to the productivity committees which he
       promoted strongly;   but the position was also greatly
       complicated by the fact that quite a number of trade
       union leaders feared that they would be entangled
       and entrapped by the mandarins, by the state
       bureaucracy;   and this they felt could be avoided if
       the institutions that were created gave prominence
       rather to the two sides of industry, the employers
       and the trade unions, and this the productivity
       committees and later the Employer -Labour Conference
       tended to do.

36. McCarthy: <u>The Decade of Upheaval</u> op.cit. p.50.

37. ibid. p.102.

38. ibid. p.95.

39. Nor was this trend evident in Northern Ireland, but there the terrible events of recent years and the honourable role of the trade union leaders in them, makes any exposition of the problem very complex (cf. Charles McCarthy: "Civil Strife and the Growth of Trade Union Unity" in <u>Government and Opposition</u> VIII, 4, 1973).

40. A development which finds a parallel throughout western Europe: See Kendall op.cit., and Schregle, <u>International Labour Review</u> op.cit.

41. cf. Clarkson op.cit.

42. page 381 above.

43. p.350 above.

44. Clarkson would have seen in the early years of the nineteenth century, in any event, common cause between nationalist Ireland and workingclass Britain. 'The quarrel between (Fergus) O'Connor and (Daniel) O'Connell arose precisely on the question of the relations of the nationalist and labour movements. O'Connor perceived, what neither Irish nationalists nor British labourites are yet able to comprehend, the identity of interest between nationalist Ireland and working class Britain. The sufferings of the mass of the English people were of the same kind and redounded to the interests of the same class as oppressed the Irish people.' (Clarkson op.cit. p.145). A not dissimilar point was made by Walter Carpenter in 1946 (See p.372a above.)

45. Conor Cruise O'Brien: <u>To Katanga and Back</u> Four Square Books 1965 p.42.

46. cf. Patrick Masterson: <u>Atheism and Alienation:</u> Pelican 1973 ch.5.

47. see p.195 above.

48. see p.195 n.57 above.

49. ITUC 1950 pp.64-65.

50. cf. Kendall op.cit.

51. McCarthy: <u>The Decade of Upheaval</u> op.cit. p.56; also Johannes Schregle: <u>Restructuring of the Irish Trade Union Movement</u>: ILO Geneva 1975, p.16.

52. idem.

53. see p. 474 above.

Appendices

Appendix One:

The 1919 reorganisation proposals

(Extract from Memorandum respecting Amalgamation:
 ILP & TUC 1919 p.61).

Objective

(1) We propose that the ultimate objective should be a
single all-inclusive Irish Workers' Union - one Union for
all workers - one authority to be finally responsible for
financing and controlling all the larger movements.

Industrial sections

(2) Subject to this ultimate authority to organise all
workers into Industrial Sections, each Section to be self-
governing, so far as the affairs of the industry alone are
involved; the Sections to be managed by an Industrial Council
or Section Committee representative of the several crafts
and callings within the Section. In effect this would mean
that the Industrial Section (comprising all crafts and
occupations in the industry) would be practically a separate
Industrial Union, except that financial control would be
retained by the governing body of the whole Union.

Local and National Sections

(3) The Sections to be organised both locally and nationally.
Every town or district to have a Section for each industry
carried on in the locality; each local Section to be linked
up with a National Council of its Industrial Section.

Trades Councils' or Workers' Councils

(4) With this form of organisation the Trades' Council would
become the Council of the Industrial Sections, and the
Delegates would be chosen by the workers at the various
crafts and occupations represented on the Sections (as at
present), with the addition, in view of future developments,
of Delegates appointed by the Works or Shop Committee of the
larger business establishments, factories, works etc. in the
locality.

Trades' Council Executive

(5) The Trades' Council would thus become a General Committee
of the local Workers' Union. Its functions would be to
control local labour movements, and act generally as the
local authority in all that concerns the workers' public
activities. Its Executive would be the Officers of the
local Industrial Sections, with such additions as might
be deemed wise.

National Governing Body

(6) The Governing Body would in the main be appointed by
and from the several Industrial Sections, with perhaps,
the President, Vice-President, Treasurer and Secretary to
be appointed by the whole Union.

Sections

(7) The following might constitute the Sections:

1. Agriculture, Land, Quarries, Roads and Fisheries:

   General Agriculture, Dairying and Cattle, Road
   Workers, Quarrymen and Fishermen.

2. Transport and Communications:

   Docks, Railway Service, Shipping and Carting,
   Motor Traction Air Service.

3. Building and Construction:

   Navvying, Structure Workers, and Furnishing.

4. Food Suppliers - Preparatory Processes:

   Flour Mills, Bakeries, Butchers, Pork Butchers,
   Confectionery Trades, Breweries and Distilleries.

5. Distributive Trades (including Catering and Personal
   Services):

   Shop Workers, Drapery Trades, Ironmongery Trades,
   Grocery Trades, Warehousing and Porters, Clerical
   Staffs, Hotel Workers, Hairdressers.

6. Engineering and Metal-Working Trades (including
   Ship-Building).

7. Clothing and Textiles:

   Spinners and Weavers, Cotton, Woollen and Flax,
   Tailors and Dressmakers, "Making-up" Trades,
   Cotton and Linen Goods, Bootmakers, Leather Workers.

8. Printing, Paper and Allied Trades:

   Printing Trades, Paper Trades, Bookbinding etc.

9. Public Service - Municipal and State:

   Post Office, Law Officers, Education, Excise and
   Customs, Land etc.

10. Miscellaneous.

Appendix Two:

The Mortished Classification: 1926.

(Extract from Journal of the Statistical and Social Inquiry
 Society of Ireland: October 1927. Part CI. Vol XV. p.221 ff.)

Perhaps the most interesting classification of Unions would
be a classification by industry, but this can only be attempted
in the sketchiest of fashions, because, apart from the by no
means simple problem of deciding what is an industry, many
Unions enrol members in several industries, and it is
impossible to ascertain their membership in any one industry.
What follows is an attempt to indicate broadly the distribution of membership in certain important industrial groups.

    The sign + indicates that the Union has members in
                several groups.

    A dash indicates that no figures of membership are
                available.

	Approximate membership
TRANSPORT	
Railways (excluding railway shops) - ...	
National Union of Railwaymen	11,700
Railway Clerks' Association	2,700
Associated Society of Locomotive Engine Drivers and Firemen	2,100
Belfast and Dublin Locomotive Engine Drivers' and Firemen's Trade Union (probably all members of other Unions) ...	600
Irish Transport and General Workers Union ...	+
Dockers, Carters, and Tramway Workers -	
Irish Transport and General Workers' Union	+
Amalgamated Transport and General Workers' Union (including a number in other industries)	8,000
Shipping -	
National Sailors and Firemen's Union ...	1,000

	Approximate membership

Building and Woodworking -

Amalgamated Society of Woodworkers
(Total membership of about 7,500
including many shipbuilding workers.)   ...   +

National Amalgamated Society of
Operative House and Ship Painters
and Decorators   ...   ...   +
(See note above. Total membership 2,000)

Irish National Union of Painters and
Decorators   1,250

United Operative Plumbers' and Domestic
Engineers' Association of Great Britain
and Ireland   1,300

Amalgamated Union of Building Trade Workers
of Great Britain and Ireland (Bricklayers
and Masons)   1,100

Ancient Guild of Incorporated Brick and
Stone Layers   600

Dublin Operative Plasterers' Society   ...   250

Slaters' and Tilers' Society   100

Various Local Craft Unions   ...   ...   -

Irish Transport and General Workers' Union   +

National Union of Municipal and General
Workers' Union   ...   ...   +

National Amalgamated Furnishing Trades'
Association   1,000
(includes members in a variety of different
branches of woodworking)

Amalgamated Society of Woodcutting
Machinists (See note above)   ...   ...   +

Engineering and Metal Working, Shipbuilding,
Coach and Motor Body Making etc. -

Irish Engineering Industrial Union   3,000

Amalgamated Engineering Union   ...   ...   -

Amalgamated Society of Woodworkers ...   ...   +
(see note under "Building")

National Union of Vehicle Builders   1,400

	Approximate membership
Associated Blacksmiths' and Iron Workers' Society of Great Britain and Ireland	-
Boilermakers' and Iron and Steel Shipbuilders' Society	-
National Society of Coppersmiths, Braziers and Metal Workers	-
National Union of Sheet Metal Workers and Braziers	-
National Union of Sheet Metal Workers and Gas Meter Makers of Ireland	-
National Union of Foundry Workers of Great Britain and Ireland	-
Irish Transport and General Workers' Union ...	+
Amalgamated Transport and General Workers' Union	+
Workers' Union	+
National Union of General and Municipal Workers	+

Printing -

Typographical Association	1,600
Dublin Typographical Provident Society ...	1,050
National Union of Printing, Bookbinding, Machine Ruling and Paper Workers	-
National Society of Electrotypers and Stereotypers	-
Bookbinders' and Machine Rulers' Association	-
Irish Women Workers' Union	+
Irish Transport and General Workers' Union	+

	Approximate membership

Clothing -

Tailors' and Garment Workers' Trade Union 3,700

Amalgamated Society of Tailors and Tailoresses 700

Irish Garment Workers' Industrial Union ... 250

Irish Union of Distributive Workers and Clerks ... ... +

Distributive Trades -

Irish Union of Distributive Workers and Clerks ... ... +
(Bulk of membership, 9,500)

National Union of Distributive and Allied Workers ... ... −

Irish National Union of Vintners', Grocers' and Allied Trades' Assistants ... −

Irish Transport and General Workers' Union... +

Milling and Baking -

Irish Bakers', Confectioners' and Allied Workers' Amalgamated Union 2,000

Irish Transport and General Workers' Union... +

Public Services - Teaching

Irish National Teachers' Organisation ...⎫

Association of Secondary Teachers of Ireland ⎬ 13,000

Irish Agricultural and Technical Instruction Officers' Organisation ⎭

Ulster National Teachers' Union ... ... −

- Civil Services

Irish Post Office Workers' Union 3,500

Union of Post Office Workers 1,000

Civil Service Clerical Association 400

Post Office Clerks' Association (Northern Ireland) −

Post Office Engineering Union ... ... −

- Local Services

Irish Municipal Employees' Trade Union ... 1,550

Irish Mental Hospital Workers Union ... 1,400

Irish Nurses' Union (section of Irish Women Workers' Union) +

Irish Transport and General Workers' Union ... +

National Union of General and Municipal Workers +

Appendix Three:

Sam Kyle in the course of the debate at the February 1939
special conference summarised the current trade union
organisation as follows:

2 unions have less than 100 members in affiliated membership to Congress

5	"	"	between	100	and	200	members	"		"
4	"	"	"	200	and	300	"	"		"
5	"	"	"	300	and	400	"	"		"
1 union has			"	400	and	500	"	"		"
2 unions have			"	600	and	700	"	"		"
1 union has			"	900	and	1,000	"	"		"
14 unions have			"	1,000	and	2,000	"	"		"
3	"	"	"	2,000	and	3,000	"	"		"
2	"	"	"	3,000	and	4,000	"	"		"
2	"	"	"	4,000	and	5,000	"	"		"
1 union has			"	6,000	and	7,000	"	"		"
1	"	"	"	8,000	and	9,000	"	"		"
3 unions have			"	9,000	and	10,000	"	"		"
1 union has			"	34,000	and	35,000	"	"		"
1	"	"	"	35,000	and	36,000	"	"		"

Trade Union Commission of Inquiry and Trade Union Conference 1939
p.23

Appendix Four:

The proposals of the 1939 Commission of Inquiry:

(Extract from Memorandum No.1 of the Report of the Trade
Union Commission of Inquiry 1939 pp. 8, 9.)

The adoption of this plan of re-organisation would mean the
re-distribution of the existing Unions into ... ten
Industrial Union Groups. The effect of the plan would be to
merge the existing Unions affiliated to Congress into
Industrial Union Groups as follows:-

1.   Building :
     Amalgamated Union of Building Trade Workers; Ancient
Guild of Incorporated Brick and Stone-Layers' Trade Union;
Cork Operative Society of Masons, Bricklayers and Paviors;
National Amalgamated Society of Painters; Irish National
Painters' and Decorators' Trade Union; United House and
Ship Painters' and Decorators' Trade Union of Ireland;
Operative Plasterers' Trades' Society, Dublin; Plumbers',
Glaziers' & Domestic Engineers' Union; Amalgamated Union
of Slaters and Tilers; Stonecutters Union of Ireland;
Amalgamated Society of Woodworkers; Irish National Union of
Woodworkers; National Amalgamated Furnishing Trades' Association.

2.   Engineering Ship Building and Vehicle Building:

     Irish Engineering Industrial Union; Association of
Engineering and Shipbuilding Draughtsmen; National Union of
Sheet Metal Workers and Gas Meter Makers of Ireland;
National Union of Vehicle Builders; Electrical Trades Union
(Ireland).

3.   Seamen and Dockers:

     National Union of Seamen; Irish Seamen's & Port Workers'
Union.

4.   Rail and Road Transport:

     Railway Clerks' Association; National Union of Railwaymen;
Associated Society of Locomotive Engineers and Firemen;
Belfast and Dublin Locomotive Engine Drivers' and Firemen's
Trade Union.

5.   Printing:

     Dublin Typographical Provident Society; Typographical
Association; Amalgamated Society of Lithographic Printers
& Auxiliaries; Irish Bookbinders & Paper Rulers' Trade
Union; Electrotypers' and Stereotypers' Society.

6. <u>Bakery Workers</u>:

   Irish Bakers', Confectioners' and Allied Workers'
Amalgamated Union.

7. <u>Distributive, Clerical and Supervisory</u>:

   Irish Union of Distributive Workers and Clerks; Irish
Local Government Officials Union; National Amalgamated
Union of Life Assurance Workers; National Federation of
Insurance Workers.

8. <u>Teachers</u>:

   Irish National Teachers' Organisation; Vocational
Education Officers' Organisation.

9. <u>Civil Service</u>:

   Civil Service Clerical Association; Post Office
Workers' Union.

10. <u>General Workers</u>:

   Irish Municipal Employees' Trade Union; Limerick
Corporation Employees' Society; Irish Transport and General
Workers' Union; Amalgamated Transport and General Workers'
Union; National Union of Boot and Shoe Operatives; National
Union of Tailors and Garment Workers; National Society of
Brushmakers; National Union of Packing Case Makers; Irish
Women Workers' Union; Cork Operative Butchers' Society.

Appendix Five:

Trade Union Membership in Ireland: 1970

	Republic	Northern Ireland	All Ireland
Number of trade unions	95	77	147
Membership of:			
general unions	216,600	103,400	320,000
white-collar unions	89,600	71,600	161,200
other unions	80,600	88,000	168,600
Total membership	386,800	263,000	649,800
men	286,800*	193,500	480,000
as percentage of total	74%	74%	74%
women	100,000*	69,500	169,500
as percentage of total	26%	26%	26%
White-collar members	130,000*	83,000*	213,000
as percentage of total	34%	31%	33%
Percentage of employees in trade unions			
men	57%	66%	61%
women	40%	36%	38%
total	52%	54%	53%
Ten biggest unions:	265,000	168,000	
as percentage of total	69%	72%	
Main unions			
ITGWU	150,400	6,400	156,800
ATGWU	18,100	83,200	101,300
AUEW(ES)	5,400	27,300	32,700
WUI	31,000	--	31,000
EETU/PTU	1,700	17,000	18,700
IUDWC	15,900	--	15,900
Unions affiliated to ICTU	371,500	231,200	602,700
as percentage of total	96%	88%	93%
Unions with head offices in Republic	322,000	27,900	359,900
as percentage of total	86%	9%	55%
Northern Ireland	--	15,400	15,400
as percentage of total	--	6%	2%
Britain	54,800	219,700	274,500
as percentage of total	14%	84%	42%

*   Rough estimate

Abbreviations: ICTU - Irish Congress of Trade Unions;

ITGWU - Irish Transport and General Workers' Union;
ATGWU - Amalgamated Transport and General Workers' Union;
AUEW (ES) - Amalgamated Union of Engineering Workers
(Engineering Section); WUI - Workers Union of Ireland:
EETU/PTU - Electrical, Electronics and Telecommunications
Union/Plumbing Trades Union; IUDWC - Irish Union of
Distributive Workers and Clerks.

Source: Irish Congress of Trade Unions, Trade Union Information,
June 1971, January 1972, February 1972.

Appendix Six:

Extract from Trade Union Information Vol.VIII, no.43,
March 1953 pp. 1-6.

The absence of comprehensive statistics of trade union
membership in Ireland has long been evident. To fill this
gap the Research Department of the Irish Trade Union Congress
has compiled details relating to trade unions in Ireland
which it is intended to summarise in this and succeeding
articles. The material has been collected from various
sources. Its compilation would not have been possible
without the co-operation of trade union officials and the
assistance of the Registrars of Friendly Societies for the
Republic of Ireland and for Northern Ireland, and the
Department of Industry and Commerce. The Research Department
readily acknowledges, with gratitude, this co-operation
and assistance and the advice which various individuals
willingly gave.

The first step in the enquiry was the compilation of a list
of all trade unions with members in Ireland. (Throughout
this article the term "trade union" is intended to refer
to a trade union of workpeople. It does not include a trade
union of employers.) For the Republic of Ireland there were
two principal sources of information. The Registrar of
Friendly Societies made available a list of trade unions
registered under the Trade Union Acts, 1871 to 1935, while
the Department of Industry and Commerce made available
a list of trade unions holding negotiation licences under
the Trade Union Act, 1941. These lists, however, do not
cover all trade unions. There are a large number of Civil
Service associations as well as trade unions with members
in State employment which are not registered and which are
not required to hold negotiation licences. There are some
other organisations of employees in a similar position.

There were also two principal sources of information for
Northern Ireland, the Report of the Registrar of Friendly
Societies (Ministry of Commerce) and the "Directory of
Principal Organisations of Employers and Workpeople in Northern
Ireland" (Ministry of Labour and National Insurance).
The former lists trade unions registered in Northern Ireland
under the Trade Union Acts, 1871 to 1940 as well as trade
unions registered in Great Britain which had recorded their
rules in Northern Ireland. Not all Northern Ireland trade
unions are registered nor have all trade unions registered
in Britain and with members in Northern Ireland recorded
their rules there.

Having compiled as complete a list as was possible of trade
unions and organisations of employees in Ireland the next
question was to decide whether any of these organisations
should be excluded from the scope of the enquiry. It was
clearly desirable that all trade unions and organisations
of employees analogous to trade unions should be included.
In practice, however, it was necessary to decide where a line
should be drawn. In general, all organisations of employees -

including those of salaried and professional workers, as
well as those of manual wage-earners - which were known
to include among their principal functions that of negotiating
with employers in connection with wages or salaries or
conditions of employment of their members, were included. All
organisations in the nature of "house" or "company" unions,
however, were excluded.

There are a number of registered trade unions which are
part of national or amalgamated unions. For example, the
Belfast Operative Bakers' Society, the Cork Operative Bakers'
Trade Union and Drogheda Operative Bakers' and Confectioners'
Trades Union, although registered as separate unions, are
part of the Irish Bakers', Confectioners' and Allied Workers'
Amalgamated Union. The Irish Air Line Pilots' Association
is affiliated to the Workers' Union of Ireland. The Belfast
Bread Servers' Trade Union, as well as several textile
unions in Northern Ireland, although registered as separate
unions are part of the Amalgamated Transport and General
Workers' Union. Such unions have been excluded from the
scope of the enquiry so as to avoid duplication of membership.
A similar question arises in the case of the Building
Workers' Trade Union. This union, which holds a negotiation
licence, has four constituent and wholly separate unions,
the Ancient Guild of Incorporated Brick and Stone Layers'
Trade Union, the Irish National Painters' and Decorators'
Trade Union, the Irish National Union of Woodworkers and the
Stonecutters' Trade Union of Ireland. None of these four
unions hold separate negotiation licences although the first
three are registered. In this case the four unions which
make up the Building Workers' Trade Union were included
in the enquiry but the Union itself was not.

In a few cases, it was necessary to make somewhat arbitrary
decisions. The Irish Sub-Postmasters' Union although
affiliated to the Congress of Irish Unions has been excluded
from the enquiry for the reason that many sub-postmasters
are not employees in the normal sense of the term. Two
registered trade unions, the Dublin Biscuit Operatives'
Labour Union and Benefit Society and the Dublin Guild of
Female Biscuit Operatives, have also been excluded as it
was considered that for the purpose of the enquiry these
may be regarded as benefit societies or social clubs rather
than as trade unions.

The number of trade unions which were included in the
final list was 161 of which 81 have members in the Republic
of Ireland only, 46 have members in Northern Ireland only and,
34 have members both in the Republic and in Northern Ireland.

Of the 161 trade unions, 85 have their chief offices in the
Republic of Ireland, 11 in Northern Ireland and 65 outside
Ireland.

Of the total, 62 trade unions are affiliated to the Irish
Trade Union Congress, 23 to the Congress of Irish Unions while

76 are not affiliated to either Congress. (Of the unaffiliated trade unions, however, 28 in the Republic of
Ireland are associations of State employees, nineteen of
which are affiliated to the Civil Service Alliance.)

The names of the trade unions are given on pages 605-08
together with a code which indicates (a) the situation of
their chief offices, (b) the part of Ireland in which they
have members and (c) the Congress to which they are
affiliated (if either).

The compilation of the membership figures of the trade unions
included in the enquiry naturally presented the greatest
difficulty. In many cases there were two or more sources
of information. For the Republic of Ireland there were
in the case of trade unions with their chief offices in the
Republic, the returns made to the Registrar of Friendly
Societies and in the case of trade unions holding negotiation
licences, the returns made to the Department of Industry
and Commerce. The membership of unregistered trade unions
without negotiation licences was in some cases available
in published reports and in others was obtained direct from
the unions. For Northern Ireland there were in the case
of registered trade unions and trade unions registered
in Britain which had recorded their rules in Northern
Ireland, the returns made to the Registrar of Friendly
Societies.

The latest available returns made to the two Registrars
of Friendly Societies in Ireland relate to the end of
December, 1950. The dates of the returns made to the
Department of Industry and Commerce varied. Of the 73
returns of trade unions holding negotiation licences 2
related to 1949, 10 to 1950, 51 to 1951 and 10 to 1952.

Needless to say, when information concerning membership
was available from more than one source, there were often
two and sometimes more different figures. An example –
admittedly an extreme one – will serve to illustrate the
problem confronting the investigator. According to the
return made to the Registrar of Friendly Societies, the
membership of the Irish Transport and General Workers'
Union at the end of 1950 was 116,257. The membership
returned to the Department of Industry and Commerce as
at April, 1951, was 140,439. The membership given in the
seventh annual report of the Congress of Irish Unions for
1951 was 130,000.

It must be said that it is extremely difficult for certain
unions – especially general unions – to give an accurate
return of membership due to the fluctuations in numbers of
members which occur. Again, some unions return only benefit
members and exclude those who because they have fallen into
arrears with their contributions are not in benefit while
other unions return all who are on the books. There is often
a substantial difference between what may be called "gross"
and "net" membership.

Number and Membership of Trade Unions in Ireland

	Total		Affiliated to Irish TUC		CIU		Unaffiliated	
	Unions	Members	Unions	Members	Unions	Members	Unions	Members
Trade Unions with Chief Offices in:								
Republic of Ireland	85	281,429	19	83,070	23	172,454	43	25,995
Northern Ireland	6	10,123	2	1,000	--	--	4	9,123
Outside Ireland	62	220,259	41	213,796	--	--	21	6,463
Total	153	511,811	62	297,866	23	172,454	68	41,491
of which								
ITGWU	1	130,000	--	--	1	130,000	--	--
ATGWU	1	90,000	1	90,000	--	--	--	--
Others	151	291,811	61	207,866	22	42,454	68	41,491
Trade Unions with Membership of:								
100 or less	31	1,356	3	208	2	135	26	1,013
101 to 250	26	4,148	6	816	3	452	17	2,880
251 to 500	16	5,554	6	2,086	3	1,069	7	2,399
501 to 1,000	20	13,458	10	6,671	2	1,475	8	5,312
1,001 to 1,500	12	14,161	5	5,852	3	3,416	4	4,893
1,501 to 2,000	9	15,387	5	7,969	3	5,434	1	1,984
2,001 to 3,000	7	17,680	5	12,296	2	5,384	--	--
3,001 to 5,000	17	68,317	10	41,017	3	10,510	4	16,700
5,001 to 7,500	5	31,612	4	25,302	--	--	1	6,310
7,501 to 10,000	2	17,022	2	17,022	--	--	--	--
10,001 to 15,000	3	39,770	2	25,191	1	14,579	--	--
15,001 to 25,000	3	63,346	3	63,346	--	--	--	--
Over 25,000	2	220,000	1	90,000	1	130,000	--	--
Total	153	511,811	62	297,866	23	172,454	68	41,491

	Total		Affiliated to Irish TUC		CIU		Unaffiliated	
	Unions	Members	Unions	Members	Unions	Members	Unions	Members
General Unions	6	267,907	4	134,407	1	130,000	1	3,500
Manual Workers:								
Craft	46	89,395	21	74,593	12	11,091	13	3,711
Mixed	24	57,946	14	42,236	5	12,649	5	3,070
Postal Service	9	13,247	4 }	15,808	--	--	5 }	13,675
Civil Service	31	16,236	1 }		--	--	30 }	
Distribution, Offices	9	33,808	3	12,040	2	18,339	4	3,429
Insurance, Banking	5	10,429	3	2,781	--	--	2	7,648
Professions, Services	23	22,843	12	16,001	3	384	8	6,458
Total	153	511,811	62	297,866	23	172,454	68	41,491

Note:- The figures in the above table relate to the whole of Ireland.

Abbreviations:- Irish TUC: Irish Trade Union Congress; CIU: Congress of Irish Unions;
ITGWU: Irish Transport and General Workers' Union;
ATGWU: Amalgamated Transport and General Workers' Union.

It will be apparent from the foregoing that there are
serious difficulties in the way of compiling accurate
figures of trade union membership. The figures finally
used in the present enquiry were not necessarily those
returned to the Registrars or to the Department of Industry
and Commerce or in connection with affiliation to the Irish
TUC or to the CIU. In each case what was considered, in all
the circumstances, the best available estimate was taken.
Frequently, this was after consultation with officials of
the unions concerned or where this was not possible, with
other competent persons. In very many cases, of course, the
figures as returned to the Registrars, to the Department
or to the Congresses were taken where these were known
to be approximately in line with the present actual
membership.

Taken generally, the figures may be taken to relate to the
end of 1952 or the beginning of 1953.

There were eight organisations in respect of which
membership figures were not ascertainable: all have members
in Northern Ireland only. These organisations have, naturally,
been excluded from the statistics which follow.

Statistics of membership were available for 153 trade unions
and organisations of employees. Eighty-five of these which
had their chief offices in the Republic of Ireland had a
total membership of 281,429. Six with chief offices in
Northern Ireland had a membership of 10,123. Sixtytwo with
chief offices situated outside Ireland had a membership of
220,259. The total membership of all the trade unions and
organisations covered by the enquiry was 511,811. Two
general unions made up 43 per cent of the total, viz. the
Irish Transport and General Workers' Union (ITGWU)
with an estimated 130,000 members and the Amalgamated
Transport and General Workers' Union (ATGWU) with an
estimated 90,000 members.

Sixty-two unions with a total membership of 297,866 were
affiliated to the Irish Trade Union Congress (ITUC) and
twenty-three with a membership of 172,454 were affiliated
to the Congress of Irish Unions (CIU) - 130,000 of them in
a single union, the ITGWU. The sixty-eight unaffiliated
organisations had a membership of 41,491. Of Ireland's
511,811 trade unionists, 58 per cent are in unions affiliated
to the ITUC, 34 per cent in unions affiliated to the CIU and
8 per cent in unaffiliated unions.

Size of Unions

There were fifty-seven unions with fewer than 250 members
(thirty-one of these had 100 members or less).
Another sixteen had between 251 and 500 members. Thus 73
out of the total of 153 unions had fewer than 500 members.
Although nearly half the total number of trade unions are
in this category, their aggregate membership amounts to a
mere 2 per cent of total membership.

There were 20 unions of 501 to 1,000 members each with an
aggregate membership of 13,458: 21 unions of 1,001 to 2,000
members each with an aggregate membership of 29,548; 7
unions of 2,001 to 3,000 members each with an aggregate membership of 17,680 and 17 unions of 3,001 to 5,000 members each
with an aggregate membership of 68,317. Thus unions with
less than 5,001 members numbered 137 and had a total
membership of 140,061 which is 27 per cent of the total in all
unions.

There were only 15 unions with more than 5,000 members
though these comprised 73 per cent of all trade unionists.
Seven of these had between 5,001 and 10,000 members each,
with an aggregate membership of 47,634.* The three unions
with a membership between 10,001 and 15,000 were the Irish
Union of Distributive Workers and Clerks, National Union
of General and Municipal Workers and National Union of
Tailors and Garment Workers. Their aggregate membership was
39,770.

The five unions with more than 15,000 members were: ITGWU
(130,000), ATGWU (90,000), Workers' Union of Ireland (25,000),
Amalgamated Engineering Union (21,500) and the Amalgamated
Society of Woodworkers (16,900).

It will be noted that fully three quarters of the membership
of unions affiliated to the CIU are in a single union. On
the other hand, the largest union affiliated to the ITUC
constitutes only 30 per cent of the total membership of unions
affiliated to that Congress. The contrast is more remarkable
when it is realised that while a single union makes up 75 per
cent of the total membership of CIU, the twelve biggest
unions affiliated to the ITUC in fact make up a rather
smaller proportion of its total membership.

Type of Union

The table on page 602 gives the number and membership of
the different types of unions. In many cases no definite
or firm classification was possible and it was necessary
in these instances to adopt somwhat arbitrary classifications.
General unions, of which there are six, have members in a large
number of industries and services and in many non-industrial and
non-manual occupations. General unions account for 267,907
members which is more than half the total membership of all
trade unions - one out of two trade unionists in Ireland are,
therefore, members of a general union.

The 46 unions of craft workers, with a total membership of
89,395, cover those unions which cater solely or almost
exclusively for craft workers, that is, in general, crafts with
a recognised system of apprenticeship. The 24 unions of "mixed"
manual workers, with a membership of 57,946 include industrial
unions with members in all industrial occupations of a
particular industry (e.g. National Union of Tailors and Garment
Workers) as well as unions which take in skilled, semi-
skilled and unskilled workers (e.g. Irish Engineering
and Foundry Union.)   There were nine unions, with

13,247 members, in the Postal Service classification and
31 associations with 16,236 members, in the Civil Service
classification. The 9 unions with members in distributive
trades and in clerical occupations (outside the Civil Service)
had a membership of 33,808. Five unions in banking and
insurance had 10,429 members. The 23 unions with 22,843
members classified under "Professions, Services" include
those organising teachers, musicians, commercial travellers,
nurses, hairdressers, journalists, etc. Unions catering
solely for transport workers are included in the table under
the appropriate categories, clerical staff under
"Distribution, Offices" and operative grades under
"Manual Workers."

*   These seven unions were Electrical Trades Union, Irish
Bank Officials' Association, Irish National Teachers'
Organisation, Irish Women Workers' Union, National
Association of Transport Employees (formerly the National
Union of Railwaymen), Post Office Workers' Union and the
Union of Shop, Distributive and Allied Workers.

A   Chief Office in Republic of Ireland
B   Chief Office in Northern Ireland
C   Chief Office outside Ireland
 D   Members in Republic of Ireland only
 E   Members in Northern Ireland only
 F   Members both in Republic of Ireland and in Northern Ireland
  G   Affiliated to Irish Trade Union Congress
  H   Affiliated to Congress of Irish Unions
  J   Not affiliated to either Congress

ADJ   Air Traffic Control Officers' Association
CFG   Amalgamated Engineering Union
CFG   Amalgamated Slaters', Tilers' & Roofing Operatives' Society
CFG   Amalgamated Society of Lithographic Printers
CEJ   Amalgamated Society of Woodcutting Machinists
CFG   Amalgamated Society of Woodworkers
CFG   Amalgamated Transport and General Workers' Union
CEG   Amalgamated Union of Building Trade Workers
CEG   Amalgamated Union of Foundry Workers
CFG   Associated Blacksmiths', Forge and Smithy Workers' Society
CFG   Associated Society of Locomotive Engineers and Firemen
ADJ   Association of Attendants (Dundrum Asylum)
CEJ   Association of Building Technicians
CFG   Association of Engineering and Shipbuilding Draughtsmen
BEJ   Association of Local Government Officers*
ADJ   Association of Officers of Taxes
ADJ   Association of Printing and Binding Clerks
CEG   Association of Scientific Workers
CEG   Association of Supervisory Staffs, Executives and Technicians

ADJ	Association of Surveyors of Customs and Excise
ADH	Ancient Guild of Incorporated Brick and Stone Layers' Trade Union
ADG	Assurance Representatives' Organisation
BEJ	Belfast Coopers' Trade Union
ADG	Civil Service Clerical Association
ADJ	Civil Service Executive and Higher Officers' Association
ADJ	Civil Service Staff Officers' Association
ADJ	Civil Service Temporary Clerks' Association
CEJ	Civil Service Union
CEG	Clerical and Administrative Workers' Union
ADJ	Comhaltas Cana
ADG	Cork Coopers' Benevolent Society
ADH	Cork Housepainters' Society
ADG	Cork Operative Butchers' Society
ADJ	Cumann Aisteoiri Radio Eireann
ADJ	Cumann Cigiri Canach
ADJ	Cumann Lucht Meteoruiochta na h-Eireann
ADJ	Cumann Oifigeach an Oireachtais
ADJ	Customs and Excise Clerical Association
ADJ	Customs and Excise Controlling Grades Association
ADJ	Customs and Excise Preventive Staff Association
ADJ	Customs and Excise Watchers' Association
ADH	Dublin and District Electrotypers' & Stereotypers' Society
ADJ	Dublin Port and Docks Board Officers' Association
ADH	Dublin Typographical Provident Society
CFJ	Electrical Power Engineers' Association
CEG	Electrical Trades Union
ADH	Electrical Trades Union (Ireland)
CEJ	Engineer Surveyors' Association
ADJ	Federation of Government Employees
ADG	Federation of Rural Workers
CEG	Fire Brigades Union
BEJ	Flax and Other Textile Workers' Trade Union
ADJ	G.P.O. Departmental Officers' Association
CFJ	Guild of Insurance Officials
ADH	Guild of Irish Journalists
CEJ	Guild of Radio Service Engineers
ADJ	High and Supreme Court Clerks' Association
CEJ	Inland Revenue Staff Federation
CFJ	Institute of Journalists
ADJ	Institute of Professional Civil Servants
ADH	Irish Actors' Equity Association
ADH	Irish Automobile Drivers' and Automobile Mechanics' Union
AFG	Irish Bakers', Confectioners' and Allied Workers' Amalgamated Union
AFJ	Irish Bank Officials' Association
ADH	Irish Bookbinders' and Allied Trades Union
ADJ	Irish Civil Aviation Radio Officers' Union
ADJ	Irish Creamery Managers' Association
ADH	Irish Engineering and Foundry Union
ADH	Irish Engineering, Industrial and Electrical Trade Union
ADG	Irish Federation of Commercial Travellers
ADG	Irish Federation of Musicians
ADJ	Irish Local Government Officials' Union
ADG	Irish Municipal Employees' Trade Union
ADG	Irish National League of the Blind

ADH	Irish National Painters' and Decorators' Trade Union
AFG	Irish National Teachers' Organisation
ADH	Irish National Union of Vintners', Grocers' and Allied Trades' Assistants
ADH	Irish National Union of Woodworkers
ADJ	Irish Nurses' Organisation
ADJ	Irish Pilots' and Marine Officers Association
ADG	Irish Post Office Engineering Union
ADH	Irish Racecourse Bookmakers' Assistants' Association
ADJ	Irish Railwaymen's Union
ADH	Irish Seamen and Port Workers' Union
ADG	Irish Shoe and Leather Workers' Union
ADH	Irish Society of Woodcutting Machinists
BEJ	Irish Textile Overlookers' Trade Society*
ADH	Irish Transport and General Workers' Union
ADJ	Irish Transport Officers' Guild
ADH	Irish Union of Distributive Workers and Clerks
ADG	Irish Union of Hairdressers and Allied Workers
ADJ	Irish Vehicle and General Woodworkers' Trade Union
ADG	Irish Women Workers' Union
CEJ	Iron, Steel and Metal Dressers' Trade Society
CEJ	Medical Practitioners' Union
CFG	National Amalgamated Union of Life Assurance Workers
CFG	National Association of Operative Plasterers
CEG	National Association of Theatrical and Kine Employees
AFG	National Association of Transport Employees **
CFG	National Federation of Insurance Workers
CEG	National League of the Blind
CFG	National Society of Brushmakers
CFG	National Society of Coppersmiths, Braziers and Metal Workers
CEJ	National Society of Electrotypers and Stereotypers
CFG	National Society of Painters
CEJ	National Society of Pottery Workers*
CEG	National Union of Boot and Shoe Operatives
CEJ	National Union of Cooperative Officials
CFG	National Union of Furniture Trade Operatives
CEG	National Union of General and Municipal Workers
CFJ	National Union of Gold, Silver and Allied Trades
CEJ	National Union of Hosiery Workers
CFG	National Union of Journalists
CEJ	National Union of Musical Instrument Makers*
CEJ	National Union of Operative Heating, Domestic and Ventilating Engineers and General Metal Workers
CEG	National Union of Packing Case Makers
CEJ	National Union of Press Telegraphists
CEG	National Union of Printing, Bookbinding and Paper Workers
CFG	National Union of Scalemakers
CFG	National Union of Seamen
CEG	National Union of Sheet Metal Workers and Braziers
ADH	National Union of Sheet Metal Workers and Gas Meter Makers of Ireland
CFG	National Union of Tailors and Garment Workers
CFG	National Union of Vehicle Builders
BEG	North of Ireland Operative Butchers' and Allied Workers' Association
BEJ	Northern Ireland Civil Service Association
BEG	Northern Ireland Musicians' Association

BEJ	Northern Union of Teachers in Technical Institutes*
ADH	Operative Plasterers' Trade Society of Dublin
ADJ	Ordnance Survey Staff Association
ADJ	Packing Case Makers' Trade Union
CFG	Plumbing Trades Union
ADJ	Post Office Clerical Association
BEJ	Post Office Clerks' Association*
ADJ	Post Office Controlling Officers' Association
CEG	Post Office Engineering Union
ADG	Post Office Workers' Union
ADJ	Postal Inspectors' Association
ADJ	Postmasters' Association
ADJ	Prison Officers' Association
CFJ	Prison Officers' Association*
ADH	Regular Dublin Operative Coopers' Society
CFJ	Shipconstructors' and Shipwrights' Association
ADJ	Social Welfare Officers' Association
ADJ	Social Welfare Supervisors' Association
CFJ	Society of Lithographic Artists, Designers, Engravers and Process Workers
CEJ	Society of Technical Civil Servants
ADJ	Stamping Branch Association
ADJ	Stonecutters' Trade Union of Ireland
CFG	Transport Salaried Staffs Association
CFG	Typographical Association
BEJ	Ulster Teachers' Union*
BEJ	Ulster Transport and Allied Operatives' Union
CEG	Union of Post Office Workers
CEG	Union of Shop, Distributive and Allied Workers
ADH	United House and Ship Painters' and Decorators' Trade Union of Ireland
CEJ	United Patternmakers' Association
CFG	United Society of Boilermakers' and Iron and Steel Ship Builders
ADJ	United Stationery Engine Drivers', Cranemen, Firemen, Motormen and Machinemen's Trade Union
ADG	Vocational Education Officers' Association
ADG	Workers' Union of Ireland

*   Membership not ascertainable when statistics were being compiled

** Formerly the National Union of Railwaymen.

Appendix Seven

Extract from <u>Trade Union Information</u> Vol.VIII, no.44 April 1953
pp.1-4.

The Trade Union Movement

At the beginning of the century there were less than 50,000
trade unionists in Ireland. Since then the numbers have
been multiplied ten times and today there are about 513,000
men and women in the ranks of the trade union movement,
319,000 of them in the Republic of Ireland and 194,000 in
Northern Ireland. These trade unionists are organised in
157 trade unions, of which 80 have members in the Republic
of Ireland only, 42 have members in Northern Ireland only
and 35 have members both in the Republic of Ireland and
in Northern Ireland.

The progress made in organising workers into trade unions
and the development of the movement generally represents
an achievement of which Irish workers may well be proud
but still more is it a testimonial to the vision of the
pioneers of trade unions in this country who despite the
bitter opposition of the enemies of the working class laid
the foundation for what is now the largest and most widespread movement in our land, a movement, which, above all
others, unites workers of the north and the south, bringing
them together in bonds of fraternity and common interest.

Great as has been the progress already made, much remains
to be done in the field of organisation. The half million
or so workers organised in trade unions represent little
more than half the potential membership. While the proportion
of eligible workpeople organised in this country compares
very favourably with most other countries it is obvious
that there still is ample scope for the expansion of the
movement.

The reunification of the trade union movement in Ireland
with a single national centre would permit of the full strength
of the organised workers being brought to bear towards the
solution of the serious economic and social questions facing
the working class in both parts of our country. At present
about 298,000 trade unionists are in unions affiliated to
the Irish Trade Union Congress, 172,000 in unions affiliated
to the Congress of Irish Unions and 42,000 in unaffiliated unions.

Another main task facing the movement is to raise the trade
union consciousness of members so that they become active
participants in the work of their organisations and not
merely dues-paying or card-carrying members. To achieve
this it is necessary to further the education of trade
unionists in the fundamental principles of trade unionism
and the philosophy of the working class movement.

Trade Unions in Ireland

Before dealing with the breakdown of trade union membership
between the Republic of Ireland and Northern Ireland some
amendments and revisions to the figures for Ireland given
in our last issue are necessary in the light of additional
information received by the Research Department. The
changes are of a minor nature. Membership figures have
been received in respect of two unions which were not
available when the statistics were being compiled, viz.
the National Society of Pottery Workers and the Prison
Officers' Association both of which have members in Northern
Ireland only; the membership of two other unions the names
of which were not included in the list published in our
last issue have also been ascertained, viz. Belfast
Corporation Senior Officers' Association (BEJ) and the
Ulster Chemists' Association (Associates' section) (BEJ)*;
finally, revised membership figures have been received for
two other unions. Although this additional and revised
information does not seriously affect the figures given in
the table on page 3 of our last issue, it is considered
desirable, for the convenience of readers, to summarise
the revised figures.

The total membership of 153 trade unions in Ireland was
given as 511,811. The amended figure in respect of 157
trade unions is 513,212. Eighty-five unions with chief offices
in the Republic of Ireland had a membership of 281,429; eight
unions with chief offices in Northern Ireland had 10,681
members and 64 unions with chief offices outside Ireland
had 221,102 members. There were 62 unions affiliated to
the Irish Trade Union Congress with a membership of
298,418, made up of nineteen unions with chief offices in the
Republic with 83,070 members, two unions with chief offices
in Northern Ireland with 1,000 members and 41 unions with
chief offices outside Ireland with 214,348 members. There
were 23 unions affiliated to the Congress of Irish Unions
with a membership of 172,454: all of these unions have
their chief offices in the Republic. The 72 unaffiliated
unions had a membership of 42,340; forty-three of these
with chief offices in the Republic had 25,905 members, six
with chief offices in Northern Ireland had 9,681 members while
23 with chief offices outside Ireland had 6,754 members.

The breakdown of these revised statistics of trade union
membership in Ireland as between the Republic of Ireland
and Northern Ireland is given below. The scope of the
survey and the sources of the membership figures were dealt
with in some detail in our last issue.

---

* The code letters shown indicate the situation of the chief
offices of the unions, the part of Ireland in which they have
members and the Congress to which they are affiliated (if either).
The code-key was given at the head of the list of unions in
Ireland on page 5 of the March issue of this journal.

There was an error in the coding of the ITGWU on page 6 of the
March issue. The code should have been AFH and not ADH.

Republic of Ireland

The table on the opposite page shows the number and membership
of trade unions in the Republic of Ireland classified in
accordance with the location of their chief offices, size
of membership and type of union. It is in similar form
to the table relating to the whole of Ireland published
in our last issue.

The total membership of the 115 trade unions in the Republic
of Ireland was 319,343. The eighty-five unions with chief
offices in the Republic had a membership of 273,252 or
86 per cent of the total. The remaining thirty unions with
chief offices outside Ireland had 46,091 members or 14 per
cent of the total.** It will be noted that the membership in
the Republic of Ireland of the Irish Transport and General
Workers' Union, estimated at 128,000, represents exactly
two-fifths of total trade union membership.

There were fifty unions with fewer than 250 members each
(twenty-seven of these had 100 members or less) with an
aggregate membership of 4,952. Another eleven unions with
between 251 and 500 members each had 3,812 in all. Thus 61
out of the total of 115 unions had less than 500 members.
Although representing more than half the total number of
unions, their aggregate membership amounted to less than
3 per cent of total membership.

There were thirteen unions with 501 to 1,000 members each,
with an aggregate membership of 10,078; fifteen with 1,001 to
2,000 members each, with a total of 21,048 members; five
with 2,001 to 3,000 members each, totalling 12,793; eleven
with 3,001 to 5,000 members each, with a total of 44,093.
Unions with less than 5,001 members, therefore, numbered
105 and had 96,776 members or just 30 per cent of the total in
all unions.

There were only ten unions with more than 5,000 members each
though these represented 70 per cent of all trade unionists.
Eight of these, with between 5,001 and 15,000 members each, had
an aggregate membership of 69,567, viz. Amalgamated Society
of Woodworkers, Amalgamated Transport and General Workers' Union,
Irish National Teachers' Organisation, Irish Union of
Distributive Workers and Clerks, Irish Women Workers' Union,
National Union of Tailors and Garment Workers, Post Office
Workers' Union, National Association of Transport Employees,
(formerly the National Union of Railwaymen).

The two trade unions with more than 15,000 members were the
Irish Transport and General Workers' Union with an estimated
membership of 128,000 (in the Republic) and the Workers'
Union of Ireland with 25,000 members.

** The Ministry of Labour Gazette for November 1952 gives the
membership in the Republic of Ireland of trade unions with
chief offices in the United Kingdom as 55,000 at the end of
1951. Since then, however, the National Union of Railwaymen
(in Ireland) has become the National Association of Transport
Employees and the membership in the Republic of Ireland of the
National Union of Boot and Shoe Operatives has become the Irish
Shoe and Leather Workers Unions. Both these unions have their
chief offices in the Republic.

There were four general unions with 171,966 members or 54
per cent of the total. The 35 unions of craft workers, with
a total membership of 37,412, cover those unions which
cater solely or almost exclusively for craft workers. The
16 unions of "mixed" manual workers had 40,707 members:
these unions include industrial unions as well as unions
organising skilled, semi-skilled and unskilled manual
workers. There were seven unions, with 9,839 members,
in the Postal Service classification and 27 associations with
10,467 members in the Civil Service classification. The
six unions organising workers in the distributive trades
and clerical occupations (outside the Civil Service) had
a total membership of 24,203 while five unions in banking
and insurance had 7,538 members. The fifteen unions with
17,211 members classified under "Professions, Services"
include those organising teachers, musicians, commercial
travellers, nurses, hairdressers, journalists, etc. (Unions
organising transport workers only are included in the table
under the appropriate classifications, clerical staff
under "Distribution, Offices" and operative grades under
"Manual Workers").

Northern Ireland

The total membership of the 77 trade unions with members in
Northern Ireland was 193,869.*** Eight of these which had
their chief offices in Northern Ireland had a total membership of 10,681; five with chief offices in the Republic
of Ireland had 8,177 members. The remaining sixty-four
unions with chief offices outside Ireland had 175,011
members or 90 per cent of the total. The membership of
the Amalgamated Transport and General Workers' Union
represents exactly two-fifths of total union membership.

There were twenty-nine unions with fewer than 250 members
(seventeen of these had 100 members or less). Another
seven unions had between 251 and 500 members. Thus 36
out of the total of 77 unions had less than 500 members.
Although these represented nearly half the total number
of unions their aggregate membership amounted to only
5,380 or less than 3 per cent of total membership.

There were eleven unions with 501 to 1,000 members each
with an aggregate membership of 7,620; sixteen unions
with 1,001 to 2,000 members each with a total of 23,810
members; four unions with 2,001 or 3,000 members each with
10,435 members in all and three unions with 3,001 to 5,000
members each, with a total membership of 12,144. Therefore,
unions with less than 5,001 members numbered 70 and had a total

---

*** The Ministry of Labour Gazette for November 1952
gives the membership of trade unions in Northern Ireland
as 196,000 at the end of 1951.

Number and Membership of Trade Unions in the Republic of Ireland

	Total		Affiliated to				Unaffiliated	
			Irish TUC		CIU			
	Unions	Members	Unions	Members	Unions	Members	Unions	Members
Trade Unions with Chief Offices in								
Republic of Ireland	85	273,252	19	78,520	23	170,454	43	24,278
of which ITGWU	1	128,000	--	--	1	128,000	--	--
Outside Ireland	30	46,091	24	44,645	--	--	6	1,446
Total	115	319,343	43	123,165	23	170,454	49	25,724
Trade Unions with Membership of:								
100 or less	27	1,308	5	303	2	135	20	870
101 to 250	23	3,644	7	1,126	3	452	13	2,066
251 " 500	11	3,812	3	935	3	1,069	5	1,808
501 " 1,000	13	10,078	6	4,586	2	1,475	5	4,017
1,001 " 1,500	9	10,430	4	4,918	3	3,416	2	2,096
1,501 " 2,000	6	10,618	2	3,200	3	5,434	1	1,984
2,001 " 3,000	5	12,793	3	7,409	2	5,384	--	--
3,001 " 5,000	11	44,093	5	20,700	3	10,510	3	12,883
5,001 " 7,500	4	25,916	4	25,916	--	--	--	--
7,501 " 15,000	4	43,651	3	29,072	1	14,579	--	--
Over 15,000	2	153,000	1	25,000	1	128,000	--	--
Total	115	319,343	43	123,165	23	170,454	49	25,724
General Unions	4	171,966	3	43,966	1	128,000	--	--
Manual Workers:								
Craft	35	37,412	18	25,485	12	11,091	5	836
Mixed	16	40,707	8	26,114	5	12,640	3	1,953
Postal Service	7	9,839	2 }	} 12,400	--	--	5 }	} 7,906
Civil Service	27	10,467	1 }		--	--	26 }	
Distribution, Offices	6	24,203	1 }	} 4,339	2	18,339	3 }	} 9,063
Insurance, Banking	5	7,538	3 }		--	--	2 }	
Professions, Services	15	17,211	7	10,861	3	384	5	5,966
Total	115	319,343	43	123,165	23	170,454	49	25,724

Abbreviations: Irish TUC: Irish Trade Union Congress; CIU: Congress of Irish Unions; ITGWU: Irish Transport and General Workers' Union

membership of 59,389, that is, 31 per cent of the total in all trade unions.

The seven unions with more than 5,000 members in Northern Ireland were the Amalgamated Engineering Union, the Amalgamated Society of Woodworkers, Amalgamated Transport and General Workers' Union, Electrical Trades Union, National Union of General and Municipal Workers, National Union of Tailors and Garment Workers and the Union of Shop, Distributive and Allied Workers. These seven unions with a total membership of 134,480 represented 69 per cent of all trade unionists.

There were four general unions with 95,941 members or almost exactly half the total membership of all trade unions. The thirty craft unions had 52,135 members and the thirteen "mixed" unions, 17,334 members. Seven unions in the Post Office and Civil Service classifications had 9,373 members and the five unions with members in the distributive trades and in clerical occupations had 10,135 members. There were four unions in insurance and banking with a membership of 2,891. The fourteen unions classified under "Professions, Services" had 6,060 members.

Number and Membership of Trade Unions in Northern Ireland----------

	Unions	Members
Unions with Chief Offices in		
Republic of Ireland	5	8,177
Northern Ireland	8	10,681
Outside Ireland	64	175,011
Total	77	193,869
Unions affiliated to Irish TUC	46	175,253
Other Trade Unions	31	18,616
Unions with Membership of		
100 or less	17	778
101 to 250	12	1,965
251 " 500	7	2,637
501 " 1,000	11	7,620
1,001 " 1,500	9	11,132
1,501 " 2,000	7	12,678
2,001 " 3,000	4	10,435
3,001 " 5,000	3	12,144
5,001 " 7,500	4	25,853
Over 7,500	3	108,627
Total	77	193,869
General Unions	4	95,941
Manual Workers		
Craft	30	52,135
Mixed	13	17,334
Postal Service	2	} 9,373
Civil Service	5	
Distribution, Offices	5	10,135
Insurance, Banking	4	2,891
Professions, Services	14	6,060
Total	77	193,869

Appendix Eight

Source: Joint Memorandum on Trade Union Unity 1954

CIU annual report 1954

CONGRESS OF IRISH UNIONS

LIST OF AFFILIATED UNIONS

Union	Membership
Actors' Equity Association, Irish	210
Automobile Drivers' & Automobile Mechanics' Union	1,500
Bookbinders' and Allied Trades' Union, Irish	1,075
Building Workers' Trade Union	1,700
Distributive Workers' and Clerks, Irish Union of	14,697
Electrical Trades' Union (Ireland)	2,500
Electrotypers' and Stereotypers' Society	83
Engineering and Foundry Union, Irish	2,960
Engineering, Industrial & Electrical Trade Union, Irish	1,978
Guild of Irish Journalists	46
Painters' & Decorators' Trade Union of Ireland, United House and Ship	423
Plasterers' Trade Society, Operative	1,300
Racecourse Bookmakers' Assistants Association	200
Regular Dublin Coopers' Society	254
Seamen's and Port Workers' Union, Irish	2,950
Sheet Metal Workers' and Gas Meter Makers of Ireland, The National Union of	300
Sub-Postmasters' Union, Irish	1,500
Transport and General Workers' Union, Irish	148,442
Typographical Provident Society, Dublin	1,267
Vintners', Grocers' & Allied Trades' Assistants, Irish National Union of	3,844
Wood-cutting Machinists, Irish Society of	750
Woodworkers, Irish National Union of	950
TOTAL	188,929

List of Unions Affiliated to the Irish Trade Union
Congress with affiliated Membership

(Note: Unions with less than one hundred and forty-four members
are not required to state their membership and accordingly
in these cases the figures are estimated).

Union	Membership
Assurance Representatives' Organisation	1,201
Assurance Workers, National Amalgamated Union of Life	100
Bakers', Confectioners' and Allied Workers' Amalgamated Union, Irish	5,000

Union	Membership
Blacksmiths', Forge and Smithy Workers' Society, Associated	479
Blind of Ireland, Irish National League of the	100
Blind of Great Britain and Ireland, The National League of the	124
Boilermakers' and Iron and Steel Shipbuilders, United Society of	3,656
Boot and Shoe Operatives, National Union of	500
Brushmakers, National Society of	192
Building Trade Workers of Great Britain and Ireland, Amalgamated Union of	1,980
Butchers' and Allied Workers' Association, North of Ireland Operative	489
Butchers' Society, Cork Operative	91
Civil Service Clerical Association	3,600
Clerical and Administrative Workers' Union	2,000
Commercial Travellers' Federation, Irish	600
Coopers' Society, Cork	47
Coppersmiths, Braziers and Metalworkers, National Society of	360
Electrical Trades' Union	5,453
Enginering Union, Amalgamated	21,486
Engineering and Shipbuilding Draughtsmen, Association of	1,216
Fire Brigade Union, The	100
Foundry Workers, Amalgamated Union of	882
Furniture Trade Operatives, National Union of	2,934
General and Municipal Workers, National Union of	2,400
Hairdressers and Allied Workers, The Irish Union of	411
Insurance Workers, National Federation of	1,158
Journalists, National Union of	508
Locomotive Engineers and Firemen, Associated Society of	1,483
Municipal Employees' Trade Union, Irish	1,500
Musicians, Irish Federation of	788
Musicians' Association, Northern Ireland	300
Packing Case Makers, National Union of	50
Painters, National Society of	3,884
Pilots' and Marine Officers' Association	200
Plasterers, National Association of Operative	1,011
Plumbing Trades' Union	3,323
Post Office Engineering Union	545
Post Office Engineering Union, Irish	1,500
Post Office Workers' Union	6,000
Post Office Workers, Union of	2,742
Printers, Amalgamated Society of Lithographic	288
Printing, Bookbinding and Paper Workers, National Union of	1,487
Rural Workers, Federation of	1,000
Scalemakers, National Union of	100
Scientific Workers, Association of	59
Seamen, National Union of	1,000
Sheet Metal Workers and Braziers, National Union of	900
Shoe and Leather Workers' Union, Irish	3,000
Shop, Distributive and Allied Workers, Union of	6,335
Slaters, Tilers and Roofing Operatives, Amalgamated	102

Union	Membership
Supervisory Staffs, Executives and Technicians, Association of	1,206
Tailors and Garment Workers, National Union of	6,651
Teachers' Organisation, Irish National	7,414
Theatrical and Kine Employees, National Association of	492
Transport and General Workers' Union, Amalgamated	40,000
Transport Employees, National Association of	3,000
Transport Salaried Staffs' Association	4,147
Typographical Association	2,138
Vehicle Builders, National Union of	2,000
Vocational Education Officers' Organisation	600
Women Workers' Union, Irish	6,500
Woodworkers, Amalgamated Society of	16,860
Workers' Union of Ireland	25,000
TOTAL	210,663

Appendix Nine:

From: Jerome J. Judge: 'Trade Union Organisation in the
Republic of Ireland': M.Econ.Sc. thesis 1951

In view of the Report on Vocational Organisation[1] and
the efforts of the Irish Trade Union Congress to bring
about a reorganisation within the Trade Union movement,
the same suggestions as contained in the 1939 Report of
the Irish Trade Union Congress[2] are set out herewith, but
in terms of present day numbers and types of trade unions.
Its chief purpose is for any comparison with what has been
done or what would have to be done, if there was a
reorganisation along the same or similar lines.

Building and Furnishing:[3]

ITUC

Painters & Decorators, National Society of Operative House and Ship	1,300
Plasterers, National Association of Operative	500
Plumbing Trades Union	1,400
Slaters, Tilers and Roofing Operatives, Amalgamated Society of	135
Woodworkers, Amalgamated Society of	8,000
Furniture Trade Operatives, National Union of	5,000
Amalgamated Transport & General Workers Union	--
Workers Union of Ireland	--
Amalgamated Engineering Union	--
National Society of Brushmakers	290

IND

Packing Case Makers Trade Union	118
Irish Vehicle & General Woodworkers Union	300

CIU

Brick & Stone Layers' Trade Union, Ancient Guild of Incorporated	2,500
Engineering & Foundry Union, Irish	4,200
Engineering, Industrial & Electrical T.U., Irish	4,000
Painters & Decorators, Irish National Union	750
Painters & Decorators Trade Union of Ireland, United House and Ship	450
Painters Society, Cork House	--
Plasterers Trade Society of Dublin, Operative	1,900
Woodworkers, Irish National Union of	1,500
Woodcutting Machinists, Irish Society of	750
Regular Dublin Operative Coopers Society	260

[* Some footnotes in the original text are omitted here. C.McC.]

ENGINEERING, SHIP BUILDING, VEHICLE BUILDING:
ITUC

Amalgamated Engineering Union	4,500
Blacksmiths, Forge & Smithy Workers Society	150
Boilermakers & Iron & Steel Shipbuilders, United Society of	400
Coppersmiths, Braziers & Metal Workers, National Society of	170
Plumbing Trades Union	--
Vehicle Builders, National Union of	3,000
National Union of Scale Makers	71

IND

Gold, Silver & Allied Trade, National Union	200
Engineers Association, The Electrical Power	30

CIU

Electrical Trades Union (Ireland)	3,000
Engineering & Foundry Union, Irish	4,200
Engineering, Industrial & Electrical, Irish	4,000
Sheetmetal Makers & Gas Meter Makers of Ireland, National Union of	460
Automobile Drivers, Automobile Mechanics Union, Irish	4,000

IND

Engine Drivers, Cranemen, Firemen & Machinemen's Trade Union, United Stationery	1,036

SEAMEN & DOCKERS:

ITUC

National Union of Seamen	--

CIU

Irish Seamen's & Port Workers' Union	--

IND

Pilots & Marine Officers Association	250

RAIL & ROAD TRANSPORT:

ITUC

Locomotive Engineers & Firemen, Associated Society	900
National Union of Railwaymen	4,550
Transport Salaried Staffs Association (RCA)	2,388

CIU

Irish Railwaymen's Union	2,500

IND

Transport Officers Guild	115

PRINTING & PUBLISHING:

ITUC

Typographical Association	879
Society of Lithographic Artists, Designers, Engravers, & Process Workers	100
Amalgamated Society of Lithographic Printers & Auxiliaries thereto of G.B. & Ireland	160
National Union of Journalists	300

IND

Institute of Journalists	100

CIU

Irish Bookbinders & Allied Trades Union	1,000
Electrotypers & Stereotypers Society, Dublin & District	80
The Dublin Typographical Provident Society	1,300
The Guild of Irish Journalists	70

BAKERY:

ITUC

Irish Bakers, Confectioners and Allied Workers Amalgamated Union	3,600

DISTRIBUTIVE, CLERICAL, SUPERVISORY:

ITUC

National Amalgamated Union of Life Assurance Workers	80
National Federation of Insurance Workers	550
Commercial Travellers Federation, Irish	900

IND

Guild of Insurance Officials	1,000
Irish Local Government Officials	3,500

CIU

Irish National Union of Vintners, Grocers and Allied Assistants	4,000
Irish Union of Distributive Workers & Clerks	14,000

TEACHERS:

ITUC

Irish National Teachers Organisation	11,000
Vocational Educational Officers Association	650

CIVIL SERVICE:

ITUC

Post Office Workers Union	7,000
Irish Post Office Engineering Union	2,000
Civil Service Clerical Association	4,000

CIU

Irish Sub-Postmasters Union	1,571

GENERAL WORKERS:

ITUC

Amalgamated Transport & General Workers Union	12,500
Workers Union of Ireland	25,000
Tailors & Garment Workers, National Union of	5,500
Boot & Shoe Operatives, National Union of	5,387
Cigarette Machine Operators Society	40
Irish Women Workers Union	6,000
Federation of Rural Workers	9,000
Blind, National League of the	185
Municipal Employees Trade Union, Irish	2,500
Musicians, Irish Federation of	450
Butchers Society, Cork Operative	90

IND

Cigarette Machine Operators Society	40
Hairdressers Assistants, Irish Union of	600

CIU

Irish Transport & General Workers Union	130,000
Bookmakers Assistants Association, The Irish Racecourse	200
Actors Equity Association, Irish	200

It appears that the task of reorganising the trade unions
along similar lines as those proposed by the Irish Trade
Union Congress in 1939 or according to the Report of
Vocational Organisation has been still further complicated
by the formation of a separate Congress, representing
entirely Irish unions, which Congress appears to be
building up along similar organisational lines as the
Irish Trade Union Congress, thus, in effect, having "at
least two of each type of Union."

Appendix Ten:

The statements of membership submitted by affiliated unions
up to the date of writing this report show little change
on last year's figures, when the total membership
affiliated was 210,000. Affiliation figures for some
preceding years are given hereunder. Trades Council
membership is excluded.

1922:	189,000	1932:	95,000	1942:	164,000
1923:	183,000	1933:	95,000	1943:	183,000
1924:	175,000	1934:	115,000	1944:	187,000
1925:	149,000	1935:	125,000	1945:	146,000
1926:	123,000	1936:	134,000	1946:	147,000
1927:	113,000	1937:	146,000	1947:	163,000
1928:	103,000	1938:	161,000	1948:	187,000
1929:	92,000	1939:	162,000	1949:	196,000
1930:	102,000	1940:	163,000	1950:	197,000
1931:	102,000	1941:	173,000	1951:	211,000

Source: ITUC annual report 1954 p.27.

Appendix Eleven:

TRADE UNION MEMBERSHIP
(% of total membership)

Union Type	1945	1950	1955	1960	1965	1970	Increase
General	80,000 (46.67)	163,038 (57.16)	179,941 (57.96)	180,619 (56.7)	201,065 (56.31)	217,452 (54.52)	137,117 (+171)
White-Collar	40,195 (23.35)	48,673 (17.06)	55,054 (17.73)	61,785 (19.39)	72,292 (20.24)	91,127 (22.85)	50,932 (+127)
Craft	17,942 (10.42)	26,481 (9.28)	27,955 (9.0)	26,273 (8.25)	30,453 (8.53)	32,481 (8.15)	14,543 (+81)
Other	33,673 (19.56)	47,061 (16.5)	47,506 (15.3)	49,895 (15.66)	53,287 (14.92)	57,754 (14.48)	24,081 (+72)
TOTAL	172,145	285,253	310,456	318,572	357,097	398,818	226,673 (+132)

Source: B. Hillery and A. Kelly: 'Aspects of trade union membership' in Management
XXI, 4 April 1974

Appendix Twelve:

MEMBERSHIP OF BRITISH-BASED UNIONS IN THE REPUBLIC

Year	1945	1950	1955	1960	1965	1970
Membership	39,429	47,474	42,242	40,511	50,292	53,407
% of Total Membership	22.9	16.64	13.61	12.72	14.0	13.3

Source: B. Hillery and A. Kelly: 'Aspects of trade union membership' Management XXI, 4 April 1974

Appendix Thirteen:

Extract from:

D.W. Bleakley: "The Northern Ireland Trade Union Movement":
Journal of the Statistical & Social Inquiry Society of
Ireland, XIX 1953-54 pp.158-161.

Membership of T.U.'s. registered in N.I. or G.B.*

Year	No. of Unions	Membership
1927	71	65,500
1929	67	63,000
1933	67	56,000
1941	72	109,000
1945	78	142,000
1953 (all unions, British, N. Ireland and Eire based)	92	200,000

The 92 unions which organise in Northern Ireland divide
into three groups: those registered in Great Britain, those
registered in Northern Ireland, and those with headquarters
in Eire.

About 90% of Northern Ireland trade unionists belong to
British based unions and the following list shows their
composition:-

English and Scottish Unions Operating in Northern Ireland
(69 in number)

Union	Membership
Amalgamated Engineering Union	17,190
Amalgamated Slaters', Tilers & Roofing Operatives Society	119
Amalgamated Society of Lithographic Printers of G.B. & Ir.	288
Amalgamated Society of Woodcutting Machinists	656
Amalgamated Society of Woodworkers	7,568
Amalgamated Transport and General Workers' Union	73,260
Amalgamated Union of Building Trade Workers of G.B. & Ir.	2,139
Amalgamated Union of Foundry Workers of G.B. & Ir.	873

* cf. Ulster Year Books, and Reports of Registrar of
   Friendly Societies (N.I.).

Union	Membership
Associated Blacksmiths', Forge and Smithy Workers' Society	373
Associated Society of Locomotive Engineers and Firemen	not available
Association of Building Technicians	6
Association of Engineering & Shipbuilding Draughtsmen	1,216
Association of Scientific Workers	53
Association of Supervisory Staffs, Executives and Technicians	1,206
British Broadcasting Corporation Staff Association	147
Civil Service Clerical Association	not available
Civil Service Union	349
Clerical and Administrative Workers' Union	2,000
Electrical Power Engineers' Association	216
Electrical Trades Union	5,453
Engineer Surveyors' Association	42
Fire Brigades Union	501
Guild of Insurance Officials	387
Inland Revenue Staff Federation	510
Iron, Steel & Metal Dressers' Trade Society	76
Medical Practitioners' Union	210
National Society of Painters	2,538
National Society of Life Assurance Workers	27
National Association of Theatrical & Kine Employees	492
National Federation of Insurance Workers	1,158
National Association of Operative Plasterers	964
National League of the Blind, G.B. & Ireland	146
National Society of Brushmakers	90
National Society of Coppersmiths, Braziers and Metal Workers	360
National Society of Electrotypers and Stenographers	35
National Society of Pottery Workers	not available
National Union of Boot and Shoe Operatives	500
National Union of Co-operative Officials	34
National Union of Furniture Trade Operatives	1,383
National Union of General and Municipal Workers	12,434
National Union of Gold, Silver and Allied Trades	49
National Union of Hosiery Workers	550
National Union of Journalists	114
National Union of Operative Heating, Domestic and Ventilating Engineers and General Metal Workers	167
National Union of Packing Case Makers	not available
National Union of Press Telegraphists	21
National Union of Printing, Bookbinding and Paper Workers	1,487
National Union of Scalemakers	29
National Union of Seamen	3,000
National Union of Sheetmetal Workers and Braziers	900
National Union of Tailors and Garment Workers	6,651
National Union of Vehicle Builders	1,006

Union	Membership
Plumbing Trades Union	1,944
Post Office Engineering Union	545
Prison Officers' Association	29
Shipconstructors' and Shipwrights' Association	1,347
Society of Lithographic Artists, Designers, Engravers and Process Workers	70
Society of Technical Civil Servants	29
Transport Salaried Staffs Association	1,695
Typographical Association	1,129
Union of Shop, Distributive and Allied Workers	6,335
United Patternmakers' Association	329
United Society of Boilermakers' and Iron and Steel Ship Builders	3,664
Union of Post Office Workers	2,742
Pearl Federation	35
Prudential Staff Union	370
Refuge Field Staff Association	109
Royal Liver Employers Union	130

This list comprises the most important section of Northern Irish trade unionism, and, except for a few "company" unions, all come within Webb's definition of a trade union as: "A continuous association of wage - or salary - earners for the purpose of maintaining or improving the conditions of their working lives."

The next grouping is that of trade unions with registered or chief offices in Northern Ireland. There are 18 such unions and their membership is 27,000.

Northern Ireland Unions

(18 in number).

Union	Membership
Belfast Bread Servers' Trade Union	750
Belfast Coopers' Trade Union	59
Belfast Operative Bakers Society	1,180
Clothpassers and Winding Masters Trade Society	59
Flax and Other Textile Workers Trade Union	570
Loom-overlookers, Trade Union	590
Lurgan Hemmers and Veiners and General Workers, Trade Union	999
Northern Ireland Musicians' Association	319
Northern Ireland Textile Workers' Trade Union	2,407
Portadown, Banbridge and District Textile Workers' Trade Union	373
Power-loom Yarndressers' Trade Society	191
Ulster Transport and Allied Operatives' Union	8,031
Ulster Teachers' Union	2,730

Union	Membership
Northern Ireland Civil Service Association	5,058
North of Ireland Operative Butchers and Allied Workers' Association	480
Belfast Corporation Senior Officers' Association	not available
Ulster Chemists' Association	not available
Ulster Public Officers' Association	2,700

In addition to this group of 18 unions, 9 small teaching associations join with the two main teaching organisations in the work of the Federal Council of Teachers in Northern Ireland. It should also be noted that some of the Northern Ireland textile unions, and the unions in the bread and baking trades, form part of larger unions.

Most Northern Ireland based unions tend to be regional in outlook and take little part in the work of the trade union movement as a whole. The four largest local unions, U.T. & A.O.U., N.I.C.S.A., U.T.U., and U.P.O.A. are not affiliated to the Irish T.U.C. or the Belfast Trades Council, though, in the case of the civil servants there are legal reasons preventing co-operation with other trade unions.

The final group of unions covers those with headquarters in Eire. There are 5 such unions and total membership is 8,700.

Trade Unions with Headquarters in Eire
and Operating in N.I.
(5 in number).

Union	Membership
Irish National Teachers' Organisation	1,288
Irish Bank Officials' Association	1,604
Irish Transport & General Workers' Union	2,825
Irish Bakers', Confectioners' and Allied Workers Amalgamated Union	not available
National Association of Transport Employees	2,961

The final union in this list is an interesting newcomer that last year replaced the British National Union of Railwaymen. The N.U.R., after 67 years in Ireland, decided to withdraw from the country, and it co-operated in the formation of the new association, giving it a substantial sum of money to set it on its feet. This was a most important decision from the point of view of Northern Ireland trade unionists, and it has given rise to a great deal of discussion.

Analysis of Numbers

It will be seen from these figures that the A.T.G.W.U.
dominates the Northern Ireland trade union scene as it does
in Britain. 40% of our trade unionists are in the Transport
Union, and the A.E.U., as second largest union, has only
17,190 members, while the N.U.G.M.W. is third with 12,434.
Six other unions have more than 5,000 members. These are
(4 British based) N.U.T.G.W., U.S.D.A.W., A.S.W., and E.T.U.,
and (2 Northern Ireland based) U.T.A.O.U., and N.I.C.S.A.
A recent break-down of the union figures** by the Irish T.U.C.
reveals the following pattern:-

No. in Union.	No. of such Unions.	Total Membership
100 or less	17	778
101 - 250	12	1,965
251 - 500	7	2,637
501 - 1,000	11	7,620
1,001 - 1,500	9	11,132
1,501 - 2,000	7	12,678
2,001 - 3,000	4	10,435
3,001 - 5,000	3	12,144

The tendency in Northern Ireland, as elsewhere, is towards
concentration of numbers into a few organisations. Thus, out
of the 92 unions operating in this region, 70 had memberships
below 5,000, and 47 had less than 1,000. With the rising
costs of administration, and the growth of large scale and
highly mechanised industries, this trend is inevitable and
is likely to continue. The following table shows the
industrial classification of unions operating in Northern
Ireland as recorded by the Irish T.U.C.:-

Industry	No. of Unions	Membership
General unions	4	95,941
Manual workers:		
(a) craft	30	52,135
(b) mixed	13	17,334
Postal Services }	2 }	9,373 }
Civil Service }	5 }	
Distribution, Offices	5	10,135
Insurance,Banking	4	2,891
Professions, Services	14	6,060
		193,869

** Trade Union Information (Irish T.U.C.). April 1953, p.4.

Appendix Fourteen:

Office of the Minister for Industry and Commerce, Dublin,
9th April, 1947.

Secretary,
Irish Trade Union Congress,
32 Nassau Street,
Dublin.

A Chara,

I am desired by the Minister for Industry and Commerce to
say that he has under consideration the revision of the
Trade Union Act, 1941-42, arising out of the decision of the
Supreme Court in the case of the National Union of Railwaymen v. Daniel Sullivan and others, the expiration in
September next of the power to reduce the deposits prescribed in the schedule of the Act, and his general desire
to secure effective and, if possible, agreed legislation
for the regulation of Trade Unions. I have set down
hereunder, in rough form, the Minister's present views as
to the main objects which legislation in connection with
Trade Unions shall seek to attain:-

(a)   An organisation should not be entitled to call itself
      a Trade Union, or hold itself out as being such,
      unless its constitution and rules are so framed as to
      make the organisation of workers (or masters) for
      the purpose of carrying on negotiations and entering
      into agreements concerning the conditions of their
      employment the primary purpose of the organisation.
      A Trade Union should have known and suitable rules,
      and known officers and offices.

(b)   It is desirable that there should be some formal
      act of registration or certification, following on
      the examination of the purposes and rules of the
      organisation by a competent and independent authority
      and possibly the lodgment of a deposit as evidence of
      its bona fides before an organisation can describe
      itself as a Trade Union, or practise as such.

(c)   While protecting the position of existing Trade Unions,
      it is desirable to provide that the foundation of a
      new Union should not be facilitated, until it has
      been established to the satisfaction of the competent
      and independent authority that the proposed new Union
      will promote the organisation of workers not previously
      organised effectively or is desired by a substantial
      number of workers previously organised in another Union,
      and will not tend to promote undesirable conflict between
      Trade Unions. A new Union should have its headquarters'
      control within the State.

(d)   The continued registration or certification of an organ-
      isation as a Trade Union should be conditional on the
      maintenance of its constitution and rules in an
      approved form, on its conducting its business in
      accordance with its rules, and the absence of com-
      plaint from other Trade Unions that its activities
      have tended to promote the disorganisation of workers,
      or have improperly prejudiced the position of workers
      organised by another Trade Union.

(e)   There should be protection for individual workers
      against the inequitable acts of Trade Unions of
      which they are members, or membership of which is
      necessary to procure employment.

(f)   A Trade Union, like any other person, should be
      bound by the agreements into which it enters, and
      parties with whom such agreements are made should
      have right of legal redress if a Trade Union breaks
      an agreement or permits its members to do so.

(g)   The amalgamation of existing Unions catering for
      similar classes of workers should be encouraged and
      facilitated.

It will be clear that in regard to some of the matters
indicated above, the framing of legislation might be a
matter of some difficulty in view of the Supreme Court's
judgement that 'a law which takes away the right of
citizens at their choice to form Associations and Unions not
contrary to public order and morality is not a law which
can validly be made under the Constitution'. The Minister
has not yet sought legal advice in this connection but
he believes that the general aims could be secured by con-
fining the protection and privileges conferred by legislation
to Unions formed and acting in accordance with the proposed
law, and perhaps, also, by control of the use of the name
Trade Union or cognate names.

The Minister desires to obtain the views of your Council on
this matter as a preliminary to discussion. It is his
view that there is no necessary conflict between the aims
which the Government should endeavour to achieve by legislation,
in the control of Trade Unions, and the aims which, it
appears to him, would naturally be regarded as desirable
by the leaders of Irish Trade Unionism. He would hope,
therefore, to be able to obtain general agreement on the
main lines of proposals for legislation to amend the Trade
Union Act.

Your Council will appreciate that owing to the expiration
of the powers given under Section 8 of the Trade Union Act,
1941, there is some element of urgency in the preparation of
amending legislation.

Mise le meas,
        (Signed)   B. CULLIGAN,
                   Runai Aire.

(reproduced from ITUC 1947 pp. 75-77).

Appendix Fifteen:

1947:

Replies from the members of the Central Council
on the Revision of the Trade Union Act.

Extract:

(William O'Brien papers: Ms.13974)

BUILDING WORKERS' TRADE UNION - FURTHER REPORT:

In making the following suggestions for the amendment
of the Trade Union Act 1941-42, or the Industrial Relations
Act as the case may be, you will understand that our main
concern at the moment is the improvement in the system of
organisation and the method of negotiation for the building
industry or such like industries, there may be many other
aspects of these Acts which need careful consideration,
but that would mean detailed examination of almost every
section.

As you are aware, the Group system has done very useful
work, but has many weaknesses, amongst the most notable
of which is the lack of control, lack of finance, multiplicity of unions, and the unbusiness-like method of
attending to correspondence etc. which was due to the
fact that we were dependent on the goodwill of one or other
of the whole time officials, who in addition to carrying
on his own job undertook to do the work of the Group.
Another feature of the Group System as at present constituted,
is the fact that we have had to include the Cross Channel
Unions amongst those taking part in our deliberations.
It is with a view to the remedying of these defects that
we make the following suggestions:-

INDUSTRIAL GROUPS

An Industrial Group means a Standing Body substantially
representative of each section of workers or employers in
a scheduled industry, whether throughout the whole State
or in a particular part thereof.

Each section of workers or employers in a scheduled
industry shall be designated by Craft or Occupation.

Where more than one Trade Union caters for a
particular Craft or Occupation they shall be regarded as
being members of the one section for the purpose of the Act.

Each section shall have the power to appoint delegates to
the Industrial Group.

JOINT INDUSTRIAL COUNCILS

Each Industrial Group constituted in accordance with the
provisions of the preceding paragraph shall have the power
to appoint an appropriate number of delegates as members
of the Joint Industrial Council of their industry, provided
always that every member of such Joint Industrial Council
is drawn from an enterprise or trade union whose headquarters control is situated within the State. The
delegates representative of the workers and employers
appointed as members of the Joint Industrial Council shall
be designated as the Negotiating Committee for the workers
and employers respectively in their industry, and shall
have the same powers as the holders of a negotiating licence.

A registered Joint Industrial Council shall be a board
in relation to which section 3 of the Trade Union Act '42
is applicable.

A Joint Industrial Council may operate in respect of the
whole State and shall be called a National Joint Industrial
Council.

A Joint Industrial Council may operate in respect of a
clearly defined area and shall be called an Area Joint
Industrial Council.

Every National Industrial Council, Area Joint Industrial
Council and Industrial Group shall have registered offices,
officials and staff required to conduct the business carried
on by such body.

The expenses incurred for the payment of the officers and
staff, and registered offices to be defrayed out of a tax
imposed on the particular industry.

This tax might also be utilised as a guarantee fund against
any loss of office or benefit by any member of an outside
controlled trade union which decides to merge with an
existing Irish controlled union, or to establish a new
Irish Union.

OWEN HYNES.

Appendix Sixteen:

THE NATIONAL WAGE ROUNDS

1946-47 (first round) Increases varied but, on average, wage rates rose by about one-fourth.

1948 (second round) Average increase on the basis of a national agreement resulted in £0.40 to £0.50 per week for men and about half these amounts for women.

1951 (third round) A general movement resulting in various increases ranging for men from £0.50 to £0.90, women getting about two-thirds of the men's increase.

1952 (fourth round) A national agreement, partially negotiated on the trade union side but generally implemented, resulted in an increase of £0.625 per week, women getting about two-thirds of this.

1955 (fifth round) A general increase, with some workers during the round coming back for more; there was great diversity in the increases, ranging from £0.55 to £0.85 per week.

1957 (sixth round) A national agreement for £0.50 per week, women getting from £0.25 to £0.375 per week.

1959 (seventh round) A general movement took place resulting in increases for men of from £0.50 to £0.75 per week and for women £0.325 to £0.50. It was followed in 1960 by a movement for a reduction in working hours and for the five-day week.

1961 (eighth round) By the summer of 1961, increases of up to £0.70 per week had been negotiated, but settlements for electricians and building workers pushed up the rates; and by the end of the year, they ranged from £1.00 to £1.25 a week for men and from £0.50 to £0.75 for women.

1964 (ninth round). A nationally negotiated increase gave increases to everyone of 12 per cent subject to a minimum increase of £1.00 for men.

1966 (tenth round) In the absence of a national agreement, the ICTU recommended a maximum of £1.00 a week, which was later supported by the Labour Court and generally applied.

1968 (eleventh round) During 1967, the practice of negotiating two-year comprehensive agreements began, and this became the feature of the eleventh round, the increases being £1.75 to £2.00 per week for men, in two or three phases; women got about 75 per cent of this.

1969-70 (twelfth round) Electricians in November 1968 and,
in particular, maintenance craftsmen in April 1969 led the
way for settlements which were of the order of £4.00 a
week in two or three phases over an eighteen-month period.
Women's increases averaged about 80 per cent of men's.
There was a very wide spread of termination dates by this time.

1971 (thirteenth round) This was a national agreement
concluded on December 21 1970, providing for a phased
agreement over eighteen months, the first phase being £2.00
per week (women a minimum of £1.70) and the second phase
4 per cent with an automatic adjustment for increases in
the consumer price index figure.

1972 (fourteenth round) This was a national agreement
concluded on July 31 1972, providing for a phased agreement
of (in general) seventeen months, the first phase giving
9 per cent on basic pay up to £30 a week, 7½ per cent on
next £10 and 4 per cent on the remainder (with some additional
provisions), and the second phase, which arises after twelve
months, giving 4 per cent on basic pay with an automatic
adjustment for increases in the consumer price index figure.

1974 (fifteenth round) This was a national agreement amended
on March 7 1974 providing for a phased agreement of from
twelve to fifteen months, with in the first phase increases
of from 5% to 9% with a floor of £2.40, and a second phase
of 4% with a supplement in both phases of 60p. a week.
There were some complex provisions aimed at compensating
for the shorter term.

1975 (sixteenth round) This was a national agreement concluded on April 22 1975 providing for a phased agreement
of twelve months duration, each phase being of three months
duration, the first being 8% (the CPI increases) with a
floor of £2, the second being 4%, or 5% if the CPI rises
to that level or higher, subject to a floor of £1; the
third phase and the fourth phase being similar to the
second, subject to an overriding maximum for the year of
26%. On September 24 1975 the agreement was adjusted,
in its third and fourth phases, by linking it directly to
the CPI providing neither a minimum or a maximum.

Appendix Seventeen:

Year	ITUC	CIU
1922	189,000	
1923	183,000	
1924	175,000	
1925	149,000	
1926	123,000	
1927	113,000	
1928	103,000	
1929	92,000	
1930	102,000	
1931	102,000	
1932	95,000	
1933	95,000	
1934	115,000	
1935	125,000	
1936	134,000	
1937	146,000	
1938	161,000	
1939	162,000	
1940	163,000	
1941	173,000	
1942	164,000	
1943	183,000	
1944	187,000	
1945	146,000	77,500
1946	147,000	80,000
1947	163,000	104,315
1948	187,000	132,097
1949	196,000	159,609
1950	197,000	170,202
1951	211,000	170,601
1952	214,000	180,893
1953	208,000	188,929
1954	211,141	194,138
1955	218,000	194,138
1956	221,000	192,905
1957	222,000	192,991
1958	226,333	187,969
	(66 unions)	(21 unions)

Source: R. Roberts, Journal of the Statistical and
Social Inquiry Society of Ireland XX: 2 :   p.95 (1958-59).

Appendix Eighteen:

International Labour Organisation

(a)   Convention 87:   Freedom of Association and
        Protection of the Right to Organise

Article 2

Workers and employers, without distinction whatsoever,
shall have the right to establish and, subject only
to the rules of the organisation concerned, to join
organisations of their own choosing without previous
authorisation.

Article 3

1.   Workers' and employers' organisations shall have
the right to draw up their constitutions and rules,
to elect their representatives in full freedom, to
organise their administration and activities and to
formulate their programmes.

2.   The public authorities shall refrain from any
interference which would restrict this right or impede
the lawful exercise thereof.

Article 4

Workers' and employers' organisations shall not be
liable to be dissolved or suspended by administrative
authority.

Article 5

Workers' and employers' organisations shall have the
right to establish and join federations and confederations
and any such organisation, federation or confederation,
shall have the right to affiliate with international
organisations of workers and employers.

Article 6

The provisions of Articles 2, 3 and 4 hereof apply
to federations and confederations of workers' and
employers' organisations.

Article 7

The acquisition of legal personality by workers' and
employers' organisations, federations and confederations
shall not be made subject to conditions of such a
character as to restrict the application of the provisions
of Articles 2, 3 and 4 hereof.

Article 8

1.   In exercising the rights provided for in this
Convention workers and employers and their respective
organisations, like other persons or organised
collectivities, shall respect the law of the land.

2.   The law of the land shall not be such as to impair,
nor shall it be so applied as to impair, the guarantees
provided for in this Convention.

Article 9

1.   The extent to which the guarantees provided for
in this Convention shall apply to the armed forces
and the police shall be determined by national laws or
regulations.

2. In accordance with the principle set forth in
paragraph 8 of Article 19 of the Constitution of
the International Labour Organisation the ratification
of this Convention by any Member shall not be deemed
to affect any existing law, award, custom or agreement
in virtue of which members of the armed forces or the
police enjoy any right guaranteed by this Convention.

Article 10

In this Convention the term "organisation" means any
organisation of workers or of employers for furthering
and defending the interests of workers or of employers,

Article 11

Each Member of the International Labour Organisation
for which this Convention is in force undertakes to take
all necessary and appropriate measures to ensure that
workers and employers may exercise freely the right to
organise.

(b)   Convention 98 concerning the Application of the
       Principles of the Right to Organise and to
       Bargain Collectively.

Article 1

1.   Workers shall enjoy adequate protection against
acts of anti-union discrimination in respect of their
employment.

2.   Such protection shall apply more particularly
in respect of acts calculated to:

(a)   make the employment of a worker subject to the condition that he shall not join a union or shall relinquish trade union membership;

(b)   cause the dismissal of or otherwise prejudice a worker by reason of union membership or because of participation in union activities outside working hours or, with the consent of the employer, within working hours.

Article 2

1.   Workers' and employers' organisations shall enjoy adequate protection against any acts of interference by each other or each other's agents or members in their establishment, functioning or administration.

2.   In particular, acts which are designed to promote the establishment of workers' organisations under the domination of employers or employers' organisations, or to support workers' organisations by financial or other means, with the object of placing such organisations under the control of employers or employers' organisations, shall be deemed to constitute acts of interference within the meaning of this Article.

Article 3

Machinery appropriate to national conditions shall be established, where necessary, for the purpose of ensuring respect for the right to organise as defined in the preceding articles.

Article 4

Measures appropriate to national conditions shall be taken, where necessary, to encourage and promote the full development and utilisation of machinery for voluntary negotiation between employers or employers' organisations and workers' organisations, with a view to the regulation of terms and conditions of employment by means of collective agreements.

Article 5

1.   The extent to which the guarantees provided for in this Convention shall apply to the armed forces and the police shall be determined by national laws or regulations.

2.   In accordance with the principle set forth in paragraph 8 of Article 19 of the Constitution of the International Labour Organisation the ratification of this Convention by any Member shall not be deemed to affect any existing law, award, custom or agreement in virtue of which members of the armed forces or the police enjoy any right guaranteed by this Convention.

Article 6

"This Convention does not deal with the position of
public servants engaged in the administration of
the State, nor shall it be construed as prejudicing
their rights or status in any way."

(Source: ITUC 1955 p.114).

[Note: The conventions still remain to trouble
the government;   and the Irish Congress of Trade
Unions in the light of their provisions has queried
recent Irish legislation, to the point that the
matter has been transmitted to the ILO Committee
of Experts.   See Maurice Cashell: Influence on
Irish Law and Practice of International Labour
Standards   in International Labour Review:
Vol. CVI, 1, July 1972.   pp.57-58.   For a
brief discussion on the general acceptability of
the convention see: Freedom of Association:
an International Survey: International Labour
Office Geneva 1975 pp.38-40.   C.McC.]

SOURCES

PRIMARY SOURCES

Manuscript material:

Alexander, Paul: Letter of August 21 1975 concerning
the establishment in 1951 of the
Irish Shoe and Leather Workers' Union.

Commission on   Manuscript submissions to the Commission
Vocational Organ-   which have been deposited in the National
isation 1943:   Library, in particular the following:
Volume 12, document 17A; Volume 16,
documents 92,92A and 92B; Volume 18,
document 136 and 165.

Johnson, Thomas: Private papers deposited in the National
Library and in particular Mss. 17124,
17149(1), 17149 (11), 19197, 17265,17267.

Mortished, R.J.P.:   "Irish Trade Union Law November 1951";
paper delivered to the Civics Institute;
among the Johnson papers.

Northern Ireland   Restricted access in Trinity College
Committee minutes: Library: November 30 1945, August 27
1948, August 13 1954.

Northern Ireland   Restricted access in Trinity College
annual conference   Library: all years from 1946 to
reports: 1958 inclusive.

Northern Ireland   Restricted access in Trinity College
special conference   Library.
February 17 1951:

O'Brien, William: Private papers deposited in the National
Library and in particular Mss. 13951,
13970, 13971, 13974, 15675, 15676, 15676(1),
15704(1).

Roberts, Ruaidhri: Memorandum on Trade Union Structure in
Ireland 1954: files of the Irish
Congress of Trade Unions.

Theses

Boyle, J.W.:   The Rise of the Irish Labour Movement
1888-1907: Ph.D. thesis University
of Dublin, Trinity College 1961.

Judge, Jerome J.:   Trade Union Organisation in the Republic
of Ireland: dissertation for M.Econ.Sc.
University College Dublin 1951.

Judge, Jerome J.:   The Labour Movement in the Republic of
                     Ireland Ph.D. thesis, University
                     College Dublin 1955.

Printed material: Trade Union Reports:

Congress of Irish   Reports of annual meetings 1945 to 1959
Unions: inclusive.

Irish Trades Union   Reports of annual conferences   1901 to
Congress: 1914 inclusive.

Irish Trades Union   Reports of annual meetings 1916 and 1917.
Congress and Labour
Party:

Irish Labour Party   Reports of annual conferences 1918
and Trade Union   to 1929 inclusive.
Congress:

Irish Trade Union   Reports of annual congresses 1930
Congress: to 1959 inclusive.

Provisional United   Report of Drafting Sub-committee 1955,
Organisation: second and third reports, and draft
                         constitution 1957.

Irish Congress of   First Annual Report 1959.
Trade Unions:

National Union of   Irish Union Delegate Conference
Boot and Shoe   December 1951.
Operatives:

Trades Union Congress (UK): Trade Union Structure and Closer
                                                  Unity 1946

Printed material: other trade union publications:

Trade Union   Irish Trade Union Congress and later
Information: Irish Congress of Trade Unions: 1953,
                         vol.8, 43 and 44; 1954, vol.9, 52, 53 and
                         54; 1955, vol.10 and 60; Vol.11, 55
                         and 56; 1957, Vol.13, 74, 78 and 79.
                         1972, no.168.

Printed material: the Labour Party:

Labour Party: Annual conference reports: 1936, 1937, 1944.

Labour Party: Official statement relating to the dis-
                         affiliation of the Irish Transport and
                         General Workers Union Dublin, February 1944.

Statutory Instruments:

Bunreacht na hEireann 1937
Emergency Powers (no.83) Order 1941
Emergency Powers (no.166) Order 1942
Emergency Powers (no.38) Order 1942
Emergency Powers (no.260) Order 1943
Industrial Relations Act 1946
Trade Union Act 1871
Trade Union Act 1876
Trade Union Act 1913
Trade Union Act 1935
Trade Union Act 1941
Trade Union Act 1942
Trade Disputes Act 1906

Parliamentary Debates:

Dail Debates: June 1941, vols. 83, 84 and 85
Dail Debates: June 26 1945
Dail Debates:October 15 1947
Dail Debates:October 16 1948
Dail Debates:June 25 1946, July 9 and July 16 1946
Seanad Debates: March 14 1940
Seanad Debates: April 24 1940
Parliamentary Debates: House of Commons Northern Ireland
    October 5 and October 17 1950.

Reports of Commissions:

Commission on Vocational Organisation Dublin 1943
Royal Commission on Trade Unions 1869
Royal Commission on Trade Unions and Employers' Associations
    1965-1968 Cmnd. 3623 1968.

Cases:

Allen v. Flood [1898] A.C.1
B.&.I. Steampacket Co. v. Brannigan [1958] I.R. 128
Brendan Dunne v. Fitzpatrick [1958] I.R. 29
Cooper v. Millea [1938] I.R. 749
Educational Company v. Fitzpatrick [1961] I.R. 345
Esplanade Pharmacy Ltd. v. Larkin [1957] I.R. 285
I.T. & G.W.U. v. A.T. & G.W.U. [1936] I.R. 471
Larkin v. Long [1915] A.C. 814
Leathem v. Craig [1899] I.R. 667
N.U.R. v. Sullivan [1947] I.R. 77
Osborne v. A.S.R.S. [1910] A.C. 87
Quinn v. Leathem [1901] A.C. 495

R.(I.U.D.W.&C.) v. Rathmines U.D.C. [1928] I.R. 260
Roundabout Ltd. v. Beirne [1959] I.R. 423
Ryan v. Cooke and Quinn [1938] I.R. 512
Sherriff v. McMullen [1952] I.R. 236
Smith v. Beirne [1955] 89 I.L.T.R. 24
Taff Vale Rly. v. A.S.R.S. [1901] A.C. 426
Valentine v. Hyde [1919] 2 Ch. 129
White v. Riley [1921] 1 Ch.1.

Newspapers:

Irish Independent May 17 1949
Irish Press: June 23 1949
               April 9 1953
               April 10 1953
Irish Times: May 14 1949
               May 16 1949

SECONDARY   SOURCES

Studies directly concerned with the trade union and labour
    movement

Bagwell, Philips: The Railwaymen: The History of the
                         National Union of Railwaymen, 1963.

Bleakley, D.W.:   "The Northern Ireland Trade Union
                         Movement" in Journal of the Statistical
                         and Social Inquiry Society of Ireland,
                         XIX, 1953-1954.

Browne, M.H.:   "Industrial Labour and Incomes Policy
                         in the Republic of Ireland": in
                         British Journal of Industrial Relations,
                         III, 1965.

Bundock, Clement J.:   The National Union of Printing, Bookbinding,
                         and Paper Workers, 1959.

Cashell, Maurice: "Influence on Irish Law and Practice of
                         International Labour Standards" in
                         International Labour Review, Vol.CVI, 1,
                         July 1972.

Chronicle: British Journal of Industrial Relations,
                         issues from March 1972 to July 1974 inclusive

Clarkson, J.Dunsmore: Labour and Nationalism in Ireland:
                         New York, 1925.

Connolly, James: The Axe to the Root: Dublin 1921

     —   Erin's Hope. The End and the Means:
                         The New Evangel: Dublin 1972 edition.

Delany   V.T.H.:   "Immunity in Tort and the Trade Disputes
                         Act - a New Limitation": in Modern Law
                         Review XVIII 1955 and XIX 1956.

Erle, Sir William: The Law Relating to Trade Unions:
                         Macmillan 1868: also published in the
                         eleventh and final report of the Royal
                         Commission on Trade Unions 1869,
                         Sessional papers vol.XXXI 1868-9(20).

Fox, Alan: A History of the National Union of Boot
                         and Shoe Operatives 1894-1957, 1958.

Fox, R.M.:   Louie Bennett: Her Life and Times,
                         Dublin 1958.

Frow, Edmund and   1868 Year of the Unions, 1968.
Katanka, Michael:

Heuston, R.F.V.:   "Trade Unions and the Law": in The Irish
                         Jurist IV, 1969.

Higgenbottam, S.:   Our Society's History, 1939 (concerning
                         the Amalgamated Society of Woodworkers.)

Hillery, Brian J.:   "Trade Union Finance in the Republic of
                         Ireland": Economic and Social Review
                         V, 3, April 1974.

Hillery, B. and   "Aspects of Trade Union Membership",
Kelly, A.:   Management, XX1, 4, April 1974.

International Labour   Freedom of Association: an International
Office: Survey, Geneva, 1975.

Irish Transport and   Fifty Years of Liberty Hall: Dublin 1959.
General Workers'
Union:

Johnson, Thomas: "The Corporate State and Fascism": in
                         The Distributive Worker, June 1934.

Kahn-Freund, O.:   "Trade Unions, the Law and Society": in
                         Modern Law Review, XXXIII, 3, 1970.

Kelly, Aidan: "Changes in Occupational Structure and
                         Industrial Relations in Ireland":
                         in Management Vol.XX11, 6/7 1975.

Kendall, Walter: The Labour Movement in Europe, 1975.

Larkin, Emmet: James Larkin: Irish Labour Leader:
                         1876-1947, 1965.

McCarthy, Charles: The Decade of Upheaval: Irish Trade
                       Unions in the Nineteen Sixties: Dublin 1973.

    -        - :   "Civil Strife and the Growth of Trade Union
                       Unity": The Case of Ireland: in
                       Government and Opposition, Vol.VIII,4, 1973.

    -        - :   "Trade Unions and Economic Planning in
                       Ireland": International Labour Review
                       Vol.94, 1, Geneva,1966.

McCarthy, W.E.J. and   Management by Agreement: 1973.
Ellis, N.D.:

McCartney, J.B.:   "Strike Law and the Constitution": in The
                       Irish Jurist, Vol.XXX, 1964.

MacKechnie, Geoffrey: Labour Relations Policies within the
                       Firm, Dublin 1975.

McMullen, William: Preface to James Connolly: The Workers'
                       Republic, 1951.

Mitchell, Arthur: Labour in Irish Politics 1890-1930, 1974.

Mortished, R.J.P.:   "Trade Union Organisation in Ireland": in
                       Journal of the Statistical and Social
                       Inquiry Society of Ireland: Part CI,
                       Vol.XV,1927.

    -        - :   "The Industrial Relations Act, 1946":
                       in Journal of the Statistical and
                       Social Inquiry Society of Ireland:
                       Vol.XV11, 1947.

Nevin, Donal: "Radical Movements in the Twenties and
                       Thirties": in (ed.) T. Desmond Williams,
                       Secret Societies in Ireland, 1973.

O'Brien, William   Forth the Banners Go: Dublin 1969.
(as told to Edward
MacLysaght):

O'Mahony, David: Industrial Relations in Ireland:
                       The Background: ERI, Dublin 1964.

    -        - :   Economic Aspects of Industrial Relations,
                       ERI, Dublin 1965.

Pelling, Henry: A History of British Trade Unionism, 1971.

Roberts, Ruaidhri: "Trade Union Organisation in Ireland":
                       in Journal of the Statistical
                       and Social Inquiry Society of Ireland,
                       XX, II, 1958-59.

Ryan, W.P.:   The Irish Labour Movement, Dublin 1919.

Schregle, Johannes: Restructuring of the Irish Trade Union Movement, ILO, Geneva 1975.

   -      -   :   "Labour Relations in Western Europe: Some topical issues": in International Labour Review Vol.CIX:1: Geneva, 1974.

Shillman, Bernard: Trade Unionism and Trade Disputes in Ireland, Dublin 1960.

Swift, John: History of the Dublin Bakers and Others: Dublin 1948.

Toynbee, Arnold: "A State within the State": in he Observer, October 26 1975.

Van Beinum, Hans: The Morale of the Dublin Busmen, Irish National Productivity Committee, Dublin,1966

Wedderburn, K.W.:   The Worker and the Law, Pelican 1971.

Other Studies

Abrahamson, Max W.:   "Strict Interpretation in Ireland": in Modern Law Review, Vol.24, 1961.

Barraclough, Geoffrey: An Introduction to Contemporary History: Pelican, 1974.

Beloff, Michael: "Legal Education and the New Universities": in The Irish Jurist, 1959.

Berger, Berger and Kellner: The Homeless Mind: Penguin 1974.

Beth, Loren P.:   The Development of Judicial Review in Ireland 1937-1966: Institute of Public Administration 1967.

Breathnach, Seamus: The Irish Police, Anvil Books 1974

Budge, Ian and O'Leary, Cornelius: Approach to Crisis: A Study of Belfast Policies 1613-1970: 1973.

Cruise-O'Brien, Conor: To Katanga and Back: 1965.

Cullen, L.M.:   An Economic History of Ireland since 1660: London 1972.

Desmond, Barry: "The Johnson thesis in Ireland (q.v.)": in Management Vol. XXII, 6/7, 1975.

Dumont, Louis: Homo Hierarchicus, 1972.

Ehrlich, Eugen: tr. Moll, Walter L,: Fundamental Principles of the Sociology of Law, 1936.

Hobhouse, L.T.:	Morals in Evolution: London, 1951.
Johnson, Paul:	"A Brotherhood of National Misery": in Management Vol. XXII, 6/7, 1975.
Kelly, John Maurice:	Fundamental Rights in the Irish Law and Constitution, 1961.
Kennedy, David:	in Ireland in the War Years and After 1939-51 ed.Nowlan, Kevin B., and Williams, T. Desmond, 1969.
Lloyd, Dennis:	The Idea of Law, Penguin 1974.
Lyons, F.S.L.:	Ireland Since the Famine, 1971.
- - :	in Ireland in the War Years and After 1939-51 ed.Nowlan, Kevin B., and Williams, T. Desmond, 1969.
Maine, Sir Henry Sumner:	Ancient Law, London 1878.
Masterson, Patrick:	Atheism and Alienation: Pelican 1973.
Meenan, James:	The Irish Economy since 1922: Liverpool University Press, 1970.
Moynihan, Maurice:	Currency and Central Banking in Ireland, Gill and Macmillan, 1975.
Pound, Roscoe:	Justice According to Law, 1951.
Strauss, Emile:	Irish Nationalism and British Democracy, London 1951.
Whyte, J.H.	Church and State in Modern Ireland, 1923-1970: Gill and Macmillan 1971.

INDEX

Abrahamson, Max, 507

Adaptations of Enactments Act 1922, 132

Aer Rianta, 547

Alexander, Paul, 407, 412

Aliens Act, 169

Allen v. Flood, 497

Amalgamated Engineering Union, 73, 107, 109, 110, 119, 199, 315, 323, 337, 341

Amalgamated Society of Carpenters and Joiners (see also Amalgamated Society of Woodworkers), 58, 59

Amalgamated Society of Engineers (see also Amalgamated Engineering Union), 53

Amalgamated Society of Woodworkers, 54, 72, 119, 121A-124, 127, 130, 156, 199, 315, 372A

Amalgamated Transport and General Workers Union, 52, 72-75, 81, 82, 119-121A, 124-129, 132-134, 146-149, 199, 212, 213, 216, 220, 239, 259, 262, 263, 302, 303, 305, 306, 314, 315, 342, 410, 411, 426, 472

amalgamated unions (see also British-based unions) 1-9, 12-19, 30-34, 46-56, 71-74, 81, 83, 105, 110, 118-128, 131-134, 144, 150-153, 159, 161, 164-169, 180, 186, 189, 200-220, 229-238, 259, 263-277, 278-280, 303-307, 315, 349, 362-379, 382-388, 395-412, 428-437, 455-457, 467, 528

American Federation of Labour, 35

Anglo-Irish Trade Agreement, 99

Anglo-Irish Treaty, 60-63, 80, 173, 408

Anthony, R.S., 64

apprenticeship, 403, 530-532

Ardnacrusha, 68

Army Comrades Association, 101

Asquith, H.H., 25

Assurance Representatives
  Organisation, 392

Athlone, 11

Athlone Trades Council, 76

Ballymena and District Trades and
  Labour Council, 318, 324

Bambridge, Major General, 58

Bangor Trades Council, 324

Banking Commission 1938, 193

Barraclough, Geoffrey, 580

Barron, T., 127

Barry, J., 238, 276

Beattie, J., 261

Beirne, Walter, 325, 410, 443, 508-
  511, 540, 541

Belfast, 1-5, 13-16, 19, 29, 30, 42, 44, 46,
  50, 52, 56-60, 69, 71, 78, 79, 82,
  104, 121A, 124, 257, 262

Belfast Protestant Association, 10

Belfast Socialist Party, 11

Belfast trades council (various
  titles) v, 5-16, 29, 76, 107, 119,
  144, 156, 178, 213, 260, 272, 323-
  325, 335, 337, 349, 426, 457

Bell, Councillor, 318

Beloff, Michael, 488

Bennett, Louie, v, 98, 106, 107, 112,
  113, 116, 123, 238, 280, 315

Bentham, Jeremy, 483

Berne, 43, 44

Beth, Loren P., 489

Bevin, Ernest, 121, 270

Binks, Harold, 262, 317, 318, 327,
  332-337, 343, 344, 347, 349, 441

Black and Tans, 41, 56, 408

Bleakley, David, v, 306, 324

Blease, William, 319

Blueshirts, 101, 102, 115, 116

Bord na Mona, 562

Bowman, Alexander, 10

Boyle, J.W., v, 8

Bridlington Agreement, 460, 468,
   470-472

British-based unions (see under
   amalgamated unions)

British and Irish Steam Packet Co. v.
   Brannigan (Carlingford Lough case)
   507, 508

British Trade Union Congress, 2-8, 15,
   20, 23, 55, 59, 60, 80, 81, 119,
   157, 264, 362-369, 434-436, 439,
   459, 461, 467, 557; London Conference
   1945: 267, 269, 270-274

Brooke, Basil, 313, 335

Browne, Michael Bishop, 371

Browne, Noel, 297, 401

Broy Harriers, 101, 103

Brugha, Cathal, 65

Budd J., 484, 485, 493, 513, 515, 516

Building Workers Trade Union, 379-382

Busteed, John, 432

Cairns, P.J., 205, 241

Calvert, Lilian, 333, 334

Campbell, D.R., 16, 29, 32

Campbell, Sean P., 114, 116, 127,
   200, 201, 240, 242, 276

Canty, Michael, 6

Capital Grants to Industries Acts, 313

Capital Investment Advisory Committee,
   547

Carlow, 130

Carpenter, Walter, 372A

Carson, Sir Edward, 23, 30, 43, 57

Cassidy, Tom, 42

Catholic Standard, 257, 258, 389

Central Bank, 560

Chamberlain, Neville, 172

Chapman, W.T., 410, 412

Chenevix, H., 318, 411

Childers, E.H., 189

Civil Service Clerical Association, 249

Civil service conciliation and
  arbitration scheme, 543-56, 561

Civil service staff, 249, 543-546

Civil service unions, 54, 561

Clann na Poblachta, 294, 295, 386

Clarkson, J.D., v, 10, 31, 47, 53, 57, 59

Clonmel, 20, 22

Coleraine Trades Council, 324

Colgan, Michael, 184, 200, 201, 221,
  234, 236, 239, 245, 261, 276, 297

Collins, Michael, 62, 65

Comintern, 256

Commission on Vocational Organisation
  1939-1943, 4, 116, 117, 155, 169,
  186, 189, 191, 192, 195, 197, 199,
  210, 297, 371, 379-382, 391, 393,
  570, 579

Committee on Congress membership in
  Northern Ireland, 261-262

Committee on Industrial Organisation,
  573

communism, 102, 118, 172, 255-259,
  269, 338, 377, 441, 442

Conditions of Employment Act 1936, 182

Confederation of Shipbuilding and
  Engineering Unions, 306, 323, 324,
  334, 335

Congested Districts Board, 2

Connolly, Con, 318, 393

Connolly, James, 10, 11, 14, 17-22,
  25, 29, 30, 36, 37, 85, 94-96, 111,
  115, 116, 130, 147, 155, 191, 193,
  210, 255, 271, 299, 306, 395, 441, 459,
  461, 558, 570, 579, 581

Conroy, John, 404, 426, 444, 453,
  510, 575, 576, 578

Control of Prices Act 1937, 383

Cooper, John, 506

Cooper v. Millea, 484-502, 506

Coras Iompair Eireann, 242, 280, 400,
  403, 409, 472, 473, 540

Corish, Brendan, 400, 401, 429

Cork, 7, 15, 16, 23, 50, 60, 64, 69,
  230, 248, 405, 407

Cork Brewery Workers, 54

Cork Commercial Travellers
  Association, 123

Cork Employers Association, 15, 19

Cork Operative Butchers Society, 146

Cork School of Commerce, 389

Cork trades councils(various titles),
  5, 8, 15, 76, 200, 318, 325, 393

corporate state, 114, 116, 172, 209,
  210, 269

Cosgrave, William, 79, 80, 101, 102,
  104

Costello, John A., 294, 387

Council of Ireland, 70

Council of Irish Unions, 167, 168

County and City Managers Association,
  576

Courtney, M., 82, 83

Coyne, E.J., 390-392

Craig, Sir James, 103

Crawford, Leo, 209, 231, 232, 234,
  246, 252, 276, 292, 297, 367, 380,
  388, 395, 396, 398, 399, 435, 436,
  474

Crowley, Patrick, 392

Cruise-O'Brien, Conor, 579

Cullen, Denis, 106, 111, 250

Cullen, L.M., 3, 41, 42, 99

Cumann na nGaedheal, 65, 79, 92, 101

Curlis, H.J., 341

Dail Eireann (see also Oireachtas), 41, 43, 56, 60-64, 79, 93, 95, 116, 121, 156, 164, 166, 167, 169, 190, 204, 209, 211, 218, 230, 254, 257, 295, 296, 373, 386, 526, 533, 548

Daly, P.T., 12, 17, 19, 23, 29, 155, 156, 158-163, 192, 218, 219, 579

Davitt, Michael, 2, 6

Deakin, Arthur, 368, 372

Delany, V.T.H., 507

Department of Finance, 250

Department of Industry and Commerce, 182, 197, 201, 237, 302

Department of Local Government, 68

Department of Supplies, 182

Derry (see also Londonderry) 19, 32, 33, 46, 76, 313, 364

Derry trades council (various titles), 324

de Valera, Eamon, 38, 40, 65, 67, 68, 79, 99-104, 112, 168-173, 178, 179, 202, 249, 293, 295, 358, 386, 387, 525, 526, 529, 545, 561-563

Devlin, Joseph, 104

Diamond, Harry, 321, 333, 334

Dillon, James, 279, 560

Dillon, John, 171

Disputes Committee of Congress (see also trade union organisation), 82, 83, 124, 212, 213, 216, 470, 471, 531

Distributive Worker, The, 115

Dixon J., 488, 508, 509

Dixon, Sir Owen, 499

Donegal, 182, 183, 185, 186

Douglas, Senator James, 181, 184, 196

Doyle, Gerry, 240, 547

Drogheda, 44

Drogheda trades council (various titles), 5, 8, 76

Drumgoole, Michael, 160, 161, 167, 200, 220, 276

Dublin, 1, 3, 4, 6, 15, 16, 20, 22, 23, 29, 35, 43, 44, 50, 54, 64, 106, 123, 124, 129, 185, 212, 236, 248, 253

Dublin Council of Action, 206, 208-211, 218, 230, 232

Dublin and District Electrotypers, 54

Dublin Employers' Federation, 19

Dublin Exhibition 1864, 5

Dublin trades councils (various titles), 5-9, 12, 15, 29, 31, 54, 76, 81, 93, 111, 119, 130, 131, 134, 156, 208, 213, 215, 217, 218, 230, 250-254, 325, 364, 372A, 426

Dublin Typographical and Provident Society, 160, 162, 167, 276

Dublin Unemployed Association, 358, 438

Dublin United Tramway Company, 212

Duffy, Luke, 112, 113

Duffy, Michael, 102

Dundalk, 16, 405

Dunne v. Fitzpatrick, 508

Dunne, Sean, 328

Educational Company of Ireland v. Fitzpatrick, 464, 482, 484, 485, 488, 490, 507, 512-516, 549

Edward VIII, abdication, 169

Ehrlich, Eugen, 525, 526

Electrical Trade Union (England), 123

Electrical Trade Union (Ireland), 54, 81

Electricity (Special Provisions) Act, 1966, 512

Electricity Supply Board, 377, 472, 529, 562, 569

Elger, William, 157

Ellis, N.D. 538

Elvin, H.H., 157

Emergency Powers Act, 169, 375

Emergency Powers Act (Northern Ireland) 1926, 345

Employment and Training Act, 318, 321, 333-337, 341, 342

Enniskillen Trades Council, 324

Erle, Sir William, 484, 485, 489, 490-498, 514, 517, 525

Esplanade Pharmacy Ltd. v. Larkin, 522

European Recovery Programme, 296, 388, 402

Everett, James, 387, 395, 401

Farmers Party, 80, 179

Farrell, Terry, 458

fascism, 102, 103, 105, 111-118, 124, 195, 266, 267, 269, 462

Federated Union of Employers, 384, 401, 439, 536, 540

Federation of Irish Manufacturers, 186-190, 195

Federation of Road and Rail Workers, 506

Federation of Rural Workers, 328

Ferguson, R.C., 237

Fermanagh, 60

Fianna Fail, 40, 79, 80, 92, 100, 101, 117, 167, 179, 196, 201, 202, 246, 258, 293-296, 358, 360, 386, 401, 405, 525, 527, 548

Fine Gael, 40, 102, 114, 179, 180, 258, 294, 386

Fitzpatrick, W.J., 511

Foran, Thomas, 29, 51, 55

Forristal, J.P., 435

Fox, R.M., iv, 111

Franchise Acts, 38

Franco, 102, 172

Gallagher, T., 14

Galway, 20

Gavan Duffy J., 243, 280, 484, 487,
  501-506, 516, 517, 525

General Federation of Trade Unions, 12

Getgood, Robert, 180, 220, 260, 262,
  275, 276, 327

Gladstone, William, 10

Good, John, 20

Gordon, Dawson, 156

Gould, F., 160

Government of Ireland Bill (1914), 24

Green, Ernest, 390

Griffith, Arthur, 3, 13, 14, 17, 38,
  61, 62, 64, 65

guild socialists, 116

Hallsworth, Joseph, 364

Hanna, J., 500

Hardie, Keir, 10

Harkin, Brendan, 341

Harland and Wolff, 100, 343

Healy, T.M., 171

Heery, J.D., 328

Henderson, Arthur, 43

Heuston, R.F.V., 499, 507, 512

Hickey, James, 259, 400, 401, 429

High Court, 204, 243, 280, 371, 500,
  505, 509, 513, 517, 535, 540

Hillery, Brian, 304-305

Hobhouse, L.T., 493, 494

Hogan, James, 102

Hollywood and District Trades
  Council, 324

Holy Year (1950),296, 385

Hudson, Larry, 299

Hurley, Jerry, 157

Hynes, Owen, 167, 205, 241, 379-382,
  395, 397, 461

Income Tax Commission, 547

Independent Labour Party, 11

individualism, 494-496, 505-507,
514-516

Industrial Courts Act 1919, 130

Industrial Development Authority, 547

Industrial Efficiency and Prices Bill,
383, 384, 548, 563

Industrial Organisation and
Development Act, 332, 549

industrial rationalisation, 106-108

Industrial Relations Act 1946, 360,
368, 372A, 374, 510, 527, 531-
533, 540-544

Industrial Workers of the World, 18

Industries Development Acts, 313

International Confederation of Free
Trade Unions, 394

International Federation of Christian
Trade Unions, 393, 394

International Federation of Trade
Unions, 117, 118

International Labour Organisation,
266, 346, 361-365, 387, 388, 398,
402, 432, 462, 583

Ireland Act 1949, 294, 295, 385,
395, 396, 398, 399, 405

Ireland, John, 257

Irish Agricultural and General
Workers Union, 54

Irish Bakers, Confectionery and
Allied Workers Union, iv, 81, 200,
250

Irish-based unions, 9, 19, 23, 32,
34, 46, 51, 54, 55, 70, 71, 72,
105, 110, 118-121A, 122, 123,
124-128, 150, 159, 161, 164, 167,
168, 186, 189, 201, 204, 205, 206,
211, 218, 229, 231, 236, 243, 259,
263, 270, 273-280, 300, 303, 305,
316, 347-349, 362, 364, 376, 379,
380, 382, 385, 396-411, 428-437,
444, 445, 453-456, 528

Irish Bookbinders and Allied Trades
  Union, 54, 234

Irish Citizen Army Comrades' Association, 372A

Irish Conference of Professional and
  Service Associations, 571, 576

Irish Constitution, 170, 171, 463,
  500, 504, 505, 513-517, 524-526

Irish Democratic Trade and Labour
  Federation, 6

Irish Drapers' Assistants Association,
  34, 46, 50, 53

Irish Electrical Industrial Union, 54

Irish Engineering and Foundry Union, 54

Irish Engineering and Industrial
  Union, 81, 130

Irish Engineering, Shipbuilding and
  Foundry Trades Union, 53

Irish Federated Trade and Labour
  Union, 6

Irish Independent, 11

Irish Labour League, 6

Irish Municipal Employees Trade
  Union, 146, 160, 328

Irish National Federation, 7

Irish National League, 5

Irish National League of the Blind, 54

Irish National Painters' & Decorators'
  Trade Union, 51
Irish National Productivity Committee,
  573

Irish National Teachers Organisation,
  118, 199, 261, 443, 444

Irish National Union of Vintners',
  Grocers', and Allied Trades
  Assistants, 54, 277, 508, 509

Irish National Union of Woodworkers,
  54, 121A-123, 130

Irish Nationality and Citizenship
  Act, 169

Irish Party, 11, 13, 22, 38, 41

Irish Republican Army, 42, 56, 59, 60,
  63, 54, 100-103, 169, 238, 258,
  296, 298, 299, 330, 349, 438, 440

Irish Shoe and Leather Workers Union,
  404-407, 410-412

Irish Socialist Republican Party, 11

Irish Tourist Board, 547

Irish Transport and General Workers
  Union, iv, 14-19, 26, 29, 31, 32,
  46, 49, 51-55, 58, 61, 65, 66,
  70-82, 97, 119, 120-121A, 124-129,
  130-134, 144-151, 156, 157, 182,
  183, 197-200, 208, 211-215, 220,
  230, 231, 235, 239, 242, 243, 250,
  253-259, 262, 263, 266, 271-279,
  302, 305, 324, 325, 346, 387, 397,
  398, 400, 404-409, 411, 426, 472,
  506, 510, 575

Irish Union of Distributive Workers
  and Clerks, 72, 81, 123, 167, 199,
  200, 276, 277, 499, 509, 512-516

Irish Women Workers Union, 71, 76, 78,
  83, 97, 106-109, 146, 150, 232, 236,
  460

Jackson, Archie, 218

Johnson J., 501

Johnson, Thomas, 29-40, 46, 50, 51,
  64, 65, 67, 71, 77-79, 82, 85, 94-
  96, 115, 122, 128, 129, 192, 211,
  212, 260, 270, 271, 361, 362, 366, 369,
  370, 430, 469, 579

Joint Memorandum on Trade Union Unity
  1954, 301, 302

Joint Production Council, 331

Judge, Jerome J., v, 54, 201, 304

Kahn-Freund, O., 529

Keady, Martin, 542

Keane, T.P., 244

Kelly, Aidan, 304, 305, 571

Kelly, John, 525

Kendall, Walter, iii

Kennedy, Norman, 411, 426

Kennedy, Tom, 121A, 200, 220, 235,
  274, 275, 276

Keyes, Michael, 156, 165, 218, 220, 273, 275

Kilkenny, 10, 81

Kingsmill Moore J., 515

Kyle, Sam, 29, 98, 118, 127, 129, 133, 143, 150, 153, 154, 156, 160, 161, 166, 193, 194, 200, 212, 213, 214, 216, 231, 233, 236, 240, 247, 251, 262, 267, 269, 270, 273-275, 320, 328, 399, 400, 429, 580

Kyne, T., 401

Labour Court, 375-377, 384, 401, 402, 483, 527, 531, 533-545, 548, 561

Labour Party, 22, 24, 39, 40, 43, 63-70, 77, 78, 80, 85, 92, 93, 94, 97, 98, 101, 115, 116, 154, 164, 179, 192, 194, 207, 209, 214, 218, 219, 230, 236, 237, 246, 253, 254, 255-259, 265, 269, 294, 383, 384, 386, 389, 395, 399, 400, 406

Labour Party (United Kingdom), 10, 22, 29, 37, 43, 56, 69

Labour Representation Committee, 11

Land and Labour Associations, 32

Land League, 2, 5

Larkin, Delia, 155

Larkin, Denis, 411, 442

Larkin, Emmet, iv

Larkin, James (Junior), 79, 192, 206, 209, 210, 253-257, 276, 320, 332, 364, 365, 369-378, 395, 396, 398, 399, 404, 426, 427, 435, 442, 453, 462, 575, 578

Larkin, James (Senior), iv, 10-25, 29, 36, 52, 65, 66, 78-81, 109, 120, 130, 131, 135, 150, 151, 155, 158, 199, 206, 208-210, 215,217,,220, 230, 232, 248, 250-259, 292, 325, 373, 426, 570

Larne Trades Council, 324

Lavery J., 488-491

Law, Bonar, 26

Lawlor, T., 160

Leader, The, 211

League of Nations, 43, 173

Leathem v. Craig, 496

Leeburn, W.J., 319, 321

Lemass, Sean, 163, 182, 190, 202, 232,
   233, 237, 238, 245, 246, 248, 278,
   279, 315, 316, 358, 360, 365-370,
   372A-379, 383, 384, 396, 402-404,
   432, 462, 463, 469, 470, 527-536,
   539, 541, 548-550, 563, 572, 573, 575

Limerick, 12, 16, 42, 248, 298

Limerick Corporation Employees
   Society, 146

Limerick trades council (various
   titles), 8, 55, 76, 107, 110, 276

Lisburn Trades Council, 324

Litvinoff, 32, 37

Lloyd, Dennis, 484, 488, 525, 531

Lloyd George, David, 30, 31, 408

London, 24

London Agreement 1925, 70

Londonderry (see also Derry), 60

Luxemburg, Rosa, 66

Lynch, Eamonn, 85, 142, 143, 153, 154,
   156, 158, 159, 201

Lynch, Gilbert, 215, 265, 273, 274, 276, 393

Lyons, F.S.L., 178, 293, 313

McAteer, John, 318, 331, 335, 337

MacBride, Sean, 295, 296, 388, 560

McCabe, John, 157

M'Carron, James, 17, 19, 34

McCarthy, W.E.J., 538

McCullough, Billy, 263

MacDonald, Ramsay, 10

McDowell, Kay, 236

MacEntee, Sean, 163-167, 182, 185, 202

Macgougan, Jack, 262, 318, 350, 579

MacLysaght, Edward, iv

McMullan, Gordon, v

McMullen, William, 70, 97, 121A, 197,
   200, 246, 255, 262, 264, 268, 276,
   316, 346, 347, 348, 387, 397, 398,
   402, 411, 540

MacPartlin, Thomas, 32

Madden, D., 337, 341

Maine, Sir Henry, 494

Mansion House Conference 1918, 36

Marchbank, John, 159-162, 165

Marshall, George C., 388

Martin, John, 6

Meredith J., 120, 121, 129, 132-134, 204

Mervyn, Michael, 440, 442, 443

Mid-Ulster Trades Council, 324

Mirchell, Arthur H., v

Molony, Helena, 77, 97, 122, 127,
   150, 153, 154

Montesquieu, baron de, 486

Morrissey, Dan, 93, 387, 549

Morrow, Robert, 144, 160

Mortished, R.J.P., 69, 71-76, 78,
   80, 85, 117, 146, 170, 266, 474, 535,
   538, 539, 541, 542, 543, 583

Muintir na Tire, 103

Mullingar trades council, 76

Murnaghan J., 487, 500

Murphy, Thomas, 22

Mussolini, 102, 116

Napier, Sam, 328-329

National Amalgamated Furnishing
   Trades Association, 73, 110

National Amalgamated Union of Shop
   Assistants, 52, 54

National Association of Operative
   Plasterers, 123

National Centre Party, 101

National Corporate Party, 102

National Council of Labour Colleges,
96, 390

National Economic and Social Council,
560

National Employer-Labour Conference,
468, 543, 546, 573, 576

National Federation of Building
Trade Operatives, 306, 334, 335

National Guard, 101

National Industrial Development
Council, 342

National Industrial Economic
Council, 560, 573, 576

National Labour Party, 254, 259, 384,
385, 386, 395, 399, 400

National League, 80

National Sailors' and Firemen's
Union, 73

National Society of Painters, 337

National Union of Boot and Shoe
Operatives, 146, 397, 404-407,
410-412

National Union of Distributive and
Allied Workers, 119

National Union of Dock Labourers,
15, 16, 52

National Union of General and
Municipal Workers, 119, 341

National Union of Railwaymen, 35, 51,
52, 53, 58, 60, 72, 73, 82, 119,
127, 152, 156, 159, 200, 218, 220,
242, 243, 280, 397, 400, 407-412,
502, 506

National Union of Railwaymen v.
Sullivan and Ors., 371, 373, 376,
409, 469, 483, 487, 504, 507, 514,
515, 549

National Union of Sheetmetal Makers
and Gas Meter Makers, 54

National Union of Tailors and Garment
Makers, 146, 324

National Union of Transport Employees,
407-412

nationalism, 9, 13, 24, 25, 26, 33,
  37, 39, 44, 47, 54, 55, 66, 72,
  105, 122, 123, 125, 127, 128, 135,
  148, 150, 166, 187, 210, 263-272,
  277-279, 292, 295, 297-301, 307,
  314, 362, 364-367, 371, 372, 385,
  389-396, 407-409, 441, 442, 446,
  459, 526, 530, 556, 570, 577, 579

Navan Trades Council, 76

Neill, Ivan, 333-335

Nevin, Donal, v, 319

New Way, 52

Newry, 10

Newry trades council, v, 76, 324

Newtownards trades council, 324

Northern Ireland Board of Trade, 331

Northern Ireland Committee of
  Congress (see also trade union
  organisation), 262, 306, 314-350

Northern Ireland Electricity Board, 333

Northern Ireland Hospital Authority, 335

Northern Ireland Labour Party, 69, 98,
  326-329, 332

Northern Ireland Tourist Board, 331, 334

Norton, William, 85, 92, 94, 113, 114,
  154, 164-166, 209, 219, 230, 235,
  256, 360, 363, 367, 372A, 388, 395,
  396, 399-401, 439, 462, 541

O'Brien, George, 389

O'Brien J., 497

O'Brien, P.J., 230, 234, 236, 238,
  243, 257, 300

O'Brien, William, iv, 10, 20-22, 29,
  30, 33, 36, 37, 38, 40, 46, 54, 65,
  66, 94, 119-123, 128, 130, 131, 135,
  143-165, 197, 200-220, 229-233, 240,
  250-259, 263, 264, 273-280, 292,
  304, 316, 346, 364, 426, 459, 579,
  582

O'Carroll, E., 127

O'Connell, Daniel, 526

O'Connell, T.J., 92, 94, 121

O'Duffy, Eoin, 101, 102, 114

O'Farrell, J.T., 55, 73, 152, 160,
  196, 215, 217, 218, 276, 393, 394

Offences Against the State Act, 169,
  299

O'Higgins, Kevin, 61, 78, 79

O'Higgins, T.F., 101

Oireachtas (see also Dail Eireann and
  Seanad Eireann), 504, 505, 524, 525

O'Lehane, M.J., 46, 50-53

Omagh trades council, 324

O Murchu, Sean, 299

O'Neill, Terence, ii, 556

Operative Plasterers' Trade Society
  of Dublin, 123, 240

O'Rahilly, Alfred, 115, 257, 389,
  390-392

O'Reilly, T.J., 6

Osborne case (Osborne v. Amalgamated
  Society of Railway Servants), 20, 345

O'Shannon, Cathal, 65, 69, 97, 183,
  201, 216, 231, 246, 248, 264, 265,
  268, 270, 276, 277, 364, 380

Pallas, Christopher, Lord Chief Baron, 497

Parker J., 498, 507

Parnell, James Stewart, 5, 6, 8, 171

Pearse, Padraig, 66

People's College, Adult Education
  Association, 390, 392

Pius XII, 102

Planning for the Crisis, 194

Plunkett, Horace, 5, 38

Porter, G., 337

Post Office Workers' Union, 80, 200,
  205, 244, 249

Pound, Roscoe, 485, 493, 512

prices and incomes policy, 374, 383, 536-538

Profintern, 256

Public Safety Act, 80, 100

Quadragessimo Anno, 102

Quinn v. Leathem, 170

Railway Clerks Association, 55, 72, 73, 127, 152, 218, 276

Rathmines Urban District Council, 499

Redmond, John, iv, 11, 21, 25, 30, 38, 56

Redmond, William, 80

Reform Act 1832, 491

Registrar of Friendly Societies, 302

Registrar of Trade Unions, 80, 81

Republican Party, 64, 65

Rerum Novarum, 297

Restriction of Employment Order 1942, 260

Rex (I.U.D.W. & C.) v. Rathmines U.D.C., 483, 499

Richardson, E.L., 17, 570

Roberts, Ruaidhri, 318, 332, 336-339, 392, 399, 432, 455, 456, 458-473, 547

Roman Catholic Church, 96, 171, 172, 195, 296-298, 381, 385, 389-394, · 559

Roundabout Ltd. v. Beirne, 487, 508

Royal Commission on Trade Unions 1869, 496

Royal Commission on Trade Unions and Employers Associations 1965-1968, (Donovan Commission) 529

Royal Ulster Constabulary, 60

Ryan v. Cooke & Quinn (the Monument Creamery case), 501

Ryan, W.P., 45

Schregle, Johannes, 432

Scott, W.A., 134

Scottish TUC, 20, 56, 119, 157, 219

Seanad Eireann (see also Oireachtas),
  184, 185, 196, 230

Sexton, James, 15, 52, 58, 120

Sherriff v. McMullen, 508

Shipbuilding and Engineering Federation
  (see Confederation of Shipbuilding
  and Engineering Workers), 76

Short Brothers and Harland, 342

Sinclair, Betty, 325, 337, 339, 340

Sinn Fein, 3, 5, 9-23, 26, 31, 35, 38,
  39, 41, 57, 79, 94, 307

Sligo, 25, 29, 30

Sligo trades council, 76

Smith v. Beirne, 508, 509

Smith, Bob, 317, 348, 349, 445

Socialist Party of Ireland, 10, 18

socialists and socialism, 2, 8, 9, 10,
  14, 17, 37, 38, 40-43, 47, 56, 67,
  94-98, 105, 113, 115, 116, 192, 210,
  256, 263, 264, 269-272, 292, 326,
  327, 329, 338, 372A, 385, 394, 441,
  442, 575-578

Somerville, Michael, 156, 160

South, Sean, 298

soviets, 61, 66

Spartacists, 66

Special Powers Act, 60

Statistical and Social Inquiry Society
  of Ireland, 71, 455, 461, 464, 538

Statistics of Trade Advisory
  Committee, 332

Stewart, E.W., 21

Stormont (Northern Ireland Parliament),
  59, 60, 69, 70, 74, 103, 104,
  314-350

Strabane trades council, 324

Suicre Eireann, 547

Supreme Court, 202, 242, 280, 360,
   371-378, 409, 464, 487, 500,
   505-509, 513, 515, 517, 524,
   530, 549

Swift, John, iv, 160, 208, 235,
   236, 239, 547

syndicalism, 14, 17, 19, 20, 26, 40,
   42, 46, 47, 51, 70, 74, 75, 85, 93,
   94-97, 111, 115, 116, 146, 191, 210,
   306, 345, 459-461, 558, 579, 581

Taff Vale Ry. v. Amalgamated Society
   of Railway Servants, 10, 170, 500,
   501

Tailor and Garment Workers Trade Union
   (see also National Union of Tailors
   and Garment Workers), 72, 81

Tewson, Vincent, 388, 435, 467

Thomas, J.H., 408

Thorne, Will, 6

Tierney, Michael, 102

Tipperary Workingmen's Union, 54

Toynbee, Arnold, 557-578

Trade Disputes Act 1906, 11, 170, 184,
   203, 247, 483-487, 498-501, 507-510,
   513, 515, 528

Trade Disputes and Trade Unions Act
   (Northern Ireland) 1927, 133, 327,
   344-346

Trade Union Act 1871, 132, 133, 197,
   496

Trade Union Act Amendment Act, 1876,
   132

Trade Union Acts 1871-1935, 203, 204,
   345

Trade Union Acts 1941-1942, 151, 163,
   165, 167, 179, 181, 200-221, 229-
   243, 249, 252, 253, 259, 274, 278,
   280, 360, 374, 378, 382, 405, 409,
   462, 463, 487, 503-506, 528, 530,
   532, 582

Trade Unions and Trade Disputes Act
   1927, 80

Trade Union Information, 1953, 301-307

trade union organisation, (see also
  Committee on Congress membership
  in NI and Disputes Committee)

  classification: Mortished's: 71-76

  classification: Trade Union
    Information, 1953, 301-307

  commission of inquiry 1936-1939,
    98, 105, 119, 134, 142-173,
    181, 304, 397

  committee on trade union organisation
    1962, 583

  conference (1927) 83, 84

  congress 1919, 46-52

  congress 1930, 85, 92-94, 97

  congress 1953, 468-471

  delegates to congresses: their
    character, 149-150

  education: trade unions, 389-393

  freedom of association, 346, 461-465

  functions of congress, 459, 467,
    468; CIU functions of congress:
    473-474

  industrial councils, 111

  industry-based unions (see also
    syndicalism), 432

  international affiliation, 393, 394

  leadership in trade unions, 426-428

  legal status, 131-134, 170; in
    Northern Ireland, 133-134

  Lemass proposals 1947, 378, 402

  Provisional United Organisation,
    437, 440-447, 453-459, 468, 469

  Roberts's memorandum 1954, 432,
    461-468

  trades councils (see also Mortished),
    110, 111, 131, 152, 324, 325

  unity conference 1953, 404

  unity memorandum 1954, 433

Treason Act, 169

Typographical Association, 31, 34, 73, 435

Tyrone, 60

Ulster covenant, 57

Ulster Protestant League, 104

Ulster Volunteer Force, 57

unionists (understood politically), 17, 24, 35, 36, 41, 59, 66, 79, 103, 300, 314-350, 445, 446

United Irish League, 17

United Trades Congress, 23

University College Cork, 389, 432

University College Dublin, 389, 390

Valentine v. Hyde, 513

Vance, Cecil, 342

Vocational Education Officers' Organisation, 389

vocational organisation, (see also corporate state), 102, 103, 115-117, 377, 379-382

Wages Councils Act, 344

wages standstill orders, 179, 200, 206-217, 237, 239, 243-250, 251, 253, 527, 532

Walker, William, 10-12, 17, 22

Walsh, Sean, 276

Waterford, 34, 36

Watters, C.D., 82, 152, 153, 160

Weldon, A. (Gus), 389

Westport, 182

Wexford, 10, 23

Wexford trades council, 76

Whelan, Billy, 160, 162, 167, 387

white-collar unionism, 571, 572, 575

White v. Riley, 490, 491, 513

Whitley, H.T., 31, 34

Williams J., 363

Wilson, T., 318

Woodcock, George, 435, 436

Workers Educational Association,
  390, 391

Workers Union, 15

Workers Union of Ireland, 65, 66, 81,
  130, 131, 150, 151, 191, 192, 199,
  206, 215, 250, 276, 411, 426

Workman, Clark & Co., 100

World Federation of Trade Unions,
  393, 394

Wyndham Act, 3